CREDITS

The editor of this text would like to acknowledge the authors and publishers who graciously granted permission to reprint the following selections:

1. "Social Psychological Inquiry" by Arthur G. Neal. Used by permission of the author from *Social Psychology: A Sociological Perspective*, Simon and Schuster, 1983.

2. "What Is Social Psychology" by Elliot Aronson. Used by permission of the author and publisher. From *The Social Animal*, sixth edition, by Elliot Aronson. Copyright © 1992 by W. H. Freeman and Company. Reprinted with permission.

3. "Pathology of Imprisonment" by Philip G. Zimbardo. Used by permission of the author and publisher from *Society*, Vol. 9, No. 6, 1972, pp. 4–8. Copyright © 1972 by Transaction, Inc.

4. "On Being Sane in Insane Places" by D. L. Rosenhan. Used by permission of the author and publisher from *Science*, Vol. 179 (January 19, 1973), pp. 250–258. Copyright © 1973 by the American Association for the Advancement of Science.

5. "Society as Symbolic Interaction" by Herbert Blumer. From Arnold M. Rose (editor), *Human Behavior and Social Processes: An Interactionist Approach.* Copyright © 1962 by Houghton Mifflin Company. Used with permission.

6. "On the Social Psychology of the Psychological Experiment: With Particular Reference to Demand Characteristics and Their Implications" by Martin T. Orne. Used by permission of the author from *American Psychologist*, 17, November 1962, pp. 776–783.

7. "Birthdate and Mortality: An Evaluation of the Death-Dip/Death-Rise Phenomenon" by Bryan Byers, Richard A. Zeller, and Peggy Y. Byers. From *Sociological Focus*, Vol. 24, No. 1, 1991, pp. 13–28. Used by permission.

8. "Techniques of Neutralization" by Gresham M. Sykes and David Matza. Used by permission of the principal author from the *American Sociological Review*, Vol. 22, December 1957, pp. 664–670.

9. "The Social Self" by Charles Horton Cooley. Excerpt reprinted from *Human Nature and the Social Order* by Charles Horton Cooley, Charles Scribner's Sons, 1902, pp. 179–185, 259–260.

10. "Attitudes" by Gordon W. Allport. Used by permission of Clark University Press from *The Handbook of Social Psychology* edited by C. Murchison. Worcester, Mass.: Clark University Press, 1935.

11. "The Social Psychology of George Herbert Mead" by Bernard N. Meltzer of Western Michigan University, Kalamazoo, Michigan. Used by permission of the author, Center for

35. "Hanging Tongues: A Sociological Encounter with the Assembly Line" by William E. Thompson. Used by permission of the author and Human Sciences Press from *Qualitative Sociology*, Vol. 6, No. 3, 1983, pp. 215–237.

36. "The Social Construction of Deviance: Experts on Battered Women" by Donileen R. Loseke and Spencer E. Cahill. Copyright © 1984 by the Society for the Study of Social Problems. Reprinted from *Social Problems*, Vol. 31, No. 3, February 1984, pp. 296–310, by permission of the publisher and authors.

37. "Towards a Sociological Understanding of Psychoanalysis" by Peter L. Berger. Used by permission of the author and the New School for Social Research from *Social Research*, 32:1, Spring 1965.

38. "Psychological Modernity" by Arthur G. Neal. Used by permission of the author from *Social Psychology: A Sociological Perspective*, Simon and Schuster, 1983.

Contents

PREFACE

It is with great satisfaction and delight that I introduce *Readings in Social Psychology: Perspective and Method*. I am confident that the book will provide those interested in social psychology with a suitable supplemental reader. In particular, it should have the most appeal for social psychologists who have both sociological training and an appreciation for the contributions that psychology has made to the discipline of social psychology. The book will hopefully appeal to psychologists as well.

When I began to think seriously about compiling this collection of readings, I asked myself an important question: Other than a primary text, what would I need to teach a social psychology course? The answer came quite easily: a collection of readings that represent the domain of social psychology.

This book represents the perspective and methods of the discipline in many ways. It examines the contributions of sociology and psychology to the field; it represents qualitative and quantitative approaches; it makes important connections between macro-level social phenomena and the micro-level world of the individual; and it explores the discipline's theoretical and applied dimensions. In addition, the book continually emphasizes the relevance of social psychology not only as an academic discipline but also as an area of applicability to everyday life.

Readings in Social Psychology: Perspective and Method serves as the companion reader to *Social Psychology: Shaping Identity, Thought, and Conduct* by Michael C. Kearl and Chad Gordon. It is also a supplement to other social psychology texts. A correlation chart is provided in the appendix as an aid to those wishing to match specific chapters in other social psychology texts with selections in this book.

The book is divided into four parts: Introducing Social Psychology; The Self, Society, and Social Patterns of Human Experience; Reality Negotiation with Others; and Institutional Social Psychology. Part One provides an introduction to social psychology in terms of important substantive areas, theory, and methodology that derive from the field's basis in both sociology and psychology. Part Two emphasizes the interconnectedness among the self, the individual, society, and social structures. Part Three addresses reality negotiation through understanding, interpretation, social perception, and reality construction. The final part makes specific micro- and macro-social psychological connections that present and emphasize the significant linkages between individual behavior and the societal and institutional structures within which individuals live and operate. Each part discusses major theoretical, practical, and research-supported views on each theme. Overall, the book demonstrates how social psychology is a product of both psychology and sociology and, as a discipline, is applicable to almost any aspect of daily life. The field's reach is vast and ranges from the everyday social interaction to the most complex and intricate social structures.

I hope that I have accomplished my goal: to provide a useful, thorough, thoughtful, and applicable supplemental text for teaching social psychology. The journey has not been without help. Many individuals have given important support, assistance, and advice. Without them, this project would not have been possible.

I would first like to thank the superb staff at Allyn and Bacon. In particular, I would like to recognize those in the Editorial Office who provided me with much assistance and support. I would like to show my appreciation to Bill Barke, Vice President and Editorial Director at Allyn and Bacon. I would also like to thank Senior Editor Karen Hanson for having faith in me and my project, and for providing me with much needed feedback and critical review on earlier content. Without Karen, this project would not have been possible. I would also like to thank Laura Lynch and Deborah Brown for helping to facilitate this project and for fielding my many questions. Thanks are also due to Barbara Tsantinis of the Permission Department for guidance and advice on copyright issues. Last, but certainly not least, I would like to thank Joyce Nilsen for listening to my original idea and assisting me in beginning this project.

This project was also aided on other fronts as well. First, I would like to thank Valparaiso University and Saint Mary's College, Notre Dame, Indiana. I am grateful to Celia Fallon for clerical assistance. I also owe thanks to the Cushwa-Leighton Library at Saint Mary's College and to Head Librarian Sister Bernice Hollenhorst, Robert Hohl, Julia Long, and Leonore Klee for their assistance with my research. I appreciate the assistance of psychologist Rebecca Stoddart of Saint Mary's College, who provided me with additional social psychology textbooks. Thanks also to the telecommunications staff, who played such a vital role with fax transmittals in the final stages of this project. Finally, I would like to thank those social psychology students at Saint Mary's College who used earlier versions of this reader. In particular, I would like to recognize those students who provided specific feedback on selections and content: Lori Corirossi, Angela Cutrona, Christine Delaney, Deb Lohman, Mary Barger, Kelly Flynn, Heidi Fuhr, Elizabeth Martin, Rena Sauer, and Rachel Verdick.

I would also like to recognize and thank other important individuals: at the University of Notre Dame, sociologists Penny Briner, Richard Lamanna, Andrew Weigert, Kevin Christiano, Ronald Vander Griend, and Richard Williams; at Bowling Green State University, sociologists Richard A. Zeller, Arthur G. Neal, and Ralph Wahrman. Additionally, I would like to show my appreciation to Professors Whitney Gordon (Sociology), James E. Hendricks (Criminal Justice), and David Hines (Psychology) of Ball State University, and Professor Peter Venturelli of the Sociology Department at Valparaiso University.

I would like to thank my wife, Dr. Peggy Y. Byers, for her unending optimism, support, and encouragement. I could not have a better friend, colleague, and spouse. Thank you, Peggy, for all you have given me.

Finally, I would like to thank each of the authors featured within this book for allowing me to reprint their work, as well as all of the copyright holders who so promptly answered my reprint requests.

B. B.

PART ONE

Introducing Social Psychology

The field of social psychology is indeed vast, drawing on such diverse areas as sociology, psychology, communications, physiology, sociobiology, human development, religion, history, and political science. In spite of the eclectic theoretical and methodological background that might be considered under the purview of social psychology, it is securely situated within the social and behavioral sciences, especially psychology and sociology.

Social psychology is concerned with many aspects of human behavior. Certain assumptions guide the discipline in its quest for understanding. The field assumes that the individual is influenced by and at the same time reciprocally influences the environment and social situations. In a sense, one can say that society is within the individual, and the individual is within society. This unique, reciprocal relationship between society and the individual makes social psychology particularly useful in explaining many forms of human behavior.

It may also be suggested that societies have certain needs that are characteristic of social systems. As a result, one's behavior will be governed to a certain extent by the needs of the larger social system within a given society, the most notable of which may be the need of a society to govern the conduct of its individual members. Out of such an expectation emerge social structures which are patterned ways in which people behave in the company of others. These may include simple conversational gestures (e.g., "Hi! How are you?") to behavioral expectations within a crowd.

The examination of this reciprocity between the environment and the individual and of the presence of social structures within society may be addressed from two different vantage points. It has been suggested that there may actually be two types of social psychology: sociological social psychology (SSP) and psychological social psychology (PSP). Social psychology does have two origins, sociological and psychological. Out of this merger has come a field of study that aligns aspects of both disciplines. However, both sociology and psychology often claim their own brand of social psychology, with distinct theoretical and methodological preferences. In spite of this, the two fields tend to merge in many ways that may be found in their offspring.

In addition to the issues of theory and method, the two social psychologies do share some intellectual tradition. Early works of William James, Sigmund Freud, Thomas Dewey, Charles Horton Cooley, William I. Thomas, and George

1

Herbert Mead have influenced both psychological and sociological social psychology. Due to this shared intellectual history, much of what the two social psychologies address is more alike than different. These commonalities run deep. First, both are interested in explaining social behavior. That is, they attempt to explain behavior that emerges out of the influence of others within society. Second, although to a certain degree both fields recognize intrapersonal processes (such as self-definitions and feelings), their main emphasis is on interpersonal processes, or the behavior that occurs among people in social groups. Both disciplines also recognize the contributions of intrapersonal behavior to interpersonal behavior.

Both social psychologies observe behavior using quantitative and qualitative approaches. The psychological brand of social psychology will tend toward quantitative empirical methodology more than its counterpart, and is also likely to give more attention to intrapersonal processes than its sociological partner. Further, the psychological approach will emphasize cognitive, social learning, and psychoanalytic theory. Although never discounting the social experience of the individual, the psychological side of social psychology may place more focus on the individual than the social group. However, both varieties of social psychology will be interested in the emphasis of structure upon individual behavior.

The sociological side of social psychology has adopted theoretical and methodological approaches that are different from those of its psychological partner. Rather than experimental methodologies, the sociological brand will tend to utilize more naturalistic techniques of empirical observation or even survey methodology. For instance, the Chicago School of Symbolic Interaction emphasizes the richness of detail that one can derive from observing behavior in its natural setting. In fact, this school may at times reject any predetermined methodology for observing behavior. Herein lies the essence of the qualitative approach to social psychology. Yet direct observation is not the only methodology used by sociological social psychology. Those adopting the Iowa School orientation may prefer a more quantitative approach that uses surveys and sophisticated social research scales for measuring attitudinal behavior. In this way, social behavior is described, analyzed, and explained with methods and approaches more like those employed in the hard sciences.

The relationship between theory and method is important for both traditions of social psychology. While each has traditionally opted for certain methodologies with the ultimate goal of explaining human behavior or finding its "causes" (while of course social psychologists may "crossover" and use the methods of their colleagues), both maintain, as all sciences do, that there is a necessary and crucial link between theory and research. The reciprocal relationship of theory and method within social psychology provides a foundation for current and future research. Without theory, research questions cannot be adequately formulated. Without research, the theory that is used to formulate the original question and guides future research can be neither supported nor rejected. Although such reasoning may sound circular, this relationship suggests a mutual dependency between theory and research that has long been recognized by the social and behavioral sciences.

Conducting research on human behavior is fraught with issues that are unlike those faced by the scientist of the biology, chemistry, or physics laboratory. It is assumed that humans are thinking, intentional, acting beings who have values, feelings, attitudes, opinions, and beliefs. While these characteristics are the lifeblood of social psychological research, they do present special problems. It is rather unrealistic to attempt to provide conclusive explanations of the reasons behind human behavior. At best, one may show that a certain independent variable (presumed cause) is correlated, or associated with, a certain dependent variable (presumed effect). However, to say that certain elements of the social world coincide or occur together certainly does not automatically mean that one causes the other. Therefore, the terms "cause" and "effect" are somewhat misleading in the social sciences, because they suggest that one may be quite sure that certain social variables are the causes and that others are the effects.

Research on human behavior is challenging for other reasons as well. First, research subjects do not merely respond to a particular experimental stimulus or an attitudinal questionnaire. Rather, they respond to these from their own unique circumstances or cultural milieu, and one cannot easily or adequately separate the task from the behavioral and attitudinal predispositions the subject might bring into the research or observation setting. Second, human subjects have intentions, desires, and self-perceptions that may influence a particular set of findings. A subject may wish to be cast in a favorable light or perhaps try to find out what the social psychologist is hoping to discover, and attempt to oblige him or her. Finally, there are obvious ethical issues that prevent certain forms of research from being conducted. One must always assure that informed consent has been given, and the subject will suffer no physical or psychological harm. Without such safeguards, there would is no place for work done by social psychologists. The costs of social science research should always be weighed against its probable benefits.

Of central concern to the social psychologist as a social scientist is the issue of human conduct or behavior and the motivations for engaging in certain action. Humans must coexist within the larger structures of society, which place certain expectations and restrictions upon behavior. In order for these conduct norms to be followed, social learning must take place. This learning may involve reinforcement, observation, and vicarious mechanisms for incorporating life's lessons. Once the standards of conduct are learned, they must be incorporated within the individual. This incorporation, often called "internalization," means that the person has come to understand the norm and the expectations associated with it. The individual is free to act yet only *within* certain boundaries. Understanding the combined nature of social system needs and individual needs is central to understanding the nature of conduct within society. Through an appreciation of such duality, one can better explain the human social condition.

THE SELECTIONS

The readings chosen for this first section of the book speak to the duality and vast nature of social psychology as a discipline. Each addresses a slightly different social psychological topic or issue. Some selections represent the sociological side of the discipline, while others offer the psychological perspective. Regardless of the social psychology represented, the common traits of society, social structure, and the individual remain constant.

The first two selections provide an introduction to the two "faces" of social psychology. The first, "Social Psychological Inquiry," is written by the sociological social psychologist Arthur G. Neal, who briefly and succinctly outlines the field. He not only discusses the sociological side of the discipline but also describes its psychological component. The second, "What Is Social Psychology?" by the psychological social psychologist Elliot Aronson, is a unique and thought-provoking presentation of social psychology that uses anecdotal and empirical examples.

The next two selections illustrate the impact of structure upon an individual's behavior. Both provide powerful testimony to the potential influence of environmental pressures on human behavior. Philip G. Zimbardo, in his now-famous prison study, "Pathology of Imprisonment," outlines the results of a mock prison created to measure the effects of the prison environment on behavior. Seemingly "normal" people changed and exhibited behavior that they would not have shown in any other setting. Environment is also the focus of D. L. Rosenhan's "On Being Sane in Insane Places." Rosenhan deals with people's social perceptions of others based on studies in actual mental hospitals rather than a mock setting.

As outlined above, theory is central to the understanding of social behavior. Herbert Blumer, who is credited with coining the term "symbolic interaction" to describe a prominent sociological social psychology theory, discusses in "Society as Symbolic Interaction" how symbol and social gesture are essential to understanding human social interaction, theory, and method.

The relationship between theory and method is an essential marriage for the purposes of social psychological research, as both branches of the field recognize. Martin T. Orne, in "On the Social Psychology of the Psychological Experiment," discusses the difficulties in conducting research on humans. He deals with social psychological research using experimentation, predominantly that done by psychologists, and possible demand characteristics that may influence the research setting.

The final two selections in the first part of this book also deal with research but in slightly different ways. In "Birthdate and Mortality," Bryan Byers, Richard A. Zeller, and Peggy Y. Byers combine social psychological theory with a quantitative research method in an attempt to understand better the influence of ceremonial occasions on mortality patterns. "Techniques of Neutralization" by Gresham M. Sykes and David Matza is a qualitative piece that proposes a theory of delinquency involving the use of rationalizations to excuse individual behavior in an attempt to avoid social control. This article is based in part on landmark theorizing conducted by the criminologist and social psychologist Edwin Sutherland. While the latter two present different approaches and issues, both share the domain of social psychology.

FOR FURTHER READING

Arthur Aron and Elaine N. Aron. *The Heart of Social Psychology.* Lexington, MA: Lexington Books, 1986.

Bernard Asbell. *What They Know About You.* New York: Random House, 1991.

Clyde W. Franklin. *Theoretical Perspectives in Social Psychology.* Boston: Little, Brown and Company, 1982.

Morton Hunt. *Profiles of Social Research: The Scientific Study of Human Interactions.* New York: Russell Sage Foundation, 1985.

Jay M. Jackson. *Social Psychology, Past and Present: An Integrative Orientation.* Hillsdale, NJ: Lawrence Earlbaum and Associates, Publishers, 1988.

1

Social Psychological Inquiry

ARTHUR G. NEAL

Social psychology is a legitimate child of the twentieth century. Its parents are respectable, genderless, and of equal status: each contributes to the qualities and attributes of the child, but the child has its own distinctive identity. The sociological parent makes a contribution through its emphasis on social structure, group membership, and social change. We are all a part of the structures studied by the sociologist, and the qualities of our lives are shaped by them. The psychological parent emphasizes thought processes, cognition, conditioning, and reinforcement. Psychology provides images of ourselves as thinking, minded, information-processing creatures. The field of social psychology can be thought of as representing the overlap between sociology and psychology; it draws on the characteristics of the two without being a carbon copy of either.

While social psychology has clearly established its legitimacy, it is also an oddity. Some say that social psychology has "a split personality"; others say that there are really two social psychologies rather than one (Stryker, 1977). A good deal of evidence could be assembled to support either view. That social psychology is a divided field is suggested in several ways. Many colleges and universities offer two courses bearing the identical label of social psychology but offer them in two separate departments. The faculty member who thinks of himself or herself as a social psychologist could have received graduate training exclusively in either a psychology or a sociology department.

Sociologists and psychologists have their own separate journals in social psychology. The psychologists publish in the *Journal of Social Psychology* and the sociologists publish in the *Social Psychological Quarterly*.

The divisions in social psychology are an outgrowth of the compartmentalization that has occurred in the modern university. Knowledge has become fragmented, broken down into small units, and extensively elaborated. There are both advantages and disadvantages to this process. The advantages are that one can explore topics in depth, that one can develop high levels of expertise in limited areas, and that one can direct resources toward solving specific, identifiable problems. The main disadvantages are that compartmentalization tends to draw boundaries, to generate vested interests, and to produce schisms within the academic community. Problems develop in communication across departmental boundaries; sociologists and psychologists fail to interact with each other; and researchers working on related problems frequently fail to exchange ideas or to share the excitement of their research. Students are also affected by the compartmentalization process. Knowledge is packaged in bits and pieces and frequently contained within the boundaries of a specific course and its requirements. If knowledge is to be integrated at all, the responsibility is left entirely up to the student.

We may understand the development of social psychology during the twentieth century as an outgrowth of the desire for insights into many facets of human behavior. Why do people do the things they do? Are there identifiable qualities underlying human nature? Are humans unique in the animal kingdom? Why do people go to war? What is the basis for human aggression? How do people differ in their personality characteristics? Is human behavior predictable? Why do people respond differently to similar situations? These are among the many questions still associated with social psychology in popular thinking. They are not among the basic questions social psychologists raise today, although these questions did receive a great deal of attention in the historical development of the field. We now know that many of these questions are unanswerable, or that we can give credible answers to them only through highly qualified restatements of the questions.

We have rejected many of the early theories in social psychology because they presented static models of human behavior. Today we recognize that social life is always in the process of change and development. What we see and do in the world around us is shaped by interactions with the many people in our lives, and these interactions continue throughout the life course. The study of social psychology today begins with an appreciation of the diversity of human behavior and with a recognition that humans construct their realities from their relationships with one another.

The unity of social psychology as a field lies in the objectives of inquiry. The overriding concerns are with understanding group processes and the many ways in which groups influence individual thought and behavior. Both psychologists and sociologists are concerned with relationships between the individual and society, with thought processes, with social learning, and with the situations in which social behavior occurs. We can clarify each of these major concerns through a comparison and contrast of some

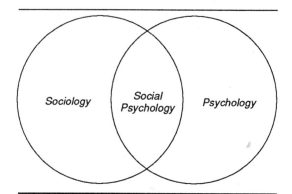

FIGURE 1   The Two Social Psychologies. The psychological version of social psychology bears an affinity to biology with its emphasis on physiological responses to environmental stimuli. In contrast, the sociological version of social psychology bears an affinity to history and anthropology with its emphasis on social organization and culture. The common domain of the two social psychologies lies with the overlapping interests in environmental context, cognitive processes, and social learning.

of the major theoretical perspectives within psychology and sociology.

The diversity within the field stems from variations in theoretical perspectives, in agendas for research, and in levels of analysis. Some social psychologists place primary emphasis on cognition and thought processes, while others emphasize behavior and the learning process; some prefer to concentrate on small groups, while others like to deal with broader social structures; some prefer the methods of experimental research, while others choose naturalistic observations or survey research. But whatever the differences among them, social psychologists are oriented toward describing, explaining, and understanding human behavior. The research of social psychology should enable us to see more clearly the social influences that guide and shape our own behavior as well as the behavior of those with whom we interact.

THE FACES OF SOCIAL PSYCHOLOGY

Thomas Kuhn (1970) emphasized the importance of paradigms for the growth and development of the various sciences. According to Kuhn, a *paradigm* is a constellation of assumptions, beliefs, values, theories, and research techniques shared by the members of a scientific community. In effect, "a paradigm is the fundamental images of a subject matter within a science" (Ritzer, 1975: 7). The paradigm identifies the topics for investigation, specifies the kinds of questions to raise, points to the rules or methods to follow, and suggests what will be found and why it is important. The conduct of research is thus a social enterprise that is guided by a set of principles based on consensus within a scientific community.

Social psychology is not comprised of a single scientific community but of several subcommunities. There is no single paradigm to serve as a guide to inquiry; instead, there are multiple paradigms and theoretical perspectives shared by some but not all social psychologists. As a multiple paradigm science, social psychology is characterized by multiple and overlapping theoretical perspectives that vary in degrees of compatibility with each other. The differences in paradigms are why we have at least two social psychologies rather than one. Even within psychology and sociology there are substantial variations in assumptions and topics for investigation. We can note the multiple theoretical perspectives by drawing on the topics that have emerged as the central ones for social psychological inquiry. These topics include concern for cognition, social learning, and social situations....

... The field of social psychology can be thought of as representing the overlap between psychology and sociology; it draws on the characteristics of the two fields without being a carbon copy or duplicate of either. The overriding concerns of social psychology are with understanding group processes and the many ways in which social interactions shape individual thought and behavior. The relationship between the individual and society, the social construction of reality, and the situational basis of human behavior are among the topics encompassed in the overlap between the two fields.

Social psychology is a multiple-paradigm science, in which several theoretical perspectives have been elaborated to serve as guides to inquiry. The major theoretical approaches, however, deal with some aspect or another of cognition, social learning, and social situations. Social psychologists are concerned with describing, predicting, and explaining human behavior. Cognitive theories emphasize mental processes and the content of ideas, while learning theories emphasize the contingencies of conditioning and reinforcement. The field of social psychology today is dominated by cognitive theories, both in psychology and sociology, although there are still many social psychologists who place primary emphasis on theories of learning. Symbolic interactionism is the major cognitive theory in sociology, while attribution theory and cognitive consistency theory occupy prominent places in psychology. Although there are major differences among them, each theory concentrates on reality construction as a major theme.

Social psychology offers a major set of perspectives on the multiple aspects of reality construction in social relationships. The scope of inquiry is broad enough to encompass the processes by which people form self-identities, by which they develop social attachments, by which the behavior of individuals results in rates or trends within the larger society. Through communication and interaction, individuals become both the producers and the products of social life in its varied forms.

Investigators use a variety of methods in social psychological inquiry. In each case, however, they emphasize systematic observation as a basis for drawing dependable conclusions about human behavior. Using participant observation, the researcher observes social life directly in natural settings, and obtains information through active involvement. Experimental studies, by way of contrast, use the laboratory to create the social conditions of concern and to test for the effects of variables on each other. Through survey research the social psychologist taps the distribution of attitudes and behavior in the general population by carefully drawing representative samples and using questionnaires. There are advantages and disadvantages to each of these methods, but all are directed toward clarifying some of the basic principles in the social construction of reality.

REFERENCES

Kuhn, Thomas. 1970. *The Structure of Scientific Revolutions*. Chicago: University of Chicago Press.

Ritzer, George. 1975. *Sociology: A Multiple Paradigm Science*. Englewood Cliffs, N.J.: Prentice-Hall.

Stryker, Sheldon. 1977. "Developments in 'Two Social Psychologies': Toward an Appreciation of Mutual Relevance," *Sociometry* 40 (June): 145–160.

2

What Is Social Psychology?

ELLIOT ARONSON

As far as we know, Aristotle was the first person to formulate some of the basic principles of social influence and persuasion; but, although he did say that man is a social animal, he was probably *not* the first person to make that observation. Moreover, chances are he was not the first person to marvel at the truth of that statement while simultaneously puzzling over its triteness and insubstantiality. Although it is certainly true that people are social animals, so are a host of other creatures, from ants and bees to monkeys and apes. What does it mean to say that humans are "social animals"? Let's look at some concrete examples:

A college student named Sam and four of his acquaintances are watching a presidential candidate make a speech on television. Sam is favorably impressed; he likes him better than the opposing candidate because of his sincerity. After the speech, one of the other students asserts that she was turned off by the candidate—that she considered him to be a complete phony—and that she prefers the opposing candidate. All of the others are quick to agree with her. Sam looks puzzled and a trifle distressed. Finally, he mumbles to his acquaintances, "I guess he didn't come across as sincere as I would have hoped."

A second-grade teacher stands before her class and asks, "What is the sum of six, nine, four, and eleven?" A boy in the third row puzzles over the question for several seconds, hesitates, raises his hand tentatively, and when called on, haltingly answers, "Thirty?" The teacher nods, smiles at him, says, "Nice work, Ted," and pastes a gold star on his forehead. She then asks the class, "What is the sum of seven, four, eight, three, and ten?" Without wasting a moment, Ted leaps to his feet and shouts, "Thirty-two!"

A four-year-old girl is given a toy drum for her birthday. After pounding on it for a few minutes, she casts it aside and studiously ignores it for the next several weeks. One day a friend comes to visit, picks up the drum, and is about to play with it. Suddenly the young "owner" tears the drum from her friend's grasp and proceeds to play with it as if it had always been her favorite toy.

A ten-year-old girl avidly consumes two bowls of Wheaties daily because an Olympic gymnastics champion endorses the product and implies that she owes her athletic prowess, in part, to the consumption of that particular brand of cereal.

A shopkeeper who has lived his entire life in a small town in Montana has never had any contact with real, live black people, but he "knows" they are shiftless, lazy, and oversexed.

Charlie, a high-school senior, has recently moved to a new city. He used to be quite popular, but not anymore. Although the kids at school are civil to him, they have not been particularly friendly. He is feeling lonely, insecure, and unattractive. One day, during lunch period, he finds himself at a table with two of his female classmates. One of them is warm, attractive, brilliant, and vivacious; he has been admiring her and daydreaming about her. For several weeks he has been longing for an opportunity to talk to her. The other young woman is not nearly as appealing. Charlie ignores the vivacious woman of his dreams and begins an earnest conversation with her companion.

Following the 1970 tragedy at Kent State University, in which four students were shot and killed by Ohio National Guardsmen while demonstrating against the war in Southeast Asia, a high-school teacher from Kent, Ohio, asserted that the slain students deserved to die. She made this statement even though she was well aware of the fact that at least two of the victims were not participating in the demonstration but were peacefully walking across campus at the time of the shooting. Indeed, she went on to say, "Anyone who appears on the streets of a city like Kent with long hair, dirty clothes, or barefooted deserves to be shot."[1]

When the Reverend Jim Jones sounded the alert, over 900 members of the People's Temple settlement in Guyana gathered before him. He knew that some of the members of a congressional investigation party had been murdered and that the sanctity and isolation of Jonestown would soon be violated. Jones proclaimed that it was time for them to die. Vats of poison were prepared, and amidst only scattered shouts of protest or acts of resistance, mothers and fathers administered the fatal mixture to their infants and children, drank it themselves, and lay down, arm in arm, waiting to die.

Mary has just turned nine. For her birthday, she received a Suzie Homemaker baking and cooking set, complete with "her own little oven." Her parents chose this present because she seems very interested in culinary things and is forever helping mommy set the table, prepare the meals, and clean the house. "Isn't it wonderful," says Mary's father, "how at age nine she is already interested in being a housewife? Little girls must have housewifery built into their genes. Those feminists don't know what they're talking about."

George Woods is black. When he and I were growing up together in Massachusetts in the 1940s, he considered himself a "colored boy" and felt inferior to his white friends. There were many reasons for this feeling. That George was treated like an inferior by the white community had a direct influence upon him, of course; a number of other forces influenced him less directly. In those days, George could entertain himself by turning on the radio and listening to "Amos 'n Andy," a radio show in which black adults were portrayed as naive children, as stupid, lazy, and illiterate, but rather cute—not unlike friendly domesticated animals. The black characters were, of course, played by white actors. In films, George could see the stereotyped "colored man," usually a chauffeur or some other menial. A standard plot would have the "colored man" accompany the white hero into a haunted house, where they would hear a strange and ominous noise: The camera pans in on the "colored man's" face; his eyes grow large with fright; he screams, "Feets, do your stuff!" and dashes through the door, not taking time to open it first. We can only guess what George experienced while viewing these films in the company of his white friends.

Most of George's acquaintances were blacks who "knew their place." They were obsequious to whites, used hair straightener in an attempt to look less black, and cared little about their African heritage. The idea was to be white, a goal which, of course, was unattainable. I would be amazed if this climate did not lower George's self-concept because such changes in self-concept are not atypical: A famous study of black children in the forties by Kenneth and Mamie Clark showed that, as early as age three, many of the children had learned to feel inferior to whites.[2]

Things change. Although discrimination and unfairness are still very much a part of our society, George Woods's children, growing up in the 1970s and 1980s, did not face quite the same prospect as George himself did. The mass media now depict blacks in roles that are not exclusively menial; and a new pride in blackness has emerged, along with an interest in, and enthusiasm about, Afro-American history and culture. The society is influencing George's children in a much different way than it influenced George.

Although things do change, we should not be complacent in the belief that all changes are in a linear, humanistic direction.

On August 30, 1936, during the Spanish Civil War, a single plane bombed Madrid. There were several casualties, but no one was killed. The world was profoundly shocked by the idea of a congested city being attacked from the air. Newspaper editorials around the world expressed the general horror and indignation of the citizenry. Only nine years later, U.S. planes dropped nuclear bombs on Hiroshima and Nagasaki. More than one hundred thousand people were killed and countless thousands suffered severe injuries. Shortly thereafter, a poll indicated that only 4.5 percent of the U.S. population felt we should not have used those weapons, and an astonishing 22.7 percent felt we should have used many more of them before Japan had a chance to surrender.[3] Clearly, something had happened during those nine years to influence opinion.

A DEFINITION

What is social psychology? There are almost as many definitions of social psychology as there are social psychologists. Instead of listing some of these definitions, it might be more informative to let the subject matter define the field. The examples presented in the preceding pages are all illustrations of sociopsychological situations. As diverse as these situations may be, they do contain one common factor: social influence. The opinion of Sam's friends on the merits of the presidential candidate influenced Sam's judgment (or at least his public statement regarding that judgment). The rewards emanating from the teacher influenced the speed and vigor of Ted's classroom responses. The four-year-old seemed to find her toy drum more attractive because of the inadvertent influence of her friend's interest. The Olympic athlete's influence on our Wheaties-eating youngster, on the other hand, was far from inadvertent; rather, it was intentionally designed to motivate her to convince her mother to buy Wheaties. That Charlie ig-

nored the woman of his dreams almost certainly has something to do with his fear of rejection, the way he was feeling about himself, and his implicit assumption about the relative likelihood of being rejected by either of the two women. The Montana shopkeeper was certainly not born with an unflattering stereotype of black people in his head—somebody, somehow, put it there. Exactly how the high-school teacher in Kent, Ohio, came to believe that innocent people deserved to die is a fascinating and frightening question; for now, let us simply say that this belief was probably influenced by her own indirect complicity in the tragic events on campus. A still more disturbing question arises from Jonestown: What forces could compel parents to help poison their children? Again, this is a complex question to which I hope to provide some partial answers and insights as this text unfolds. Turning to little Mary and her Suzie Homemaker set, it is conceivable, as Mary's father says, that "housewifery" is genetic, but it is far more likely that, from infancy onward, Mary was rewarded and encouraged every time she expressed an interest in such traditionally "feminine" things as cooking, sewing, and dolls—to a far greater extent than if she expressed an interest in football, boxing, and chemistry. It is also reasonable to assume that, if Mary's kid brother had shown an interest in "housewifery," he would *not* have received a Suzie Homemaker set for *his* birthday. Also, as with young George Woods, who felt inferior to his playmates, Mary's self-image could have been shaped by the mass media, which tend to depict women in roles that the culture encourages them to play: housewife, secretary, nurse, schoolteacher—the mass media rarely depict women as biochemists, college professors, or business executives. If we compare the young George Woods with his children, we will see that the self-images of minority-group members can change, and these changes can influence and be influenced by changes in the mass media and changes in the attitudes of the general population. This, of course, is graphically illustrated by the opinions of Americans about the use of nuclear weapons in 1945.

The key phrase in the preceding paragraph is "social influence." And this becomes our working definition of social psychology: the influences that people have upon the beliefs or behavior of others. Using this is our definition, we will attempt to understand many of the phenomena described in the preceding illustrations. How are people influenced? Why do they accept influence—or, put another way, what's in it for them? What are the variables that increase or decrease the effectiveness of social influence? Does such influence have a permanent effect, or is it merely transitory? What are the variables that increase or decrease the permanence of the effects of social influence? Can the same principles be applied equally to the attitudes of the high-school teacher in Kent, Ohio, and to the toy preferences of young children? How does one person come to like another person? Is it through these same processes that we come to like our new sports car or a box of Wheaties? How does a person develop prejudices against an ethnic or racial group? Is it akin to liking—but in reverse—or does it involve an entirely different set of psychological processes?

Most people are interested in questions of this sort; in a sense, therefore, most people are social psychologists. Because most of us spend a good deal of our time interacting with other people—being influenced by them, influencing them, being delighted, amused, and angered by them—it is natural that most of us develop hypotheses about social behavior. Although most amateur social psychologists test these hypotheses to their own satisfaction, these "tests" lack the rigor and impartiality of careful scientific investigation. Often, the results of scientific research are identical with what most people

"know" to be true. This is not surprising; conventional wisdom is usually based upon shrewd observation that has stood the test of time.

In fact, when you are reading the experiments in this volume, you may occasionally find yourself thinking: "That's obvious— why did they spend time and money to find that out?" There are several reasons why we do experiments, even though the findings often seem unsurprising. For one thing, we are all susceptible to the *hindsight effect*, which refers to our tendency to overestimate our powers of prediction, once we know the outcome of a given event. For example, research has shown that on the day after an election, when people are asked which candidate they would have picked to win, they almost always believe they would have picked the actual winners—even though the day *before* the election, their predictions wouldn't have been nearly as accurate.[4] Similarly, the outcome of an experiment almost always seems more predictable once we have the results in hand, than if we had been asked to predict the results without the benefit of hindsight.

In addition, it is important to conduct research—even if the results seem obvious— because many of the things we "know" to be true turn out to be false when carefully investigated. Although it seems reasonable, for example, to assume that people who are threatened with severe punishment for engaging in a certain behavior might eventually learn to despise that behavior, it turns out that when this question is studied scientifically, just the reverse is true: People who are threatened with mild punishment develop a dislike for the forbidden behavior; people who are severely threatened show, if anything, a slight *increase* in liking for the forbidden behavior. Likewise, most of us, from our own experience, would guess that, if we overheard someone saying nice things about us (behind our backs), we would tend to like that person—all other things being equal. This turns out to be true. But what is equally true is that we tend to like that person even more if some of the remarks we overhear are anything *but* nice.

In their attempts to understand human social behavior, professional social psychologists have a great advantage over most amateur social psychologists. Although, like the amateur, they usually begin with careful observation, they can go far beyond that. They do not need to wait for things to happen so that they can observe how people respond; they can, in fact, *make* things happen. That is, they can conduct an experiment in which scores of people are subjected to particular conditions (for example, a severe threat or a mild threat; overhearing nice things or overhearing a combination of nice and nasty things). Moreover, they can do this in situations in which everything can be held constant except the particular conditions being investigated. Professional social psychologists can, therefore, draw conclusions based on data far more precise and numerous than those available to the amateur social psychologist, who must depend upon observations of events that occur randomly and under complex circumstances. . . .

PEOPLE WHO DO CRAZY THINGS ARE NOT NECESSARILY CRAZY

The social psychologist studies social situations that affect people's behavior. Occasionally, these natural situations become focused into pressures so great they cause people to behave in ways easily classifiable as abnormal. When I say "people" I mean very large numbers of people. To my mind, it does not increase our understanding of human behavior to classify these people as psychotic. It is much more useful to try to understand the nature of the situation and the processes that were operating to produce the behavior. This leads us to Aronson's first law: "People

who do crazy things are not necessarily crazy."

Let us take, as an illustration, the Ohio schoolteacher who asserted that the four Kent State students deserved to die. I don't think she was alone in this belief—and although all the people who hold this belief *may* be psychotic, I seriously doubt it, and I doubt that so classifying them does much to enhance our understanding of the phenomenon. Similarly, in the aftermath of the Kent slayings, the rumor spread that the slain girls were pregnant anyway—so that it was a blessing they died—and that all four of the students were filthy and so covered with lice that the mortuary attendants became nauseated while examining the bodies. These rumors, of course, were totally false. But, according to James Michener,[5] they spread like wildfire. Were all the people who believed and spread these rumors insane?

Ellen Berscheid[6] has observed that people have a tendency to explain unpleasant behavior by attaching a label to the perpetrator ("crazy," "sadistic," or whatever), thereby excluding that person from the rest of "us nice people." In that way, we need not worry about the unpleasant behavior, because it has nothing to do with us nice folks. According to Berscheid, the danger in this kind of thinking is that it tends to make us smug about our own susceptibility to situational pressures producing unpleasant behavior, and it leads to a rather simple-minded approach to the solution of social problems. Specifically, such a simple-minded solution might include the development of a set of diagnostic tests to determine who is a liar, who is a sadist, who is corrupt, who is a maniac; social action might then consist of identifying these people and relegating them to the appropriate institutions. Of course, this is not to say psychosis does not exist or that psychotics should never be institutionalized. Nor am I saying all people are the same and respond exactly as crazily to the same intense social pressures. To repeat, what I am saying is that some situational variables can move a great proportion of us "normal" adults to behave in very unappetizing ways. It is of paramount importance that we attempt to understand these variables and the processes producing unpleasant behavior.

An illustration might be useful. Think of a prison. Consider the guards. What are they like? Chances are, most people would imagine prison guards to be tough, callous, unfeeling people. Some might even consider them to be cruel, tyrannical, and sadistic. People who take this kind of *dispositional* view of the world might suggest that the reason people become guards is to have an opportunity to exercise their cruelty with relative impunity. Picture the prisoners. What are they like? Rebellious? Docile? No matter what specific pictures exist inside our heads, the point is there *are* pictures there—and most of us believe that the prisoners and the guards are quite different from us in character and personality.

This *may* be true, but don't be too sure. In a dramatic piece of research, Philip Zimbardo and his students created a simulated prison in the basement of the Psychology Department at Stanford University. Into this "prison" he brought a group of normal, mature, stable, intelligent young men. By flipping a coin, Zimbardo designated one-half of them prisoners and one-half of them guards, and they lived as such for several days. What happened? Let's allow Zimbardo to tell us in his own words:

> At the end of only six days we had to close down our mock prison because what we saw was frightening. It was no longer apparent to us or most of the subjects where they ended

and their roles began. The majority had indeed become "prisoners" or "guards," no longer able to clearly differentiate between role-playing and self. There were dramatic changes in virtually every aspect of their behavior, thinking and feeling. In less than a week, the experience of imprisonment undid (temporarily) a lifetime of learning; human values were suspended, self-concepts were challenged, and the ugliest, most base, pathological side of human nature surfaced. We were horrified because we saw some boys ("guards") treat other boys as if they were despicable animals, taking pleasure in cruelty, while other boys ("prisoners") became servile, dehumanized robots who thought only of escape, of their own individual survival, and of their mounting hatred of the guards.[7]

NOTES

1. Michener, J. (1971). *Kent State: What happened and why*. New York: Random House.
2. Clark, K., & Clark, M. (1947). Racial identification and preference in Negro children. In T. M. Newcomb & E. L. Hartley (Eds.), *Readings in social psychology* (pp. 169–178). New York: Holt.
3. Harris, J. (1970). *Hiroshima: A study in science, politics, and the ethics of war*. Menlo Park, CA: Addison-Wesley.
4. Powell, J. L. (1988). A test of the knew-it-all-along effect in the 1984 presidential and statewide elections. *Journal of Applied Social Psychology, 18*, 760–773.
5. Michener, *Kent State*.
6. Ellen Berscheid; personal communication.
7. Zimbardo, P. (1971, October 25). *The psychological power and pathology of imprisonment* (p. 3). Statement prepared for the U.S. House of Representatives Committee on the Judiciary; Subcommittee No. 3: Hearings on Prison Reform, San Francisco, CA.

3

Pathology of Imprisonment

PHILIP G. ZIMBARDO

I was recently released from solitary confinement after being held therein for 37 months [months!]. A silent system was imposed upon me and to even whisper to the man in the next cell resulted in being beaten by guards, sprayed with chemical mace, black-jacked, stomped and thrown into a strip-cell naked to sleep on a concrete floor without bedding, covering, wash basin or even a toilet. The floor served as toilet and bed, and even there the silent system was enforced. To let a moan escape your lips because of the pain and discomfort ... resulted in another beating. I spent not days, but months there during my 37 months in solitary. ... I have filed every writ possible against the administrative acts of brutality. The state courts have all denied the petitions. Because of my refusal to let the things die down and forget all that happened during my 37 months in solitary ... I am the most hated prisoner in [this] penitentiary, and called a "hard-core incorrigible."

Maybe I am an incorrigible, but if true, it's because I would rather die than to accept being treated as less than a human being. I have never complained of my prison sentence as being unjustified except through legal means of appeals. I have never put a knife on a guard's throat and demanded my release. I know that thieves must be punished and I don't justify stealing, even though I am a thief myself. But now I don't think I will be a thief when I am released. No, I'm not rehabilitated. It's just that I no longer think of becoming wealthy by stealing. I now only think of killing—killing those who have beaten me and treated me as if I were a dog. I hope and pray for the sake of my own soul and future life of freedom that I am able to overcome the bitterness and hatred which eats daily at my soul, but I know to overcome it will not be easy.

This eloquent plea for prison reform—for humane treatment of human beings, for the basic dignity that is the right of every American—came to me secretly in a letter from a prisoner who cannot be identified because he is still in a state correctional institution. He sent it to me because he read of an experiment I recently conducted at Stanford University. In an attempt to understand just what it means psychologically to be a prisoner or a prison guard, Craig Haney, Curt Banks, Dave Jaffe and I created our own prison. We carefully screened over 70 volunteers who answered an ad in a Palo Alto city newspaper and ended up with about two dozen young men who were selected to be part of this study. They were mature, emotionally stable, normal, intelligent college students from middle-class homes throughout the United States and Canada. They appeared to represent the cream of the crop of this generation. None had any criminal record and all were relatively homogeneous on many dimensions initially.

Half were arbitrarily designated as prisoners by a flip of a coin, the others as guards. These were the roles they were to play in our simulated prison. The guards were made aware of the potential seriousness and danger of the situation and their own vulnerability. They made up their own formal rules for maintaining law, order and respect, and were generally free to improvise new ones during their eight-hour, three-man shifts. The prisoners were unexpectedly picked up at their homes by a city policeman in a squad car, searched, handcuffed, fingerprinted, booked at the Palo Alto station house and taken blindfolded to our jail. There they were stripped, deloused, put into a uniform, given a number and put into a cell with two other prisoners where they expected to live for the next two weeks. The pay was good ($15 a day) and their motivation was to make money.

We observed and recorded on videotape the events that occurred in the prison, and we interviewed and tested the prisoners and guards at various points throughout the study. Some of the videotapes of the actual encounters between the prisoners and guards were seen on the NBC News feature "Chronolog" on November 26, 1971.

At the end of only six days we had to close down our mock prison because what we saw was frightening. It was no longer apparent to most of the subjects (or to us) where reality ended and their roles began. The majority had indeed become prisoners or guards, no longer able to clearly differentiate between role playing and self. There were dramatic changes in virtually every aspect of their behavior, thinking and feeling. In less than a week the experience of imprisonment undid (temporarily) a lifetime of learning; human values were suspended, self-concepts were challenged and the ugliest, most base, pathological side of human nature surfaced. We were horrified because we saw some boys (guards) treat others as if they were despicable animals, taking pleasure in cruelty, while other boys (prisoners) became servile, dehumanized robots who thought only of escape, of their own individual survival and of their mounting hatred for the guards.

We had to release three prisoners in the first four days because they had such acute situational traumatic reactions as hysterical crying, confusion in thinking and severe de-

pression. Others begged to be paroled, and all but three were willing to forfeit all the money they had earned if they could be paroled. By then (the fifth day) they had been so programmed to think of themselves as prisoners that when their request for parole was denied, they returned docilely to their cells. Now, had they been thinking as college students acting in an oppressive experiment, they would have quit once they no longer wanted the $15 a day we used as our only incentive. However, the reality was not quitting an experiment but "being paroled by the parole board from the Stanford County Jail." By the last days, the earlier solidarity among the prisoners (systematically broken by the guards) dissolved into "each man for himself." Finally, when one of their fellows was put in solitary confinement (a small closet) for refusing to eat, the prisoners were given a choice by one of the guards: give up their blankets and the incorrigible prisoner would be let out, or keep their blankets and he would be kept in all night. They voted to keep their blankets and to abandon their brother.

About a third of the guards became tyrannical in their arbitrary use of power, in enjoying their control over other people. They were corrupted by the power of their roles and became quite inventive in their techniques of breaking the spirit of the prisoners and making them feel they were worthless. Some of the guards merely did their jobs as tough but fair correctional officers, and several were good guards from the prisoners' point of view since they did them small favors and were friendly. However, no good guard ever interfered with a command by any of the bad guards; they never intervened on the side of the prisoners, they never told the others to ease off because it was only an experiment, and they never even came to me as prison superintendent or experimenter in charge to complain. In part, they were good because the others were bad; they needed the others to help establish their own egos in a positive light. In a sense, the good guards perpetuated the prison more than the other guards because their own needs to be liked prevented them from disobeying or violating the implicit guards' code. At the same time, the act of befriending the prisoners created a social reality which made the prisoners less likely to rebel.

By the end of the week the experiment had become a reality, as if it were a Pirandello play directed by Kafka that just keeps going after the audience has left. The consultant for our prison, Carlo Prescott, an ex-convict with 16 years of imprisonment in California's jails, would get so depressed and furious each time he visited our prison, because of its psychological similarity to his experiences, that he would have to leave. A Catholic priest who was a former prison chaplain in Washington, D. C. talked to our prisoners after four days and said they were just like the other first-timers he had seen.

But in the end, I called off the experiment not because of the horror I saw out there in the prison yard, but because of the horror of realizing that *I* could have easily traded places with the most brutal guard or become the weakest prisoner full of hatred at being so powerless that I could not eat, sleep or go to the toilet without permission of the authorities. *I* could have become Calley at My Lai, George Jackson at San Quentin, one of the men at Attica or the prisoner quoted at the beginning of this article.

Individual behavior is largely under the control of social forces and environmental contingencies rather than personality traits, character, will power or other empirically unvalidated constructs. Thus we create an illusion of freedom by attributing more internal control to ourselves, to the individual, than actually exists. We thus underestimate the power and pervasiveness of situational controls over behavior because: a) they are often non-obvious and subtle, b) we can often avoid entering situations where we might be so controlled, c) we label as "weak"

or "deviant" people in those situations who do behave differently from how we believe we would.

Each of us carries around in our heads a favorable self-image in which we are essentially just, fair, humane and understanding. For example, we could not imagine inflicting pain on others without much provocation or hurting people who had done nothing to us, who in fact were even liked by us. However, there is a growing body of social psychological research which underscores the conclusion derived from this prison study. Many people, perhaps the majority, can be made to do almost anything when put into psychologically compelling situations—regardless of their morals, ethics, values, attitudes, beliefs or personal convictions. My colleague, Stanley Milgram, has shown that more than 60 percent of the population will deliver what they think is a series of painful electric shocks to another person even after the victim cries for mercy, begs them to stop and then apparently passes out. The subjects complained that they did not want to inflict more pain but blindly obeyed the command of the authority figure (the experimenter) who said that they must go on. In my own research on violence, I have seen mild-mannered co-eds repeatedly give shocks (which they thought were causing pain) to another girl, a stranger whom they had rated very favorably, simply by being made to feel anonymous and put in a situation where they were expected to engage in this activity.

Observers of these and similar experimental situations never predict their outcomes and estimate that it is unlikely that they themselves would behave similarly. They can be so confident only when they were outside the situation. However, since the majority of people in these studies do act in non-rational, non-obvious ways, it follows that the majority of observers would also succumb to the social psychological forces in the situation.

With regard to prisons, we can state that the mere act of assigning labels to people and putting them into a situation where those labels acquire validity and meaning is sufficient to elicit pathological behavior. This pathology is not predictable from any available diagnostic indicators we have in the social sciences, and is extreme enough to modify in very significant ways fundamental attitudes and behavior. The prison situation, as presently arranged, is guaranteed to generate severe enough pathological reactions in both guards and prisoners as to debase their humanity, lower their feelings of self-worth and make it difficult for them to be part of a society outside of their prison.

For years our national leaders have been pointing to the enemies of freedom, to the fascist or communist threat to the American way of life. In so doing they have overlooked the threat of social anarchy that is building within our own country without any outside agitation. As soon as a person comes to the realization that he is being imprisoned by his society or individuals in it, then, in the best American tradition, he demands liberty and rebels, accepting death as an alternative. The third alternative, however, is to allow oneself to become a good prisoner—docile, cooperative, uncomplaining, conforming in thought and complying in deed.

Our prison authorities now point to the militant agitators who are still vaguely referred to as part of some communist plot, as the irresponsible, incorrigible troublemakers. They imply that there would be no trouble, riots, hostages or deaths if it weren't for this small band of bad prisoners. In other words, then, everything would return to "normal" again in the life of our nation's prisons if they could break these men.

The riots in prison are coming from within—from within every man and woman who refuses to let the system turn them into an object, a number, a thing or a no-thing. It is not communist inspired, but inspired by the spirit of American freedom. No man

wants to be enslaved. To be powerless, to be subject to the arbitrary exercise of power, to not be recognized as a human being is to be a slave.

To be a militant prisoner is to become aware that the physical jails are but more blatant extensions of the forms of social and psychological oppression experienced daily in the nation's ghettos. They are trying to awaken the conscience of the nation to the ways in which the American ideals are being perverted, apparently in the name of justice but actually under the banner of apathy, fear and hatred. If we do not listen to the pleas of the prisoners at Attica to be treated like human beings, then we have all become brutalized by our priorities for property rights over human rights. The consequence will not only be more prison riots but a loss of all those ideals on which this country was founded.

The public should be aware that they own the prisons and that their business is failing. The 70 percent recidivism rate and the escalation in severity of crimes committed by graduates of our prisons are evidence that current prisons fail to rehabilitate the inmates in any positive way. Rather, they are breeding grounds for hatred of the establishment, a hatred that makes every citizen a target of violent assault. Prisons are a bad investment for us taxpayers. Until now we have not cared, we have turned over to wardens and prison authorities the unpleasant job of keeping people who threaten us out of our sight. Now we are shocked to learn that their management practices have failed to improve the product and instead turn petty thieves into murderers. We must insist upon new management or improved operating procedures.

The cloak of secrecy should be removed from the prisons. Prisoners claim they are brutalized by the guards, guards say it is a lie. Where is the impartial test of the truth in such a situation? Prison officials have forgotten that they work for us, that they are only public servants whose salaries are paid by our taxes. They act as if it is their prison, like a child with a toy he won't share. Neither lawyers, judges, the legislature nor the public is allowed into prisons to ascertain the truth unless the visit is sanctioned by authorities and until all is prepared for their visit. I was shocked to learn that my request to join a congressional investigating committee's tour of San Quentin and Soledad was refused, as was that of the news media.

There should be an ombudsman in every prison, not under the pay or control of the prison authority, and responsible only to the courts, state legislature and the public. Such a person could report on violations of constitutional human rights.

Guards must be given better training than they now receive for the difficult job society imposes upon them. To be a prison guard as now constituted is to be put in a situation of constant threat from within the prison, with no social recognition from the society at large. As was shown graphically at Attica, prison guards are also prisoners of the system who can be sacrificed to the demands of the public to be punitive and the needs of politicians to preserve an image. Social scientists and business administrators should be called upon to design and help carry out this training.

The relationship between the individual (who is sentenced by the courts to a prison term) and his community must be maintained. How can a prisoner return to a dynamically changing society that most of us cannot cope with after being out of it for a number of years? There should be more community involvement in these rehabilitation centers, more ties encouraged and promoted between the trainees and family and friends, more educational opportunities to prepare them for returning to their communities as more valuable members of it than they were before they left.

Finally, the main ingredient necessary to effect any change at all in prison reform, in the rehabilitation of a single prisoner or even in the optimal development of a child is caring. Reform must start with people—especially people with power—caring about the well-being of others. Underneath the toughest, society-hating convict, rebel or anarchist is a human being who wants his existence to be recognized by his fellows and who wants someone else to care about whether he lives or dies and to grieve if he lives imprisoned rather than lives free.

4

On Being Sane in Insane Places

D. L. ROSENHAN

If sanity and insanity exist, how shall we know them?

The question is neither capricious nor itself insane. However much we may be personally convinced that we can tell the normal from the abnormal, the evidence is simply not compelling. It is commonplace, for example, to read about murder trials wherein eminent psychiatrists for the defense are contradicted by equally eminent psychiatrists for the prosecution on the matter of the defendant's sanity. More generally, there are a great deal of conflicting data on the reliability, utility, and meaning of such terms as "sanity," "insanity," "mental illness," and "schizophrenia" (1). Finally, as early as 1934, Benedict suggested that normality and abnormality are not universal (2). What is viewed as normal in one culture may be seen as quite aberrant in another. Thus, notions of normality and abnormality may not be quite as accurate as people believe they are.

To raise questions regarding normality and abnormality is in no way to question the fact that some behaviors are deviant or odd. Murder is deviant. So, too, are hallucinations. Nor does raising such questions deny the existence of the personal anguish that is often associated with "mental illness." Anxiety and depression exist. Psychological suffering exists. But normality and abnormality, sanity and insanity, and the diagnoses that flow from them may be less substantive than many believe them to be.

At its heart, the question of whether the sane can be distinguished from the insane (and whether degrees of insanity can be distinguished from each other) is a simple matter: do the salient characteristics that lead to diagnoses reside in the patients themselves or in the environments and contexts in which observers find them? From Bleuler, through Kretchmer, through the formulators of the recently revised *Diagnostic and Statistical Manual* of the American Psychiatric Association, the belief has been strong that patients present symptoms, that those symptoms can be categorized, and, implicitly, that the sane are distinguishable from the insane. More recently, however, this belief has been questioned. Based in part on theoretical and anthropological considerations, but also on philosophical, legal, and therapeutic ones, the view has grown that psychological categorization of mental illness is useless at best and downright harmful, misleading, and pejorative at worst. Psychiatric diagnoses, in this view, are in the minds of the observers and are not valid summaries of characteristics displayed by the observed (3–5).

Gains can be made in deciding which of these is more nearly accurate by getting normal people (that is, people who do not have, and have never suffered, symptoms of serious psychiatric disorders) admitted to psychiatric hospitals and then determining whether they were discovered to be sane and, if so, how. If the sanity of such pseudopatients were always detected, there would be prima facie evidence that a sane individual can be distinguished from the insane context in which he is found. Normality (and presumably abnormality) is distinct enough that it can be recognized wherever it occurs, for it is carried within the person. If, on the other hand, the sanity of the pseudopatients were never discovered, serious difficulties would arise for those who support traditional modes of psychiatric diagnosis. Given that the hospital staff was not incompetent, that the pseudopatient had been behaving as sanely as he had been outside of the hospital, and that it had never been previously suggested that he belonged in a psychiatric hospital, such an unlikely outcome would support the view that psychiatric diagnosis betrays little about the patient but much about the environment in which an observer finds him.

This article describes such an experiment. Eight sane people gained secret admission to 12 different hospitals (6). Their diagnostic experiences constitute the data of the first part of this article; the remainder is devoted to a description of their experiences in psychiatric institutions. Too few psychiatrists and psychologists, even those who have worked in such hospitals, know what the experience is like. They rarely talk about it with former patients, perhaps because they distrust information coming from the previously insane. Those who have worked in psychiatric hospitals are likely to have adapted so thoroughly to the settings that they are insensitive to the impact of that experience. And while there have been occasional reports of researchers who submitted themselves to psychiatric hospitalization (7), these researchers have commonly remained in the hospitals for short periods of time, often with the knowledge of the hospital staff. It is difficult to know the extent to which they were treated like patients or like research colleagues. Nevertheless, their reports about the inside of the psychiatric hospital have been valuable. This article extends those efforts.

PSEUDOPATIENTS AND THEIR SETTINGS

The eight pseudopatients were a varied group. One was a psychology graduate student in his 20's. The remaining seven were older and "established." Among them were three psychologists, a pediatrician, a psychiatrist, a painter, and a housewife. Three pseudopatients were women, five were men. All of them employed pseudonyms, lest their alleged diagnoses embarrass them later. Those who were in mental health professions alleged another occupation in order to avoid the special attentions that might be accorded by staff, as a matter of courtesy or caution, to ailing colleagues (8). With the exception of myself (I was the first pseudopatient and my presence was known to the hospital administrator and chief psychologist and, so far I can tell, to them alone), the presence of pseudopatients and the nature of the research program was not known to the hospital staffs (9).

The settings were similarly varied. In order to generalize the findings, admission into a variety of hospitals was sought. The 12 hospitals in the sample were located in five different states on the East and West coasts. Some were old and shabby, some were quite new. Some were research-oriented, others not. Some had good staff-patient ratios, others were quite understaffed. Only one was a strictly private hospital. All of the others were supported by state or federal funds or, in one instance, by university funds.

After calling the hospital for an appointment, the pseudopatient arrived at the admissions office complaining that he had been hearing voices. Asked what the voices said, he replied that they were often unclear, but as far as he could tell they said "empty," "hollow," and "thud." The voices were unfamiliar and were of the same sex as the pseudopatient. The choice of these symptoms was occasioned by their apparent similarity to existential symptoms. Such symptoms are alleged to arise from painful concerns about the perceived meaninglessness of one's life. It is as if the hallucinating person were saying, "My life is empty and hollow." The choice of these symptoms was also determined by the *absence* of a single report of existential psychoses in the literature.

Beyond alleging the symptoms and falsifying name, vocation, and employment, no further alterations of person, history, or circumstances were made. The significant events of the pseudopatient's life history were presented as they had actually occurred. Relationships with parents and siblings, with spouse and children, with people at work and in school, consistent with the aforementioned exceptions, were described as they were or had been. Frustrations and upsets were described along with joys and satisfactions. These facts are important to remember. If anything, they strongly biased the subsequent results in favor of detecting sanity, since none of their histories or current behaviors were seriously pathological in any way.

Immediately upon admission to the psychiatric ward, the pseudopatient ceased simulating *any* symptoms of abnormality. In some cases, there was a brief period of mild nervousness and anxiety, since none of the pseudopatients really believed that they would be admitted so easily. Indeed, their shared fear was that they would be immediately exposed as frauds and greatly embarrassed. Moreover, many of them had never visited a psychiatric ward; even those who had, nevertheless had some genuine fears about what might happen to them. Their nervousness, then, was quite appropriate to the novelty of the hospital setting, and it abated rapidly.

Apart from that short-lived nervousness, the pseudopatient behaved on the ward as he "normally" behaved. The pseudopatient spoke to patients and staff as he might ordinarily. Because there is uncommonly little to do on a psychiatric ward, he attempted to engage others in conversation. When asked by staff how he was feeling, he indicated that he was fine, that he no longer experienced symptoms. He responded to instructions from attendants, to calls for medication (which was not swallowed), and to dining-hall instructions. Beyond such activities as were available to him on the admissions ward, he spent his time writing down his observations about the ward, its patients, and the staff. Initially these notes were written "secretly," but as it soon became clear that no one much cared, they were subsequently written on standard tablets of paper in such public places as the dayroom. No secret was made of these activities.

The pseudopatient, very much as a true psychiatric patient, entered a hospital with no foreknowledge of when he would be discharged. Each was told that he would have to get out by his own devices, essentially by convincing the staff that he was sane. The psychological stresses associated with hospitalization were considerable, and all but one of the pseudopatients desired to be discharged almost immediately after being admitted. They were, therefore, motivated not only to behave sanely, but to be paragons of cooperation. That their behavior was in no way disruptive is confirmed by nursing reports, which have been obtained on most of the patients. These reports uniformly indicate that the patients were "friendly," "cooperative," and "exhibited no abnormal indications."

THE NORMAL ARE NOT DETECTABLY SANE

Despite their public "show" of sanity, the pseudopatients were never detected. Admitted, except in one case, with a diagnosis of schizophrenia (10), each was discharged with a diagnosis of schizophrenia "in remission." The label "in remission" should in no way be dismissed as a formality, for at no time during any hospitalization had any question been raised about any pseudo-patient's simulation. Nor are there any indications in the hospital records that the pseudopatient's status was suspect. Rather, the evidence is strong that, once labeled schizophrenic, the pseudopatient was stuck with that label. If the pseudopatient was to be discharged, he must naturally be "in remission"; but he was not sane, nor, in the institution's view, had he ever been sane.

The uniform failure to recognize sanity cannot be attributed to the quality of the hospitals, for, although there were considerable variations among them, several are considered excellent. Nor can it be alleged that there was simply not enough time to observe the pseudopatients. Length of hospitalization ranged from 7 to 52 days, with an average of 19 days. The pseudopatients were not, in fact, carefully observed, but this failure clearly speaks more to traditions within psychiatric hospitals than to lack of opportunity.

Finally, it cannot be said that the failure to recognize the pseudopatients' sanity was due to the fact that they were not behaving sanely. While there was clearly some tension present in all of them, their daily visitors could detect no serious behavioral consequences—nor, indeed, could other patients. It was quite common for the patients to "detect" the pseudopatients' sanity. During the first three hospitalizations, when accurate counts were kept, 35 of a total of 118 patients on the admissions ward voiced their suspicions, some vigorously. "You're not crazy. You're a journalist, or a professor [referring to the continual note-taking]. You're checking up on the hospital." While most of the patients were reassured by the pseudopatient's insistence that he had been sick before he came in but was fine now, some continued to believe that the pseudopatient was sane throughout his hospitalization (11). The fact that the patients often recognized normality when staff did not raises important questions.

Failure to detect sanity during the course of hospitalization may be due to the fact that physicians operate with a strong bias toward what statisticians call the type 2 error (5). This is to say that physicians are more inclined to call a healthy person sick (a false positive, type 2) than a sick person healthy (a false negative, type 1). The reasons for this are not hard to find: it is clearly more dangerous to misdiagnose illness than health. Better to err on the side of caution, to suspect illness even among the healthy.

But what holds for medicine does not hold equally well for psychiatry. Medical illnesses, while unfortunate, are not commonly pejorative. Psychiatric diagnoses, on the contrary, carry with them personal, legal, and social stigmas (12). It was therefore important to see whether the tendency toward diagnosing the sane insane could be reversed. The following experiment was arranged at a research and teaching hospital whose staff had heard these findings but doubted that such an error could occur in their hospital. The staff was informed that at some time during the following 3 months, one or more pseudopatients would attempt to be admitted into the psychiatric hospital. Each staff member was asked to rate each patient who presented himself at admissions or on the ward according to the likelihood that the patient was a pseudopatient. A 10-point scale was used, with a 1 and 2 reflecting high confidence that the patient was a pseudopatient.

Judgments were obtained on 193 patients who were admitted for psychiatric treatment. All staff who had had sustained contact with or primary responsibility for the patient—attendants, nurses, psychiatrists, physicians, and psychologists—were asked to make judgments. Forty-one patients were alleged, with high confidence, to be pseudopatients by at least one member of the staff. Twenty-three were considered suspect by at least one psychiatrist. Nineteen were suspected by one psychiatrist *and* one other staff member. Actually, no genuine pseudo-patient (at least from my group) presented himself during this period.

The experiment is instructive. It indicates that the tendency to designate sane people as insane can be reversed when the stakes (in this case, prestige and diagnostic acumen) are high. But what can be said of the 19 people who were suspected of being "sane" by one psychiatrist and another staff member? Were these people truly "sane," or was it rather the case that in the course of avoiding the type 2 error the staff tended to make more errors of the first sort—calling the crazy "sane"? There is no way of knowing. But one thing is certain: any diagnostic process that lends itself so readily to massive errors of this sort cannot be a very reliable one.

THE STICKINESS OF PSYCHODIAGNOSTIC LABELS

Beyond the tendency to call the healthy sick—a tendency that accounts better for diagnostic behavior on admission than it does for such behavior after a lengthy period of exposure—the data speak to the massive role of labeling in psychiatric assessment. Having once been labeled schizophrenic, there is nothing the pseudopatient can do to overcome the tag. The tag profoundly colors others' perceptions of him and his behavior.

From one viewpoint, these data are hardly surprising, for it has long been known that elements are given meaning by the context in which they occur. Gestalt psychology made this point vigorously, and Asch (13) demonstrated that there are "central" personality traits (such as "warm" versus "cold") which are so powerful that they markedly color the meaning of other information in forming an impression of a given personality (14). "Insane," "schizophrenic," "manic-depressive," and "crazy" are probably among the most powerful of such central traits. Once a person is designated abnormal, all of his other behaviors and characteristics are colored by that label. Indeed, that label is so powerful that many of the pseudopatients' normal behaviors were overlooked entirely or profoundly misinterpreted. Some examples may clarify this issue.

Earlier I indicated that there were no changes in the pseudopatient's personal history and current status beyond those of name, employment, and, where necessary, vocation. Otherwise, a veridical description of personal history and circumstances was offered. Those circumstances were not psychotic. How were they made consonant with the diagnosis of psychosis? Or were those diagnoses modified in such a way as to bring them into accord with the circumstances of the pseudopatient's life, as described by him?

As far as I can determine, diagnoses were in no way affected by the relative health of the circumstances of a pseudopatient's life. Rather, the reverse occurred: the perception of his circumstances was shaped entirely by the diagnosis. A clear example of such translation is found in the case of a pseudopatient who had had a close relationship with his mother but was rather remote from his father during his early childhood. During adolescence and beyond, however, his father became a close friend, while his relationship with his mother cooled. His present relationship with his wife was characteristically close and warm. Apart from occasional angry exchanges, friction was minimal. The children had rarely been spanked. Surely there is nothing especially pathological about such a history. Indeed, many readers may see a similar pattern in their own experiences, with no markedly deleterious consequences. Observe, however, how such a history was translated in the psychopathological context, this from the case summary prepared after the patient was discharged.

This white 39-year-old male . . . manifests a long history of considerable ambivalence in close relationships, which begins in early childhood. A warm relationship with his mother cools during his adolescence. A distant relationship to his father is described as becoming very intense. Affective stability is absent. His attempts to control emotionality with his wife and children are punctuated by angry outbursts and, in the case of the children, spankings. And while he says that he has several good friends, one senses considerable ambivalence embedded in those relationships also. . . .

The facts of the case were unintentionally distorted by the staff to achieve consistency with a popular theory of the dynamics of a schizophrenic reaction (15). Nothing of an ambivalent nature had been described in relations with parents, spouse, or friends. To the extent that ambivalence could be inferred, it was probably not greater than is found in all human relationships. It is true the pseudopatient's relationships with his parents changed over time, but in the ordinary context that would hardly be remarkable—indeed, it might very well be expected. Clearly, the meaning ascribed to his verbalizations (that is, ambivalence, affective instability) was determined by the diagnosis: schizophrenia. An entirely different meaning would have been ascribed if it were known that the man was "normal."

All pseudopatients took extensive notes publicly. Under ordinary circumstances, such behavior would have raised questions in the minds of observers, as, in fact, it did among patients. Indeed, it seemed so certain that the notes would elicit suspicion that elaborate precautions were taken to remove them from the ward each day. But the precautions proved needless. The closest any staff member came to questioning these notes occurred when one pseudopatient asked his physician what kind of medication

he was receiving and began to write down the response. "You needn't write it," he was told gently. "If you have trouble remembering, just ask me again."

If no questions were asked of the pseudopatients, how was their writing interpreted? Nursing records for three patients indicate that the writing was seen as an aspect of their pathological behavior. "Patient engages in writing behavior" was the daily nursing comment on one of the pseudopatients who was never questioned about his writing. Given that the patient is in the hospital, he must be psychologically disturbed. And given that he is disturbed, continuous writing must be a behavioral manifestation of that disturbance, perhaps a subset of the compulsive behaviors that are sometimes correlated with schizophrenia.

One tacit characteristic of psychiatric diagnosis is that it locates the sources of aberration within the individual and only rarely within the complex of stimuli that surrounds him. Consequently, behaviors that are stimulated by the environment are commonly misattributed to the patient's disorder. For example, one kindly nurse found a pseudopatient pacing the long hospital corridors. "Nervous, Mr. X?" she asked. "No, bored," he said.

The notes kept by pseudopatients are full of patient behaviors that were misinterpreted by well-intentioned staff. Often enough, a patient would go "berserk" because he had, wittingly or unwittingly, been mistreated by, say, an attendant. A nurse coming upon the scene would rarely inquire even cursorily into the environmental stimuli of the patient's behavior. Rather, she assumed that his upset derived from his pathology, not from his present interactions with other staff members. Occasionally, the staff might assume that the patient's family (especially when they had recently visited) or other patients had stimulated the outburst. But never were the staff found to assume that one of themselves or the structure of the hospital had anything to do with a patient's behavior. One psychiatrist pointed to a group of patients who were sitting outside the cafeteria entrance half an hour before lunchtime. To a group of young residents he indicated that such behavior was characteristic of the oral-acquisitive nature of the syndrome. It seemed not to occur to him that there were very few things to anticipate in a psychiatric hospital besides eating.

A psychiatric label has a life and an influence of its own. Once the impression has been formed that the patient is schizophrenic, the expectation is that he will continue to be schizophrenic. When a sufficient amount of time has passed, during which the patient has done nothing bizarre, he is considered to be in remission and available for discharge. But the label endures beyond discharge, with the unconfirmed expectation that he will behave as a schizophrenic again. Such labels, conferred by mental health professionals, are as influential on the patient as they are on his relatives and friends, and it should not surprise anyone that the diagnosis acts on all of them as a self-fulfilling prophecy. Eventually, the patient himself accepts the diagnosis, with all of its surplus meanings and expectations, and behaves accordingly (5).

The inferences to be made from these matters are quite simple. Much as Zigler and Phillips have demonstrated that there is enormous overlap in the symptoms presented by patients who have been variously diagnosed (16), so there is enormous overlap in the behaviors of the sane and the insane. The sane are not "sane" all of the time. We lose our tempers "for no good reason." We are occasionally depressed or anxious, again for no good reason. And we may find it difficult to get along with one or another person—again for no reason that we can specify. Similarly, the insane are not always insane. Indeed, it was the impression of the pseudopatients while living with them that

they were sane for long periods of time—that the bizarre behaviors upon which their diagnoses were allegedly predicated constituted only a small fraction of their total behavior. If it makes no sense to label ourselves permanently depressed on the basis of an occasional depression, then it takes better evidence than is presently available to label all patients insane or schizophrenic on the basis of bizarre behaviors or cognitions. It seems more useful, as Mischel (17) has pointed out, to limit our discussions to *behaviors*, the stimuli that provoke them, and their correlates.

It is not known why powerful impressions of personality traits, such as "crazy" or "insane," arise. Conceivably, when the origins of and stimuli that give rise to a behavior are remote or unknown, or when the behavior strikes us as immutable, trait labels regarding the *behavior* arise. When, on the other hand, the origins and stimuli are known and available, discourse is limited to the behavior itself. Thus, I may hallucinate because I am sleeping, or I may hallucinate because I have ingested a peculiar drug. These are termed sleep-induced hallucinations, or dreams, and drug-induced hallucinations, respectively. But when the stimuli to my hallucinations are unknown, that is called craziness, or schizophrenia—as if that inference were somehow as illuminating as the others.

THE EXPERIENCE OF PSYCHIATRIC HOSPITALIZATION

The term "mental illness" is of recent origin. It was coined by people who were humane in their inclinations and who wanted very much to raise the station of (and the public's sympathies toward) the psychologically disturbed from that of witches and "crazies" to one that was akin to the physically ill. And they were at least partially successful, for the treatment of the mentally ill *has* improved considerably over the years. But while treatment has improved, it is doubtful that people really regard the mentally ill in the same way that they view the physically ill. A broken leg is something one recovers from, but mental illness allegedly endures forever (18). A broken leg does not threaten the observer, but a crazy schizophrenic? There is by now a host of evidence that attitudes toward the mentally ill are characterized by fear, hostility, aloofness, suspicion, and dread (19). The mentally ill are society's lepers.

That such attitudes infect the general population is perhaps not surprising, only upsetting. But that they affect the professionals—attendants, nurses, physicians, psychologists, and social workers—who treat and deal with the mentally ill is more disconcerting, both because such attitudes are self-evidently pernicious and because they are unwitting. Most mental health professionals would insist that they are sympathetic toward the mentally ill, that they are neither avoidant nor hostile. But it is more likely that an exquisite ambivalence characterizes their relations with psychiatric patients, such that their avowed impulses are only part of their entire attitude. Negative attitudes are there too and can easily be detected. Such attitudes should not surprise us. They are the natural offspring of the labels patients wear and the places in which they are found.

Consider the structure of the typical psychiatric hospital. Staff and patients are strictly segregated. Staff have their own living space, including their dining facilities, bathrooms, and assembly places. The glassed quarters that contain the professional staff, which the pseudopatients came to call "the cage," sit out on every dayroom. The staff emerge primarily for caretaking purposes—to give medication, to conduct a therapy or group meeting, to instruct or reprimand a patient. Otherwise, staff keep to themselves, almost as if the disorder that afflicts their charges is somehow catching.

So much is patient-staff segregation the rule that, for four public hospitals in which

an attempt was made to measure the degree to which staff and patients mingle, it was necessary to use "time out of the staff cage" as the operational measure. While it was not the case that all time spent out of the cage was spent mingling with patients (attendants, for example, would occasionally emerge to watch television in the dayroom), it was the only way in which one could gather reliable data on time for measuring.

The average amount of time spent by attendants outside of the cage was 11.3 percent (range, 3 to 52 percent). This figure does not represent only time spent mingling with patients, but also includes time spent on such chores as folding laundry, supervising patients while they shave, directing ward cleanup, and sending patients to off-ward activities. It was the relatively rare attendant who spent time talking with patients or playing games with them. It proved impossible to obtain a "percent mingling time" for nurses, since the amount of time they spent out of the cage was too brief. Rather, we counted instances of emergence from the cage. On the average, daytime nurses emerged from the cage 11.5 times per shift, including instances when they left the ward entirely (range, 4 to 39 times). Late afternoon and night nurses were even less available, emerging on the average 9.4 times per shift (range, 4 to 41 times). Data on early morning nurses, who arrived usually after midnight, and departed at 8 a.m., are not available because patients were asleep during most of this period.

Physicians, especially psychiatrists, were even less available. They were rarely seen on the wards. Quite commonly, they would be seen only when they arrived and departed, with the remaining time being spent in their offices or in the cage. On the average, physicians emerged on the ward 6.7 times per day (range, 1 to 17 times). It proved difficult to make an accurate estimate in this regard, since physicians often maintained hours that allowed them to come and go at different times.

The hierarchical organization of the psychiatric hospital has been commented on before (20), but the latent meaning of that kind of organization is worth noting again. Those with the most power have least to do with patients, and those with the least power are most involved with them. Recall, however, that the acquisition of role-appropriate behaviors occurs mainly through the observation of others, with the most powerful having the most influence. Consequently, it is understandable that attendants not only spend more time with patients than do any other members of the staff—that is required by their station in the hierarchy—but also, insofar as they learn from their superiors' behavior, spend as little time with patients as they can. Attendants are seen mainly in the cage, which is where the models, the action, and the power are.

I turn now to a different set of studies, these dealing with staff response to patient-initiated contact. It has long been known that the amount of time a person spends with you can be an index of your significance to him. If he initiates and maintains eye contact, there is reason to believe that he is considering your requests and needs. If he pauses to chat or actually stops and talks, there is added reason to infer that he is individuating you. In four hospitals, the pseudopatient approached the staff member with a request which took the following form: "Pardon me, Mr. [or Dr. or Mrs.] X, could you tell me when I will be eligible for grounds privileges?" (or "... when I will be presented at the staff meeting?" or "... when I am likely to be discharged?"). While the content of the question varied according to the appropriateness of the target and the pseudopatient's (apparent) current needs the form was always a courteous and relevant request for information. Care was taken never to approach a particular member of the staff more than once a day, lest the staff member become suspicious or irritated. In examining these data, remember that the behavior of the pseudopatients was neither bizarre nor disruptive. One could indeed engage in good conversation with them.

The data for these experiments are shown in Table 1, separately for physicians (column 1) and for nurses and attendants (column 2). Minor differences between these four institutions were overwhelmed by the degree to which staff avoided continuing contacts that patients had initiated. By far, their most common response consisted of either a brief response to the question, offered while they were "on the move" and with head averted, or no response at all.

The encounter frequently took the following bizarre form: (pseudopatient) "Pardon me, Dr. X. Could you tell me when I am eligible for grounds privileges?" (physician) "Good morning, Dave. How are you today?" (Moves off without waiting for a response.)

It is instructive to compare these data with data recently obtained at Stanford University. It has been alleged that large and eminent universities are characterized by faculty who are so busy that they have no time for students. For this comparison, a young lady approached individual faculty members who seemed to be walking purposefully to some meeting or teaching engagement and asked them the following six questions.

1. "Pardon me, could you direct me to Encina Hall?" (at the medical school: "... to the Clinical Research Center?").
2. "Do you know where Fish Annex is?" (there is no Fish Annex at Stanford).
3. "Do you teach here?"
4. "How does one apply for admission to the college?" (at the medical school: "... to the medical school?").
5. "Is it difficult to get in?"
6. "Is there financial aid?"

Without exception, as can be seen in Table 1 (column 3), all of the questions were

TABLE 1 Self-Initiated Contact by Pseudopatients with Psychiatrists and Nurses and Attendants, Compared to Contact with Other Groups.

CONTACT	PSYCHIATRIC HOSPITALS		UNIVERSITY CAMPUS (NONMEDICAL)	UNIVERSITY MEDICAL CENTER PHYSICIANS		
	(1) Psychiatrists	(2) Nurses and Attendants	(3) Faculty	(4) "Looking for a Psychiatrist"	(5) "Looking for an Internist"	(6) No Additional Comment
Responses						
Moves on, head averted (%)	71	88	0	0	0	0
Makes eye contact (%)	23	10	0	11	0	0
Pauses and chats (%)	2	2	0	11	0	10
Stops and talks (%)	4	0.5	100	78	100	90
Mean number of questions answered (out of 6)	*	*	6	3.8	4.8	4.5
Respondents (No.)	13	47	14	18	15	10
Attempts (No.)	185	1283	14	18	15	10

*Not applicable.

answered. No matter how rushed they were, all respondents not only maintained eye contact, but stopped to talk. Indeed, many of the respondents went out of their way to direct or take the questioner to the office she was seeking, to try to locate "Fish Annex," or to discuss with her the possibilities of being admitted to the university.

Similar data, also shown in Table 1 (columns 4, 5, and 6), were obtained in the hospital. Here too, the young lady came prepared with six questions. After the first question, however, she remarked to 18 of her respondents (column 4), "I'm looking for a psychiatrist," and to 15 others (column 5), "I'm looking for an internist." Ten other respondents received no inserted comment (column 6). The general degree of co-operative responses is considerably higher for these university groups than it was for pseudopatients in psychiatric hospitals. Even so, differences are apparent within the medical school setting. Once having indicated that she was looking for a psychiatrist, the degree of cooperation elicited was less than when she sought an internist.

POWERLESSNESS AND DEPERSONALIZATION

Eye contact and verbal contact reflect concern and individuation; their absence, avoidance and depersonalization. The data I have presented do not do justice to the rich daily encounters that grew up around matters of depersonalization and avoidance. I have records of patients who were beaten by staff for the sin of having initiated verbal contact. During my own experience, for example, one patient was beaten in the presence of other patients for having approached an attendant and told him, "I like you." Occasionally, punishment meted out to patients for misdemeanors seemed so excessive that it could not be justified by the most radical interpretations of psychiatric canon. Nevertheless, they appeared to go unquestioned. Tempers

were often short. A patient who had not heard a call for medication would be roundly excoriated, and the morning attendants would often wake patients with, "Come on, you m———f———s, out of bed!"

Neither anecdotal nor "hard" data can convey the overwhelming sense of powerlessness which invades the individual as he is continually exposed to the depersonalization of the psychiatric hospital. It hardly matters *which* psychiatric hospital—the excellent public ones and the very plush private hospital were better than the rural and shabby ones in this regard, but, again, the features that psychiatric hospitals had in common overwhelmed by far their apparent differences.

Powerlessness was evident everywhere. The patient is deprived of many of his legal rights by dint of his psychiatric commitment (21). He is shorn of credibility by virtue of his psychiatric label. His freedom of movement is restricted. He cannot initiate contact with the staff, but may only respond to such overtures as they make. Personal privacy is minimal. Patient quarters and possessions can be entered and examined by any staff member, for whatever reason. His personal history and anguish is available to any staff member (often including the "grey lady" and "candy striper" volunteer) who chooses to read his folder, regardless of their therapeutic relationship to him. His personal hygiene and waste evacuation are often monitored. The water closets may have no doors.

At times, depersonalization reached such proportions that pseudopatients had the sense that they were invisible, or at least unworthy of account. Upon being admitted, I and other pseudopatients took the initial physical examinations in a semipublic room, where staff members went about their own business as if we were not there.

On the ward, attendants delivered verbal and occasionally serious physical abuse to patients in the presence of other observing patients, some of whom (the pseudopatients) were writing it all down. Abusive behavior, on the other hand, terminated quite abruptly when other staff members were known to be coming. Staff are credible witnesses. Patients are not.

A nurse unbuttoned her uniform to adjust her brassiere in the presence of an entire ward of viewing men. One did not have the sense that she was being seductive. Rather, she didn't notice us. A group of staff persons might point to a patient in the dayroom and discuss him animatedly, as if he were not there.

One illuminating instance of depersonalization and invisibility occurred with regard to medications. All told, the pseudopatients were administered nearly 2100 pills, including Elavil, Stelazine, Compazine, and Thorazine, to name but a few. (That such a variety of medications should have been administered to patients presenting identical symptoms is itself worthy of note.) Only two were swallowed. The rest were either pocketed or deposited in the toilet. The pseudopatients were not alone in this. Although I have no precise records on how many patients rejected their medications, the pseudopatients frequently found the medications of other patients in the toilet before they deposited their own. As long as they were cooperative, their behavior and the pseudopatients' own in this matter, as in other important matters, went unnoticed throughout.

Reactions to such depersonalization among pseudopatients were intense. Although they had come to the hospital as participant observers and were fully aware that they did not "belong," they nevertheless found themselves caught up in and fighting the process of depersonalization. Some examples: a graduate student in psychology asked his wife to bring his textbooks to the hospital so he could "catch up on his homework"—this despite the elaborate precautions taken to conceal his professional association. The same student, who had trained for quite some time to get into the

hospital, and who had looked forward to the experience, "remembered" some drag races that he had wanted to see on the weekend and insisted that he be discharged by that time. Another pseudopatient attempted a romance with a nurse. Subsequently, he informed the staff that he was applying for admission to graduate school in psychology and was very likely to be admitted, since a graduate professor was one of his regular hospital visitors. The same person began to engage in psychotherapy with other patients—all of this as a way of becoming a person in an impersonal environment.

THE SOURCES OF DEPERSONALIZATION

What are the origins of depersonalization? I have already mentioned two. First are attitudes held by all of us toward the mentally ill—including those who treat them—attitudes characterized by fear, distrust, and horrible expectations on the one hand, and benevolent intentions on the other. Our ambivalence leads, in this instance as in others, to avoidance.

Second, and not entirely separate, the hierarchical structure of the psychiatric hospital facilitates depersonalization. Those who are at the top have least to do with patients, and their behavior inspires the rest of the staff. Average daily contact with psychiatrists, psychologists, residents, and physicians combined ranged from 3.9 to 25.1 minutes, with an overall mean of 6.8 (six pseudopatients over a total of 129 days of hospitalization). Included in this average are time spent in the admissions interview, ward meetings in the presence of a senior staff member, group and individual psychotherapy contacts, case presentation conferences, and discharge meetings. Clearly, patients do not spend much time in interpersonal contact with doctoral staff. And doctoral staff serve as models for nurses and attendants.

There are probably other sources. Psychiatric installations are presently in serious financial straits. Staff shortages are pervasive, staff time at a premium. Something has to give, and that something is patient contact. Yet, while financial stresses are realities, too much can be made of them. I have the impression that the psychological forces that result in depersonalization are much stronger than the fiscal ones and that the addition of more staff would not correspondingly improve patient care in this regard. The incidence of staff meetings and the enormous amount of record-keeping on patients, for example, have not been as substantially reduced as has patient contact. Priorities exist, even during hard times. Patient contact is not a significant priority in the traditional psychiatric hospital, and fiscal pressures do not account for this. Avoidance and depersonalization may.

Heavy reliance upon psychotropic medication tacitly contributes to depersonalization by convincing staff that treatment is indeed being conducted and that further patient contact may not be necessary. Even here, however, caution needs to be exercised in understanding the role of psychotropic drugs. If patients were powerful rather than powerless, if they were viewed as interesting individuals rather than diagnostic entities, if they were socially significant rather than social lepers, if their anguish truly and wholly compelled our sympathies and concerns, would we not *seek* contact with them, despite the availability of medications? Perhaps for the pleasure of it all?

THE CONSEQUENCES OF LABELING AND DEPERSONALIZATION

Whenever the ratio of what is known to what needs to be known approaches zero, we tend to invent "knowledge" and assume that we understand more than we actually do. We seem unable to acknowledge that we simply don't know. The needs for diagnosis and remediation of behavioral and emotional problems are enormous. But rather than ac-

knowledge that we are just embarking on understanding, we continue to label patients "schizophrenic," "manic-depressive," and "insane," as if in those words we had captured the essence of understanding. The facts of the matter are that we have known for a long time that diagnoses are often not useful or reliable, but we have nevertheless continued to use them. We now know that we cannot distinguish insanity from sanity. It is depressing to consider how that information will be used.

Not merely depressing, but frightening. How many people, one wonders, are sane but not recognized as such in our psychiatric institutions? How many have been needlessly stripped of their privileges of citizenship, from the right to vote and drive to that of handling their own accounts? How many have feigned insanity in order to avoid the criminal consequences of their behavior, and, conversely, how many would rather stand trial than live interminably in a psychiatric hospital—but are wrongly thought to be mentally ill? How many have been stigmatized by well-intentioned, but nevertheless erroneous, diagnoses? On the last point, recall again that a "type 2 error" in psychiatric diagnosis does not have the same consequences it does in medical diagnosis. A diagnosis of cancer that has been found to be in error is cause for celebration. But psychiatric diagnoses are rarely found to be in error. The label sticks, a mark of inadequacy forever.

Finally, how many patients might be "sane" outside the psychiatric hospital but seem insane in it—not because craziness resides in them, as it were, but because they are responding to a bizarre setting, one that may be unique to institutions which harbor nether people? Goffman (4) calls the process of socialization to such institutions "mortification"—an apt metaphor that includes the processes of depersonalization that have been described here. And while it is impossible to know whether the pseudopatients' responses to these processes are characteristic of all inmates—they were, after all, not real patients—it is difficult to believe that these processes of socialization to a psychiatric hospital provide useful attitudes or habits of response for living in the "real world."

SUMMARY AND CONCLUSIONS

It is clear that we cannot distinguish the sane from the insane in psychiatric hospitals. The hospital itself imposes a special environment in which the meanings of behavior can easily be misunderstood. The consequences to patients hospitalized in such an environment—the powerlessness, depersonalization, segregation, mortification, and self-labeling—seem undoubtedly countertherapeutic.

I do not, even now, understand this problem well enough to perceive solutions. But two matters seem to have some promise. The first concerns the proliferation of community mental health facilities, of crisis intervention centers, of the human potential movement, and of behavior therapies that, for all of their own problems, tend to avoid psychiatric labels, to focus on special problems and behaviors, and to retain the individual in a relatively nonpejorative environment. Clearly, to the extent that we refrain from sending the distressed to insane places, our impressions of them are less likely to be distorted. (The risk of distorted perceptions, it seems to me, is always present, since we are much more sensitive to an individual's behaviors and verbalizations than we are to the subtle contextual stimuli that often promote them. At issue here is a matter of magnitude. And, as I have shown, the magnitude of distortion is exceedingly high in the extreme context that is a psychiatric hospital.)

The second matter that might prove promising speaks to the need to increase the sensitivity of mental health workers and researchers to the *Catch 22* position of psychiatric patients. Simply reading materials in this area will be of help to some such workers and researchers. For others, directly experiencing the impact of psychiatric hospitalization will be of enormous use. Clearly, further research into the social psychology of such total institutions will both facilitate treatment and deepen understanding.

I and the other pseudopatients in the psychiatric setting had distinctly negative reactions. We do not pretend to describe the subjective experiences of true patients. Theirs may be different from ours, particularly with the passage of time and the necessary process of adaptation to one's environment. But we can and do speak to the relatively more objective indices of treatment within the hospital. It could be a mistake, and a very unfortunate one, to consider that what happened to us derived from malice or stupidity on the part of the staff. Quite the contrary, our overwhelming impression of them was of people who really cared, who were committed and who were uncommonly intelligent. Where they failed, as they sometimes did painfully, it would be more accurate to attribute those failures to the environment in which they, too, found themselves than to personal callousness. Their perceptions and behavior were controlled by the situation, rather than being motivated by a malicious disposition. In a more benign environment, one that was less attached to global diagnosis, their behaviors and judgments might have been more benign and effective.

REFERENCES AND NOTES

1. P. Ash, *J. Abnorm. Soc. Psychol.* **44,** 272 (1949); A. T. Beck, *Amer. J. Psychiat.* **119,** 210 (1962); A. T. Boisen, *Psychiatry* **2,** 233 (1938); N. Kreitman, *J. Ment. Sci.* **107,** 876 (1961); N. Kreitman, P. Sainsbury, J. Morrisey, J. Towers, J. Scrivener, *ibid.,* p. 887; H. O. Schmitt and C. P. Fonda, *J. Abnorm. Soc. Psychol.* **52,** 262 (1956); W. Seeman, *J. Nerv. Ment. Dis.* **118,** 541 (1953). For an analysis of

these artifacts and summaries of the disputes, see J. Zubin, *Annu. Rev. Psychol.* **18**, 373 (1967); L. Phillips and J. G. Draguns, *ibid.* **22**, 447 (1971).

2. R. Benedict, *J. Gen. Psychol.* **10**, 59 (1934).

3. See in this regard H. Becker, *Outsiders: Studies in the Sociology of Deviance* (Free Press, New York, 1963); B. M. Braginsky, D. D. Braginsky, K. Ring, *Methods of Madness: The Mental Hospital as a Last Resort* (Holt, Rinehart & Winston, New York, 1969); G. M. Crocetti and P. V. Lemkau, *Amer. Sociol. Rev.* **30**, 577 (1965); E. Goffman, *Behavior in Public Places* (Free Press, New York, 1964); R. D. Laing, *The Divided Self: A Study of Sanity and Madness* (Quadrangle, Chicago, 1960); D. L. Phillips, *Amer. Sociol. Rev.* **28**, 963 (1963); T. R. Sarbin, *Psychol. Today* **6**, 18 (1972); E. Schur, *Amer. J. Sociol.* **75**, 309 (1969); T. Szasz, *Law, Liberty and Psychiatry* (Macmillan, New York, 1963); *The Myth of Mental Illness: Foundations of a Theory of Mental Illness* (Hoeber-Harper, New York, 1963). For a critique of some of these views, see W. R. Gove, *Amer. Sociol. Rev.* **35**, 873 (1970).

4. E. Goffman, *Asylums* (Doubleday, Garden City, N.Y., 1961).

5. T. J. Scheff, *Being Mentally Ill: A Sociological Theory* (Aldine, Chicago, 1966).

6. Data from a ninth pseudopatient are not incorporated in this report because, although his sanity went undetected, he falsified aspects of his personal history, including his marital status and parental relationships. His experimental behaviors therefore were not identical to those of the other pseudopatients.

7. A. Barry, *Bellevue Is a State of Mind* (Harcourt Brace Jovanovich, New York, 1971); I. Belknap, *Human Problems of a State Mental Hospital* Mc-Graw-Hill, New York, 1956); W. Caudill, F. C. Redlich, H. R. Gilmore, E. B. Brody, *Amer. J. Orthopsychiat.* **22**, 314 (1952); A. R. Goldman, R. H. Bohr, T. A. Steinberg, *Prof. Psychol.* **1**, 427 (1970); unauthored, *Roche Report* **1** (No. 13), 8 (1971).

8. Beyond the personal difficulties that the pseudopatient is likely to experience in the hospital, there are legal and social ones that, combined, require considerable attention before entry. For example, once admitted to a psychiatric institution it is difficult, if not impossible, to be discharged on short notice, state law to the contrary notwithstanding. I was not sensitive to these difficulties at the outset of the project, nor to the personal and situational emergencies that can arise, but later a writ of habeas corpus was prepared for each of the entering pseudopatients and an attorney was kept "on call" during every hospitalization. I am grateful to John Kaplan and Robert Bartels for legal advice and assistance in these matters.

9. However distasteful such concealment is, it was a necessary first step to examining these questions. Without concealment, there would have been no way to know how valid these experiences were; nor was there any way of knowing whether whatever detections occurred were a tribute to the diagnostic acumen of the staff or to the hospital's rumor network. Obviously, since my concerns are general ones that cut across individual hospitals and staffs, I have respected their anonymity and have eliminated clues that might lead to their identification.

10. Interestingly, of the 12 admissions, 11 were diagnosed as schizophrenic and one, with the identical symptomatology, as manic-depressive psychosis. This diagnosis has a more favorable prognosis, and it was given by the only private hospital in our sample. On the relations between social class and psychiatric diagnosis, see A. deB. Hollingshead and F. C. Redlich, *Social Class and Mental Illness: A Community Study* (Wiley, New York, 1958).

11. It is possible, of course, that patients have quite broad latitudes in diagnosis and therefore are inclined to call many people sane, even those whose behavior is patently aberrant. However, although we have no hard data on this matter, it was our distinct impression that this was not the case. In many instances, patients not only singled us out for attention, but came to imitate our behaviors and styles.

12. J. Cumming and E. Cumming, *Community Ment. Health* **1**, 135 (1965); A. Farina and K. Ring, *J. Abnorm. Psychol.* **70**, 47 (1965); H. E. Freeman and O. G. Simmons, *The Mental Patient Comes Home* (Wiley, New York, 1963); W. J. Johannsen, *Ment. Hygiene* **53**, 218 (1969); A. S. Linsky, *Soc. Psychiat.* **5**, 166 (1970).

13. S. E. Asch, *J. Abnorm. Soc. Psychol.* **41**, 258 (1946); *Social Psychology* (Prentice-Hall, New York, 1952).

14. See also I. N. Mensh and J. Wishner, *J. Personality* **16**, 188 (1947); J. Wishner, *Psychol. Rev.* **67**, 96 (1960); J. S. Bruner and R. Tagiuri, in *Handbook of Social Psychology*, G. Lindzey, Ed. (Addison-Wes-

ley, Cambridge, Mass., 1954), vol. 2, pp. 634–654; J. S. Bruner, D. Shapiro, R. Tagiuri, in *Person Perception and Interpersonal Behavior*, R. Tagiuri and L. Petrullo, Eds. (Stanford Univ. Press, Stanford, Calif., 1958), pp. 277–288.

15. For an example of a similar self fulfilling prophecy, in this instance dealing with the "central" trait of intelligence, see R. Rosenthal and L. Jacobson, *Pygmalion in the Classroom* (Holt, Rinehart & Winston, New York, 1968).

16. E. Zigler and L. Phillips, *J. Abnorm. Soc. Psychol.* **63,** 69 (1961). See also R. K. Freudenberg and J. P. Robertson, *A.M.A. Arch. Neurol. Psychiatr.* **76,** 14 (1956).

17. W. Mischel, *Personality and Assessment* (Wiley, New York, 1968).

18. The most recent and unfortunate instance of this tenet is that of Senator Thomas Eagleton.

19. T. R. Sarbin and J. C. Mancuso, *J. Clin. Consult. Psychol.* **35,** 159 (1970); T. R. Sarbin, *ibid.* **31,** 447 (1967); J. C. Nunnally, Jr., *Popular Conceptions of Mental Health* (Holt, Rinehart & Winston, New York, 1961).

20. A. H. Stanton and M. S. Schwartz, *The Mental Hospital: A Study of Institutional Participation in Psychiatric Illness and Treatment* (Basic, New York, 1954).

21. D. B. Wexler and S. E. Scoville, *Ariz. Law Rev.* **13,** 1 (1971).

22. I thank W. Mischel, E. Orne, and M. S. Rosenhan for comments on an earlier draft of this manuscript.

5

Society as Symbolic Interaction

HERBERT BLUMER

A view of human society as symbolic interaction has been followed more than it has been formulated. Partial, usually fragmentary, statements of it are to be found in the writings of a number of eminent scholars, some inside the field of sociology and some outside. Among the former we may note such scholars as Charles Horton Cooley, W. I. Thomas, Robert E. Parks, E. W. Burgess, Florian Znaniecki, Ellsworth Faris, and James Mickel Williams. Among those outside the discipline we may note William James, John Dewey, and George Herbert Mead. None of these scholars, in my judgment, has presented a systematic statement of the nature of human group life from the standpoint of symbolic interaction. Mead stands out among all of them in laying bare the fundamental premises of the approach, yet he did little to develop its methodological implications for sociological study. Students who seek to depict the position of symbolic interaction may easily give different pictures of it. What I have to present should be regarded as my personal version. My aim is to present the basic premises of the point of view and to develop their methodological consequences for the study of human group life.

The term "symbolic interaction" refers, of course, to the peculiar and distinctive character of interaction as it takes place between human beings. The peculiarity consists in the fact that human beings interpret or "define" each other's actions instead of merely reacting to each other's actions. Their "response" is not made directly to the actions of one another but instead is based on the meaning which they attach to such actions. Thus, human interaction is mediated by the use of symbols, by interpretation, or by ascertaining the meaning of one another's actions. This mediation is equivalent to inserting a process of interpretation between stimulus and response in the case of human behavior.

The simple recognition that human beings interpret each other's actions as the means of acting toward one another has permeated the thought and writings of many scholars of human conduct and of human group life. Yet few of them have endeavored to analyze what such interpretation implies about the nature of the human being or about the nature of human association. They are usually content with a mere recognition that "interpretation" should be caught by the student, or with a simple realization that symbols, such as cultural norms or values, must be introduced into their analyses. Only G. H. Mead, in my judgment, has sought to think through what the act of interpretation implies for an understanding of the human being, human action, and human association. The essentials of his analysis are so penetrating and profound and so important for an understanding of human group life that I wish to spell them out, even though briefly.

The key feature in Mead's analysis is that the human being has a self. This idea should not be cast aside as esoteric or glossed over as something that is obvious and hence not worthy of attention. In declaring that the human being has a self, Mead had in mind chiefly that the human being can be the object of his own actions. He can act toward himself as he might act toward others. Each of us is familiar with actions of this sort in which the human being gets angry with himself, rebuffs himself, takes pride in himself, argues with himself, tries to bolster his own courage, tells himself that he should "do this" or not "do that," sets goals for himself, makes compromises with himself, and plans what he is going to do. That the human being acts toward himself in these and countless other ways is a matter of easy empirical observation. To recognize that the human being can act toward himself is no mystical conjuration.

Mead regards this ability of the human being to act toward himself as the central mechanism with which the human being faces and deals with his world. This mechanism enables the human being to make indications to himself of things in his surroundings and thus to guide his actions by what he notes. Anything of which a human being is conscious is something which he is indicating to himself—the ticking of a clock, a knock at the door, the appearance of a friend, the remark made by a companion, a recognition that he has a task to perform, or the realization that he has a cold. Conversely, anything of which he is not conscious is, *ipso facto*, something which he is not indicating to himself. The conscious life of the human being, from the time that he awakens until he falls asleep, is a continual flow of self-indications—notations of the things with which he deals and takes into account. We are given, then, a picture of the human being as an organism which confronts its world with a mechanism for making indications to itself. This is the mechanism that is involved in interpreting the actions of others. To interpret the actions of another is to point out to oneself that the action has this or that meaning or character.

Now, according to Mead, the significance of making indications to oneself is of paramount importance. The importance lies along two lines. First, to indicate something is to extricate it from its setting, to hold it apart, to give it a meaning or, in Mead's language, to make it into an object. An object—that is to say, anything that an individual indicates to himself—is different from a stimulus; instead of having an intrinsic character which acts on the individual and which can be identified apart from the individual, its character or meaning is conferred on it by the individual. The object is a product of the individual's disposition to act instead of being an antecedent stimulus which evokes the act. Instead of the individual being surrounded by an environment of pre-existing objects which play upon him and call forth his behavior, the proper picture is that he constructs his objects on the basis of his on-going activity. In any of his countless acts—whether minor, like dressing himself, or major, like organizing himself for a professional career—the individual is designating different objects to himself, giving them meaning, judging their suitability to his action, and making decisions on the basis of the judgment. This is what is meant by interpretation or acting on the basis of symbols.

The second important implication of the fact that the human being makes indications to himself is that his action is constructed or built up instead of being a mere release. Whatever the action in which he is engaged, the human individual proceeds by pointing out to himself the divergent things which have to be taken into account in the course of his action. He has to note what he wants to do and how he is to do it; he has to point out to himself the various conditions which may be instrumental to his action and those which may obstruct his action; he has to take account of the demands, the expectations, the prohibitions, and the threats as they may arise in the situation in which he is acting. His action is built up step by step through a process of such self-indication. The human individual pieces together and guides his action by taking account of different things and interpreting their significance for his prospective action. There is no instance of conscious action of which this is not true.

The process of constructing action through making indications to oneself cannot be swallowed up in any of the conventional psychological categories. This process is distinct from and different from what is spoken of as the "ego"—just as it is different from any other conception which conceives of the self in terms of composition or organization. Self-indication is a moving communicative process in which the individual notes things, assesses them, gives them a meaning, and decides to act on the basis of the meaning. The human being stands over against the world, or against "alters," with such a process and not with a mere ego. Further, the process of self-indication cannot be subsumed under the forces, whether from the outside or inside, which are presumed to play upon the individual to produce his behavior. Environmental pressures, external stimuli, organic drives, wishes, attitudes, feelings, ideas, and their like do not cover or explain the process of self-indication. The process of self-indication stands over against them in that the individual points out to himself and interprets the appearance or expression of such things, noting a given social demand that is made on him, recognizing a command, observing that he is hungry, realizing that he wishes to buy something, aware that he has a given feeling, conscious that he dislikes eating with someone he despises, or aware that he is thinking of doing some given thing. By virtue of indicating such things to himself, he places himself over against them and is able to act back against them, accepting them, rejecting them, or transforming them in accordance with how he defines or interprets them. His behavior, accordingly, is not a result of such things as environmental pressures, stimuli, motives, attitudes, and ideas but arises instead from how he interprets and handles these things

in the action which he is constructing. The process of self-indication by means of which human action is formed cannot be accounted for by factors which precede the act. The process of self-indication exists in its own right and must be accepted and studied as such. It is through this process that the human being constructs his conscious action.

Now Mead recognizes that the formation of action by the individual through a process of self-indication always takes place in a social context. Since this matter is so vital to an understanding of symbolic interaction it needs to be explained carefully. Fundamentally, group action takes the form of a fitting together of individual lines of action. Each individual aligns his action to the action of others by ascertaining what they are doing or what they intend to do—that is, by getting the meaning of their acts. For Mead, this is done by the individual "taking the role" of others—either the role of a specific person or the role of a group (Mead's "generalized other"). In taking such roles the individual seeks to ascertain the intention or direction of the acts of others. He forms and aligns his own action on the basis of such interpretation of the acts of others. This is the fundamental way in which group action takes place in human society.

The foregoing are the essential features, as I see them, in Mead's analysis of the bases of symbolic interaction. They presuppose the following: that human society is made up of individuals who have selves (that is, make indications to themselves); that individual action is a construction and not a release, being built up by the individual through noting and interpreting features of the situations in which he acts; that group or collective action consists of the aligning of individual actions, brought about by the individuals' interpreting or taking into account each other's actions. Since my purpose is to present and not to defend the position of symbolic interaction I shall not endeavor in this essay to advance support for the three premises which I have just indicated. I wish merely to say that the three premises can be easily verified empirically. I know of no instance of human group action to which the three premises do not apply. The reader is challenged to find or think of a single instance which they do not fit.

I wish now to point out that sociological views of human society are, in general, markedly at variance with the premises which I have indicated as underlying symbolic interaction. Indeed, the predominant number of such views, especially those in vogue at the present time, do not see or treat human society as symbolic interaction. Wedded, as they tend to be, to some form of sociological determinism, they adopt images of human society, of individuals in it, and of group action which do not square with the premises of symbolic interaction. I wish to say a few words about the major lines of variance.

Sociological thought rarely recognizes or treats human societies as composed of individuals who have selves. Instead, they assume human beings to be merely organisms with some kind of organization, responding to forces which play upon them. Generally, although not exclusively, these forces are lodged in the make-up of the society, as in the case of "social system," "social structure," "culture," "status position," "social role," "custom," "institution," "collective representation," "social situation," "social norm," and "values." The assumption is that the behavior of people as members *of a society* is an expression of the play on them of these kinds of factors or forces. This, of course, is the logical position which is necessarily taken when the scholar explains their behavior or phases of their behavior in terms of one or another of such social factors. The individuals who compose a human society are treated as the media through which such factors operate, and the social action of such individuals is regarded as an expression of

such factors. This approach or point of view denies, or at least ignores, that human beings have selves—that they act by making indications to themselves. Incidentally, the "self" is not brought into the picture by introducing such items as organic drives, motives, attitudes, feelings, internalized social factors, or psychological components. Such psychological factors have the same status as the social factors mentioned: they are regarded as factors which play on the individual to produce his action. They do not constitute the process of self-indication. The process of self-indication stands over against them, just as it stands over against the social factors which play on the human being. Practically all sociological conceptions of human society fail to recognize that the individuals who compose it have selves in the sense spoken of.

Correspondingly, such sociological conceptions do not regard the social actions of individuals in human society as being constructed by them through a process of interpretation. Instead, action is treated as a product of factors which play on and through individuals. The social behavior of people is not seen as built up by them through an interpretation of objects, situations, or the actions of others. If a place is given to "interpretation," the interpretation is regarded as merely an expression of other factors (such as motives) which precede the act, and accordingly disappears as a factor in its own right. Hence, the social action of people is treated as an outward flow or expression of forces playing on them rather than as acts which are built up by people through their interpretation of the situations in which they are placed.

These remarks suggest another significant line of difference between general sociological views and the position of symbolic interaction. These two sets of views differ in where they lodge social action. Under the perspective of symbolic interaction, social action is lodged in acting individuals who fit their respective lines of action to one another through a process of interpretation; group action is the collective action of such individuals. As opposed to this view, sociological conceptions generally lodge social action in the action of society or in some unit of society. Examples of this are legion. Let me cite a few. Some conceptions, in treating societies or human groups as "social systems," regard group action as an expression of a system, either in a state of balance or seeking to achieve balance. Or group action is conceived as an expression of the "functions" of a society or of a group. Or group action is regarded as the outward expression of elements lodged in society or the group, such as cultural demands, societal purposes, social values, or institutional stresses. These typical conceptions ignore or blot out a view of group life or of group action as consisting of the collective or concerted actions of individuals seeking to meet their life situations. If recognized at all, the efforts of people to develop collective acts to meet their situations are subsumed under the play of underlying or transcending forces which are lodged in society or its parts. The individuals composing the society or the group become "carriers," or media for the expression of such forces; and the interpretative behavior by means of which people form their actions is merely a coerced link in the play of such forces.

The indication of the foregoing lines of variance should help to put the position of symbolic interaction in better perspective. In the remaining discussion I wish to sketch somewhat more fully how human society appears in terms of symbolic interaction and to point out some methodological implications.

Human society is to be seen as consisting of acting people, and the life of the society is to be seen as consisting of their actions. The acting units may be separate individuals, collectivities whose members are acting together on a common quest, or organizations acting on behalf of a constituency. Respective examples are individual purchasers in a market, a play group or missionary band, and a business corporation or a national professional association. There is no empirically observable activity in a human society that does not spring from some acting unit. This banal statement needs to be stressed in light of the common practice of sociologists of reducing human society to social units that do not act—for example, social classes in modern society. Obviously, there are ways of viewing human society other than in terms of the acting units that compose it. I merely wish to point out that in respect to concrete or empirical activity human society must necessarily be seen in terms of the acting units that form it. I would add that any scheme of human society claiming to be a realistic analysis has to respect and be congruent with the empirical recognition that a human society consists of acting units.

Corresponding respect must be shown to the conditions under which such units act. One primary condition is that action takes place in and with regard to a situation. Whatever be the acting unit—an individual, a family, a school, a church, a business firm, a labor union, a legislature, and so on—any particular action is formed in the light of the situation in which it takes place. This leads to the recognition of a second major condition, namely, that the action is formed or constructed by interpreting the situation. The acting unit necessarily has to identify the things which it has to take into account—tasks, opportunities, obstacles, means, demands, discomforts, dangers, and the like; it has to assess them in some fashion and it has to make decisions on the basis of the assessment. Such interpretative behavior may take place in the individual guiding his own action, in a collectivity of individuals acting in concert, or in "agents" acting on behalf of a group or organization. Group life consists of acting units developing acts to meet the situations in which they are placed.

Usually, most of the situations encountered by people in a given society are defined or "structured" by them in the same way. Through previous interaction they develop and acquire common understandings or definitions of how to act in this or that situation. These common definitions enable people to act alike. The common repetitive behavior of people in such situations should not mislead the student into believing that no process of interpretation is in play; on the contrary, even though fixed, the actions of the participating people are constructed by them through a process of interpretation. Since ready-made and commonly accepted definitions are at hand, little strain is placed on people in guiding and organizing their acts. However, many other situations may not be defined in a single way by the participating people. In this event, their lines of action do not fit together readily and collective action is blocked. Interpretations have to be developed and effective accommodation of the participants to one another has to be worked out. In the case of such "undefined" situations, it is necessary to trace and study the emerging process of definition which is brought into play.

Insofar as sociologists or students of human society are concerned with the behavior of acting units, the position of symbolic interaction requires the student to catch the process of interpretation through which they construct their actions. This process is not to be caught merely by turning to conditions which are antecedent to the process. Such antecedent conditions are helpful in understanding the process insofar as they enter into it, but as mentioned previously they do not constitute the process. Nor can one catch the process merely by inferring its nature from the overt action which is its product. To catch the process, the student must take the role of the acting unit whose behavior he is studying. Since the interpretation is being made by the acting unit in terms of objects designated and appraised, meanings acquired, and decisions made, the process has to be seen from the standpoint of the acting unit. It is the recognition of this fact that makes the research work of such scholars as R. E. Park and W. I. Thomas so notable. To try to catch the interpretative process by remaining aloof as a so-called "objective" observer and refusing to take the role of the acting unit is to risk the worst kind of subjectivism—the objective observer is likely to fill in the process of interpretation with his own surmises in place of catching the process as it occurs in the experience of the acting unit which uses it.

By and large, of course, sociologists do not study human society in terms of its acting units. Instead, they are disposed to view human society in terms of structure or organization and to treat social action as an expression of such structure or organization. Thus, reliance is placed on such structural categories as social system, culture, norms, values, social stratification, status positions, social roles and institutional organization. These are used both to analyze human society and to account for social action within it. Other major interests of sociological scholars center around this focal theme of organization. One line of interest is to view organization in terms of the functions it is supposed to perform. Another line of interest is to study societal organization as a system seeking equilibrium; here the scholar endeavors to detect mechanisms which are indigenous to the system. Another line of interest is to identify forces which play upon organization to bring about changes in it; here the scholar endeavors, especially through comparative study, to isolate a relation between causative factors and structural results. These various lines of sociological perspective and interest, which are so strongly entrenched today, leap over the acting units of a society and bypass the interpretative process by which such acting units build up their actions.

These respective concerns with organization on one hand and with acting units on the other hand set the essential difference between conventional views of human society and the view of it implied in symbolic interaction. The latter view recognizes the presence of organization to human society and respects its importance. However, it sees and treats organization differently. The difference is along two major lines. First, from the standpoint of symbolic interaction the organization of a human society is the framework inside of which social action takes place and is not the determinant of that action. Second, such organization and changes in it are the product of the activity of acting units and not of "forces" which leave such acting units out of account. Each of these two major lines of difference should be explained briefly in order to obtain a better understanding of how human society appears in terms of symbolic interaction.

From the standpoint of symbolic interaction, social organization is a framework inside of which acting units develop their actions. Structural features, such as "culture," "social systems," "social stratification," or "social roles," set conditions for their action but do not determine their action. People—that is, acting units—do not act toward culture, social structure or the like; they act toward situations. Social organization enters into action only to the extent to which it shapes situations in which people act, and to the extent to which it supplies fixed sets of symbols which people use in interpreting their situations. These two forms of influence of social organization are important. In the case of settled and stabilized societies, such as isolated primitive tribes and peasant communities, the influence is certain to be profound. In the case of human societies, particularly modern societies, in which streams of new situations arise

and old situations become unstable, the influence of organization decreases. One should bear in mind that the most important element confronting an acting unit in situations is the actions of other acting units. In modern society, with its increasing crisscrossing of lines of action, it is common for situations to arise in which the actions of participants are not previously regularized and standardized. To this extent, existing social organization does not shape the situations. Correspondingly, the symbols or tools of interpretation used by acting units in such situations may vary and shift considerably. For these reasons, social action may go beyond, or depart from, existing organization in any of its structural dimensions. The organization of a human society is not to be identified with the process of interpretation used by its acting units; even though it affects that process, it does not embrace or cover the process.

Perhaps the most outstanding consequence of viewing human society as organization is to overlook the part played by acting units in social change. The conventional procedure of sociologists is (a) to identify human society (or some part of it) in terms of an established or organized form, (b) to identify some factor or condition of change playing upon the human society or the given part of it, and (c) to identify the new form assumed by the society following upon the play of the factor of change. Such observations permit the student to couch propositions to the effect that a given factor of change playing upon a given organized form results in a given new organized form. Examples ranging from crude to refined statements are legion, such as that an economic depression increases solidarity in the families of workingmen or that industrialization replaces extended families by nuclear families. My concern here is not with the validity of such propositions but with the methodological position which they presuppose. Essentially, such propositions either ignore the role of the interpretative behavior of acting units in the given instance of change, or else regard the interpretative behavior as coerced by the factor of change. I wish to point out that any line of social change, since it involves change in human action, is necessarily mediated by interpretation on the part of the people caught up in the change—the change appears in the form of new situations in which people have to construct new forms of action. Also, in line with what has been said previously, interpretations of new situations are not predetermined by conditions antecedent to the situations but depend on what is taken into account and assessed in the actual situations in which behavior is formed. Variations in interpretation may readily occur as different acting units cut out different objects in the situation, or give different weight to the objects which they note, or piece objects together in different patterns. In formulating propositions of social change, it would be wise to recognize that any given line of such change is mediated by acting units interpreting the situations with which they are confronted.

Students of human society will have to face the question of whether their preoccupation with categories of structure and organization can be squared with the interpretative process by means of which human beings, individually and collectively, act in human society. It is the discrepancy between the two which plagues such students in their efforts to attain scientific propositions of the sort achieved in the physical and biological sciences. It is this discrepancy, further, which is chiefly responsible for their difficulty in fitting hypothetical propositions to new arrays of empirical data. Efforts are made, of course, to overcome these shortcomings by devising new structural categories, by formulating new structural hypotheses, by developing more refined techniques of research, and even by formulating new methodological schemes of a structural character. These efforts continue to ignore or to explain away the interpretative process by which people act, individually and collectively, in society. The question remains whether human society or social action can be successfully analyzed by schemes which refuse to recognize human beings as they are, namely, as persons constructing individual and collective action through an interpretation of the situations which confront them.

6

On the Social Psychology of the Psychological Experiment

With Particular Reference to Demand Characteristics and Their Implications[1]

MARTIN T. ORNE[2]

> *It is to the highest degree probable that the subject['s] . . . general attitude of mind is that of ready complacency and cheerful willingness to assist the investigator in every possible way by reporting to him those very things which he is most eager to find, and that the very questions of the experimenter . . . suggest the shade of reply expected. . . . Indeed . . . it seems too often as if the subject were now regarded as a stupid automaton. . . .*
> —A. H. Pierce, 1908[3]

Since the time of Galileo, scientists have employed the laboratory experiment as a method of understanding natural phenomena. Generically, the experimental method consists of abstracting relevant variables from complex situations in nature and reproducing in the laboratory segments of these situations, varying the parameters involved so as to determine the effect of the experimental variables. This procedure allows generalization from the information obtained in the laboratory situation back to the original situation as it occurs in nature. The physical sciences have made striking advances through the use of this method, but in the behavioral sciences it has often been difficult to meet two necessary requirements for meaningful experimentation: reproducibility and ecological validity.[4] It has long been recognized that certain differences will exist between the types of experiments conducted in the physical sciences and those in the behavioral sciences because the former investi-

gates a universe of inanimate objects and forces, whereas the latter deals with animate organisms, often thinking, conscious subjects. However, recognition of this distinction has not always led to appropriate changes in the traditional experimental model of physics as employed in the behavioral sciences. Rather the experimental model has been so successful as employed in physics that there has been a tendency in the behavioral sciences to follow precisely a paradigm originated for the study of inanimate objects, i.e., one which proceeds by exposing the subject to various conditions and observing the differences in reaction of the subject under different conditions. However, the use of such a model with animal or human subjects leads to the problem that the subject of the experiment is assumed, at least implicitly, to be a *passive responder* to stimuli—an assumption difficult to justify. Further, in this type of model the experimental stimuli themselves are usually rigorously defined in terms of what *is done* to the subject. In contrast, the purpose of this paper will be to focus on what the human subject *does* in the laboratory: what motivation the subject is likely to have in the experimental situation, how he usually perceives behavioral research, what the nature of the cues is that the subject is likely to pick up, etc. Stated in other terms, what factors are apt to affect the subject's reaction to the well-defined stimuli in the situation? These factors comprise what will be referred to here as the "experimental setting."

Since any experimental manipulation of human subjects takes place within this larger framework or setting, we should propose that the above-mentioned factors must be further elaborated and the parameters of the experimental setting more carefully defined so that adequate controls can be designed to isolate the effects of the experimental setting from the effects of the experimental variables. Later in this paper we shall propose certain possible techniques of control which have been devised in the process of our research on the nature of hypnosis.

Our initial focus here will be on some of the qualities peculiar to psychological experiments. The experimental situation is one which takes place within the context of an explicit agreement of the subject to participate in a special form of social interaction known as "taking part in an experiment." Within the context of our culture the roles of subject and experimenter are well understood and carry with them well-defined mutual role expectations. A particularly striking aspect of the typical experimenter-subject relationship is the extent to which the subject will play his role and place himself under the control of the experimenter. Once a subject has agreed to participate in a psychological experiment, he implicitly agrees to perform a very wide range of actions on request without inquiring as to their purpose, and frequently without inquiring as to their duration.

Furthermore, the subject agrees to tolerate a considerable degree of discomfort, boredom, or actual pain, if required to do so by the experimenter. Just about any request which could conceivably be asked of the subject by a reputable investigator is legitimized by the quasi-magical phrase, "This is an experiment," and the shared assumption that a legitimate purpose will be served by the subject's behavior. A somewhat trivial example of this legitimization of requests is as follows:

A number of casual acquaintances were asked whether they would do the experimenter a favor; on their acquiescence, they were asked to perform five push-ups. Their response tended to be amazement, incredulity and the question "Why?" Another similar group of individuals were asked whether they would take part in an experiment of brief duration. When they agreed to do so, they too were asked to perform five push-ups. Their typical response was "Where?"

The striking degree of control inherent in the experimental situation can also be illustrated by a set of pilot experiments which were performed in the course of designing an experiment to test whether the degree of control inherent in the *hypnotic* relationship is greater than that in a waking relationship.[5] In order to test this question, we tried to develop a set of tasks which waking subjects would refuse to do, or would do only for a short period of time. The tasks were intended to be psychologically noxious, meaningless, or boring, rather than painful or fatiguing.

For example, one task was to perform serial additions of each adjacent two numbers on sheets filled with rows of random digits. In order to complete just one sheet, the subject would be required to perform 224 additions! A stack of some 2,000 sheets was presented to each subject—clearly an impossible task to complete. After the instructions were given, the subject was deprived of his watch and told, "Continue to work; I will return eventually." Five and one-half hours later, the *experimenter* gave up! In general, subjects tended to continue this type of task for several hours, usually with little decrement in performance. Since we were trying to find a task which would be discontinued spontaneously within a brief period, we tried to create a more frustrating situation as follows:

Subjects were asked to perform the same task described above but were also told that when [they] finished the additions on each sheet, they should pick up a card from a large pile, which would instruct them on what to do next. However, every card in the pile read,

> You are to tear up the sheet of paper which you have just completed into a minimum of thirty-two pieces and go on to the next sheet of paper and continue working as you did before; when you have completed this piece of paper, pick up the next card which will instruct you further. Work as accurately and as rapidly as you can.

Our expectation was that subjects would discontinue the task as soon as they realized that the cards were worded identically, that each finished piece of work had to be destroyed, and that, in short, the task was completely meaningless.

Somewhat to our amazement, subjects tended to persist in the task for several hours with relatively little sign of overt hostility. Removal of the one-way screen did not tend to make much difference. The postexperimental inquiry helped to explain the subjects' behavior. When asked about the tasks, subjects would invariably attribute considerable meaning to their performance, viewing it as an endurance test or the like.

Thus far, we have been singularly unsuccessful in finding an experimental task which would be discontinued, or, indeed, refused by subjects in an experimental set-

ting.[6,7] Not only do subjects continue to perform boring, unrewarding tasks, but they do so with few errors and little decrement in speed. It became apparent that it was extremely difficult to design an experiment to test the degree of social control in hypnosis, in view of the already *very high degree of control in the experimental situation itself.*

The quasi-experimental work reported here is highly informal and based on samples of three or four subjects in each group. It does, however, illustrate the remarkable compliance of the experimental subject. The only other situations where such a wide range of requests are carried out with little or no question are those of complete authority, such as some parent-child relationships or some doctor-patient relationships. This aspect of the experiment as a social situation will not become apparent unless one tests for it; it is, however, present in varying degrees in all experimental contexts. Not only are tasks carried out, but they are performed with care over considerable periods of time.

Our observation that subjects tend to carry out a remarkably wide range of instructions with a surprising degree of diligence reflects only one aspect of the motivation manifested by most subjects in an experimental situation. It is relevant to consider another aspect of motivation that is common to the subjects of most psychological experiments: high regard for the aims of science and experimentation.

A volunteer who participates in a psychological experiment may do so for a wide variety of reasons ranging from the need to fulfill a course requirement, to the need for money, to the unvoiced hope of altering his personal adjustment for the better, etc. Over and above these motives, however, college students tend to share (with the experimenter) the hope and expectation that the study in which they are participating will in some material way contribute to science and perhaps ultimately to human welfare in general. We should expect that many of the characteristics of the experimental situation derive from the peculiar role relationship which exists between subject and experimenter. Both subject and experimenter share the belief that whatever the experimental task is, it is important, and that as such no matter how much effort must be exerted or how much discomfort must be endured, it is justified by the ultimate purpose.

If we assume that much of the motivation of the subject to comply with any and all experimental instructions derives from an identification with the goals of science in general and the success of the experiment in particular,[8] it follows that the subject has a stake in the outcome of the study in which he is participating. For the volunteer subject to feel that he has made a useful contribution, it is necessary for him to assume that the experimenter is competent and that he himself is a "good subject."

The significance to the subject of successfully being a "good subject" is attested to by the frequent questions at the conclusion of an experiment, to the effect of, "Did I ruin the experiment?" What is most commonly meant by this is, "Did I perform well in my role as experimental subject?" or "Did my behavior demonstrate that which the experiment is designed to show?" Admittedly, subjects are concerned about their performance in terms of reinforcing their self-image; nonetheless, they seem even more concerned with the utility of their performances. We might well expect then that as far as the subject is able, he will behave in an experimental context in a manner designed to play the role of a "good subject" or, in other words, *to validate the experimental hypothesis.* Viewed in this way, the student volunteer is *not* merely a passive responder in an experimental situation but rather he has a very real stake in the successful outcome of the experiment. This problem is implicitly recognized in the large number of psychological studies which attempt to conceal the true purpose of the experiment from the sub-

ject in the hope of thereby obtaining more reliable data. This maneuver on the part of psychologists is so widely known in the college population that even if a psychologist is honest with the subject, more often than not he will be distrusted. As one subject pithily put it, "Psychologists always lie!" This bit of paranoia has some support in reality.

The subject's performance in an experiment might almost be conceptualized as problem-solving behavior; that is, at some level he sees it as his task to ascertain the true purpose of the experiment and respond in a manner which will support the hypotheses being tested. Viewed in this light, the totality of cues which convey an experimental hypothesis to the subject become significant determinants of subjects' behavior. We have labeled the sum total of such cues as the *"demand characteristics of the experimental situation"* (Orne, 1959a). These cues include the rumors or campus scuttlebutt about the research, the information conveyed during the original solicitation, the person of the experimenter, and the setting of the laboratory, as well as all explicit and implicit communications during the experiment proper. A frequently overlooked, but nonetheless very significant source of cues for the subject lies in the experimental procedure itself, viewed in the light of the subject's previous knowledge and experience. For example, if a test is given twice with some intervening treatment, even the dullest college student is aware that some change is expected, particularly if the test is in some obvious way related to the treatment.

The demand characteristics perceived in any particular experiment will vary with the sophistication, intelligence, and previous experience of each experimental subject. To the extent that the demand characteristics of the experiment are clear-cut, they will be perceived uniformly by most experimental subjects. It is entirely possible to have an experimental situation with clear-cut demand characteristics for psychology undergraduates which, however, does not have the same clear-cut demand characteristics for enlisted army personnel. It is, of course, those demand characteristics which are perceived by the subject that will influence his behavior.

We should like to propose the heuristic assumption that a subject's behavior in any experimental situation will be determined by two sets of variables: *(a)* those which are traditionally defined as experimental variables and *(b)* the perceived demand characteristics of the experimental situation. The extent to which the subject's behavior is related to the demand characteristics, rather than to the experimental variable, will in large measure determine both the extent to which the experiment can be replicated with minor modification (i.e., modified demand characteristics) and the extent to which generalizations can be drawn about the effect of the experimental variables in nonexperimental contexts (the problem of ecological validity [Brunswik, 1947]).

It becomes an empirical issue to study under what circumstances, in what kind of experimental contexts, and with what kind of subject populations, demand characteristics become significant in determining the behavior of subjects in experimental situations. It should be clear that demand characteristics cannot be eliminated from experiments; all experiments will have demand characteristics, and these will always have some effect. It does become possible, however, to study the effect of demand characteristics as opposed to the effect of experimental variables. However, techniques designed to study the effect of demand characteristics need to take into account that these effects result from the subject's *active* attempt to respond appropriately to the *totality* of the experimental situation.

It is perhaps best to think of the perceived demand characteristics as a contextual variable in the experimental situation. We should like to emphasize that, at this stage, little is known about this variable. In our first study which utilized the demand characteristics concept (Orne, 1959b), we found that a particular experimental effect was present only in records of those subjects who were able to verbalize the experimenter's hypothesis. Those subjects who were unable to do so did not show the predicted phenomenon. Indeed we found that whether or not a given subject perceived the experimenter's hypothesis was a more accurate predictor of the subject's actual performance than his statement about what he thought he had done on the experimental task. It became clear from extensive interviews with subjects that response to the demand characteristics is not merely conscious compliance. When we speak of "playing the role of a good experimental subject," we use the concept analogously to the way in which Sarbin (1950) describes role playing in hypnosis: namely, largely on a nonconscious level. The demand characteristics of the situation help define the role of "good experimental subject," and the responses of the subject are a function of the role that is created.

We have a suspicion that the demand characteristics most potent in determining subjects' behavior are those which convey the purpose of the experiment effectively but not obviously. If the purpose of the experiment is not clear, or is highly ambiguous, many different hypotheses may be formed by different subjects, and the demand characteristics will not lead to clear-cut results. If, on the other hand, the demand characteristics are so obvious that the subject becomes fully conscious of the expectations of the experimenter, there is a tendency to lean over backwards to be honest. We are encountering here the effect of another facet of the college student's attitude toward science. While the student wants studies to "work," he feels he must be honest in his report; otherwise, erroneous conclusions will be drawn. Therefore, if the subject becomes acutely aware of the experimenter's expectations, there may be a tendency for biasing in the opposite direction. (This is analogous to the often observed tendency to favor individuals whom we dislike in an effort to be fair.)[9]

Delineation of the situations where demand characteristics may produce an effect ascribed to experimental variables, or where they may obscure such an effect and actually lead to systematic data in the opposite direction, as well as those experimental contexts where they do not play a major role, is an issue for further work. Recognizing the contribution to experimental results which may be made by the demand characteristics of the situation, what are some experimental techniques for the study of demand characteristics?

As we have pointed out, it is futile to imagine an experiment that could be created without demand characteristics. One of the basic characteristics of the human being is that he will ascribe purpose and meaning even in the absence of purpose and meaning. In an experiment where he knows some purpose exists, it is inconceivable for him not to form some hypothesis as to the purpose, based on some cues, no matter how meager; this will then determine the demand characteristics which will be perceived by and operate for a particular subject. Rather than eliminating this variable then, it becomes necessary to take demand characteristics into account, study their effect, and manipulate them if necessary.

One procedure to determine the demand characteristics is the systematic study of each individual subject's perception of the experimental hypothesis. If one can determine what demand characteristics are perceived by each subject, it becomes possible to determine to what extent these, rather than the experimental variables, correlate with the observed behavior. If the subject's behavior correlates better with the demand characteristics than with the experimental variables, it is probable that the demand characteristics are the major determinants of the behavior.

The most obvious technique for determining what demand characteristics are perceived is the use of postexperimental inquiry. In this regard, it is well to point out that considerable self-discipline is necessary for the experimenter to obtain a valid inquiry. A great many experimenters at least implicitly make the demand that the subject not perceive what is really going on. The temptation for the experimenter, in, say, a replication of an Asch group pressure experiment, is to ask the subject afterwards, "You didn't realize that the other fellows were confederates, did you?" Having obtained the required, "No," the experimenter breathes a sigh of relief and neither subject nor experimenter pursues the issue further.[10] However, even if the experimenter makes an effort to elicit the subject's perception of the hypothesis of the experiment, he may have difficulty in obtaining a valid report because the subject as well as he himself has considerable interest in appearing naive.

Most subjects are cognizant that they are not supposed to know any more about an experiment than they have been told and that excessive knowledge will disqualify them from participating, or, in the case of a postexperimental inquiry, [that] such knowledge will invalidate their performance. As we pointed out earlier, subjects have a real stake in viewing their performance as meaningful. For this reason, it is commonplace to find a pact of ignorance resulting from the intertwining motives of both experimenter and subject, neither wishing to create a situation where the particular subject's performance needs to be excluded from the study.

For these reasons, inquiry procedures are required to push the subject for information without, however, providing in themselves cues as to what is expected. The general question which needs to be explored is the subject's perception of the experimental purpose and the specific hypotheses of the experimenter. This can best be done by an open-ended procedure starting with the very general question of "What do you think that the experiment is about?" and only much later asking specific questions. Responses of "I don't know" should be dealt with by encouraging the subject to guess, use his imagination, and in general, by refusing to accept this response. Under these circumstances, the overwhelming majority of students will turn out to have evolved very definite hypotheses. These hypotheses can then be judged, and a correlation between them and experimental performance can be drawn.

Two objections may be made against this type of inquiry: (a) that the subject's perception of the experimenter's hypotheses is based on his own experimental behavior, and therefore a correlation between these two variables may have little to do with the determinants of behavior, and (b) that the inquiry procedure itself is subject to demand characteristics.

A procedure which has been independently advocated by Riecken (1958) and Orne (1959a) is designed to deal with the first of these objections. This consists of an inquiry procedure which is conducted much as though the subject had actually been run in the experiment, without, however, permitting him to be given any experimental data. Instead, the precise procedure of the experiment is explained, the experimental material is shown to the subject, and he is told what he would be required to do; however, he is not permitted to make any responses. He is then given a postexperimental inquiry as though he had been a subject. Thus, one would say, "If I had asked you to do all these things, what do you think that the experiment would be about, what do you think I would be trying to prove, what would my hypothesis be?" etc. This technique, which we have termed the pre-experimental inquiry, can be extended very readily to the giving of pre-experimental tests, followed by the explanation of experimental conditions and tasks, and the administration of

postexperimental tests. The subject is requested to behave on these tests as though he had been exposed to the experimental treatment that was described to him. This type of procedure is not open to the objection that the subject's own behavior has provided cues for him as to the purpose of the task. It presents him with a straight problem-solving situation and makes explicit what, for the true experimental subject, is implicit. It goes without saying that these subjects who are run on the pre-experimental inquiry conditions must be drawn from the same population as the experimental groups and may, of course, not be run subsequently in the experimental condition. This technique is one of approximation rather than of proof. However, if subjects describe behavior on the pre-inquiry conditions as similar to, or identical with, that actually given by subjects exposed to the experimental conditions, the hypothesis becomes plausible that demand characteristics may be responsible for the behavior.

It is clear that pre- and postexperimental inquiry techniques have their own demand characteristics. For these reasons, it is usually best to have the inquiry conducted by an experimenter who is not acquainted with the actual experimental behavior of the subjects. This will tend to minimize the effect of experimenter bias.

Another technique which we have utilized for approximating the effect of the demand characteristics is to attempt to hold the demand characteristics constant and eliminate the experimental variable. One way of accomplishing this purpose is through the use of simulating subjects. This is a group of subjects who are not exposed to the experimental variable to which the effect has been attributed, but who are instructed to act as if this were the case. In order to control for experimenter bias under these circumstances, it is advisable to utilize more than one experimenter and to have the experimenter who actually runs the subjects "blind" as to which group (simulating or real) any given individual belongs.

Our work in hypnosis (Damaser, Shor, & Orne, 1963; Orne, 1959b; Shor, 1959) is a good example of the use of simulating controls. Subjects unable to enter hypnosis are instructed to simulate entering hypnosis for another experimenter. The experimenter who runs the study sees both highly trained hypnotic subjects and simulators in random order and does not know to which group each subject belongs. Because the subjects are run "blind," the experimenter is more likely to treat the two groups of subjects identically. We have found that simulating subjects are able to perform with great effectiveness, deceiving even well-trained hypnotists. However, the simulating group is not exposed to the experimental condition (in this case, hypnosis) to which the given effect under investigation is often ascribed. Rather, it is a group faced with a problem-solving task: namely to utilize whatever cues are made available by the experimental context and the experimenter's concrete behavior in order to behave as they think that hypnotized subjects might. Therefore, to the extent that simulating subjects are able to behave identically, it is possible that demand characteristics, rather than the altered state of consciousness, could account for the behavior of the experimental group.

The same type of technique can be utilized in other types of studies. For example, in contrast to the placebo control in a drug study, it is equally possible to instruct some subjects not to take the medication at all, but to act as if they had. It must be emphasized that this type of control is different from the placebo control. It represents an approximation. It maximally confronts the simulating subject with a problem-solving task and suggests how much of the total effect could be accounted for by the demand characteristics—assuming that the experimental group had taken full advantage of them, an assumption not necessarily correct.

All of the techniques proposed thus far share the quality that they depend upon the active cooperation of the control subject, and in some way utilize his thinking process as an intrinsic factor. The subject does *not* just respond in these control situations but, rather, he is required *actively* to solve the problem.

The use of placebo experimental conditions is a way in which this problem can be dealt with in a more classic fashion. Psychopharmacology has used such techniques extensively, but here too they present problems. In the case of placebos and drugs, it is often the case that the physician is "blind" as to whether a drug is placebo or active, but the patient is not, despite precautions to the contrary; i.e., the patient is cognizant that he does not have the side effects which some of his fellow patients on the ward experience. By the same token, in psychological placebo treatments, it is equally important to ascertain whether the subject actually perceived the treatment to be experimental or control. Certainly the subject's perception of himself as a control subject may materially alter the situation.

A recent experiment in our laboratory illustrates this type of investigation (Orne & Scheibe, 1964). We were interested in studying the demand characteristics of sensory deprivation experiments, independent of any actual sensory deprivation. We hypothesized that the overly cautious treatment of subjects, careful screening for mental or physical disorders, awesome release forms, and, above all, the presence of a "panic (release) button" might be more significant in producing the effects reported from sensory deprivation than the actual diminution of sensory input. A pilot study (Stare, Brown, & Orne, 1959), employing pre-inquiry techniques, supported this view. Recently, we designed an experiment to test more rigorously this hypothesis.

This experiment, which we called Meaning Deprivation, had all the *accoutrements* of sensory deprivation, including release forms and a red panic button. However, we carefully refrained from creating any sensory deprivation whatsoever. The experimental task consisted of sitting in a small experimental room which was well lighted, with two comfortable chairs, as well as ice water and a sandwich, and an optional task of adding numbers. The subject did not have a watch during this time, the room was reasonably quiet, but not soundproof, and the duration of the experiment (of which the subject was ignorant) was four hours. Before the subject was placed in the experimental room, 10 tests previously used in sensory deprivation research were administered. At the completion of the experiment, the same tasks were again administered. A microphone and a one-way screen were present in the room, and the subject was encouraged to verbalize freely.

The control group of 10 subjects was subjected to the identical treatment, except that they were told that they were control subjects for a sensory deprivation experiment. The panic button was eliminated for this group. The formal experimental treatment of these two groups of subjects was the same in terms of the objective stress—four hours of isolation. However, the demand characteristics had been purposively varied for the two groups to study the effect of demand characteristics as opposed to objective stress. Of the 14 measures which could be quantified, 13 were in the predicted direction and 6 were significant at the selected 10% *alpha* level or better. A Mann-Whitney μ test has been performed on the summation ranks of all measures as a convenient method for summarizing the overall differences. The one-tailed probability which emerges is $p = .001$, a clear demonstration of expected effects.

This study suggests that demand characteristics may in part account for some of the findings commonly attributed to sensory deprivation. We have found similar significant effects of demand characteristics in accounting for a great deal of the findings reported in hypnosis. It is highly probable that careful attention to this variable, or group of variables, may resolve some of the current controversies regarding a number of psychological phenomena in motivation, learning, and perception.

In summary, we have suggested that the subject must be recognized as an active participant in any experiment, and that it may be fruitful to view the psychological experiment as a very special form of social interaction. We have proposed that the subject's behavior in an experiment is a function of the totality of the situation, which includes the experimental variables being investigated and at least one other set of variables which we have subsumed under the heading, demand characteristics of the experimental situation. The study and control of demand characteristics are not simply matters of good experimental technique; rather, it is an empirical issue to determine under what circumstances demand characteristics significantly affect subjects' experimental behavior. Several empirical techniques have been proposed for this purpose. It has been suggested that control of these variables in particular may lead to greater reproducibility and ecological validity of psychological experiments. With an increasing understanding of these factors intrinsic to the experimental context, the experimental method in psychology may become a more effective tool in predicting behavior in nonexperimental contexts.

NOTES

1. This paper was presented at the Symposium, "On the Social Psychology of the Psychological Experiment," American Psychological Association Convention, New York, 1961.

The work reported here was supported in part by a Public Health Service Research Grant, M-3369, National Institute of Mental Health.

2. I wish to thank my associates Ronald E. Shor, Donald N. O'Connell, Ulric Neisser, Karl E. Scheibe, and Emily F. Carota for their comments and criticisms in the preparation of this paper.
3. See reference list (Pierce, 1908).
4. Ecological validity, in the sense that Brunswik (1947) has used the term: appropriate generalization from the laboratory to nonexperimental situations.
5. These pilot studies were performed by Thomas Menaker.
6. Tasks which would involve the use of actual severe physical pain or exhaustion were not considered.
7. This observation is consistent with Frank's (1944) failure to obtain resistance to disagreeable or nonsensical tasks. He accounts for this "primarily by S's unwillingness to break the tacit agreement he had made when he volunteered to take part in the experiment, namely, to do whatever the experiment required of him" (p. 24).
8. This hypothesis is subject to empirical test. We should predict that there would be measurable differences in motivation between subjects who perceive a particular experiment as "significant" and those who perceive the experiment as "unimportant."
9. Rosenthal (1961) in his recent work on experimenter bias, has reported a similar type of phenomenon. Biasing was maximized by ego involvement of the experimenters, but when an attempt was made to increase biasing by paying for "good results," there was a marked reduction of effect. This reversal may be ascribed to the experimenters' becoming too aware of their own wishes in the situation.
10. Asch (1952) himself took great pains to avoid this pitfall.

REFERENCES

Asch, S. E., *Social Psychology* (New York: Prentice-Hall, 1952).
Brunswik, E., *Systematic and Representative Design of Psychological Experiments with Results in Physical and Social Perception* (Berkeley: University of California Press, 1947), Syllabus Series, no. 304.
Damaser, Esther C., Shor, R. E., and Orne, M. T., "Physiological Effects During Hypnotically-Requested Emotions," *Psychosomatic Medicine*, 25 (1963), 334–43.
Frank, J. D., "Experimental Studies of Personal Pressure and Resistance: I. Experimental Production of Resistance," *Journal of General Psychology*, 30 (1944), 23–41.
Orne, M. T., "The Demand Characteristics of an Experimental Design and Their Implications," paper read at American Psychological Association, Cincinnati, 1959a.
Orne, M. T., "The Nature of Hypnosis: Artifact and Essence," *Journal of Abnormal and Social Psychology*, 58 (1959b), 277–99.
Orne, M. T., and Scheibe, K. E., "The Contribution of Nondeprivation Factors in the Production of Sensory Deprivation Effects: The Psychology of the 'Panic Button,'" *Journal of Abnormal and Social Psychology*, 68 (1964), 3–12.
Pierce, A. H., "The Subconscious Again," *Journal of Philosophy, Psychology, and Scientific Method*, 5 (1908), 264–71.
Riecken, H. W., "A Program for Research on Experiments in Social Psychology," paper read at Behavioral Sciences Conference, University of New Mexico, 1958.
Rosenthal, R., "On the Social Psychology of the Psychological Experiment: With Particular Reference to Experimenter Bias," paper read at American Psychological Association, New York, 1961.
Sarbin, T. R., "Contributions to Role-taking Theory: I. Hypnotic Behavior," *Psychological Review*, 57 (1950), 255–70.
Shor, R. E., "Explorations in Hypnosis: A Theoretical and Experimental Study," unpublished doctoral dissertation, Brandeis University, 1959.
Stare, F., Brown, J., and Orne, M. T., "Demand Characteristics in Sensory Deprivation Studies," unpublished seminar paper, Massachusetts Mental Health Center and Harvard University, 1959.

7

Birthdate and Mortality
An Evaluation of the Death-Dip/Death-Rise Phenomenon

BRYAN BYERS
RICHARD A. ZELLER
PEGGY Y. BYERS

The timing of death has sparked inquiry and investigation. Many have made attempts at ascertaining the most likely, and least likely, time of death (Fischer and Dlin 1972; Phillips 1972; Marriott and Harshbarger 1973; Phillips and Feldman 1973; Labovitz 1974; Alderson 1975; Baltes 1977; Kunz and Summers 1980; Schulz and Bazerman 1980; Boor 1981 and 1982; Marriott and Fitzgerald 1981; Rago, Mason and Cleland 1981; Tanur 1981; Harrison and Moore 1982; Wasserman 1983; Byers 1985; Byers and Zeller 1987; and Byers and Zeller forthcoming). The quantitative search for mortality patterns has been cause for continued intrigue and study.

The timing of death and mortality patterns have been studied using statistical methods. The first such researcher in the area was David P. Phillips (1972). Phillips was the first to describe the pattern or phenomenon as the "Death-Dip/Death-Rise" hypothesis. It has been maintained that there is a significant reduction in deaths (death-dip) before certain dates and an increase in mortality (death-rise) after those important dates, for certain individuals. Hence, there will be fewer deaths before certain dates or occasions and more deaths after the date or event has passed. This position maintains, then, that certain individuals are capable of postponing or delaying their own demise until a personally significant event has been experienced. The common events considered for this hypothesis have included birthdays, Christmas, Easter, Yom Kippur and political events. . . .

[Some] authors have also contested the validity of the hypothesis. Among the most noteworthy findings from these researchers have been the relatively small effects around a criterion date (Alderson 1975). Baltes (1977) found no significant dip or rise at all. The evidence that the original Phillips data does not hold up to rigorous methodological scrutiny, and the lack of any strong theoretical statement to explain the phenomenon (Schultz and Bazerman, 1980) casts doubt on the death dip/death rise phenomenon.

Thus, the literature concerning the Death-Dip/Death-Rise hypothesis is filled with contradictions and anomalies. Phillips (1972) and Phillips and Feldman (1973) confirmed the hypothesis for famous people; Labovitz (1974) does not. However, Labovitz (1974) confirms the hypothesis significantly when examining fifty non-famous people while Alderson finds only a trivial effect for a quarter of a million. Baltes (1977) finds no Death-Dip/Death-Rise effect for deaths to people under nineteen years of age. Byers and Zeller (1987) found a death-rise after the criterion date. Time intervals for evaluation in these studies range from weeks to months to quarters.

These anomalies raise the following questions:

1. Why is the Death-Dip/Death-Rise hypothesis confirmed when the sample is small but not when the sample is large?
2. How long is an appropriate interval before and after the birth date for the hypothesis to operate?
3. Does the pattern, if it actually describes mortality behavior, apply across year, gender, race, marital status, age, and cause of death?

The present study is designed to answer these questions. Specifically, a large sample will be examined at monthly, weekly, and daily intervals and the mortality behavior within a variety of relevant contextual variables will be examined.

THEORETICAL FOUNDATION

Due to the apparent lack of a strong theoretical foundation, the present discussion will examine the few theoretical attempts which do exist to explain these findings, critique these, and offer some alternative theoretical possibilities.

Prior Research

As mentioned earlier, the first such researcher in this field was David Phillips. Theoretically, Phillips and Feldman (1973) attempted to explain the death-dip/death-rise phenomenon with a discussion of Durkheimian theory with an emphasis on the notion of social integration and the shared celebratory function which criterion dates supposedly hold for many people. That is to say, a strong death-dip/death-rise finding which Phillips claims to have found (and that was later contested by Schultz & Bazerman 1980 and others) could be indicative of the sense of belonging, solidarity, and integration an individual feels to his/her culture and society. These characteristics, Phillips and Feldman (1973) maintain, are elicited by the collective and individual importance

such events hold for people. The ideas and explanation contained within the original article tended to support an already popular notion: Individuals, if they have the internal strength, can hold on to experience a special day. This idea has remained popular mainly due to anecdotal cases which have supported this belief, and the consistent way in which the idea aligns with American ideology (i.e., you can do anything if you set your mind to it). Our explanation for the popularity of these findings may, therefore, be found on two fronts, one being related to the public appeal such findings have and the other being the ideological verification such findings provide.

While the Phillips and Feldman explanation is clearly sociological in nature, there have been attempts at psychological explanation. Researchers providing a psychological theory foundation have been Harrison and Moore (1982) and Harrison and Kroll (1985). In both studies, the authors used the "opponent process theory" of motivation. The theory is a psychological one in the stimulus-response tradition. Stated briefly, a stimulus (in this case a criterion date) elicits an emotional state for the individual. The removal of the stimulus will produce an opposite reaction. That is, when the criterion date has passed, there will be a negative response. The above authors, then, in their latest paper associate the presence of the stimulus with something "good" and its absence with something "bad," or less desirable. As a result, the criterion date of Christmas produces an affective reaction and the subsequent death dip or decrease. The removal of that stimulus elicits emotions in the opposite direction with the result of death surges.

We maintain that both theories have weaknesses as applied to the death-dip/death-rise phenomenon. There are two primary limitations we will address with the alternatives below. First, neither theory provides any strong argument concerning the manner in which different individuals may have radically divergent experiences. Instead, all individuals are placed together with the apparent expectation that there are no significant differences in experience. How can it be stated with any certainty that the social, psychological, or social-psychological experience may be so uniform? What is needed is a theoretical approach to this issue which will allow for individualized experience while being theoretically sound and generalizable. Secondly, there are no explanations for the possible control variable differences one may find in such research. Why is it that one category of individuals (the never married, the elderly, etc.) may demonstrate a mortality pattern consistent with the hypothesis while another may not? These two theoretical limitations will be addressed below.

THEORETICAL ALTERNATIVES

A promising theoretical approach to the present research problem is a social psychological one. The rationale for this approach is that the individual experience related to the death-dip/death-rise may best be situated there because of the personal significance which the date apparently contains. This assumption permeates the death-dip/death-rise literature. In order to investigate this approach the following discussion will center on the works of W. I. Thomas and Peter Berger & Thomas Luckmann.

The work of W. I. Thomas is primarily known from the now famous maxim related to the definition of the situation: "If men define situations as real, they are real in their consequences" (Thomas 1928). Individuals, according to Thomas, do not merely respond to the societal definition of events and ideas which have been provided for them. Instead, individuals also respond to the unique understanding events have for them. This idea may even come into play with regard to significant events individuals may experience.

A particularly interesting and useful idea contained within Thomas' "situational analysis" is the notion that individuals construct a reality for themselves even though there are powerful societal definitions provided *a priori*. As for significant events, society places significance on such things as birthdays, anniversaries, and Christmas. In addition, and depending on one's membership in various subcultures, certain other religious or ethnic holidays may also be situationally defined by the group as significant. Through socialization, one learns the social significance of holidays and other social events. In addition, however, situational analysis also suggests that the individual develops a "definition of the situation" which will be unique to the person and different from the societal definition. Therefore, Thomas would maintain that the societal influence always exists. Further, Thomas notes that the definition provided by society and that generated by the individual may compete. Due to the societal nature of the definition and the individual definition interaction, there may be a "rivalry" between definitions. The meaning of the rivalry for Thomas is grounded in the idea that individuals interpret situations and create reality for themselves but are also influenced by the larger social structure and the meanings contained therein.

The notion that reality is "constructed" has an appealing utility to the present discussion (Peter Berger and Thomas Luckmann 1966). As with the work of Thomas, Berger and Luckmann recognize the significance of societal influences and the individual definition. They suggest that the nature of social reality is constructed by the participant in society through interpretation and symbolic meaning. Significant events have symbolic meaning for society and individuals. The symbolic nature and interpretation of events is molded through social processes into a reality which is acted upon and accepted as the true nature of society. Individual experiences may be integrated into this reality construction, interpreted, and responded to per the reality the events represent. In this way, the social construction of reality involves the symbolic interpretive process of creating social structure through the human experience. The social construction of reality centered around the societal and personal emphasis placed on important events, then, may be another useful theoretical alternative in understanding the meaning behind the death-dip/death-rise phenomenon.

The death-dip/death-rise phenomenon may therefore be interpreted through situational analysis and the social construction of reality. The social self is influenced a great deal by the processes of society. In turn, the nature of social experience is influenced by the individual. Within this paradigm, the importance placed on experience, symbols, events, and communication cannot be underestimated as these elements relate to the significance placed on socially, and personally, important events. Through the definition of the situation and the social construction of reality, then, individuals may experience the social and personal significance of an event such as Christmas with the result being a dip and rise pattern.

METHOD

Population

The population for this study included all reported deaths in the State of Ohio for the calendar years 1979, 1980, and 1981. The population included all natural and causes by other circumstances. The definition of "death," for the purpose of this study, was any mortality recorded or registered in the official state mortality records. The record of mortality consisted of Vital Statistics for the years 1979, 1980, and 1981. The datum were Ohio Department of Health Vital Statistics.[1]

The population to be enumerated in this study includes the total number of deaths recorded in Ohio for the years cited above (N = 297,991). The population included all deaths classified by the criteria outlined in the *Manual of the International Statistical Classification of Diseases, Injuries, and Causes of Death* (World Health Organization, 1980). The listings for causes of death consisted of nineteen major headings with 138 sub-classifications and 1,280 specific disease, injury and death causes.

The population was intended to insure that every applicable case could be included. In order to conduct the study, the population was restricted to those causes of death which could be classified under "natural" or "disease" categorizations. Those causes of death which may be classified under the non-natural headings or sub-headings in the classification manual had to be excluded due to the assumed lack of control over death. The phenomenon could only be tested on natural and disease categories due to the personal mastery of control assumption which states that in order to control the timing of mortality the death must not be due to some external cause (i.e., accidents, homicides), or due to some cause in which the individual has much control (i.e., suicide). Deaths other than those due to natural cause have an unpredictable nature, thus, limiting the applicability of personal control over mortality timing. After removing non-natural and non-disease categories of death, the population consisted of 268,424 cases. This procedure left 558 specific cause of death classifications.

Statistical Technique

In order to study the Death-Dip/Death-Rise hypothesis, the year was defined by day where January 1 = 1 and December 31 = 365.[2] For each subject, the date of birth and the date of death were coded on year defined by day. Data relevant to the problem under investigation in this paper was created by subtracting the death date from the birth date.

Through this procedure, a distribution of 0-364 was obtained in which zero was the birthday for all cases with the other 364 days being the number of days after the birthday that the death occurred.

The contextual variables used in this study were as follows: *Death Year* signifies 1979, 1980 or 1981, the year the death occurred; *Gender and Race* were examined by using the categories of white male, nonwhite male, white female, and nonwhite female; *Marital Status* consisted of married, never married, widowed, and divorced; *Age* was delineated by using ten to forty-nine in one group and those fifty and over in the other.

A cause of death was given to all cases used in the present study. The classifications used came from the World Health Organization's *Manual of the International Statistical Classification of Diseases, Injuries, and Causes of Death* (World Health Organization, 1980). This was conducted after all non-natural causes of death were excluded.

The revised classification is as follows:

Category causes
1. Neoplasms (140-239);
   Nutritional and Metabolic Diseases and Immunity Disorders (240- 279);
   Diseases of Blood and Blood-Forming Organs (280-289).
2. Mental Disorder (290-319);
   Diseases of the Nervous System and Sense Organs (320-389).
3. Diseases of the Circulatory System (390-459);
   Diseases of the Respiratory System (460-519);
   Diseases of the Digestive System (520-579);
   Diseases of the Genitourinary System (580-629).
4. Diseases of the Skin and Subcutaneous Tissue (680-709);
   Diseases of the Musculoskeletal System and Connective Tissue (710- 739).
5. Symptoms, Signs and Ill-Defined Conditions (780-799).

RESULTS

. . . An examination of Table 1 reveals a death percentage significantly less than 50% in the thirty days prior to the birthday compared to the thirty days after the birthday for 1980 and 1981, but not for 1979; for white males, white females, and nonwhite males, but not for nonwhite females; for married and the never married, but not for widowed and divorced; for those fifty or more years of age but not for those ten to forty-nine years of age; and for those in cause of death categories #3 and #5, but not for cause of death categories #1, #2, and #4.

Some significant differences appear to be due to the large sample size, while some of the insignificant differences appear to be due to inadequate sample size. For example, 48.8% of the ten to forty-nine year olds and 48.9% of the fifty or older who died within thirty days of their birthday died before their birthday. However, the former is not significant but the latter is due to the larger number of cases in that category.

The most notable Death Dip/Death Rise categories in Table 1 are the never married and cause of death category #5. For the never married, of those who died within thirty days of their birthday, 45.0% died prior to the birthday while 55.0% died after the birthday. For the cause of death category #5 (Symptoms, Signs and Ill-Defined Conditions), 38.4% died prior to the birthday while 61.6% died after the birthday. These contextual categories warrant further examination. Specifically, we wish to explore whether this apparent death-dip prior to the birthday, and the death-rise after the birthday, was of more or less than one month's duration for these two contextual categories. Table 2 presents a statistical analysis of the birth minus

TABLE 1.   Statistical Analysis of Birth Minus Death Day Frequencies by
Contextual Variables Within First Month

DEATH OCCURRED WITHIN X DAYS OF BIRTH	PERCENT DYING PRIOR	PERCENT DYING AFTER	NUMBER OF DEATHS	X^2	P
Year of Death					
1979	49.4%	50.6%	14137	2.17	n.s.
1980	47.9	52.1	14703	25.89	< .01
1981	49.1	50.9	14602	4.28	< .01
Sex and Race					
White Male	48.6	51.4	20342	15.42	< .01
White Female	49.1	50.9	19086	5.71	< .05
Nonwhite Male	47.5	52.5	2179	5.25	< .05
Nonwhite Female	48.8	51.2	1835	1.10	n.s.
Marital Status					
Married	49.0	51.0	20608	8.48	< .01
Never married	45.0	55.0	3505	34.35	< .01
Widowed	49.4	50.6	16320	2.31	n.s.
Divorced	48.7	51.3	2788	1.86	n.s.
Age					
10 to 49	48.8	51.2	2703	1.56	n.s.
50 or more	48.9	51.1	40522	19.02	< .01
Cause of Death					
#1	49.3	50.7	12040	2.40	n.s.
#2	49.2	50.8	748	.19	n.s.
#3	48.7	51.3	30193	20.62	< .01
#4	47.3	52.7	203	.60	n.s.
#5	38.4	61.6	258	13.95	< .01

deathday frequencies by month for the never married and for cause of death category #5.

An examination of Table 2 reveals that the dip in deaths prior to the birthday and/or rise in deaths after the birthday occurred for the never married significantly for four months. This effect is strongest in the first month prior/after the birthday. However, this effect remains strong and significant in the second, third, and fourth months prior/after the birthday. Further examination of Table 2 reveals that the dip in deaths prior to the birthday and/or rise in deaths after the birthday occurred for cause of death #5 significantly for five months. The authors will speculate on the reasons for such a pattern in the discussion section of this paper. . . .

DISCUSSION

The foregoing discussion centered on the Death-Dip/Death-Rise Phenomenon. The premise states that individuals may have a tendency to postpone mortality in order to experience a socially, or personally, significant event. Here, the discussion dealt with date of birth as a significant event; previous research has examined other possible significant events.

TABLE 2. Statistical Analysis of Birth Minus Death Day Frequencies by Month for Never Married and Cause of Death Category #5

DEATH OCCURRED WITHIN X DAYS OF BIRTH	PERCENT DYING PRIOR	PERCENT DYING AFTER	NUMBER OF DEATHS	X^2	P
Never Married					
1 to 30	45.0%	55.0%	3505	34.35	< .01
31 to 60	47.0	53.0	3747	13.75	< .01
61 to 90	46.4	53.6	3701	19.26	< .01
91 to 120	47.0	53.0	3767	13.80	< .01
121 to 150	49.0	51.0	3575	1.33	n.s.
151 to 180	50.5	49.5	3557	.31	n.s.
1 to 120	46.4%	53.6%	14721	77.63	< .01
Cause of Death Category #5					
1 to 30	38.4%	61.6%	258	13.95	< .01
31 to 60	30.5	69.5	344	52.20	< .01
61 to 90	29.0	71.0	386	67.99	< .01
91 to 120	33.9	66.1	307	31.93	< .01
121 to 150	36.6	63.4	273	19.52	< .01
151 to 180	45.0	55.0	258	2.62	n.s.
1 to 120	32.4%	67.6%	1295	159.86	< .01

The aforementioned analysis provided new insight into this research area. . . . The authors were able to detect significant variation in mortality patterns. Several interesting findings were revealed.

First, . . . there was a greater tendency for individuals to die within thirty days after their birthday than within thirty days before their birthday (chi square = 24.99; $p < .01$). . . .

This . . . becomes ever more salient when examining the mortality patterns for the never married and cause #5 contextual variables. For these variables, there was a noteworthy and significant tendency for more individuals dying after the birth date. As earlier reported, the never married ($X^2 = 34.35$; $p < .01$) were more likely to die after the date of birth. One may expand on this finding.

For the never married category, one may speculate that the date of birth has special significance because it is "their day." In other words, the date of birth may be the more significant social event for them since they did not marry. . . .

Other authors have found similar findings. Marriott and Harshbarger (1973) found that those without family ties demonstrated a noteworthy pattern. As these authors indicated, " . . . increases in the frequency of deaths after Christmas seemed to occur among those people without family ties, especially single women (p. 263). They discovered a death-rise for those who were never married and widowed. Both studies used the criterion date of Christmas and found a death-rise after the event but no dip before. Although the criterion date . . . is not a birthday, the finding is useful nonetheless because the present study found an effect for the never married group. Further, this finding is interesting in light of Walter Gove's (1973) conclusion that married individuals fair better in terms of health and also live longer. Marital status has been found to have a significant impact on death.

One might suggest that the marital bond, and the unity created through the social construction of reality and the definition of the situation (Berger & Kellner 1964), may have an impact on the nature of the death-dip/death-rise phenomenon. In this case, the never married group may exhibit a definition of the situation and reality construction which emphasizes the celebratory importance placed on their date of birth due to the absence of marriage anniversaries and births in the family of procreation.

Another noteworthy point is the significant finding for cause #5. This category, as listed in the *World Health Organization* manual, is used for those deaths which are not clearly explainable. The authors feel that the significant X^2 (13.95; $p < .01$) coupled with the enigma surrounding this category provide an interesting point for speculation. One might contend that these apparent unexplainable deaths may be accounted for by the Death-Dip/Death-Rise premise. First, the deaths were not categorizable due to their apparent unrecognizable characteristics. Second, this cause category accounted for the largest pre- and post-deathday difference. Therefore, the unexplainable nature of the death and the degree of significance found points to the Death-Dip/Death-Rise Phenomenon.

The enigma surrounding this cause of death category begs for an explanation which can account for the dip and rise. Theoretically, the nature of this cause category being "symptoms, signs, and ill-defined conditions" suggests the presence of social psychological processes. Although one could find a dip and rise for other specific causes of death, the presence of a significant pattern around the criterion date for this category suggests the possibility of some process related to the definitional nature of the

criterion date. The nature of this cause category suggests that no categorizable cause of death could be attributed to the case. Being a sort of "catch-all" category, the deaths found there could not be fully explained through any clear organic or physiological cause. For this reason, the authors maintain that the significant finding for this cause category may support the possibility that for those individuals the social construction of reality and the definition of the situation, as related to the date of birth, had a special type of significance. . . .

NOTES

1. Special thanks to Dr. Jerry Wicks and the Population and Society Research Center of Bowling Green State University for the data used in this study.
2. In 1980, 365 death days were examined in addition to the date of birth. This accounts for the addition of February 29, 1980.

REFERENCES

Alderson, M. 1975. "The Relationship Between Month of Birth and Month of Death in the Elderly." *British Journal of Preventive Social Medicine* 29:151–156.

Baltes, M. M. 1977. "On the Relationship Between Significant Yearly Events and Time of Death: Random or Systematic Distribution?" *Omega* 8:165–172.

Berger, P. L. and H. Kellner. 1964. "Marriage and the Construction of Reality." *Diogenes* 45:1–25.

Berger, P. L. and T. Luckmann. 1966. *The Social Construction of Reality.* Garden City, NY: Anchor Books.

Boor, M. 1981. "Effects of United States Presidential Elections on Suicide and Other Causes of Death." *American Sociological Review* 46:616–618.

Boor, M. 1982. "Reduction in Deaths by Suicide, Accidents, and Homicide Prior to United States Presidential Elections." *Journal of Social Psychology* 118:135–136.

Byers, B. D. 1985. *An Empirical Exploration of the Death-Dip/Death-Rise Phenomenon.* Unpublished Master Thesis, Bowling Green State University: Bowling Green, OH.

Byers, B. D. and R. A. Zeller. 1987. "Christmas and Mortality: Death Dip, No; Death Rise, Yes." *Professional Psychology: Research and Practice* 18:394–396.

_____. forthcoming. "Death Heaping in Vital Statistics." *Omega.*

Fischer, K. H. and B. M. Dlin. 1972. "Psychogenic Determination of Time of Illness or Death by Anniversary Reactions and Emotional Deadlines." *Psychosomatics* 13:170–173.

Gove, W. 1973. "Sex, Marital Status, and Mortality." *American Journal of Sociology* 79:45–67.

Harrison, A. A. and N. E. A. Kroll. 1985. "Variations in Death Rates in the Proximity of Christmas: An Opponent Process Interpretation." *Omega* 16:181–192.

Harrison, A. A. and M. Moore. 1982. "Birth Dates and Death Dates: A Closer Look." *Omega* 13:117–125.

Kunz, P. R., and J. Summers. 1980. "A Time to Die: A Study of the Relationship of Birthdays and Time of Death." *Omega* 10:281–289.

Labovitz, S. 1974. "Control Over Death: The Canadian Case." *Omega* 5:217–221.

Marriott, C. and J. M. Fitzgerald. 1981. "Nixon's Resignation and Death Rates: Individual/Systems Interaction in America." *Omega* 12:107–115.

Marriott, C. and D. Harashbarger. 1973. "The Hollow Holiday: Christmas, A Time of Death in Appalachia." *Omega* 4:259–266.

Phillips, D. P. 1972 (1975). "Death and Birthday: An Unexpected Connection." Pp. 281–293 in Kenneth C. W. ammeyer (ed.), *Population Studies: Selected Essays and Research,* 2nd edition. Chicago: Rand McNally.

Phillips D. P. and K. A. Feldman. 1973. "A Dip in Deaths Before Ceremonial Occasions: Some New Relationships Between Social Integration and Mortality." *American Sociological Review* 38:678–696.

Rago, W. V., M. Mason, and C. C. Cleland. 1981. "Mortality and Important Events: Another Look." *Bulletin of the Psychonomic Society* 17:76–78.

Schulz, R. and M. Bazerman. 1980. "Ceremonial Occasions and Mortality: A Second Look." *American Psychologist* 35:253–261.

Tanur, J. M. 1981. "Ceremonial Occasions and Mortality: A Third Look." *American Psychologist* 36:315–316.

Thomas, W. I. and D. S. Thomas. 1928. *The Child in America.* New York: Alfred A. Knopf.

Wasserman, I. M. 1983. "Political Business Cycles, Presidential Elections, and Suicide and Mortality Patterns." *American Sociological Review* 48:711–720.

World Health Organization. 1980. *Manual of the International Classification of Diseases, Injuries, and Causes of Death.*

8

Techniques of Neutralization

GRESHAM M. SYKES
DAVID MATZA

In attempting to uncover the roots of juvenile delinquency, the social scientist has long since ceased to search for devils in the mind or stigma of the body. It is now largely agreed that delinquent behavior, like most social behavior, is learned and that it is learned in the process of social interaction.

The classic statement of this position is found in Sutherland's theory of differential association, which asserts that criminal or delinquent behavior involves the learning of (a) techniques of committing crimes and (b) motives, drives, rationalizations, and attitudes favorable to the violation of law.[1] Unfortunately, the specific content of what is learned—as opposed to the process by which it is learned—has received relatively little attention in either theory or research. Perhaps the single strongest school of thought on the nature of this content has centered on the idea of a delinquent subculture. The basic characteristic of the delinquent subculture, it is argued, is a system of values that represents an inversion of the values held by respectable, law-abiding society. The world of the delinquent is the world of the law-abiding society turned upside down and its norms constitute a countervailing force directed against the conforming social order. Cohen[2] sees the process of developing a delinquent subculture as a matter of building, maintaining, and reinforcing a code for behavior which exists by opposition, which stands in point-by-point contradiction to dominant values, particularly those of the middle class. Cohen's portrayal of delin-

quency is executed with a good deal of sophistication, and he carefully avoids overly simple explanations such as those based on the principle of "follow the leader" or easy generalizations about "emotional disturbances." Furthermore, he does not accept the delinquent subculture as something given, but instead systematically examines the function of delinquent values as a viable solution to the lower-class, male child's problems in the area of social status. Yet in spite of its virtures, this image of juvenile delinquency as a form of behavior based on competing or countervailing values and norms appears to suffer from a number of serious defects. It is the nature of these defects and a possible alternative or modified explanation for a large portion of juvenile delinquency with which this paper is concerned.

The difficulties in viewing delinquent behavior as springing from a set of deviant values and norms—as arising, that is to say, from a situation in which the delinquent defines his delinquency as "right"—are both empirical and theoretical. In the first place, if there existed in fact a delinquent subculture such that the delinquent viewed his illegal behavior as morally correct, we could reasonably suppose that he would exhibit no feelings of guilt or shame at detection or confinement. Instead, the major reaction would tend in the direction of indignation or a sense of martyrdom.[3] It is true that some delinquents do react in the latter fashion, although the sense of martyrdom often seems to be based on the fact that others "get away with it" and indignation appears to be directed against the chance events or lack of skill that led to apprehension. More important, however, is the fact that there is a good deal of evidence suggesting that many delinquents *do* experience a sense of guilt or shame, and its outward expression is not to be dismissed as a purely manipulative gesture to appease those in authority. Much of this evidence is, to be sure, of a clinical nature or in the form of impressionistic judgments of those who must deal first hand with the youthful offender. Assigning a weight to such evidence calls for caution, but it cannot be ignored if we are to avoid the gross stereotype of the juvenile delinquent as a hardened gangster in miniature.

In the second place, observers have noted that the juvenile delinquent frequently accords admiration and respect to law-abiding persons. The "really honest" person is often revered, and if the delinquent is sometimes overly keen to detect hypocrisy in those who conform, unquestioned probity is likely to win his approval. A fierce attachment to a humble, pious mother or a forgiving, upright priest (the former, according to many observers, is often encountered in both juvenile delinquents and adult criminals) might be dismissed as rank sentimentality, but at least it is clear that the delinquent does not necessarily regard those who abide by the legal rules as immoral. In a similar vein, it can be noted that the juvenile delinquent may exhibit great resentment if illegal behavior is imputed to "significant others" in his immediate social environment or to heroes in the world of sport and entertainment. In other words, if the delinquent does hold to a set of values and norms that stand in complete opposition to those of respectable society, his norm-holding is of a peculiar sort. While supposedly thoroughly committed to the deviant system of the delinquent subculture, he would appear to recognize the moral validity of the dominant normative system in many instances.[4]

In the third place, there is much evidence that juvenile delinquents often draw a sharp line between those who can be victimized and those who cannot. Certain social groups are not to be viewed as "fair game" in the performance of supposedly approved delinquent acts while others warrant a variety of attacks. In general, the potentiality for victimization would seem to be a function of the social distance between the juvenile delinquent and others and thus we find implicit maxims in the world of the delinquent such as "don't steal from friends" or "don't commit vandalism against a church of your own faith."[5] This is all rather obvious, but the implications have not received sufficient attention. The fact that supposedly valued behavior tends to be directed against disvalued social groups hints that the "wrongfulness" of such delinquent behavior is more widely recognized by delinquents than the literature has indicated. When the pool of victims is limited by considerations of kinship, friendship, ethnic group, social class, age, sex, etc., we have reason to suspect that the virtue of delinquency is far from unquestioned.

In the fourth place, it is doubtful if many juvenile delinquents are totally immune from the demands for conformity made by the dominant social order. There is a strong likelihood that the family of the delinquent will agree with respectable society that delinquency is wrong, even though the family may be engaged in a variety of illegal activities. That is, the parental posture conducive to delinquency is not apt to be a positive prodding. Whatever may be the influence of parental example, what might be called the "Fagin" pattern of socialization into delinquency is probably rare. Furthermore, as Redl has indicated, the idea that certain neighborhoods are completely delinquent, offering the child a model for delinquent behavior without reservations, is simply not supported by the data.[6]

The fact that a child is punished by parents, school officials, and agencies of the legal system for his delinquency may, as a number of observers have cynically noted, suggest to the child that he should be more careful not to get caught. There is an equal or greater probability, however, that the child will internalize the demands for conformity. This is not to say that demands for conformity cannot be counteracted. In fact, as we shall see shortly, an understanding of how internal and external demands for conformity are neutralized may be crucial for understanding delinquent behavior. But it is to say that a complete denial of the validity of demands for conformity and the substitution of a new normative system is improbable, in light of the child's or adolescent's dependency on adults and encirclement by adults inherent in his status in the social structure. No matter how deeply enmeshed in patterns of delinquency he may be and no matter how much this involvement may outweigh his associations with the law-abiding, he cannot escape the condemnation of his deviance. Somehow the demands for conformity must be met and answered; they cannot be ignored as part of an alien system of values and norms.

In short, the theoretical viewpoint that sees juvenile delinquency as a form of behavior based on the values and norms of a deviant subculture in precisely the same way as law-abiding behavior is based on the values and norms of the larger society is open to serious doubt. The fact that the world of the delinquent is embedded in the larger world of those who conform cannot be overlooked nor can the delinquent be equated with an adult thoroughly socialized into an alternative way of life. Instead, the juvenile delinquent would appear to be at least partially committed to the dominant social order in that he frequently exhibits guilt or shame when he violates its proscriptions, accords approval to certain conforming figures, and distinguishes between appropriate and inappropriate targets for his deviance. It is to an explanation for the apparently paradoxical fact of his delinquency that we now turn.

As Morris Cohen once said, one of the most fascinating problems about human behavior is why men violate the laws in which they believe. This is the problem that confronts us when we attempt to explain why delinquency occurs despite a greater or lesser commitment to the usages of conformity. A basic clue is offered by the fact that social rules or norms calling for valued behavior seldom if ever take the form of categorical imperatives. Rather, values or norms appear as qualified guides for action, limited in their applicability in terms of time, place, persons, and social circumstances. The moral injunction against killing, for example, does not apply to the enemy during combat in time of war, although a captured enemy comes once again under the prohibition. Similarly, the taking and distributing of scarce goods in a time of acute social need is felt by many to be right, although under other circumstances private property is held inviolable. The normative system of a society, then, is marked by what Williams has termed *flexibility;* it does not consist of a body of rules held to be binding under all conditions.[7]

This flexibility is, in fact, an integral part of the criminal law in that measures for "defenses to crimes" are provided in pleas such as non-age, necessity, insanity, drunkenness, compulsion, self-defense, and so on. The individual can avoid moral culpability for his criminal action—and thus avoid the negative sanctions of society—if he can prove that criminal intent was lacking. *It is our argument that much delinquency is based on what is essentially an unrecognized extension of defenses to crimes, in the form of justifications for deviance that are seen as valid by the delinquent but not by the legal system or society at large.*

These justifications are commonly described as rationalizations. They are viewed as following deviant behavior and as protecting the individual from self-blame and the blame of others after the act. But there is also reason to believe that they precede deviant behavior and make deviant behavior possible. It is this possibility that Sutherland mentioned only in passing and that other writers have failed to exploit from the viewpoint of sociological theory. Disapproval flowing from internalized norms and conforming others in the social environment is neutralized, turned back, or deflected in advance. Social controls that serve to check or inhibit deviant motivational patterns are rendered inoperative, and the individual is freed to engage in delinquency without serious damage to his self-image. In this sense, the delinquent both has his cake and eats it too, for he remains committed to the dominant normative system and yet so qualifies its imperatives that violations are "acceptable" if not "right." Thus the delinquent represents not a radical opposition to law-abiding society but something more like an apologetic failure, often more sinned against than sinning in his own eyes. We call these justifications of deviant behavior techniques of neutralization; and we believe these techniques make up a crucial component of Sutherland's "definitions favorable to the violation of law." It is by learning these techniques that the juvenile becomes delinquent, rather than by learning moral imperatives, values or attitudes standing in direct contradiction to those of the dominant society. In analyzing these techniques, we have found it convenient to divide them into five major types.

THE DENIAL OF RESPONSIBILITY

Insofar as the delinquent can define himself as lacking responsibility for his deviant actions, the disapproval of self or others is sharply reduced in effectiveness as a restraining influence. As Justice Holmes has said, even a dog distinguishes between being stumbled over and being kicked, and modern society is no less careful to draw a line

between injuries that are unintentional, i.e., where responsibility is lacking, and those that are intentional. As a technique of neutralization, however, the denial of responsibility extends much further than the claim that deviant acts are an "accident" or some similar negation of personal accountability. It may also be asserted that delinquent acts are due to forces outside of the individual and beyond his control such as unloving parents, bad companions, or a slum neighborhood. In effect, the delinquent approaches a "billiard ball" conception of himself in which he sees himself as helplessly propelled into new situations. From a psychodynamic viewpoint, this orientation toward one's own actions may represent a profound alienation from self, but it is important to stress the fact that interpretations of responsibility are cultural constructs and not merely idiosyncratic beliefs. The similarity between this mode of justifying illegal behavior assumed by the delinquent and the implications of a "sociological" frame of reference or a "humane" jurisprudence is readily apparent.[8] It is not the validity of this orientation that concerns us here, but its function of deflecting blame attached to violations of social norms and its relative independence of a particular personality structure.[9] By learning to view himself as more acted upon than acting, the delinquent prepares the way for deviance from the dominant normative system without the necessity of a frontal assault on the norms themselves.

THE DENIAL OF INJURY

A second major technique of neutralization centers on the injury or harm involved in the delinquent act. The criminal law has long made a distinction between crimes which are *mala in se* and *mala prohibita* —that is between acts that are wrong in themselves and acts that are illegal but not immoral—and the delinquent can make the same kind of distinction in evaluating the wrongfulness of his behavior. For the delinquent, however, wrongfulness may turn on the question of whether or not anyone has clearly been hurt by his deviance, and this matter is open to a variety of interpretations. Vandalism, for example, may be defined by the delinquent simply as "mischief"—after all, it may be claimed, the persons whose property has been destroyed can well afford it. Similarly, auto theft may be viewed as "borrowing," and gang fighting may be seen as a private quarrel, an agreed upon duel between two willing parties, and thus of no concern to the community at large. We are not suggesting that this technique of neutralization, labeled the denial of injury, involves an explicit dialectic. Rather, we are arguing that the delinquent frequently, and in a hazy fashion, feels that his behavior does not really cause any great harm despite the fact that it runs counter to law. Just as the link between the individual and his acts may be broken by the denial of responsibility, so may the link between acts and their consequences be broken by the denial of injury. Since society sometimes agrees with the delinquent, e.g., in matters such as truancy, "pranks," and so on, it merely reaffirms the idea that the delinquent's neutralization of social controls by means of qualifying the norms is an extension of common practice rather than a gesture of complete opposition.

THE DENIAL OF THE VICTIM

Even if the delinquent accepts the responsibility for his deviant actions and is willing to admit that his deviant actions involve an injury or hurt, the moral indignation of self and others may be neutralized by an insistence that the injury is not wrong in light of the circumstances. The injury, it may be claimed, is not really an injury; rather, it is a form of rightful retaliation or punishment. By a subtle alchemy the delinquent moves himself into the position of an avenger and the victim is transformed into a wrongdoer.

Assaults on homosexuals or suspected homosexuals, attacks on members of minority groups who are said to have gotten "out of place," vandalism as revenge on an unfair teacher or school official, thefts from a "crooked" store owner—all may be hurts inflicted on a transgressor, in the eyes of the delinquent. As Orwell has pointed out, the type of criminal admired by the general public has probably changed over the course of years and Raffles no longer serves as a hero;[10] but Robin Hood, and his latter day derivatives such as the tough detective seeking justice outside the law, still capture the popular imagination, and the delinquent may view his acts as part of a similar role.

To deny the existence of the victim, then, by transforming him into a person deserving injury is an extreme form of a phenomenon we have mentioned before, namely, the delinquent's recognition of appropriate and inappropriate targets for his delinquent acts. In addition, however, the existence of the victim may be denied for the delinquent, in a somewhat different sense, by the circumstances of the delinquent act itself. Insofar as the victim is physically absent, unknown, or a vague abstraction (as is often the case in delinquent acts committed against property), the awareness of the victim's existence is weakened. Internalized norms and anticipations of the reactions of others must somehow be activated, if they are to serve as guides for behavior; and it is possible that a diminished awareness of the victim plays an important part in determining whether or not this process is set in motion.

THE CONDEMNATION OF THE CONDEMNERS

A fourth technique of neutralization would appear to involve a condemnation of the condemners or, as McCorkle and Korn have phrased it, a rejection of the rejectors.[11] The delinquent shifts the focus of attention from his own deviant acts to the motives and behavior of those who disapprove of his violations. His condemners, he may claim, are hypocrites, deviants in disguise, or impelled by personal spite. This orientation toward the conforming world may be of particular importance when it hardens into a bitter cynicism directed against those assigned the task of enforcing or expressing the norms of the dominant society. Police, it may be said, are corrupt, stupid, and brutal. Teachers always show favoritism and parents always "take it out" on their children. By a slight extension, the rewards of conformity—such as material success—become a matter of pull or luck, thus decreasing still further the stature of those who stand on the side of the law-abiding. The validity of this jaundiced viewpoint is not so important as its function in turning back or deflecting the negative sanctions attached to violations of the norms. The delinquent, in effect, has changed the subject of the conversation in the dialogue between his own deviant impulses and the reactions of others; and by attacking others, the wrongfulness of his own behavior is more easily repressed or lost to view.

THE APPEAL TO HIGHER LOYALTIES

Fifth, and last, internal and external social controls may be neutralized by sacrificing the demands of the larger society for the demands of the smaller social groups to which the delinquent belongs such as the sibling pair, the gang, or the friendship clique. It is important to note that the delinquent does not necessarily repudiate the imperatives of the dominant normative system, despite his failure to follow them. Rather, the delinquent may see himself as caught up in a dilemma that must be resolved, unfortunately, at the cost of violating the law. One aspect of this situation has been studied by Stouffer and Toby in their research on the conflict between particularistic and universalistic demands, between the claims of friendship and general social obligations,

and their results suggest that "it is possible to classify people according to a predisposition to select one or the other horn of a dilemma in a role conflict."[12] For our purposes, however, the most important point is that deviation from certain norms may occur not because the norms are rejected but because other norms, held to be more pressing or involving a higher loyalty, are accorded precedence. Indeed, it is the fact that both sets of norms are believed in that gives meaning to our concepts of dilemma and role conflict.

The conflict between the claims of friendship and the claims of law, or a similar dilemma, has of course long been recognized by the social scientist (and the novelist) as a common human problem. If the juvenile delinquent frequently resolves his dilemma by insisting that he must "always help a buddy" or "never squeal on a friend," even when it throws him into serious difficulties with the dominant social order, his choice remains familiar to the supposedly law-abiding. The delinquent is unusual, perhaps, in the extent to which he is able to see the fact that he acts in behalf of the smaller social groups to which he belongs as a justification for violations of society's norms, but it is a matter of degree rather than of kind.

"I didn't mean it." "I didn't really hurt anybody." "They had it coming to them." "Everybody's picking on me." "I didn't do it for myself." These slogans or their variants, we hypothesize, prepare the juvenile for delinquent acts. These "definitions of the situation" represent tangential or glancing blows at the dominant normative system rather than the creation of an opposing ideology; and they are extensions of patterns of thought prevalent in society rather than something created *de novo*.

Techniques of neutralization may not be powerful enough to fully shield the individual from the force of his own internalized values and the reactions of conforming others, for as we have pointed out, juvenile delinquents often appear to suffer from feelings of guilt and shame when called into account for their deviant behavior. And some delinquents may be so isolated from the world of conformity that techniques of neutralization need not be called into play. Nonetheless, we would argue that techniques of neutralization are critical in lessening the effectiveness of social controls and that they lie behind a large share of delinquent behavior. Empirical research in this area is scattered and fragmentary at the present time, but the work of Redl,[13] Cressey,[14] and others has supplied a body of significant data that has done much to clarify the theoretical issues and enlarge the fund of supporting evidence. Two lines of investigation seem to be critical at this stage. First, there is need for more knowledge concerning the differential distribution of techniques of neutralization, as operative patterns of thought, by age, sex, social class, ethnic group, etc. On *a priori* grounds it might be assumed that these justifications for deviance will be more readily seized by segments of society for whom a discrepancy between common social ideals and social practice is most apparent. It is also possible, however, that the habit of "bending" the dominant normative system—if not "breaking" it—cuts across our cruder social categories and is to be traced primarily to patterns of social interaction within the familial circle. Second, there is need for a greater understanding of the internal structure of techniques of neutralization, as a system of beliefs and attitudes, and its relationship to various types of delinquent behavior. Certain techniques of neutralization would appear to be better adapted to particular deviant acts than to others, as we have suggested, for example, in the case of offenses against property and the denial of the victim. But the issue remains far from clear and stands in need of more information.

In any case, techniques of neutralization appear to offer a promising line of research in enlarging and systematizing the theoretical grasp of juvenile delinquency. As more information is uncovered concerning techniques of neutralization, their origins, and their consequences, both juvenile delinquency in particular, and deviation from normative systems in general may be illuminated.

NOTES

1. E. H. Sutherland, *Principles of Criminology*, revised by D. R. Cressey, Chicago: Lippincott, 1955, pp. 77–80.
2. Albert K. Cohen, *Delinquent Boys*, Glencoe, Ill.: The Free Press, 1955.
3. This form of reaction among the adherents of a deviant subculture who fully believe in the "rightfulness" of their behavior and who are captured and punished by the agencies of the dominant social order can be illustrated, perhaps, by groups such as Jehovah's Witnesses, early Christian sects, nationalist movements in colonial areas, and conscientious objectors during World Wars I and II.
4. As Weber has pointed out, a thief may recognize the legitimacy of legal rules without accepting their moral validity. Cf. Max Weber, *The Theory of Social and Economic Organization* (translated by A. M. Henderson and Talcott Parsons), New York: Oxford University Press, 1947, p. 125. We are arguing here, however, that the juvenile delinquent frequently recognizes *both* the legitimacy of the dominant social order and its moral "rightness."
5. Thrasher's account of the "Itschkies"—a juvenile gang composed of Jewish boys—and the immunity from "rolling" enjoyed by Jewish drunkards is a good illustration. Cf. F. Thrasher, *The Gang*, Chicago: The University of Chicago Press, 1947, p. 315.
6. Cf. Solomon Kobrin, "The Conflict of Values in Delinquency Areas," *American Sociological Review*, 16 (October 1951): 653–61.
7. Cf. Robin Williams, Jr., *American Society*, New York: Knopf, 1951, p. 28.
8. A number of observers have wryly noted that many delinquents seem to show a surprising awareness of sociological and psychological explanations for their behavior and are quick to point out the causal role of their poor environment.

9. It is possible, of course, that certain personality structures can accept some techniques of neutralization more readily than others, but this question remains largely unexplored.

10. George Orwell, *Dickens, Dali, and Others*, New York: Reynal, 1946.

11. Lloyd W. McCorkle and Richard Korn, "Resocialization Within Walls," *The Annals of the American Academy of Political and Social Science*, 293 (May 1954): 88–98.

12. See Samuel A. Stouffer and Jackson Toby, "Role Conflict and Personality," in *Toward a General Theory of Action*, edited by Talcott Parsons and Edward A. Shils, Cambridge: Harvard University Press, 1951, p. 494.

13. See Fritz Redl and David Wineman, *Children Who Hate*, Glencoe: The Free Press, 1956.

14. See D. R. Cressey, *Other People's Money*. Glencoe: The Free Press, 1953.

PART TWO

The Self, Society, and Social Patterns of Human Experience

The self, society, and social patterns of human experience refer to the complexity of human social conduct within a larger social structure. Human conduct does not exist within a vacuum. There are multiple influences on individuals that result in the product of human behavior. These influences may include socialization or learning experiences, one's ability to understand and respond to informal social norms, the formal rules that societies place on behavior, subcultural behavior expectations, social group membership, and social role expectations.

Although individuals are often considered to be motivated by "free will," certain social and societal constraints are placed upon behavior. Certain patterns of behavior are expected, and it is partly out of an understanding of the norms of social conduct that individuals come to develop a social self. The "self" is the term used to describe that part of the human social experience whereby one incorporates various aspects of learning, perception, and experience into an entity that characterizes a unique person. The self is intangible and constantly changing with demands from society and from those with whom one interacts. The self emerges through the process of social interaction and personifies the roles and statuses that each person possesses within society.

The self represents that which makes a person human, unique, and mutable to the social environment, and provides a foundation for social interaction and the creation of social reality. When we interact with others, we do so from our own unique perspectives, which are the product of years of learned attitudes, biases, and prejudices. Our social perceptions, which involve the interpretation of others' action, are an essential ingredient in who we are, what we become, and how we come to define ourselves. An important part of our social self, and consequently our social identity, includes these foundations.

Many factors pertinent to the social self influence and alter the nature and creation of social interaction. The self not only facilitates interaction with others but also suggests another form of interaction that is only possible for human beings. The form of interaction discussed here is the treatment of the self as an object. While most interaction occurs between people within the interpersonal domain, and consequently between social selves while occupying social roles, some forms of social interaction may only involve one person. This intrapersonal process is referred to as the treatment of the self as an object.

Just as one can treat another person, element, or entity as an object that one can respond to and interpret, the self can also become an object, and the individual may react to that object within a process of intrapersonal social interaction. The social self, with its ability to treat both other social actors and itself as an object of response, emerges through the process of symbolic interaction. This is done only through the uniquely human ability to treat others and one's self as objects and the focus of interaction. Through the social self and the process of symbolic interaction, one is able to function as an active participant within society through intrapersonal and interpersonal behavior.

Part of this active participation is the interpretation of social events. In everyday life, individuals sense, interpret, and experience events that occur within the social world. Given an individual's learned need to interact with and be in the company of others, it should be no surprise that social interaction, and the outcome of that interaction, is of central importance to the understanding of humans as societal participants. This active participation often involves the interpretation of social events in ways that reflect predictable social patterns. In a sense, the social perceptions of individuals within society may show them behaving as amateur social scientists. Since both social scientists and individuals wish to understand better the social world to which they belong, this phenomena represents an interesting and useful commonality regarding social perception.

The process of social perception is guided by many factors. Often, social perceptions involve an individual's attempt to explain some social event through the means of attribution, or the behavior of the self through a process of self-perception. However, many social factors influence this process of amateur social perception.

As amateur social scientists, individuals are continually trying to explain the behavior of others. Normally, this involves interpreting outcomes or events that are caused by an individual's behavior, an environmental factor, or a situational variable. Often, the task of explaining behavior, whether it is the behavior of others or one's self, will be reduced to some combination of dispositional factors (personal or individual traits) and situational factors (environmental influences). When explaining the behavior of others, we tend to give more credence to dispositional factors. When explaining our own behavior, we tend to place more emphasis on situational characteristics. When we are not sure of our own attitudes regarding a particular issue, we may take the processes of attribution and person perception that we use to uncover the attitudes of others and apply them to the self. Herein lies the difference between person perception in the form of attribution and self-perception.

Attitudes, beliefs, and values are beneficial in trying to explain the social world. Humans are greatly influenced by the learned attitudes that they and others hold. These cognitive positions that express preferences toward certain issues, objects, or events are a powerful social influence. Being essentially based on unconfirmed information, beliefs may also serve, as do attitudes, the important social function of guiding action. Values, which basically fulfill an evaluative purpose (often involving issues of right and wrong, good and evil, etc.), also influence thought and behavior, since it is value-laden positions that spark debate, discussion, and heated social interaction. Attitudes, beliefs, and values thus all serve important functions in understanding human cognition and behavior. Much debate has centered on the connection between attitude and behavior. Central to this discussion is whether attitudes create behavior patterns or visa versa. This could indeed be a reciprocal relationship, although the debate is far from over.

Also important to social psychology are language and symbol. Language and its shared use are essential in day-to-day communication. Without language, people and societies would be unable to engage in the process of social interaction that is so vital to the emergence and continued development of the social self. In our daily lives, without much overt recognition, we follow established, learned language and gestural patterns. Many of these patterns are so entrenched within the interaction experience that verbal and nonverbal behavior are difficult, if not impossible, to separate, since they often go hand in hand. The intertwined nature of verbal and nonverbal behavior makes for a total, or *gestalt*, experience in the social and sociological aspects of language, or sociolinguistics.

Essential to this experience and process is the use of symbols and the shared meaning that symbols have within a social group, territory, culture, or society. Symbols are objects or entities within the sociolinguistic world to which human meaning is attached. Individuals, social groups, and societies give meaning to symbols, and it is through the use of symbols that interaction is possible. Words are symbols, gestures are symbols, and objects in the social environment can be symbols. A symbol is anything that represents something else. Symbols do not have natural meaning; the social meaning attached to objects is a human creation. Human beings create symbols and the meaning attached to them in an effort to facilitate social interaction. Symbols, their shared meaning, and their continued use are essential ingredients in the analysis and understanding of human conduct.

As with language, the shared meaning of symbols is important to the flow of social interaction and communication, and thus is given additional attention here. The shared meaning of symbols, whether referring to spoken language, written material, or nonverbal communication, pertains to the similar understanding that words, gestures, and other forms of communication have for interacting individuals. It is within this similar understanding that we find the true importance of shared meaning. Social interaction would essentially be chaotic without the shared meaning of symbols in the form of words and gestures or, in the absence of shared meaning, an ability to create meaning within a social encounter.

Our ability to interpret these symbols through the social patterning of shared meaning allows individuals to coexist within the same society. Therefore, while certain aspects of society exist *a priori*, other dimensions are the product of social interaction and the social construction of reality.

THE SELECTIONS

Each selection within this part of the book pertains to the important role that the self plays within the larger societal structure. "The Social Self" by Charles Horton Cooley addresses the formation of the social self through the process of self-perception. Written in 1902, this excerpt may be one of the first comprehensive accounts of how the self emerges. Included within this piece is the notion of the "looking-glass self," which has evolved into a concept vital to sociological social psychology. Also central to social psychology are attitudes. In "Attitudes," also of classical origin, the psychological social psychologist Gordon W. Allport cogently analyzes attitudes and their social relevance. Probably the most influential theoretician in the study of the formation of the self was George Herbert Mead. Making connections among the mind, self, and society, Bernard N. Meltzer, in "The Social Psychology of George Herbert Mead," clearly outlines Mead's thinking on human symbolic communication and the role of the individual within the larger societal structure.

The contributions of Cooley, Allport, and Mead have all become timeless works on social judgment and issues pertinent to the formation of the social self, which were the major focus of social psychology in the earlier part of the twentieth century. Later research concentrated on other conceptual areas. For example, attribution theory has played an important role in social psychology in recent years. In the two selections that examine the process of perceiving others, William W. Wilmot and D. Sadow present complementary works. Wilmot offers a clear and understandable discussion of "Attribution of Causality and Responsibility," while Sadow takes these ideas further in her presentation of "Irrational Attributions of Responsibility."

Of course, person perception is not confined to our perceptions of others within the process of social interaction, for it can include both perceptions of the self as well. Russell H. Fazio, Mark P. Zanna, and Joel Cooper do a superb job of presenting two theories that pertain to this issue in "Dissonance and Self-Perception." The unique and separate contributions of the cognitive and behavioral aspects of Festinger's theory of cognitive dissonance and Bem's theory of self-perception are discussed. Both theories outline the role of the self within society from a psychological social psychological perspective by pointing to the attitude-behavior connection, the process by which we may come to have certain attitudes, and our need to understand the behavior of others and ourselves.

Human needs also come in other varieties. Charles Derber, in "Monopolizing the Conversation," shows how persons within individualistic societies may attempt to turn the focus of conversation back on themselves. This occurs out of an egocentric need to be the center of attention, which is a product of the larger social and cultural forces of individualism. Much has been written on the psychology, sociology, and social psychology of individualism, and Derber's piece brings together important conceptual and practical issues pertinent to the process of human interpersonal communication. Interpersonal relations are also characterized by other significant features. While Derber outlines how individuals may come to present themselves in unflattering ways, Arlie Russell Hochschild discusses how the social setting and its concomitant expectations can lead to a state of "Managed feeling." Hochschild explores the social construction of feeling states by distinguishing surface acting, deep acting, and verbal and nonverbal behavior within the context of self-presentation to others.

Self-presentation is often influenced by the groups to which people belong, for group membership produces certain expectations for behavior and behavioral outcomes. Sociologist Tamotsu Shibutani, in "Reference Groups as Perspectives," examines the vital role that reference groups can play in communication and social interaction. Since a reference group is a group of individuals that a person uses to measure one's own action and accomplishments, one's behavior may be governed by membership in such a group. In a similar fashion, sociologist Jennifer Hunt, in "Police

Accounts of Normal Force," shows how reference group membership can create certain emotional states, and produce certain "accounts" (justifications and excuses for behavior) and behaviors that are unique to the police subculture, which is a powerful force in an officer's life. Certain emotional states are expected within this subculture, and the appropriateness of behavior is determined by the approval and disapproval of one's peers. In other words, what is considered deviant is defined by the group.

The definition of deviance may also be a function of who is doing the defining. As Howard Becker illustrates in "Deviant Careers," the powerful force of labeling can propel a person into a life of marginalization. Deviance may be divided into that which is considered primary and secondary. The former pertains to that deviance that does not occur due to a deviant life style, while the latter suggests that the person has adopted a nonconforming stance in relation to the self and interaction within society. This sociological social psychology piece speaks not only to the behavior of individuals but also to the powerful macro social forces that can influence and elicit certain patterns of behavior.

The final selection also illustrates that which is outside the person. In "The Promise," C. Wright Mills attempts to bring together micro and macro aspects of behavior pertaining to "personal troubles" and "public issues," and social psychological connections between personal biography and history. This micro/macro link is essential to a fuller understanding of social psychology. Through a realization of the vital and intimate connections between personal difficulties and larger social problems, and of one's biographical and historical position within society, one can better understand the nature of the social self and come to generate a social psychological imagination.

FOR FURTHER READING

Herbert Blumer. *Symbolic Interactionism: Perspective and Method.* Berkeley: University of California Press, 1969.

Fritz Heider. *The Psychology of Interpersonal Relations.* New York: John Wiley and Sons, Inc., 1958.

George Herbert Mead. *Mind, Self, and Society.* Chicago: University of Chicago Press, 1934.

Kelly Shaver. *An Introduction to Attribution Processes.* Cambridge, MA: Winthrop Publishers, Inc., 1975.

9

The Social Self

CHARLES HORTON COOLEY

The social self is simply any idea, or system of ideas, drawn from the communicative life, that the mind cherishes as its own. Self-feeling has its chief scope *within* the general life, not outside of it. . . .

That the "I" of common speech has a meaning which includes some sort of reference to other persons is involved in the very fact that the word and the ideas it stands for are phenomena of language and the communicative life. It is doubtful whether it is possible to use language at all without thinking more or less distinctly of someone else, and certainly the things to which we give names and which have a large place in reflective thought are almost always those which are impressed upon us by our contact with other people. Where there is no communication there can be no nomenclature and no developed thought. What we call "me," "mine," or "myself" is, then, not something separate from the general life, but the most interesting part of it, a part whose interest arises from the very fact that it is both general and individual. That is, we care for it just because it is that phase of the mind that is living and striving in the common life, trying to impress itself upon the minds of others. "I" is a militant social tendency, working to hold and enlarge its place in the general current of tendencies. So far as it can it waxes, as all life does. To think of it as apart from society is a palpable absurdity of which no one could be guilty who really *saw* it as a fact of life. . . .

The reference to other persons involved in the sense of self may be distinct and particular, as when a boy is ashamed to have his mother catch him at something she has forbidden, or it may be vague and general, as when one is ashamed to do something which only his conscience, expressing his sense of social responsibility, detects and disapproves; but it is always there. There is no sense of "I," as in pride or shame, without its correlative sense of you, or he, or they. Even the miser gloating over his hidden gold can feel the "mine" only as he is aware of the world of men over whom he has secret power; and the case is very similar with all kinds of hid treasure. Many painters, sculptors, and writers have loved to withhold their work from the world, fondling it in seclusion until they were quite done with it; but the delight in this, as in all secrets, depends upon a sense of the value of what is concealed.

. . . We think of the body as "I" when it comes to have social function or significance, as when we say "I am looking well today," or "I am taller than you are." We bring it into the social world, for the time being, and for that reason, put our self-consciousness into it. Now it is curious, though natural, that in precisely the same way we may call any inanimate object "I" with which we are identifying our will and purpose. This is notable in games, like golf or croquet, where the ball is the embodiment of the player's fortunes. You will hear a man say, "I am in the long grass down by the third tee," or "I am in position for the middle arch." So a boy flying a kite will say "I am higher than you," or one shooting at a mark will declare that he is just below the bullseye.

and interesting class of
~ence takes the form of a
~nagination of how one's
...y idea he appropriates—ap-
...~s in a particular mind, and the kind of
self-feeling one has is determined by the attitude toward this attributed to that other
mind. A social self of this sort might be called
the reflected or looking-glass self:

"*Each to each a looking-glass*
Reflects the other that doth pass."

As we see our face, figure, and dress in the
glass, and are interested in them because
they are ours, and pleased or otherwise with
them according as they do or do not answer
to what we should like them to be; so in
imagination we perceive in another's mind
some thought of our appearance, manners,
aims, deeds, character, friends, and so on,
and are variously affected by it.

A self-idea of this sort seems to have
three principal elements: the imagination of
our appearance to the other person; the
imagination of his judgment of that appearance, and some sort of self-feeling, such as
pride or mortification. The comparison with
a looking-glass hardly suggests the second
element, the imagined judgment, which is
quite essential. The thing that moves us to
pride or shame is not the mere mechanical
reflection of ourselves, but an imputed sentiment, the imagined effect of this reflection
upon another's mind. This is evident from
the fact that the character and weight of that
other, in whose mind we see ourselves,
makes all the difference with our feeling. We
are ashamed to seem evasive in the presence
of a straightforward man, cowardly in the
presence of a brave one, gross in the eyes of a
refined one, and so on. We always imagine,
and in imagining share, the judgments of the
other mind. A man will boast to one person
of an action—say some sharp transaction in
trade—which we would be ashamed to own
to another.

It should be evident that the ideas that
are associated with self-feeling and form the
intellectual content of the self cannot be covered by any simple description, as by saying
that the body has such a part in it, friends
such a part, plans so much, etc., but will vary
indefinitely with particular temperaments
and environments. The tendency of the self,
like every aspect of personality, is expressive
of far-reaching hereditary and social factors,
and is not to be understood or predicted
except in connection with the general life.
Although special, it is in no way separate—
specialty and separateness are not only different but contradictory, since the former
implies connection with a whole. The object
of self-feeling is affected by the general
course of history, by the particular development of nations, classes, and professions,
and other conditions of this sort.

The truth of this is perhaps most decisively shown in the fact that even those ideas
that are most generally associated or colored
with the "my" feeling, such as one's idea of
his visible person, of his name, his family, his
intimate friends, his property, and so on, are
not universally so associated, but may be
separated from the self by peculiar social
conditions. . . .

The peculiar relations to other persons
attending any marked personal deficiency or
peculiarity are likely to aggravate, if not to
produce, abnormal manifestations of self-
feeling. Any such trait sufficiently noticeable
to interrupt easy and familiar intercourse
with others, and make people talk and think
about a person or *to* him rather than *with* him,
can hardly fail to have this effect. If he is
naturally inclined to pride or irritability,
these tendencies, which depend for correc-
tion upon the flow of sympathy, are likely to
be increased. One who shows signs of mental aberration is, inevitably perhaps, but cru-
elly, shut off from familiar, thoughtless
intercourse, partly excommunicated; his isolation is unwittingly proclaimed to him on

every countenance by curiosity, indifference, aversion, or pity, and in so far as he is human enough to need free and equal communication and feel the lack of it, he suffers pain and loss of a kind and degree which others can only faintly imagine, and for the most part ignore. He finds himself apart, "not in it," and feels chilled, fearful, and suspic Thus "queerness" is no sooner perceiv than it is multiplied by reflection from othe. minds. The same is true in some degree of dwarfs, deformed or disfigured persons, even the deaf and those suffering from the infirmities of old age.

10

Attitudes

GORDON W. ALLPORT

The concept of attitude is probably the most distinctive and indispensable concept in contemporary American social psychology. No other term appears more frequently in experimental and theoretical literature. Its popularity is not difficult to explain. It has come into favor, first of all, because it is not the property of any one psychological school of thought, and therefore serves admirably the purposes of eclectic writers. Furthermore, it is a concept which escapes the ancient controversy concerning the relative influence of heredity and environment. Since an attitude may combine both instinct and habit in any proportion, it avoids the extreme commitments of both the instinct-theory and environmentalism. The term likewise is elastic enough to apply either to the dispositions of single, isolated individuals or to broad patterns of culture. Psychologists and sociologists therefore find in it a meeting point for discussion and research. This useful, one might almost say peaceful, concept has been so widely adopted that it has virtually established itself as the keystone in the edifice of American social psychology. In fact several writers (cf. Bogardus, 1931; Thomas and Znaniecki, 1918; Folsom, 1931) *define* social psychology as the scientific study of attitudes.

As might be expected of so abstract and serviceable a term, it has come to signify many things to many writers. . . .

It is undeniable that the concept of 'attitude' has become something of a factotum for both psychologists and sociologists. But, in spite of all the animadversions of crit-ics, the term is now in nearly universal use and plays a central role in most of the recent systematic studies in social psychology. It is therefore a concept which students must examine with unusual care. . . .

GENESIS OF ATTITUDES

Four Common Conditions for the Formation of Attitudes

One of the chief ways in which attitudes are built up is through the accretion of experience, that is to say, through the *integration* of numerous specific responses of a similar type. It is not, as a rule, the discrete and isolated experience which engenders an attitude; for in itself the single experience lacks organization in memory, meaning, and emotion. An attitude is characteristically a fusion, or, in Burnham's terms (1924, p. 285), a "residuum of many repeated processes of sensation, perception, and feeling."

It is a favorite doctrine of mental hygiene that *wholesome* attitudes are those which are the product of *all* experience that is relevant to a certain issue, without repressions or dissociations to mar their inclusiveness. Thus Morgan writes:

> A hasty generalization based on a very few incidents should be viewed with suspicion, [whereas if the attitude] grew from actual experiences, and is a correct abstract formulation of the lessons learned from a large number of these experiences, it should be rated high. (1934, p. 49)

Important as the mechanism of integration unquestionably is in the formation of attitudes, it has in recent years been criticized for its one-sided emphasis. The motto of integration is *e pluribus unum*. It inevitably implies that the infant is totally specific and fragmentary in his responses, and that in childhood his attitudes become gradually "pieced together," and that in adulthood he becomes still more thoroughly unified.

Certain recent developments in psychology have brought a quite contrary emphasis in their train. Integration, it is said, is not the only mechanism of development.... According to this doctrine the original matrix of all attitudes is coarse, diffuse, and non-specific; it is the mass-action found in infancy, which tends only to have a general positive (adient) or negative (abient) orientation. From this point of view it might be said that in the beginning the infant has two primordial, non-specific attitudes, namely, approaching and avoiding. From this matrix, he must segregate action-patterns and conceptual systems which will supply him with adequate attitudes for the direction of his adaptive conduct.

A third important source of attitudes is the dramatic experience, or *trauma*. It is well known that a permanent attitude may be formed as the result of a compulsive organization in the mental field following a single intense emotional experience. Probably everyone can trace certain of his fears, dislikes, prejudices, and predilections to dramatic incidents of childhood. Sometimes, as Freudians have shown, the source of these early fixations are suppressed and forgotten, and the resulting attitude, though strong, seems to be of mysterious origin. But sometimes the whole process of traumatic fixation is accessible to memory. The recovery of the traumatic origins to consciousness does not necessarily weaken the attitude. The autobiography of W. E. Leonard (1927) illustrates the tenacity of early attitudes of fear in spite of the insight acquired into their origin. Although the traumatic experiences of childhood seem to be especially important, there

is all through life a susceptibility to the influence of emotional shock. In *Days without End* Eugene O'Neill traces the genesis of a young man's atheistic attitude to the death of his parents, and the restoration of his religious attitude to the critical illness of his wife many years later. Even in old age radical changes of attitude through circumstances of dramatic moment are not unknown.

There is a fourth common condition under which attitudes are formed. Through the imitation of parents, teachers, or playmates, they are sometimes adopted *ready-made*. Even before he has an adequate background of appropriate experience a child may form many intense and lasting attitudes toward races and professions, toward religion and marriage, toward foreigners and servants, and toward morality and sin. A parent's tone of voice in disapproving of the ragamuffins who live along the railroad track is enough to produce an uncritical attitude in the child who has no basis in his experience for the rational adoption of the parent's point of view. It frequently happens that *subsequent* experience is fitted into the attitude thus uncritically adopted, not—as the mental hygienist advocates—made the basis for the attitude. In such cases every contact is prejudged, contradictory evidence is not admitted, and the attitude which was borrowed second-hand is triumphant. Few men have actually encountered "tricky Japanese" or "cruel Turks," few have known tragedy to follow a dinner party of thirteen, or the lighting of three cigarettes from the same match. And yet thousands of such attitudes and beliefs are adopted ready-made and tenaciously held against all evidence to the contrary.

PREJUDGMENT AND PREJUDICE

Whenever a pre-existing attitude is so strong and inflexible that it seriously distorts perception and judgment, rendering them inappropriate to the demands of the objective situation, the social psychologist usually designates this tenacious attitude as a *stereotype, a prejudice,* or sometimes, more loosely, as a *logic-tight compartment.* These three concepts, which are more or less interchangeable, are of great value in the explanation of social phenomena. They explain why the skillful propagandist chooses solidified emotional attitudes to play upon. They tell why human beings persevere in ancient ruts of thought and action, and why "facts" are of relatively little importance in shaping public opinion, and why the dead hand of the past is permitted to fashion the social policies of the present day. They explain why the banal remarks of a famous man or woman are widely circulated and reverently quoted, and why the cleverer epigrams and shrewder pronouncements of an unknown sage are ignored or discounted. They help one to understand the characteristic conservatism and the "cultural lag" of society. . . .

RÉSUMÉ

. . . The doctrine of attitudes has almost completely captured and refashioned the science of social psychology. The nature of attitudes, however, is still in dispute, and it may correctly be questioned whether a science reared upon so amorphous a foundation can be strong. What is most urgently needed is a clarification of the doctrine of attitudes, and to this task the present chapter has been addressed.

Because of historical considerations it is necessary to include a wide range of subjective determining tendencies under the general rubric of Attitude. Yet it is both possible and desirable to distinguish between attitudes and many correlative forms of readiness-for-response. Attitudes proper may be *driving* or *directive, specific* or *general, common* or *individual.* They characteristically have a material or conceptual object of reference, and are "pointed" in some direction with respect to this object. If they are so generalized that the object and the direction are not identifiable, they then merge into what may be called the "traits" of personality. Common attitudes can be roughly classified and measured, and when abstracted from the personalities which contain them they constitute the "socius" which is that portion of the unique personality of special interest to social science.

Attitudes are never directly observed, but, unless they are admitted, through inference, as real and substantial ingredients in human nature, it becomes impossible to account satisfactorily either for the consistency of any individual's behavior, or for the stability of any society.

REFERENCES

Bogardus, E. S. (1931). *Fundamentals of social psychology* (2nd ed.). New York: Century.

Burnham, W. H. (1924). *The normal mind.* New York: Appleton.

Folsom, J. K. (1931). *Social psychology.* New York: Harper.

Leonard, W. E. (1927). *The locomotive-god.* New York: Century.

Morgan, J. J. B. (1934). *Keeping a sound mind.* New York: Macmillan.

Thomas, W. I., & Znaniecki, F. (1918). *The Polish peasant in Europe and America* (Vol. 1). Boston: Badger.

11

The Social Psychology of George Herbert Mead

BERNARD N. MELTZER

A. PRELIMINARY REMARKS

While Mead's system of Social Psychology is given its fullest exposition in *Mind, Self and Society*, each of three other books (as well as a few articles) rounds out the complete picture.

It should be pointed out at this juncture that Mead himself published no full-length systematic statement of his theory. All four of the books bearing his authorship are post-humously collected and edited works. They comprise a loose accumulation of his lecture notes, fragmentary manuscripts, and tentative drafts of unpublished essays. Since the chief aim of his editors has been completeness—rather than organization—the books consist, in considerable part, of alternative formulations, highly repetitive materials, and sketchily developed ideas.

Nevertheless, a brief description of these volumes is in order, since they constitute the major source-materials concerning Mead's social psychology.

Philosophy of the Present (1932) contains the Paul Carus Foundation lectures delivered by Mead in 1930, a year before his death. These lectures present a philosophy of history from the pragmatist's point of view. Moreover, this volume presents his ideas on the analogous developments of social experience and of scientific hypotheses.

Mind, Self and Society (1934) is chiefly a collection of lectures delivered to his classes in Social Psychology at the University of Chicago.

Movements of Thought in the 19th Century (1936) is largely a collection of lectures delivered to his classes in the History of Ideas.

Philosophy of the Act (1938), according to Paul Schilpp, represents a fairly *systematic* statement of the philosophy of pragmatism. This "systematic" statement I found (as did G. S. Lee) to be made up of essays and miscellaneous fragments, which are technical and repetitious, obscure and difficult.

A final observation regarding the content of these books should be made: Mead's orientation is generally *philosophical*. Rather than marshalling his own empirical evidence, he uses the findings of various sciences and employs frequent apt and insightful illustrations from everyday life. These illustrations usually are not used to prove points, but rather to serve as data to be analyzed in terms of his scheme.

Before launching upon a presentation of Mead's social-psychological theories, it might be wise to explain his designation of his viewpoint as that of "Social Behaviorism." By this term Mead means to refer to the description of behavior at the distinctively human level. Thus, for social behaviorism, the basic datum is the social act. As we shall see, the study of social arts entails concern with the covert aspects of behavior. Further, the concept of the "social act" implies that human conduct and experience has a fundamental social dimension—that the social context is an inescapable element in distinctively human actions.

n radial behaviorism, ʹiorism starts with the ᵼf individuals; but *un-* ial behaviorism con- ...in broad enough terms to ...clude *covert* activity. This inclusion is deemed necessary to understanding the distinctive character of human conduct, which Mead considers a qualitatively different emergent from infrahuman behavior. Watson's behaviorism, on the other hand, reduces human behavior to the very same mechanisms as are found on the infrahuman level. As a corollary, Watson sees the social dimension of human behavior as merely a sort of external influence upon the individual. Mead, by contrast, views generically human behavior as *social* behavior, human acts as *social* acts. For Mead, both the content and the very existence of distinctively human behavior are accountable only on a social basis. (These distinctions should become more clear in the course of this report.)

It can readily be inferred from this brief explanation of Mead's usage of the term "social behaviorism" that, before we can explore the nature and function of the mind—which Mead considers a uniquely human attribute—supporting theories of society, and of self—another uniquely human attribute—require elaboration. Hence, the natural, logical order of Mead's thinking seems to have been society, self, and mind— rather than "Mind, Self, and Society."

B. CONTENT OF MEAD'S SOCIAL PSYCHOLOGY

1. Society

According to Mead, all group life is essentially a matter of cooperative behavior. Mead makes a distinction, however, between infrahuman society and human society. Insects— whose society most closely approximates the complexity of human social life—act to-gether in certain ways because of their biological makeup. Thus, their cooperative behavior is physiologically determined. This is shown by many facts, among which is the fact of the fixity, the stability, of the relationships of insect-society members to one another. Insects, according to the evidence, go on for countless generations without any difference in their patterns of association. This picture of infrahuman society remains essentially valid as one ascends the scale of animal life, until we arrive at the human level.

In the case of human association, the situation is fundamentally different. Human cooperation is not brought about by mere physiological factors. The very diversity of the patterns of human group life makes it quite clear that human cooperative life cannot be explained in the same terms as the cooperative life of insects and the lower animals. The fact that human patterns are not stabilized and cannot be explained in biological terms led Mead to seek another basis of explanation of human association. Such cooperation can only be brought about by some process wherein: (a) each acting individual ascertains the *intention* of the acts of others, and then (b) makes his own response on the basis of that intention. What this means is that, in order for human beings to cooperate, there must be present some sort of mechanism whereby each acting individual: (a) can come to understand the lines of action of others, and (b) can guide his own behavior to fit in with those lines of action. Human behavior is not a matter of responding directly to the activities of others. Rather, it involves responding to the *intentions* of others, i.e., to the future, intended behavior of others—not merely to their present actions.

We can better understand the character of this distinctively human mode of interaction between individuals by contrasting it with the infrahuman "conversation of gestures." For example when a mother hen clucks, her chicks will respond by running to her. This does not imply however, that the hen clucks *in order* to guide the chicks, i.e., with the *intention* of guiding them. Clucking is a natural sign or signal—rather than a significant (meaningful) symbol—as it is not meaningful to the hen. That is, the hen (according to Mead) does not take the role, or viewpoint, of the chicks toward its own gesture and respond to it, in imagination, as they do. The hen does not envision the response of the chicks to her clucking. Thus, hens and chicks do not share the same experience.

Let us take another illustration by Mead: Two hostile dogs, in the pre-fight stage, may go through elaborate conversation of gestures (snarling, growling, baring fangs, walking stiffleggedly around one another, etc.). The dogs are adjusting themselves to one another by responding to one another's gestures. (A gesture is that portion of an act which represents the entire act; it is the initial, overt phase of the act, which epitomizes it, e.g., shaking one's fist at someone.) Now, in the case of the dogs the response to a gesture is dictated by pre-established tendencies to respond in certain ways. Each gesture leads to a direct, immediate, automatic, and unreflecting response by the recipient of the gesture (the other dog). Neither dog responds to the *intention* of the gestures. Further, each dog does not make his gestures with the intent of eliciting certain responses in the other dog. Thus, animal interaction is devoid of conscious, deliberate meaning.

To summarize: Gestures, at the nonhuman or nonlinguistic level, do not carry the connotation of conscious meaning or intent, but serve merely as cues for the appropriate responses of others. Gestural communication takes place immediately, without any interruption of the act, without the mediation of a definition or meaning. Each organism adjusts "instinctively" to the other; it does not stop and figure out which response

it will give. Its behavior is, largely, a series of direct automatic responses to stimuli.

Human beings, on the other hand, respond to one another on the basis of intentions or meanings of gestures. This renders the gesture *symbolic,* i.e., the gesture becomes a symbol to be interpreted; it becomes something which, in the imaginations of the participants, stands for the entire act.

Thus, individual A begins to act, i.e., makes a gesture: for example, he draws back an arm. Individual B (who perceives the gesture) completes, or fills in, the act in his imagination; i.e., B imaginatively projects the gesture into the future: "He will strike me." In other words, B perceives what the gesture stands for, thus getting its meaning. In contrast to the direct responses of the chicks and the dogs, the human being inserts an interpretation between the gesture of another and his response to it. Human behavior involves responses to *interpreted* stimuli.[1]

We see, then, that people respond to one another on the basis of imaginative activity. In order to engage in concerted behavior, however, each participating individual must be able to attach the same meaning to the same gesture. Unless interacting individuals interpret gestures similarly, unless they fill out the imagined portion in the same way, there can be no cooperative action. This is another way of saying what has by now become a truism in sociology and social psychology: Human society rests upon a basis of *consensus,* i.e., the sharing of meanings in the form of common understandings and expectations.

In the case of the human being, each person has the ability to respond to his own gestures; and thus, it is possible to have the same meaning for the gestures as other persons. (For example: As I say "chair," I present to myself the same image as to my hearer; moreover, the same image as when someone else says "chair.") This ability to stimulate oneself as one stimulates another, and to respond to oneself as another does, Mead ascribes largely to man's vocal-auditory mechanism. (The ability to hear oneself implies at least the potentiality for responding to oneself.) When a gesture has a shared, common meaning, when it is—in other words—a *linguistic* element, we can designate it as a "significant symbol." (Take the words, "Open the window": the pattern of action symbolized by these words must be in the mind of the speaker as well as the listener. Each must respond, in imagination, to the words in the same way. The speaker must have an image of the listener responding to his words by opening the window, and the listener must have an image of his opening the window.)

The imaginative completion of an act—which Mead calls "meaning" and which represents mental activity—necessarily takes place through *role-taking*. To complete imaginatively the total act which a gesture stands for, the individual must put himself in the position of the other person, must identify with him. The earliest beginnings of role-taking occur when an already established act of another individual is stopped short of completion, thereby requiring the observing individual to fill in, or complete, the activity imaginatively. (For example, a crying infant may have an image of its mother coming to stop its crying.)

As Mead points out, then, the relation of human beings to one another arises from the developed ability of the human being to respond to his own gestures. This ability enables different human beings to respond in the same way to the same gesture, thereby sharing one another's experience.

This latter point is of great importance. Behavior is viewed as "social" not simply when it is a response to others, but rather when it has incorporated in it the behavior of others. The human being responds to himself as other persons respond to him, and in so doing he imaginatively shares the conduct of others. That is, in imagining their response he shares that response.[2]

2. Self

To state that the human being can respond to his own gestures necessarily implies that he possesses a *self*. In referring to the human being as having a self, Mead simply means that such an individual may act socially toward himself, just as toward others. He may praise, blame, or encourage himself; he may become disgusted with himself, may seek to punish himself, and so forth. Thus, the human being may become the object of his own actions. The self is formed in the same way as other objects—through the "definitions" made by others.

The mechanism whereby the individual becomes able to view himself as an object is that of role-taking, involving the process of communication, especially by vocal gestures or speech. (Such communication necessarily involves role-taking.) It is only by taking the role of others that the individual can come to see himself as an object. The standpoint of others provides a platform for getting outside oneself and thus viewing oneself. The development of the self is concurrent with the development of the ability to take roles.

The crucial importance of language in this process must be underscored. It is through language (significant symbols) that the child acquires the meanings and definitions of those around him. By learning the symbols of his groups, he comes to internalize their definitions of events or things, including their definitions of his own conduct.

It is quite evident that, rather than assuming the existence of selves and explaining society thereby, Mead starts out from the prior existence of society as the context within which selves arise. This view contrasts with the nominalistic position of the social contract theorists and of various individualistic psychologies.

Genesis of the Self. The relationship between role-playing and various stages in the development of the self is described below:

1. *Preparatory Stage* (not explicitly named by Mead, but inferable from various fragmentary essays). This stage is one of meaningless imitation by the infant (for example, "reading" the newspaper). The child does certain things that others near it do without any understanding of what he is doing. Such imitation, however, implies that the child is incipiently taking the roles of those around it, i.e., is on the verge of putting itself in the position of others and acting like them.

2. *Play Stage.* In this stage the actual playing of roles occurs. The child plays mother, teacher, storekeeper, postman, streetcar conductor, Mr. Jones, etc. What is of central importance in such play-acting is that it places the child in the position were it is able to act back toward itself in such roles as "mother" or "teacher." In this stage, then, the child first begins to form a self, that is, to direct activity toward itself—and it does so by taking the roles of others. This is clearly indicated by use of the third person in referring to oneself instead of the first person: "John wants . . . ," "John is a bad boy."

However, in this stage the young child's configuration of roles is unstable; the child passes from one role to another in unorganized, inconsistent fashion. He has, as yet, no unitary standpoint from which to view himself, and hence, he has no unified conception of himself. In other words, the child forms a number of separate and discrete objects of itself, depending on the roles in which it acts toward itself.

3. *Game Stage.* This is the "completing" stage of the self. In time, the child finds himself in situations wherein he must take a number of roles simultaneously. That is, he must respond to the expectations of several people at the same time. This sort of situation is exemplified by the game of baseball—to use Mead's own illustration. Each player must visualize the intentions and expectations of several other players. In such situations the child must take the roles of groups of individuals as over against particular roles. The child becomes enabled to do this by abstracting a "composite" role out of the concrete roles of particular persons. In the course of his association with others, then, he builds up a *generalized other*, a generalized role or standpoint from which he views himself and his behavior. This generalized other represents, then, the set of standpoints which are common to the group.

Having achieved this generalized standpoint, the individual can conduct himself in an organized, consistent manner. He can view himself from a consistent standpoint. This means, then, that the individual can transcend the local and present expectations and definitions with which he comes in contact. An illustration of this point would be the Englishman who "dresses for dinner" in the wilds of Africa. Thus, through having a generalized other, the individual becomes emancipated from the pressures of the peculiarities of the immediate situation. He can act with a certain amount of consistency in a variety of situations because he acts in accordance with a generalized set of expectations and definitions that he has internalized.

The "I" and the "Me."   The self is essentially a social process within the individual involving two analytically distinguishable phases: The "I" and the "Me."

The "I" is the impulsive tendency of the individual. It is the initial, spontaneous, unorganized aspect of human experience. Thus, it represents the undirected tendencies of the individual.

The "Me" represents the incorporated other within the individual. Thus, it comprises the organized set of attitudes and definitions, understandings and expectations—or simply meanings—common to the group. In any given situation the "Me" comprises the generalized other and, often, some particular other.

Every act begins in the form of an "I" and usually ends in the form of the "Me."

For the "I" represents the initiation of the act prior to its coming under control of the definitions or expectations of others (the "Me"). The "I" thus gives *propulsion* while the "Me" gives *direction* to the act. Human behavior, then, can be viewed as a perpetual series of initiations of acts by the "I" and of acting-back-upon the act (that is, guidance of the act) by the "Me." The act is a resultant of this interplay.

The "I," being spontaneous and propulsive, offers the potentiality for new, creative activity. The "Me," being regulatory, disposes the individual to both goal-directed activity and conformity. In the operation of these aspects of the self, we have the basis for, on the one hand, social control and, on the other, novelty and innovation. We are thus provided with a basis for understanding the mutuality of the relationship between the individual and society.[3]

Implications of Selfhood. Some of the major implications of selfhood in human behavior are as follows:

1. The possession of a self makes of the individual a society in miniature. That is, he may engage in interaction with himself just as two or more different individuals might. In the course of this interaction, he can come to view himself in a new way, thereby bringing about changes in himself.

2. The ability to act toward oneself makes possible an inner experience which need not reach overt expression. That is, the individual, by virtue of having a self, is thereby endowed with the possibility of having a mental life: He can make indications to himself—which constitutes *mind*.

3. The individual with a self is thereby enabled to direct and control his behavior. Instead of being subject to all impulses and stimuli directly playing upon him, the individual can check, guide, and organize his behavior. He is, then, *not* a mere passive agent.

All three of these implications of selfhood may be summarized by the statement that the self and the mind (mental activity) are twin emergents in the social process.

3. Mind

Development of Mind. As in the instance of his consideration of the self, Mead rejects individualistic psychologies, in which the social process (society, social interaction) is viewed as presupposing, and being a product of, mind. In direct contrast is his view that mind presupposes, and is a product of, the social process. Mind is seen by Mead as developing correlatively with the self, constituting (in a very important sense) the self in action.

Mead's hypothesis regarding mind (as regarding the self) is that the mental emerges out of the organic life of man through communication. The mind is present only at certain points in human behavior, viz, when significant symbols are being used by the individual. This view dispenses with the substantive notion of mind as existing as a box-like container in the head, or as some kind of fixed, ever-present entity. Mind is seen as a *process*, which manifests itself whenever the individual is interacting with himself by using significant symbols.

Mead begins his discussion of the mind with a consideration of the relation of the organism to its environment. He points out that the central principle in all organic behavior is that of continuous adjustment, or adaptation, to an environing field. We cannot regard the environment as having a fixed character for all organisms, as being the same for all organisms. All behavior involves selective attention and perception. The organism accepts certain events in its field, or vicinity, as stimuli and rejects or overlooks certain others as irrelevant to its needs. (For example, an animal battling for life ignores food.) Bombarded constantly by stimuli, the organism selects those stimuli or aspects of its field which pertain to, are functional to, the acts in which the organism is engaged. Thus, the organism has a hand in determining the nature of its environment. What this means, then, is that Mead, along with Dewey, regards all life as ongoing activity, and views stimuli—not as initiators of activity—but as elements selected by the organism in the furtherance of that activity.

Perception is thus an activity that involves selective attention to certain aspects of a situation, rather than a mere matter of something coming into the individual's nervous system and leaving an impression. Visual perception, e.g., is more than a matter of just opening one's eyes and responding to what falls on the retina.

The determination of the environment by the biologic individual (infrahumans and the unsocialized infant) is not a cognitive relationship. It is selective, but does not involve consciousness, in the sense of reflective intelligence. At the distinctively human level, on the other hand, there is a hesitancy, an inhibition of overt conduct, which is *not* involved in the selective attention of animal behavior. In this period of inhibition, mind is present.

For human behavior involves inhibiting an act and trying out the varying approaches in imagination. In contrast, as we have seen, the acts of the biologic individual are relatively immediate, direct, and made up of innate or habitual ways of reacting. In other words, the unsocialized organism lacks consciousness of meaning. This being the case, the organism has no means for the abstract analysis of its field when new situations are met, and hence no means for the reorganization of action-tendencies in the light of that analysis.[4]

Minded behavior (in Mead's sense) arises around problems. It represents, to repeat an important point, a temporary inhibition of action wherein the individual is attempting to prevision the future. It consists of presenting to oneself, tentatively and in advance of overt behavior, the different possibilities or alternatives of future action with reference to a given situation. The future is, thus, present in terms of images of prospective lines of action from which the individual can make a selection. The mental process is, then, one of delaying, organizing, and selecting a response to the stimuli of the environment. This implies that the individual *constructs* his act, rather than responding in predetermined ways. Mind makes it possible for the individual purposively to control and organize his responses. Needless to say, this view contradicts the stimulus-response conception of human behavior.

When the act of an animal is checked, it may engage in overt trial and error or random activity. In the case of blocked human acts, the trial and error may be carried on covertly, implicitly. Consequences can be imaginatively "tried out" in advance. This is what is primarily meant by "mind," "reflective thinking," or "abstract thinking."

What this involves is the ability to indicate elements of the field or situation, abstract from the situation, and recombine them so that procedures can be considered in advance of their execution. Thus, to quote a well-known example, the intelligence of the detective as over against the intelligence of the bloodhound lies in the capacity of the former to isolate and indicate (to himself and to others) what the particular characters are which will call out the response of apprehending the fugitive criminal.

The mind is social in both origin and function. It arises in the social process of communication. Through association with the members of his groups, the individual comes to internalize the definitions transmitted to him through linguistic symbols, learns to assume the perspectives of others, and thereby acquires the ability to think. When the mind has risen in this process, it operates to maintain and adjust the individual in his society; and it enables the society to persist.

The persistance of a human society depends, as we have seen, upon consensus; and consensus necessarily entails minded behavior.

The mind is social in function in the sense that the individual continually indicates to himself in the role of others and controls his activity with reference to the definitions provided by others. In order to carry on thought, he must have some standpoint from which to converse with himself. He gets this standpoint by importing into himself the roles of others.

By "taking the role of the other," as I earlier pointed out, we can see ourselves as others see us, and arouse in ourselves the responses that we call out in others. It is this conversation with ourselves, between the representation of the other (in form of the "Me") and our impulses (in the form of the "I") that constitutes mind. Thus, what the individual actually does in minded behavior is to carry on an internal conversation. By addressing himself from the standpoint of the generalized other, the individual has a universe of discourse, a system of common symbols and meanings, with which to address himself. These are presupposed as the context for minded behavior.

Mead holds, then, that mental activity is a peculiar type of activity that goes on in the experience of the person. The activity is that of the person responding to himself, of indicating things to himself.

To repeat, mind originates in the social process, in association with others. There is little doubt that human beings lived together in groups before mind ever evolved. But there emerged, because of certain biological developments, the point where human beings were able to respond to their own acts and gestures. It was at this point that mind, or minded behavior, emerged. Similarly, mind comes into existence for the individual at the point where the individual is capable of responding to his own behavior, i.e., where he can designate things to himself.

Summarizing this brief treatment of mind, mental activity, or reflective thinking, we may say that it is a matter of making indications of meanings to oneself as to others. This is another way of saying that mind is the process of using significant symbols. For thinking goes on when an individual uses a symbol to call out in himself the responses which others would make. Mind, then, is symbolic behavior.[5] As such, mind is an emergent from nonsymbolic behavior and is fundamentally irreducible to the stimulus-response mechanisms which characterize the latter form of behavior.

It should be evident that Mead avoids both the behavioristic fallacy of reduction and the individualistic fallacy of taking for granted the phenomenon that is to be explained.

Objects. Returning to Mead's discussion of the organism-in-environment, we can now give more explicit attention to his treatment of *objects*. As we have seen, we cannot regard the environment as having a fixed character for all organisms. The environment is a function of the animal's own character, being greatly determined by the makeup of the animal. Each animal largely selects its own environment. It selects out the stimuli toward which it acts, its makeup and ongoing activity determining the kinds of stimuli it will select. Further, the qualities which are possessed by the objects toward which the animal acts arise from the kind of experiences that the animal has with the objects. (To illustrate, grass is not the same phenomenon for a cat and for a cow.) The environment and its qualities, then, are always functional to the structure of the animal.

As one passes on to the human level, the relation of the individual to the world becomes markedly more complicated. This is so because the human being is capable of forming objects. Animals, lacking symbols, see stimuli, such as patches of color—not objects. An object has to be detached, pointed out, "imaged" to oneself. The human being's environment is constituted largely by objects.

Now, let us look at the relation of the individual to objects. An object represents a plan of action. That is, an object doesn't exist for the individual in some pre-established form. Perception of any object has telescoped in it a series of experiences which one would have if he carried out the plan of action toward that object. The object has no qualities for the individual, aside from those which would result from his carrying out a plan of action. In this respect, the object is constituted by one's activities with reference to it. (For example, chalk is the sum of qualities which are perceived as a result of one's actions: a hard, smooth, white writing implement.)

The objects which constitute the "effective environment," the individual's experienced environment, are established by the individual's activities. To the extent that his activity varies, his environment varies. In other words, objects change as activities toward them change. (Chalk, for instance, may become a missile.)

Objects, which are constituted by the activities of the human individual, are largely *shared* objects. They stand for common patterns of activity of individuals. This is true, Mead points out, by virtue of the fact that objects arise, and are present in experience, only in the process of being indicated to oneself (and, hence, explicitly or implicitly, to others). In other words, the perspective from which one indicates an object implicates definitions by others. Needless to say, these definitions involve language, or significant symbols. The individual acquires a commonality of perspective with others by learning the symbols by which they designate aspects of the world.[6]

4. The Act

All human activity other than reflex and habitual action is built up in the process of its execution; i.e., behavior is constructed as it goes along, for decisions must be made at several points. The significance of this fact is that people act—rather than merely react.

For Mead, the unit of study is "the act," which comprises both overt and covert aspects of human action. Within the act, all the separated categories of the traditional, orthodox psychologies find a place. Attention, perception, imagination, reasoning, emotion, and so forth, are seen as parts of the act—rather than as more or less extrinsic influences upon it. Human behavior presents itself in the form of acts, rather than of concatenations of minute responses.

The act, then, encompasses the total process involved in human activity. It is viewed as a complete span of action: Its initial point is an impulse and its terminal point some objective which gives release to the impulse. In between, the individual is in the process of constructing, organizing his behavior. It is during this period that the act undergoes its most significant phase of development. In the case of human behavior, this period is marked by the play of images of possible goals or lines of action upon the impulse, thus directing the activity to its consummation.

In pointing out that the act begins with an impulse, Mead means that organisms experience disturbances of equilibrium. In the case of the lower animals, their biological makeup channelizes the impulse toward appropriate goals. In the case of the human being, the mere presence of an impulse leads to nothing but mere random, unorganized activity. This is most clearly—but definitely not exclusively—seen in the instance of the behavior of infants. Until the defining actions of others set up goals for it, the human infant's behavior is unchannelized. It is the function of images to direct, organize and construct this activity. The presence in behavior of images implies, of course, a process of indicating to oneself, or mind.

The act may have a short span (e.g., attending a particular class meeting, or starting a new page of notes) or may involve the major portion of a person's life (e.g., trying to achieve a successful career). Moreover, acts are parts of an interlacing of previous acts, are built up, one upon another. This is in contradistinction to the view that behavior is a series of discrete stimulus-response bonds. Conceiving human behavior in terms of acts, we become aware of the necessity for viewing any particular act within its psychosocial context.[7]

Using the concept of the act, Mead sets up classes of acts—the automatic act, the blocked act, the incomplete act, and the retrospective act—and analyzes them in terms of his frame of reference. Space does not permit presentation of these intriguing analyses.

C. SUMMARY

At several points in this report the reader must have been aware of the extremely close interwoven character of Mead's various concepts. In the discussions of society, or self, and of mind, certain ideas seemed to require frequent (and, perhaps, repetitious) statement. A brief summary of Mead's position may help to reveal more meaningfully the way in which his key concepts interlock and logically imply one another.

The human individual is born into a society characterized by *symbolic interaction*. The use of *significant symbols* by those around him enables him to pass from the conversation of gestures—which involves direct, unmeaningful response to the overt acts of others—to the occasional *taking of the roles* of others. This role-taking enables him to share the perspectives of others. Concurrent with role-taking, the *self* develops, i.e., the capac-

ity to act toward oneself. Action toward oneself comes to take the form of viewing oneself from the standpoint, or perspective, of the *generalized other* (the composite representative of others, of society, within the individual), which implies defining one's behavior in terms of the expectations of others. In the process of such viewing of oneself, the individual must carry on symbolic interaction with himself, involving an internal conversation between his impulsive aspect (the "I") and the incorporated perspectives of others (the "Me"). The *mind*, or mental activity, is present in behavior whenever such symbolic interaction goes on—whether the individual is merely "thinking" (in the everyday sense of the word) or is also interacting with another individual. (In both cases the individual must indicate things to himself.) Mental activity necessarily involves *meanings*, which usually attach to and define, *objects*. The meaning of an object or event is simply an image of the pattern of action which defines the object or event. That is, the completion in one's imagination of an act, or the mental picture of the actions and experiences symbolized by an object, defines the act or the object. In the unit of study that Mead calls "the act," all of the foregoing processes are usually entailed. The concluding point to be made in this summary is the same as the point with which I began: Mead's concept intertwine and mutually imply one another. To drive home this important point, I must emphasize that human society (characterized by symbolic interaction) both precedes the rise of individual selves and minds, and is maintained by the rise of individual selves and minds. This means, then, that symbolic interaction is both the medium for the development of human beings and the process by which human beings associate as human beings.

Finally, it should be clearly evident by now that any distinctively human act necessarily involves: symbolic interaction, role-taking, meaning, mind, and self. Where one of these concepts is involved, the others are, also, necessarily involved. Here we see, unmistakably, the organic unity of Mead's position.

NOTES

1. The foregoing distinctions can also be expressed in terms of the differences between "signs," or "signals," and symbols. A sign stands for something else because of the fact that it is present at approximately the same time and place with that "something else." A symbol, on the other hand, stands for something else because its users have agreed to let it stand for that "something else." Thus, signs are directly and intrinsically linked with present or proximate situations; while symbols, having arbitrary and conventional, rather than intrinsic, meanings, transcend the immediate situation. (We shall return to this important point in our discussion of "mind.") Only symbols, of course, involve interpretation, self-stimulation and shared meaning.

2. To anyone who has taken even one course in sociology it is probably superfluous to stress the importance of symbols, particularly language, in the acquisition of all other elements of culture. The process of socialization is essentially a process of symbolic interaction.

3. At first glance, Mead's "I" and "Me" may appear to bear a close affinity with Freud's concepts of Id, Ego, and Superego. The resemblance is, for the most part, more apparent than real. While the Superego is held to be harshly frustrating and repressive of the instinctual, libidinous, and aggressive Id, the "Me" is held to provide necessary direction—often of a *gratifying* nature—to the otherwise undirected impulses constituting the "I." Putting the matter in figurative terms: Freud views the Id and the Superego as locked in combat upon the battleground of the Ego; Mead sees the "I" and "Me" engaged in close collaboration. This difference in perspective may derive from different preoccupations: Freud was primarily concerned with tension, anxiety, and "abnormal" behavior; Mead was primarily concerned with behavior generically.

It is true, on the other hand, that the Id, Ego, and Superego—particularly as modified by such neoFreudians as Karen Horney, Erich Fromm,

and H. S. Sullivan—converge at a few points with the "I" and "Me." This is especially evident in the emphasis of both the Superego and "Me" concepts upon the internalization of the norms of significant others through the process of identification, or role-taking.

Incidentally, it should be noted that both sets of concepts refer to processes of behavior, *not* to concrete entities or structures. See, also, the discussion of "mind" which follows.

4. The reader should recognize here, in a new guise, our earlier distinction between signs and symbols. Signs have "intrinsic" meanings which induce direct reactions; symbols have arbitrary meanings which require interpretations by the actor prior to his response or action. The former, it will be recalled, are "tied to" the immediate situation, while the latter "transcend" the immediate situation. Thus, symbols may refer to past or future events, to hypothetical situations, to nonexistent or imaginary objects, and so forth.

5. A growing number of linguists, semanticists, and students of speech disorders are becoming aware of the central role of symbols in the *content*, as well as the process of thought. Edward Sapir and Benjamin Whorf have formulated "the principle of linguistic relativity," which holds that the structure of a language influences the manner in which the users of the language will perceive, comprehend, and act toward reality. Wendell Johnson, in the field of semantics, and Kurt Goldstein, in the study of aphasia, are representative investigators who have recognized the way in which symbols structure perception and thought. Mead's theory clearly foreshadows these developments.

6. The contrast between this view of learning and the neo-behavioristic "learning theory" of Clark Hull and other psychologists should be clearly evident. Basically, learning theorists attempt to reduce human learning to the mechanisms found in infrahuman learning. This is reflected in their tendency to ignore the role of linguistic symbols in human behavior, their conceptualization of human activity in terms of stimulus-response couplets, and their view of learning as equivalent with conditioning. (For an excellent critique of learning theory from the symbolic interactionist standpoint, see: Manford H. Kuhn, "Kinsey's View of Human Behavior," *Social Problems*, 1(April 1954), pp. 119–125.

7. The reader may have noted that this discussion makes no explicit reference to the problem of motivation. Mead had little to say regarding motives. Adherents to his general orientation have tended either to regard motives as implicit in the concept of *object* ("a plan of action") or to consider them "mere" verbal labels offered in supposed explanation of the actions of oneself or of others.

In my judgment, a conception of motivation can be formulated that is both useful and consistent with Mead's theories. Motivation can refer to "a process of defining (symbolically, of course) the goal of an act." Thus, while both human and infrahuman behavior may be viewed as goal-directed, only human behavior would be considered "motivated." Just as "motive" would be restricted to the human level, "drive" might serve a comparable function on the infrahuman level.

This would not imply that motives lie back of, or "cause," human acts. Rather, human acts are in constant process of construction, and the goal-definitions by individuals undergo constant reformulation. I mean to designate by "motive," however, the definition the individual makes, *at any given time*, of the objectives of his own specific acts. Such definitions, obviously, would be socially derived.

12

Attribution of Causality and Responsibility

William W. Wilmot

[A] perceptual regularity characteristic of person perception is the attribution of causality. As human beings, we want to come to grips with our environment; we want to make sense out of the world. One of the techniques we utilize to this end is the attribution of causality. From the general view that events are caused, we view human behavior as being caused. Most of us feel we are in part responsible for our actions, and we impose this same perspective on others. We see them as at least partly responsible for their actions [Tagiuri, 1969].

When we mentally attach causes to the behaviors of others, we essentially have two choices: attribution to *external* causes or attribution to *internal* causes; that is, we ascribe the behavior of another either to the actor (internal locus) or to the circumstances surrounding him or her (external locus) [Schopler and Compere, 1971]. We tend to attribute the person's actions to external causality under the following conditions [Baron and Byrne, 1977]:

1. *High consensus.* Other people also act in this manner in this kind of situation. For instance, if we think that most people will suffer depression when they lose a loved one, then person A's depression is seen as being caused by the loss of a loved one.
2. *High consistency.* If the person acts similarly to the way she is acting in this situation on other occasions, then we assume that the situational constraints produce the behavior.
3. *High distinctiveness.* If this person acts differently in other situations, then we as-

sume that her depression has been produced by circumstances of this situation. For instance, if someone lies when interviewed by the police for a drug charge but does not lie in other situations, we would tend to see the lying as produced by the strong arm of the law, and not by some personality trait.

The conditions leading to an attribution of internal causality are the opposite of those cited earlier. If there is low consensus (others in this situation do not act this way), then we attribute the behavior to a personality, or internal state of the person. Suppose that an out-of-work, recently divorced friend of yours has been evicted by his landlord. During the process of moving, he physically harms his ex-wife because she had come over to claim some of the furniture. You will see your friend as "aggressive" or "hostile," because most people would not act violently in such a situation. Therefore, whenever attributing causes to the other, the more unique or bizarre the behavior, the more likely we are to attribute it to some internal state. If there is low consistency (the person is in the situation often, but acts differently), we tend to attribute the behavior to internal states that are unpredictable. Take the evicted friend again. If he has been with his former mate many times before in dealing with the property, but this one time he assaults her, we are likely to conclude that he "has gone off the deep end," or some similar situation. Finally, if there is low distinctiveness (the person acts similarly in a number of situations), then we assume it is a function of personality not of the situation. If our friend has been in many physical spats with others before, we would see him as an aggressive person and would see his assault on his ex-wife as just fitting a firmly established pattern.

The key to attribution of causality is, as Kelley [1972] notes, the amount of covariation. If the behavior occurs with the presence of the person and not when the person is not present, then we conclude that the person has caused it. With the man who assaulted his former mate, if the woman has been physically assaulted many times by many former romantic partners, we would conclude that something in her behavior toward men contributes to the responses that they have toward her [Kelley, 1972].

When attributing causality, the judgment centers on whether we think the other has the power to create the effects. In most situations, we also attribute responsibility—where we impose an emotional or moral judgment along with the notion of causality. Researchers in attribution theory separate the two processes, but the preceding examples combine the notions of causality and responsibility because in most reactions to others, the two are intertwined.

The degree of responsibility we place on others for events depends on a number of factors. If external forces are not very strong or if the ability to withstand those forces is regarded as high, we tend to place causality and responsibility in the lap of the other. If the person has the ability to create effects, he is typically held responsible for those effects [Tagiuri, 1958]. When observing a disintegrating marriage, for example, if we feel that one of the partners had it in his power to cause the demise of the marriage by having an outside relationship, we place the responsibility on him. Furthermore, if we see the person intending to gain the desired goal, we are more likely to assign responsibility to him. In sum, people are held responsible for the effects they intend to create and for ef-

fects they have the ability to create [Heider, 1958].

The crux of the matter is that in analyzing social situations, we usually have two choices. We can ascribe the effects either to the person or to the environment. If we see another fail at a task, we can attribute it to a lack of ability, "a personal characteristic, or to the difficult task, an environmental factor" [Heider, 1958]. Whichever path we choose has consequences for our transactions. If, in the preceding case, we see the person as failing because of a lack of ability, we may concomitantly perceive him as a weak-willed, nonpowerful person. Our tendency will be to blame him and to take the "he-had-it-coming" attitude toward his misfortunes. This attribution often follows the "belief in a just world" notion that many people have [Shaver, 1975]. If a person is fired, has children in trouble with the law, or is experiencing any other difficulty, this belief allows people to conclude that if bad things happen to a person, he or she somehow deserves it. This attribution pins the effects of behaviors solely upon the person.

If, on the other hand, we ascribe his failure to environmental causes ("Anyone would have failed at that"), then we will see him in a friendlier light and be sympathetic to his plight. A special form of attributing causes to environmental forces occurs in the case of unconscious motivation. If you see someone's behavior as caused by circumstances beyond his understanding and control ("He had a bad childhood and that is why he is insane."), you will absolve him of blame. Our courts of law recognize that environmental forces may be so overwhelming in some cases that the individual should not be tried.

The attribution process is central to the ongoing communication transactions we have with others. If we see someone as "trustworthy" and "having to slightly bend the truth," our communication behavior toward her will be markedly different than if we view her as a "liar who cannot be trusted in any situation." In our communicative transactions with others, we make attributions, attach meanings to their communicative behaviors, and take action based on them. The process of attribution, therefore, occurs constantly in our communication with others.

REFERENCES

Baron, Robert A., and Donn Byrne, *Social Psychology: Understanding Human Interaction*, 2d ed. Boston: Allyn and Bacon, 1977.

Heider, Fritz, *The Psychology of Interpersonal Relations*. New York: Wiley, 1958.

Kelley, Harold H., "Attribution in Social Interaction," in *Attribution: Perceiving the Causes of Behavior*, Edward E. Jones et al. Morristown, NJ: General Learning Corporation, 1972.

Schopler, John, and John C. Compere, "Effects of Being Kind or Harsh to Another on Liking." *Journal of Personality and Social Psychology* 20, No. 2 (1971): 155–159.

Shaver, Kelly G., *An Introduction to Attribution Processes*. Cambridge, MA: Winthrop Publishers, 1975.

Tagiuri, Renato, "Social Preference and Its Perception," in *Person Perception and Interpersonal Behavior*, Renato Tagiuri and Luigi Petrullo (eds.). Stanford, CA: Stanford University Press, 1958, pp. 316–336.

Tagiuri, Renato, "Person Perception," in *The Handbook of Social Psychology, Vol. III: The Individual in a Social Context*, Gardner Lindzey and Elliot Aronson (eds.). Reading, MA: Addison-Wesley, 1969, pp. 395–449.

13

Irrational Attributions of Responsibility
Who, What, When, and Why

D. SADOW

Among the more disquieting of psychology's recent demonstrations of human irrationality has been the observation that people appear to hold victims responsible for the misfortunes that befall them (6, 7, 8). A variety of only partially supported explanations for this behavior has been proposed. A recent suggestion has been that these effects are exaggerations of normal attribution processes. Sadow and Laird (5) demonstrated that only some subjects blame victims and that the tendency to blame could be predicted by a measure of subjects' characteristic tendency to attribute the causes of events to persons or situational forces. This study explored additional implications of the attributional model of the process of blaming victims.

The first implication derives from the recognition that this kind of attributional process is an automatic, almost perceptual way of comprehending situations. If so, variations in characteristic locus of perceived cause should be most influential in relatively hurried, unconsidered evaluations of responsibility, like those usually obtained in Walster paradigm studies (8). In Walster's studies, subjects gave both perpetrators and victims of accidents higher ratings of responsibility when the consequences of those accidents were more severe. In situations that were identical except for less serious consequences, perpetrators and victims were both blamed less.

One might expect that when judgments are more carefully considered, the tendency to blame the victim would disappear. However, a second kind of difference among individuals may be important in more considered judgments, specifically, the level of development of moral judgment (2). Clearly, fusing consequences and culpability represents a primitive, less rational way of assigning moral responsibility, which might be observed among individuals who employ less sophisticated modes of moral judgments.

In sum, then, two linked hypotheses were tested here: (a) when judgments of responsibility are obtained under hurried conditions, victims will be blamed, but only by individuals who characteristically attribute causes of events to persons; and (b) when judgments are more carefully considered, this effect of attributional "style" will be diminished, and blaming victims will either not occur or will be observed only among subjects who employ relatively low levels of moral judgments.

METHOD

Subjects were 56 female and 51 male college students who volunteered for the experiment. In the first session each subject read one of two stories previously used (6, 8). In the Walster story, a car owner parks his car at the top of the hill, and later the car rolls down and causes either mild or severe damage to a grocer. In the Shaver story, a machine breaks down during a demonstration and causes either mild or severe injury to a child. After reading the story, subjects rated on a 20-point scale the degree to which the perpetrator-victim (car owner or machine operator) and the victim (grocer or child) were responsible for the incident.

Subjects were then asked to give reason for their judgments as well as to weigh the responsibility of the protagonists in terms of what Gutkin (1) considers the "components of responsibility." The subjects then rated, for a second "unbiased" time, the extent to which each of the protagonists in each story was responsible for the accident. This concluded the first session.

Administered in the second session were: (a) the Locus of Causal Attribution Scale (3), which measures the subjects' tendency to locate causes of events in actors or the situation (higher scores mean greater person attribution); and (b) the Defining Issues Test (4), which assesses the "relative importance attributed to principled moral considerations in making a moral decision" (higher scores mean a more sophisticated level of moral judgment).

Subjects were divided at the median on their Attribution Scale scores and on their Defining Issues Test scores. The median score on the Attribution Scale was 19, and the range was 5 to 36. The median score on the Defining Issues Test was 30, and the range was 16 to 46. The ratings of responsibility assigned to the victims were analyzed in separate four-way analyses of variance with three between factors, i.e., mild versus severe outcome, strong victim (grocer) versus weak victim (child), and either high/low Attribution Scale score or high/low Defining Issues Test score, and one within factor, i.e., the ratings of responsibility obtained before versus those obtained after consideration of the issues.

RESULTS

A three-way interaction of mild/severe × high/low Attribution Scale score × before/after was observed ($F_{1,99}$ = 10.09, p < .01). As predicted, the high person attributers blamed the victims more in the severe than the mild conditions on the first ratings, but not on the second, better considered ratings. Unexpectedly, low person attributers also blamed the victim more in the mild consequences conditions. These results are consistent with the hypothesis that Attribution Scale scores affect first but not second ratings of responsibility; see Table 1.

A four-way analysis of variance with Defining Issues Test scores rather than Locus of Causal Attribution Test scores as the individual difference variable did not show the predicted relationship between level of moral judgment and consequences. However, another kind of irrational attribution was indicated. All subjects tended to blame the weaker victim, the child, more than the grocer in the first judgments but not in the later judgments ($F_{1,99}$ = 6.03, p < .01). This effect only occurred among subjects scoring low on the Defining Issues Test; high scorers did not differ between victims ($F_{1,99}$ = 3.45, p < .06) (see Table 1, bottom). In general, no effects of consequences on judgments of perpetrators occurred in this study.

DISCUSSION

In the hurried first judgments, people who characteristically attribute the causes of actions to persons also attributed more responsibility to victims when the consequences they suffered were more severe. This supports the attribution interpretation of this effect, as does the fact that it occurred only when the judgments were hurried. The fact that more considered judgments were not affected by consequences also suggests that the social implications of this phenomenon

TABLE 1   Mean Ratings of Responsibility Assigned to Victims

| SCORES | FIRST RATING | | | | SECOND RATING | | | |
| | Mild | | Severe | | Mild | | Severe | |
	M	SD	M	SD	M	SD	M	SD
Subjects' Attribution Scale								
High Scores	1.2	46	2.6	4.23	1.4	.89	2.0	3.08
Low Scores	3.4	4.40	1.1	.52	1.4	1.04	1.7	1.97

| SCORES | Strong Victim | | Weak Victim | |
	M	SD	M	SD
Subjects' Defining Issues Test				
High Scores	1.2	.68	1.6	1.96
Low Scores	1.3	.82	3.2	4.72

are less serious than previously appeared to be the case. Certainly there are occasions in everyday life when we attribute responsibility hurriedly and thoughtlessly, and in those we may do so irrationally, but more careful consideration is sufficient to prevent this effect, as well as the other variety of irrational causal attribution observed in this study.

The differences in responsibility attributed to the grocer and child were not anticipated nor easily explained. This is not a simple difference between the Walster and Shaver stories, since the child is held more responsible only when judgments are hurried or when the judge scores low on the Defining Issues Test. Perhaps this result simply reflects an unjustified assumption that children are more likely to contribute to their problems, an assumption that does not hold up under more leisurely or sophisticated examination.

It should be noted that the effects of consequences while significant, in many cases, were always small and did not for instance, override the over-all, clearly rational view that the car owner and machine operator were more responsible than the grocer or child.

In conclusion, it seems clear that reflected decisions tend to be more rational; hence attribution of responsibility to the victim is reduced for all subjects upon consideration. The implications for human relationships seem to be that major decisions of negotiating boards, arbitrating bodies, and juries could be improved by a slow and thoughtful analysis of the different elements which determine attributions of responsibility, such as causality and intentionality. It seems of utmost importance to seriously consider any data which might improve the objectivity of our juries and court systems. Finally, the judgment of any decision-making board could be improved if level of moral sophistication is seriously considered when electing its members.

Future research might be directed at clarifying the issues and implications of the problem of irrational attribution of responsibility. Also, such research might include experiments with methods of training jury members and other decision-making bodies to have greater objectivity.

REFERENCES

1. Gutkin, D. An analysis of the concept of moral intentionality. Human Development, 1973, 16, 371–381.

2. Kohlberg, L. From is to ought: how to commit the naturalistic fallacy and get away with it in the study of moral development. In T. Mischel (Ed.), *Cognitive development and epistemology*. Part II: B. New York: Academic Press, 1971. Pp. 151–235.

3. Laird, J. D., & Berglas, S. Individual differences in the effects of engaging in counterattitudinal behavior. *Journal of Personality*, 1975, 43, 286–304.

4. Rest, J. *Manual for the Defining Issues Test: an objective test of moral judgment development*. Minneapolis: Univer. of Minnesota, 1974.

5. Sadow, D., & Laird, J. D. Irrational attributions of responsibility: who's to blame for them? *European Journal of Social Psychology*, 1981, 11, 427–430.

6. Shaver, K. G. Defensive attribution: effects of severity and relevance on the responsibility assigned for an accident. *Journal of Personality and Social Psychology*, 1970, 14, 101–113.

7. Shaw, M. E., & Sulzer, J. L. An empirical test of Heider's levels in attribution of responsibility. *Journal of Abnormal and Social Psychology*, 1964, 69, 39–46.

8. Walster, E. Assignment of responsibility for an accident. *Journal of Personality and Social Psychology*, 1966, 3, 73–79.

Dissonance and Self-Perception

An Integrative View of
Each Theory's Proper Domain of Application

RUSSELL H. FAZIO
MARK P. ZANNA
JOEL COOPER

If an individual freely chooses to perform a behavior which is discrepant from his attitude, he tends later to realign his attitude toward that behavior. For example, a subject who complies with an experimenter's request to write an attitude-discrepant essay against the legalization of marijuana is typically found to favor such legalization to a lesser degree than previously. This now classic attitude change effect is readily explained by both Festinger's theory of cognitive dissonance (1957) and Bem's self-perception theory (1972). Dissonance theory, in general, concerns the relationship between various cognitions. The theory posits the existence of a drive-like motivation to maintain consistency among relevant cognitions. Self-perception theory, on the other hand, concerns the passive inference of attitudinal dispositions from behavior. According to Bem (1972), "Individuals come to 'know' their own attitudes, emotions, and other internal states partially by inferring them from observations of their own overt behavior and/or the circumstances in which this behavior occurs" (p. 2). Social psychologists vary in which theory they endorse.

Although the underlying processes posited by each theory differ, the predictions drawn from each are very similar. According to both, individuals closely examine the be-

havior in question and the external environment. Both theories stress the importance of various situational cues, e.g., freedom of choice and level of monetary inducement, as possible external justifications (or, in the "language" of self-perception theory, external causal attributions) for the performance of attitude-discrepant behavior. In addition, both theories possess rare predictive and explanatory power in the sense that they can account for a great deal of attitude change data.

Given the similarity of dissonance and self-perception theories and the historical dominance of attitude research in social psychology, it is understandable that a controversy as to the relative superiority of one theory over the other emerged soon after Bem's (1965, 1967) proposal of self-perception theory as an alternative to cognitive dissonance theory. Social psychologists have largely conceptualized the two as "competing" theories and have expended much effort to disconfirm their nonpreferred theory. The details of the controversy need not be reviewed here. It will suffice to remark that the issue is far from settled. Neither theory has been convincingly demonstrated to be relatively superior (cf. Greenwald, 1975), despite a plethora of so-called "crucial experiments" (e.g., Snyder

& Ebbesen, 1972; Ross & Shulman, 1973; Green, 1974; Schaffer, 1975; Swann & Pittman, 1975).

It shall be the aim of this paper to provide an integrated framework for the operation of both dissonance and self-perception processes. We hope to refocus the manner in which the two theories are viewed and to suggest an integration. More specifically, we propose that they not be regarded as "competing" theories. Our basic tenet is that dissonance and self-perception are actually complementary and that, within its proper domain of application, each theory is correct. Together the two theories provide a more complete conceptual framework for explaining the manner in which, and the conditions under which, the examination of one's behavior will lead to attitude change.

DISSONANCE THEORY AND ATTITUDE-DISCREPANT BEHAVIOR

A major difference between cognitive dissonance theory and self-perception theory concerns the matter of aversive tension. A motivation to reduce cognitive discrepancies is a central part of dissonance theory but, "in the self-perception explanation, there is no aversive motivational pressure postulated" (Bem, 1972, p. 17). This difference provides the characteristic by which dissonance and self-perception processes must ultimately be distinguished.

The recent development by Zanna and Cooper (1974) of an attributional framework in which the possible occurrence of dissonance arousal can be investigated has led to research on the question of dissonance as an aversive arousal state. Given the extensive review of this research by Zanna and Cooper (1976), only two relevant studies will be summarized here. We will emphasize the relevance of these findings to our view that dissonance and self-perception theories are complementary.

Following Schachter and Singer's (1962) theory that an emotion is a combination of arousal and a cognitive label, Zanna and Cooper (1974) reasoned that the arousal which is postulated to occur when one freely chooses to write a counterattitudinal essay is also amenable to cognitive labeling. As long as an individual in an induced-compliance setting attributes this presumed arousal to his performance of a counterattitudinal behavior, he will experience dissonance and attempt to reduce it, possibly via attitude change (cf. Worchel & Arnold, 1974). However, if the situational cues provide a reasonable alternative to which he can "misattribute" this arousal, then no dissonance and no subsequent attitude change will occur.

Zanna and Cooper (1974) varied potential cognitive labels by giving subjects a placebo which ostensibly produced a side effect of relaxation or tension or no side effect. Subjects were then placed in an induced-compliance situation where they wrote a counterattitudinal essay under conditions of high or low choice. The no side effects condition demonstrated the typical effect in which high choice subjects changed their attitudes more than low choice subjects. Of particular importance is the fact that this effect failed to occur in the conditions where subjects could attribute their arousal to the pill which supposedly made them feel tense. In the relaxation conditions, the attitude change effect was accentuated—presumably because the high choice subjects experienced arousal, despite believing that they had taken a relaxing drug.

From the data of Zanna and Cooper's experiment (1974), and other studies using the "misattribution" approach (e.g., Zanna, Higgins, & Taves, 1976), it is possible to infer that aversive arousal does result when one performs a counterattitudinal behavior. Cooper, Zanna, & Taves (Note 1) went further by demonstrating that arousal is a necessary condition for attitude-discrepant behavior to lead to attitude change. In their study, counterattitudinal advocacy did not affect subjects' attitudes when they had taken a drug (phenolbarbitol) which inhibited their becoming aroused. However, when subjects had taken an arousing drug (amphetamine), they did change their attitudes. This result constitutes further evidence that arousal is associated with attitude change in counterattitudinal, induced compliance situations.

Taken together, these studies confirm the dissonance theory proposition that freely choosing to perform an attitude-discrepant behavior leads to a state of aversive arousal (cf. Kiesler & Pallak, 1976). The findings cast serious doubt on the self-perception view that people infer their attitudes from counterattitudinal behavior without experiencing aversive motivational pressure. Self-perception theory obviously remains a powerful and useful predictive tool in the domain of attitude-discrepant behaviors. It well predicts the occurrence of attitude change and, furthermore, suggests the attributional process involved in the identification of arousal as dissonance. However, the theory cannot be considered to accurately capture and depict the process by which a person who behaves counterattitudinally is led to make a change of cognition. The research described demonstrates that cognitive inconsistency is accompanied by aversive arousal.

SELF-PERCEPTION THEORY AND ATTITUDE-CONGRUENT BEHAVIOR

An additional major difference between dissonance and self-perception theories concerns the theories' implications for attitude-congruent behavior. Self-perception theory predicts that a new attitude will emerge if an individual performs a behavior which is more extreme than is implied by his attitude. It is not necessary for the behavior to be attitude-discrepant. That is, self-per-

ception theory leads to the expectation that attitude change will occur if the behavioral advocacy lies anywhere along the attitudinal continuum other than the person's preferred position.

Dissonance theory, on the other hand, predicts attitude change only if the behavior performed is discrepant with the attitude. The theory is not applicable to situations in which pro-attitudinal advocacy occurs. In fact, one might argue that the theory leads to a prediction of no attitude change in such situations on the basis that the two cognitions—attitude and the behavioral advocacy—form a consonant relationship.

There now exists much independent evidence supporting the basic self-perception notion concerning the inference of attitude from behavior (e.g., Bandler, Madaras, & Bem, 1968; Salancik, 1974). Also, in what has become a research area of increasing interest, it has been reliably demonstrated that an individual's interest in an activity can actually be undermined if he is provided with oversufficient external justification for the performance of a behavior he would normally freely engage in (e.g., Deci, 1971; Lepper, Greene, & Nisbett, 1973; Benware & Deci, 1975; Ross, 1976). Such "overjustification effects" are easily interpretable from a self-perception analysis, but are outside the realm of dissonance theory.

Most relevant to our concerns is the fact that Kiesler, Nisbett, and Zanna (1969) demonstrated attitude change in the direction of *more* favorability to the position advocated. Subjects committed themselves to argue against air pollution (a behavior generally consistent with their attitudes) to passers-by in the street. In addition, some of the subjects were led to believe that the performance of this behavior had implications for belief, while other subjects were led to believe that there was no such link between beliefs and behavior. Belief-relevant subjects were found to be more favorable to the position they were to advocate than were belief-irrelevant subjects or control subjects who were not committed to the behavior.

In the Kiesler et al. study (1969; cf. also Zanna & Kiesler, 1971), it is important to note the extremity of the behavior relative to the attitude. Although subjects committed themselves to perform a behavior which was generally consistent with their attitudes, proselytizing against pollution to passers-by on a street corner is probably a more extreme behavior than was implied by the subjects' attitudes. That is, while the subjects did hold antipollution attitudes, their attitudes were unlikely to have been of such an extreme nature that they would typically, and without request, proselytize against pollution. Any action which appears as ordinary behavior in relation to an individual's attitude should not lead to attitude change. The act implies nothing new about attitude and will not result in a self-attribution of a new, more extreme attitude. Only if the overt action is more extreme than implied by an individual's attitude will a self-attribution result in a shift to a more extreme position (cf. Pallak & Kleinhesselink, 1976).

LATITUDES OF ACCEPTANCE AND REJECTION

Thus far, we have argued that dissonance theory is appropriately applied to attitude-discrepant behaviors and self-perception theory to attitude-congruent behaviors. In conjunction, we suggest, the two theories can account for attitude change effects which result from the full range of behaviors. However, each theory has its proper and specialized domain of application.

In order to define each theory's domain, we have used such terms as attitude-congruent vs. attitude-discrepant, proattitudinal vs. counter-attitudinal, and consistent vs. inconsistent. In fact, such vague terms permeate the entire literature in this area. How are these terms to be defined? Operationally, at least, social psychologists have defined them

by dichotomizing the attitudinal continuum. Any position on the same side of the midpoint as the subject's expressed attitude is typically considered congruent and any position on the opposite side is considered discrepant. Such an operational definition obscures some important distinctions. After all, is it not basically attitude-congruent for someone who is only slightly in favor of a given proposal to write an essay pointing out a few of the disadvantages of the proposal? Similarly, would it not be just as attitude-discrepant for this person to write an essay favoring an extreme version of the proposal as to write an essay arguing against the adoption of the proposal?

Festinger's (1957) original statement merely proposed that two cognitions are dissonant or discrepant with one another when one does not "follow from" the other. An endorsement of an extreme radical position does not follow from a slightly liberal attitude any more so than an endorsement of a conservative position does. That is, it may be just as counterattitudinal for a person who views himself as occupying a center-left position to favor a radical proposal as it is to favor a conservative one.

A more precise and psychologically meaningful definition than the typical midpoint dichotomy seems necessary. Such a definition may be garnered from the work of Sherif and his colleagues (Sherif, Sherif, & Nebergall, 1965; Sherif & Hovland, 1961; Hovland, Harvey, & Sherif, 1957) who developed a useful and relevant technique of attitude measurement. In their research, the investigators had subjects indicate which one of a continuum of extreme pro- to extreme con-attitudinal statements they found most acceptable, which additional positions they found acceptable, and which they found objectionable. The range of acceptable positions, including the most acceptable position, was termed the latitude of acceptance; the range of objectionable positions, the latitude of rejection.

We propose that attitude-congruent behavior be defined as the endorsement of any position within an individual's latitude of acceptance. This procedure avoids the arbitrariness of a midpoint dichotomy and permits each individual to define for him or herself those positions deemed to be attitude-congruent. It is within the latitude of acceptance, we suggest, that self-perception theory applies. The endorsement of a position, other than the most acceptable position, within this latitude may lead to a self-attributional inference that one holds that newly-endorsed position as his attitude. Correspondingly, attitude-discrepant behavior is defined as the endorsement of any position within an individual's latitude of rejection—regardless of whether this region is on the same side of the midpoint as the individual's most acceptable position, on the opposite side, or on both sides. We propose that this latitude of rejection defines the domain to which dissonance theory is applicable. Writing an essay in support of a statement within one's latitude of rejection may lead to dissonance arousal and subsequent attitude change.

The following experiment was designed and conducted to test the above theoretical notions. After completing a latitudes measure, and provided his latitudes met certain a priori criteria necessitated by the experimental procedure, each subject was committed to write an essay supporting either the most extreme position within his latitude of acceptance (Accept conditions) or the least extreme position within his latitude of rejection (Reject conditions). These two positions were always adjacent ones (see Fig. 1). In addition, subjects were committed under conditions of low choice or high choice. Within the Reject condition, high choice subjects should change their attitudes more than low choice subjects via a dissonance reduction process. Within the Accept conditions, high choice subjects should infer more extreme attitudes than low choice subjects via a self-perception process.

In order to examine the crucial question of arousal and to identify the attitude change process as dissonance or self-perception, one further variable, the presence of a stimulus to which dissonance could potentially be misattributed, was included. Because disso-

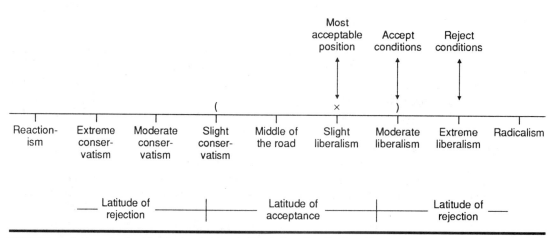

FIGURE 1   A Hypothetical Latitudes Measure Depicting the Position That Individual Would Have Been Assigned to Support in Either the Accept or Reject Conditions.

nance is not aroused in low choice settings, this misattribution stimulus was paired only with high choice Accept and Reject conditions. Within the Reject conditions, we have argued that dissonance theory is applicable. Thus, subjects in the high choice–misattribution condition should experience dissonance arousal, misattribute that arousal, and exhibit no attitude change (cf. Zanna & Cooper, 1974). The prediction for the Reject conditions, then, is that final attitudes in the high choice–no misattribution condition should be more extreme than both those in the low choice condition and those in the high choice–misattribution condition. Within the Accept conditions, we have argued that self-perception theory is applicable. Since no arousal is expected to occur, the opportunity to misattribute arousal should not obviate attitude change. Thus, the prediction in the Accept conditions is that the final attitudes of both the high choice–misattribution subjects and the high choice–no misattribution subjects should be more extreme than the attitudes of the low choice subjects.

METHOD

Subjects

Seventy-five male and female freshmen at Princeton University were recruited for a survey of people's political attitudes, for which they were promised $1.50. Of these subjects, 48 met the a priori criteria that had been established concerning the latitudes measure (see below) and were included in the experiment. Subjects were randomly assigned to condition with the restriction that there be an equal number ($n = 8$) in each condition. They were run in individual booths in groups of two to five.

Procedure

After all subjects for a given experimental period arrived, the experimenter began by explaining the alleged purpose of the experiment. He indicated that he and a professor in the department were beginning a research program in order to study voting behavior in the '76 presidential election and that the present study was concerned with political attitudes. After these introductory remarks, each subject was told to enter a 4 ft 4 in × 3 ft 4 in × 6 ft 4 in (133 cm × 103 cm × 195 cm) soundproof booth where the subject completed the latitudes measure.

Latitudes. The measure consisted of nine statements, each of which began with the phrase "The socio-political philosophy of this nation should be one of..." and concluded with one of the following nine terms: radicalism, extreme liberalism, moderate liberalism, slight liberalism, middle of the road, slight conservatism, moderate conservatism, extreme conservatism, reactionism. The subject was instructed to place a symbol by the one statement he found most acceptable, another symbol by any other statements he found acceptable, and yet another symbol by any he found objectionable. The instructions asked him to judge each and every statement.[1]

In order to be included as a subject the individual's latitudes were required to meet certain criteria. Since the majority of Princeton students held liberal positions, we chose to have all subjects argue in the liberal direction so as to compare the endorsement of statements on the same side of the midpoint as the subject's preferred position. The following criteria were necessary: (1) The most acceptable position had to be no more conservative than middle of the road. (2) At least one statement more liberal than the most acceptable had to be checked as acceptable. (3) At least one statement more liberal than any acceptable positions had to be checked as objectionable. Employing these criteria insured that each subject would be capable of assignment to any experimental condition.

At this point, the experimenter explained that the purpose of the study, the first in a program of research which was to culminate in our investigation of voting behavior, was to ascertain what distinctions people made between various political philosophies and what arguments they perceived to support those positions. The subjects were told that in past research of this sort concerning such issues as the legalization of marijuana and the military draft, we had discovered that one of the best ways to find out what the relevant arguments were was to have people write short, forceful essays supporting a given position. Subjects were told that the same procedure was to be employed in this study.

The experimenter continued by remarking that the essays would be content analyzed in order to discover what the relevant arguments in support of a position were. In order to associate the essay with a foreseeable and possibly undesired consequence (cf. Cooper & Worchel, 1970; Nel, Helmreich, & Aronson, 1969), one further use to which the essay would be put was detailed. A local high school teacher who had four or five classes of sophomores had supposedly heard about the study and asked that we help him in a class project. The teacher intended to have a few members of his class engage in a debate concerning political philosophies before an assembly of all his classes. The essays the subjects wrote were ostensibly to be sent to the debaters who would use those arguments in the debate. Thus, the subjects were led to believe that their arguments might possibly convince some high school sophomores to adopt that position.

Subjects were also told that "in order to avoid any systematic bias," they would be randomly assigned to a position to write about. The experimenter commented that such random assignment was one of the few methods of control a social scientist could employ in a study of this sort.

After randomly assigning each subject to experimental condition and preparing the necessary materials, the experimenter handed each subject a booklet, entitled "1975 Princeton University Political Survey." The first page of the booklet asked for the subject's name and class. The second page informed the subject of the position he was to support in his essay. Printed on this page was either the most extreme liberal position within the subject's latitude of acceptance (Accept conditions) or the least extreme liberal position within his latitude of rejection (Reject conditions). The instructions on this page told the subject to complete the questions on the following pages and to then "write a short, forceful and persuasive essay" supporting the position he had been assigned on the blank sheet at the end of the booklet.

Choice Manipulation. The presence or absence of a "Subject Consent Form" as the next page constituted the choice manipulation. This form began with the following paragraph.

> I understand the nature of the study in which I am being asked to participate. I am aware that my essay will be used in a high school government class. I further understand that I will be paid $1.50 for simply appearing here today, regardless of whether or not I actually decide to participate in the entire study. In addition, I understand that I can leave at any time, if I so desire.

The form then asked the subject to check whether he chose to participate and to allow the release of his essay to the high school class or whether he chose not to participate, and to sign his name and fill in the date. The form concluded with two sentences thanking the subject, if he chose to participate, "for your voluntary agreement to write an essay supporting the position assigned to you" or, if he chose not to participate, "for taking the time to come here today." Also printed in large letters on the bottom of this page, as a reminder to the subject of what he was agreeing to write, was the position the subject had been assigned. All subjects, in fact, chose to participate. This form appeared in the high choice booklets, but was absent in the low choice booklets.

Misattribution Stimulus. In the two high choice misattribution conditions, a one page questionnaire entitled "Departmental Equipment Inquiry" followed the subject consent forms. The booth each subject was seated in was to serve as the stimulus to which dissonance arousal might be misattributed. The page began by explaining that the booths had been recently purchased and installed by the psychology department and that this was, in fact, the first time the booths were being used. The department was supposedly interested in people's assessments of the new booths. The inquiry was supposedly "unrelated to the actual study" and "had been placed in a random position in each booklet in order to assess the effect of duration of time spent in the booth on evaluations of the booth."

The questionnaire began with an item labeled "general measure" which asked subjects to rate on a 31-point scale "To what degree do the booths make you feel tense or uncomfortable?" The endpoints of the scale were labeled "Not tense or uncomfortable at all" and "Very tense or uncomfortable." Three specific measures, each a 31-point scale with endpoints labeled "Not at all adequate" and "Perfectly adequate" followed. These items asked the subject to rate the lighting, air ventilation, and size of the booth. Thus, this questionnaire provided subjects in the booth conditions with an opportunity to "blame" any aversive arousal they might be feeling on the booths, rather than on their decision to write the essay.

Dependent Variable. The next page of the booklet contained the dependent variable. In the low choice conditions, this page followed the notification of the position the subject was to support. In the high choice–no booth conditions, it followed the subject consent form. In the high choice–booth conditions, it appeared immediately after the booth questionnaire. The measure was a 31-point scale with endpoints labeled "Extremely Conservative" and "Extremely Liberal". The question asked, "To what degree do you perceive yourself to be politically conservative or liberal?"

The last page of the booklet was a blank sheet of paper on which the subject was to write the essay. Since the critical behavior was the commitment to write the essay (Wicklund, Cooper, & Linder, 1967), no subject was required to actually complete the essay. As soon as all the subjects in a group had completed the measures and had begun to write, the experimenter interrupted, informed the subjects that the experiment had ended, and carefully debriefed them.

RESULTS

Preliminary examination of the data indicated that, on the average, subjects held a slight to moderate liberal position as their most acceptable position. The initial position mean was 6.44 on a scale where reactionism was scored as 1 and radicalism as 9. Subjects assigned to the Accept conditions endorsed either a moderate or extreme liberal position. Those assigned to the Reject conditions endorsed either an extreme liberal or radical position.

Because the initial and final attitude scales differed markedly, it was not possible to compute a change score. Hence, the data were analyzed in a 2 × 3 analysis of covariance, with the subject's most acceptable position in the latitudes scale serving as the covariate.[2] The adjusted means are presented in Table 1. Attitudes were more extreme in the Accept than in the Reject conditions (Accept M = 21.77, Reject M = 19.60; $F(1,41)$ = 13.22, p < .001). This main effect indicates that Accept subjects were more willing to agree with the position they committed themselves to endorsing than were Reject subjects. In addition, the analysis revealed a main effect for the conditions under which subjects committed themselves to writing the essay ($F(2,41)$ = 5.61, p < .01). Overall, high choice–no booth subjects (M = 21.92) tended to express more extreme attitudes than high choice–booth subjects (M = 20.59) who, in turn, expressed more extreme attitudes than low choice subjects (M = 19.55). The interaction effect was not statistically significant ($F(2,41)$ = 1.10).

The overall analysis of covariance does not, however, allow an exact test of the hypothesis. The critical test is provided by the a priori t-ratio comparisons of the adjusted means (Kerlinger & Pedhazur, 1973) within the Accept and Reject conditions. As predicted, within the Accept conditions, the mean in the high choice–no booth condition is significantly greater than that in the low choice condition ($t(41)$ = 2.35, p < .05).[3] Also, in accordance with expectation, attitude scores in the high choice–booth condition tended to be more extreme than those in the low choice condition ($t(41)$ = 1.94, p = .06). The statistical marginality of this latter effect is understandable given the fact that there was in the high choice–booth condition one highly aberrant subject whose adjusted final score fell 3.5 standard deviations below the

mean of the remaining seven scores in this condition. Were this subject's data deleted from the analysis, the high choice–booth condition (M = 22.60) would differ significantly from the low choice condition ($t(40)$ = 2.16, p < .05), indicating that the opportunity to misattribute arousal did not attenuate attitude change. These data are consistent with the proposition that a self-perception process must have served as the attitude change mechanism.

Within the Reject conditions, the mean in the high choice–no booth condition was significantly greater than both the mean in the low choice condition ($t(41)$ = 2.35, p < .05) and the mean in the high choice–booth condition ($t(41)$ = 2.23, p < .05). Thus, in the case of objectionable positions, the opportunity to attribute one's arousal to the booth obviated attitude change—a finding that is indicative of a dissonance process.

Also informative is the fact that a weighted contrast revealed the mean in the high choice–booth–Reject condition to be significantly different from the average of the means of the other three high choice conditions ($t(41)$ = 3.12, p < .01). Thus, as expected, final attitudes were less extreme in the one condition where subjects were both experiencing dissonance and given an opportunity to misattribute that arousal.

Within the two high choice–booth conditions, subjects' assessments of the booth were also examined. The prediction, of course, is that the Reject subjects, since they are the ones who are misattributing dissonance arousal, should evaluate the booths

TABLE 1   Adjusted Means

LATITUDE	LOW CHOICE	HIGH CHOICE–NO BOOTH	HIGH CHOICE–BOOTH
Accept	20.33ab	22.70c	22.29c
Reject	18.77a	21.14bc	18.89a

Note. The higher the mean, the more liberal subjects perceived themselves to be. Cell means not sharing a common subscript differ beyond the 5% significance level (except the low choice–Accept vs. high choice–booth–Accept comparison which is at p = .06).

more negatively than the Accept subjects. Because the data were highly skewed, they were analyzed by a nonparametric arcsine transformation of the proportion of subjects in each condition who fell below the overall median (Langer & Abelson, 1972). The only dimension on which the booths were judged differently by Accept and Reject subjects was that concerning the adequacy of the air ventilation. Apparently, air ventilation was the most salient dimension on which the booths could plausibly be considered inadequate. Six of the eight Reject subjects, compared to two of the eight Accept subjects, rated the air ventilation below the overall median ($z = 2.09$, $p < .04$). Thus, it was those subjects whom we suggested were experiencing dissonance arousal who found the booths relatively inadequate. This judgment served to "explain" the cause of their discomfort and to obviate what would otherwise have been motivational pressure to change their attitudes.

DISCUSSION

The results of the experiment provide support for the conceptual framework that was developed earlier in this paper. Subjects who endorsed an acceptable position more extreme than their most acceptable position shifted their attitudes towards that endorsement when they had decision freedom. This effect occurred even when subjects were provided with an arousal misattribution cue. Since the cue did not attenuate attitude change, it is reasonable to assume that dissonance arousal did not occur. Instead, the attitude change occurred via a self-perception process. In addition, subjects who freely chose to endorse a position within their latitude of rejection subsequently expressed more extreme attitudes. In the context of objectionable positions, the misattribution cue was employed and served to attenuate attitude change, indicating that dissonance arousal occurred. By "blaming" the booths

for their discomfort, subjects were able to avoid the need to adjust their attitudes to justify their behavior (cf. Zanna & Cooper, 1974, 1976).

Can either self-perception or dissonance theory explain the data in both the Accept and the Reject conditions? We doubt that either theory is capable of that. Self-perception theory has difficulty with the attenuation of attitude change which was found to occur in the Reject conditions. Dissonance theory, on the other hand, finds the lack of attenuation of attitude change in the Accept conditions difficult to explain. However, dissonance theory might maintain that endorsing any position along the continuum, other than the most acceptable one, does not "follow from" one's attitude. The more extreme this endorsement, relative to one's most acceptable position, the greater the arousal which is experienced. Such an explanation would be forced to assume that the likelihood of misattribution to some external stimulus changes as a function of level of arousal. At lower levels of arousal, as in the Accept conditions, an individual is more likely to attribute that arousal to his own behavior rather than to some external stimulus. Thus, no misattribution nor the subsequent attenuation of attitude change occurred in the Accept conditions. At higher levels of arousal, as in the Reject conditions, misattribution to some external cue is more likely than attribution to the agreement to write the essay. Thus, attitude change was attenuated in the Reject conditions.

Such an explanation cannot be rejected completely by the data since we are concerned in the Accept conditions with the lack of a difference between the high choice–no booth and the high choice–booth conditions. However, there seems to be no compelling reason to assume that the likelihood of misattribution to some external stimulus changes as a function of level of arousal. Also, this explanation, since it asserts that there is more arousal in the Reject condition than in the Accept condition, leads to the prediction of greater attitude change in the high choice–Reject condition than in the high choice–Accept condition. The fact that the data tend in the opposite direction casts serious doubt upon this explanation.

Thus, the findings provide evidence for the notion that both dissonance and self-perception processes occur. However, each theory can be appropriately applied only to its own specialized domain. Self-perception theory convincingly explains attitudinal shifts within an individual's latitude of acceptance. Correspondingly, dissonance theory provides an accurate account for attitude change effects within the latitude of rejection.

Unfortunately, in order to maintain random assignment, our procedure could not differentiate the amount of discrepancy between the most acceptable position and the endorsed position from the latitudes of acceptance and rejection. In order to argue within their randomly assigned latitude, subjects in the Reject conditions tended to endorse a position about one step more extreme than those in the Accept conditions. We are not, however, suggesting that a certain, specifiable amount of discrepancy is necessary to arouse dissonance processes. Large or small discrepancies could arouse dissonance, if the endorsed position were to fall within the latitude of rejection. It is our position that these individually defined latitudes delineate whether dissonance or self-perception processes will occur. In fact, when one examines only those subjects in the high choice–booth conditions who endorsed a position two units from their most acceptable positions, one finds that the final adjusted attitude scores of the two subjects in the Accept condition are higher than any of the scores of the seven subjects from the Reject condition. Equalizing for discrepancy, then, there still seems to be a difference between the conditions—more change in the Accept–booth

condition than in the Reject–booth condition. Although necessarily based upon a small number of cases, this internal analysis suggests that even if discrepancy were equalized, one would find latitudinal position to serve as an indicator of the attitudinal process occurring.

What periods during the history of an attitude favor the likelihood of self-perception or dissonance processes operating? Latitudes of acceptance and rejection provide the key through which some meaningful implications can be drawn. A wide latitude of acceptance will increase the likelihood of a self-perception process occurring, while a wide latitude of rejection will make a dissonance process more likely. We might speculate that the period during which attitudes are formed is characterized by a broad latitude of acceptance. After all, when an individual has little information about, or experience with an attitude object, he is likely to endorse a number of positions as acceptable ones. On the other hand, firmly established attitudes regarding attitude objects toward which an individual has had much relevant experience are likely to be characterized by the acceptability of relatively few positions and, hence, by a wide latitude of rejection. In short, while self-perception seems applicable to the early stages of attitude development, dissonance theory may be most relevant to later stages when an individual is more certain of his feelings toward an attitude object.

It should be noted that our experimental procedure involved what we considered to be the simplest method of operationalizing acceptable vs. objectionable behaviors. Subjects were committed to endorsing attitudinal positions within or beyond their latitudes of acceptance. The behavior itself, and the consequences of that behavior, were held constant. That is, all subjects were to write an essay which they were led to believe might convince some high school students to adopt the position advocated.

However, it is reasonable to assume that the same pattern of data would accrue if the position endorsed where held constant and the extremity of the behavior and/or consequences varied. One can imagine a behavioral latitudes measure on which individuals could indicate which behaviors they found acceptable and which objectionable. Performance of a behavior more extreme than implied by one's attitude yet within the behavioral latitude of acceptance may lead to the self-perception of a new attitude. Performance of a behavior within the behavioral latitude of rejection may lead to dissonance-induced attitude change. For example, for an individual who favors the legalization of marijuana, signing a petition to that effect may be within the latitude of acceptance, and, therefore, evoke a self-perception process. On the other hand, marching on the state capital may fall within the latitude of rejection, and, therefore, produce dissonance. These different processes may occur even though the position endorsed is identical for the two behaviors. Further research is necessary to examine the extent of the similarity between a methodology employing behavioral latitudes and the methodology used in this study.

Hopefully, our conceptualization and the data that accompany it will serve to call a truce between dissonance and self-perception theorists. Within its proper domain of application, each theory is superior to the other, but, in general, no such relative superiority exists. Alone neither theory can explain all the data. Together, they provide social psychology with provocative and convincing explanations of the effects of overt behavior on attitudes.

NOTES

1. In their more recent work, Sherif et al. (1965), also measured a latitude of noncommitment—the range of positions to which an individual is indifferent—which intervenes between latitudes of acceptance and rejection. In the present experiment the latitude of noncommittment was ignored, because it does not permit a clear prediction of which attitude change process will occur.

2. Two points should be noted. First, the relationship between initial and final attitude scores was virtually identical in each condition. Thus, the critical analysis of covariance requirement concerning homogeneity of within-group regression coefficients was met. Second, no significant differences on the covariate existed between the various conditions. Indeed, the analysis of covariance was performed, not in order to equalize initial differences, but in order to allow initial position to "explain" what in an analysis of variance would be considered error variance (Cohen & Cohen, 1975). The proportion of variance on the dependent measure accounted for by the covariate was, in fact, highly significant ($F(1,41) = 75.93$, $p < .001$).

3. All significance levels reported in this paper are based on two-tailed comparisons.

REFERENCES

Bandler, R. J., Madaras, G. R., & Bem, D. J. Self-observation as a source of pain perception. *Journal of Personality and Social Psychology*, 1968, **9**, 205–209.

Bem, D. J. An experimental analysis of self-persuasion. *Journal of Experimental Social Psychology*, 1965, **1**, 199–218.

Bem, D. J. Self-perception: An alternative interpretation of cognitive dissonance phenomena. *Psychological Review*, 1967, **74**, 183–200.

Bem, D. J. Self-perception theory. *In* L. Berkowitz (Ed.), *Advances in experimental social psychology* (Vol. 6). New York: Academic Press, 1972, 1–62.

Benware, C., & Deci, E. L. Attitude change as a function of the inducement for espousing a proattitudinal communication. *Journal of Experimental Social Psychology*, 1975, **11**, 271–278.

Cohen, J., & Cohen, P. *Applied multiple regression/correlation analysis for the behavioral sciences.* Hillsdale, New Jersey: Lawrence Erlbaum Associates, 1975.

Cooper, J., & Worchel, S. Role of undesired consequences in arousing cognitive dissonance. *Journal of Personality and Social Psychology*, 1970, **16**, 199–206.

Deci, E. L. Effects of externally mediated rewards on intrinsic motivation. *Journal of Personality and Social Psychology*, 1971, **18**, 105–115.

Festinger, L. *A theory of cognitive dissonance.* Stanford: Stanford University Press, 1957.

Green, D. Dissonance and self-perception analyses of "forced-compliance": When two theories make competing predictions. *Journal of Personality and Social Psychology*, 1974, **29**, 819–828.

Greenwald, A. G. On the inconclusiveness of "crucial" cognitive tests of dissonance vs. self-perception theories. *Journal of Experimental Social Psychology*, 1975, **11**, 490–499.

Hovland, C. I., Harvey, O. J., & Sherif, M. Assimilation and contrast effects in reactions to communication and attitude change. *Journal of Abnormal and Social Psychology*, 1957, **55**, 244–252.

Kerlinger, F. N., & Pedhazur, E. J. *Multiple regression in behavioral research.* New York: Holt, Rinehart, and Winston, 1973.

Kiesler, C. A., Nisbett, R. E., & Zanna, M. P. On inferring one's beliefs from one's behavior. *Journal of Personality and Social Psychology*, 1969, **11**, 321–327.

Kiesler, C. A., & Pallak, M. S. Arousal properties of dissonance manipulations. *Psychological Bulletin*, 1976, **83**, 1014–1025.

Langer, E. J., & Abelson, R. P. The semantics of asking a favor: How to succeed in getting help without really dying. *Journal of Personality and Social Psychology*, 1972, **24**, 26–32.

Lepper, M. R., Greene, D., & Nisbett, R. E. Undermining children's intrinsic interest with extrinsic reward: A test of the "overjustification" hypothesis. *Journal of Personality and Social Psychology*, 1973, **28**, 129–137.

Nel, E., Helmreich, R., & Aronson, E. Opinion change in the advocate as a function of the persuasibility of his audience: A clarification of the meaning of dissonance. *Journal of Personality and Social Psychology*, 1969, **12**, 117–124.

Pallak, M. S., & Kleinhesselink, R. R. Polarization of attitudes: Belief inference from consonant behavior. *Personality and Social Psychology Bulletin*, 1976, **2**, 55–58.

Ross, M. The self-perception of intrinsic motivation. *In* J. H. Harvey, W. J. Ickes, & R. F. Kidd (Eds.), *New directions in attribution research.* Hillsdale, New Jersey: Lawrence Erlbaum Associates, 1976.

Ross, M., & Shulman, R. F. Increasing the salience of initial attitudes: Dissonance versus self-perception theory. *Journal of Personality and Social Psychology*, 1973, **28**, 138–144.

Salancik, J. R. Inference of one's attitude from behavior recalled under linguistically manipulated cognitive sets. *Journal of Experimental Social Psychology*, 1974, **10**, 415–427.

Schachter, S., & Singer, J. E. Cognitive, social, and physiological determinants of emotional state. *Psychological Review*, 1962, **69**, 379–399.

Schaffer, D. R. Some effects of consonant and dissonant attitudinal advocacy on initial attitude salience and attitude change. *Journal of Personality and Social Psychology*, 1975, **32**, 160–168.

Sherif, C. W., Sherif, M., & Nebergall, R. E. *Attitude and attitude change: The social judgment-involvement approach.* Philadelphia: Saunders, 1965.

Sherif, M., & Hovland, C. I. *Social judgment: Assimilation and contrast effects in communication and attitude change.* New Haven: Yale University Press, 1961.

Snyder, M., & Ebbesen, E. Dissonance awareness: A test of dissonance theory versus self-perception theory. *Journal of Experimental Social Psychology*, 1972, **8**, 502–517.

Swann, W. B., & Pittman, T. S. Salience of initial ratings and attitude change in the "forbidden toy" paradigm. *Personality and Social Psychology Bulletin*, 1975, **1**, 493–496.

Wicklund, R. A., Cooper, J., & Linder, D. E. Effects of expected effort on attitude change prior to exposure. *Journal of Experimental Social Psychology*, 1967, **3**, 416–428.

Worchel, S., & Arnold, S. E. The effect of combined arousal states on attitude change. *Journal of Experimental Social Psychology*, 1974, **10**, 549–560.

Zanna, M. P., & Cooper, J. Dissonance and the pill: An attribution approach to studying the arousal properties of dissonance. *Journal of Personality and Social Psychology*, 1974, **29**, 703–709.

Zanna, M. P., & Cooper, J. Dissonance and the attribution process. *In* J. H. Harvey, W. J.

Ickes, & R. F. Kidd, (Eds.), *New directions in attribution research.* Hillsdale, New Jersey: Lawrence Erlbaum Associates, 1976.

Zanna, M. P., Higgins, E. T., & Taves, P. A. Is dissonance phenomenologically aversive? *Journal of Experimental Social Psychology,* 1976, **12,** 530–538.

Zanna, M. P., & Kiesler, C. A. Inferring one's beliefs from one's behavior as a function of belief relevance and consistency of behavior. *Psychonomic Science,* 1971, **24,** 283–285.

REFERENCE NOTE

1. Cooper, J., Zanna, M. P., & Taves, P. A. *On the necessity of arousal for attitude change in the induced compliance paradigm.* Unpublished manuscript, Princeton University, 1975.

15

Monopolizing the Conversation
On Being Civilly Egocentric

CHARLES DERBER

"Conversation indeed" said the Rocket. "You have talked the whole time yourself. That is not conversation."
"Somebody must listen" answered the Frog, "and I like to do all the talking myself."'
"You are a very irritating person" said the Rocket, "and very ill bred. I hate people who talk about themselves, as you do, when one wants to talk about oneself, as I do . . . "
—Oscar Wilde, from "The Remarkable Rocket"

Individualism has a counterpart in American psychology. People tend to seek attention for themselves in face-to-face interactions. This attention-getting psychology reflects an underlying character structure of "self-orientation" that emerges in highly individualistic societies.[1] Erich Fromm has theorized that a shared character structure develops in each society, a "social character" that is a response to the requirements of the social order and best suited for survival and success within it. The self-oriented character type develops a highly egocentric view of the world and is motivated primarily by self-interest. To cope with social and economic insecurity bred by individualism, he becomes preoccupied with himself. His "attention-getting" psychology is thus rooted in a broad self-absorption engendered by social conditions highly developed in contemporary America.[2]

In informal conversation, the self-oriented person repeatedly seeks to turn attention to himself. This "conversational narcissism" is closely related to the individualistic norms already discussed. . . . Attention is allocated according to norms in which each individual is responsible for himself, and is free, within limits of civility, to take as much as he can. These norms legitimate focusing on one's own needs in informal talk and are consistent with the effort by self-oriented conversationalists to gain predominant attention for themselves.

THE FORMS OF CONVERSATIONAL NARCISSISM

Conversational narcissism is the key manifestation of the dominant attention-getting psychology in America. It occurs in informal conversations among friends, family and co-workers. The profusion of popular literature about listening and the etiquette of managing those who talk constantly about themselves suggests its pervasiveness in everyday life; its contemporary importance is indicated by the early appearance of these problems in the most recent edition of Emily Post's etiquette manual.[3]

In observations of ordinary conversations, I have found a set of extremely common conversational practices which show an unresponsiveness to others' topics and involve turning them into one's own. Because of norms prohibiting blatantly egocentric behavior, these practices are often exquisitely subtle; ritual forms of civility and face-saving have evolved to limit the overt expression of egoism in social life.[4] Although conversationalists are free to introduce topics about themselves, they are expected to maintain an appearance of genuine interest in those about others in the conversation. A delicate face-saving system requires that people refrain from openly disregarding others' concerns and keep expressions of disinterest from becoming visible. Practices of conversational narcissism are normally, then, driven underground and expressed in disguised forms where they are not readily discerned by any member of the conversation.[5]

To explore the narcissistic practices that occur most often, we must distinguish between two kinds of attention-response: the *shift-response* and the *support-response*. The shift- and support-responses are alternative ways one can react to others' conversational initiatives. The differences between the two can be seen in the following examples:[6]

JOHN: I'm feeling really starved.
MARY: Oh, I just ate. (shift-response)

JOHN: I'm feeling really starved.
MARY: When was the last time you ate? (support-response)

JOHN: God, I'm feeling so angry at Bob.
MARY: Yeah, I've been feeling the same way toward him (shift-response)

JOHN: God, I'm feeling so angry at Bob.
MARY: Why, what's been going on between the two of you? (support-response)

JOHN: My mother would pack me melted cheese sandwiches every day.
MARY: My mom never made me a lunch I could stand to eat. (shift-response)

JOHN: My mother would pack me melted cheese sandwiches every day.
MARY: Hey, your mother was all right. (support-response)

JOHN: I saw Jane today on the street.
MARY: I haven't seen her in a week. (shift-response)

JOHN: I saw Jane today on the street.
MARY: Oh, how's she doing? (support-response)

JOHN: I just love Brahms.
MARY: Chopin's my favorite. (shift-response)

JOHN: I just love Brahms.
MARY: Which is your favorite piece? (support-response)

The shift-response and support-response are both commonly used. They are superficially so little different that few conversationalists notice the distinction. Yet they affect the flow of attention and the development of topics in markedly different ways. When Mary uses the shift-response, she temporarily shifts the attention to herself and creates the potential for a change in topic. When using the support-response, she keeps the attention and topic securely focused on John.

Of the two responses, only the shift-response changes who is the subject of the conversation. For example, if Mary says to John, "I'm going to the movies tonight," John can temporarily make himself the subject with any of the following replies:

> That reminds me, I've got to go home tonight.
> I'm sick of movies these days.
> Gee, I wonder what I'm going to do tonight.

With each of these shift-responses, John introduces the dilemma of whether the conversation will continue with Mary as the subject or will turn to him. Alternatively, he could offer the following kinds of support responses:

> What movie?
> Great, you deserve a break.
> Are you feeling good enough to go?

These support-responses are attention-giving ones not in competition with Mary's initial assertion. They keep the conversation clearly focused on her and give her license to continue as the subject. Support-responses, unlike shift-responses, cannot normally be introduced to transfer attention to the self.[7]

Conversational narcissism involves preferential use of the shift-response and under-utilization of the support-response. We can distinguish between active and passive narcissistic practices. The active practices involve repeated use of the shift-response to subtly turn the topics of others into topics about oneself. The passive practices involve minimal use of support-responses so that others' topics are not sufficiently reinforced and so are terminated prematurely.

Active Practices

The shift-response is the one response to another's initiative through which one can introduce one's own topic. While it does not necessarily change the topic—and is frequently not so intended—it nonetheless always creates the possibility. The following dialogue illustrates how the shift-response is typically used by self-oriented conversationalists to bring attention to themselves:

MARY: My summer place has been such a blessing this year.
JOHN: I know, I sure would like a place like that, the way I've been feeling, but I've got to earn the bread first, you know?
MARY: Yeah.
JOHN: I figure that if I work enough this year and next, I'll be able to check that place out in Vermont again and maybe . . .

Although John appears, in his first response, to have expanded on Mary's topic, he has subtly shifted the attention to himself. He has not responded directly to her feelings, but has shifted the conversation to his own state of mind, his problems with money,

and his desires for a summer place of his own. Rather than returning to her topic, Mary then responds with a support-response allowing John in the following turn to consolidate his earlier topical initiative.

While changing the topic, John links his response to Mary's and prefaces his own with an acknowledgment of hers. The preface is a token gesture of recognition of what the other has said. Numerous other prefaces such as "oh really," "huh," "isn't that something," "same here," and "I can't believe it" recur in conversations. They soften the transition in topic and help to protect the individual against charges of unresponsiveness. A preface acknowledges that one is paying attention to the previous statement and adds legitimacy to an assertion in which the individual suddenly introduces himself as the subject. It also presents the interjection of oneself as not simply an effort to gain attention, but rather a form of responsiveness to share personal experience or information.[8]

Although important for maintaining civility, a shift-response does not require a preface. For example:

JOHN: I've got such a huge appetite.
BILL: I couldn't eat a thing.

JOHN: My father would take me every two weeks to a game and I spent every minute looking forward to it.
BILL: I remember the first game my father took me to. I made so much noise that he didn't want to take me anymore.

Here, the shifts in focus are legitimized by the appearance of a topical connection. The subtlety of the shift-response is that it is always based on a connection to the previous subject. This creates an opening for the respondent to shift the topic to himself while still preserving the "face" of the other.

While repeating the shift-response is the most common way self-oriented conversationalists seek attention, it does not always imply conversational narcissism. The shift-response can serve either as a sharing-response or as a narcissistic topical initiative. The major difference lies not in introducing the shift-response, but in the intent and the statements which follow. When serving narcissistic ends, shift-responses are repeated until a clear shift in subject has transpired. When meant only as sharing-responses, interjecting oneself is temporary and is quickly followed by returning to the original topic. In these instances, the shift-response only briefly brings attention to oneself as a means of furthering the conversation.

The effectiveness of the shift-response as an attention-getting device lies partly in the difficulty in distinguishing immediately whether a given response is a sharing one or a narcissistic initiative. At a certain stage in the development of another's topic, it becomes appropriate to introduce information about oneself, but normally not until the other has introduced most of his information or narrative. The earlier the initial shift-response, the more likely it foreshadows an effort to seize the conversation.[9] This is illustrated in the following conversation:

MARY: I saw the most beautiful rainbow today.
JOHN: Wow, I saw a lovely one just last week.

At this point, Mary cannot know whether John actually is interested in her experience or in simply turning the talk to himself. His statement is connected to hers and may well represent an honest attempt to share his experience or to highlight hers. But it may also signal a narcissistic initiative, which would be confirmed if he persists in using the shift response.

MARY: I saw the most beautiful rainbow today.
JOHN: Wow, I saw a lovely one just last week.

MARY: It had such a magnificent blend of blues and golds.
JOHN: Huh, the one I saw was all reds and yellows.

John's repeated shift responses have now become a competing initiative that make it more difficult for Mary to sustain her own subject. A decisive topical shift occurs in the next turn as Mary, despite her option to continue with her own topic, accommodates John's initiative with a support-response:

MARY: I saw the most beautiful rainbow today.
JOHN: Wow, I saw such a lovely one last week.
MARY: It had such a magnificent blend of blues and golds.
JOHN: Huh, the one I saw was all reds and yellows.
MARY: What time of day did you see it?
JOHN: Early afternoon. I was walking near the river and . . .

The active narcissistic practice always follows some variation of this pattern, in which repetitions of the shift-response turns the conversation to oneself. The shift-response functions as a gaining-initiative which introduces one's own topic. It sets the stage for a topic competition which will persist as long as each conversationalist continues to use a shift-response. The self-oriented conversationalist triumphs in this competition when his shift-response succeeds in eliciting a succession of support-responses from others, thus securing their acquiescence to his topic.

Incessant use of the shift-response is not typical because it is too baldy egoistic and disruptive. A more acceptable—and more pervasive—approach is one where a conversationalist makes temporary responsive concessions to others' topics before intervening to turn the focus back to himself. The self-oriented conversationalist mixes shift-responses with support-responses, leaving the impression that he has interest in others as well as himself.

JIM: You know, I've been wanting to get a car for so long.

BILL: Yeah. (support-response)

JIM: Maybe when I get the job this summer, I'll finally buy one. But they're so expensive.

BILL: I was just thinking about how much I spend on my car. I think over $1500 a year. You know I had to lay out over $750 for insurance. And $250 for that fender job. (shift-response)

JIM: Yeah, it's absurd. (support-response)

BILL: I'm sick of cars. I've been thinking of getting a bicycle and getting around in a healthy way. I saw a great red racer up in that bike shop on Parkhurst Ave.

JIM: I love bikes. But I'm just really feeling a need for a car now. I want to be able to drive up the coast whenever I want. (shift-response)

BILL: Uh huh . . . (support-response)

JIM: I could really get into a convertible.

BILL: Oh, you can go anywhere on a bike. I'm going to borrow John's bike and go way up north next weekend. You know, a couple of weekends ago Sue and I rented bikes and rode down toward the Cape . . . (shift-response)

The narcissistic initiative and the ensuing topic competition is subtle here. From a casual reading of the transcript there appears to be a responsive exchange with no readily discernible egocentricity. But a more careful examination reveals the familiar narcissistic pattern. Bill responds initially to Jim's topic with a support-response that indicates acknowledgment and at least minimal interest. Most of his subsequent responses, however, are shift-responses that change the topic from Jim's desires for a new car to a discussion of his own car and then to his own interest in bicycles. Jim makes several efforts to

steer the conversation back to his original concern, but Bill's attention-getting initiatives are successful. In the end, he launches into a story about his bike trip, which decisively shifts the topic to himself.

This interchange exemplifies the pattern of active conversational narcissism. One conversationalist transforms another's topic into one pertaining to himself through persistent use of the shift-response. The topic-shift is accomplished prematurely, before the first speaker has had the opportunity to complete what he regards as the full development of his subject. Yet it is accomplished without violation of the ritual obligations of responsiveness and occasions no blatant injuries of face.

Passive Practices

Passive practices constitute a more subtle expression of narcissism, characterized not by the grabbing of attention but by miserliness in the responses given to others. Such practices involve under-utilization of the support responses that normally allow others to pursue their topics. The effect is to let the other's topics die through lack of encouragement, thereby opening the floor to the initiation of one's own topics.

To analyze the passive practices which recur most frequently, we must first distinguish between three different kinds of support-responses, which I call: *the background acknowledgment, the supportive assertion,* and *the supportive question. Background acknowledgments* are abbreviated responses such as "uh huh," "yeah," "oh really," and "umm." They are the weakest of the support-responses, but their use is important because they give the appearance that one is listening and wants the speaker to continue. *Supportive assertions* are complete declarative responses to the topic initiatives of others, and include evaluative statements ("I think that's great"), comments ("I never would have thought of him"), and suggestions ("You must see her right away"). A supportive assertion is a stronger response than the background acknowledgment, for it not only confirms that one is listening but indicates active engagement in the topic. *Supportive questions* are queries which draw out a speaker on his topic. They are the most encouraging of all support responses and the most active way of assuring that another's topic will be sustained.[10]

Passive practices involve *minimal use* and *differential use* of these three types of support-responses so that the topics of others are prematurely concluded. Minimal use contributes to the termination of a topic by withholding or delaying support-responses. Differential use means that a weaker support-response is chosen when a stronger one could be used.

Minimal Use. Conversationalists cannot refrain from making any support-responses in the course of a conversation, as this would indicate too blatant an indifference to the other's topic.[11] Minimal use entails, then, a subtle unresponsiveness, where there is compliance with ritual expressions of attentiveness, but nevertheless a relative neglect of support-responses.

The most devastating form is the avoidance of the supportive question. While not all topics depend on such questions for their perpetuation, a high percentage are carried, particularly in the early phases, by others' queries. While a topic can be aborted at any point by lack of interest, a lack of support and interest when it is first initiated most effectively kills it. One can speak of the take-off points or critical thresholds which shape the life-expectancy of the topic. If, in the first several turns of talk, the topic reaches take-off, it is far less vulnerable to derailment by minimal use. Prior to takeoff, topics die if they do not elicit either enthusiastic background acknowledgments or responsive questions which give explicit indication of support and interest. A string of supportive

questions at the opening of a topic will normally guarantee a respectable life-expectancy for the topic, while the absence of any questions at this stage can be an ominous sign which signals premature termination.

Despite their importance, supportive questions are typically discretionary; under most circumstances, conversationalists are free to ask questions but are also at liberty not to. While there are certain initiatives which call for a mandatory response (if someone says, "I'm feeling so terrible," a supportive question like "What's wrong?" would normally be expected in return), most initiatives allow for far greater discretion. If John makes a topical initiative by saying, "I saw my friend Bill today," Jim can show active interest with a supportive question such as "How's he feeling?" or "How did it go?" He commits no offense, however, if he simply offers a background acknowledgment such as "hummm" or volunteers no support-response whatsoever.

Passive conversational narcissism entails neglect of supportive questions at all such discretionary points and extremely sparse use of them throughout conversation. Listening behavior takes place, but is passive. There is little attempt to draw others out or assume other forms of active listening. This creates doubt in the others regarding the interest of their topics or their rights to attention while, however, providing no clear basis for complaint about either inattentiveness or narcissism.

A second very common minimal-use practice involves the underutilization or delay of background acknowledgments. Although weaker than supportive questions, background acknowledgments such as "yeah" or "uh huh" are nonetheless critical cues by which speakers gauge the degree of interest in their topics. A variety of studies suggest that background acknowledgments facilitate the unfolding of topics and that their absence or delay can easily disrupt the development of the speaker's topic.[12]

Ritual restraints preclude withholding all background acknowledgments. Every conversationalist is expected to extend such minimal support even when he has no interest whatsoever in the topic.[13] Speakers can exploit this expectation by interjecting expressions such as "you know," subtle requests for immediate affirmations that indicate the other is paying attention. This is a way that conversationalists insecure about others' attention or interest can actively solicit support.

Despite the ritual constraints, there is sufficient freedom to permit a potent form of minimal response. While this can involve avoiding the background acknowledgment, it most often assumes the form of a delay in its insertion so that the speaker does not receive the immediate reinforcement that permits smooth continuation of his line of thought.[14] Studies have shown that background acknowledgments can be placed with precision timing and are often perfectly inserted during split-second pauses of the other's speech.[15] Conversationalists who delay their responses for up to several seconds after another speaker has paused can throw him off-balance, disrupting his flow of speech and causing him to wonder whether his listeners are genuinely interested. Repetition of the delayed response creates more gaps in the rhythm, slowing the momentum of the conversation further and suggesting the need for a change in topic.[16] Such passive narcissism is rarely a conscious device to gain attention, but is nonetheless a common means by which self-oriented conversationalists "underrespond" to the topics of others and thus open the floor to their own.

Differential Use. Differential use involves the offering of the weakest support-response consistent with the demands of civility.[17] By exercising his discretion to select the least encouraging support-response, the self-oriented conversationalist hastens the termina-

tion of others' topics. This is often accomplished by the use of background acknowledgments where far stronger responses, especially a supportive question, might be more appropriate:

MARY: Oh, I had the most awful headache all day. Tom was awful at work and, uh, just kept bothering me and bothering me. And Louise, too, more of the same. I'm so sick of it.

JOHN: Yeah.

In this instance, Mary has opened with a complaint calling for a stronger, more supportive response than the one offered. Typically, with such openings, a supportive question to draw out the speaker's feelings or experiences sets the stage for fully playing out the topic.[18] By substituting the minimal acknowledgment where a question could have been asked, John discourages Mary's initiative. She has the option to continue, but will find it difficult to do so in the face of repeated discouragement of this form.

Different conversationalists vary in their vulnerability to such discouragement, depending on their assertiveness, security, and other personality factors affecting their need for responsiveness from others. Those most vulnerable are those dependent on the strongest support-responses, on being drawn out through supportive questioning. Differential use will effectively silence these speakers. At the other extreme, the most aggressive conversationalists will pursue their topics even when their initiatives elicit only weak background acknowledgments or none at all. The only effective narcissistic practice with such speakers is an active one, through aggressive use of the shift-response in one's own behalf.

Successfully aborting others' topics does not always insure a turning of conversation to oneself, but, at minimum, prepares the stage for this possibility. At topic termination any speaker may seek to initiate his or her own topic. A second topic competition can then follow which may or may not reproduce the characteristics of the one just completed. In the pure narcissistic pattern, a conversationalist will act to discourage every topic and initiate continuing competition until he or she succeeds in securely establishing his or her own. In practice, few conversationalists remain unresponsive to *all* topics of others, but will exercise selective discretion, reinforcing with support-responses a limited number that are of interest and discouraging the others with minimal and differential use.

NOTES

1. In contrast, an "attention-giving" psychology is based on the tendency for the individual to focus attention on the needs and concerns of others as well as himself in social life. While the attention-getting psychology is more consistent with the individualistic norms of the dominant culture and is more pervasive in the society, the attention-giving psychology is expected of members of subordinate groups, especially women, and tends to characterize their behavior in face-to-face interactions with those more powerful.

While a dominant psychology of attention develops in every culture, there is thus significant variation by sex and social status. I am concerned in this chapter only with the dominant form in American culture.

2. In his classic work, *Escape from Freedom*, Fromm discussed the concept of social character and emphasized the primacy of individualism in shaping character structure in modern capitalist cultures. The theme of egoism has been central in many analyses of the psychology bred by individualism. In his work on suicide, Durkheim treated egoism as a response to the weakening of social bonds and traditional collectivities. The disaffiliated individual is centrally self-oriented as his isolation breeds self-absorption and his individualized social and economic position erodes collective purposes and engenders preoccupation with his own needs.

Several American social theorists have recently pointed to the emergence of self-orientation as a central element in American social character. Philip Reiff has discussed "psychological man"—a character type bred by modern individualism and concerned primarily with his own personal growth and gratification. Richard Sennett has discussed the fall of "public man" and the rise of the more self-oriented and private man of contemporary culture. Christopher Lasch has spoken of the growth of the narcissistic character as a response to the survival pressures of contemporary individualism. The breakdown of family life and other community supports and the burdening of each individual with economic and social responsibilities formerly shared with others necessarily generates a focus on oneself and preoccupation with one's own needs. These themes are elaborated in the last chapter. See Émile Durkheim, *Suicide*, Philip Reiff, *The Triumph of the Therapeutic*, Richard Sennett, *The Fall of Public Man*, Christopher Lasch, *The Culture of Narcissism*.

3. See Emily Post, *Etiquette*, Chapter 1.

4. The ritual order has been richly described by Erving Goffman, "Face-Work," in *Interaction Ritual*.

5. This unawareness may extend to the self-oriented individual himself. Conversational narcissism is typically not conscious behavior but reflects rather a habitual focus on or absorption with oneself that is non-self-consciously expressed in conversational patterns. Use of terminology such as conversational initiatives or strategies should thus not be understood as always referring to willful or manipulative behavior but to unreflective behavior that has the effect of creating shifts in topic and attention.

6. The illustrations of shift-responses here are drawn from the transcriptions of the dinner conversations. The support-responses here are hypothetical, presented in this format to highlight the contrast with shift-responses. Unless otherwise indicated, all examples presented in the text in this chapter are drawn from the transcripts. For purposes of readability, the presentation of the transcripts is nontechnical and does not include special markings denoting pauses or interruptions.

7. Under special circumstances, a support-response can be used as an attention-getting initiative by subtly redirecting the conversation. By asking a certain form of question about the other, for example, the respondent may steer the talk toward new ideas, leading eventually toward a

focus on himself. However, it cannot lead to a shift in the next turn in the conversation, and normally sustains the talk on the other's topic for at least several successive turns.

8. That the shift-response is, in fact, often intended as a sharing-response and not as a vehicle to shift topics renders this more plausible. The distinction between the shift-response as a sharing response and as an attention-getting initiative is considered in the following pages. It can be pointed out here that when used for narcissistic purposes of topical initiative, it has attributes of what Reusch has called a tangential response, a speech act which gives the impression of being responsive but does not actually affirm or validate what the other has just said. See Reusch, "The Tangential Response," in Hoch and Zubin (eds.), *Psychopathology of Communication.*

9. There may be certain topics where it is legitimate to introduce oneself into the conversation immediately (for example, to provide certain necessary information for the further unfolding of the topic). The openness in the unfolding of topics and the looseness in the rules regarding the phase at which it is legitimate to introduce the self as subject in talk about others' topics creates the possibility for the exploitation of the shift-response for narcissistic ends.

10. All support-responses are attention-giving responses which allow another conversationalist to hold the topical focus. I have characterized the "strength" of these responses in terms of how active a form of attention they suggest in the listener and how much support they provide for the other to remain as the focus of attention.

11. The absence of all such support-responses entitles the offended party to either inquire directly as to whether the other is listening or to directly express annoyance at the inattentiveness and to expect an apology.

12. See especially Don H. Zimmerman and Candace West, "Sex-Roles, Interruptions and Silences in Conversation," in Barrie Thorne and Nancy Henley (eds.), *Language and Sex.*

13. This leads to one of the most common deceptive practices in conversation, with the respondents mumbling "yeah" "uh huh" or other affirmations while paying only minimal attention and impatiently waiting to introduce their own concerns into the talk.

14. *Relative* discretion is permitted in frequency of use; conversationalists vary in the frequency with which they make background acknowledgments, both because of differences in personality and interactional style and in their characteristic responsiveness. It is worth noting that certain conversationalists who have strong need for validation may find their topics undermined not only by narcissistic others who extend relatively infrequent acknowledgments, but also others who may be responsive but whose conversational style does not involve frequent responses of this kind. Speakers who differ significantly in their use of background acknowledgments or other support-responses may find it difficult to talk to one another, not understanding the forms of validation which facilitate each other's speech.

15. See Gail Jefferson, "A Case of Precision Timing in Ordinary Conversation: Overlapped Tag-Positioned Address Terms in Closing Sequences," *Semiotica* (1969), pp. 48–96. See also Zimmerman and West, "Sex-Roles."

16. The study by Zimmerman and West, "Sex-Roles," shows a linking of delayed response with premature topic termination and topic change-over, reporting that in at least three of ten transcripts topic closure follows regularly on the heels of a sequence of such repeated delayed responses.

17. Jessie Bernard uses the more general term "minimal response" to refer to what I have called differential use. Her notion of minimal response includes elements of my categories of minimal use as well as differential use. See Bernard, *The Sex Game,* especially Chapter 6.

18. A topic carried by questions is as follows:

> MARY: What a day at school.
> JOHN: What happened?
> MARY: Oh, the kids were just impossible.
> JOHN: Was it Ann and Larry again?
> MARY: Yeah, plus a few others. They were all . . .

Here a comparable topical initiative receives the stronger support-response and is brought to "takeoff" by repetition of supportive questions. The importance of the supportive question in securing the topic of others suggests why narcissistic practice involves a very low reliance on such questions.

REFERENCES

Bernard, Jessie. "Talk, Conversation, Listening, Silence," In *The Sex Game*. New York: Atheneum, 1972, pp. 153–64.

Durkheim, Emile. *Suicide*. New York: The Free Press, 1951.

Fromm, Erich. *Escape from Freedom*. New York: Avon, 1941.

Goffman, Erving. *Interaction Ritual*. New York: Anchor, 1967.

Hoch, G., and R. Zubin (eds.). *Psychopathology of Communication*. New York: Grune and Stratton, 1958.

Lasch, Christopher. *The Culture of Narcissism*. New York: Basic Books, 1978.

Post, Emily. *Etiquette*. New York: Funk and Wagnalls, 1973.

Reiff, Philip. *The Triumph of the Therapeutic*. New York: Harper & Row, 1966.

Sennett, Richard. *The Fall of Public Man*. New York: Knopf, 1977.

Thorne, Barrie, and Nancy Henley (eds.). *Language and Sex*. Rowley, Mass.: Newbury House Publishers, 1975.

Wilde, Oscar. *The Fairy Tales of Oscar Wilde*. New York: Hart, 1975.

Zimmerman, Don H., and Candace West. "Sex Roles, Interruptions and Silences in Conversation." In Barrie Thorne and Nancy Henley (eds.), *Language and Sex*. Rowley, Mass.: Newbury House Publishers, 1975, pp. 105–129.

16

Managing Feeling

ARLIE RUSSELL HOCHSCHILD

He who always wears the mask of a friendly man must at last gain a power over friendliness of disposition, without which the expression itself of friendliness is not to be gained—and finally friendliness of disposition gains the ascendancy over him—he is benevolent.
—Nietzsche

"Sincerity" is detrimental to one's job, until the rules of salesmanship and business become a "genuine" aspect of oneself.
—C. Wright Mills

We all do a certain amount of acting. But we may act in two ways. In the first way, we try to change how we outwardly appear. As it is for the people observed by Erving Goffman, the action is in the body language, the put-on sneer, the posed shrug, the controlled sigh. This is surface acting.[1] The other way is deep acting. Here, display is a natural result of working on feeling; the actor does not try to *seem* happy or sad but rather expresses spontaneously, as the Russian director Constantin Stanislavski urged, a real feeling that has been self-induced. Stanislavski offers this illustration from his own experience:

At a party one evening, in the house of friends, we were doing various stunts and they decided, for a joke, to operate on me. Tables were carried in, one for operating, the other supposedly containing surgical instruments. Sheets were draped around; bandages, basins, various vessels were brought. The "surgeons" put on white coats and I was dressed in a hospital gown. They laid me on the operating table and bandaged my eyes. What disturbed me was the extremely solicitous manner of the doctors. They treated me as if I were in a desperate condition and did everything with utmost seriousness. Suddenly the thought flashed through my mind, "What if they really should cut me open?!"

Now and then a large basin made a booming noise like the toll of a funeral bell.

"Let us begin!" someone whispered.

Someone took a firm hold on my right wrist. I felt a dull pain and then three sharp stabs. I couldn't help trembling. Something that was harsh and smarted was rubbed on my wrist. Then it was bandaged, people rustled around handing things to the surgeon.

Finally, after a long pause, they began to speak out loud, they laughed, congratulated me. My eyes were unbandaged and on my left arm lay a new-born baby made out of my right hand, all swaddled in gauze. On the back of my hand they had painted a silly, infantile face.[2]

The "patient" above is not pretending to be frightened at his "operation." He is not trying to fool others. He is really scared. Through deep acting he has managed to scare himself. Feelings do not erupt spontaneously or automatically in either deep acting or surface acting. In both cases the actor has learned to intervene—either in creating the inner shape of a feeling or in shaping the outward appearance of one.

In surface acting, the expression on my face or the posture of my body feels "put on." It is not "part of me." In deep acting, my conscious mental work—the effort to imagine a tall surgeon looming over me, for example—keeps the feeling that I conjure up from being part of "myself." Thus in either method, an actor may separate what it takes to act from the idea of a central self.

But whether the separation between "me" and my face or between "me" and my feeling counts as estrangement depends on something else—the outer context. In the world of the theater, it is an honorable art to make maximum use of the resources of memory and feeling in stage performance. In private life, the same resources can be used to advantage, though to a lesser extent. But when we enter the world of profit-and-loss statements, when the psychological costs of emotional labor are not acknowledged by the company, it is then that we look at these otherwise helpful separations of "me" from my face and my feeling as potentially estranging.

SURFACE ACTING

To show through surface acting the feelings of a Hamlet or an Ophelia, the actor operates countless muscles that make up an outward gesture. The body, not the soul, is the main tool of the trade. The actor's body evokes passion in the *audience's* soul, but the actor is only *acting* as if he had feeling. Stanislavski, the originator of a different type of acting—called Method acting—illustrates surface acting in the course of disparaging it:

[The actor portrayed] an important general [who] accidentally found himself alone at home with nothing to do. Out of boredom he lined up all the chairs in the place so that they looked like soldiers on parade. Then he made neat piles of everything on all the tables. Next he thought of something rather spicy; after that he looked aghast over a pile of business correspondence. He signed several letters without reading them, yawned, stretched himself, and then began his silly activities all over again.

All the while [the actor] was giving the text of the soliloquy with extraordinary clarity; about the nobility of highly placed persons and the dense ignorance of everyone else. He did it in a cold, impersonal way, indicating the outer form of the scene without any attempt to put life or depth into it. In some places he rendered the text with technical crispness, in others he underscored his pose, gesture, play, or emphasized some special detail of his characterization. Meantime he was watching his public out of the corner of his eye to see whether what he was doing carried across.[3]

This is surface acting—the art of an eyebrow raised here, an upper lip tightened there. The actor does not really experience the world from an imperial viewpoint, but he works at seeming to. What is on the actor's mind? Not the chairs that he has commanded to line up at attention, but the audience, which is the nearest mirror to his own surface.

Stanislavski described the limitations of surface acting as follows:

This type of art (of the Coquelin school) is less profound than beautiful. It is more immediately effective than truly powerful; [its] form is more interesting than its content. It acts more on your sense of sound and sight than on your soul. Consequently it is more likely to delight than to move you. You can receive great impressions through this art. But they will neither warm your soul nor penetrate deeply into it. Their effect is sharp but not lasting. Your astonishment rather than your faith is aroused. Only what can be accomplished through surprising theatrical beauty or picturesque pathos lies within the bounds of this art. But delicate and deep human feelings are not subject to such technique. They call for natural emotions at the very moment in which they appear before you in the flesh. They call for the direct cooperation of nature itself.[4]

DEEP ACTING

There are two ways of doing deep acting. One is by directly exhorting feeling, the other by making indirect use of a trained imagination.[5] Only the second is true Method acting. But in either case, Stanislavski argued, the acting of passions grows out of living in them.

People sometimes talk as much about their *efforts* to feel (even if these efforts fail) as they do about having feelings.[6] When I asked students simply to describe an event in which they experienced a deep emotion, the responses were sprinkled with such phrases as "I psyched myself up, I squashed my anger down, I tried hard not to feel disappointed, I forced myself to have a good time, I mustered up some gratitude, I put a damper on my love for her, I snapped myself out of the depression."[7] In the flow of experience, there were occasional common but curious shades of will—will to evoke, will to suppress, and will to somehow allow a feeling, as in "I finally let myself feel sad about it."[8]

Sometimes there was only a social custom in mind—as when a person wished to feel sad at a funeral. But other times there was a desperate inner desire to avoid pain. Herbert Gold describes a man's effort to prevent himself from feeling love for a wife he no longer has:

He fought against love, he fought against grief, he fought against anger. They were all linked. He reminded himself when touched, moved, overwhelmed by the sights and smell of her, or a sight and smell which recalled her, or passing their old house or eating their foods, or walking on their streets; don't do this, don't feel. First he succeeded in removing her from the struggle. . . . He lost his love. He lost his anger. She became a limited

idea, like a newspaper death notice. He did not lose her entirely, but chipped away at it: don't, don't, don't, he would remind himself in the middle of the night; don't feel; and then dream what he could.[9]

These are almost like orders to a contrary horse (whoa, giddyup, steady now), attempts to exhort feeling as if feeling can listen when it is talked to.[10] And sometimes it does. But such coaching only addresses the capacity to duck a signal, to turn away from what evokes feeling.[11] It does not move to the home of the imagery, to that which gives power to a sight, a sound, or a smell. It does not involve the deeper work of retraining the imagination.

Ultimately, direct prods to feeling are not based on a deep look into how feeling works, and for this reason Stanislavski advised his actors against them: "On the stage there cannot be, under any circumstances, action which is directed immediately at the arousing of a feeling for its own sake. . . . Never seek to be jealous, or to make love, or to suffer for its own sake. All such feelings are the result of something that has gone before. Of the thing that goes before you should think as you can. As for the result, it will produce itself."[12]

Stanislavski's alternative to the direct prodding of feeling is Method acting. Not simply the body, or immediately accessible feeling, but the entire world of fantasy, of subconscious and semiconscious memory, is conceived as a precious resource.[13]

If he were in the hands of Stanislavski, the man who wanted to fight off love for his former wife would approach his task differently. First, he would use "emotion memory": he would remember all the times he had felt furious at his wife's thoughtlessness or cruelty. He would focus on one most exasperating instance of this, reevoking all the circumstances. Perhaps she had forgotten his birthday, had made no effort to remember, and failed to feel badly about it afterwards. Then he would use the "if" supposition and say to himself: "How would I feel about her if this is what she really was like?" He would not prompt himself not to feel love; rather he would keep alive the cruel episode of the forgotten birthday and sustain the "if." He would not, then, fall naturally out of love. He would actively conduct himself out of love through deep acting.

The professional actor simply carries this process further for an artistic purpose. His goal should be to accumulate a rich deposit of "emotion memories"—memories that recall feelings. Thus, Stanislavski explains, the actor must relearn how to remember:

> Two travelers were marooned on some rocks by high tide. After their rescue they narrated their impressions. One remembered every little thing he did; how, why, and where he went, where he climbed up and where he climbed down; where he jumped up or jumped down. The other man had no recollection of the place at all. He remembered only the emotions he felt. In succession came delight, apprehension, fear, hope, doubt, and finally panic.[14]

To store a wealth of emotion memories, the actor must remember experiences emotively. But to remember experiences emotively, he or she must first experience them in that way too, perhaps with an eye to using the feelings later.[15] So the conceiving of emotion memory as a noun, as something one *has*, brings with it a conceiving of memory and of spontaneous experience itself as also having the qualities of a usable, nounlike thing. Feeling—whether at the time, or as it is recalled, or as it is later evoked in acting—is an object. It may be a valuable object in a worthy pursuit, but it is an object nonetheless.

Some feelings are more valuable objects than others, for they are more richly associated with other memorable events; a terrifying train ride may recall a childhood fall or a nightmare. Stanislavski recalled, for example, seeing an old beggar killed by a trolley car but said that the memory of this event was less valuable to him as an actor than another one:

> It was long ago—I came upon an Italian, leaning over a dead monkey on the sidewalk. He was weeping and trying to push a bit of orange rind into the animal's mouth. It would seem that this scene had affected my feelings more than the death of the beggar. It was buried more deeply into my memory. I think that if I had to stage the street accident I would search for emotional material for my part in my memory of the scene of the Italian with the dead monkey rather than in the tragedy itself.[16]

But emotion memory is not enough. The memory, like any image drawn to mind, must *seem real now*. The actor must *believe* that an imagined happening *really is happening now*. To do this, the actor makes up an "as if," a supposition. He actively suspends the usual reality testing, as a child does at play, and allows a make-believe situation to seem real. Often the actor can manage only a precarious belief in *all* of an illusion, and so he breaks it up into sturdier small details, which taken one by one are easier to believe: "*if* I were in a terrible storm" is chopped up into "*if* my eyebrows were wet and *if* my shoes were soaked." The big *if* is broken into many little ones.[17]

The furnishings of the physical stage—a straight horse-hair chair, a pointer leaning against the wall—are used to support the actor's *if*. Their purpose is not to influence the audience, as in surface acting, but to help convince the person doing deep acting that the *if* events are really happening.

EVERYDAY DEEP ACTING

In our daily lives, offstage as it were, we also develop feeling for the parts we play; and along with the workday props of the kitchen table or office restroom mirror we also use deep acting, emotion memory, and the sense of "as if this were true" in the course of trying to feel what we sense we ought to feel or want to feel. Usually we give this little thought, and we don't name the momentary acts involved. Only when our feeling does not fit the situation, and when we sense this as a problem, do we turn our attention to the inward, imagined mirror, and ask whether we are or should be acting.

Consider, for example, the reaction of this young man to the unexpected news that a close friend had suffered a mental breakdown:

> I was shocked, yet for some reason I didn't think my emotions accurately reflected the bad news. My roommate appeared much more shaken than I did. *I thought that I should be more upset by the news than I was.* Thinking about this conflict I realized that one reason for my emotional state might have been the spatial distance separating me from my friend, who was in the hospital hundreds of miles away. I then tried to focus on his state . . . and began to picture my friend as I thought he then existed.

Sensing himself to be less affected than he should be, he tried to visualize his friend—perhaps in gray pajamas, being led by impassive attendants to the electric-shock room. After bringing such a vivid picture to mind, he might have gone on to recall smaller private breakdowns in his own life and thereby evoked feelings of sorrow and empathy. Without at all thinking of this as acting, in complete privacy, without audience or stage, the young man can pay, in the currency of deep acting, his emotional respects to a friend.

Sometimes we try to stir up a feeling we wish we had, and at other times we try to block or weaken a feeling we wish we did not have. Consider this young woman's report of her attempt to keep feelings of love in check.

> Last summer I was going with a guy often, and I began to feel very strongly about him. I knew, though, that he had broken up with a girl a year ago because she had gotten too

serious about him, so I was afraid to show any emotion. I also was afraid of being hurt, so I attempted to change my feelings. *I talked myself into not caring about him* . . . but I must admit it didn't work for long. To sustain this feeling I had to *invent bad things about him and concentrate on them* or continue to tell myself he didn't care. It was a hardening of emotions, I'd say. It took a lot of work and was unpleasant because I had to concentrate on anything I could find that was irritating about him.

In this struggle she hit upon some techniques of deep acting. "To invent bad things about him and concentrate on them" is to make up a world she could honestly respond to. She could tell herself, "If he is self-absorbed, then he is unlovable, and *if* he is unlovable, which at the moment I believe, then I don't love him." Like Stanislavski during his make-believe "operation," she wavers between belief and doubt, but she nevertheless reaches for the inner token of feeling that it is her part to offer. She wavers between belief and doubt in her beloved's "flaws." But her temporary effort to prevent herself from falling in love may serve the grander purpose of waiting for him to reciprocate. So in a way, her act of momentary restraint, as she might see it, was an offering to the future of their love.

We also set a personal stage with personal props, not so much for its effect on our audience as for the help it gives us in believing in what we imagine. Serving almost as stage props, often, are fellow members of the cast—friends or acquaintances who prod our feelings in a desired direction. Thus, a young woman who was trying not to love a man used her supporting cast of friends like a Greek chorus: "I could only say horrible things about him. My friends thought he was horrible because of this and reinforced my feelings of dislike for him."

Sometimes the stage setting can be a dismayingly powerful determinant of feeling. Consider this young woman's description of her ambivalent feelings about a priest forty years her senior: "I started trying to make myself like him and fit the whole situation. When I was with him I did like him, but then I'd go home and write in my journal how much I couldn't stand him. I kept changing my feelings." What she felt while facing the priest amid the props of a living room and two cups of afternoon tea collapsed when she left that setting. At home with her diary, she felt free of her obligation to please her suitor by trying to like him. There, she felt another obligation—to be honest to her diary. What changed between the tea party and the diary session was her sense of which feeling was real. Her sense of realness seemed to shift disconcertingly with the stage setting, as if her feeling of liking the priest gained or lost its status as "real" depending on its context.

Sometimes the realness of a feeling wavers more through time. Once a love story is subject to doubt, the story is rewritten; falling in love comes to seem like the work of convincing each other that this had been true love. A nineteen-year-old Catholic college student recalled:

> Since we both were somewhat in need of a close man-woman relationship and since we were thrown together so often (we lived next door to each other and it was summertime), I think that we convinced ourselves that we loved each other. I had to try to convince myself that I loved him in order to justify or somehow make "right" sleeping with him, which I never really wanted to do. We ended up living together supposedly because we "loved" each other. But I would say instead that we did it for other reasons which neither of us wanted to admit. What pretending that I loved him meant to me was having a secret nervous breakdown.

This double pretending—pretending to him and pretending to herself that she loved him—created two barriers to reflection and spontaneous feeling. First, she tried to feel herself in love—intimate, deeply enhanced, and exquisitely vulnerable—in the face of

contrary evidence. Second, she tried not to feel irritation, boredom, and a desire to leave. By this effort to orchestrate feeling—to keep some feelings above consciousness and some below, and to counter inner resistances on a daily basis—she tried to suppress reality testing. She both nurtured an illusion about her lover and doubted the truth of it. It was the strain of this effort that led to her "secret nervous breakdown."

In the theater, the illusion that the actor creates is recognized beforehand as an illusion by actor and audience alike. But in real life we more often participate in the illusion. We take it into ourselves, where it struggles against the sense we ordinarily make of things. In life, illusions are subtle, changeable, and hard to define with certainty, and they matter far more to our sanity.

The other side of the matter is to live with a dropped illusion and yet want to sustain it. Once an illusion is clearly defined as an illusion, it becomes a lie. The work of sustaining it then becomes redefined as lying to oneself so that one becomes self-stigmatized as a liar. This dilemma was described by a desperate wife and mother of two:

> I am desperately trying to change my feelings of being trapped [in marriage] into feelings of wanting to remain with my husband voluntarily. Sometimes I think I'm succeeding—sometimes I know I haven't. *It means I have to lie to myself and know I am lying.* It means I don't like myself very much. It also makes me wonder whether or not I'm a bit of a masochist. I feel responsible for the children's future and for my husband's, and there's the old self-sacrificer syndrome. I know what I'm doing. I just don't know how long I can hold out.

On stage, the actress doing Method acting tries to delude herself; the more voluntary, the more richly detailed the lie, the better. No one thinks she actually *is* Ophelia or even pretending to be. She is borrowing Ophelia's reality or something from her own personal life that resembles it. She is trying to delude herself and create an illusion for the audience, who accept it as a gift. In everyday life there is also illusion, but how to define it is chronically unclear; the matter needs constant attention, continual questioning and testing. In acting, the illusion starts out as an illusion. In everyday life, that definition is always a possibility and never quite a certainty. On stage, the illusion leaves as it came, with the curtain. Off stage, the curtains close, too, but not at our bidding, not when we expect, and often to our dismay. On stage, illusion is a virtue. But in real life, the lie to oneself is a sign of human weakness, of bad faith. It is far more unsettling to discover that we have fooled ourselves than to discover that we have been fooling others.

This is because for the professional actor the illusion takes on meaning only in relation to a professional role whereas in real life the illusion takes on meaning with reference to living persons. When in private life we recognize an illusion we have held, we form a different relation to what we have thought of as ourself. We come to distrust our sense of what is true, as we know it through feeling. And if our feelings have lied to us, they cannot be part of our good, trustworthy, "true" self. To put it another way, we may recognize that we distort reality, that we deny or suppress truths, but we rely on an observing ego to comment on these unconscious processes in us and to try to find out what is going on despite them.

At the same time, everyday life clearly requires us to do deep acting. We must dwell on what it is that we want to feel and on what we must do to induce the feeling. Consider, for example, this young man's efforts to counter an apathy he dreaded:

> I was a star halfback in high school. [But in my senior year] before games I didn't feel the surge of adrenalin—in a word, I wasn't "psyched-up." This was due to emotional difficulties I was experiencing at the time, and still experience. Also, I had been an A student but my grades were dropping. Be-

cause in the past I had been a fanatical, emotional, intense player—a "hitter," recognized by coaches as a hard worker and a player with "desire"—this was very upsetting. I did everything I could to get myself "up." I tried to be outwardly rah-rah, I tried to get myself scared of my opponents—anything to get the adrenalin flowing. I tried to look nervous and intense before games, so at least the coaches wouldn't catch on . . . when actually I was mostly bored, or in any event, not "up." Before one game I remember wishing I was in the stands watching my cousin play for his school.

This young man felt a slipping sense of realness; he was clear that he felt "basically" bored, not "really" up. What also seemed real to him was the sense that he should feel driven to win and that he wanted to feel that way. What also felt real to him in hindsight was his effort to seem to the coaches like a "hitter" (surface acting) and his effort to make himself fearful of his opponents (deep acting).

As we look back at the past, we may alternate between two understandings of "what really happened." According to one, our feeling was genuine and spontaneous. According to the other, it seemed genuine and spontaneous, but in fact it was covertly managed. In doubt about which understanding will ultimately make sense, we are led to ask about our present feelings: "Am I acting now? How do I know?" One basic appeal of the theater is that the stage decides that question for us: we know for sure who is acting.

In sum, what distinguishes theater from life is not illusion, which both have, need, and use. What distinguishes them is the honor accorded to illusion, the ease in knowing when an illusion *is* an illusion, and the consequences of its use in making feeling. In the theater, the illusion dies when the curtain falls, as the audience knew it would. In private life, its consequences are unpredictable and possibly fateful: a love is killed, a suitor rejected, another hospital bed filled.

INSTITUTIONAL EMOTION MANAGEMENT

The professional actress has a modest say over how the stage is assembled, the props selected, and the other characters positioned, as well as a say over her own presence in the play. This is also true in private life. In both cases the person is the *locus* of the acting process.

But something more operates when institutions are involved, for within institutions various elements of acting are taken away from the individual and replaced by institutional mechanisms. The locus of acting, of emotion management, moves up to the level of the institution. Many people and objects, arranged according to institutional rule and custom, together accomplish the act. Companies, prisons, schools, churches—institutions of virtually any sort—assume some of the functions of a director and alter the relation of actor to director. Officials in institutions believe they have done things right when they have established illusions that foster the desired feelings in workers, when they have placed parameters around a worker's emotion memories, a worker's use of the *as if*. It is not that workers are allowed to see and think as they like and required only to show feeling (surface acting) in institutionally approved ways. The matter would be simpler and less alarming if it stopped there. But it doesn't. Some institutions have become very sophisticated in the techniques of deep acting; they suggest how to imagine and thus how to feel.

As a farmer puts blinders on his workhorse to guide its vision forward, institutions manage how we feel.[18] One of the ways in which they do this is to prearrange what is available to the worker's view. A teaching hospital, for example, designs the stage for medical students facing their first autopsy. Seeing the eye of a dead person might call to mind a loved one or oneself; to see this organ coldly violated by a knife might lead a student to faint, or flee in horror, or quit medicine then and there. But this seldom happens. In their study of medical training, Lief and Fox report:

> The immaculate, brightly lit appearance of the operating room, and the serious professional behavior required, justify and facilitate a clinical and impersonal attitude toward death. Certain parts of the body are kept covered, particularly the face and genitalia, and the hands, which are so strongly connected with human, personal qualities, are never dissected. Once the vital organs have been taken out, the body is removed from the room, bringing the autopsy down to tissues, which are more easily depersonalized. The deft touch, skill, and professional attitude of the prosector makes the procedure neater and more bloodless than might otherwise be the case, and this increases intellectual interest and makes it possible to approach the whole thing scientifically rather than emotionally. Students appear to avoid talking about the autopsy, and when they do talk about it, the discussion is impersonal and stylized. Finally, whereas in laboratory dissection humor appears to be a wide-spread and effective emotional control device, it is absent in the autopsy room, perhaps because the death has been too recent and [humor] would appear too insensitive.[19]

Covering the corpse's face and genitalia, avoiding the hands, later removing the body, moving fast, using white uniforms, and talking in uniformed talk—these are customs designed to manage the human feeling that threatens order.[20]

Institutions arrange their front stages. They guide the way we see and what we are likely to feel spontaneously. Consider the inevitable institutional halls, especially those near the areas where people wait. Often in medical, academic, and corporate settings we find on the walls a row of photographs or oil paintings of persons in whom we should have full confidence. Consider Allen Wheelis's description of a waiting-room picture of a psychiatrist:

With the crossed legs you claim repose, tranquility. . . . Everything is under control. With the straight shoulders you say dignity, *status*. No matter what comes up, this guy has nothing to fear, is calmly certain of his worth and of his ability. With the head turned sharply to the left you indicate that someone is claiming his attention. No doubt hundreds of people would like this guy's attention. He was engrossed in his book, but now he's being interrupted. And what was he reading? *Playboy? Penthouse?* The funny papers? Oh, no; he's into something heavy. We can't see the title, but we know it's plenty important. . . . Usually it's Osler's *Principles and Practice of Medicine.* And the finger marking his place? Why, he's been at it so intently, so diligently, he's already halfway through. And the other hand, lying so lightly, so gracefully, on the book. That shows intelligence, experience, mastery. He's not scratching his head trying to figure out what the hell the author is getting at. . . . Anytime you knock on this guy's door, you'll find him just like that, dressed to the nines, tie up tight in his buttoned-down collar, freshly pressed jacket, deeply immersed in one of these heavy tomes.[21]

The professional's own office, of course, should be done up in a pleasant but impersonal decor, not too messy and colorful but not too cold and bare; it should reflect just the amount of professional warmth the doctor or lawyer or banker himself ought to show. Home is carefully distinguished from office, personal flair from professional expertise. This stage setting is intended to inspire our confidence that the service is, after all, worth paying a lot for.

Airlines seem to model "stage sets" on the living rooms seen on daytime television serials; the Muzak tunes, the TV and movie screens, and the smiling flight attendants serving drinks are all calculated to "make you feel at home." Even fellow passengers are considered part of the stage. At Delta Airlines, for example, flight attendants in training are advised that they can prevent the boarding of certain types of passengers—

a passenger with "severe facial scars," for example. The instructor elaborated: "You know, the other passengers might be reminded of an airplane crash they had read about." The bearer of a "severe facial scar," then, is not deemed a good prop. His or her effect on the emotion memory of other money-paying passengers might be all wrong.[22]

Sometimes props are less important than influential directors. Institutions authorize stage directors to coach the hired cast in deep acting. Buttressed with the authority of a high office or a specialized degree, the director may make suggestions that are often interpreted at lower levels as orders.

The director's role may be simple and direct, as in the case of a group of college students training to be clinicians in a camp for emotionally disturbed children, studied by Albert Cohen. These students, who composed the junior staff, did not know at first how they were supposed to feel or think about the wild behavior of the disturbed children. But in the director's chair sat the senior counselors, advising them on how to see the children: "They were expected to see the children as victims of uncontrollable impulses somehow related to their harsh and depriving backgrounds, and in need of enormous doses of kindliness and indulgence in order to break down their images of the adult world as hateful and hostile."[23]

They were also taught how to *feel* properly toward them: "The clinician must never respond in anger or with intent to punish, although he might sometimes have to restrain or even isolate children in order to prevent them from hurting themselves or one another. Above all, the staff were expected to be warm and loving and always to be governed by a 'clinical attitude.'"[24] To be warm and loving toward a child who kicks, screams, and insults you—a child whose problem is unlovability—requires emotion work. The art of it is passed down from senior to junior counselor, as in other settings it passes from judge to law clerk, professor to graduate student, boss to rising subordinate.

The professional worker will implicitly frown on certain uses of emotion memory. The senior counselor of disturbed children will not allow herself to think, "Tommy reminds me of the terrible brat I had to babysit when I was thirteen, and if he's like that I'll end up hating him." Instead, she will reconceive Tommy in another way: "Tommy is really like the other kid I used to babysit when I was fourteen. He was difficult but I got to like him, so I expect I'll get to like Tommy despite the way he pushes me away suspiciously."

A proper way to *experience* the child, not simply a proper way to seem to feel, was understood by everyone as part of the job. And Cohen reports that the young caretakers did admirably: "To an extraordinary degree they fulfilled these expectations, including, I am convinced, the expectation that they *feel* sympathy and tenderness and love toward their charges, despite their animal-like behavior. The speed with which these college students learned to behave in this way cannot be easily explained in terms of gradual learning through a slow process of 'internalization.'"[25]

In more circuitous ways, too, the formal rules that prop up an institution set limits to the emotional possibilities of all concerned. Consider, for example, the rules that guard access to information. Any institution with a bit of hierarchy in it must suppress democracy to some extent and thus must find ways to suppress envy and resentment at the bottom. Often this is done by enforcing a hierarchy of secrets. The customary rule of secrecy about pay is a case in point: those at the bottom are almost never allowed to know how much money those at the top get each month, nor, to the fullest extent, what privileges they enjoy. Also kept secret are deliberations that determine when and to what level an individual is likely to rise or fall within the organization. As one University

of California administrative memorandum explained: "Letters concerning the disposition of tenure review cases will be kept confidential, in order that those involved not hold grudges or otherwise harbor resentment toward those unfavorably disposed in their case." In this situation, where the top depends upon being protected from the middle and the bottom—from "those involved" as the memo put it—leaks can cause panic.[26]

Finally, drugs of various sorts can be used to stimulate or depress mood, and companies are not above engineering their use. Just as the plow displaced manual labor, in some reported instances drug use seems to be displacing emotional labor. The labor that it takes to withstand stress and boredom on the job can be performed, some workers have found, by Darvon and Valium. Workers at the American Telephone and Telegraph Company, for example, found that nurses in its medical department gave out Valium, Darvon, codeine, and other drugs free and without prescription. There are a number of ways, some of them company-sponsored, to "have a nice day" on the job, as part of the job.[27]

AN INSTRUMENTAL STANCE TOWARD FEELING

The stage actor makes the finding and expressing of feeling his main professional task. In Stanislavski's analogy, he seeks it with the dedication of a prospector for precious metal. He comes to see feeling as the object of painstaking internal mining, and when he finds it, he processes it like gold. In the context of the theater, this use of feeling is considered exciting and honorable. But what happens when deep and surface acting become part of a day's work, part of what we sell to an employer in return for a day's wage? What happens when our feelings are processed like raw ore?

In the Recurrent Training class for experienced flight attendants at Delta Airlines, I observed borrowings from all types of acting. These can be seen in the ways students answered when the instructor asked how they tried to stop feeling angry and resentful at passengers:

> If I pretend I'm feeling really up, sometimes I actually get into it. The passenger responds to me as though I were friendly, and then more of me responds back [surface acting].
>
> Sometimes I purposely take some deep breaths. I try to relax my neck muscles [deep acting with the body].
>
> I may just talk to myself: "Watch it. Don't let him get to you. Don't let him get to you. Don't let him get to you." And I'll talk to my partner and she'll say the same thing to me. After a while, the anger goes away [deep acting, self-prompting].
>
> I try to remember that if he's drinking too much, he's probably scared of flying. I think to myself, "he's like a little child." Really, that's what he is. And when I see him that way, I don't get mad that he's yelling at me. He's like a child yelling at me then. [deep acting, Method acting].

Surface and deep acting in a commercial setting, unlike acting in a dramatic, private, or therapeutic context, make one's face and one's feelings take on the properties of a resource. But it is not a resource to be used for the purposes of art, as in drama, or for the purposes of self-discovery, as in therapy, or for the pursuit of fulfillment, as in everyday life. It is a resource to be used to make money. Outside of Stanislavski's parlor, out there in the American marketplace, the actor may wake up to find himself actually operated upon.

NOTES

Epigraphs: F. W. Nietzsche (1874), cited in Gellhorn (1964): C. Wright Mills, *White Collar*, p. 183.
1. As suggested by Goffman's description of "Preedy" on the beach, in *The Presentation of Self in Everyday Life* (1959), surface acting is alive and well in Goffman's work. But the second method of acting, deep acting, is less apparent in his illustrations, and the theoretical statement about it is correspondingly weak. Goffman posits a self capable of surface acting, but not one capable of deep acting.
2. Stanislavski (1965), p. 268.
3. Ibid., p. 196.
4. Ibid., p.22.
5. There is actually another distinguishable way of doing deep acting—by actively altering the body so as to change conscious feeling. This surface-to-center approach differs from surface acting. Surface acting uses the body to *show* feeling. This type of deep acting uses the body to *inspire* feeling. In relaxing a grimace or unclenching a fist, we may actually make ourselves feel less angry (ibid., p. 93). This insight is sometimes used in bio-feedback therapy (see Brown 1974, p. 50).
6. The direct method of cognitive emotion work is known not by the result (see Peto 1968) but by the effort made to achieve the result. The result of any given act is hard enough to discern. But if we were to identify emotion work by its results, we would be in a peculiar bind. We might say that a "cooled-down anger" is the result of an effort to reduce anger. But then we would have to assume that we have some basis for knowing what the anger "would have been like" had the individual not been managing his anger. We are on theoretically safer ground if we define emotion management as a set of acts *addressed* to feeling. (On the nature of an act of will, as separate from its effect, see Jean Piaget in Campbell 1976, p. 87).
7. In each instance the individual indicates awareness of acting on a feeling. A passive stance toward feeling was reflected in other examples: "I found myself filled with pride," "My stomach did a trapeze act all by itself."
8. By definition, each method of emotion work is active, but just how active, varies. At the active end of the continuum we contort reality and grip our bodily processes as though gripping the steering wheel of a car. At the passive extreme we may simply perform an act upon an act—as in deliberately relaxing already existing controls or issuing permission to "let" ourselves feel sad. (For a discussion of active versus passive concentration in autogenic training, see Wolfgang Luthe, quoted in Pelletier 1977, p. 237). In addition we may "ride over" a feeling (such as a nagging sense of depression) in the attempt to feel cheerful. When we

meet an inward resistance, we "put on" the cheer. When we meet no inward resistance, we amplify a feeling: we "put it out."

9. Gold (1979), p. 129.

10. It also presupposes an *aspiration* to feel. The man who fought against love wanted to feel the same about his former wife as he thought she felt about him; if he was a limited idea to her, he wanted her to be that for him. A courtly lover in twelfth-century France or a fourteen-year-old American female rock fan might have been more disposed to aspire to one-sided love, to want it that way. Deep acting comes with its social stories about what we aspire to feel.

11. Stanislavski (1965), p. 38. Indeed, an extra effort is required *not to focus* on the intent, the effort of trying to feel. The point, rather, is to focus on seeing the situation. Koriat et al. (1972) illustrated this second approach in a laboratory experiment in which university students were shown films of simulated wood-chopping accidents. In one film a man lacerates the tips of his fingers; in another a woodworker cuts off his middle finger; in a third, a worker dies after a plank of wood is thrust through his midsection by a circular saw. Subjects were instructed to detach themselves when first viewing the films and then, on another viewing, to involve themselves. To deintensify the effect of the films, the viewers tried to remind themselves that they were just films and often focused on technical aspects of production to reinforce this sense of unreality. Others tried to think of the workers in the films as being responsible for their own injuries through negligence. Such detachment techniques may be common in cases when people victimize others (see Latane and Darley 1970). To intensify the films' effect, the viewers reported trying to imagine that the accidents were happening to them, or to someone they knew, or were similar to experiences they had had or had witnessed; some tried to think about and exaggerate the consequences of accidents. Koriat et al. conceive of these deintensifying or intensifying devices as aspects of appraisal that precede a "coping response." Such devices may also be seen as mental acts that adjust the "if supposition" and draw on the "emotional memory" described in Stanislavski (1965).

12. Stanislavski (1965), p. 57.

13. In *An Actor Prepares*, Stanislavski points out an apparent contradiction: "We are supposed to create under inspiration; only our subconscious gives us inspiration; yet we apparently can use this subconscious only through our consciousness, which kills it" (1965, p. 13). The solution to this problem is the indirect method. The subconscious is induced. As Stanislavski notes: "The aim of the actor's preparation is to cross the threshold of the subconscious. . . . Beforehand we have 'true-seeming feeling,' afterwards 'sincerity of emotion.' On this side of it, we have the simplicity of a limited fantasy; beyond, the simplicity of the larger imagination, [where] the creative process differs each time it is repeated" (p. 267).

14. Ibid., p. 163.

15. The mind acts as a magnet to reusable feeling. Stanislavski advises actors: "Imagine that you have received some insult in public, perhaps a slap in the face, that makes your cheek burn whenever you think of it. The inner shock was so great that it blotted out all the details of this harsh incident. But some insignificant thing will instantly revive the memory of the insult, and the emotion will recur with redoubled violence. Your cheek will grow red or you will turn pale and your heart will pound. If you possess such sharp and easily aroused emotional material, you will find it easy to transfer it to the stage and play a scene analogous to the experience you had in real life which left such a shocking impression on you. To do this you will not need any technique. It will play itself because nature will help you" (1965, p. 176).

16. Ibid., p. 127.

17. Stanislavski once admonished his actors: "You do not get hold of this exercise because . . . you are anxious to believe all of the terrible things I put into the plot. But do not try to do it all at once; proceed bit by bit, helping yourselves along by small truths. If every little auxiliary act is executed truthfully, then the whole action will unfold rightly" (Ibid., p. 126).

18. We commonly assume that institutions are called in when individual controls fail: those who cannot control their emotions are sent to mental hospitals, homes for disturbed children, or prisons. But in looking at the matter this way, we may ignore the fact that individual failures of control often signal a prior institutional failure to shape feeling. We might ask instead what sort of church, school, or family influence was unavailable to the parents of institutionalized patients, who pre-

sumably tried to make their children into adequate emotion managers.

19. Lief and Fox (1963) quoted in Lazarus (1975), p. 55.

20. Scientific writing, like scientific talk, has a function similar to that of covering the face and genitalia. It is an extension of institutional control over feeling. The overuse of passive verb forms, the avoidance of "I," the preference for Latinate nouns, and for the abstract over the concrete, are customs that distance the reader from the topic and limit emotionality. In order to seem scientific, writers obey conventions that inhibit emotional involvement. There is a purpose in such "poor" writing.

21. Wheelis (1980), p. 7.

22. I heard the rationale for this company regulation discussed in class on February 19, 1980. (It was also stated in the training manual.) Whether it has ever been enforced, and with what result, I don't know.

23. Cohen, (1966), p. 105.

24. Ibid.

25. Ibid.

26. The very way most institutions conduct the dirty work of firing, demotion, and punishment also assures that any *personal* blame aimed at those who fire, demote, and punish is not legitimized. It becomes illegitimate to interpret an "impersonal act" of firing as a personal act, as in "You did that to me, you bastard!" See Wolff (1950), pp. 345–378.

27. See Robert Howard, "Drugged, Bugged, and Coming Unplugged," *Mother Jones*, August 1981.

REFERENCES

Brown, Barbara. 1974. *New Mind, New Body*. New York: Harper & Row.

Campbell, Sarah F. (ed.). 1976. *Piaget Sampler*. New York: Wiley.

Cohen, Albert. 1966. *Deviance and Control*. Englewood Cliffs, NJ: Prentice-Hall.

Gellhorn, E. 1964. "Motion and emotion: the role of proprioception in the physiology and pathology of emotions." *Psychological Review* 71: 457–472.

Goffman, Erving. 1959. *The Presentation of Self in Everyday Life*. New York: Doubleday Anchor.

Gold, Herbert. 1979. "The smallest part," pp. 203–212. In William Abrahams (ed.), *Prize Stories, 1979*. The O'Henry Award. Garden City, NY: Doubleday.

Koriat, A., R. Melkman, J. R. Averill, and Richard Lazarus. 1972. "The self-control of emotional reactions to a stressful film." *Journal of Personality* 40: 601–619.

Latane', Bibb, and John Darley, 1970. *The Unresponsive Bystander*. New York: Appleton-Century-Crofts.

Lazarus, Richard. 1975. "The self-regulation of emotion," pp. 47–67. In L. Levi (ed.), *Emotions, Their Parameters and Measurement*. New York: Raven Press.

Lief, H. I., and R. C. Fox, 1963. "Training for a 'detached concern' in medical studies," pp. 12–35. In H. I. Lief, V. F. Lief, and N. R. Lief (eds.), *The Psychological Basis of Medical Practice*. New York: Harper & Row.

Mills, C. Wright. 1956. *White Collar*. New York: Oxford University Press.

Nietzsche, F. W. 1876. *Menschliches alzumenschliches*, Vol. 1. Leipzig: Kroner.

Pelletier, Kenneth. 1977. *Mind as Healer, Mind as Slayer? A Holistic Approach to Preventing Stress Disorders*. New York: Dell.

Peto, Andrew, 1968. "On affect control." *International Journal of Psychoanalysis* 49 (parts 2–3): 471–473.

Stanislavski, Constantin. 1965. *An Actor Prepares*. Tr. Elizabeth Reynolds Hapgood. New York: Theatre Arts Books. First published 1948.

Wheelis, Allen. 1980. *The Scheme of Things*. New York and London: Harcourt Brace Jovanovich.

Wolff, Kurt H. 1950. *The Sociology of Georg Simmel*. New York: Free Press.

17

Reference Groups as Perspectives

TAMOTSU SHIBUTANI

Although Hyman coined the term . . . , the concept of reference group has become one of the central analytic tools in social psychology. . . . The inconsistency in behavior as a person moves from one social context to another is accounted for in terms of a change in reference groups; the exploits of juvenile delinquents, especially in interstitial areas, are being explained by the expectations of peer-group gangs; modifications in social attitudes are found to be related to changes in associations. The concept has been particularly useful in accounting for the choices made among apparent alternatives, particularly where the selections seem to be contrary to the "best interests" of the actor. Status problems—aspirations of social climbers, conflicts in group loyalty, the dilemmas of marginal men—have also been analyzed in terms of reference groups, as have the differential sensitivity and reaction of various segments of an audience to mass communication. It is recognized that the same generic processes are involved in these phenomenally diverse events, and the increasing popularity of the concept attests to its utility in analysis. . . .

. . . It is the contention of this paper that the restriction of the concept of reference group to the . . . group whose perspective constitutes the frame of reference of the actor will increase its usefulness in research. Any group or object may be used for comparisons, and one need not assume the role of those with whom he compares his fate. . . . Under some circumstances, however, group loyalties and aspirations are related to perspectives assumed, and the character of this relationship calls for further exploration. Such a discussion necessitates a restatement of the familiar, but, in view of the difficulties in some of the work on reference groups, repetition may not be entirely out of order. In spite of the enthusiasm of some proponents there is actually nothing new in reference-group theory.

CULTURE AND PERSONAL CONTROLS

Thomas pointed out many years ago that what a man does depends largely upon his definition of the situation. One may add that the manner in which one consistently defines a succession of situations depends upon his organized perspective. A perspective is an ordered view of one's world—what is taken for granted about the attributes of various objects, events, and human nature. It is an order of things remembered and expected as well as things actually perceived, an organized conception of what is plausible and what is possible; it constitutes the matrix through which one perceives his environment. The fact that men have such ordered perspectives enables them to conceive of their ever changing world as relatively stable, orderly, and predictable. As Riezler puts it, one's perspective is an outline scheme which, running ahead of experience, defines and guides it.

There is abundant experimental evidence to show that perception is selective; that the organization of perceptual experience depends in part upon what is antici-

139

pated and what is taken for granted. Judgments rest upon perspectives, and people with different outlooks define identical situations differently, responding selectively to the environment. Thus, a prostitute and a social worker walking through a slum area notice different things; a sociologist should perceive relationships that others fail to observe. Any change of perspectives—becoming a parent for the first time, learning that one will die in a few months, or suffering the failure of well-laid plans—leads one to notice things previously overlooked and to see the familiar world in a different light. As Goethe contended, history is continually rewritten, not so much because of the discovery of new documentary evidence, but because the changing perspectives of historians lead to new selections from the data.

Culture, as the concept is used by Redfield, refers to a perspective that is shared by those in a particular group; it consists of those "conventional understandings, manifest in act and artifact, that characterize societies."[1] Since these conventional understandings are the premises of action, those who share a common culture engage in common modes of action. Culture is not a static entity but a continuing process; norms are creatively reaffirmed from day to day in social interaction. Those taking part in collective transactions approach one another with set expectations, and the realization of what is anticipated successively confirms and reinforces their perspectives. In this way, people in each cultural group are continuously supporting one another's perspectives, each by responding to the others in expected ways. In this sense culture is a product of communication.

In his discussion of endopsychic social control Mead spoke of men "taking the role of the generalized other," meaning by that that each person approaches his world from the standpoint of the culture of his group. Each perceives, thinks, forms judgments, and controls himself according to the frame of reference of the group in which he is participating. Since he defines objects, other people, the world, and himself from the perspective that he shares with others, he can visualize his proposed line of action from this generalized standpoint, anticipate the reactions of others, inhibit undesirable impulses, and thus guide his conduct. The socialized person is a society in miniature; he sets the same standards of conduct for himself as he sets for others, and he judges himself in the same terms. He can define situations properly and meet his obligations, even in the absence of other people, because, as already noted, his perspective always takes into account the expectations of others. Thus, it is the ability to define situations from the same standpoint as others that makes personal controls possible.[2] When Mead spoke of assuming the role of the generalized other, he was not referring to people but to perspectives shared with others in a transaction.

The consistency in the behavior of a man in a wide variety of social contexts is to be accounted for, then, in terms of his organized perspective. Once one has incorporated a particular outlook from his group, it becomes his orientation toward the world, and he brings this frame of reference to bear on all new situations. Thus, immigrants and tourists often misinterpret the strange things they see, and a disciplined Communist would define each situation differently from the non-Communist. Although reference-group behavior is generally studied in situations where choices seem possible, the actor himself is often unaware that there are alternatives.

The proposition that men think, feel, and see things from a standpoint peculiar to the group in which they participate is an old one, repeatedly emphasized by students of anthropology and of the sociology of knowledge.... The concept of reference group actually introduces a minor refinement in the long familiar theory, made necessary by the special characteristics of modern mass societies. First of all, in modern societies special problems arise from the fact that men some-times use the standards of groups in which they are *not* recognized members, sometimes of groups in which they have never partici-pated directly, and sometimes of groups that do not exist at all. Second, in our mass society, characterized as it is by cultural pluralism, each person internalizes several perspectives, and this occasionally gives rise to embarrassing dilemmas which call for sys-tematic study. Finally, the development of reference-group theory has been facilitated by the increasing interest in social psychol-ogy and the subjective aspects of group life, a shift from a predominant concern with ob-jective social structures to an interest in the experiences of the participants whose regu-larized activities make such structures dis-cernible.

A reference group, then, is that group whose outlook is used by the actor as the frame of reference in the organization of his perceptual field. All kinds of groupings, with great variations in size, composition, and structure, may become reference groups. Of greatest importance for most people are those groups in which they participate di-rectly—what have been called membership groups—especially those containing a num-ber of persons with whom one stands in a primary relationship. But in some transac-tions one may assume the perspective attrib-uted to some social category—a social class, an ethnic group, those in a given community, or those concerned with some special inter-est. On the other hand, reference groups may be imaginary, as in the case of artists who are "born ahead of their times," scientists who work for "humanity," or philanthropists who give for "posterity." Such persons esti-mate their endeavors from a postulated per-spective imputed to people who have not yet been born. There are others who live for a distant past, idealizing some period in history and longing for "the good old days," criticizing current events from a standpoint imputed to people long since dead. Reference groups, then, arise through

the internalization of norms; they constitute the structure of expectations imputed to some audience for whom one organizes his conduct.

THE CONSTRUCTION OF SOCIAL WORLDS

As Dewey emphasized, society exists in and through communication; common perspec-tives—common cultures—emerge through participation in common communication channels. It is through social participation that perspectives shared in a group are inter-nalized. Despite the frequent recitation of this proposition, its full implications, espe-cially for the analysis of mass societies, are not often appreciated. . . .

Modern mass societies, indeed are made up of a bewildering variety of social worlds. Each is an organized outlook, built up by people in their interaction with one another; hence, each communication channel gives rise to a separate world. Probably the great-est sense of identification and solidarity is to be found in the various communal struc-tures—the underworld, ethnic minorities, the social elite. Such communities are fre-quently spatially segregated, which isolates them further from the outer world, while the "grapevine" and foreign-language presses provide internal contacts. Another common type of social world consists of the associa-tional structures—the world of medicine, of organized labor, of the theater, of café soci-ety. These are held together not only by var-ious voluntary associations within each locality but also by periodicals like *Variety*, specialized journals, and feature sections in newspapers. Finally, there are the loosely connected universes of special interest—the world of sports, of the stamp collector, of the daytime serial—serviced by mass media pro-grams and magazines like *Field and Stream*. Each of these worlds is a unity of order, a universe of regularized mutual response. Each is an area in which there is some struc-ture which permits reasonable anticipation of the behavior of others, hence, an area in which one may act with a sense of security and confidence.[3] Each social world, then, is a culture area, the boundaries of which are set neither by territory nor by formal group membership but by the limits of effective communication.

Since there is a variety of communication channels, differing in stability and extent, social worlds differ in composition, size, and the territorial distribution of the participants. Some, like local cults, are small and concentrated; others, like the intellectual world, are vast and the participants dispersed. Worlds differ in the extent and clarity of their boundaries; each is confined by some kind of horizon, but this may be wide or narrow, clear or vague. The fact that social worlds are not coterminous with the universe of men is recognized; those in the underworld are well aware of the fact that outsiders do not share their values. Worlds differ in exclusiveness and in the extent to which they demand the loyalty of their participants. Most important of all, social worlds are not static entities; shared perspectives are continually being reconstituted. Worlds come into existence with the establishment of communication channels; when life conditions change, social relationships may also change, and these worlds may disappear.

Every social world has some kind of communication system—often nothing more than differential association—in which there develops a special universe of discourse, sometimes an argot. Special meanings and symbols further accentuate differences and increase social distance from outsiders. In each world there are special norms of conduct, a set of values, a special prestige ladder, characteristic career lines, and a common outlook toward life—a Weltanschauung. In the case of elites there may even arise a code of honor which holds only for those who belong, while others are dismissed as beings somewhat less than human from whom bad manners may be expected. A social world, then, is an order conceived which

serves as the stage on which each participant seeks to carve out his career and to maintain and enhance his status.

One of the characteristics of life in modern mass societies is simultaneous participation in a variety of social worlds. Because of the ease with which the individual may expose himself to a number of communication channels, he may lead a segmentalized life, participating successively in a number of unrelated activities. Furthermore, the particular combination of social worlds differs from person to person; this is what led Simmel to declare that each stands at that point at which a unique combination of social circles intersects. The geometric analogy is a happy one, for it enables us to conceive the numerous possibilities of combinations and the different degrees of participation in each circle. To understand what a man does, we must get at his unique perspective—what he takes for granted and how he defines the situation—but in mass societies we must learn in addition the social world in which he is participating in a given act. . . .

NOTES

1. R. Redfield, *The Folk Culture of Yucatan* (Chicago: University of Chicago Press, 1941), p. 132. For a more explicit presentation of a behavioristic theory of culture see *The Selected Writings of Edward Sapir in Language, Culture and Personality,* ed. D. G. Mandelbaum (Berkeley: University of California Press, 1949), pp. 104–9, 308–31, 544–59.
2. G. H. Mead, "The Genesis of the Self and Social Control," *International Journal of Ethics,* XXXV (1925), 251–77, and *Mind, Self and Society* (Chicago: University of Chicago Press, 1934), pp. 152–64. Cf. T. Parsons, "The Superego and the Theory of Social Systems," *Psychiatry,* XV (1952), 15–25.
3. Cf. K. Riezler, *Man: Mutable and Immutable* (Chicago: Henry Regnery Co., 1950), pp. 62–72; L. Landgrebe, "The World as a Phenomenological Problem," *Philosophy and Phenomenological Research,* I (1940), 38–58; and A. Schuetz, "The Stranger: An Essay in Social Psychology," *American Journal of Sociology,* XLIX (1944), 499–507.

18

Police Accounts of Normal Force

JENNIFER HUNT

The police are required to handle a variety of peacekeeping and law enforcement tasks including settling disputes, removing drunks from the street, aiding the sick, controlling crowds, and pursuing criminals. What unifies these diverse activities is the possibility that their resolution might require the use of force. Indeed, the capacity to use force stands at the core of the police mandate (Bittner, 1980).

The bulk of the sociological literature on the use of force by police is concerned with analyzing the objective causes of "excessive" force. Some social scientists, for example, suggest that the incidence of extra-legal force correlates with characteristics of individual officers—in particular, their authoritarianism, age, or length of service (Niederhoffer, 1967; Blumberg, 1983). Others emphasize the relevance of the behavior and characteristics of the target population, including demeanor, sex, race, and class (Reiss, 1970; Friedrich, 1980; Lee, 1981). Still others investigate the legal and organizational roots of force. They are concerned with how formal rules and/or subcultural norms may influence the police officer's decision to employ force (Fyfe, 1983; Waegel, 1984).

Although representing diverse perspectives, these approaches share a similar underlying orientation to use of force by police. First, they all specify, in advance of study, formal or legal definitions of permissible force, definitions that are then used to identify deviations legally classifiable as brutal or "excessive." This procedure disregards the understandings and standards police officers actively employ in using and evaluating force in the course of their work. Second, these studies are primarily concerned with identifying the objective conditions held to determine "excessive" force defined in this way. As a result, they minimize the active role of consciousness in police decisions to use force, tending to depict such decisions as mere passive responses to external determinants.

In contrast, sociologists working within the symbolic interactionist tradition have displayed particular interest in the police officer's own assessment of what constitutes necessary force. This research has varied in how such assessments are conceptualized. Rubinstein (1973: 302), for example, suggests that police use force instrumentally to control persons whom they perceive as presenting a physical threat. In contrast, Van Maanen (1978) explores how police, in reacting to others, are highly attentive to symbolic violation of their authority, dispensing harsh treatment to categories of persons who commit such violations.

The following research departs from and seeks to extend the symbolic interactionist concern with police officers' own assessments of the use of force. It explores how

AUTHOR'S NOTE: I am deeply indebted for both substantive and editorial assistance to Michael Brown and Robert M. Emerson. I would also like to thank Peter Manning, Bill DiFazio, Jim Birch, and Marie DeMay Della Guardia for their comments on an earlier draft of this article.

police themselves classify and evaluate acts of force as either legal, normal, or excessive. Legal force is that coercion necessary to subdue, control, and restrain a suspect in order to take him into custody. Although force not accountable in legal terms is technically labelled excessive by the courts and the public, the police perceive many forms of illegal force as normal. Normal force involves coercive acts that specific "cops" on specific occasions formulate as necessary, appropriate, reasonable, or understandable. Although not always legitimated or admired, normal force is depicted as a necessary or natural response of normal police to particular situational exigencies.

Most officers are expected to use both legal and normal force as a matter of course in policing the streets. In contrast, excessive force or brutality exceeds even working police notions of normal force. These are acts of coercion that cannot be explained by the routine police accounting practices ordinarily used to justify or excuse force. Brutality is viewed as illegal, illegitimate, and often immoral violence, but the police draw the lines in extremely different ways and at different points than do either the court system or the public.

These processes of assessing and accounting for the use of force, with special reference to the critical distinction between normal and excessive force as drawn by the police, will be explored in what follows. The study begins by examining how rookie police learn on the street to use and account for force in a manner that contradicts what they were taught at the academy. It then considers "normal force" and the accounting processes whereby police discriminatively judge when and how much force is appropriate in specific situations and incidents. It concludes with a discussion of excessive force and peer reactions to those who use it frequently.

The article is based on approximately eighteen months of participant observation in a major urban police department referred to as the Metro City P.D. I attended the police academy with male and female recruits and later rode with individual officers in one-person cars on evening and night shifts in high crime districts.[1] The female officers described in this research were among the first 100 women assigned to the ranks of uniformed patrol as a result of a discrimination suit filed by the Justice Department and a police-woman plaintiff.

LEARNING TO USE NORMAL FORCE

The police phrase "it's not done on the street the way that it's taught at the academy" underscores the perceived contradiction between the formal world of the police academy and the informal world of the street. This contradiction permeates the police officer's construction of his world, particularly his view of the rational and moral use of force.

In the formal world of the police academy, the recruit learns to account for force by reference to legality. He or she is issued the regulation instruments and trained to use them to subdue, control, and restrain a suspect. If threatened with great bodily harm, the officer learns that he can justifiably use deadly force and fire his revolver. Yet the recruit is taught that he cannot use his baton, jack, or gun, unnecessarily to torture, maim, or kill a suspect.

When recruits leave the formal world of the academy and are assigned to patrol a district, they are introduced to an informal world in which police recognize normal as well as legal and brutal force. Through observation and instruction, rookies gradually learn to apply force and account for its use in terms familiar to the street cop. First, rookies learn to adjust their arsenals to conform to street standards. They are encouraged to buy the more powerful weapons worn by veteran colleagues as these colleagues point out the inadequacy of a wooden baton or compare their convoy jacks to vibrators. They quickly discover that their department-issued equipment marks them as new recruits. At any rate, within a few weeks, most rookies have dispensed with the wooden baton and convoy jack and substituted them with the more powerful plastic nightstick and flat headed slapjack.[2]

Through experience and informal instruction, the rookie also learns the street use of these weapons. In school, for example, recruits are taught to avoid hitting a person on the head or neck because it could cause lethal damage. On the street, in contrast, police conclude that they must hit wherever it causes the most damage in order to incapacitate the suspect before they themselves are harmed. New officers also learn that they will earn the respect of their veteran coworkers not by observing legal niceties in using force, but by being "aggressive" and using whatever force is necessary in a given situation.

Peer approval helps neutralize the guilt and confusion that rookies often experience when they begin to use force to assert their authority. One female officer, for example, learned she was the object of a brutality suit while listening to the news on television. At first, she felt so mortified that she hesitated to go to work and face her peers. In fact, male colleagues greeted her with a standing ovation and commented, "You can use our urinal now." In their view, any aggressive police officer regularly using normal force might eventually face a brutality suit or civilian complaint. Such accusations confirm the officer's status as a "street cop" rather than an "inside man" who doesn't engage in "real police work."[3]

Whereas male rookies are assumed to be competent dispensers of force unless proven otherwise, women are believed to be physically weak, naturally passive, and emotionally vulnerable.[4] Women officers are assumed to be reluctant to use physical force and are viewed as incompetent "street cops"

until they prove otherwise. As a result, women rookies encounter special problems in learning to use normal force in the process of becoming recognized as "real street cops." It becomes crucial for women officers to create or exploit opportunities to display their physical abilities in order to overcome sexual bias and obtain full acceptance from coworkers. As a result, women rookies are encouraged informally to act more aggressively and to display more machismo than male rookies. Consider the following incident where a young female officer reflects upon her use of force during a domestic disturbance:

> And when I get there, if goddamn, there isn't a disturbance going on. So Tom comes, the guy that I went to back up. The male talks to him. I take the female and talk to her. And the drunk (cop) comes and the sergeant comes and another guy comes. So while we think we have everything settled, and we have the guy calmed down, he turns around and says to his sister, no less, that's who it is, "Give me the keys to my car!" And with that, she rips them out of her pocket and throws them at him. Now, he goes nuts. He goes into a Kung fu stance and says he's gonna kill her. The drunk cop says, "Yo, knock it off!" and goes to grab him and the guy punches him. So Mike (the drunk cop) goes down. Tommy goes to grab him and is wrestling with him. And all the cops are trying to get in there. So I ran in with my stick and I stick the guy in the head. But I just missed Tommy's face and opened him (the suspect) up. So all of a sudden everybody's grabbin' him and I'm realizing that if we get him down, he won't hurt anybody. So I pushed the sergeant out of the way and I got my stick under the guy's legs and I pulled his legs out from under him and I yelled, "Tommy, take him down." I pulled his legs and he went down and I sat on him. So Tommy says, "Well, cuff him." And I says, "I can't find my goddamned cuffs." I molested my body trying to get my cuffs. . . .
>
> So, when I [finally] get my cuffs, we cuff him. And we're sitting there talking. And Tommy, he has no regard for me whatsoever.

... The guy's opened up and he bled all over Tommy's shirt. And I turned around and said, "Tommy, look at your shirt. There's blood all over your shirt." He said, "Who the hell almost clobbered me?" I said, "I'm sorry Tom, that was me." He said, "You're the one that opened him up? And I said, "Yeh, I'm sorry, I didn't mean to get so close to you." ...

So when the sergeant came out he said, "And you, what do you mean telling me to get outta the way." He said, "Do you know you pushed me outta your way...." And I said, "I didn't want you to get hurt ... and I was afraid he was gonna kick one of you." And he says, "I still can't believe you pushed me outta your way. You were like a little dynamo." And I found after that I got respect from the sergeant. He doesn't realize it but he treated me differently after that.

Her colleagues' reactions provided informal instruction in the use of normal force, confirming that her actions under these circumstances were reasonable and even praiseworthy.

For a street cop, it is often a graver error to use too little force and develop a "shaky" reputation than it is to use too much force and be told to calm down. Thus officers, particularly rookies, who do not back up their partners in appropriate ways or who hesitate to use force in circumstances where it is deemed necessary are informally instructed regarding their aberrant ways. If the problematic incident is relatively insignificant and his general reputation is good, a rookie who "freezes" one time is given a second chance before becoming generally known as an untrustworthy partner. However, such incidents become the subject of degrading gossip, gossip that pressures the officer either to use force as expected or risk isolation. Such talk also informs rookies about the general boundaries of legal and normal force.

For example, a female rookie was accused of "freezing" in an incident that came to be referred to as a "Mexican standoff." A pedestrian had complained that "something funny is going on in the drugstore." The officer walked into the pharmacy where she found an armed man committing a robbery. Although he turned his weapon on her when she entered the premises, she still pulled out her gun and pointed it at him. When he ordered her to drop it, claiming that his partner was behind her with a revolver at her head, she refused and told him to drop his.[5] He refused, and the stalemate continued until a sergeant entered the drugstore and ordered the suspect to drop his gun.

Initially, the female officer thought she had acted appropriately and even heroically. She soon discovered, however, that her hesitation to shoot had brought into question her competence with some of her fellow officers. Although many veterans claimed that "she had a lot a balls" to take her gun out at all when the suspect already had a gun on her, most contended "she shoulda shot him." Other policemen confirmed that she committed a "rookie mistake"; she had failed to notice a "lookout" standing outside the store and hence had been unprepared for an armed confrontation. Her sergeant and lieutenant, moreover, even insisted that she had acted in a cowardly manner, despite her reputation as a "gung-ho cop," and cited the incident as evidence of the general inadequacy of policewomen.

In the weeks that followed, this officer became increasingly depressed and angry. She was particularly outraged when she learned that she would not receive a commendation, although such awards were commonly made for "gun pinches" of this nature. Several months later, the officer vehemently expressed the wish that she had killed the suspect and vowed that next time she would "shoot first and ask questions later." The negative sanctions of supervisors and colleagues clearly encouraged her to adopt an attitude favorable to using force with less restraint in future situations.

Reprimand, gossip, and avoidance constitute the primary means by which police try to change or control the behavior of co-workers perceived as unreliable or cowardly. Formal accusations, however, are discouraged regardless of the seriousness of the misconduct. One male rookie, for example, earned a reputation for cowardice after he allegedly had to be "dragged" out of the car during an "assist officer." Even then, he apparently refused to help the officers in trouble. Although no formal charges were field, everyone in the district was warned to avoid working with this officer.

Indeed, to initiate formal charges against a coworker may discredit the accuser. In one incident a male rookie, although discouraged by veteran officers and even his district captain, filed charges of cowardice against a female rookie. The rookie gained the support of two supervisors and succeeded in having the case heard before the Board of Inquiry. During the trial he claimed the woman officer failed to aid him in arresting a man who presented physical resistance and had a knife on his person. In rebuttal, the woman testified that she perceived no need to participate in a physical confrontation because she saw no knife and the policeman was hitting the suspect. Inspite of conflicting testimony, she was found guilty of "Neglect of Duty." Although most veterans thought the woman was "flaky" and doubted her competence, they also felt the male rookie had exaggerated his story. Moreover, they were outraged that he filed formal charges and he quickly found himself ostracized.

At the same time that male and female rookies are commended for using force under appropriate circumstances, they are reprimanded if their participation in force is viewed as excessive or inappropriate. In this way, rookies are instructed that although many acts of coercion are accepted and even demanded, not everything goes. They thereby learn to distinguish between normal and brutal force. In the following incident, for example, a policewoman describes how she instructed a less experienced officer that her behavior was unreasonable and should be checked. Here, the new officer is chastised for misreading interactional cues and overreacting to minor affronts when treating a crazy person involved in a minor dispute as if he were a serious felon.[6]

> But like I said, when I first heard about it (another fight) I'd wondered if Mary had provoked it any because we'd gone on a disturbance and it was a drunk black guy who called to complain that the kid who lived upstairs keeps walking through his apartment. The kid to me looks wacky. He's talking crazy. He's saying they shoulda sent men. What are you women going to do. Going on and on. And to me it was a bullshit job. But Mary turns around and says, "We don't have to take that from him. Let's lock him up." I said, "Mary forget it." And the kid has numchuck sticks on him and when he turned his back . . . he had them in his back pocket. So, as he's pulling away saying you're scared, like a little kid, I turned around and said, "I've got your sticks." And I go away. Mary . . . so Mary was . . . I looked at her and she was so disappointed in me . . . like I'd turned chicken on her. So I tried to explain to her, I said, "Mary, all we have is disorderly conduct. That's a summary offense. That's bullshit." I said, "Did you want to get hurt for a summary offense?" I said, "The guy was drunk who called to complain. It wasn't even a legit complaint." I said, "It's just . . . You've got to use discretion. If you think I'm chicken think of the times when a 'man with a gun' comes over the air and I'm the first car there." I said, "When it's worth it, I'll do anything. When it's not worth it, I'll back off." And I think she tries to temper herself some because Collette and her, they finally had a talk about why they hated each other. And Collette said to her, "I think you're too physical. I think you look for fights." And I think maybe Mary hearing it twice, once from me and once from Collette, might start to think that maybe she does pro-

voke. Instead of going up . . . I always go up to them friendly and then if they act shitty I get shitty.

In summary, when rookies leave the academy, they begin to familiarize themselves with street weapons and to gain some sense of what kinds of behavior constitute too little or too much force. They also begin to develop an understanding of street standards for using and judging appropriate and necessary force. By listening to and observing colleagues at work and by experiencing a variety of problematic interactions with the public, newcomers become cognizant of the occasions and circumstances in which to use various degrees and kinds of force. But at the same time, they are learning not only when and how to use force, but also a series of accounting practices to justify and to legitimate as "normal" (and sometimes to condemn) these acts of coercion. Normal force is thus the product of the police officers' accounting practices for describing what happened in ways that prefigure or anticipate the conclusion that it was in some sense justified or excusable and hence "normal." It is to a consideration of the ways in which officers learn to provide such accounts for normal force that I now turn.

ACCOUNTING FOR NORMAL FORCE

Police routinely normalize the use of force by two types of accounts: excuses and justifications. Excuses deny full responsibility for an act of force but acknowledge its inappropriateness. Acts of force become excusable when they are depicted as the natural outcome of strong, even uncontrollable emotions normally arising in certain routine sorts of police activities. Through such accounts, officers excuse force by asserting that it is a "natural," "human" reaction to certain extreme, emotionally trying situations. Justifications accept responsibility for the coercive act in question but deny that the act was

wrongful or blameworthy (Scott and Lyman, 1968; Emerson, 1969: 142–171). Police justify force through two analytically distinct kinds of accounts: situational and abstract. In the former, the officer represents force as a response in some specific situation needed to restore immediate control or to reestablish the local order of power in the face of a threat to police authority. In contrast, abstract accounts justify force as a morally appropriate response to certain categories of crime and criminals who symbolize a threat to the moral order. As an account, abstract justification does not highlight processes of interactional provocation and threats to immediate control, but rather legitimates force as a means of obtaining some higher moral purpose, particularly the punishment of heinous offenders.

None of these accounts are mutually exclusive, and are often combined in justifying and excusing the use of force in any specific instance. For example, police consider it justifiable to use force to regain control of someone who has challenged an officer's authority. However, an officer may also excuse his behavior as an "overreaction," claiming he "snapped out" and lost control, and hence used more force or different kinds of force than were required to regain control. Mixed accounts involving situational and abstract justifications of force are also frequent: force may be depicted as necessary to regain control when an officer is physically assaulted; but at the same time it may also be justified as punishment appropriate to the kind of morally unworthy person who would challenge an officer's authority.

Excuses and Normal Force

Excuses are accounts in which police deny full responsibility for an act but recognize its inappropriateness. Excuses therefore constitute socially approved vocabularies for relieving responsibility when conduct is questionable. Police most often excuse morally problematic force by referring to emotional or physiological states that are precipitated by some circumstances of routine patrol work. These circumstances include shootouts, violent fights, pursuits, and instances in which a police officer mistakenly comes close to killing an unarmed person.

Policework in these circumstances can generate intense excitement in which the officer experiences the "combat high" and "adrenaline rush" familiar to the combat soldier.[7] Foot and car pursuits not only bring on feelings of danger and excitement from the chase, but also a challenge to official authority. As one patrolman commented about a suspect: "Yeh, he got tuned up (beaten) . . . you always tune them up after a car chase." Another officer normalized the use of force after a pursuit in these terms:

> It's my feeling that violence inevitably occurs after a pursuit. . . . The adrenaline . . . and the insult involved when someone flees increases with every foot of the pursuit. I know the two or three times that I felt I lost control of myself . . . was when someone would run on me. The further I had to chase the guy the madder I got. . . . The funny thing is the reason for the pursuit could have been for something as minor as a traffic violation or a kid you're chasing who just turned on a fire hydrant. It always ends in violence. You feel obligated to hit or kick the guy just for running.

Police officers also excuse force when it follows an experience of helplessness and confusion that has culminated in a temporary loss of emotional control. This emotional combination occurs most frequently when an officer comes to the brink of using lethal force, drawing a gun and perhaps firing, only to learn there were no "real" grounds for this action. The officer may then "snap out" and hit the suspect.[8] In one such incident, for example, two policemen picked up a complainant who positively identified a suspect as a man who just tried to shoot him. Just as the officers approached the suspect, he suddenly reached for his back pocket for what the officers assumed to be a gun. One officer was close enough to jump the suspect before he pulled his hand from his pocket. As it turned out, the suspect had no weapon, having dropped it several feet away. Although he was unarmed and under control, the suspect was punched and kicked out of anger and frustration by the officer who had almost shot him.[9]

Note that in both these circumstances—pursuit and near-miss mistaken shootings—officers would concede that the ensuing force is inappropriate and unjustifiable when considered abstractly. But although abstractly wrong, the use of force on such occasions is presented as a normal, human reaction to an extreme situation. Although not every officer might react violently in such circumstances, it is understandable and expected that some will.

Situational Justifications

Officers also justify force as normal by reference to interactional situations in which an officer's authority is physically or symbolically threatened. In such accounts, the use of force is justified instrumentally—as a means of regaining immediate control in a situation where that control has become tenuous. Here, the officer depicts his primary intent for using force as a need to reestablish immediate control in a problematic encounter, and only incidentally as hurting or punishing the offender.

Few officers will hesitate to assault a suspect who physically threatens or attacks them. In one case, an officer was punched in the face by a prisoner he had just apprehended for allegedly attempting to shoot a friend. The incident occurred in the stationhouse and several policemen observed the exchange. Immediately, one officer hit the prisoner in the jaw and the rest immediately joined the brawl.

Violations of an officer's property such as his car or hat may signify a more symbolic assault on the officer's authority and self, thus justifying a forceful response to maintain control. Indeed, in the police view, almost any person who verbally challenges a police officer is appropriately subject to force.[10] In the following extract, a female officer accounts in these ways for a colleague's use of force against an escaping prisoner:

> And so Susan gets on the scene (of the fight). They cuff one of the girls, and she throws her in the back seat of the car. She climbs over the back seat, jumps out of the car with cuffs on and starts running up the stairs. Susan and Jane are trying to cuff the other girl and all of a sudden Susan looks up and sees her cuffs running away. She (Jane) said Susan turned into an animal. Susan runs up the steps grabs the girl by the legs. Drags her down the five steps. Puts her in the car. Kicks her in the car. Jane goes in the car and calls her every name she can think of and waves her stick in her face.[11]

On rare occasions, women officers encounter special problems in these regards. Although most suspects view women in the same way as policemen, some seem less inclined to accord female officers de facto and symbolic control in street encounters, and on a few occasions seem determined to provoke direct confrontations with such officers, explicitly denying their formal authority and attempting none too subtly to sexualize the encounter. Women officers, then, might use force as a resource for rectifying such insults and for establishing control over such partially sexualized interactions. Consider the following woman officer's extended account providing such situational justifications for the use of force:

> Well, the day before the lieutenant had a rollcall announcement that there had been a pursuit in one of the districts and, as a result, a fireman was killed. And he said, "Why

pursue them? In court nothing is gonna happen anyway and being as it was a taxi cab that was involved it would be returned." He said, "What I'm trying to say . . ." "So one of the guys said, "What's a pursuit?" He said, "Exactly."

So Goddamn, if not the next day, about three o'clock in the morning, three thirty, I heard Anne go out with a carstop at Second and Madison. And I heard Joan back her up, and she (Anne) ran the car through (the computer) and I heard, "Hold me out for TVRs (traffic tickets)." So, I'm sitting at Second Street, Second and Nassau, writing curfews up. And this silver Thunderbird (the same car) blows right by a stop sign where I'm sitting. And I look up and think to myself, "Now, do I want to get involved." And I figure, it was really belligerent doing it right in front of me. So I take off after him, put my lights on and he immediately pulls over. So he jumps out of the car. I jump out of the car right away and I say, "I'm stopping you for that stop sign you just blew through." And he says, "Aw come on, I just got stopped. I'm sick of this shit." So I said to him, "Look, I don't care how many times you got stopped." He said, "Well, I'm sick of this shit." And I said, "I'm stopping you right now for the stop sign you went through at Second and Nassau. Let me see your cards please." Then he starts making these lip smacking noises at me everytime he begins to talk. He said, (smack) "The only way you're seeing my cards is if you lock me up and the only way you're gonna lock me up is if you chase me." And I said to him, "Well, look, I will satisfy you on one account. Now go to your car because I will lock you up. . . . And just sit in your car. I'll be right with you." He smacks his lips, turns around and goes to his car and he sits. And I call a wagon at Second and Nassau. They ask me what I have. I say, "I've got one to go." So as the wagon acknowledges, the car all of a sudden tears out of its spot. And I get on the air and say, "I'm in pursuit." And I give them a description of the car and the direction I'm going. And I heard a couple of other cars coming in and they're comin' in. And all of a sudden he pulls over about a block and a half after I started the pursuit. So I got on the air and I said, "I got him at Second and Washington." I jumped out of my car and as I jumped out he tears away again. Now I'm ready to die of embarrassment. I have to get back on the air as say no I don't have him. So I got on the air and said, "Look, he's playing games with me now. He took off again." I said, "I'm still heading South on Second street." He gets down to Lexington. He pulls over again. Well, this time I pulled the police car in front of him. I jumped out of the car and as I'm jumping out of the car I hear two female voices screaming, "Lock him up, lock him up!" I go over to the car and I hear him lock the doors. I pull out my gun and I put it right in his window. I say, "Unlock that door." Well, he looked at the gun. He nearly like to shit himself. He unlocked the door. I holster my gun. I go to grab his arms to pull him out and all of a sudden I realize Anne's got him. So we keep pulling him out of the car. Throw him on the trunk of his car and kept pounding him back down on the trunk. She's punching his head. I'm kicking him. Then I take out my blackjack. I jack him across the shoulder. Then I go to jack him in the head and I jack Anne's fingers. We're being so rough. Then the wagon comes and we're kicking the shit out of him. Trying to . . . dragging him over to the wagon. This poor sucker don't have a chance. The next thing they know is we're throwing him bodily into the wagon. And they said, "Did you search him?" We go to the wagon, drag him out again. Now we're tearing through his pockets throwing everything on the ground. Pick him up bodily again, threw him in. . . . So I straightened it out with the sergeant and he said, "By the way what were you doing?" I said, "I was in a pursuit." (He said) "A pursuit! Thank God the Lieutenant wasn't there. He said there's no such thing as a pursuit." I said, "I tried to call it another name but I couldn't think of any other name to call it. All I know of it is as a pursuit. I'm following some guy at fast speed who refuses to pull over." So I said, "What did you want me to do? Let any citizen on the street get stopped and pull away and that's the end of it?"

In this instance, a male suspect manages to convey a series of affronts to the officer's authority. These affronts become explicitly and insultingly sexual,[12] turning the challenge from the claim that "no cop will stop me" to the more gender specific one, "no woman cop will stop me." Resistance ups the ante until the suspect backs down in the face of the officer's drawn revolver. The force to which the culprit was then subjected is normalized through all the accounts considered to this point—it is situationally justified as a means to reestablish and maintain immediate and symbolic control in a highly problematic encounter and it is excused as a natural, collective outburst following resolution of a dangerous, tension-filled incident. And finally, it is more implicitly justified as appropriate punishment, an account building upon standard police practices for abstract justification, to which I now turn.

Abstract Justifications

Police also justify the use of extreme force against certain categories of morally reprehensible persons. In this case, force is not presented as an instrumental means to regain control that has been symbolically or physically threatened. Instead, it is justified as an appropriate response to particularly heinous offenders. Categories of such offenders include: cop haters who have gained notoriety as persistent police antagonizers; cop killers or any person who has attempted seriously to harm a police officer (Westley, 1970: 131); sexual deviants who prey on children and "moral women";[13] child abusers; and junkies and other "scum" who inhabit the street. The more morally reprehensible the act is judged, the more likely the police are to depict any violence directed toward its perpetrator as justifiable. Thus a man who exposes himself to children in a playground is less likely to experience police assault than one who rapes or sexually molests a child.

"Clean" criminals, such as high level mafiosi, white-collar criminals, and professional burglars, are rarely subject to abstract force. Nor are perpetrators of violent and nonviolent street crimes who prey on adult males, prostitutes, and other categories of persons who belong on the street.[14] Similarly, the "psycho" or demented person is perceived as so mentally deranged that he is not responsible for his acts and hence does not merit abstract, punitive force (Van Maanen, 1978: 233–4).

Police justify abstract force by invoking a higher moral purpose that legitimates the violation of commonly recognized standards.[15] In one case, for example, a nun was raped by a 17-year-old male adolescent. When the police apprehended the suspect, he was severely beaten and his penis put in an electrical outlet to teach him a lesson. The story of the event was told to me by a police officer who, despite the fact that he rarely supported the use of extralegal force, depicted this treatment as legitimate. Indeed, when I asked if he would have participated had he been present, he responded, "I'm Catholic. I would have participated."

EXCESSIVE FORCE AND PEER RESPONSES

Although police routinely excuse and justify many incidents where they or their coworkers have used extreme force against a citizen or suspect, this does not mean that on any and every occasion the officer using such force is exonerated. Indeed, the concept of normal force is useful because it suggests that there are specific circumstances under which police officers will not condone the use of force by themselves or colleagues as reasonable and acceptable. Thus, officer-recognized conceptions of normal force are subject to restrictions of the following kinds:

(1) Police recognize and honor some rough equation between the behavior of the suspect and the harmfulness of the force to which it is subject. There are limits, there-

fore, to the degree of force that is acceptable in particular circumstances. In the following incident, for example, an officer reflects on a situation in which a "symbolic assailant" (Skolnick, 1975: 45) was mistakenly subject to more force than he "deserved" and almost killed:

One time Bill Johnson and I, I have more respect for him than any other policeman. . . . He and I, we weren't particularly brutal. If the guy deserved it, he got it. It's generally the attitude that does it. We had a particularly rude drunk one day. He was really rude and spit on you and he did all this stuff and we even had to cuff him lying down on the hard stretcher, like you would do an epileptic. . . . We were really mad at this guy. So, what you normally do with drunks is you take them to the district cell. . . . So we were really mad. We said let's just give him one or two shots . . . slamming on the brakes and having him roll. But we didn't use our heads. He's screaming and hollering "You lousy cops" and we slammed on the brakes and we didn't use our heads and we heard the stretcher go nnnnnnBam and then nothing. We heard nothing and we realized we had put this man in with his head to the front so when we slammed on the brakes this stretcher. . . . I guess it can roll four foot. Well, it was his head that had hit the front of it and we heard no sounds and my God, I've never been so scared. Me and Bill we thought we killed him. So I'm saying "Bill, what are we gonna do? How are we gonna explain this one." The guy's still saying nothing. So, we went to Madison Street and parked. It's a really lonely area. And we unlocked the wagon and peeked in. We know he's in there. We were so scared and we look in and there's not a sound and we see blood coming in front of the wagon and think "Oh my God we killed this man. What am I gonna do? What am I gonna tell my family?" And to make a long story short, he was just knocked out. But boy was I scared. From then on we learned, feet first.

(2) Although it is considered normal and natural to become emotional and angry in

highly charged, taut encounters, officers nonetheless prefer to minimize the harmful consequences of the use of force. As a result, officers usually acknowledge that emotional reactions that might lead to extreme force should be controlled and limited by co-workers if at all possible. In the following account, for example, an officer justified the use of force as a legitimate means to regain situational control when physically challenged. Nonetheless, he expressed gratitude to his partner for stopping him from doing serious harm when he "snapped out" and lost control:

> Well, I wasn't sure if she was a girl until I put my hand on her shoulder and realized it was a woman's shoulder. I was trying to stop her. But it happened when she suddenly kicked me in the balls. Then everything inside of me exploded and I grabbed her and pushed her against the car and started pressing her backwards and kept pressing her backwards. All of a sudden something clicked inside of me because I noticed her eyes changed and her body caved in and she looked frightened because she knew that I was gonna kill her. And I stopped. I think I stopped because Susan was on the scene. She must have said something. But anyway she (Susan) told me later that I should calm down. And I snapped at her and told her to mind her own business because she didn't know what happened. The girl kicked me in the balls. But she was right about it. I mean it was getting to me. I'd never hit a woman before.

(3) Similarly, even in cases where suspects are seen as deserving some violent punishment, this force should not be used randomly and without control. Thus, in the following incident, an officer who "snapped out" and began to beat a child abuser clearly regarded his partner's attempt to stop the beating as reasonable:

> We get a call "meet complainant" and I drive up and there's a lady standing out in front of the house and she's saying, "Listen officer, I don't know what the story is but the neigh-bors in there. They're screaming and hollering and there's kicking going on in there and I can't take it. I can't sleep. There's too much noise." Nothing unusual about that. Just a typical day in the district. So the next thing you do is knock on the door and tell them to please keep the noise down or whatever you do. You say to yourself it's probably a boy friend–girl friend fight. So I knock on the door and a lady answers just completely hysterical. And I say, "Listen, I don't know what's going on in here," but then I hear this, just this screeching. You know. And I figure well I'm just going to find out what's going on so I just go past the lady and what's happening is that the husband had.... The kid was being potty trained and the way they were potty training this kid, this two-year-old boy, was that the boyfriend of this girl would pick up this kid and he would sit him down on top of the stove. It was their method of potty training. Well, first of all you think of your own kids. I mean afterwards you do. I mean I've never been this mad in my whole life. You see this little two-year-old boy seated on top of the stove with rings around it being absolutely scalding hot. And he's saying "I'll teach you to go...." It just triggered something. An uncontrollable.... It's just probably the most violent I ever got. Well you just grab that guy. You hit him ten, fifteen times ... you don't know how many. You just get so mad. And I remember my partner eventually came in and grabbed me and said, "Don't worry about it. We got him. We got him." And we cuffed him and we took him down. Yeah that was bad.

Learning these sorts of restrictions on the use of normal force and these informal practices of peer control are important processes in the socialization of newcomers. This socialization proceeds both through ongoing observation and experience and, on occasion, through explicit instruction. For example, one veteran officer advised a rookie, "The only reason to go in on a pursuit is not to get the perpetrator but to pull the cop who gets there first offa the guy before he kills him."

It is against this background that patrol officers identify excessive force and the existence of violence-prone peers. Some officers become known for recurrently committing acts of coercion that exceed working notions of normal force and that cannot be excused or justified with routine accounting practices. In contrast to the officer who makes a "rookie mistake" and uses excessive force from inexperience, the brutal cop does not honor the practices of normal force. Such an officer is also not effectively held in check by routine means of peer control. As a result, more drastic measures must be taken to prevent him from endangering the public and his colleagues.

One rookie gained a reputation for brutality from frequent involvement in "unnecessary" fights. One such incident was particularly noteworthy: Answering a call on a demented male with a weapon, he came upon a large man pacing the sidewalk carrying a lead pipe. The officer got out of the patrol car and yelled in a belligerent tone of voice, "What the fuck are you doing creep?" At this point "the creep" attacked the officer and tried to take away his gun. A policewoman arrived on the scene, joined the fight, called an assist, and rescued the patrolman. Although no one was hurt, colleagues felt the incident was provoked by the officer who aggressively approached a known crazy person who should have been assumed to be unpredictable and nonresponsible.

When colleagues first began to doubt this officer's competence, he was informally instructed to moderate his behavior by veteran and even rookie partners. When his behavior persisted, confrontations with fellow officers became explosive. When peers were unable to check his behavior, complaints were made to superiors. Officially, colleagues indicated they did not want to work with him because of "personality problems." Informally, however, supervisors were informed of the nature of his provocative and dangerous behavior. The sergeant responded by putting the rookie in a wagon with a responsible partner whom he thought might succeed in controlling him. When this strategy proved unsuccessful, he was eventually transferred to the subway unit. Such transfers to "punishment districts," isolated posts, "inside units," or the subway are typical means of handling police officers deemed dangerous and out of control.

As this discussion indicates, the internal control of an exceptionally or inappropriately violent police officer is largely informal. With the exception of civilian complaints and brutality suits, the behavior of such officers rarely becomes the subject of formal police documents. However, their reputations are often well known throughout the department and the rumors about their indiscretions educate rookies about how the line between normal force and brutality is drawn among working police officers.

It takes more than one incident of excessively violent behavior for a police officer to attain a brutal reputation. The violent officer is usually involved in numerous acts of aggressive behavior that are not accountable as normal force either because of their frequency or because of their substance. However, once identified as "brutal," a "head beater," and so on, an officer's use of force will be condemned by peers in circumstances in which competent officers would be given the benefit of the doubt. For example, one officer gained national notoriety during a federal investigation into a suspicious shooting. Allegedly, a local resident had thrown an axe at the patrol wagon. According to available accounts, the police pursued the suspect inside a house and the officer in question shot him in the head. Although witnesses claimed the victim was unarmed, the officer stated that he fired in self defense. The suspect reportedly attacked him with a metal pipe. This policeman had an established reputation for being "good with his hands," and many colleagues assumed he had brutally shot an unarmed man in the aftermath of a pursuit."

CONCLUSION

The organization of policework reflects a poignant moral dilemma: for a variety of reasons, society mandates to the police the right to use force but provides little direction as to its proper use in specific, "real life" situations. Thus, the police, as officers of the law, must be prepared to use force under circumstances in which its rationale is often morally, legally, and practically ambiguous. This fact explains some otherwise puzzling aspects of police training and socialization.

The police academy provides a semblance of socialization for its recruits by teaching formal rules for using force. It is a semblance of socialization because it treats the use of force as capable of rationalization within the moral and legal conventions of the civilian world. The academy also, paradoxically, trains recruits in the use of tools of violence with potential for going far beyond the limitations of action imposed by those conventions. Consequently, the full socialization of a police officer takes place outside the academy as the officer moves from its idealizations to the practicalities of the street. This movement involves several phases: (1) a decisive, practical separation from the formal world established within the academy; (2) the cultivation of a working distinction between what is formally permissible and what is practically and informally required of the "street cop"; and (3) the demonstration of competence in using and accounting for routine street practices that are morally and legally problematic for those not working the street.

The original dilemma surrounding the use of force persists throughout the socialization process, but is increasingly dealt with by employing accounts provided by the police community that reduce and neutralize the moral tension. The experienced "street cop" becomes an expert at using techniques of neutralization (Sykes and Matza, 1957) to characterize the use of force on the streets, at judging its use by others, and at evaluating the necessity for using force by standards those techniques provide. Use of these techniques also reinforces the radical separation of the formal and informal worlds of policework, duplicating within the context of the organization itself the distinction between members and outsiders. This guarantees that members will be able to distinguish between those who can and cannot be trusted to use force and to understand the conditions under which its use is reasonable.

As accounts neutralizing the use of force, justifications and excuses both serve—though each in a different way—to manage the tension inherent in situations fraught with moral insecurity. They conventionalize but do not reform situations that are inherently charged and morally ambiguous. In this way they simultaneously preserve the self-image of police as agents of the conventional order, provide ways in which individual officers can resolve their personal doubts as to the moral status of their action and those of their colleagues, and reinforce the solidarity of the police community.

NOTES

1. Nonetheless masculine pronouns are generally used to refer to the police in this article, because the Metro P.D. remained dominated by men numerically, in style and in tone.
My fieldwork experience is discussed in detail in a forthcoming paper (Hunt, 1984).
2. Some officers also substitute a large heavy duty flashlight for the nightstick. If used correctly, the flashlight can inflict more damage than the baton and is less likely to break when applied to the head or other parts of the body.
3. For a discussion of the cultural distinction between "inside men" who handle desk and administrative tasks and "real cops" who work outside on the street, see Hunt (1984).

4. As the Metro City Police Commissioner commented in an interview: "In general, they (women) are physically weaker than males. . . . I believe they would be inclined to let their emotions all to frequently overrule their good judgment . . . there are periods in their life when they are psychologically unbalanced because of physical problems that are occurring within them."

5. The woman officer later explained that she did not obey the suspect's command because she saw no reflection of the partner in the suspect's glasses and therefore assumed he was lying.

6. Patrol officers do not view demented people as responsible for their acts and therefore do not hold them strictly culpable when they challenge an officer's authority (see Van Maanen, 1978: 231). In dealing with such persons, coercion other than that narrowly required for control and self-protection tends to be viewed as inappropriate and unjustifiable.

7. The combat high is a state of controlled exhilaration in which the officer experiences a heightened awareness of the world around him. Officers report that perception, smell, and hearing seem acute; one seems to stand outside oneself and the world appears extraordinarily vivid and clear. At the same time, officers insist that they are able to think rationally and instantly translate thoughts into action; when experienced, fear is not incapacitating but instead enhances the ability to act.

8. This police experience of fear and helplessness, leading to a violent outburst, may be analogized to a parent's reaction on seeing his child almost die in an accident. Imagine a scene in which a father is walking with his six-year-old son. Suddenly, the boy runs into the street to get a red ball on the pavement. The father watches a car slam on the brakes and miss the boy by two inches. He grabs his son and smacks him on the face before he takes him in his arms and holds him.

9. Rubinstein (1973: 304–305) describes a similar instance of police use of force.

10. According to Van Maanen (1978: 224), such persons tend to be labeled "assholes." The "asshole," who symbolically challenges an officer's control and thereby defies his definition of a situation, provokes the officer's wrath and becomes a likely candidate for street justice (Van Maanen, 1978: 224).

11. Note that this account employs both the justifications of reestablishing real and symbolic control, and the excuse of emotionally snapping out in response to this symbolic challenge and to the resulting pursuit.

12. Again, such affronts arise with different frequency and have different impact depending upon gender. Although policemen are occasionally subjected to sexual insults by women and teenage girls, this kind of harassment is more commonly experienced by women and thus constitutes a special type of affront to the female officer.

13. For a discussion of the significance of "the moral woman," see Hunt (1984).

14. The categories of persons who merit violence are not unique to the police. Prisoners, criminals, and hospital personnel appear to draw similar distinctions between morally unworthy persons; on the latter, see Sudnow (1967: 105).

15. Abstract force constitutes what Emerson (1969: 149) calls a "principled justification."

Here one depicts the act as an attempt to realize some absolute moral or social value that has precedence over the value violated by the act.

16. The suspect was known to other officers from prior encounters as a slightly demented cop antagonizer. Consequently, the officer's actions appeared completely unnecessary because he was not dealing with an unpredictable stranger. The suspect's neighbors depicted him as a mentally disturbed person who was deathly afraid of the police because he had been a frequent target of harassment.

REFERENCES

Bittner, E. (1980) *The Functions of the Police in Modern Society.* Cambridge, MA: Oelgeschlager, Gunn & Hain.

Blumberg, M. (1983) *The Use of Firearms by Police Officers: The Impact of Individuals, Communities, and Race.* Ph.D. dissertation. School of Criminal Justice, State University of New York at Albany.

Emerson, R. M. (1969) *Judging Delinquents: Context and Process in Juvenile Court.* Chicago: Aldine.

Friedrich, R. (1980) "Police use of force: Individuals, situations, and organizations." *The Annals* 452: 82–97.

Fyfe, J. J. (1983) "Police shootings: Environment, license and individuals." Presented at the Annual Meeting of the Amer. Society of Criminology.

Hunt, J. (forthcoming) "The development of rapport through the negotiation of gender in field work among police." *Human Organization*.

Lee, J. A. (1981) "Some structural aspects of police deviance in relation to minority groups," in C. D. Shearing (ed.) *Organizational Police Deviance*. Toronto: Butterworths.

Niederhoffer, A. (1967) *Behind the Shield: The Police in Urban Society*. Garden City, NY: Anchor-Doubleday.

Reiss, A. J. (1970) "Police brutality—answers to key questions," in A. Niederhoffer and A. S. Blumberg (eds.) *The Ambivalent Force: Perspectives on the Police*. Toronto: Xerox College Publishing.

Rubinstein, J. (1973) *City Police*. New York: Ballentine.

Scott, M. B. and S. M. Lyman (1968) "Accounts." *Amer. Soc. Rev.* 33: 46–62.

Skolnick, J. (1975) *Justice Without Trial*. New York: John Wiley.

Sudnow, D. (1967) *Passing On: The Social Organization of Dying*. Englewood Cliffs NJ: Prentice-Hall.

Sykes, G. M. and D. Matza (1957) "Techniques of neutralization: A theory of delinquency." *Amer. Soc. Rev.* 22: 664–70.

Van Maanen, J. (1978). "The asshole," in P. K. Manning and J. Van Maanen (eds.) *Policing: A View From the Street*. Santa Monica, CA: Goodyear.

Waegel, W. B. (1984) "The use of deadly force by police: The effect of statutory change." *Crime and Delinquency* 30: 121–140.

Westley, W. A. (1970) *Violence and the Police: A Sociological Study of Law, Custom and Morality*. Cambridge, MA: MIT.

19

Deviant Careers

HOWARD BECKER

The first step in most deviant careers is the commission of a nonconforming act, an act that breaks some particular set of rules. How are we to account for the first step?

People usually think of deviant acts as motivated. They believe that the person who commits a deviant act, even for the first time (and perhaps especially for the first time), does so purposely. His purpose may or may not be entirely conscious, but there is a motive force behind it. We shall turn to the consideration of cases of intentional nonconformity in a moment, but first I must point out that many nonconforming acts are committed by people who have no intention of doing so; these clearly require a different explanation.

Unintended acts of deviance can probably be accounted for relatively simply. They imply an ignorance of the existence of the rule, or of the fact that it was applicable in this case, or to this particular person. But it is necessary to account for the lack of awareness. How does it happen that the person does not know his act is improper? Persons deeply involved in a particular subculture (such as a religious or ethnic subculture) may simply be unaware that everyone does not act "that way" and thereby commit an impropriety. There may, in fact, be structured areas of ignorance of particular rules. Mary Haas has pointed out the interesting case of interlingual word taboos.[1] Words which are perfectly proper in one language have a "dirty" meaning in another. So the person, innocently using a word common in his own language, finds that he has shocked and horrified his listeners who come from a different culture.

In analyzing cases of intended nonconformity, people usually ask about motivation: why does the person want to do the deviant thing he does? The question assumes that the basic difference between deviants and those who conform lies in the character of their motivation. Many theories have been propounded to explain why some people have deviant motivations and others do not. Psychological theories find the cause of deviant motivations and acts in the individual's early experiences, which produce unconscious needs that must be satisfied if the individual is to maintain his equilibrium. Sociological theories look for socially structured sources of "strain" in the society, social positions which have conflicting demands placed upon them such that the individual seeks an illegitimate way of solving the problems his position presents him with. (Merton's famous theory of anomie fits into this category.)[2]

But the assumption on which these approaches are based may be entirely false. There is no reason to assume that only those who finally commit a deviant act actually have the impulse to do so. It is much more likely that most people experience deviant impulses frequently. At least in fantasy, people are much more deviant than they appear. Instead of asking why deviants want to do things that are disapproved of, we might better ask why conventional people do not follow through on the deviant impulses they have.

Something of an answer to this question may be found in the process of commitment through which the "normal" person becomes progressively involved in conventional institutions and behavior. In speaking of commitment,[3] I refer to the process through which several kinds of interests become bound up with carrying out certain lines of behavior to which they seem formally extraneous. What happens is that the individual, as a consequence of actions he has taken in the past or the operation of various institutional routines, finds he must adhere to certain lines of behavior, because many other activities than the one he is immediately engaged in will be adversely affected if he does not. The middle-class youth must not quit school, because his occupational future depends on receiving a certain amount of schooling. The conventional person must not indulge his interests in narcotics, for example, because much more than the pursuit of immediate pleasure is involved; his job, his family, and his reputation in his neighborhood may seem to him to depend on his continuing to avoid temptation.

In fact, the normal development of people in our society (and probably in any society) can be seen as a series of progressively increasing commitments to conventional norms and institutions. The "normal" person, when he discovers a deviant impulse in himself, is able to check that impulse by thinking of the manifold consequences acting on it would produce for him. He has staked too much on continuing to be normal to allow himself to be swayed by unconventional impulses.

This suggests that in looking at cases of intended nonconformity we must ask how the person manages to avoid the impact of conventional commitments. He may do so in one of two ways. First of all, in the course of growing up the person may somehow have avoided entangling alliances with conventional society. He may, thus, be free to follow his impulses. The person who does not have a reputation to maintain or a conventional job he must keep may follow his impulses. He has nothing staked on continuing to appear conventional.

However, most people remain sensitive to conventional codes of conduct and must deal with their sensitivities in order to engage in a deviant act for the first time. Sykes and Matza have suggested that delinquents actually feel strong impulses to be law-abiding, and deal with them by techniques of neutralization: "justifications for deviance that are seen as valid by the delinquent but not by the legal system or society at large." They distinguish a number of techniques for neutralizing the force of law-abiding values.

> In so far as the delinquent can define himself as lacking responsibility for his deviant actions, the disapproval of self or others is sharply reduced in effectiveness as a restraining influence. . . . The delinquent approaches a "billiard ball" conception of himself in which he sees himself as helplessly propelled into new situations. . . . By learning to view himself as more acted upon than acting, the delinquent prepares the way for deviance from the dominant normative system without the necessity of a frontal assault on the norms themselves. . . .
> A second major technique of neutralization centers on the injury or harm involved in the delinquent act. . . . For the delinquent . . . wrongfulness may turn on the question of whether or not anyone has clearly been hurt by his deviance, and this matter is open to a variety of interpretations. . . . Auto theft may be viewed as "borrowing," and gang fighting may be seen as a private quarrel, an agreed upon duel between two willing parties, and thus of no concern to the community at large. . . .
> The moral indignation of self and others may be neutralized by an insistence that the injury is not wrong in light of the circumstances. The injury, it may be claimed, is not really an injury; rather, it is a form of rightful retaliation or punishment. . . . Assaults on homosexuals or suspected homosexuals, at-

tacks on members of minority groups who are said to have gotten "out of place," vandalism as revenge on an unfair teacher or school official, thefts from a "crooked" store owner—all may be hurts inflicted on a transgressor, in the eyes of the delinquent. . . .

A fourth technique of neutralization would appear to involve a condemnation of the condemners. . . . His condemners, he may claim, are hypocrites, deviants in disguise, or impelled by personal spite. . . . By attacking others, the wrongfulness of his own behavior is more easily repressed or lost to view. . . .

Internal and external social controls may be neutralized by sacrificing the demands of the larger society for the demands of the smaller social groups to which the delinquent belongs such as the sibling pair, the gang, or the friendship clique. . . . The most important point is that deviation from certain norms may occur not because the norms are rejected but because other norms, held to be more pressing or involving a higher loyalty, are accorded precedence.[4]

In some cases a nonconforming act may appear necessary or expedient to a person otherwise law-abiding. Undertaken in pursuit of legitimate interests, the deviant act becomes, if not quite proper, at least not quite improper. In a novel dealing with a young Italian-American doctor we find a good example.[5] The young man, just out of medical school, would like to have a practice that is not built on the fact of his being Italian. But, being Italian, he finds it difficult to gain acceptance from the Yankee practitioners of his community. One day he is suddenly asked by one of the biggest surgeons to handle a case for him and thinks that he is finally being admitted to the referral system of the better doctors in town. But when the patient arrives at his office, he finds the case is an illegal abortion. Mistakenly seeing the referral as the first step in a regular relationship with the surgeon, he performs the operation. This act, although improper, is thought necessary to building his career.

But we are not so much interested in the person who commits a deviant act once as in the person who sustains a pattern of deviance over a long period of time, who makes of deviance a way of life, who organizes his identity around a pattern of deviant behavior. It is not the casual experimenters with homosexuality (who turned up in such surprisingly large numbers in the Kinsey Report) that we want to find out about, but the man who follows a pattern of homosexual activity throughout his adult life.

One of the mechanisms that lead from casual experimentation to a more sustained pattern of deviant activity is the development of deviant motives and interests. We shall examine this process in detail later, when we consider the career of the marihuana user. Here it is sufficient to say that many kinds of deviant activity spring from motives which are socially learned. Before engaging in the activity on a more or less regular basis, the person has no notion of the pleasures to be derived from it; he learns these in the course of interaction with more experienced deviants. He learns to be aware of new kinds of experiences and to think of them as pleasurable. What may well have been a random impulse to try something new becomes a settled taste for something already known and experienced. The vocabularies in which deviant motivations are phrased reveal that their users acquire them in interaction with other deviants. The individual *learns*, in short, to participate in a subculture organized around the particular deviant activity.

Deviant motivations have a social character even when most of the activity is carried on in a private, secret, and solitary fashion. In such cases, various media of communication may take the place of face-to-face interaction in inducting the individual into the culture. The pornographic pictures I mentioned earlier were described to prospective buyers in a stylized language. Ordinary words were used in a technical shorthand designed to whet specific tastes. The word "bondage," for instance, was used repeatedly to refer to pictures of women restrained in handcuffs or straitjackets. One does not acquire a taste for "bondage photos" without having learned what they are and how they may be enjoyed.

One of the most crucial steps in the process of building a stable pattern of deviant behavior is likely to be the experience of being caught and publicly labeled as a deviant. Whether a person takes this step or not depends not so much on what he does as on what other people do, on whether or not they enforce the rule he has violated. Although I will consider the circumstances under which enforcement takes place in some detail later, two notes are in order here. First of all, even though no one else discovers the nonconformity or enforces the rules against it, the individual who has committed the impropriety may himself act as enforcer. He may brand himself as deviant because of what he has done and punish himself in one way or another for his behavior. This is not always or necessarily the case, but may occur. Second, there may be cases like those described by psychoanalysts in which the individual really wants to get caught and perpetrates his deviant act in such a way that it is almost sure he will be.

In any case, being caught and branded as deviant has important consequences for one's further social participation and self-image. The most important consequence is a drastic change in the individual's public identity. Committing the improper act and being publicly caught at it place him in a new status. He has been revealed as a different kind of person from the kind he was supposed to be. He is labeled a "fairy," "dope fiend," "nut" or "lunatic," and treated accordingly.

In analyzing the consequences of assuming a deviant identity let us make use of Hughes' distinction between master and auxiliary status traits.[6] Hughes notes that most statuses have one key trait which serves to distinguish those who belong from those who do not. Thus the doctor, whatever else he may be, is a person who has a certificate stating that he has fulfilled certain requirements and is licensed to practice medicine; this is the master trait. As Hughes points out, in our society a doctor is also informally expected to have a number of auxiliary traits: most people expect him to be upper middle class, white, male, and Protestant. When he is not there is a sense that he has in some way failed to fill the bill. Similarly, though skin color is the master status trait determining who is Negro and who is white, Negroes are informally expected to have certain status traits and not to have others; people are surprised and find it anomalous if a Negro turns out to be a doctor or a college professor. People often have the master status trait but lack some of the auxiliary, informally expected characteristics; for example, one may be a doctor but be female or Negro.

Hughes deals with this phenomenon in regard to statuses that are well thought of, desired and desirable (noting that one may have the formal qualifications for entry into a status but be denied full entry because of lack of the proper auxiliary traits), but the same process occurs in the case of deviant statuses. Possession of one deviant trait may have a generalized symbolic value, so that people automatically assume that its bearer possesses other undesirable traits allegedly associated with it.

To be labeled a criminal one need only commit a single criminal offense, and this is all the term formally refers to. Yet the word carries a number of connotations specifying auxiliary traits characteristic of anyone bearing the label. A man who has been convicted of housebreaking and thereby labeled criminal is presumed to be a person likely to break into other houses; the police, in rounding up known offenders for investigation after a crime has been committed, operate on this premise. Further, he is considered likely to commit other kinds of crimes as well, because he has shown himself to be a person without "respect for the law." Thus, apprehension for one deviant act exposes a person to the likelihood that he will be regarded as deviant or undesirable in other respects.

There is one other element in Hughes' analysis we can borrow with profit: the distinction between master and subordinate statuses.[7] Some statuses, in our society as in others, override all other statuses and have a certain priority. Race is one of these. Membership in the Negro race, as socially defined, will override most other status considerations in most other situations; the fact that one is a physician or middle-class or female will not protect one from being treated as a Negro first and any of these other things second. The status of deviant (depending on the kind of deviance) is this kind of master status. One receives the status as a result of breaking a rule, and the identification proves to be more important than most others. One will be identified as a deviant first, before other identifications are made. The question is raised: "What kind of person would break such an important rule?" And the answer is given: "One who is different from the rest of us, who cannot or will not act as a moral human being and therefore might break other important rules." The deviant identification becomes the controlling one.

Treating a person as though he were generally rather than specifically deviant produces a self-fulfilling prophecy. It sets in motion several mechanisms which conspire to shape the person in the image people have of him.[8] In the first place, one tends to be cut off, after being identified as deviant, from participation in more conventional groups, even though the specific consequences of the particular deviant activity might never of themselves have caused the isolation had there not also been the public knowledge and reaction to it. For example, being a ho-

mosexual may not affect one's ability to do office work, but to be known as a homosexual in an office may make it impossible to continue working there. Similarly, though the effects of opiate drugs may not impair one's working ability, to be known as an addict will probably lead to losing one's job. In such cases, the individual finds it difficult to conform to other rules which he had no intention or desire to break, and perforce finds himself deviant in these areas as well. The homosexual who is deprived of a "respectable" job by the discovery of his deviance may drift into unconventional, marginal occupations where it does not make so much difference. The drug addict finds himself forced into other illegitimate kinds of activity, such as robbery and theft, by the refusal of respectable employers to have him around.

When the deviant is caught, he is treated in accordance with the popular diagnosis of why he is that way, and the treatment itself may likewise produce increasing deviance. The drug addict, popularly considered to be a weak-willed individual who cannot forego the indecent pleasures afforded him by opiates, is treated repressively. He is forbidden to use drugs. Since he cannot get drugs legally, he must get them illegally. This forces the market underground and pushes the price of drugs up far beyond the current legitimate market price into a bracket that few can afford on an ordinary salary. Hence the treatment of the addict's deviance places him in a position where it will probably be necessary to resort to deceit and crime in order to support his habit.[9] The behavior is a consequence of the public reaction to the deviance rather than a consequence of the inherent qualities of the deviant act.

Put more generally, the point is that the treatment of deviants denies them the ordinary means of carrying on the routines of everyday life open to most people. Because of this denial, the deviant must of necessity develop illegitimate routines. The influence of public reaction may be direct, as in the instances considered above, or indirect, a consequence of the integrated character of the society in which the deviant lives.

Societies are integrated in the sense that social arrangements in one sphere of activity mesh with other activities in other spheres in particular ways and depend on the existence of these other arrangements. . . .

Many varieties of deviance create difficulties by failing to mesh with expectations in other areas of life. Homosexuality is a case in point. Homosexuals have difficulty in any area of social activity in which the assumption of normal sexual interests and propensities for marriage is made without question. In stable work organizations such as large business or industrial organizations there are often points at which the man who would be successful should marry; not to do so will make it difficult for him to do things that are necessary for success in the organization and will thus thwart his ambitions. The necessity of marrying often creates difficult enough problems for the normal male, and places the homosexual in an almost impossible position. Similarly, in some male work groups where heterosexual prowess is required to retain esteem in the group, the homosexual has obvious difficulties. Failure to meet the expectations of others may force the individual to attempt deviant ways of achieving results automatic for the normal person.

Obviously, everyone caught in one deviant act and labeled a deviant does not move inevitably toward greater deviance in the way the preceding remarks might suggest. The prophecies do not always confirm themselves, the mechanisms do not always work. What factors tend to slow down or halt the movement toward increasing deviance? Under what circumstances do they come into play?

One suggestion as to how the person may be immunized against increasing deviance is found in a recent study of juvenile

delinquents who "hustle" homosexuals.[10] These boys act as homosexual prostitutes to confirmed adult homosexuals. Yet they do not themselves become homosexual. Several things account for their failure to continue this kind of sexual deviancy. First, they are protected from police action by the fact that they are minors. If they are apprehended in a homosexual act, they will be treated as exploited children, although in fact they are the exploiters; the law makes the adult guilty. Second, they look on the homosexual acts they engage in simply as a means of making money that is safer and quicker than robbery or similar activities. Third, the standards of their peer group, while permitting homosexual prostitution, allow only one kind of activity, and forbid them to get any special pleasure out of it or to permit any expressions of endearment from the adult with whom they have relations. Infractions of these rules, or other deviations from normal heterosexual activity, are severely punished by the boy's fellows.

Apprehension may not lead to increasing deviance if the situation in which the individual is apprehended for the first time occurs at a point where he can still choose between alternate lines of action. Faced, for the first time, with the possible ultimate and drastic consequences of what he is doing, he may decide that he does not want to take the deviant road, and turn back. If he makes the right choice, he will be welcomed back into the conventional community; but if he makes the wrong move, he will be rejected and start a cycle of increasing deviance.

Ray has shown, in the case of drug addicts, how difficult it can be to reverse a deviant cycle.[11] He points out that drug addicts frequently attempt to cure themselves and that the motivation underlying their attempts is an effort to show nonaddicts whose opinions they respect that they are really not as bad as they are thought to be. On breaking their habit successfully, they find, to their dismay, that people still treat them as though they were addicts (on the premise, apparently, of "once a junkie, always a junkie").

A final step in the career of a deviant is movement into an organized deviant group. When a person makes a definite move into an organized group—or when he realizes and accepts the fact that he has already done so—it has a powerful impact on his conception of himself. A drug addict once told me that the moment she felt she was really "hooked" was when she realized she no longer had any friends who were not drug addicts.

Members of organized deviant groups of course have one thing in common: their deviance. It gives them a sense of common fate, of being in the same boat. From a sense of common fate, from having to face the same problems, grows a deviant subculture: a set of perspectives and understandings about what the world is like and how to deal with it, and a set of routine activities based on those perspectives. Membership in such a group solidifies a deviant identity.

Moving into an organized deviant group has several consequences for the career of the deviant. First of all, deviant groups tend, more than deviant individuals, to be pushed into rationalizing their position. At an extreme, they develop a very complicated historical, legal, and psychological justification for their deviant activity. The homosexual community is a good case. Magazines and books by homosexuals and for homosexuals include historical articles about famous homosexuals in history. They contain articles on the biology and physiology of sex, designed to show that homosexuality is a "normal" sexual response. They contain legal articles, pleading for civil liberties for homosexuals.[12] Taken together, this material provides a working philosophy for the active homosexual, explaining to him why he is the way he is, that other people have also been that way, and why it is all right for him to be that way.

Most deviant groups have a self-justifying rationale (or "ideology"), although seldom is it as well worked out as that of the homosexual. While such rationales do operate, as pointed out earlier, to neutralize the conventional attitudes that deviants may still find in themselves toward their own behavior, they also perform another function. They furnish the individual with reasons that appear sound for continuing the line of activity he has begun. A person who quiets his own doubts by adopting the rationale moves into a more principled and consistent kind of deviance than was possible for him before adopting it.

The second thing that happens when one moves into a deviant group is that he learns how to carry on his deviant activity with a minimum of trouble. All the problems he faces in evading enforcement of the rule he is breaking have been faced before by others. Solutions have been worked out. Thus, the young thief meets older thieves who, more experienced than he is, explain to him how to get rid of stolen merchandise without running the risk of being caught. Every deviant group has a great stock of lore on such subjects and the new recruit learns it quickly.

Thus, the deviant who enters an organized and institutionalized deviant group is more likely than ever before to continue in his ways. He has learned, on the one hand, how to avoid trouble and, on the other hand, a rationale for continuing. . . .

NOTES

1. Mary R. Haas, "Interlingual Word Taboos," *American Anthropologist*, 53 (July-September, 1951), 338–344.
2. Robert K. Merton, *Social Theory and Social Structure* (New York: The Free Press of Glencoe, 1957), pp. 131–194.
3. I have dealt with this concept at greater length in "Notes on the Concept of Commitment," *American Journal of Sociology*, LXVI (July, 1960), 32–40.

See also Erving Goffman, *Encounters: Two Studies in the Sociology of Interaction* (Indianapolis: The Bobbs-Merrill Co., Inc., 1961), pp. 88–110; and Gregory P. Stone, "Clothing and Social Relations: A Study of Appearance in the Context of Community Life" (unpublished Ph.D. dissertation, Department of Sociology, University of Chicago, 1959).

4. Gresham M. Sykes and David Matza, "Techniques of Neutralization: A Theory of Delinquency," *American Sociological Review*, 22 (December, 1957), 667–669.

5. Guido D'Agostino, *Olives on the Apple Tree* (New York: Doubleday, Doran, 1940). I am grateful to Everett C. Hughes for calling this novel to my attention.

6. Everett C. Hughes, "Dilemmas and Contradictions of Status," *American Journal of Sociology*, L (March, 1945), 353–359.

7. *Ibid.*

8. See Marsh Ray, "The Cycle of Abstinence and Relapse Among Heroin Addicts," *Social Problems*, 9 (Fall, 1961), 132–140.

9. See *Drug Addiction: Crime or Disease?* Interim and Final Reports of the Joint Committee of the American Bar Association and the American Medical Association on Narcotic Drugs (Bloomington, Indiana: Indiana University Press, 1961).

10. Albert J. Reiss, Jr., "The Social Integration of Queers and Peers," *Social Problems*, 9 (Fall, 1961), 102–120.

11. Ray, *op. cit.*

12. *One* and *The Mattachine Review* are magazines of this type that I have seen.

20

The Promise

C. WRIGHT MILLS

Nowadays, men often feel that their private lives are a series of traps. They sense that, within their everyday worlds, they cannot overcome their troubles, and, in this feeling, they are quite correct: What ordinary men are directly aware of and what they try to do are bounded by the private orbits in which they live; their visions and their powers are limited to the close-up scenes of job, family, neighborhood; in other milieux, they move vicariously and remain spectators. And the more aware they become, however vaguely, of ambitions and of threats that transcend their immediate locales, the more trapped they seem to feel.

Underlying this sense of being trapped are seemingly impersonal changes in the very structure of continent-wide societies. The facts of contemporary history are also facts about the success and the failure of individual men and women. When a society is industrialized, a peasant becomes a worker; a feudal lord is liquidated or becomes a businessman. When classes rise or fall, a man is employed or unemployed; when the rate of investment goes up or down, a man takes new heart or goes broke. When wars happen, an insurance salesman becomes a rocket launcher; a store clerk, a radar man; a wife lives alone; a child grows up without a father. Neither the life of an individual nor the history of a society can be understood without understanding both.

Yet, men do not usually define the troubles they endure in terms of historical change and institutional contradiction. The well-being they enjoy, they do not usually impute to the big ups and downs of the societies in which they live. Seldom aware of the intricate connection between the patterns of their own lives and the course of world history, ordinary men do not usually know what this connection means for the kinds of men they are becoming and for the kinds of history-making in which they might take part. They do not possess the quality of mind essential to grasp the interplay of man and society, of biography and history, of self and world. They cannot cope with their personal troubles in such ways as to control the structural transformations that usually lie behind them.

Surely, it is no wonder. In what period have so many men been so totally exposed at so fast a pace to such earthquakes of change? That Americans have not known such catastrophic changes as have the men and women of other societies is due to historical facts that are now quickly becoming "merely history." The history that now affects every man is world history. Within this scene and this period, in the course of a single generation, one-sixth of mankind is transformed from all that is feudal and backward into all that is modern, advanced, and fearful. Political colonies are freed; new and less visible forms of imperialism, installed. Revolutions occur; men feel the intimate grip of new kinds of authority. Totalitarian societies rise, and are smashed to bits—or succeed fabulously. After two centuries of ascendancy, capitalism is shown up as only one way to make society into an industrial apparatus. After two centuries of hope, even formal democracy is restricted to a quite small portion of mankind. Everywhere in the underdeveloped world, ancient ways of life are broken up and vague expectations become urgent demands. Everywhere in the overdeveloped world, the means of authority and of violence become total in scope and bureaucratic in form. Humanity itself now lies before us, the supernation at either pole concentrating its most coordinated and massive efforts upon the preparation of World War III.

The very shaping of history now outpaces the ability of men to orient themselves in accordance with cherished values. And which values? Even when they do not panic, men often sense that older ways of feeling and thinking have collapsed, and that newer beginnings are ambiguous to the point of moral stasis. Is it any wonder that ordinary men feel they cannot cope with the larger worlds with which they are so suddenly confronted? That they cannot understand the meaning of their epoch for their own lives? That—in defense of selfhood—they become morally insensible, trying to remain altogether private men? Is it any wonder that they come to be possessed by a sense of the trap?

It is not only information that they need—in this Age of Fact, information often dominates their attention and overwhelms their capacities to assimilate it. It is not only the skills of reason that they need—although their struggles to acquire these often exhaust their limited moral energy.

What they need, and what they feel they need, is a quality of mind that will help them to use information and to develop reason in order to achieve lucid summations of what is going on in the world and of what may be happening within themselves. It is this quality, I am going to contend, that journalists and scholars, artists and publics, scientists and editors are coming to expect of what may be called the sociological imagination.

The sociological imagination enables its possessor to understand the larger historical scene in terms of its meaning for the inner life and the external career of a variety of individuals. It enables him to take into account how individuals, in the welter of their daily experience, often become falsely conscious of their social positions. Within that welter, the framework of modern society is sought, and within that framework the psychologies of a variety of men and women are formulated. By such means, the personal uneasiness of individuals is focused upon explicit troubles, and the indifference of publics is transformed into involvement with public issues.

The first fruit of this imagination—and the first lesson of the social science that embodies it—is the idea that the individual can understand his own experience and gauge his own fate only by locating himself within his period, that he can know his own chances in life only by becoming aware of those of all individuals in his circumstances. In many ways, it is a terrible lesson; in many ways, a magnificent one. We do not know the limits of man's capacities for supreme effort or willing degradation, for agony or glee, for pleasurable brutality or the sweetness of reason. But in our time we have come to know that the limits of "human nature" are frighteningly broad. We have come to know that every individual lives, from one generation to the next, in some society; that he lives out a biography, and that he lives it out within some historical sequence. By the fact of his living he contributes, however minutely, to the shaping of this society and to the course of its history, even as he is made by society and by its historical push and shove.

The sociological imagination enables us to grasp history and biography and the relations between the two within society. That is its task and its promise. To recognize this task and this promise is the mark of the classic social analyst. It is characteristic of Herbert Spencer—turgid, polysyllabic, comprehensive; of E. A. Ross—graceful, muckraking, upright; of Auguste Comte and

Emile Durkheim; of the intricate and subtle Karl Mannheim. It is the quality of all that is intellectually excellent in Karl Marx; it is the clue to Thorstein Veblen's brilliant and ironic insight, to Joseph Schumpeter's many-sided constructions of reality; it is the basis of the psychological sweep of W. E. H. Lecky no less than of the profundity and clarity of Max Weber. And it is the signal of what is best in contemporary studies of man and society.

No social study that does not come back to the problems of biography, of history, and of their intersections within a society has completed its intellectual journey. Whatever the specific problems of the classic social analysts, however limited or however broad the features of social reality they have examined, those who have been imaginatively aware of the promise of their work have consistently asked three sorts of questions:

1. What is the structure of this particular society as a whole? What are its essential components, and how are they related to one another? How does it differ from other varieties of social order? Within it, what is the meaning of any particular feature for its continuance and for its change?

2. Where does this society stand in human history? What are the mechanics by which it is changing? What is its place within, and its meaning for, the development of humanity as a whole? How does any particular feature we are examining affect, and how is it affected by, the historical period in which it moves? And this period—what are its essential features? How does it differ from other periods? What are its characteristic ways of history-making?

3. What varieties of men and women now prevail in this society and in this period? And what varieties are coming to prevail? In what ways are they selected and formed, liberated and repressed, made sensitive and blunted? What kinds of "human nature" are revealed in the conduct and character we observe in this society in this period? And

what is the meaning for "human nature" of each and every feature of the society we are examining?

Whether the point of interest is a great power state or a minor literary mood, a family, a prison, a creed—these are the kinds of questions the best social analysts have asked. They are the intellectual pivots of classic studies of man in society—and they are the questions inevitably raised by any mind possessing the sociological imagination. For that imagination is the capacity to shift from one perspective to another—from the political to the psychological; from examination of a single family to comparative assessment of the national budgets of the world; from the theological school to the military establishment; from considerations of an oil industry to studies of contemporary poetry. It is the capacity to range from the most impersonal and remote transformations to the most intimate features of the human self—and to see the relations between the two. Back of its use, there is always the urge to know the social and historical meaning of the individual in the society and in the period in which he has his quality and his being.

That, in brief, is why it is by means of the sociological imagination that men now hope to grasp what is going on in the world, and to understand what is happening in themselves as minute points of the intersections of biography and history within society. In large part, contemporary man's self-conscious view of himself as at least an outsider, if not a permanent stranger, rests upon an absorbed realization of social relativity and of the transformative power of history. The sociological imagination is the most fruitful form of this self-consciousness. By its use, men whose mentalities have swept only a series of limited orbits often come to feel as if suddenly awakened in a house with which they had only supposed themselves to be familiar. Correctly or incorrectly, they often come to feel that they can now provide themselves with adequate summations, cohesive assessments, comprehensive orientations. Older decisions that once appeared sound now seem to them products of a mind unaccountably dense. Their capacity for astonishment is made lively again. They acquire a new way of thinking, they experience a transvaluation of values: In a word, by their reflection and by their sensibility, they realize the cultural meaning of the social sciences.

Perhaps the most fruitful distinction with which the sociological imagination works is between the "personal troubles of milieu" and the "public issues of social structure." This distinction is an essential tool of the sociological imagination and a feature of all classic work in social science.

Troubles occur within the character of the individual and within the range of his immediate relations with others; they have to do with his self and with those limited areas of social life of which he is directly and personally aware. Accordingly, the statement and the resolution of troubles properly lie within the individual as a biographical entity and within the scope of his immediate milieu— the social setting that is directly open to his personal experience and, to some extent, his willful activity. A trouble is a private matter: Values cherished by an individual are felt by him to be threatened.

Issues have to do with matters that transcend these local environments of the individual and the range of his inner life. They have to do with the organization of many such milieux into the institutions of a historical society as a whole, with the ways in which various milieux overlap and interpenetrate to form the larger structure of social and historical life. An issue is a public matter: Some value cherished by publics is felt to be threatened. Often, there is a debate about what that value really is and about what it is that really threatens it. This debate is often without focus, if only because it is the very nature of an issue, unlike even widespread

trouble, that it cannot very well be defined in terms of the immediate and everyday environments of ordinary men. An issue, in fact, often involves a crisis in institutional arrangements, and often, too, it involves what Marxists call "contradictions" or "antagonisms."

In these terms, consider unemployment. When, in a city of 100,000, only one man is unemployed, that is his personal trouble, and for its relief we properly look to the character of the man, his skills, and his immediate opportunities. But when, in a nation of 50 million employees, 15 million men are unemployed, that is an issue, and we may not hope to find its solution within the range of opportunities open to any one individual. The very structure of opportunities has collapsed. Both the correct statement of the problem and range of possible solutions require us to consider the economic and political institutions of the society, and not merely the personal situation and character of a scatter of individuals.

Consider war. The personal problem of war, when it occurs, may be how to survive it or how to die in it with honor; how to make money out of it; how to climb into the higher safety of the military apparatus; or how to contribute to the war's termination. In short, according to one's values, to find a set of milieux and within it to survive the war or make one's death in it meaningful. But the structural issues of war have to do with its causes; with what types of men it throws up into command; with its effects upon economic and political, family and religious institutions, with the unorganized irresponsibility of a world of nation-states.

Consider marriage. Inside a marriage, a man and a woman may experience personal troubles; but, when the divorce rate during the first four years of marriage is 250 out of every 1,000 attempts, this is an indication of a structural issue having to do with the institutions of marriage and the family and other institutions that bear upon them.

Or consider the metropolis—the horrible, beautiful, ugly, magnificent sprawl of the great city. For many upper-class people, the personal solution to the problem of the city is to have an apartment with private garage under it in the heart of the city, and forty miles out, a house by Henry Hill, garden by Garrett Eckbo, on a hundred acres of private land. In these two controlled environments—with a small staff at each end and a private helicopter connection—most people could solve many of the problems of personal milieux caused by the facts of the city. But all this, however splendid, does not solve the public issues that the structural fact of the city poses. What should be done with this wonderful monstrosity? Break it all up into scattered units, combining residence and work? Refurbish it as it stands? Or, after evacuation, dynamite it and build new cities according to new plans in new places? What should those plans be? And who is to decide and to accomplish whatever choice is made? These are structural issues; to confront them and to solve them requires us to consider political and economic issues that affect innumerable milieux.

Insofar as an economy is so arranged that slumps occur, the problem of unemployment becomes incapable of personal solution. Insofar as war is inherent in the nation-state system and in the uneven industrialization of the world, the ordinary individual in his restricted milieu will be powerless—with or without psychiatric aid—to solve the troubles this system or lack of system imposes upon him. Insofar as the family as an institution turns women into darling little slaves and men into their chief providers and unweaned dependents, the problem of a satisfactory marriage remains incapable of purely private solution. Insofar as the overdeveloped megalopolis and the overdeveloped automobile are built-in features of the overdeveloped society, the issues of urban living will not be solved by personal ingenuity and private wealth.

What we experience in various and specific milieux, I have noted, is often caused by structural changes. Accordingly, to understand the changes of many personal milieux, we are required to look beyond them. And the number and variety of such structural changes increase as the institutions within which we live become more embracing and more intricately connected with one another. To be aware of the idea of social structure and to use it with sensibility is to be capable of tracing such linkages among a great variety of milieux. To be able to do that is to possess the sociological imagination.

What are the major issues for publics and the key troubles of private individuals in our time? To formulate issues and troubles, we must ask what values are cherished yet threatened, and what values are cherished and supported, by the characterizing trends of our period. In the case both of threat and of support, we must ask what salient contradictions of structure may be involved.

When people cherish some set of values and do not feel any threat to them, they experience *well-being*. When they cherish values but *do* feel them to be threatened, they experience a crisis—either as a personal trouble or as a public issue. And, if all their values seem involved, they feel the total threat of panic.

But suppose people are neither aware of any cherished values nor experience any threat? That is the experience of *indifference*, which, if it seems to involve all their values, becomes apathy. Suppose, finally, they are unaware of any cherished values, but still are very much aware of a threat? That is the experience of *uneasiness*, of anxiety, which, if it is total enough, becomes a deadly, unspecified malaise.

Ours is a time of uneasiness and indifference—not yet formulated in such ways as to permit the work of reason and the play of sensibility. Instead of troubles—defined in terms of values and threats—there is often the misery of vague uneasiness; instead of explicit issues, there is often merely the beat feeling that all is somehow not right. Neither the values threatened nor whatever threatens them has been stated; in short, they have not been carried to the point of decision. Much less have they been formulated as problems of social science.

In the 1930s, there was little doubt—except among certain deluded business circles—that there was an economic issue that was also a pack of personal troubles. In these arguments about the "crisis of capitalism," the formulations of Marx and the many unacknowledged reformulations of his work probably set the leading terms of the issue, and some men came to understand their personal troubles in these terms. The values threatened were plain to see and cherished by all; the structural contradictions that threatened them also seemed plain. Both were widely and deeply experienced. It was a political age.

But the values threatened in the era after World War II are often neither widely acknowledged as values nor widely felt to be threatened. Much private uneasiness goes unformulated; much public malaise and many decisions of enormous structural relevance never become public issues. For those who accept such inherited values as reason and freedom, it is the uneasiness itself that is the trouble; it is the indifference itself that is the issue. And it is the condition, of uneasiness and indifference, that is the signal feature of our period.

All this is so striking that it is often interpreted by observers as a shift in the very kinds of problems that need now to be formulated. We are frequently told that the problems of our decade, or even the crises of our period, have shifted from the external realm of economics and now have to do with the quality of individual life—in fact, with the question of whether there is soon going to be anything that can properly be called individual life. Not child labor but comic books, not poverty but mass leisure, are at the center of concern. Many great public issues as well as many private troubles are described in terms of "psychiatric"—often, it seems in a pathetic attempt to avoid the large issues and problems of modern society. Often, this statement seems to rest upon a provincial narrowing of interest to the Western societies, or even to the United States—thus ignoring two-thirds of mankind; often, too, it arbitrarily divorces the individual life from the larger institutions within which that life is enacted, and which on occasion bear upon it more grievously than do the intimate environments of childhood.

Problems of leisure, for example, cannot even be stated without considering problems of work. Family troubles over comic books cannot be formulated as problems without considering the plight of the contemporary family in its new relations with the newer institutions of the social structure. Neither leisure nor its debilitating uses can be understood as problems without recognition of the extent to which malaise and indifference now form the social and personal climate of contemporary American society. In this climate, no problems of the "private life" can be stated and solved without recognition of the crisis of ambition that is part of the very career of men at work in the incorporated economy.

It is true, as psychoanalysts continually point out, that people do often have the "increasing sense of being moved by obscure forces within themselves that they are unable to define." But it is *not* true, as Ernest Jones asserted, that "man's chief enemy and danger is his own unruly nature and the dark forces pent up within him." On the contrary: "Man's chief danger" today lies in the unruly forces of contemporary society itself, with its alienating methods of production, its enveloping techniques of political domination, its international anarchy—in a word, its pervasive transformations of the very "nature" of man and the conditions and aims of his life.

It is now the social scientist's foremost political and intellectual task—for here the two coincide—to make clear the elements of contemporary uneasiness and indifference. It is the central demand made upon him by other cultural workmen—by physical scientists and artists, by the intellectual community in general. It is because of this task and these demands, I believe, that the social sciences are becoming the common denominator of our cultural period, and the sociological imagination, our most needed quality of mind.

The Definition of the Situation

WILLIAM I. THOMAS

Preliminary to any self-determined act of behavior, there is always a stage of examination and deliberation which we may call *the definition of the situation*. And actually not only concrete acts are dependent on the definition of the situation, but gradually a whole life-policy and the personality of the individual himself follow from a series of such definitions.

But the child is always born into a group of people among whom all the general types of situation which may arise have already been defined and corresponding rules of conduct developed, and where he has not the slightest chance of making his definitions and following his wishes without interference. Men have always lived together in groups. Whether mankind has a true herd instinct or whether groups are held together because this has worked out to advantage is of no importance. Certainly the wishes in general are such that they can be satisfied only in a society. But we have only to refer to the criminal code to appreciate the variety of ways in which the wishes of the individual may conflict with the wishes of society. And the criminal code takes no account of the many unsanctioned expressions of the wishes which society attempts to regulate by persuasion and gossip.

There is therefore always a rivalry between the spontaneous definitions of the situation made by the member of an organized society and the definitions which his society has provided for him. The individual tends to a hedonistic selection of activity, pleasure first; and society to a utilitarian selection, safety first. Society wishes its member to be laborious, dependable, regular, sober, orderly, self-sacrificing; while the individual wishes less of this and more of new experience. And organized society seeks also to regulate the conflict and competition inevitable between its members in the pursuit of their wishes. The desire to have wealth, for example, or any other socially sanctioned wish, may not be accomplished at the expense of another member of the society—by murder, theft, lying, swindling, blackmail, etc.

It is in this connection that a moral code arises, which is a set of rules or behavior norms regulating the expression of the wishes, and which is built up by successive definitions of the situation. In practice the abuse arises first and the rule is made to prevent its recurrence. Morality is thus the generally accepted definition of the situation, whether expressed in public opinion and the unwritten law, in a formal legal code, or in religious commandments and prohibitions.

The family is the smallest social unit and the primary defining agency. As soon as the child has free motion and begins to pull, tear, pry, meddle, and prowl, the parents begin to define the situation through speech and other signs and pressures: "Be quiet," "Sit up straight," "Blow your nose," "Wash your face," "Mind your mother," "Be kind to sister," etc. This is the real significance of Wordsworth's phrase, "Shades of the prison house begin to close upon the growing child." His wishes and activities begin to be inhibited, and gradually, by definitions within the family, by playmates, in the school, in the Sunday school, in the community, through reading, by formal instruction, by informal signs of approval and disapproval, the growing member learns the code of his society.

In addition to the family we have the community as a defining agency. At present the community is so weak and vague that it gives us no idea of the former power of the local group in regulating behavior. Originally the community was practically the whole world of its members. It was composed of families related by blood and marriage and was not so large that all the members could not come together; it was a face-to-face group. I asked a Polish peasant what was the extent of an *"okolica"* or neighborhood—how far it reached. "It reaches," he said, "as far as the report of a man reaches—as far as a man is talked about." And it was in communities of this kind that the moral code which we now recognize as valid originated. The customs of the community are "folkways," and both state and church have in their more formal codes mainly recognized and incorporated these folkways. . . .

A less formal but not less powerful means of defining the situation employed by the community is gossip. The Polish peasant's statement that a community reaches as far as a man is talked about was significant, for the community regulates the behavior of its members largely by talking about them. Gossip has a bad name because it is sometimes malicious and false and designed to improve the status of the gossiper and degrade its object, but gossip is in the main true and is an organizing force. It is a mode of defining the situation in a given case and of attaching praise or blame. It is one of the means by which the status of the individual and of his family is fixed.

The community also, particularly in connection with gossip, knows how to attach opprobrium to persons and actions by using epithets which are at the same time brief and emotional definitions of the situation.

"Bastard," "whore." "traitor," "coward," "skunk," "scab," "snob," "kike," etc., are such epithets. In "Faust" the community said of Margaret, "She stinks." The people are here employing a device known in psychology as the "conditioned reflex." If, for example, you place before a child (say six months old) an agreeable object, a kitten, and at the same time pinch the child, and if this is repeated several times, the child will immediately cry at the sight of the kitten without being pinched; of if a dead rat were always served beside a man's plate of soup he would eventually have a disgust for soup when served separately. If the word "stinks" is associated on people's tongues with Margaret, Margaret will never again smell sweet. Many evil consequences, as the psychoanalysts claim, have resulted from making the whole of sex life a "dirty" subject, but the device has worked in a powerful, sometimes a paralyzing way on the sexual behavior of women.

Winks, shrugs, nudges, laughter, sneers, haughtiness, coldness, "giving the once-over" are also language defining the situation and painfully felt as unfavorable recognition. The sneer, for example, is incipient vomiting, meaning, "you make me sick."

And eventually the violation of the code even in an act of no intrinsic importance, as in carrying food to the mouth with the knife, provokes condemnation and disgust. The fork is not a better instrument for conveying food than the knife, at least it has no moral superiority, but the situation has been defined in favor of the fork. To smack with the lips in eating is bad manners with us, but the Indian has more logically defined the situation in the opposite way; with him smacking is a compliment to the host.

In this whole connection fear is used by the group to produce the desired attitudes in its member. Praise is used also but more sparingly. And the whole body of habits and emotions is so much a community and family product that disapproval or separation is almost unbearable.

PART THREE

Reality Negotiation with Others

One might contend that the process of living within society consists of a series of reality negotiations. Reality negotiation refers to the process whereby individuals interpret, try to make sense of, and cognitively process events that occur around them. The outcome, a negotiation of social reality, is based on the combination of objective social events and the subjective interpretation of those events. Important aspects of reality negotiation include both understanding and creation. In terms of understanding, people process different kinds of information in the day-to-day social world in an overall attempt to create a sense of understanding that is motivated in part by a desire to have order and stability in one's personal life. Individuals often create social reality through a similar process. In this sense, social reality is not a constant, but instead is defined and redefined continually by societal participants. In essence, social reality is not an objective feature within society, but is based on human and social group needs through the subjective experience.

Central to reality construction is how individuals are thought to define situations. An important aspect of this particular line of reasoning involves "The Definition of the Situation" as first proposed by William I. Thomas. This definition is usually referred to as the unique interpretation of a situation that humans obtain through the process of social interaction and sometimes pass on to others through socialization. Therefore, some definitions are provided for us *a priori*, while others occur through the process of social interaction. The source of definitions provided for us often come from significant others and pertain to social expectations of conformity and morality. These are taught to us through the process of socialization. Therefore, how individuals come to define situations is central to an understanding of human behavior and social interaction.

As suggested earlier, social interaction necessarily involves reality construction, part of which includes emergent definitions of the situation. An emergent situational definition is the product of a complex social interchange that usually involves two individuals but may also occur within a small group. Whatever the case, the definition of the situation, as traditionally described in social psychology, pertains to the micro level. Within the micro-level context of social interaction, people engage in social intercourse and leave the encounter with some type of understanding of the exchange. During the exchange, however, the participants negotiate social reality with one another based on the dynamics of the encounter, the definition of the situation, and their own interpretation ability. Since the definition of the situation is concerned not only with the objective features of the situation (words, setting, appearance, images, etc.), subjective elements (interpretation, attachment of meaning, etc.) are of equal importance to understanding the social construction of reality. The latter, the subjective dimension to social reality, is essential, because it is here that the emergent definition of the situation derives and social meaning originates. Given that the social construction of reality is largely based on this subjective dimension, it is important to ascertain the effect of accuracy on situational definitions. In other words, how correct are our social perceptions that emerge during and after social interaction?

Accuracy, as applied to social reality and its creation, is in the eye of the beholder. That is, since social reality is constructed, and since this construction involves a subjective interpretation of objective features of the situation, it is accurate to the interpreter if this understanding serves his or her purposes. Given the subjective element and the human tendency to place immense faith in social perceptions of others and situations, true accuracy will seldom be achieved (nor is it important to the interpreter). However, if the individual places faith in social perceptions, he or she will define them as accurate. Therefore, social reality is emergent, allusive, and open to each individual's unique understanding of the social world.

As mentioned above, our understanding of the social world is based on interpretation, situational definitions, and the social construction of reality. It is also couched in experience, social learning, and a desire for society to appear a certain way to us. In addition, we often want others to see us in a certain way. In our day-to-day granted social interaction with others, we attempt to "put our best foot forward," or give others a certain impression of ourselves. As a common denominator in the process of social interaction and reality construction, our ability and desire to manage the impressions of us that others have makes us uniquely human. Self-presentation involves projecting to others the image of us that we want them to have. In response, others will interpret our actions or behavior and create their own definitions of the situation using the information provided to them combined with their ability to construct situational definitions based on our actions. It is the social actor's hope that the social exchange, or social interaction, will proceed smoothly without a breakdown in the image that is projected or the definition of the situation constructed by others. In this sense, then, two definitions of the situation are operating. The first is the definition of the situation that social actors wish others to receive, and the other is the definition that is constructed by those receiving the information through social interaction.

The concepts of the definition of the situation, the social construction of reality, and the presentation of self are all essential in achieving a better understanding of human behavior from a social psychological perspective. These ideas become yet more complex when applied to day-to-day social experience. In particular, there are several areas where these ideas lay important foundations for a clearer understanding of social processes and social behavior, namely in reality negotiation between unequal social participants, in specific interpersonal relationship forms, and in certain social settings. These three domains of application are addressed below.

First, it is essentially a given that society is made of unequal participants. Individuals are not born into an equal field of play, and such inequality often follows a person throughout life. While this is frequently considered a social structural issue since it affects large groups of people, inequality has a profound microscopic or social psychological influence as well. The impact of social class, ethnic and racial group membership, gender, and other forms of superordinate and subordinate relations will affect the process of interaction between social actors. These influences offer a glimpse into how social psychology can bridge the gulf between the macro and micro dimensions of human existence.

Human existence is made up of dominant and subordinate positions within the larger social structure. There are many people who may share aspects of their dominant or subordinate positions, but the central question for social psychology is how these macro relationships show up on the more micro social psychological level with regard to the process of reality negotiation.

Second, social psychology and reality negotiation have important and relevant applications to interpersonal relationships. With a broader conception of the social dynamic than is suggested above, the social nature of interpersonal relationships may or may not involve an overt demonstration of dominance and subordination. Nonetheless, the social construction of reality is a constant element in human interpersonal interactions, with intimate relations being no exception. One may speak of two social realities within the simplest interpersonal experience, the dyad. Each participant will possess a unique understanding of the social nature of that relationship and that definition will be determined in part by whether the needs of each participant are satisfied.

Needs come in many forms, including belonging, loving, and attachment. These and other needs are met through the creation and maintenance of interpersonal bonds. Each person may determine whether his or her psychological and social needs are being met within a relationship. Sometimes, however, interpersonal relations do not continue if the social exchange does not involve equity. In this sense, interpersonal relationship bonds can, and do, end at different levels, such as marriage, friendship, and acquaintance. Regardless of the level, reality negotiation and creation will influence the continued vitality of the relationship. One can say with a degree of surety that interpersonal relationships in the form of a dyad are characterized by two reality perceptions. This is often at the center of describing the interpersonal marital dyad as a combination of "her marriage" and "his marriage."

Finally, social setting greatly influences the reality negotiation process. This particular proposition pertains to the environmental influences, which at least partially cause certain behaviors. Depending on the social setting, social expectations for behavior differ. For instance, one will not observe the same behavior at a wedding ceremony as at a wedding reception. Social setting can both elicit and inhibit certain forms of behavior. In terms of prosocial behavior, social psychologists know that increased group size inhibits people from assisting someone in a crisis or an emergency due to a diffusion of responsibility. Therefore, motive and motivation to act are tied to the social setting, as are the origins of motive as they materialize in behavior. It has been said that an individual uses a "vocabulary of motive" to explain behavior, regardless of the person's motive for engaging in a given behavior. This "vocabulary" need not, however, be concerned with the actual motive or motivation for the behavior. As a social construction, then, vocabularies of motive are used to explain behavior. It is assumed that we have reasons, or motivations for our behavior. By understanding these motives, which albeit are sometimes self-serving, social psychologists may be better able to explain why a person follows a particular course of action.

THE SELECTIONS

Each of the selections in this part of the book in some way address the theme of reality negotiation between social actors within society. The first piece, Thomas's "Definition of the Situation," which is an excerpt from a larger work, may be the definitive statement on reality negotiation. Thomas describes how our interpretation of social information guides our interpretation of events and person perceptions. In addition to its interpretive ability, the definition of the situation is also the benchmark for what has been come to be known as the "Thomas Theorem," which states that "If men (people) define situations as real, they are real in their consequences." This essentially means that people respond not only to the objective features of a given situation, but also to their subjective interpretation of the situation. The social psychological importance of this unassuming statement cannot be overstated. The definition of the situation and Thomas's work have truly had a profound impact on social psychology and the topic of reality negotiation, as each of the articles within this section will demonstrate.

The second selection, which also deals directly with the definition of the situation, combines social psychology, clinical sociology, and crisis intervention. In "Uses of Clinical Sociology in Crisis Intervention Practice," I discuss the contribution that social psychology, and in particular the work of Thomas and the definition of the situation, can have for crisis intervention as a helping profession. I outline how the definition of the situation is instrumental in crisis formation.

The next two selections both address the nature of power and reality negotiation within interpersonal relations. The first, "Negotiating Reality" by Thomas J. Scheff, describes the complex process that ends in a shared definition of responsibility between participants of unequal social stature as applied to legal and psychiatric settings. In "The Doctor-Nurse Game" by Leonard I. Stein, which illustrates social identity and subordination, an additional superordinate-subordinate dimension of the negotiation of reality is examined. Stein cleverly demonstrates how nurses have been taught through their medical socialization not only to show deference to doctors in their professional conduct, but also to give doctors positive reinforcement in order to help the doctors maintain their social identity and poise. In addition to these dimensions, Stein provides examples of how reality is negotiated between doctors and nurses so that each participant can save face, and how nurses may actually wield power over doctors within certain contexts.

The next two selections, both by Erving Goffman, also address the notion of situational definitions and go further in discussing the intricate nature of self-presentation within society. Written only a few years apart, both deal quite effectively with the process of reality negotiation between social actors. The first, "Presenting the Self to Others," is an excerpt from a larger work, outlines how humans purposefully attempt to present themselves in a certain fashion. Goffman maintains that everyone wishes to be perceived in a certain way, which involves the image we wish to project to others, or "expressions given." However, the interaction process is much more complex because social actors have the ability to interpret the symbols of such images and create their own definitions of the situation. These are "expressions given off," or those impressions that others really receive, based on our overt behavior. Goffman also illustrates the process of self-presentation in "Stigma" from the book by the same name. He defines stigma and explains how those possessing a social stigma might manage their impressions for others. As Goffman points out, the perceptions of those who have a social stigma leads the perceiver to believe that the stigma is somehow connected to the stigmatized person's character or personality. The social perception that others have about those who are defined as having flawed selves is a powerful interpersonal dimension within reality negotiation.

Reality is also negotiated and constructed within important interpersonal relations. The two selections pertaining to creating, maintaining, and ending interpersonal bonds deal with the social institution of marriage. Just as any relationship has objective features, marital dyads and other forms of close interpersonal attachment are governed largely by the participants' individual and shared definitions of the situation. The selection by Peter L. Berger and Hansfried Kellner, "Marriage and the Construction of Reality," illustrates this process in the most common interpersonal dyad found within society. The second selection speaks of the end rather than the beginning of this interpersonal bond. Diane Vaughan's "Uncoupling: The Social Construction of Divorce" analyzes the very difficult process of undoing the social construction of marriage. Both coupling and uncoupling involve the process of reality construction as applied to this interpersonal dyad.

The final two selections keep with the reality construction theme, and deal with aspects of situational definitions and the motives for action and inaction. In the selection on prosocial behavior, "Social Determinants of Bystander Intervention in Emergencies," Bibb Latané and John M. Darley present experiments that uncover possible reasons for bystander apathy and inaction in the face of a crisis or emergency. Although most people might say they would assist a person in need without hesitancy or any expectation for reciprocity (normally referred to as altruism), there are situational factors that may actually impede one's motivation to offer assistance. The authors discuss how emergency situations involve definitions of the situation and what factors influence helping behavior.

In "Situated Actions and Vocabularies of Motive," C. Wright Mills discusses the importance of interpreting behavior as a complex vocabulary of motive used to explain human behavior. Mills, like Latané and Darley, places much emphasis on the influence of the social setting or situation. For Mills, the influence emerges with regard to eliciting certain vocabularies of motive. Here, he attempts to outline an analytic model, which he calls a "sociological psychology," for use in examining the role of language and motive.

FOR FURTHER READING

Peter L. Berger and Thomas Luckmann. *The Social Construction of Reality: A Treatise in the Sociology of Knowledge.* Garden City, NY: Doubleday Anchor Books, 1966.

Erving Goffman. *Interaction Ritual: Essays on Face-to-Face Behavior.* Garden City, NY: Doubleday Anchor Books, 1967.

Burkart Holzner. *Reality Construction in Society.* Cambridge, MA: Schenkman Publishing Company, Inc., 1968.

Harold Kelley. *Personal Relationships: Their Structures and Processes.* Hillsdale, NJ: Lawrence Erlbaum Associates, Publishers, 1979.

Howard Schwartz and Jerry Jacobs. *Qualitative Sociology: A Method to the Madness.* New York: The Free Press, 1979.

Diane Vaughan. *Uncoupling: Turning Points in Intimate Relationships.* New York: Vintage Books, 1986.

22

Uses of Clinical Sociology in Crisis Intervention Practice

BRYAN BYERS

For many years, crisis intervention has been a viable helping strategy. Beginning as a formal approach some 40 years ago (Lindemann, 1944), the field began to flourish. Crisis intervention was primarily attached to the medical profession so it employed a medical model. Logically, then, the major emphasis has been on psychiatric-psychological approaches of crisis definition and resolution. Recently, however, it has become apparent that there was a valuable social component to crises, which could be used in crisis intervention theory and practice.

As a helping strategy, crisis intervention includes theory (how crises are produced, types of crisis, etc.) and practice (skills for effective crisis resolution). This paper will present practical considerations for theory and practice while integrating principles of clinical sociology. The typology of crisis, crisis event interpretation, and crisis formation will be examined. . . .

CRISIS INTERVENTION AND CLINICAL SOCIOLOGY

In approaching crisis intervention, it is useful to integrate some of the ideas of "sociological intervention" (Straus, 1984) and "social behavioral intervention" (Straus, 1982) into the existing operational framework (Byers and Hendricks, 1985; Hendricks, 1984). Clinical sociology is the use of sociological knowledge and concepts for positive change, while crisis intervention is emergency emotional first-aid. Although distinctively different in definition, the two areas can be usefully integrated. The ideas of the sociological tradition are compatible with crisis intervention practice; it should prove beneficial to integrate sociological knowledge with the existing psychological and psychiatric tradition. This will not only broaden the eclectic nature of the approach, it will also offer the client more effective treatment. In other words, using interventionist strategies from different perspectives increases the likelihood that the client will receive appropriate and effective attention. Intervention strategies are situational. No one approach is appropriate at all times. However, coupling sociological practice and crisis intervention allows for an effective effort. The contention that clinical sociology should be used in company with other counseling, therapeutic, change, and intervention strategies was posited early (Jaques, 1947; Lee, 1955; Link, 1948; White, 1947; Wirth, 1931). Furthermore, the utility of sociology in therapy has been suggested in a number of recent publications (Black and Enos, 1980; Church, 1985; Glassner and Freedman, 1979; Hurvitz, 1979; Moreno and Glassner, 1979; Polak, 1971; Straus, 1979, . . . 1982, 1984). A unidisciplinary approach to the problem of personal crisis runs the risk of possibly missing important information that knowledge from another discipline might provide. As Glassner and Freedman (1979:12) have noted, "The work of crisis interventionists can be quite instructive for some aspects of clinical sociological practice." Taking this position a step further, there is a reciprocal benefit to be gained from the combined use of crisis intervention and clinical sociology. Individuals do not experience crises in a psychological vacuum; personal crises must be examined from a perspective which recognizes the role of society and the social forces which influence the individual.

Most people are thrust into crisis many times throughout a normal life cycle. The intervener must be prepared to tend to individuals in crisis in order to help restore them, at the very least, to a stable level of functioning. This is an explicit goal of crisis intervention. Stable functioning may be defined as a constitutional state where the client is capable of understanding the crisis, demonstrating effective social and psychological functioning, and learning from the crisis and the intervention. This will leave the client better equipped for future crises. Intervention is on the micro level and should entail an understanding of the client's social environment as well as psychological, affective, and behavioral aspects. This understanding of the social realm is evidence of the importance of integration, as are themes that characterize clinical sociology and that are also well suited for crisis intervention. These include a practice orientation, focus on case studies, a diagnostic nature, change-orientation, a humanistic position (Freedman, 1982), and "minimal intervention" (Straus, 1982:63). In a minimal intervention the intervener monitors and keeps at a minimum the span of interventions, the helper's authoritarian role, and the expectations for change placed on clients. (See Straus, 1982:6–7, for a complete description of "minimal intervention.") These concepts help the intervener understand the dynamics that must be dealt with within the client's social environment.

Clinical sociology offers the intervener a wide array of interpretive strategies for problem identification and solution. These include such concepts as socialization, status, role, in-group/out-group, group dynamics, conflict, interactionism, situational analysis, definition of the situation, etc. Through a utilization of the sociological perspective, then, the intervener will gain necessary insight into the social nature and function of interpersonal and intrapersonal crisis. With this understanding, the intervener may step into the crisis situation with more than the customary level of knowledge associated with crisis intervention.

Although the intervener deals directly with the individual, the social reality of the client must be recognized. This may entail intervention which not only leads to change in the individual but also to change within a dyad, a family or a social group. The orientation of the clinical sociological approach affects the group level even when an individual is being treated (Glass, 1979; Lee, 1979; Moreno and Glassner, 1979). This type of influence may be desired as part of the intervention strategy, or it may be a therapeutic by-product of the encounter. The intervener must treat the individual as a social being on the micro level while taking into account the social and/or sociological variables which influence behavior and affect. Crisis intervention and clinical sociology are both intervention strategies, and both can be applied on the micro or individual level. Further, crisis intervention is active rather than passive or neutral, as is clinical sociology. As Fritz (1985) states, "Clinical sociology is intervention work." Both approaches are defined by explicit intervention, that is, intervention for positive change.

PERSONAL CRISIS

A crisis might emerge when an individual experiences unpleasant socioemotional feelings, which result from the onset of a perceived insurmountable stressful life event. This is accompanied by an inability to cope with or adjust to the event. These are common components of personal *crisis defini-tion* (Rapaport, 1962; Smith, 1978). The "socioemotional" basis of feelings assumes that there is a close connection between social reality and one's affective state. For our use, a crisis may be defined as:

> The unpleasant psychological and social feelings/sensations, which result from the onset of a perceived insurmountable stressful life event, disrupting stability, and accompanied by an inability to adjust or cope.

According to Morrice (1976), emotional crises may present themselves in two generic forms: "accidental" or "developmental." These typologies aid the intervener in ascertaining the nature of the crisis and the appropriate intervention. The accidental form of crisis has been described by Morrice as those events in life which create an emotional impasse, cause emotional turmoil, and are temporarily incapacitating. Accidental crises are unexpected or unintended. This typology includes crises which result from sudden traumatic stress. Examples include: divorce, relationship conflict, school failure, loss of health, loss of work, death of a loved one. We all have ideals concerning how life should flow; however, the ideal is not always the reality. Even if one expects a crisis to materialize (e.g., a long-troubled marriage, terminal illness), the degree of trauma experienced when the event happens is not necessarily less. For instance, one may know cognitively that a loved one is dying of cancer, but that might not necessarily soften the impact of the stress produced by the loss. On the other hand, experiencing the long-term death of a loved one might produce more stress than the final demise. The death may be a relief rather than an incapacitating experience. Accidental crises include impasses that are not expected during an ideal life course. It is important to remember that individuals respond to stressful life events through a complex socialization process. Learning takes place through a myriad of life experiences and conditions. The response to stressful life events might hinge on how one's life situations and life chances have been formed.

The developmental category of crisis is characterized as consisting of events which are normal life experiences, but which may also produce crisis reactions. Some examples of developmental crises include growing old, getting married, sexual identity, graduation from school (high school or college), children leaving home (empty nest), value conflict, dominant-subordinate relationships. These events will not produce crisis in everyone experiencing them, of course. However, they may produce a crisis reaction under certain circumstances. The social and/or sociological nature of these two types of crisis is obvious. As stated by Burgess and Baldwin (1981:31): "Every emotional crisis is an interpersonal event involving at least one significant other person who is represented in the crisis situation directly, indirectly, or symbolically." Crises are produced in the individual through social circumstances. Social life is, at times, stressful. A certain degree of life stress is required and desirable. On a clinical level, the majority of clients treated by counselors and psychotherapists have stress-related problems (Straus, 1979). Social circumstances set the stage for individual stress reactions and crisis event interpretation.

CRISIS EVENT INTERPRETATION

Events which occur in one's life do not, alone, produce crisis. An *interpretation of the event* must take place. That is, the situation must be perceived as a crisis before the individual will react to the crisis. The concept of the "definition of the situation" is quite applicable here (Thomas, 1931). (Lydia Rapaport, 1962:211, a prominent crisis theorist, also cites W. I. Thomas as a useful social theorist in this area.) An individual presented with a potential crisis-producing situation must first define the situation or the context of the crisis. The situation may be interpreted as one of crisis or one of normalcy. It is through a definitional process that situations will be interpreted as a threat to emotional stability or as an event which poses no threat. As See and Straus (1985:66) have described, in order to understand another human being one must "discover (a) how he or she actually interprets the meaning of different kinds of situations; and (b) how he or she has come to analyze situations in that particular way." This type of analysis is useful because it enables the crisis intervener to make sense of the situation based on the social characteristics of the case. As mentioned above, the crises which characteristically affect individuals have either social influences or social causes. Individuals react to external stressors by cognitively internalizing the meaning of the crisis precipitator (hazardous event) according to personal interpretation. The crisis precipitator is any social event which has the potential to be perceived as a threat to socioemotional stability. The event is termed a "precipitator" because it precedes the crisis onset. For example, the death of a loved one may not be a crisis event until 1) the death notification has been made, and 2) the information is situationally defined. Points such as these make it important to examine the crisis situation from a clinical sociological perspective.

When describing the onset of crisis and the circumstances that produce the crisis, much of the literature describes the hazardous event, the perception of that event, the resulting feelings, and the inability to find immediate solutions (Smith, 1978). Thus, the nature of the crisis event and its interpretation, although commonly found in the psychological or psychiatric literature, may be described well through the components of interactionism or sociological social psychology. The precipitating event is commonly a social event, or at least has repercussions on the social level, which provides a basis for a social psychological interpretation of the process.

CRISIS FORMATION PROCESS

In order to intervene effectively in a crisis situation, one must have an accurate understanding of the process through which a crisis is produced. This is the crisis formation process. Also, the intervener needs to utilize an effective and efficient intervention process, that is, a procedure designed specifically as a guide to intervention while providing help to the client in crisis.

Crisis Formation Process

This is the course through which the client progresses on the way to emotional instability. Before the process begins, it is often assumed that the individual has a balanced state of affect and thought. As mentioned earlier, this is not always the case. Examples include families which have been slowly destroyed by terminal illness, domestic violence, or an alcoholic family member. In these instances, structural factors within the family must be taken into account as possible and probable contributors to a crisis. Individuals do not go untouched by prior or current events. Crisis is not experienced in a psychological vacuum. Although the client may have exhibited precrisis emotional stability, other factors often come into play to form a crisis.

Many early crisis theorists referred to the stress-producing nature of crisis situations. Partly due to ties to the medical profession, homeostasis and physiological reactions to stress were used to explain crisis (Caplan, 1964; Lindemann, 1944). It was not until the work of Howard J. Parad that it was recognized that "the event precipitating the crisis must be perceived by the person as a stressful situation before it can become a crisis" (Smith, 1978:397).

The *precipitating event,* or hazardous event, presents a threat to emotional stability. These events come in a variety of forms, such as the death of a loved one, relationship failure (divorce, breakup), interpersonal conflict, unfair social structure, or professional practices. However, it is not the event per se that produces the state of crisis. It is through a *definition of the situation* (Thomas, 1931) that the event is defined as an unpleasant occurrence. The individual first interprets the event in terms of its emotional and social consequences. Different events carry different levels of social and emotional impact depending on the nature of the event and the person experiencing it. For example, a relationship breakup might be very devastating for one person while for another it might be considered a blessing. The death of someone with a terminal illness may be a blessing, a relief, an end to a stressful life period for both the family and the patient. These reactions depend on the circumstances of the event, the actors involved, and situational definitions. Although some events will probably be quite stressful for most persons, the definitional nature of the event largely determines the degree of the emotional reaction. The interpretation of precipitating events and the resulting definition occur on the cognitive level, which, in turn, becomes transmitted to the emotional level. The definition may be made in terms of how the event will affect the individual, how the event will be seen by others, or how the event will influence others' perceptions of the individual. One not only reacts in terms of the emotional component but also according to the interpretation by others. This is most likely when the event could result in some form of social stigma, such as legal arrest, divorce, mental hospital incarceration, cancer, AIDS. Here, one can incorporate Cooley's (1956) concept of the Looking-Glass Self, which claims that people develop self-images through a perception of how others view them. The notion is that individuals mirror, in affect and cog-

nition, the believed perceptions of others. Thus, crisis formation has a major social component, and the sociological perspective offers the intervener a vantage point for examining these social aspects.

The next phase of the process, *internalization of the definition of the situation,* has already been touched upon. Internalization takes place when the client incorporates the definition of the precipitating event. In other words, the definition becomes part of the individual. The perceived nature of the precipitating event and a weighing of the personal and social consequences are incorporated into the client's behavior and thought repertoire. Once the client tests regular coping mechanisms and discovers that regular adjustment strategies prove inadequate, the emotional turmoil is overwhelming. When this is realized, the client will often engage in self-destructive behavior which only perpetuates the already present emotional hazard. It is at this point that the crisis becomes manifest. The individual knows that the sensations experienced are not normal, but is unable to provide the necessary coping behavior to resolve the crisis and restore emotional stability. . . .

SUMMARY

Many sociological concepts are applicable to crisis intervention practice. The two approaches are quite compatible. Individuals are social beings, affected by social circumstances. Crisis is not experienced in a psychological vacuum; social forces aid in the formation of crisis. Personal crisis is formed through an interpretive and definitional framework. Precipitating events are given meaning through interpretation which, in turn, leads to a crisis state through a perceived threat to socioemotional stability. It is through the precipitating events and the definition of the situation that the crisis is produced.

Once the clinician understands the social psychological basis of crisis formation, effective intervention strategy can be developed. . . .

REFERENCES

Benjamin, Alfred D. 1981. The Helping Interview, 3rd ed. Boston: Houghton Mifflin.

Black, C. M. and R. Enos. 1980. "Sociological precedents and contributions to the understanding and facilitation of individual behavior change: the case for counseling sociology," Journal of Sociology and Social Welfare 7:648–664.

Blumer, H. 1972. "Symbolic interaction: an approach to human communication," in Richard Budd and Brent Ruben, eds., Approaches to Human Communication. Rochelle Park, NJ: Hayden.

Burgess, A. W. and B. A. Baldwin. 1981. Crisis Intervention Theory and Practice. Englewood Cliffs, NJ: Prentice-Hall.

Byers, B. D. and J. E. Hendricks. 1985. "Suicide intervention with the elderly: analytical and interactional aspects." Unpublished manuscript.

Caplan, G. 1964. Principles of Preventive Psychiatry. New York: Basic Books.

Church, N. 1985. "Sociotherapy with marital couples: incorporating dramaturgical and social constructionist elements of marital interaction," Clinical Sociology Review 3:116–128.

Cooley, C. H. 1956. Social Organization: A Study of the Larger Mind. Glencoe, IL: Free Press.

Freedman, J. 1982. "Clinical sociology: what it is and what it isn't," Clinical Sociology Review 1:34–49.

Fritz, J. M. 1985. Colloquium on Clinical Sociology. Bowling Green State University, October 7.

Glass, J. 1979. "Renewing an old profession: clinical sociology," American Behavioral Scientist 22:513–530.

Glassner, B. and J. A. Freedman. 1979. Clinical Sociology. New York: Longman.

Hendricks, J. E. 1984. "Death notification: the theory and practice of informing survivors,"

Journal of Police Science and Administration 12:109–116.

Hurvitz, N. 1979. "The sociologist as a marital and family therapist," American Behavioral Scientist 22:557–576.

Jaques, E. 1947. "Social therapy: technocracy or collaboration?" Journal of Social Issues 3:59–66.

Lee, A. M. 1955. "The clinical study of society," American Sociological Review 20:648–653.

_____. 1979. "The services of clinical sociology," American Behavioral Scientist 22:487–511.

Lindemann, E. 1944. "Symptomatology and management of acute grief," American Journal of Psychiatry 101:141–148.

Link, E. P. 1948. "A note on sociosomatics," American Sociological Review 13:757–758.

Moreno, J. D. and B. Glassner. 1979. "Clinical sociology: a social ontology for therapy," American Behavioral Scientist 22:531–541.

Morrice, J. K. W. 1976. Crisis Intervention: Studies in Community Care. Oxford: Pergamon.

Polak, P. 1971. "Social systems intervention," Archives of General Psychiatry 25:110–117.

Rapaport, L. 1962. "The state of crisis: some theoretical considerations," Social Service Review 36:211–217.

See, P. and R. Straus. 1985. "The sociology of the individual," in Roger A. Straus, ed., Using Sociology: An Introduction From The Clinical Perspective. Bayside, NY: General Hall.

Smith, L. L. 1978. "A review of crisis intervention theory," Social Casework 59:396–405.

Straus, R. A. 1979. "Clinical sociology: an idea whose time has come . . . again," Case Analysis 1:21–43.

_____. 1982. "Clinical sociology on the one-to-one level: a social behavioral approach to counseling," Clinical Sociology Review 1:59–74.

_____. 1984. "Changing the definition of the situation: toward a theory of sociological intervention," Clinical Sociology Review 2:51–63.

Thomas, W. I. 1931. The Unadjusted Girl. Boston: Little, Brown.

White, L. A. 1947. "Culturological vs. psychological interpretations of human behavior," American Sociological Review 12:686–698.

Wirth, L. 1931. "Clinical sociology," American Journal of Sociology 37:49–66.

23

Negotiating Reality

Notes on Power in the Assessment of Responsibility

THOMAS J. SCHEFF

The use of interrogation to reconstruct parts of an individual's past history is a common occurrence in human affairs. Reporters, jealous lovers, and policemen on the beat are often faced with the task of determining events in another person's life, and the extent to which he was responsible for those events. The most dramatic use of interrogation to determine responsibility is in criminal trials. As in everyday life, criminal trials are concerned with both act and intent. Courts, in most cases, first determine whether the defendant performed a legally forbidden act. If it is found that he did so, the court then must decide whether he was "responsible" for the act. Reconstructive work of this type goes on less dramatically in a wide variety of other settings, as well. The social worker determining a client's eligibility for unemployment compensation, for example, seeks not only to establish that the client actually is unemployed, but that he has actively sought employment, i.e., that he himself is not responsible for being out of work.

This paper will contrast two perspectives on the process of reconstructing past events for the purpose of fixing responsibility. The first perspective stems from the common sense notion that interrogation, when it is sufficiently skillful, is essentially neutral.

Responsibility for past actions can be fixed absolutely and independently of the method of reconstruction. This perspective is held by the typical member of society, engaged in his day-to-day tasks. It is also held, in varying degrees, by most professional interrogators. The basic working doctrine is one of *absolute* responsibility. This point of view actually entails the comparison of two different kinds of items: first, the fixing of actions and intentions, and secondly, comparing these actions and intentions to some predetermined criteria of responsibility. The basic premise of the doctrine of absolute responsibility is that both actions and intentions, on the one hand, and the criteria of responsibility, on the other, are absolute, in that they can be assessed independently of social context.[1]

An alternative approach follows from the sociology of knowledge. From this point of view, the reality within which members of society conduct their lives is largely of their own construction.[2] Since much of reality is a construction, there may be multiple realities, existing side by side, in harmony or in competition. It follows, if one maintains this stance, that the assessment of responsibility involves the construction of reality by members; construction both of actions and intentions, on the one hand, and of criteria of

The author wishes to acknowledge the help of the following persons who criticized earlier drafts: Aaron Cicourel, Donald Cressey, Joan Emerson, Erving Goffman, Michael Katz, Lewis Kurke, Robert Levy, Sohan Lal Sharma, and Paul Weubben. The paper was written during a fellowship provided by the Social Science Research Institute, University of Hawaii.

responsibility, on the other. The former process, the continuous reconstruction of the normative order, has long been the focus of sociological concern.[3] The discussion in this paper will be limited, for the most part, to the former process, the way in which actions and intentions are constructed in the act of assessing responsibility.

My purpose is to argue that responsibility is at least partly a product of social structure. The alternative to the doctrine of absolute responsibility is that of relative responsibility: the assessment of responsibility always includes a process of negotiation. In this process, responsibility is in part constructed by the negotiating parties. To illustrate this thesis, excerpts from two dialogues of negotiation will be discussed: a real psychotherapeutic interview, and an interview between a defense attorney and his client, taken from a work of fiction. Before presenting these excerpts it will be useful to review some prior discussions of negotiation, the first in courts of law, the second in medical diagnosis.[4]

The negotiation of pleas in criminal courts, sometimes referred to as "bargain justice," has been frequently noted by observers of legal processes.[5] The defense attorney, or (in many cases, apparently) the defendant himself, strikes a bargain with the prosecutor—a plea of guilty will be made, provided that the prosecutor will reduce the charge. For example, a defendant arrested on suspicion of armed robbery may arrange to plead guilty to the charge of unarmed robbery. The prosecutor obtains ease of conviction from the bargain, the defendant, leniency.

Although no explicit estimates are given, it appears from observers' reports that the great majority of criminal convictions are negotiated. Newman states:

A major characteristic of criminal justice administration, particularly in jurisdictions characterized by legislatively fixed sentences, is charge reduction to elicit pleas of guilty. Not only does the efficient functioning of criminal justice rest upon a high proportion of guilty pleas, but plea bargaining is closely linked with attempts to individualize justice, to obtain certain desirable conviction consequences, and to avoid undesirable ones such as "undeserved" mandatory sentences.[6]

It would appear that the bargaining process is accepted as routine. In the three jurisdictions Newman studied, there were certain meeting places where the defendant, his client, and a representative of the prosecutor's office routinely met to negotiate the plea. It seems clear that in virtually all but the most unusual cases, the interested parties expected to, and actually did, negotiate the plea.

From these comments on the routine acceptance of plea bargaining in the courts, one might expect that this process would be relatively open and unambiguous. Apparently, however, there is some tension between the fact of bargaining and moral expectations concerning justice. Newman refers to this tension by citing two contradictory statements: an actual judicial opinion, "Justice and liberty are not the subjects of bargaining and barter;" and an off-the-cuff statement by another judge, "All law is compromise." A clear example of this tension is provided by an excerpt from a trial and Newman's comments on it.

The following questions were asked of a defendant after he had pleaded guilty to unarmed robbery when the original charge was armed robbery. This reduction is common, and the judge was fully aware that the plea was negotiated:

JUDGE: You want to plead guilty to robbery unarmed?

DEFENDANT: Yes, Sir.

JUDGE: Your plea of guilty is free and voluntary?

DEFENDANT: Yes, Sir.

JUDGE: No one has promised you anything?

DEFENDANT: No.

JUDGE: No one has induced you to plead guilty?

DEFENDANT: No.

JUDGE: You're pleading guilty because you are guilty?

DEFENDANT: Yes.

JUDGE: I'll accept your plea of guilty to robbery unarmed and refer it to the probation department for a report and for sentencing Dec. 28.[7]

The delicacy of the relationship between appearance and reality is apparently confusing, even for the sociologist-observer. Newman's comment on this exchange has an Alice-in-Wonderland quality:

> This is a routine procedure designed to satisfy the statutory requirement and is not intended to disguise the process of charge reduction.[8]

If we put the tensions between the different realities aside for the moment, we can say that there is an explicit process of negotiation between the defendant and the prosecution which is a part of the legal determination of guilt or innocence, or in the terms used above, the assessment of responsibility.

In medical diagnosis, a similar process of negotiation occurs, but is much less self-conscious than plea bargaining. The English psychoanalyst Michael Balint refers to this process as one of "offers and responses":

> Some of the people who, for some reason or other, find it difficult to cope with problems of their lives resort to becoming ill. If the doctor has the opportunity of seeing them in the first phases of their being ill, i.e. before they settle down to a definite "organized" illness, he may observe that the patients, so to speak, offer or propose various illnesses, and that they have to go on offering new illnesses until between doctor and patient an agreement can be reached resulting in the acceptance by both of them of one of the illnesses as justified.[9]

Balint gives numerous examples indicating that patients propose reasons for their coming to the doctor which are rejected, one by one, by the physician, who makes counter-proposals until an "illness" acceptable to both parties is found. If "definition of the situation" is substituted for "illness," Balint's observations become relevant to a wide variety of transactions, including the kind of interrogation discussed above. The fixing of responsibility is a process in which the client offers definitions of the situation, to which the interrogator responds. After a series of offers and responses, a definition of the situation acceptable to both the client and the interrogator is reached.

Balint has observed that the negotiation process leads physicians to influence the outcome of medical examinations, independently of the patient's condition. He refers to this process as the "apostolic function" of the doctor, arguing that the physician induces patients to have the kind of illness that the physician thinks is proper:

> Apostolic mission or function means in the first place that every doctor has a vague, but almost unshakably firm, idea of how a patient ought to behave when ill. Although this idea is anything but explicit and concrete, it is immensely powerful, and influences, as we have found, practically every detail of the doctor's work with his patients. It was almost as if every doctor had revealed knowledge of what was right and what was wrong for patients to expect and to endure, and further, as if he had a sacred duty to convert to his faith all the ignorant and unbelieving among his patients.[10]

Implicit in this statement is the notion that interrogator and client have unequal power in determining the resultant definition of the situation. The interrogator's definition of the situation plays an important part in the joint definition of the situation which is finally negotiated. Moreover, his definition is more important than the client's in determining the final outcome of the negotiation, principally because he is well trained, secure, and self-confident in his role in the transaction, whereas the client is untutored, anxious, and uncertain about his role. Stated simply, the subject, because of these conditions, is likely to be susceptible to the influence of the interrogator.

Note that plea bargaining and the process of "offers and responses" in diagnosis differ in the degree of self-consciousness of the participants. In plea bargaining the process is at least partly visible to the participants themselves. There appears to be some ambiguity about the extent to which the negotiation is morally acceptable to some of the commentators, but the parties to the negotiations appear to be aware that bargaining is going on, and accept the process as such. The bargaining process in diagnosis, however, is much more subterranean. Certainly neither physicians nor patients recognize the offers and responses process as being bargaining. There is no commonly accepted vocabulary for describing diagnostic bargaining, such as there is in the legal analogy, e.g. "copping out" or "copping a plea." It may be that in legal processes there is some appreciation of the different kinds of reality, i.e. the difference between the public (official, legal) reality and private reality, whereas in medicine this difference is not recognized.

The discussion so far has suggested that much of reality is arrived at by negotiation. This thesis was illustrated by materials presented on legal processes by Newman, and medical processes by Balint. These processes are similar in that they appear to represent clear instances of the negotiation of reality. The instances are different in that the legal bargaining processes appear to be more open and accepted than the diagnostic process. In order to outline some of the dimensions of the negotiation process, and to establish some of the limitations of the analyses by Newman and Balint, two excerpts of cases

of bargaining will be discussed: the first taken from an actual psychiatric "intake" interview, the second from a fictional account of a defense lawyer's first interview with his client.

THE PROCESS OF NEGOTIATION

The psychiatric interview to be discussed is from the first interview in *The Initial Interview in Psychiatric Practice*.[11] The patient is a thirty-four year old nurse, who feels, as she says, "irritable, tense, depressed." She appears to be saying from the very beginning of the interview that the external situation in which she lives is the cause of her troubles. She focuses particularly on her husband's behavior. She says he is an alcoholic, is verbally abusive, and won't let her work. She feels that she is cooped up in the house all day with her two small children, but that when he is home at night (on the nights when he *is* at home) he will have nothing to do with her and the children. She intimates, in several ways, that he does not serve as a sexual companion. She has thought of divorce, but has rejected it for various reasons (for example, she is afraid she couldn't take proper care of the children, finance the baby sitters, etc.). She feels trapped.[12]

In the concluding paragraph of their description of this interview, Gill, Newman, and Redlich give this summary:

> The patient, pushed by we know not what or why at the time (the children—somebody to talk to) comes for help apparently for what she thinks of as help with her external situation (her husband's behavior as she sees it). The therapist does not respond to this but seeks her role and how it is that she plays such a role. Listening to the recording it sounds as if the therapist is at first bored and disinterested and the patient defensive. He gets down to work and keeps asking, "What is it all about?" Then he becomes more interested and sympathetic and at the same time very active (participating) and demanding. *It*

sounds as if she keeps saying "This is the trouble." He says, "No! Tell me the trouble." She says, "This is it!" He says, "No, tell me," until the patient finally says, "Well I'll tell you." Then the therapist says, "Good! I'll help you."[13]

From this summary it is apparent that there is a close fit between Balint's idea of the negotiation of diagnosis through offers and responses, and what took place in this psychiatric interview. It is difficult, however, to document the details. Most of the psychiatrist's responses, rejecting the patient's offers, do not appear in the written transcript, but they are fairly obvious as one listens to the recording. Two particular features of the psychiatrist's responses especially stand out: (1) the flatness of intonation in his responses to the patient's complaints about her external circumstances; and (2) the rapidity with which he introduces new topics, through questioning, when she is talking about her husband.

Some features of the psychiatrist's coaching are verbal, however:

T. 95: Has anything happened recently that makes it...you feel that...ah... you're sort of coming to the end of your rope? I mean I wondered what led you...
P. 95: (Interrupting.) It's nothing special. It's just everything in general.
T. 96: What led you to come to a...
P. 96: (Interrupting.) It's just that I...
T. 97: ...a psychiatrist just now? (1)
P. 97: Because I felt that the older girl was getting tense as a result of ...of my being stewed up all the time.
T. 98: Mmmhnn.
P. 98: Not having much patience with her.
T. 99: Mmmhnn. (Short Pause.) Mmm. And how had you imagined that a psychiatrist could help with this? (Short pause.) (2)
P. 99: Mmm...maybe I could sort of get straightened out...

straighten things out in my own mind. I'm confused. Sometimes I can't remember things that I've done, whether I've done 'em or not or whether they happened.

T. 100: What is it that you want to straighten out? (Pause.)
P. 100: I think I seem mixed up.
T. 101: Yeah? You see that, it seems to me, is something that we really should talk about because...ah...from a certain point of view somebody might say, "Well now, it's all very simple. She's unhappy and disturbed because her husband is behaving this way, and unless something can be done about that how could she expect to feel any other way." But, instead of that, you come to the psychiatrist, and you say that you think there's something about you that needs straightening out. (3) I don't quite get it. Can you explain that to me? (Short pause.)
P. 101: I sometimes wonder if I'm emotionally grown up.
T. 102: By which you mean what?
P. 102: When you're married you should have one mate. You shouldn't go around and look at other men.
T. 103: You've been looking at other men?
P. 103: I look at them, but that's all.
T. 104: Mmmhnn. What you mean...you mean a grown-up person should accept the marital situation whatever it happens to be?
P. 104: That was the way I was brought up. Yes. (Sighs.)
T. 105: You think that would be a sign of emotional maturity?
P. 105: No.
T. 106: No. So?
P. 106: Well, if you rebel against the laws of society you have to take the consequences.
T. 107: Yes?
P. 107: And it's just that I...I'm not willing to take the consequences. I...I don't think it's worth it.

T. 108:   Mmhnn. So in the meantime then while you're in this very difficult situation, you find yourself reacting in a way that you don't like and that you think is . . . ah . . . damaging to your children and yourself? Now what can be done about that?

P. 108:   (Sniffs; sighs.) I dunno. That's why I came to see you.

T. 109:   Yes. I was just wondering what you had in mind. Did you think a psychiatrist could . . . ah . . . help you face this kind of a situation calmly and easily and maturely? (4) Is that it?

P. 109:   More or less. I need somebody to talk to who isn't emotionally involved with the family. I have a few friends, but I don't like to bore them. I don't think they should know . . . ah . . . all the intimate details of what goes on.

T. 110:   Yeah?

P. 110:   It becomes food for gossip.

T. 111:   Mmmhnn.

P. 111:   Besides they're in . . . they're emotionally involved because they're my friends. They tell me not to stand for it, but they don't understand that if I put my foot down it'll only get stepped on.

T. 112:   Yeah.

P. 112:   That he can make it miserable for me in other ways. . . .

T. 113:   Mmm.

P. 113:   . . . which he does.

T. 114:   Mmmhnn. In other words, you find yourself in a situation and don't know how to cope with it really.

P. 114:   I don't.

T. 115:   You'd like to be able to talk that through and come to understand it better and learn how to cope with it or deal with it in some way. Is that right?

P. 115:   I'd like to know how to deal with it more effectively.

T. 116:   Yeah. Does that mean you feel convinced that the way you're dealing with it now . . .

P. 116:   There's something wrong of course.

T. 117:   . . . something wrong with that. Mmmhnn.

P. 117:   There's something wrong with it.[14]

Note that the therapist reminds her *four times* in this short sequence that she has come to see a *psychiatrist*. Since the context of these reminders is one in which the patient is attributing her difficulties to an external situation, particularly her husband, it seems plausible to hear these reminders as subtle requests for analysis of her own contributions to her difficulties. This interpretation is supported by the therapist's subsequent remarks. When the patient once again describes external problems, the therapist tries the following tack:

T. 125:   I notice that you've used a number of psychiatric terms here and there. Were you specially interested in that in your training, or what?

P. 125:   Well, my great love is psychology.

T. 126:   Psychology?

P. 126:   Mmmhnn.

T. 127:   How much have you studied?

P. 127:   Oh (Sighs.) what you have in your nurse's training, and I've had general psych, child and adolescent psych, and the abnormal psych.

T. 128:   Mmmhnn. Well, tell me . . . ah . . . what would you say if you had to explain yourself what is the problem?

P. 128:   You don't diagnose yourself very well, at least I don't.

T. 129:   Well you can make a stab at it. (Pause.)[15]

This therapeutic thrust is rewarded: the patient gives a long account of her early life which indicates a belief that she was not "adjusted" in the past. The interview continues:

T. 135:   And what conclusions do you draw from all this about why you're not adjusting now the way you think you should?

P. 135: Well, I wasn't adjusted then. I feel that I've come a long way, but I don't think I'm still . . . I still don't feel that I'm adjusted.

T. 136: And you don't regard your husband as being the difficulty? You think it lies within yourself?

P. 136: Oh he's a difficulty all right, but I figure that even . . . ah . . . had . . . if it had been other things that . . . that this probably—this state—would've come on me.

T. 137: Oh you do think so?

P. 137: (Sighs.) I don't think he's the sole factor. No.

T. 138: And what are the factors within . . .

P. 138: I mean . . .

T. 139: . . . yourself?

P. 139: Oh it's probably remorse for the past, things I did.

T. 140: Like what? (Pause.) It's sumping' hard to tell, hunh? (Short pause.)[16]

After some parrying, the patient tells the therapist what he wants to hear. She feels guilty because she was pregnant by another man when her present husband proposed. She cries. The therapist tells the patient she needs, and will get psychiatric help, and the interview ends, the patient still crying. The negotiational aspects of the process are clear: After the patient has spent most of the interview blaming her current difficulties on external circumstances, she tells the therapist a deep secret about which she feels intensely guilty. The patient, and not the husband, is at fault. The therapist's tone and manner change abruptly. From being bored, distant, and rejecting, he becomes warm and solicitous. Through a process of offers and responses, the therapist and patient have, by implication, negotiated a shared definition of the situation—the patient, not the husband, is responsible.

A CONTRASTING CASE

The negotiation process can, of course, proceed on the opposite premise, namely that the client is not responsible. An ideal example would be an interrogation of a client by a skilled defense lawyer. Unfortunately, we have been unable to locate a verbatim transcript of a defense lawyer's initial interview with his client. There is available, however, a fictional portrayal of such an interview, written by a man with extensive experience as defense lawyer, prosecutor, and judge. The excerpt to follow is taken from the novel, *Anatomy of a Murder.*[17]

The defense lawyer, in his initial contact with his client, briefly questions him regarding his actions on the night of the killing. The client states that he discovered that the deceased, Barney Quill, had raped his wife; he then goes on to state that he then left his wife, found Quill and shot him.

"... How long did you remain with your wife before you went to the hotel bar?"
"I don't remember."
"I think it is important, and I suggest you try."
After a pause. "Maybe an hour."
"Maybe more?"
"Maybe."
"Maybe less?"
"Maybe."

I paused and lit a cigar. I took my time. I had reached a point where a few wrong answers to a few right questions would leave me with a client—if I took his case—whose cause was legally defenseless. Either I stopped now and begged off and let some other lawyer worry over it or I asked him the few fatal questions and let him hang himself. Or else, like any smart lawyer, I went into the Lecture. I studied my man, who sat as inscrutable as an Arab, delicately fingering his Ming holder, daintily sipping his dark mustache. He apparently did not realize how close I had him to admitting that he was guilty of first degree murder, that is, that he "feloniously, wilfully and of his malice aforethought did kill and murder one Barney Quill." The man was a sitting duck.[18]

The lawyer here realizes that his line of questioning has come close to fixing the responsibility for the killing on his client. He therefore shifts his ground by beginning "the lecture":

The Lecture is an ancient device that lawyers use to coach their clients so that the client won't quite know he has been coached and his lawyer can still preserve the face-saving illusion that he hasn't done any coaching. For coaching clients, like robbing them, is not only frowned upon, it is downright unethical and bad, very bad. Hence the Lecture, an artful device as old as the law itself, and one used constantly by some of the nicest and most ethical lawyers in the land. "Who, me" I didn't tell him what to say," the lawyer can later comfort himself. "I merely explained the law, see." It is a good practice to scowl and shrug here and add virtuously: "That's my duty, isn't it?"

... "We will now explore the absorbing subject of legal justification or excuse," I said.

... "Well, take self-defense," I began. "That's the classic example of justifiable homicide. On the basis of what I've so far heard and read about your case I do not think we need pause too long over that. Do you?"

"Perhaps not," Lieutenant Manion conceded. "We'll pass it for now."

"Let's," I said dryly. "Then there's the defense of habitation, defense of property, and the defense of relatives or friends. Now there are more ramifications to these defenses than a dog has fleas, but we won't explore them now. I've already told you at length why I don't think you can invoke the possible defense of your wife. When you shot Quill her need for defense had passed. It's as simple as that."

"Go on," Lieutenant Manion said, frowning.

"Then there's the defense of a homicide committed to prevent a felony—say you're being robbed—; to prevent the escape of the felon—suppose he's getting away with your wallet—; or to arrest a felon—you've caught up with him and he's either trying to get away or has actually escaped." ...

... "Go on, then; what are some of the other legal justifications or excuses?"

"Then there's the tricky and dubious defense of intoxication. Personally I've never seen it succeed. But since you were not drunk when you shot Quill we shall mercifully not dwell on that. Or were you?"

"I was cold sober. Please go on."

"Then finally there's the defense of insanity." I paused and spoke abruptly, airily: "Well, that just about winds it up." I arose as though making ready to leave.

"Tell me more."

"There is no more." I slowly paced up and down the room.

"I mean about this insanity."

"Oh, insanity," I said, elaborately surprised. It was like luring a trained seal with a herring. "Well, insanity, where proven, is a complete defense to murder. It does not legally justify the killing, like self-defense, say, but rather excuses it." The lecturer was hitting his stride. He was also on the home stretch. "Our law requires that a punishable killing—in fact, any crime—must be committed by a sapient human being, one capable, as the law insists, of distinguishing between right and wrong. If a man is insane, legally insane, the act of homicide may still be murder but the law excuses the perpetrator."

Lieutenant Manion was sitting erect now, very still and erect. "I see—and this—this perpetrator, what happens to him if he should—should be excused?"

"Under Michigan law—like that of many other states—if he is acquitted of murder on the grounds of insanity it is provided that he must be sent to a hospital for the criminally insane until he is pronounced sane." ...

... Then he looked at me. "Maybe," he said, "maybe I was insane."

... Thoughtfully: "Hm.... Why do you say that?"

"Well, I can't really say," he went on slowly. "I—I guess I blacked out. I can't remember a thing after I saw him standing behind the bar that night until I got back to my trailer."

"You mean—you mean you don't remember shooting him?" I shook my head in wonderment.

"Yes, that's what I mean."

"You don't even remember driving home?"

"No."

"You don't remember threatening Barney's bartender when he followed you outside after the shooting—as the newspaper says you did?" I paused and held my breath. "You don't remember telling him, 'Do you want some, too, Buster?' ?"

The smoldering dark eyes flickered ever so little. "No, not a thing."

"My, my," I said blinking my eyes, contemplating the wonder of it all. "Maybe you've got something there."

The Lecture was over; I had told my man the law; and now he had told me things that might possibly invoke the defense of insanity. . . . [19]

The negotiation is complete. The ostensibly shared definition of the situation established by the negotiation process is that the defendant was probably not responsible for his actions.

Let us now compare the two interviews. The major similarity between them is their negotiated character: they both take the form of a series of offers and responses that continue until an offer (a definition of the situation) is reached that is acceptable to both parties. The major difference between the transactions is that one, the psychotherapeutic interview, arrives at an assessment that the client is responsible; the other, the defense attorney's interview, reaches an assessment that the client was not at fault, i.e., not responsible. How can we account for this difference in outcome?

DISCUSSION

Obviously, given any two real cases of negotiation which have different outcomes, one might construct a reasonable argument that the difference is due to the differences between the cases—the finding of responsibility in one case and lack of responsibility in the other, the only outcomes which are reasonably consonant with the facts of the respective cases. Without rejecting this argument, for the sake of discussion only, and without claiming any kind of proof or demonstration, I wish to present an alternative argument; that the difference in outcome is largely due to the differences in technique used by the interrogators. This argument will allow us to suggest some crucial dimensions of negotiation processes.

The first dimension, consciousness of the bargaining aspects of the transaction, has already been mentioned. In the psychotherapeutic interview, the negotiational nature of the transaction seems not to be articulated by either party. In the legal interview, however, certainly the lawyer, and perhaps to some extent the client as well, is aware of, and accepts the situation as one of striking a bargain, rather than as a relentless pursuit of the absolute facts of the matter.

The dimension of shared awareness that the definition of the situation is negotiable seems particularly crucial for assessments of responsibility. In both interviews, there is an agenda hidden from the client. In the psychotherapeutic interview, it is probably the psychiatric criteria for acceptance into treatment, the criterion of "insight." The psychotherapist has probably been trained to view patients with "insight into their illness" as favorable candidates for psychotherapy, i.e., patients who accept, or can be led to accept, the problems as internal, as part of their personality, rather than seeing them as caused by external conditions.

In the legal interview, the agenda that is unknown to the client is the legal structure of defenses or justifications for killing. In both the legal and psychiatric cases, the hidden agenda is not a simple one. Both involve fitting abstract and ambiguous criteria (insight, on the one hand, legal justification, on the other) to a richly specific, concrete case. In the legal interview, the lawyer almost immediately broaches this hidden agenda; he states clearly and concisely the major legal justifications for killing. In the psychiatric interview, the hidden agenda is never revealed. The patient's offers during most of the interview are rejected or ignored. In the last part of the interview, her last offer is accepted and she is told that she will be given treatment. In no case are the reasons for these actions articulated by either party.

The degree of shared awareness is related to a second dimension which concerns the format of the conversation. The legal interview began as an interrogation, but was quickly shifted away from that format when the defense lawyer realized the direction in which the questioning was leading the client, i.e., toward a legally unambiguous admission of guilt. On the very brink of such an admission, the defense lawyer stopped asking questions and started, instead, to make statements. He listed the principal legal justifications for killing, and, in response to the *client's* questions, gave an explanation of each of the justifications. This shift in format put the client, rather than the lawyer, in control of the crucial aspects of the negotiation. It is the client, not the lawyer, who is allowed to pose the questions, assess the answers for their relevance to his case, and most crucially, to determine himself the most advantageous tack to take. Control of the definition of the situation, the evocation of the events and intentions relevant to the assessment of the client's responsibility for the killing, was given to the client by the lawyer. The resulting client-controlled format of negotiation gives the client a double advantage. It not only allows the client the benefit of formulating his account of actions and intentions in their most favorable light, it also allows him to select, out of a diverse and ambiguous set of normative criteria concerning killing, that criteria which is most favorable to his own case.

Contrast the format of negotiation used by the psychotherapist. The form is consistently that of interrogation. The psychother-apist poses the questions; the patient answers. The psychotherapist then has the answers at his disposal. He may approve or disapprove, accept or reject, or merely ignore them. Throughout the entire interview, the psychotherapist is in complete control of the situation. Within this framework, the tactic that the psychotherapist uses is to reject the patient's "offers" that her husband is at fault, first by ignoring them, later, and ever more insistently, by leading her to define the situation as one in which she is at fault. In effect, what the therapist does is to reject her offers, and to make his own counteroffers.

These remarks concerning the relationship between technique of interrogation and outcome suggest an approach to assessment of responsibility somewhat different than that usually followed. The common sense approach to interrogation is to ask how accurate and fair is the outcome. Both Newman's and Balint's analyses of negotiation raise this question. Both presuppose that there is an objective state of affairs that is independent of the technique of assessment. This is quite clear in Newman's discussion, as he continually refers to defendants who are "really" or "actually" guilty or innocent.[20] The situation is less clear in Balint's discussion, although occasionally he implies that certain patients are really physically healthy, but psychologically distressed.

The type of analysis suggested by this paper seeks to avoid such presuppositions. It can be argued that *independently* of the facts of the case, the technique of assessment plays a part in determining the outcome. In particular, one can avoid making assumptions about actual responsibility by utilizing a technique of textual criticism of a transaction. The key dimension in such work would be the relative power and authority of the participants in the situation.[21]

As an introduction to the way in which power differences between interactants shape the outcome of negotiations, let us take as an example an attorney in a trial dealing with "friendly" and "unfriendly" witnesses. A friendly witness is a person whose testimony will support the definition of the situation the attorney seeks to convey to the jury. With such a witness the attorney does not employ power, but treats him as an equal. His questions to such a witness are open, and allow the witness considerable freedom. The attorney might frame a question such as "Could you tell us about your actions on the night of ———?"

The opposing attorney, however, interested in establishing his own version of the witness' behavior on the same night, would probably approach the task quite differently. He might say: "You felt angry and offended on the night of ———, didn't you?" The witness frequently will try to evade so direct a question with an answer like: "Actually, I had started to. . . ." The attorney quickly interrupts, addressing the judge: "Will the court order the witness to respond to the question, yes or no?" That is to say, the question posed by the opposing attorney is abrupt and direct. When the witness attempts to answer indirectly, and at length, the attorney quickly invokes the power of the court to coerce the witness to answer as he wishes, directly. The witness and the attorney are not equals in power; the attorney used the coercive power of the court to force the witness to answer in the manner desired.

The attorney confronted by an "unfriendly" witness wishes to control the format of the interaction, so that he can retain control of the definition of the situation that is conveyed to the jury. It is much easier for him to neutralize an opposing definition of the situation if he retains control of the interrogation format in this manner. By allowing the unfriendly witness to respond only by yes or no to his own verbally conveyed account, he can suppress the ambient details of the opposing view that might sway the jury, and thus maintain an advantage for his definition over that of the witness.

In the psychiatric interview discussed above, the psychiatrist obviously does not invoke a third party to enforce his control of the interview. But he does use a device to impress the patient that she is not to be his equal in the interview, that is reminiscent of the attorney with an unfriendly witness. The device is to pose abrupt and direct questions to the patient's open-ended accounts, implying that the patient should answer briefly and directly; and, through that implication, the psychiatrist controls the whole transaction. Throughout most of the interview the patient seeks to give detailed accounts of her behavior and her husband's, but the psychiatrist almost invariably counters with a direct and, to the patient, seemingly unrelated question.

The first instance of this procedure occurs at T6, the psychiatrist asking the patient, "what do you do?" She replies "I'm a nurse, but my husband won't let me work." Rather than responding to the last part of her answer, which would be expected in conversation between equals, the psychiatrist asks another question, changing the subject: "How old are you?" This pattern continues throughout most of the interview. The psychiatrist appears to be trying to teach the patient to follow his lead. After some thirty or forty exchanges of this kind, the patient apparently learns her lesson; she cedes control of the transaction completely to the therapist, answering briefly and directly to direct questions, and elaborating only on cue from the therapist. The therapist thus implements his control of the interview not by direct coercion, but by subtle manipulation.

All of the discussion above, concerning shared awareness and the format of the negotiation, suggests several propositions concerning control over the definition of the situation. The professional interrogator, whether lawyer or psychotherapist, can maintain control if the client cedes control to him because of his authority as an expert, because of his manipulative skill in the transaction, or merely because the interrogator controls access to something the client wants, e.g., treatment, or a legal excuse. The propositions are:

1a. Shared awareness of the participants that the situation is one of negotiation. (The greater the shared awareness the more control the client gets over the resultant definition of the situation.)

b. Explicitness of the agenda. (The more explicit the agenda of the transaction, the more control the client gets over the resulting definition of the situation.)

2a. Organization of the format of the transaction, offers and responses. (The party to a negotiation who responds, rather than the party who makes the offers, has relatively more power in controlling the resultant shared definition of the situation.)

b. Counter-offers. (The responding party who makes counter-offers has relatively more power than the responding party who limits his response to merely accepting or rejecting the offers of the other party.)

c. Directness of questions and answers. (The more direct the questions of the interrogator, and the more direct the answers he demands and receives, the more control he has over the resultant definition of the situation.)

These concepts and hypotheses are only suggestive until such times as operational definitions can be developed. Although such terms as offers and responses seem to have an immediate applicability to most conversation, it is likely that a thorough and systematic analysis of any given conversation would show the need for clearly stated criteria of class inclusion and exclusion. Perhaps a good place for such research would be in the transactions for assessing responsibility discussed above. Since some 90 percent of all criminal convictions in the United States are based on guilty pleas, the extent to which

techniques of interrogation subtly influence outcomes would have immediate policy implication. There is considerable evidence that interrogation techniques influence the outcome of psychotherapeutic interviews also.[22] Research in both of these areas would probably have implications for both the theory and practice of assessing responsibility.

CONCLUSION: NEGOTIATION IN SOCIAL SCIENCE RESEARCH

More broadly, the application of the sociology of knowledge to the negotiation of reality has ramifications which may apply to all of social science. The interviewer in a survey, or the experimenter in a social psychological experiment, is also involved in a transaction with a client—the respondent or subject. Recent studies by Rosenthal and others strongly suggest that the findings in such studies are negotiated, and influenced by the format of the study.[23] Rosenthal's review of bias in research suggests that such bias is produced by a pervasive and subtle process of interaction between the investigator and his source of data. Those errors which arise because of the investigator's influence over the subject (the kind of influence discussed in this paper as arising out of power disparities in the process of negotiation), Rosenthal calls "expectancy effects." In order for these errors to occur, there must be direct contact between the investigator and the subject.

A second kind of bias Rosenthal refers to as "observer effects." These are errors of perception or reporting which do not require that the subject be influenced by investigation. Rosenthal's review leads one to surmise that even with techniques that are completely non-obtrusive, observer error could be quite large.[24]

The occurrence of these two kinds of bias poses an interesting dilemma for the lawyer, psychiatrist, and social scientist. The investigator of human phenomena is usually interested in more than a sequence of events, he wants to know why the events occurred. Usually this quest for an explanation leads him to deal with the motivation of the persons involved. The lawyer, clinician, social psychologist, or survey researcher try to elicit motives directly, by questioning the participants. But in the process of questioning, as suggested above, he himself becomes involved in a process of negotiation, perhaps subtly influencing the informants through expectancy effects. A historian, on the other hand, might try to use documents and records to determine motives. He would certainly avoid expectancy effects in this way, but since he would not elicit motives directly, he might find it necessary to collect and interpret various kinds of evidence which are only indirectly related, at best, to determine motives of the participants. Thus through his choice in the selection and interpretation of the indirect evidence, he may be as susceptible to error as the interrogator, survey researcher, or experimentalist—his error being due to observer effects, however, rather than expectancy effects.

The application of the ideas outlined here to social and psychological research need to be developed. The five propositions suggested above might be used, for example, to estimate the validity of surveys using varying degrees of open-endedness in their interview format. If some technique could be developed which would yield an independent assessment of validity, it might be possible to demonstrate, as Aaron Cicourel has suggested, the more reliable the technique, the less valid the results.

The influence of the assessment itself on the phenomena to be assessed appears to be an ubiquitous process in human affairs, whether in ordinary daily life, the determination of responsibility in legal or clinical interrogation, or in most types of social science research. The sociology of knowledge perspective, which suggests that people go through their lives constructing reality, offers a framework within which the negotia-

tion of reality can be seriously and constructively studied. This paper has suggested some of the avenues of the problem that might require further study. The prevalence of the problem in most areas of human concern recommends it to our attention as a substantial field of study, rather than as an issue that can be ignored or, alternatively, be taken as the proof that rigorous knowledge of social affairs is impossible.

NOTES

1. The doctrine of absolute responsibility is clearly illustrated in psychiatric and legal discussions of the issue of "criminal responsibility," i.e., the use of mental illness as an excuse from criminal conviction. An example of the assumption of absolute criteria of responsibility is found in the following quotation, "The finding that someone is criminally responsible means to the psychiatrist that the criminal must change his behavior before he can resume his position in society. *This injunction is dictated not by morality, but, so to speak, by reality.*" See Edward J. Sachar, "Behavioral Science and Criminal Law," *Scientific American,* 209 (1963), pp. 39-45 (emphasis added).

2. *Cf.* Peter L. Berger and Thomas Luckmann, *The Social Construction of Reality: A Treatise in the Sociology of Knowledge,* New York: Doubleday, 1966.

3. The classic treatment of this issue is found in E. Durkheim, *The Elementary Forms of the Religious Life.*

4. A sociological application of the concept of negotiation, in a different context, is found in Anselm Strauss, *et al.,* "The Hospital and its Negotiated Order," in Eliot Freidson, editor, *The Hospital in Modern Society,* New York: Free Press, 1963, pp. 147-169.

5. Newman reports a study in this area, together with a review of earlier work, in "The Negotiated Plea," Part III of Donald J. Newman, *Conviction: The Determination of Guilt or Innocence Without Trial,* Boston: Little, Brown, 1966, pp. 76-130.

6. *Ibid.,* p. 76.

7. *Ibid.,* p. 83.

8. *Idem.*

9. Michael Balint, *The Doctor, His Patient, and the Illness,* New York: International Universities Press, 1957, p. 18. A description of the negotia-

tions between patients in a tuberculosis sanitarium and their physicians is found in Julius A. Roth, *Timetables: Structuring the Passage of Time in Hospital Treatment and Other Careers*. Indianapolis: Bobbs-Merrill, 1963, pp. 48-59. Obviously, some cases are more susceptible to negotiation than others. Balint implies that the great majority of cases in medical practice are negotiated.

10. Balint, *op. cit.*, p. 216.

11. Merton Gill, Richard Newman, and Fredrick C. Redlich, *The Initial Interview in Psychiatric Practice,* New York: International Universities Press, 1954.

12. Since this interview is complex and subtle, the reader is invited to listen to it himself, and compare his conclusions with those discussed here. The recorded interview is available on the first L.P. record that accompanies Gill, Newman, and Redlich, *op. cit.*

13. *Ibid.*, p. 133. (Italics added.)

14. *Ibid.*, pp. 176-182. (Numbers in parenthesis added.)

15. *Ibid.*, pp. 186-187.

16. *Ibid.*, pp. 192-194.

17. Robert Traver, *Anatomy of a Murder*, New York: Dell, 1959.

18. *Ibid.*, p. 43.

19. *Ibid.*, pp. 46-47, 57, 58-59, and 60.

20. In his Foreword the editor of the series, Frank J. Remington, comments on one of the slips that occurs frequently, the "acquittal of the guilty," noting that this phrase is contradictory from the legal point of view. He goes on to say that Newman is well aware of this, but uses the phrase as a convenience. Needless to say, both Remington's comments and mine can both be correct: the phrase is used as a convenience, but it also reveals the author's presuppositions.

21. Berger and Luckman *op. cit.*, p. 100, also emphasize the role of power, but at the societal level. "The success of particular conceptual machineries is related to the power possessed by those who operate them. The confrontation of alternative symbolic universes implies a problem of power—which of the conflicting definitions of reality will be "made to stick" in the society." Haley's discussions of control in psychotherapy are also relevant. See Jay Haley, "Control in Psychoanalytic Psychotherapy," *Progress in Psychotherapy*, 4, New York: Grune and Stratton, 1959, pp. 48-65; see also by the same author, "The Power Tactics of Jesus Christ" (in press).

22. Thomas J. Scheff, *Being Mentally Ill*, Chicago: Aldine, 1966.

23. Robert Rosenthal, *Experimenter Effects in Behavioral Research*, New York: Appleton-Century Crofts, 1966. Friedman, reporting a series of studies of expectancy effects, seeks to put the results within a broad sociological framework; Neil Friedman, *The Social Nature of Psychological Research: The Psychological Experiment as Social Interaction*, New York: Basic Books, 1967.

24. Critics of "reactive techniques" often disregard the problem of observer effects. See, for example, Eugene J. Webb, Donald T. Campbell, Richard D. Schwartz, and Lee Sechrest, *Unobtrusive Measures: Nonreactive Research in Social Science*, Chicago: Rand-McNally, 1966.

24

The Doctor-Nurse Game

LEONARD I. STEIN

The relationship between the doctor and the nurse is a very special one. There are few professions where the degree of mutual respect and cooperation between co-workers is as intense as that between the doctor and nurse. Superficially, the stereotype of this relationship has been dramatized in many novels and television serials. When, however, it is observed carefully in an interactional framework, the relationship takes on a new dimension and has a special quality which fits a game model. The underlying attitudes which demand that this game be played are unfortunate. These attitudes create serious obstacles in the path of meaningful communications between physicians and nonmedical professional groups.

The physician traditionally and appropriately has total responsibility for making the decisions regarding the management of his patients' treatment. To guide his decisions he considers data gleaned from several sources. He acquires a complete medical history, performs a thorough physical examination, interprets laboratory findings, and at times, obtains recommendations from physician-consultants. Another important factor in his decision-making are the recommendations he receives from the nurse. The interaction between doctor and nurse through which these recommendations are communicated and received is unique and interesting.

THE GAME

One rarely hears a nurse say, "Doctor I would recommend that you order a retention enema for Mrs. Brown." A physician, upon hearing a recommendation of that nature, would gape in amazement at the effrontery of the nurse. The nurse, upon hearing the statement, would look over her shoulder to see who said it, hardly believing the words actually came from her own mouth. Nevertheless, if one observes closely, nurses make recommendations of more import every hour and physicians willingly and respectfully consider them. If the nurse is to make a suggestion without appearing insolent and the doctor is to seriously consider that suggestion, their interaction must not violate the rules of the game.

Object of the Game

The object of the game is as follows: the nurse is to be bold, have initiative, and be responsible for making significant recommendations, while at the same time she must appear passive. This must be done in such a manner so as to make her recommendations appear to be initiated by the physician.

Both participants must be acutely sensitive to each other's nonverbal and cryptic verbal communications. A slight lowering of the head, a minor shifting of position in the

Mrs. Gertrude Hermsmeier, RN, Mrs. Joyce McCollum, RN, Arnold M. Ludwig, MD, and Arnold J. Marx, MD, of Mendota State Hospital, aided in this report.

chair, or a seemingly nonrelevant comment concerning an event which occurred eight months ago must be interpreted as a powerful message. The game requires the nimbleness of a high wire acrobat, and if either participant slips the game can be shattered; the penalties for frequent failure are apt to be severe.

Rules of the Game

The cardinal rule of the game is that open disagreement between the players must be avoided at all costs. Thus, the nurse must communicate her recommendations without appearing to be making a recommendation statement. The physician, in requesting a recommendation from a nurse, must do so without appearing to be asking for it. Utilization of this technique keeps anyone from committing themselves to a position before a sub rosa agreement on that position has already been established. In that way open disagreement is avoided. The greater the significance of the recommendation, the more subtly the game must be played.

To convey a subtle example of the game with all its nuances would require the talents of a literary artist. Lacking these talents, let me give you the following example which is unsubtle, but happens frequently. The medical resident on hospital call is awakened by telephone at 1 AM because a patient on a ward, not his own, has not been able to fall asleep. Dr. Jones answers the telephone and the dialogue goes like this:

> This is Dr. Jones.
> (An open and direct communication.)
> Dr. Jones, this is Miss Smith on 2 W—Mrs. Brown, who learned today of her father's death, is unable to fall asleep.
> (This message has two levels. Openly, it describes a set of circumstances, a woman who is unable to sleep and who that morning received word of her father's death. Less openly, but just as directly, it is a diagnostic and recommendation statement; ie, Mrs.

Brown is unable to sleep because of her grief, and she should be given a sedative. Dr. Jones, accepting the diagnostic statement and replying to the recommendation statement, answers.)

> What sleeping medication has been helpful to Mrs. Brown in the past?
> (Dr. Jones, not knowing the patient, is asking for a recommendation from the nurse, who does know the patient, about what sleeping medication should be prescribed. Note, however, his question does not appear to be asking her for a recommendation. Miss Smith replies.)
> Pentobarbital mg 100 was quite effective night before last.
> (A disguised recommendation statement. Dr. Jones replies with a note of authority in his voice.)
> Pentobarbital mg 100 before bedtime as needed for sleep, got it?
> (Miss Smith ends the conversation with the tone of a grateful supplicant.)
> Yes I have, and thank you very much doctor.

The above is an example of a successfully played doctor-nurse game. The nurse made appropriate recommendations which were accepted by the physician and were helpful to the patient. The game was successful because the cardinal rule was not violated. The nurse was able to make her recommendation without appearing to, and the physician was able to ask for recommendations without conspicuously asking for them.

The Scoring System

Inherent in any game are penalties and rewards for the players. In game theory, the doctor-nurse game fits the nonzero sum game model. It is not like chess, where the players compete with each other and whatever one player loses the other wins. Rather, it is the kind of game in which the rewards and punishments are shared by both players. If they play the game successfully they both win rewards, and if they are unskilled and the game is played badly, they both suffer the penalty.

The most obvious reward from the well-played game is a doctor-nurse team that operates efficiently. The physician is able to utilize the nurse as a valuable consultant, and the nurse gains self-esteem and professional satisfaction from her job. The less obvious rewards are not less important. A successful game creates a doctor-nurse alliance; through this alliance the physician gains the respect and admiration of the nursing service. He can be confident that his nursing staff will smooth the path for getting his work done. His charts will be organized and waiting for him when he arrives, the ruffled feathers of patients and relatives will have been smoothed down, his pet routines will be happily followed, and he will be helped in a thousand and one other ways.

The doctor-nurse alliance sheds its light on the nurse as well. She gains a reputation for being a "damn good nurse." She is respected by everyone and appropriately enjoys her position. When physicians discuss the nursing staff it would not be unusual for her name to be mentioned with respect and admiration. Their esteem for a good nurse is no less than their esteem for a good doctor.

The penalties for a game failure, on the other hand, can be severe. The physician who is an unskilled gamesman and fails to recognize the nurses' subtle recommendation messages is tolerated as a "clod." If, however, he interprets these messages as insolence and strongly indicates he does not wish to tolerate suggestions from nurses, he creates a rocky path for his travels. The old truism "If the nurse is your ally you've got it made, and if she has it in for you, be prepared for misery," takes on life-sized proportions. He receives three times as many phone calls after midnight than his colleagues. Nurses will not accept his telephone orders because "telephone orders are against the rules." Somehow, this rule gets sus-

pended for the skilled players. Soon he becomes like Joe Bfstplk in the "Li'l Abner" comic strip. No matter where he goes, a black cloud constantly hovers over his head.

The unskilled gamesman nurse also pays heavily. The nurse who does not view her role as that of a consultant, and therefore does not attempt to communicate recommendations, is perceived as a dullard and is mercifully allowed to fade into the woodwork.

The nurse who does see herself as a consultant but refuses to follow the rules of the game in making her recommendations, has hell to pay. The outspoken nurse is labeled a "bitch" by the surgeon. The psychiatrist describes her as unconsciously suffering from penis envy and her behavior is the acting out of her hostility towards men. Loosely translated, the psychiatrist is saying she is a bitch. The employment of the unbright outspoken nurse is soon terminated. The outspoken bright nurse whose recommendations are worthwhile remains employed. She is, however, constantly reminded in a hundred ways that she is not loved.

GENESIS OF THE GAME

To understand how the game evolved, we must comprehend the nature of the doctors' and nurses' training which shaped the attitudes necessary for the game.

Medical Student Training

The medical student in his freshman year studies as if possessed. In the anatomy class he learns every groove and prominence on the bones of the skeleton as if life depended on it. As a matter of fact, he literally believes just that. He not infrequently says, "I've got to learn it exactly, a life may depend on me knowing that." A consequence of this attitude, which is carefully nurtured throughout medical school, is the development of a phobia: the overdetermined fear of making a mistake. The development of this fear is quite understandable. The burden the physician must carry is at times almost unbearable. He feels responsible in a very personal way for the lives of his patients. When a man dies leaving young children and a widow, the doctor carries some of her grief and despair inside himself; and when a child dies, some of him dies too. He sees himself as a warrior against death and disease. When he loses a battle, through no fault of his own, he nevertheless feels pangs of guilt, and he relentlessly searches himself to see if there might have been a way to alter the outcome. For the physician a mistake leading to a serious consequence is intolerable, and any mistake reminds him of his vulnerability. There is little wonder that he becomes phobic. The classical way in which phobias are managed is to avoid the source of the fear. Since it is impossible to avoid making some mistakes in an active practice of medicine, a substitute defensive maneuver is employed. The physician develops the belief that he is omnipotent and omniscient, and therefore incapable of making mistakes. This belief allows the phobic physician to actively engage in his practice rather than avoid it. The fear of committing an error in a critical field like medicine is unavoidable and appropriately realistic. The physician, however, must learn to live with the fear rather than handle it defensively through a posture of omnipotence. This defense markedly interferes with his interpersonal professional relationships.

Physicians, of course, deny feelings of omnipotence. The evidence, however, renders their denials to whispers in the wind. The slightest mistake inflicts a large narcissistic wound. Depending on his underlying personality structure the physician may obsess for days about it, quickly rationalize it away, or deny it. The guilt produced is usually exaggerated and the incident is handled

defensively. The ways in which physicians enhance and support each other's defenses when an error is made could be the topic of another paper. The feelings of omnipotence become generalized to other areas of his life. A report of the Federal Aviation Agency (FAA), as quoted in *Time Magazine* (Aug 5, 1966), states that in 1964 and 1965 physicians had a fatal-accident rate four times as high as the average for all other private pilots. Major causes of the high death rate were risk-taking attitudes and judgments. Almost all of the accidents occurred on pleasure trips, and were therefore not necessary risks to get to a patient needing emergency care. The trouble, suggested an FAA official, is that too many doctors fly with "the feeling that they are omnipotent." Thus, the extremes to which the physician may go in preserving his self-concept of omnipotence may threaten his own life. This overdetermined preservation of omnipotence is indicative of its brittleness and its underlying foundation of fear of failure.

The physician finds himself trapped in a paradox. He fervently wants to give his patient the best possible medical care, and being open to the nurses' recommendations helps him accomplish this. On the other hand, accepting advice from nonphysicians is highly threatening to his omnipotence. The solution for the paradox is to receive sub rosa recommendations and make them appear to be initiated by himself. In short, he must learn to play the doctor-nurse game.

Some physicians never learn to play the game. Most learn in their internship, and a perceptive few learn during their clerkships in medical school. Medical students frequently complain that the nursing staff treats them as if they had just completed a junior Red Cross first-aid class instead of two years of intensive medical training. Interviewing nurses in a training hospital sheds considerable light on this phenomenon. In their words they said,

A few students just seem to be with it, they are able to understand what you are trying to tell them, and they are a pleasure to work with; most, however, pretend to know everything and refuse to listen to anything we have to say and I guess we do give them a rough time.

In essence, they are saying that those students who quickly learn the game are rewarded, and those that do not are punished.

Most physicians learn to play the game after they have weathered a few experiences like the one described below. On the first day of his internship, the physician and nurse were making rounds. They stopped at the bed of a 52-year-old woman who, after complimenting the young doctor on his appearance, complained to him of her problem with constipation. After several minutes of listening to her detailed description of peculiar diets, family home remedies, and special exercises that have helped her constipation in the past, the nurse politely interrupted the patient. She told her the doctor would take care of the problem and that he had to move on because there were other patients waiting to see him. The young doctor gave the nurse a stern look, turned toward the patient, and kindly told her he would order an enema for her that very afternoon. As they left the bedside, the nurse told him the patient has had a normal bowel movement every day for the past week and that in the 23 days the patient has been in the hospital she had never once passed up an opportunity to complain of her constipation. She quickly added that if the doctor wanted to order an enema, the patient would certainly receive one. After hearing this report the intern's mouth fell open and the wheels began turning in his head. He remembered the nurse's comment to the patient that, "the doctor had to move on," and it occurred to him that perhaps she was really giving him a message. This experience and a few more like it, and the young doctor learns to listen

for the subtle recommendations the nurses make.

Nursing Student Training

Unlike the medical student, who usually learns to play the game after he finishes medical school, the nursing student begins to learn it early in her training. Throughout her education she is trained to play the doctor-nurse game.

Student nurses are taught how to relate to physicians. They are told he has infinitely more knowledge than they, and thus he should be shown the utmost respect. In addition, it was not many years ago when nurses were instructed to stand whenever a physician entered a room. When he would come in for a conference the nurse was expected to offer him her chair, and when both entered a room the nurse would open the door for him and allow him to enter first. Although these practices are no longer rigidly adhered to, the premise upon which they were based is still promulgated. One nurse described that premise as, "He's God almighty and your job is to wait on him."

To inculcate subservience and inhibit deviancy, nursing schools, for the most part, are tightly run, disciplined institutions. Certainly there is great variation among nursing schools, and there is little question that the trend is toward giving students more autonomy. However, in too many schools this trend has not gone far enough, and the climate remains restrictive. The student's schedule is firmly controlled and there is very little free time. Classroom hours, study hours, meal time, and bedtime with lights out are rigidly enforced. In some schools meaningless chores are assigned, such as cleaning bed springs with cotton applicators. The relationship between student and instructor continues this military flavor. Often their relationship is more like that between recruit and drill sergeant than between student and teacher. Open dialogue is inhibited by attitudes of strict black and white, with few, if any, shades of gray. Straying from the rigidly outlined path is sure to result in disciplinary action.

The inevitable result of these practices is to instill in the student nurse a fear of independent action. This inhibition of independent action is most marked when relating to physicians. One of the students' greatest fears is making a blunder while assisting a physician and being publicly ridiculed by him. This is really more a reflection of the nature of their training than the prevalence of abusive physicians. The fear of being humiliated for a blunder while assisting in a procedure is generalized to the fear of humiliation for making any independent act in relating to a physician, especially the act of making a direct recommendation. Every nurse interviewed felt that making a suggestion to a physician was equivalent to insulting and belittling him. It was tantamount to questioning his medical knowledge and insinuating he did not know his business. In light of her image of the physician as an omniscient and punitive figure, the questioning of his knowledge would be unthinkable.

The student, however, is also given messages quite contrary to the ones described above. She is continually told that she is an invaluable aid to the physician in the treatment of the patient. She is told that she must help him in every way possible, and she is imbued with a strong sense of responsibility for the care of her patient. Thus she, like the physician, is caught in a paradox. The first set of messages implies that the physician is omniscient and that any recommendation she might make would be insulting to him and leave her open to ridicule. The second set of messages implies that she is an important asset to him, has much to contribute, and is duty-bound to make those contributions. Thus, when her good sense tells her a recommendation would be helpful to him she is not allowed to communicate it di-

rectly, nor is she allowed not to communicate it. The way out of the bind is to use the doctor-nurse game and communicate the recommendation without appearing to do so.

FORCES PRESERVING THE GAME

Upon observing the indirect interactional system which is the heart of the doctor-nurse game, one must ask the question, "Why does this inefficient mode of communication continue to exist?" The forces mitigating against change are powerful.

Rewards and Punishments

The doctor-nurse game has a powerful, innate self-perpetuating force—its system of rewards and punishments. One potent method of shaping behavior is to reward one set of behavioral patterns and to punish patterns which deviate from it. As described earlier, the rewards given for a well-played game and the punishments meted out to unskilled players are impressive. This system alone would be sufficient to keep the game flourishing. The game, however, has additional forces.

The Strength of the Set

It is well recognized that sets are hard to break. A powerful attitudinal set is the nurse's perception that making a suggestion to a physician is equivalent to insulting and belittling him. An example of where attempts are regularly made to break this set is seen on psychiatric treatment wards operating on a therapeutic community model. This model requires open and direct communication between members of the team. Psychiatrists working in these settings expend a great deal of energy in urging for and rewarding openness before direct patterns of communication become established. The rigidity of the resistance to break this set is impressive. If the physician himself is a prisoner of the set and therefore does not actively try to destroy it, change is near impossible.

The Need for Leadership

Lack of leadership and structure in any organization produces anxiety in its members. As the importance of the organization's mission increases, the demand by its members for leadership commensurately increases. In our culture human life is near the top of our hierarchy of values, and organizations which deal with human lives, such as law and medicine, are very rigidly structured. Certainly some of this is necessary for the systematic management of the task. The excessive degree of rigidity, however, is demanded by its members for their own psychic comfort rather than for its utility in efficiently carrying out its mission. The game lends support to this thesis. Indirect communication is an inefficient mode of transmitting information. However, it effectively supports and protects a rigid organizational structure with the physician in clear authority. Maintaining an omnipotent leader provides the other members with a great sense of security.

Sexual Roles

Another influence perpetuating the doctor-nurse game is the sexual identity of the players. Doctors are predominately men and nurses are almost exclusively women. There are elements of the game which reinforce the stereotyped roles of male dominance and female passivity. Some nursing instructors explicitly tell their students that their femininity is an important asset to be used when relating to physicians.

COMMENT

The doctor and nurse have a shared history and thus have been able to work out their game so that it operates more efficiently than one would expect in an indirect system. Major difficulty arises, however, when the physician works closely with other disciplines which are not normally considered part of the medical sphere. With expanding medical horizons encompassing cooperation with sociologists, engineers, anthropologists, computer analysts etc, continued expectation of a doctor-nurselike interaction by the physician is disastrous. The sociologist, for example, is not willing to play that kind of game. When his direct communications are rebuffed the relationship breaks down.

The major disadvantage of a doctor-nurselike game is its inhibitory effect on open dialogue which is stifling and anti-intellectual. The game is basically a transactional neurosis, and both professions would enhance themselves by taking steps to change the attitudes which breed the game.

25

Presenting the Self to Others

ERVING GOFFMAN

When an individual enters the presence of others, they commonly seek to acquire information about him or to bring into play information about him already possessed. They will be interested in his general socio-economic status, his conception of self, his attitude toward them, his competence, his trustworthiness, etc. Although some of this information seems to be sought almost as an end in itself, there are usually quite practical reasons for acquiring it. Information about the individual helps to define the situation, enabling others to know in advance what he will expect of them and what they may expect of him. Informed in these ways, the others will know how best to act in order to call forth a desired response from him.

For those present, many sources of information become accessible and many carriers (or "sign-vehicles") become available for conveying this information. If unacquainted with the individual, observers can glean clues from his conduct and appearance which allow them to apply their previous experience with individuals roughly similar to the one before them or, more important, to apply untested stereotypes to him. They can also assume from past experience that only individuals of a particular kind are likely to be found in a given social setting. They can rely on what the individual says about himself or on documentary evidence he provides as to who and what he is. If they know, or know of, the individual by virtue of experience prior to the interaction, they can rely on assumptions as to the persistence and gener-

ality of psychological traits as a means of predicting his present and future behavior.

However, during the period in which the individual is in the immediate presence of the others, few events may occur which directly provide the others with the conclusive information they will need if they are to direct wisely their own activity. Many crucial facts lie beyond the time and place of interaction or lie concealed within it. For example, the "true" or "real" attitudes, beliefs, and emotions of the individual can be ascertained only indirectly, through his avowals or through what appears to be involuntary expressive behavior. Similarly, if the individual offers the others a product or service, they will often find that during the interaction there will be no time and place immediately available for eating the pudding that the proof can be found in. They will be forced to accept some events as conventional or natural signs of something not directly available to the senses. In Ichheiser's terms,[1] the individual will have to act so that he intentionally or unintentionally *expresses* himself, and the others will in turn have to be *impressed* in some way by him.

The expressiveness of the individual (and therefore his capacity to give impressions) appears to involve two radically different kinds of sign activity: the expression that he *gives*, and the expression that he *gives off*. The first involves verbal symbols or their substitutes which he uses admittedly and solely to convey the information that he and the others are known to attach to these symbols. This is communication in the traditional and narrow sense. The second involves a wide range of action that others can treat as symptomatic of the actor, the expectation being that the action was performed for reasons other than the information conveyed in this way. As we shall have to see, this distinction has an only initial validity. The individual does of course intentionally convey misinformation by means of both of these types of communication, the first involving deceit, the second feigning.

Taking communication in both its narrow and broad sense, one finds that when the individual is in the immediate presence of others, his activity will have a promissory character. The others are likely to find that they must accept the individual on faith, offering him a just return while he is present before them in exchange for something whose true value will not be established until after he has left their presence. (Of course, the others also live by inference in their dealings with the physical world, but it is only in the world of social interaction that the objects about which they make inferences will purposely facilitate and hinder this inferential process.) The security that they justifiably feel in making inferences about the individual will vary, of course, depending on such factors as the amount of information they already possess about him, but no amount of such past evidence can entirely obviate the necessity of acting on the basis of inferences. As William I. Thomas suggested:

> It is also highly important for us to realize that we do not as a matter of fact lead our lives, make our decisions, and reach our goals in everyday life either statistically or scientifically. We live by inference, I am, let us say, your guest. You do not know, you cannot determine scientifically, that I will not steal your money or your spoons. But inferentially I will not, and inferentially you have me as a guest.[2]

Let us now turn from the others to the point of view of the individual who presents himself before them. He may wish them to think highly of him, or to think that he thinks highly of them, or to perceive how in fact he feels toward them, or to obtain no clear-cut impression; he may wish to ensure sufficient harmony so that the interaction can be sustained, or to defraud, get rid of, confuse, mislead, antagonize, or insult them. Regardless of the particular objective which the individual has in mind and of his motive for having this objective, it will be in his interests to control the conduct of the others, especially their responsive treatment of him.[3] This control is achieved largely by influencing the definition of the situation which the others come to formulate, and he can influence this definition by expressing himself in such a way as to give them the kind of impression that will lead them to act voluntarily in accordance with his own plan. Thus, when an individual appears in the presence of others, there will usually be some reason for him to mobilize his activity so that it will convey an impression to others which it is in his interests to convey. Since a girl's dormitory mates will glean evidence of her popularity from the calls she receives on the phone, we can suspect that some girls will arrange for calls to be made, and Willard Waller's finding can be anticipated:

> It has been reported by many observers that a girl who is called to the telephone in the dormitories will often allow herself to be called several times, in order to give all the other girls ample opportunity to hear her paged.[4]

Of the two kinds of communication—expressions given and expressions given off—this report will be primarily concerned with the latter, with the more theatrical and contextual kind, the non-verbal, presumably unintentional kind, whether this communication be purposely engineered or not. As an example of what we must try to examine, I would like to cite at length a novelistic incident in which Preedy, a vacationing Englishman, makes his first appearance on the beach of his summer hotel in Spain:

> But in any case he took care to avoid catching anyone's eye. First of all, he had to make it clear to those potential companions of his holiday that they were of no concern to him whatsoever. He stared through them, round them, over them—eyes lost in space. The beach might have been empty. If by chance a ball was thrown his way, he looked surprised; then let a smile of amusement lighten his face (Kindly Preedy), looked round dazed to see that there *were* people on the beach, tossed it back with a smile to himself and not a smile *at* the people, and then resumed carelessly his nonchalant survey of space.
>
> But it was time to institute a little parade, the parade of the Ideal Preedy. By devious handlings he gave any who wanted to look a chance to see the title of his book—a Spanish translation of Homer, classic thus, but not daring, cosmopolitan too—and then gathered together his beachwrap and bag into a neat sand-resistant pile (Methodical and Sensible Preedy), rose slowly to stretch at ease his huge frame (Big-Cat Preedy), and tossed aside his sandals (Carefree Preedy, after all).
>
> The marriage of Preedy and the sea! There were alternative rituals. The first involved the stroll that turns into a run and a dive straight into the water, thereafter smoothing into a strong splashless crawl towards the horizon. But of course not really to the horizon. Quite suddenly he would turn on to his back and thrash great white splashes with his legs, somehow thus showing that he could have swum further had he wanted to, and then would stand up a quarter out of water for all to see who it was.
>
> The alternative course was simpler, it avoided the cold-water shock and it avoided the risk of appearing too high-spirited. The point was to appear to be so used to the sea, the Mediterranean, and this particular beach, that one might as well be in the sea as out of it. It involved a slow stroll down and into the edge of the water—not even noticing his toes were wet, land and water all the same to *him!*—with his eyes up at the sky gravely surveying portents, invisible to others, of the weather (Local Fisherman Preedy).[5]

The novelist means us to see that Preedy is improperly concerned with the extensive impressions he feels his sheer bodily action is giving off to those around him. We can malign Preedy further by assuming that he has acted merely in order to give a particular impression, that this is a false impression, and that the others present receive either no impression at all, or, worse still, the impression that Preedy is affectedly trying to cause them to receive this particular impression. But the important point for us here is that the kind of impression Preedy thinks he is making is in fact the kind of impression that others correctly and incorrectly glean from someone in their midst.

I have said that when an individual appears before others his actions will influence the definition of the situation which they come to have. Sometimes the individual will act in a thoroughly calculating manner, expressing himself in a given way solely in order to give the kind of impression to others that is likely to evoke from them a specific response he is concerned to obtain. Sometimes the individual will be calculating in his activity but be relatively unaware that this is the case. Sometimes he will intentionally and consciously express himself in a particular way, but chiefly because the tradition of his group or social status requires this kind of expression and not because of any particular response (other than vague acceptance or approval) that is likely to be evoked from those impressed by the expression. Sometimes the traditions of an individual's role will lead him to give a well-designed impression of a particular kind and yet he may be neither consciously nor unconsciously disposed to create such an impression. The others, in their turn, may be suitably impressed by the individual's efforts to convey something, or may misunderstand the situation and come to conclusions that are warranted neither by the individual's intent nor by the facts. In any case, in so far as the others act *as if* the individual had conveyed a particular impression, we may take a functional or pragmatic view and say that the individual has "effectively" projected a given definition of the situation and "effectively" fostered the understanding that a given state of affairs obtains.

There is one aspect of the others' response that bears special comment here. Knowing that the individual is likely to present himself in a light that is favorable to him, the others may divide what they witness into two parts: a part that is relatively easy for the individual to manipulate at will, being chiefly his verbal assertions, and a part in regard to which he seems to have little concern or control, being chiefly derived from the expressions he gives off. The others may then use what are considered to be the ungovernable aspects of his expressive behavior as a check upon the validity of what is conveyed by the governable aspects. In this a fundamental asymmetry is demonstrated in the communication process, the individual presumably being aware of only one stream of his communication, the witnesses of this stream and one other. For example, in Shetland Isle one crofter's wife, in serving native dishes to a visitor from the mainland of Britain, would listen with a polite smile to his polite claims of liking what he was eating; at the same time she would take note of the rapidity with which the visitor lifted his fork or spoon to his mouth, the eagerness with which he passed food into his mouth, and the gusto expressed in chewing the food, using these signs as a check on the stated feelings of the eater. The same woman, in order to discover what one acquaintance (A) "actually" thought of another acquaintance (B), would wait until B was in the presence of A but engaged in conversation with still another person (C). She would then covertly examine the facial expressions of A as he regarded B in conversation with C. Not being in conversation with B, and not being directly observed by him, A would sometimes relax usual constraints and tactful deceptions, and freely express what he was "actually" feeling about B. This Shetlander, in short, would observe the unobserved observer.

Now given the fact that others are likely to check up on the more controllable aspects of behavior by means of the less controllable, one can expect that sometimes the individual will try to exploit this very possibility, guiding the impression he makes through behavior felt to be reliably informing.[6] For example, in gaining admission to a tight social circle, the participant observer may not only wear an accepting look while listening to an informant, but may also be careful to wear the same look when observing the informant talking to others; observers of the observer will then not as easily discover where he actually stands. A specific illustration may be cited from Shetland Isle. When a neighbor dropped in to have a cup of tea, he would ordinarily wear at least a hint of an expectant warm smile as he passed through the door into the cottage. Since lack of physical obstructions outside the cottage and lack of light within it usually made it possible to observe the visitor unobserved as he approached the house, islanders sometimes took pleasure in watching the visitor drop whatever expression he was manifesting and replace it with a sociable one just before reaching the door. However, some visitors, in appreciating that this examination was occurring, would blindly adopt a social face a long distance from the house, thus ensuring the projection of a constant image.

This kind of control upon the part of the individual reinstates the symmetry of the communication process, and sets the stage for a kind of information game—a potentially infinite cycle of concealment, discovery, false revelation, and rediscovery. It should be added that since the others are likely to be relatively unsuspicious of the presumably unguided aspect of the individual's conduct, he can gain much by controlling it. The others of course may sense that the individual is manipulating the presumably spontaneous aspects of his behavior, and seek in this very act of manipulation some shading of conduct that the individual has not managed to control. This again provides a check upon the individual's behavior, this time his presumably uncalculated behavior, thus reestablishing the asymmetry of the communication process. Here I would like only to add the suggestion that the arts of piercing an individual's effort at calculated unintentionality seem better developed than our capacity to manipulate our own behavior, so that regardless of how many steps have occurred in the information game, the witness is likely to have the advantage over the actor, and the initial asymmetry of the communication process is likely to be retained.

When we allow that the individual projects a definition of the situation when he appears before others, we must also see that the others, however passive their role may seem to be, will themselves effectively project a definition of the situation by virtue of their response to the individual and by virtue of any lines of action they initiate to him. Ordinarily the definitions of the situation projected by the several different participants are sufficiently attuned to one another so that open contradiction will not occur. I do not mean that there will be the kind of consensus that arises when each individual present candidly expresses what he really feels and honestly agrees with the expressed feelings of the others present. This kind of harmony is an optimistic ideal and in any case not necessary for the smooth working of society. Rather, each participant is expected to suppress his immediate heart-felt feelings, conveying a view of the situation which he feels the others will be able to find at least temporarily acceptable. The maintenance of this surface of agreement, this veneer of consensus, is facilitated by each participant concealing his own wants behind statements which assert values to which everyone present feels obliged to give lip service. Further, there is usually a kind of division of definitional labor. Each participant is allowed to establish the tentative official ruling regarding matters which are vital to him but not immediately important to others, e.g., the rationalizations and justifications by which he accounts for his past activity. In exchange for this courtesy he remains silent or non-committal on matters important to others but not immediately important to him. We have then a kind of interactional *modus vivendi*. Together the participants contribute to a single over all definition of the situation which involves not so much a real agreement as to what exists but rather a real agreement as to whose claims concerning what issues will be temporarily honored. Real agreement will also exist concerning the desirability of avoiding an open conflict of definitions of the situation.[7] I will refer to this level of agreement as a "working consensus." It is to be understood that the working consensus established in one interaction setting will be quite different in content from the working consensus established in a different type of setting. Thus, between two friends at lunch, a reciprocal show of affection, respect, and concern for the other is maintained. In service occupations, on the other hand, the specialist often maintains an image of disinterested involvement in the problem of the client, while the client responds with a show of respect for the competence and integrity of the specialist. Regardless of such differences in content, however, the general form of these working arrangements is the same.

In noting the tendency for a participant to accept the definitional claims made by the others present, we can appreciate the crucial importance of the information that the individual *initially* possesses or acquires concerning his fellow participants, for it is on the basis of this initial information that the individual starts to define the situation and starts to build up lines of responsive action. The individual's initial projection commits him to what he is proposing to be and requires him to drop all pretenses of being other things. As the interaction among the participants progresses, additions and modifications in this initial informational state will of course occur, but it is essential that these later developments be related without contradiction to, and even built up from, the initial positions taken by the several participants. It would seem that an individual can more easily make a choice as to what line of treatment to demand from and extend to the others present at the beginning of an encounter than he can alter the line of treatment that is being pursued once the interaction is underway.

In everyday life, of course, there is a clear understanding that first impressions are important. Thus, the work adjustment of those in service occupations will often hinge upon a capacity to seize and hold the initiative in the service relation, a capacity that will require subtle aggressiveness on the part of the server when he is of lower socioeconomic status than his client. W. F. Whyte suggests the waitress as an example:

> The first point that stands out is that the waitress who bears up under pressure does not simply respond to her customers. She acts with some skill to control their behavior. The first question to ask when we look at the customer relationship is, "Does the waitress get the jump on the customer, or does the customer get the jump on the waitress?" The skilled waitress realizes the crucial nature of this question. . . .
>
> The skilled waitress tackles the customer with confidence and without hesitation. For example, she may find that a new customer has seated himself before she could clear off the dirty dishes and change the cloth. He is now leaning on the table studying the menu.

She greets him, says, "May I change the cover, please?" and without waiting for an answer, takes his menu away from him so that he moves back from the table, and she goes about her work. The relationship is handled politely but firmly, and there is never any question as to who is in charge.[8]

When the interaction that is initiated by "first impressions" is itself merely the initial interaction in an extended series of interactions involving the same participants, we speak of "getting off on the right foot" and feel that it is crucial that we do so. Thus, one learns that some teachers take the following view:

> You can't ever let them get the upper hand on you and you're through. So I start out tough. The first day I get a new class in, I let them know who's boss . . . You've got to start off tough, then you can ease up as you go along. If you start out easy-going, when you try to be tough, they'll just look at you and laugh.[9]

Similarly, attendants in mental institutions may feel that if the new patient is sharply put in his place the first day on the ward and made to see who is boss, much future difficulty will be prevented.[10]

Given the fact that the individual effectively projects a definition of the situation when he enters the presence of others, we can assume that events may occur within the interaction which contradict, discredit, or otherwise throw doubt upon this projection. When these disruptive events occur, the interaction itself may come to a confused and embarrassed halt. Some of the assumptions upon which the responses of the participants had been predicated become untenable, and the participants find themselves lodged in an interaction for which the situation has been wrongly defined and is now no longer defined. At such moments the individual whose presentation has been discredited may feel ashamed while the others present may feel hostile, and all the participants may come to feel ill at ease, nonplussed, out of countenance, embarrassed, experiencing the kind of anomie that is generated when the minute social system of face-to-face interaction breaks down.

In stressing the fact that the initial definition of the situation projected by an individual tends to provide a plan for the co-operative activity that follows—in stressing this action point of view—we must not overlook the crucial fact that any projected definition of the situation also has a distinctive moral character. It is this moral character of projections that will chiefly concern us in this report. Society is organized on the principle that any individual who possesses certain social characteristics has a moral right to expect that others will value and treat him in an appropriate way. Connected with this principle is a second, namely that an individual who implicitly or explicitly signifies that he has certain social characteristics ought in fact to be what he claims he is. In consequence, when an individual projects a definition of the situation and thereby makes an implicit or explicit claim to be a person of a particular kind, he automatically exerts a moral demand upon the others, obliging them to value and treat him in the manner that persons of his kind have a right to expect. He also implicitly forgoes all claims to be things he does not appear to be[11] and hence forgoes the treatment that would be appropriate for such individuals. The others find, then, that the individual has informed them as to what is and as to what they *ought* to see as the "is."

One cannot judge the importance of definitional disruptions by the frequency with which they occur, for apparently they would occur more frequently were not constant precautions taken. We find that preventive practices are constantly employed to avoid these embarrassments and that corrective practices are constantly employed to compensate for discrediting occurrences that have not been successfully avoided. When the individual employs these strategies and tactics to protect his own projections, we may refer to them as "defensive practices"; when a participant employs them to save the definition of the situation projected by another, we speak of "protective practices" or "tact." Together, defensive and protective practices comprise the techniques employed to safeguard the impression fostered by an individual during his presence before others. It should be added that while we may be ready to see that no fostered impression would survive if defensive practices were not employed, we are less ready perhaps to see that few impressions could survive if those who received the impression did not exert tact in their reception of it.

In addition to the fact that precautions are taken to prevent disruption of projected definitions, we may also note that an intense interest in these disruptions comes to play a significant role in the social life of the group. Practical jokes and social games are played in which embarrassments which are to be taken unseriously are purposely engineered.[12] Fantasies are created in which devastating exposures occur. Anecdotes from the past—real, embroidered, or fictitious— are told and retold, detailing disruptions which occurred, almost occurred, or occurred and were admirably resolved. There seems to be no grouping which does not have a ready supply of these games, reveries, and cautionary tales, to be used as a source of humor, a catharsis for anxieties, and a sanction for inducing individuals to be modest in their claims and reasonable in their projected expectations. The individual may tell himself through dreams of getting into impossible positions. Families tell of the time a guest got his dates mixed and arrived when neither the house nor anyone in it was ready for him. Journalists tell of times when an all-too-meaningful misprint occurred, and the paper's assumption of objectivity or decorum was humorously discredited. Public servants tell of times a client ridiculously misunderstood form instructions, giving answers which implied an unanticipated and bizarre definition of the situation.[13] Seamen, whose home away from home is rigorously he-man, tell stories of coming back home and inadvertently asking mother to "pass the fucking butter."[14] Diplomats tell of the time a near-sighted queen asked a republican ambassador about the health of his king.[15]

To summarize, then, I assume that when an individual appears before others he will have many motives for trying to control the impression they receive of the situation. . . .

NOTES

1. Gustav Ichheiser, "Misunderstandings in Human Relations," Supplement to *The American Journal of Sociology*, LV (September, 1949), pp. 6–7.

2. Quoted in E. H. Volkart, editor, *Social Behavior and Personality*, Contributions of W. I. Thomas to Theory and Social Research (New York: Social Science Research Council, 1951), p. 5.

3. Here I owe much to an unpublished paper by Tom Burns of the University of Edinburgh. He presents the argument that in all interaction a basic underlying theme is the desire of each participant to guide and control the responses made by the others present. A similar argument has been advanced by Jay Haley in a recent unpublished paper, but in regard to a special kind of control, that having to do with defining the nature of the relationship of those involved in the interaction.

4. Willard Waller, "The Rating and Dating Complex," *American Sociological Review*, II, p. 730.

5. William Sansom, *A Contest of Ladies* (London: Hogarth, 1956), pp. 230–32.

6. The widely read and rather sound writings of Stephen Potter are concerned in part with signs that can be engineered to give a shrewd observer the apparently incidental cues he needs to discover concealed virtues the gamesman does not in fact possess.

7. An interaction can be purposely set up as a time and place for voicing differences in opinion, but in such cases participants must be careful to agree not to disagree on the proper tone of voice, vocabulary, and degree of seriousness in which all arguments are to be phrased, and upon the mutual respect which disagreeing participants must carefully continue to express toward one another. This debaters' or academic definition of the situation may also be involved suddenly and judiciously as a way of translating a serious conflict of views into one that can be handled within a framework acceptable to all present.

8. W. F. Whyte, "When Workers and Customers Meet," Chap. VII, *Industry and Society*, ed. W. F. Whyte (New York: McGraw-Hill, 1946), pp. 132–33.

9. Teacher interview quoted by Howard S. Becker, "Social Class Variations in the Teacher-Pupil Relationship," *Journal of Educational Sociology*, XXV, p. 459.

10. Harold Taxels, "Authority Structure in a Mental Hospital Ward" (unpublished Master's thesis, Department of Sociology, University of Chicago, 1953).

11. This role of the witness in limiting what it is the individual can be has been stressed by Existentialists, who see it as a basic threat to individual freedom. See Jean-Paul Sartre, *Being and Nothingness*, trans. by Hazel E. Barnes (New York: Philosophical Library, 1956), p. 365ff.

12. Goffman, op. cit., pp. 319–27.

13. Peter Blau, "Dynamics of Bureaucracy" (Ph.D. dissertation, Department of Sociology, Columbia University, forthcoming, University of Chicago Press), pp. 127–29.

14. Walter M. Beattie, Jr., "The Merchant Seaman" (unpublished M. A. Report, Department of Sociology, University of Chicago, 1950), p. 35.

15. Sir Frederick Ponsonby, *Recollections of Three Reigns* (New York: Dutton, 1952), p. 46.

26

Stigma

ERVING GOFFMAN

The Greeks, who were apparently strong on visual aids, originated the term *stigma* to refer to bodily signs designed to expose something unusual and bad about the moral status of the signifier. The signs were cut or burnt into the body and advertised that the bearer was a slave, a criminal, or a traitor—a blemished person, ritually polluted, to be avoided, especially in public places. Later, in Christian times, two layers of metaphor were added to the term: the first referred to bodily signs of holy grace that took the form of eruptive blossoms on the skin; the second, a medical allusion to this religious allusion, referred to bodily signs of physical disorder. Today the term is widely used in something like the original literal sense, but is applied more to the disgrace itself than to the bodily evidence of it. Furthermore, shifts have occurred in the kinds of disgrace that arouse concern. Students, however, have made little effort to describe the structural preconditions of stigma, or even to provide a definition of the concept itself. It seems necessary, therefore, to try at the beginning to sketch in some very general assumptions and definitions.

PRELIMINARY CONCEPTIONS

Society establishes the means of categorizing persons and the complement of attributes felt to be ordinary and natural for members of each of these categories. Social settings establish the categories of persons likely to be encountered there. The routines of social intercourse in established settings allow us to deal with anticipated others without special attention or thought. When a stranger comes into our presence, then, first appearances are likely to enable us to anticipate his category and attributes, his "social identity"—to use a term that is better than "social status" because personal attributes such as "honesty" are involved, as well as structural ones, like "occupation."

We lean on these anticipations that we have, transforming them into normative expectations, into righteously presented demands.

Typically, we do not become aware that we have made these demands or aware of what they are until an active question arises as to whether or not they will be fulfilled. It is then that we are likely to realize that all along we had been making certain assumptions as to what the individual before us ought to be. Thus, the demands we make might better be called demands made "in effect," and the character we impute to the individual might better be seen as an imputation made in potential retrospect—a characterization "in effect," a *virtual social identity*. The category and attributes he could in fact be proved to possess will be called his *actual social identity*.

While the stranger is present before us, evidence can arise of his possessing an attribute that makes his different from others in the category of persons available for him to be, and of a less desirable kind—in the extreme, a person who is quite thoroughly bad, or dangerous, or weak. He is thus reduced in our minds from a whole and usual person to a tainted, discounted one. Such an attribute is a stigma, especially when its discrediting effect is very extensive; sometimes it is also called a failing, a shortcoming, a handicap. It constitutes a special discrepancy between virtual and actual social identity. Note that there are other types of discrepancy between virtual and actual social identity, for example the kind that causes us to reclassify an individual from one socially anticipated category to a different but equally well-anticipated one, and the kind that causes us to alter our estimation of the individual upward. Note, too, that not all undesirable attributes are at issue, but only those which are incongruous with our stereotype of what a given type of individual should be.

The term stigma, then, will be used to refer to an attribute that is deeply discrediting, but it should be seen that a language of relationships, not attributes, is really needed. An attribute that stigmatizes one type of possessor can confirm the usualness of another, and therefore is neither creditable nor discreditable as a thing in itself. For example, some jobs in America cause holders without the expected college education to conceal this fact; other jobs, however, can lead the few of their holders who have a higher education to keep this a secret, lest they be marked as failures and outsiders. Similarly, a middle class boy may feel no compunction in being seen going to the library; a professional criminal, however, writes:

> I can remember before now on more than one occasion, for instance, going into a public library near where I was living, and looking over my shoulder a couple of times before I actually went in just to make sure no one who knew me was standing about and seeing me do it.[1]

So, too, an individual who desires to fight for his country may conceal a physical defect, lest his claimed physical status be discredited; later, the same individual, embittered and trying to get out of the army, may suc-

ceed in gaining admission to the army hospital, where he would be discredited if discovered in not really having an acute sickness.[2] A stigma, then, is really a special kind of relationship between attribute and stereotype, although I don't propose to continue to say so, in part because there are important attributes that almost everywhere in our society are discrediting.

The term stigma and its synonyms conceal a double perspective: does the stigmatized individual assume his differentness is known about already or is evident on the spot, or does he assume it is neither known about by those present nor immediately perceivable by them? In the first case one deals with the plight of the *discredited*, in the second with that of the *discreditable*. This is an important difference, even though a particular stigmatized individual is likely to have experience with both situations. I will begin with the situation of the discredited and move on to the discreditable but not always separate the two.

Three grossly different types of stigma may be mentioned. First there are abominations of the body—the various physical deformities. Next there are blemishes of individual character perceived as weak will, domineering or unnatural passions, treacherous and rigid beliefs, and dishonesty, these being inferred from a known record of, for example, mental disorder, imprisonment, addiction, alcoholism, homosexuality, unemployment, suicidal attempts, and radical political behavior. Finally there are the tribal stigma of race, nation, and religion, these being stigma that can be transmitted through lineages and equally contaminate all members of a family.[3] In all of these various instances of stigma, however, including those the Greeks had in mind, the same sociological features are found: an individual who might have been received easily in ordinary social intercourse possesses a trait that can obtrude itself upon attention and turn those of us whom he meets away from him, breaking the claim that his other attributes have on us. He possesses a stigma, an undesired differentness from what we had anticipated. We and those who do not depart negatively from the particular expectations at issue I shall call the *normals*.

The attitudes we normals have toward a person with a stigma, and the actions we take in regard to him, are well known, since these responses are what benevolent social action is designed to soften and ameliorate. By definition, of course, we believe the person with a stigma is not quite human. On this assumption we exercise varieties of discrimination, through which we effectively, if often unthinkingly, reduce his life chances. We construct a stigma-theory, an ideology to explain his inferiority and account for the danger he represents, sometimes rationalizing an animosity based on other differences, such as those of social class.[4] We use specific stigma terms such as cripple, bastard, moron in our daily discourse as a source of metaphor and imagery, typically without giving thought to the original meaning.[5] We tend to impute a wide range of imperfections on the basis of the original one,[6] and at the same time to impute some desirable but undesired attributes often of a supernatural cast, such as "sixth sense," or "understanding."[7]

> For some, there may be a hesitancy about touching or steering the blind, while for others, the perceived failure to see may be generalized into a gestalt of disability, so that the individual shouts at the blind as if they were deaf or attempts to lift them as if they were crippled. Those confronting the blind may have a whole range of belief that is anchored in the stereotype. For instance, they may think they are subject to unique judgment, assuming the blinded individual draws on special channels of information unavailable to others.[8]

Further, we may perceive his defensive response to his situation as a direct expression of his defect, and then see both defect and response as just retribution for something he or his parents or his tribe did, and hence a justification of the way we treat him.[9]

Now turn from the normal to the person he is normal against. It seems generally true that members of a social category may strongly support a standard of judgment that they and others agree does not directly apply to them. Thus it is that a businessman may demand womanly behavior from females or ascetic behavior from monks, and not construe himself as someone who ought to realize either of these styles of conduct. The distinction is between realizing a norm and merely supporting it. The issue of stigma does not arise here, but only where there is some expectation on all sides that those in a given category should not only support a particular norm but also realize it.

Also, it seems possible for an individual to fail to live up to what we effectively demand of him, and yet be relatively untouched by this failure; insulated by his alienation, protected by identity beliefs of his own, he feels that he is a full-fledged normal human being, and that we are the ones who are not quite human. He bears a stigma but does not seem to be impressed or repentant about doing so. This possibility is celebrated in exemplary tales about Mennonites, Gypsies, shameless scoundrels, and very orthodox Jews.

In America at present, however, separate systems of honor seem to be on the decline. The stigmatized individual tends to hold the same beliefs about identity that we do; this is a pivotal fact. His deepest feelings about what he is may be his sense of being a "normal person," a human being like anyone else, a person, therefore, who deserves a fair chance and a fair break.[10] (Actually, however phrased, he bases his claims not on what he thinks is due *everyone*, but only everyone of a selected social category into which he unquestionably fits, for example, anyone of his age, sex, profession, and so forth.) Yet he may perceive, usually quite correctly, that whatever others profess, they do not really "accept" him and are not ready to make contact with him on "equal grounds."[11] Further, the standards he has incorporated from the wider society equip him to be intimately alive to what others see as his failing, inevitably causing him, if only for moments, to agree that he does indeed fall short of what he really ought to be. Shame becomes a central possibility, arising from the individual's perception of one of his own attributes as being a defiling thing to possess, and one he can readily see himself as not possessing.

NOTES

1. T. Parker and R. Allerton, *The Courage of His Convictions* (London: Hutchinson & Co., 1962), p. 109.
2. In this connection see the review by M. Meltzer, "Countermanipulation through Malingering," in A. Biderman and H. Zimmer, eds., *The Manipulation of Human Behavior* (New York: John Wiley & Sons, 1961), pp. 277–304.
3. In recent history, especially in Britain, low class status functioned as an important tribal stigma, the sins of the parents, or at least their milieu, being visited on the child, should the child rise improperly far above his initial station. The management of class stigma is of course a central theme in the English novel.
4. D. Riesman, "Some Observations Concerning Marginality," *Phylon*, Second Quarter, 1951, 122.
5. The case regarding mental patients is presented by TG. J. Scheff in a forthcoming paper.

6. In regard to the blind, see E. Henrich and L. Kriegel, eds., *Experiments in Survival* (New York: Association for the Aid of Crippled Children, 1961), pp. 152 and 186; and H. Chevigny, *My Eyes Have a Cold Nose* (New Haven, Conn.: Yale University Press, paperbound, 1962), p. 201.
7. In the words of one blind woman, "I was asked to endorse a perfume, presumably because being sightless my sense of smell was super-discriminating." See T. Keitlen (with N. Lobsenz), *Farewell to Fear* (New York: Avon, 1962), p. 10.
8. A. G. Gowman, *The War Blind in American Social Structure* (New York: American Foundation for the Blind, 1957), p. 198.
9. For examples, see Macgregor *et al.*, *op. cit.*, throughout.
10. The notion of "normal human being" may have its source in the medical approach to humanity or in the tendency of large-scale bureaucratic organizations, such as the nation state, to treat all members in some respects as equal. Whatever its origins, it seems to provide the basic imagery through which laymen currently conceive of themselves. Interestingly, a convention seems to have emerged in popular life-story writing where a questionable person proves his claim to normalcy by citing his acquisition of a spouse and children, and, oddly, by attesting to his spending Christmas and Thanksgiving with them.
11. A criminal's view of this nonacceptance is presented in Parker and Allerton, *op. cit.*, pp. 110–111.

27

Marriage and the Construction of Reality

PETER L. BERGER
HANSFRIED KELLNER

Ever since Durkheim it has been a commonplace of family sociology that marriage serves as a protection against anomie [normlessness] for the individual. Interesting and pragmatically useful though this insight is, it is but the negative side of a phenomenon of much broader significance. If one speaks of *anomic* states, then one ought properly to investigate also the *nomic* processes that, by their absence, lead to the aforementioned states. If, consequently, one finds a negative correlation between marriage and anomie, then one should be led to inquire into the character of marriage as a *nomos*-building instrumentality, that is, of marriage as a social arrangement that creates for the individual the sort of order in which he can experience his life as making sense. It is our intention here to discuss marriage in these terms. While this could evidently be done in a macrosociological perspective, dealing with marriage as a major social institution related to other broad structures of society, our focus will be microsociological, dealing primarily with the social processes affecting the individuals in any specific marriage, although, of course, the larger framework of these processes will have to be understood. In what sense this discussion can be described as microsociology of knowledge will hopefully become clearer in the course of it.[1]

Marriage is obviously only *one* social relationship in which this process of *nomos*-building takes place. It is, therefore, necessary to first look in more general terms at the character of this process. In doing so, we are influenced by three theoretical perspectives—the Weberian perspective on society as a network of meanings, the Meadian perspective on identity as a social phenomenon, and the phenomenological analysis of the social structuring of reality especially as given in the work of Schutz and Merleau-Ponty.[2] Not being convinced, however, that theoretical lucidity is necessarily enhanced by terminological ponderosity, we shall avoid as much as possible the use of the sort of jargon for which both sociologists and phenomenologists have acquired dubious notoriety.

The process that interests us here is the one that constructs, maintains and modifies a consistent reality that can be meaningfully experienced by individuals. In its essential forms this process is determined by the society in which it occurs. Every society has its specific way of defining and perceiving reality—its world, its universe, its overarching organization of symbols. This is already given in the language that forms the symbolic base of the society. Erected over this base, and by means of it, is a system of ready-made *typifications* [stereotypical explanations of events in the world], through which the innumerable experiences of reality come to be ordered.[3] These typifications and their order are held in common by the members of society, thus acquiring not only the character of objectivity, but being taken for granted as *the* world *tout court*, the only world that normal men can conceive of.[4] The seemingly objective and taken-for-granted character of the social definitions of reality can be seen most clearly in the case of language itself, but it is important to keep in mind that the latter forms the base and instrumentality of a much larger world-erecting process.

The socially constructed world must be continually mediated to and actualized by the individual, so that it can become and remain indeed *his* world as well. The individual is given by his society certain decisive cornerstones for his everyday experience and conduct. Most importantly, the individual is supplied with specific sets of typifications and criteria of relevance, predefined for him by the society and made available to him for the ordering of his everyday life. This ordering or (in line with our opening considerations) nomic apparatus is biographically cumulative. It begins to be formed in the individual from the earliest stages of socialization on, then keeps on being enlarged and modified by himself throughout his biography.[5] While there are individual biographical differences making for differences in the constitution of this apparatus in specific individuals, there exists in the society an overall consensus on the range of differences deemed to be tolerable. Without such consensus, indeed, society would be impossible as a going concern, since it would then lack the ordering principles by which alone experience can be shared and conduct can be mutually intelligible. This order, by which the individual comes to perceive and define his world, is thus not chosen by him, except perhaps for very small modifications. Rather, it is discovered by him as an external datum, a ready-made world that simply is *there* for him to go ahead and live in, though he modifies it continually in the process of living in it. Nevertheless, this world is in need of *validation*, perhaps precisely because of an ever-present glimmer of suspicion as to its social manufacture and relativity. This validation, while it must be undertaken by the individual himself, requires ongoing interaction with others who co-inhabit this same socially

constructed world. In a broad sense, *all* the other co-inhabitants of this world serve a validating function. Every morning the newspaper boy validates the widest coordinates of my world and the mailman bears tangible validation of my own location within these coordinates. However, some validations are more significant than others. Every individual requires the ongoing validation of his world, including crucially the validation of his identity and place in this world, by those few who are his truly significant others.[6] Just as the individual's deprivation of relationship with his significant others will plunge him into anomie, so their continued presence will sustain for him that *nomos* by which he can feel at home in the world at least most of the time. Again in a broad sense, all the actions of the significant others and even their simple presence serve this sustaining function. In everyday life, however, the principal method employed is speech. In this sense, it is proper to view the individual's relationship with his significant others as an ongoing conversation. As the latter occurs, it validates over and over again the fundamental definitions of reality once entered into, not, of course, so much by explicit articulation, but precisely by taking the definitions silently for granted and conversing about all conceivable matters on this taken-for-granted basis. Through the same conversation the individual is also made capable of adjusting to changing and new social contexts in his biography. In a very fundamental sense it can be said that one converses one's way through life.

If one concedes these points, one can now state a general sociological proposition: the plausibility and stability of the world, as socially defined, is dependent upon the strength and continuity of significant relationships in which conversation about this world can be continually carried on. Or, to put it a little differently: *the reality of the world is sustained through conversation with significant others.* This reality, of course, includes not only the imagery by which fellowmen are viewed, but also includes the way in which one views oneself. The reality-bestowing force of social relationships depends on the degree of their nearness,[7] that is, on the degree to which social relationships occur in face-to-face situations and to which they are credited with primary significance by the individual. In any empirical situation, there now emerge obvious sociological questions out of these considerations, namely, questions about the patterns of the world-building relationships, the social forms taken by the conversation with significant others. Sociologically, one must ask how these relationships are *objectively* structured and distributed, and one will also want to understand how they are *subjectively* perceived and experienced.

With these preliminary assumptions stated we can now arrive at our main thesis here. Namely, we would contend that marriage occupies a privileged status among the significant validating relationships for adults in our society. Put slightly differently: marriage is a crucial nomic instrumentality in our society. We would further argue that the essential social functionality of this institution cannot be fully understood if this fact is not perceived.

. . . Marriage in our society is a *dramatic* act in which two strangers come together and redefine themselves. The drama of the act is internally anticipated and socially legitimated long before it takes place in the individual's biography, and amplified by means of a pervasive ideology, the dominant themes of which (romantic love, sexual fulfillment, self-discovery and self-realization through love and sexuality, the nuclear family as the social site for these processes) can be found distributed through all strata of the society. The actualization of these ideologically predefined expectations in the life of the individual occurs to the accompaniment of one of the few traditional rites of passage that are still meaningful to almost all members of the society. It should be added that, in using the term "strangers," we do not mean, of course, that the candidates for the marriage come from widely discrepant social backgrounds—indeed, the data indicate that the contrary is the case. The strangeness rather lies in the fact that, unlike marriage candidates in many previous societies, those in ours typically come from different face-to-face contexts—in the terms used above, they come from different areas of conversation. They do not have a shared past, although their pasts have a similar structure. In other words, quite apart from prevailing patterns of ethnic, religious, and class endogamy [or marriage within the same group], our society is typically exogamous [involving marriage between those who differ] in terms of nomic relationships. Put concretely, in our mobile society the significant conversation of the two partners previous to the marriage took place in social circles that did not overlap. With the dramatic redefinition of the situation brought about by the marriage, however, all significant conversation for the two new partners is now centered in their relationship with each other—and, in fact, it was precisely with this intention that they entered upon their relationship.

It goes without saying that this character of marriage has its root in much broader structural configurations of our society. The most important of these, for our purposes, is the crystallization of a so-called private sphere of existence, more and more segregated from the immediate controls of the public institutions (especially the economic and political ones), and yet defined and utilized as the main social area for the individual's self-realization.[8] It cannot be our purpose here to inquire into the historical forces that brought forth this phenomenon, beyond making the observation that these are closely connected with the industrial revolution and its institutional consequences. The public institutions now confront the individual as an immensely powerful and alien world, incomprehensible in its inner workings, anonymous in its human character. If only through his work in some nook of the economic machinery, the individual must find a way of living in this alien world, come to terms with its power over him, be satisfied with a few conceptual rules of thumb to guide him through a vast reality that otherwise remains opaque to his understanding, and modify its anonymity by whatever *human relations* he can work out in his involvement with it. It ought to be emphasized, against some critics of "mass society," that this does not inevitably leave the individual with a sense of profound unhappiness and lostness. It would rather seem that large numbers of people in our society are quite content with a situation in which their public involvements have little subjective importance, regarding work as a not too bad necessity and politics as at best a spectator sport. . . . The individual in this situation, no matter whether he is happy or not, will turn elsewhere for the experiences of self-realization that do have importance for him. The private sphere, this interstitial area created (we would think) more or less haphazardly as a by-product of the social metamorphosis [or unfolding] of industrialism, is mainly where he will turn. It is here that the individual will seek power, intelligibility and, quite literally, a name—the apparent power to fashion a world, however Lilliputian, that will reflect his own being: a world that, seemingly having been shaped by himself and thus unlike those other worlds that insist on shaping him, is translucently intelligible to him (or so he thinks); a world in which, consequently, he is *somebody* —perhaps even, within its charmed circle, a lord and master. What is more, to a considerable extent these expectations are not unrealistic. The public institutions have no need to control the individual's adventures in the private sphere, as long as they really stay within the latter's circumscribed limits. The private sphere is perceived, not without

justification, as an area of individual choice and even autonomy. This fact has important consequences for the shaping of identity in modern society that cannot be pursued here. All that ought to be clear here is the peculiar location of the private sphere within and between the other social structures. In sum, it is above all and, as a rule, only in the private sphere that the individual can take a slice of reality and fashion it into his world.[9] . . .

The private sphere includes a variety of social relationships. Among these, however, the relationships of the family occupy a central position and, in fact, serve as a focus for most of the other relationships (such as those with friends, neighbors, fellow-members of religious and other voluntary associations). . . . [T]he central relationship in this whole area is the marital one. It is on the basis of marriage that, for most adults in our society, existence in the private sphere is built up. It will be clear that this is not at all a universal or even a cross culturally wide function of marriage. Rather . . . marriage in our society [has] taken on a very peculiar character and functionality. It has been pointed out that marriage in contemporary society has lost some of its older functions and taken on new ones instead.[10] This is certainly correct, but we would prefer to state the matter a little differently. Marriage and family used to be firmly embedded in a matrix of wider community relationships, serving as extensions and particularizations of the latter's social controls. There were few separating barriers between the world of the individual family and the wider community, a fact even to be seen in the physical conditions under which the family lived before the industrial revolution.[11] The same social life pulsated through the house, the street and the community. In our terms, the family and within it the marital relationship were part and parcel of a considerably larger area of conversation. In our contemporary society, by contrast, each family constitutes its own segregated subworld, with its own controls and its own closed conversation.

This fact requires a much greater effort on the part of the marriage partners. Unlike an earlier situation in which the establishment of the new marriage simply added to the differentiation and complexity of an already existing social world, the marriage partners now are embarked on the often difficult task of constructing for themselves the little world in which they will live. To be sure, the larger society provides them with certain standard instructions as to how they should go about this task, but this does not change the fact that considerable effort of their own is required for its realization. The monogamous character of marriage enforces both the dramatic and the precarious nature of this undertaking. Success or failure hinges on the present idiosyncrasies and the fairly unpredictable future development of these idiosyncrasies of *only two individuals* (who, moreover, do not have a shared past)—as Simmel has shown, the most unstable of all possible social relationships.[12] Not surprisingly, the decision to embark on this undertaking has a critical, even cataclysmic connotation in the popular imagination, which is underlined as well as psychologically assuaged by the ceremonialism that surrounds the event.

Every social relationship requires *objectivation*, that is, requires *a process by which subjectively experienced meanings become objective to the individual and*, in interaction with others, *become common property* and thereby massively objective.[13] The degree of objectivation will depend on the number and the intensity of the social relationships that are its carriers. A relationship that consists of only two individuals called upon to sustain, by their own efforts, an ongoing social world will have to make up in intensity for the numerical poverty of the arrangement. This, in turn, accentuates the drama and the precariousness. The later addition of children will add to the . . . "density" of objectivation

taking place within the nuclear family, thus rendering the latter a good deal less precarious. . . .

The attempt can now be made to outline the ideal-typical process that takes place as marriage functions as an instrumentality for the social construction of reality. The chief protagonists of the drama are two individuals, each with a biographically accumulated and available stock of experience.[14] As members of a highly mobile society, these individuals have already internalized a degree of readiness to redefine themselves and to modify their stock of experience, thus bringing with them considerable psychological capacity for entering new relationships with others.[15] Also, coming from broadly similar sectors of the larger society (in terms of region, class, ethnic and religious affiliations), the two individuals will have organized their stock of experience in similar fashion. In other words, *the two individuals have internalized the same overall world, including the general definitions and expectations of the marriage relationship itself*. Their society has provided them with a taken-for-granted image of marriage and has socialized them into an anticipation of stepping into the taken-for-granted roles of marriage. All the same, *these relatively empty projections now have to be actualized, lived through and filled with experiential content* by the protagonists. This will require a dramatic change in their definitions of reality and of themselves.

As of the marriage, most of each partner's actions must now be projected in conjunction with those of the other. Each partner's definitions of reality must be continually correlated with the definitions of the other. The other is present in nearly all horizons of everyday conduct. Furthermore, the identity of each now takes on a new character, having to be constantly matched with that of the other, indeed being typically perceived by the people at large as being symbiotically conjoined with the identity of the other. In each partner's psychological econ-

omy of significant others, the marriage partner becomes the other *par excellence*, the nearest and most decisive co-inhabitant of the
world. Indeed, all other significant relationships have to be almost automatically
reperceived and regrouped in accordance
with this drastic shift.

In other words, from the beginning of
the marriage each partner has new modes in
his meaningful experience of the world in
general, of other people and of himself. By
definition, then, marriage constitutes a
nomic rupture. In terms of each partner's
biography, the event of marriage initiates a
new nomic process. Now, the full implications of this fact are rarely apprehended by
the protagonists with any degree of clarity.
There rather is to be found the notion that
one's world, one's other-relationships and,
above all, oneself have remained what they
were before—only, of course, that world,
others and self will now be shared with the
marriage partner. It should be clear by now
that this notion is a grave misapprehension.
Just because of this fact, marriage now pro-
pels the individual into an unintended and
unarticulated development, in the course of
which the nomic transformation takes place.
What typically *is* apprehended are certain
objective and concrete problems arising out
of the marriage—such as tensions with in-
laws, or with former friends, or religious differences between the partners, as well as
immediate tensions between them. These are
apprehended as external, situational and
practical difficulties. What is *not* apprehended is the subjective side of these difficulties, namely, the transformation of *nomos*
and identity that has occurred and that continues to go on, so that all problems and
relationships are experienced in a quite new
way, that is, experienced within a new and
ever-changing reality.

Take a simple and frequent illustration—the male partner's relationships with
male friends before and after the marriage. It
is a common observation that such relation-

ships, especially if the extramarital partners
are single, rarely survive the marriage, or, if
they do, are drastically redefined after it.
This is typically the result of neither a deliberate decision by the husband nor deliberate
sabotage by the wife. What rather happens,
very simply, is a slow process in which the
husband's image of his friend is transformed
as he keeps talking about this friend with his
wife. Even if no actual talking goes on, the
mere presence of the wife forces him to see
his friend differently. This need not mean
that he adopts a negative image held by the
wife. Regardless of what image she holds or
is believed by him to hold, it will be different
from that held by the husband. This difference will enter into the joint image that now
must needs be fabricated in the course of the
ongoing conversation between the marriage
partners—and, in due course, must act pow-
erfully on the image previously held by the
husband. Again, typically, this process is
rarely apprehended with any degree of lucidity. The old friend is more likely to fade
out of the picture by slow degrees, as new
kinds of friends take his place. The process, if
commented upon at all within the marital
conversation, can always be explained by socially available formulas about "people
changing," "friends disappearing" or oneself "having become more mature." This
process of conversational liquidation is especially powerful because it is one-sided—the
husband typically talks with his wife about
his friend, but *not* with his friend about his
wife. Thus the friend is deprived of the defense of, as it were, counterdefining the relationship. *This dominance of the marital
conversation over all others is one of its most
important characteristics.* It may be mitigated
by a certain amount of protective segregation of some non-marital relationships (say
"Tuesday night out with the boys," or
"Saturday lunch with mother"), but even
then there are powerful emotional barriers
against the sort of conversation (conversation *about* the marital relationship, that is)

that would serve by way of counterdefinition.

Marriage thus posits a new reality. The individual's relationship with this new reality, however, is a dialectical one—he acts upon it, in collusion with the marriage partner, and it acts back upon both him and the partner, welding together their reality. Since, as we have argued before, the objectivation that constitutes this reality is precarious, the groups with which the couple associates are called upon to assist in co-defining the new reality. The couple is pushed towards groups that strengthen their new definition of themselves and the world, avoids those that weaken this definition. This in turn releases the commonly known pressures of group association, again acting upon the marriage partners to change their definitions of the world and of themselves. Thus the new reality is not posited once and for all, but goes on being redefined not only in the marital interaction itself but also in the various maritally based group relationships into which the couple enters.

In the individual's biography marriage, then, brings about a decisive phase of socialization that can be compared with the phases of childhood and adolescence. This phase has a rather different structure from the earlier ones. There the individual was in the main socialized into already existing patterns. Here he actively collaborates rather than passively accommodates himself. Also, in the previous phases of socialization, there was an apprehension of entering into a new world and being changed in the course of this. In marriage there is little apprehension of such a process, but rather the notion that the world has remained the same, with only its emotional and pragmatic connotations having changed. This notion, as we have tried to show, is illusionary.

The reconstruction of the world in marriage occurs principally in the course of conversation, as we have suggested. *The implicit problem of this conversation is how to match two individual definitions of reality.* By the very logic of the relationship, a common overall definition must be arrived at—otherwise the conversation will become impossible and, *ipso facto,* the relationship will be endangered. Now, this conversation may be understood as the working away of an ordering and typifying apparatus—if one prefers, an objectivating apparatus. Each partner ongoingly contributes his conceptions of reality, which are then "talked through," usually not once but many times, and in the process become objectivated by the conversational apparatus. The longer this conversation goes on, the more massively real do the objectivations become to the partners. In the marital conversation a world is not only built, but it is also kept in a state of repair and ongoingly refurnished. The subjective reality of this world for the two partners is sustained by the same conversation. The nomic instrumentality of marriage is concretized over and over again, from bed to breakfast table, as the partners carry on the endless conversation that feeds on nearly all they individually or jointly experience. Indeed, it may happen eventually that no experience is fully real unless and until it has been thus "talked through."

This process has a very important result—namely, *a hardening or stabilization of the common objectivated reality.* It should be easy to see now how this comes about. The objectivations ongoingly performed and internalized by the marriage partners become ever more massively real, as they are confirmed and reconfirmed in the marital conversation. The world that is made up of these objectivations at the same time gains in stability. For example, the images of other people, which before or in the earlier stages of the marital conversation may have been rather ambiguous and shifting in the minds of the two partners, now become hardened into definite and stable characterizations. A casual acquaintance, say, may sometimes have appeared as lots of fun and sometimes as quite a bore to the wife before her marriage. Under the influence of the marital conversation, in which this other person is frequently "discussed," she will now come down more firmly on one *or* the other of the two characterizations, or on a reasonable compromise between the two. In any of these three options, though, she will have concocted with her husband a much more stable image of the person in question than she is likely to have had before her marriage, when there may have been no conversational pressure to make a definite option at all. The same process of stabilization may be observed with regard to self-definitions as well. In this way, the wife in our example will not only be pressured to assign stable characterizations to others but also to herself. Previously uninterested politically, she now identifies herself as liberal. Previously alternating between dimly articulated religious positions, she now declares herself an agnostic. Previously confused and uncertain about her sexual emotions, she now understands herself as an unabashed hedonist in this area. And so on and so forth, with the same reality—and identity—stabilizing process at work on the husband. Both world and self thus take on a firmer, more reliable character for both partners.

Furthermore, it is not only the ongoing experience of the two partners that is constantly shared and passed through the conversational apparatus. The same *sharing extends into the past.* The two distinct biographies, as subjectively apprehended by two individuals who have lived through them, are overruled and reinterpreted in the course of their conversation. Sooner or later, they will "tell all"—or, more correctly, they will tell it in such a way that it fits into the self-definitions objectivated in the marital relationship. The couple thus construct not only present reality but reconstruct past reality as well, fabricating a common memory that integrates the recollections of the two individual pasts.[16] The comic fulfillment of this process may be seen in those cases when one partner "remembers" more clearly what happened in the other's past than the other does—and corrects him accordingly. Similarly, there occurs a *sharing of future horizons,* which leads not only to stabilization, but inevitably to a narrowing of the future projections of each partner. Before marriage the individual typically plays with quite discrepant daydreams in which his future self is projected.[17] Having now considerably stabilized his self-image, the married individual will have to project the future in accordance with this maritally defined identity. This narrowing of future horizons begins with the obvious external limitation that marriage entails, as, for example, with regard to vocational and career plans. However, it extends also the more general possibilities of the individual's biography. To return to a previous illustration, the wife, having "found herself" as a liberal, an agnostic and a "sexually healthy" person, *ipso facto* liquidates the possibilities of becoming an anarchist, a Catholic or a Lesbian. At least until further notice she has decided upon who she is—and, by the same token, upon who she will be. The stabilization brought about by marriage thus affects that total reality in which the partners exist. In the most far-reaching sense of the word, the married individual "settles down"—and *must* do so, if the marriage is to be viable, in accordance with its contemporary institutional definition.

It cannot be sufficiently strongly emphasized that this process is typically unapprehended, almost automatic in character. The protagonists of the marriage drama do *not* set out deliberately to create their world. Each continues to live in a world that is taken for granted—and keeps its taken-for-granted character even as it is metamorphosed. The new world that the married partners, Prometheuslike, have called into being is perceived by them as the normal world in which they have lived before. Reconstructed present and reinterpreted past are perceived as a continuum, extending forward into a commonly projected future. *The dramatic change that has occurred remains in bulk, unapprehended and unarticulated.* And where it forces itself upon the individual's attention, it is retrojected into the past, explained as having always been there, though perhaps in a hidden way. Typically, the reality that has been "invented" within the marital conversation is subjectively perceived as a "discovery." Thus the partners "discover" themselves and the world, "who they really are," "what they really believe," "how they really feel, and always have felt, and so-and-so." This retrojection of the world being produced all the time by themselves serves to enhance the stability of this world and at the same time to assuage the "existential anxiety" that, probably inevitably, accompanies the perception that nothing but one's own narrow shoulders supports the universe in which one has chosen to live. . . .

The use of the term "stabilization" should not detract from the insight into the difficulty and precariousness of this world-building enterprise. Often enough, the new universe collapses *in statu nascendi.* Many more times it continues over a period, swaying perilously back and forth as the two partners try to hold it up, finally to be abandoned as an impossible undertaking. If one conceives of the marital conversation as the principal drama and the two partners as the principal protagonists of the drama, then one can look upon the other individuals involved as the supporting chorus for the central dramatic action. Children, friends, relatives and casual acquaintances all have their part in reinforcing the tenuous structure of the new reality. It goes without saying that the *children form the most important part of this supporting chorus.* Their very existence in predicated on the maritally established world. The marital partners themselves are in charge of their socialization *into* this world, which to them has a pre-existent and self-evident character. They are taught from the beginning to speak precisely those lines that lend themselves to a supporting chorus, from their first invocations of "Daddy" and "Mummy" on to their adoption of the parents' ordering and typifying apparatus that now defines *their* world as well. The marital conversation is now in the process of becoming a family symposium, with the necessary consequence that its objectivations rapidly gain in density, plausibility and durability.

In sum: the process that we have been inquiring into is, ideal-typically, one in which reality is crystallized, narrowed and stabilized. Ambivalences are converted into certainties. Typifications of self and of others become settled. Most generally, possibilities become facticities. What is more, this process of transformation remains, most of the time, unapprehended by those who are both its authors and its objects.[18]

NOTES

1. The present article has come out of a larger project on which the authors have been engaged in collaboration with three colleagues in sociology and philosophy. The project is to produce a systematic treatise that will integrate a number of now separate theoretical strands in the sociology of knowledge.
2. Cf. especially Max Weber, *Wirtschaft und Gesellschaft* (Tuebingen: Mohr 1956), and *Gesammelte Aufsaetze zur Wissenschaftslehre* (Tuebingen: Mohr 1951); George H. Mead, *Mind, Self and Society* (University of Chicago Press 1934); Alfred Schutz, *Der sinnhafte Aufbau der sozialen Welt* (Vienna: Springer, 2nd ed. 1960) and *Collected Papers,* 1(The Hague: Nijhoff 1962); Maurice Merleau-Ponty, *Phenomenologie de la perception* (Paris: Gallimard 1945) and *La Structure du comportement* (Paris: Presses universitaires de France 1953).
3. Cf. Schutz, *Aufbau,* 202–20 and *Collected Papers,* I, 3–27, 283–6.
4. Cf. Schutz, *Collected Papers,* I, 207–28.
5. Cf. especially Jean Piaget, *The Child's Construction of Reality* (Routledge & Kegan Paul 1955).
6. Cf. Mead, *op. cit.,* 135–226.
7. Cf. Schutz, *Aufbau,* 181–95.

8. Cf. Arnold Gehlen, *Die Seele im technischen Zeitalter* (Hamburg: Rowohlt 1957), 57–69 and *Anthropologische Forschung* (Hamburg: Rowohlt 1961), 69–77, 127–40; Helmut Schelsky, *Soziologie der Sexualitaet* (Hamburg: Rowohlt 1955), 102–33. Also cf. Thomas Luckmann, "On religion in modern society," *Journal for the Scientific Study of Religion* (Spring 1963), 147–62.

9. In these considerations we have been influenced by certain presuppositions of Marxian anthropology as well as by the anthropological work of Max Scheler, Helmuth Plessner and Arnold Gehlen. We are indebted to Thomas Luckmann for the clarification of the social-psychological significance of the private sphere.

10. Cf. Talcott Parsons and Robert Bales, *Family: Socialization and Interaction Process* (London: Routledge & Kegan Paul 1956), 3–34, 353–96.

11. Cf. Philippe Aries, *Centuries of Childhood* (New York: Knopf 1962), 339–410.

12. Cf. Georg Simmel (Kurt Wolff ed.), *The Sociology of Georg Simmel* (New York: Collier-Macmillan 1950), 118–44.

13. Cf. Schutz, *Aufbau*, 29–36, 149–53.

14. Cf. Schutz, *Aufbau*, 186–92, 202–10.

15. David Riesman's well-known concept of "other-direction" would also be applicable here.

16. Cf. Maurice Halbwachs, *Les Cadres sociaux de la memoire* (Paris: Presses universitaires de France 1952), especially 146–77; also cf. Peter Berger, *Invitation to Sociology—A Humanistic Perspective* (Garden City, N.Y.: Doubleday-Anchor 1963), 54–65 (available in Penguin).

17. Cf. Schutz, *Collected Papers*, I, 72–3, 79–82.

18. The phenomena here discussed could also be formulated effectively in terms of the Marxian categories of reification and false consciousness. Jean-Paul Sartre's recent work, especially *Critique de la raison dialectique*, seeks to integrate these categories within a phenomenological analysis of human conduct. Also cf. Henri Lefebvre, *Critique de la vie quotidienne* (Paris: l'Arche 1958–61).

28

Uncoupling: The Social Construction of Divorce

DIANE VAUGHAN

Berger and Kellner (1964) Describe Marriage As a Definitional Process. Two autonomous individuals come together with separate and distinct biographies and begin to construct for themselves a subworld in which they will live as a couple. A redefinition of self occurs as the autonomous identity of the two individuals involved is reconstructed as a mutual identity. This redefinition is externally anticipated and socially legitimated before it actually occurs in the individual's biography.

Previously, significant conversation for each partner came from non-overlapping circles, and self-realization came from other sources. Together, they begin to construct a private sphere where all significant conversation centers in their relationship with each other. The coupled identity becomes the main source of their self-realization. Their definitions of reality become correlated, for each partner's actions must be projected in conjunction with the other. As their worlds come to be defined around a relationship with a significant other who becomes *the* significant other, all other significant relationships have to be reperceived, regrouped. The result is the construction of a joint biography and a mutually coordinated common memory.

Were this construction of a coupled identity left only to the two participants, the coupling would be precarious indeed. However, the new reality is reinforced through objectivation, that is, "a process by which subjectively experienced meanings become objective to the individual, and, in interac-

tion with others, become common property, and thereby massively objective" (Berger and Kellner, 1964:6). Hence, through the use of language in conversation with significant others, the reality of the coupling is constantly validated.

Of perhaps greater significance is that this definition of coupledness becomes taken for granted and is validated again and again, not by explicit articulation, but by conversing around the agreed [upon] definition of reality that has been created. In this way a consistent reality is maintained, ordering the individual's world in such a way that it validates his identity. Marriage, according to Berger and Kellner, is a constructed reality which is "nomosbuilding" (1964:1). That is, it is a social arrangement that contributes order to individual lives, and therefore should be considered as a significant validating relationship for adults in our society.

Social relationships, however, are seldom static. Not only do we move in and out of relationships, but the nature of a particular relationship, though enduring, varies over time. Given that the definitions we create become socially validated and hence constraining, *how do individuals move from a mutual identity, as in marriage, to assume separate, autonomous identities again?* What is the process by which new definitions are created and become validated?

The Berger and Kellner analysis describes a number of interrelated yet distinguishable stages that are involved in the social construction of a mutual identity; for example, the regrouping of all other significant relationships. In much the same way, the *demise* of a relationship should involve distinguishable social processes. Since redefinition of self is basic to both movement into and out of relationships, the social construction of a singular identity also should follow the patterns suggested by Berger and Kellner. This paper is a qualitative examination of this process. Hence, the description that follows bears an implicit test of Berger and Kellner's ideas.

The dimensions of sorrow, anger, personal disorganization, fear, loneliness, and ambiguity that intermingle every separation are well know.[1] Their familiarity does not diminish their importance. Though in real life these cannot be ignored, the researcher has the luxury of selectivity. Here, it is not the pain and disorganization that are to be explored, but the existence of an underlying orderliness.

Though the focus is on divorce, the process examined appears to apply to *any* heterosexual relationship in which the participants have come to define themselves and be defined by others as a couple. The work is exploratory and, as such, not concerned with generalizability. However, the process may apply to homosexual couples as well. Therefore, the term "uncoupling" will be used because it is a more general concept than divorce. Uncoupling applies to the redefinition of self that occurs as mutual identity unravels into singularity, regardless of marital status or sex of the participants.

The formal basis from which this paper developed was in-depth, exploratory interviews. The interviews, ranging from two to six hours, were taped and later analyzed. All of the interviewees were at different stages in the uncoupling process. Most were divorced, though some were still in stages of consideration of divorce. Two of the interviews were based on long-term relationships that never resulted in marriage. All of the relationships were heterosexual. The quality of these interviews has added much depth to the under-

standing of the separation process. The interviewees were of high intellectual and social level, and their sensitivity and insight have led to much valuable material, otherwise unavailable.

A more informal contribution to the paper comes from personal experiences and the experiences of close friends. Further corroboration has come from autobiographical accounts, newspapers, periodicals, and conversations, which have resulted in a large number of cases illustrating certain points. Additional support has come from individuals who have read or heard the paper with the intent of proving or disproving its contentions by reference to their own cases.

Since the declared purpose here is to abstract the essential features of the process of uncoupling, some simplification is necessary. The separation of a relationship can take several forms. To trace all of them is beyond the scope of this study. Therefore, to narrow the focus, we must first consider the possible variations.

Perhaps the coupled identity was not a major mechanism for self-validation from the outset of the union. Or the relationship may have at one time filled that function, but, as time passed, this coupled identity was insufficient to meet individual needs. Occasionally this fact has implications for both partners simultaneously, and the uncoupling process is initiated by both. More frequently, however, one partner still finds the marriage a major source of stability and identity, while the other finds it inadequate. In this form, one participant takes the role of initiator of the uncoupling process. However, this role may not consistently be held by one partner, but instead may alternate between them, due to the difficulty of uncoupling in the face of external constraints, social pressure not to be the one responsible for the demise of the marriage, and the variability in the self-validating function of the union over time. For the purpose of this study, the form of uncoupling under consideration is that which results when one partner, no longer finding the coupled identity self-validating, takes the role of initiator in the uncoupling process. The other partner, the significant other, still finds the marriage a major source of stability and identity.

UNCOUPLING: THE INITIATION OF THE PROCESS

> I was never psychologically married. I always felt strained by attempts that coupled me into a marital unit. I was just never comfortable as "Mrs." I never got used to my last name. I never wanted it. The day after my marriage was probably the most depressed day of my life, because I had lost my singularity. The difference between marriage and a deep relationship, living together, is that you have this ritual, and you achieve a very definite status, and it was *that* that produced my reactions—because I became in the eyes of the world a man's wife. And I was never comfortable and happy with it. It didn't make any difference who the man was.

An early phase in the uncoupling process occurs as one or the other of the partners begins to question the coupled identity. At first internal, the challenging of the created world remains for a time as a doubt within one of the partners in the coupling. Though there is a definition of coupledness, subjectively the coupledness may be experienced differently by each partner. Frequently, these subjective meanings remain internal and unarticulated. Thus, similarly, the initial recognition of the coupling as problematic may be internal and unarticulated, held as a secret. The subworld that has been constructed, for some reason, doesn't "fit."

A process of definition negotiation is begun, initiated by the one who finds the mutual identity an inadequate definition of self. Attempts to negotiate the definition of the coupledness are likely to result in the subjective meaning becoming articulated for the first time, thus moving the redefinition

process toward objectivation. The secret, held by the initiator, is shared with the significant other. When this occurs, it allows both participants to engage in the definitional process.

Though the issue is made "public" in that private sphere shared by the two, the initiator frequently finds that a lack of shared definitions of the coupled identity stalemates the negotiations. While the initiator defines the marriage as a problem, the other does not. The renegotiation of the coupled identity cannot proceed unless both agree that the subworld they have constructed needs to be redefined. Perhaps for the significant other, the marriage as it is still provides important self-validation. If so, the initiator must bring the other to the point of sharing a common definition of the marriage as "troubled."

ACCOMPANYING RECONSTRUCTIONS

Though this shared definition is being sought, the fact remains that, for the initiator, the coupled identity fails to provide self-validation. In order to meet this need, the initiator engages in other attempts at redefining the nature of the relationship. Called "accompanying reconstructions," these *may* or *may not* be shared with the significant other. They may begin long before the "secret" of the troubled marriage is shared with the other, in an effort to make an uncomfortable situation more comfortable without disrupting the relationship. Or they may occur subsequent to sharing the secret with the significant other, as a reaction to the failure to redefine the coupledness satisfactorily. Time order for their occurrence is not easily imposed—thus, "accompanying reconstructions."

The initiator's accompanying reconstructions may be directed toward the redefinition of (1) the coupledness itself, (2) the identity of the significant other, or (3) the identity of the initiator. A change in definition of either of the three implies a change in at least one of the others. Though they are presented here separately, they are interactive rather than mutually exclusive and are not easily separable in real life.

The first form of accompanying reconstruction to be considered is the initiator's redefinition of the coupledness itself. One way of redefining the coupledness is by an unarticulated conversion of the agreed-upon norms of the relationship.

> I had reconceptualized what marriage was. I decided sexual fidelity was not essential for marriage. I never told her that. And I didn't even have anyone I was interested in having that intimate a relationship with—I just did a philosophical thing. I just decided it was O.K. for me to have whatever of what quality of other relationship I needed to have. Something like that—of that caliber—was something I could never talk to her about. So I did it all by myself. I read things and decided it. I was at peace with me. I knew that we could stay married, whatever that meant. O.K., I can stay legally tied to you, and I can probably live in this house with you, and I can keep working the way I have been. I decided I can have my life and still be in this situation with you, but you need some resources, because I realize now I'm not going to be all for you. I don't want to be all for you, and I did tell her that. But I couldn't tell her this total head trip I'd been through because she wouldn't understand.

Or, the coupledness may be redefined by acceptance of the relationship with certain limitations. Boundaries can be imposed on the impact that the relationship will have on the total life space of the initiator.

> I finally came to the point where I realized I was never going to have the kind of marriage I had hoped for, the kind of relationship I had hoped for. I didn't want to end it, because of the children, but I wasn't going to let it hurt me any more. I wasn't going to depend on him any more. The children and I were going to be the main unit, and, if he occasionally wanted to participate, fine—and if not, we

would go ahead without him. I was no longer willing to let being with him be the determining factor as to whether I was happy or not. I ceased planning our lives around his presence or absence and began looking out for myself.

A second form of accompanying reconstruction occurs when the initiator attempts to redefine the significant other in a way that is more compatible with his own self-validation needs. The initiator may direct efforts toward specific behaviors, such as drinking habits, temper, sexual incompatibilities, or finance management. Or, the redefinition attempt may be of a broader scope.

> I was aware of his dependence on the marriage to provide all his happiness, and it wasn't providing it. I wanted him to go to graduate school, but he postponed it, against my wishes. I wanted him to pursue his own life. I didn't want him to sacrifice for me. I wanted him to become more exciting to me in the process. I was aware that I was trying to persuade him to be a different person.

Redefinition of the significant other may either be directed toward maintaining the coupledness, as above, or moving away from it, as is the case following.

> The way I defined being a good wife and the way John defined being a good wife were two different quantities. He wanted the house to look like a hotel and I didn't see it that way. He couldn't see why I couldn't meet his needs. . . . When he first asked for a divorce and I refused, he suggested I go back to school. I remembered a man who worked with John who had sent his wife back to school so she could support herself, so he could divorce her. I asked John if he was trying to get rid of me. He didn't answer that. He insisted I go, and I finally went.

A third form of accompanying reconstruction may be directed toward the definition of the initiator. Intermingled with attempts at redefinition of the significant other and redefinition of the coupledness itself is the seeking of self-validation outside the marriage by the initiator. A whole set of other behaviors may evolve that have the ultimate effect of moving the relationship away from the coupledness toward a separation of the joint biography.

SELF-VALIDATION OUTSIDE THE MARRIAGE

What was at first internally experienced and recognized as self-minimizing takes a more concrete form and becomes externally expressed in a search for self-maximization. Through investment of self in career, in a cause requiring commitment, in a relationship with a new significant other, in family, in education, or in activities and hobbies, the initiator develops new sources of self-realization. These alternative sources of self-realization confirm not the coupled identity but the singularity of the initiator.

Furthermore, in the move toward a distinct biography, the initiator finds ideological support that reinforces the uncoupling process. Berger and Kellner (1964:3) note the existence of a supporting ideology which lends credence to marriage as a significant validating relationship in our society. That is, the nuclear family is seen as the site of love, sexual fulfillment, and self-realization. In the move toward uncoupling, the initiator finds confirmation for a belief in *self* as a first priority.

> I now see my break with religion as a part of my developing individuality. At the time I was close friends with priests and nuns, most of whom have since left the church. I felt a bitterness toward the church for its definition of marriage. I felt constrained toward a type of marriage that was not best for me.

Whether this ideology first begins within the individual, who then actively *seeks* sources of self-realization that are ideologically congruent, or whether the initiator's own needs come to be met by a serendipitous "elective affinity" of ideas (Weber: 1930), is difficult to say. The interconnections are subtle. The supporting ideology may come from the family of orientation, the women's movement, the peer group, or a new significant other. It may grow directly, as through interaction, or indirectly, as through literature. No matter what the source, the point is that, in turning away from the marriage for self-validation, a separate distinct biography is constructed in interaction with others, and this beginning autonomy is strengthened by a supporting belief system.

The initiator moves toward construction of a separate subworld wherein significant conversation comes from circles which no longer overlap with those of the significant other. And, the significant other is excluded from that separate subworld.

> I shared important things with the children that I didn't share with him. It's almost as if I purposefully punished him by not telling him. Some good thing would happen and I'd come home and tell them and wouldn't tell him.

The initiator's autonomy is further reinforced as the secret of the troubled marriage is shared with others in the separate subworld the initiator is constructing. It may be directly expressed as a confidence exchanged with a close friend, family member, or children, or it may be that the sharing is indirect. Rather than being expressed in significant conversation, the definition of the marriage as troubled is created for others by a variety of mechanisms that relay the message that the initiator is not happily married. The definition of the marriage as problematic becomes further objectivated as the secret, once held only by the initiator, then shared with the significant other, moves to a sphere beyond the couple themselves.

Other moves away occur that deeply threaten the coupled identity for the significant other and at the same time validate the autonomy of the initiator.

> I remember going to a party by myself and feeling comfortable. She never forgot that. I never realized the gravity of that to her.

> Graduate school became a symbolic issue. I was going to be a separate entity. That's probably the one thing I wanted to do that got the biggest negative emotional response from him.

> All that time I was developing more of a sense of being away from her. I didn't depend on her for any emotional feedback, companionship. I went to plays and movies with friends.

The friendship group, rather than focusing on the coupledness, relies on splintered sources that support separate identities. Though this situation can exist in relationships in which the coupled identity is validating for both participants, the distinction is that, in the process of uncoupling, there may not be shared conversation to link the separate subworld of the initiator with that of the significant other.

These movements away by the initiator heighten a sense of exclusion for the significant other. Deep commitment to other than the coupled identity—to a career, to a cause, to education, to a hobby, to another person—reflects a lessened commitment to the marriage. The initiator's search for self-validation outside the marriage even may be demonstrated symbolically to the significant other by the removal of the wedding ring or by the desire, if the initiator is a woman, to revert to her maiden name. If the initiator's lessened commitment to the coupled identity is reflected in a lessened desire for sexual intimacy, the challenge to the identity of the significant other and the coupledness becomes undeniable. As the significant other recognizes the growing autonomy of the initiator, he, too, comes to accept the definition of the marriage as "troubled."

The roles assumed by each participant have implications for the impact of the uncoupling on each. Whereas the initiator has found other sources of self-realization outside the marriage, usually the significant other has not. The marriage still performs the major self-validating function. The significant other is committed to an ideology that supports the coupled identity. The secret of the "troubled" marriage has not been shared with others as it has by the initiator, meaning for the significant other the relationship in its changed construction remains unobjectivated. The challenge to the identity of the significant other and to the coupledness posed by the initiator may result in increased commitment to the coupled identity for the significant other. With the joint biography already separated in these ways, the couple enters into a period of "trying."

TRYING

Trying is a stage of intense definition negotiation by the partners. Now both share a definition of the marriage as troubled. However, each partner may seek to construct a new reality that is in opposition to that of the other. The significant other tries to negotiate a shared definition of the marriage as savable, whereas the initiator negotiates toward a shared definition that marks the marriage as unsavable.[2]

For the initiator, the uncoupling process is well underway. At some point the partner who originally perceived the coupled identity to be problematic and sought self-validation outside the coupled identity has experienced "psychological divorce." Sociologically, this can be defined as the point at which the individual's newly constructed separate subworld becomes the major nomos-building mechanism in his life space, replacing the nomos-building function of the coupled identity.

The initiator tries subtly to prepare the significant other to live alone. By encouraging the other to make new friends, find a job, get involved in outside activities, or seek additional education, the initiator hopes to decrease the other's commitment to and dependence upon the coupled identity for self-validation and move the other toward autonomy. This stage of preparation is not simply one of cold expediency for the benefit of the initiator, but is based on concern for the significant other and serves to mitigate the pain of the uncoupling process for both the initiator and the other.

For both, there is a hesitancy to sever the ties. In many cases, neither party is fully certain about the termination of the marriage. Mutual uncertainty may be more characteristic of the process. The relationship may weave back and forth between cycles of active trying and passive acceptance of the status quo due to the failure of each to pull the other to a common definition and the inability of either to make the break.

> I didn't want to hurt him. I didn't want to be responsible for the demise of a marriage I no longer wanted. I could have forced him into being the one to achieve the breach, for I realized it was never going to happen by itself.

> I didn't want to be the villain—the one to push her our into the big, bad world. I wanted to make sure she was at the same point I was.

> I kept hoping some alternative would occur so that he would be willing to break. I kept wishing it would happen.

Frequently, in the trying stage, the partners turn to outside help for formal negotiation of the coupled identity. Counseling, though entered into with apparent common purpose, becomes another arena in which the partners attempt to negotiate a shared definition from their separately held definitions of the marriage as savable or unsavable. For the initiator, the counseling may serve as a step in the preparation of the significant other to live alone. Not only does it serve to bring the other to the definition of the marriage as unsavable, but also the counseling provides a resource for the significant other, in the person of the counselor. Often it happens that the other has turned to no one for comfort about the problem marriage. The initiator, sensitive to this need and unable to fill it himself, hopes the counselor will fill this role. The counseling has yet another function. It further objectivates the notion of the coupled identity as problematic.

At some point during this period of trying, the initiator may suggest separation. Yet, separation is not suggested as a formal leave-taking but as a *temporary* separation meant to clarify the relationship for both partners. Again, the concern on the part of the initiator for the significant other appears. Not wanting to hurt, yet recognizing the coupled identity as no longer valid, the temporary separation is encouraged as a further means of bringing the other to accept a definition of the marriage as unsavable, to increase reliance of the other on outside resources of self-realization, and to initiate the physical breach gently.

> Even at that point, at initial separation, I wasn't being honest. I knew fairly certainly that when we separated, it was for good. I let her believe that it was a means for us first finding out what was happening and then eventually possibly getting back together.

Should the initiator be hesitant to suggest a separation, the significant other may finally tire of the ambiguity of the relationship. No longer finding the coupling as it exists self-validating, the significant other may be the one to suggest a separation. The decision to separate may be the result of discussion and planning, or it may occur spontaneously, in a moment of anger. It may be mutually agreed upon, but more often it is not. However it emerges, the decision to separate is a difficult one for both partners.

OBJECTIVATION: RESTRUCTURING OF THE PRIVATE SPHERE

The separation is a transitional state in which everything needs definition, yet very little is capable of being defined. Economic status, friendship networks, personal habits, and sex life are all patterns of the past which need simultaneous reorganization. However, reorganization is hindered by the ambiguity of the relationship. The off-again, on-again wearing of her wedding rings is symbolic of the indecision in this stage. Each of the partners searches for new roles, without yet being free of the old.

For the initiator who has developed outside resources, the impact of this uncertainty is partially mitigated. For the significant other, who has not spent time in preparation for individual existence, the major self-validating function of the marriage is gone and nothing has emerged as a substitute.

> I had lost my identity somewhere along the way. And I kept losing my identity. I kept letting him make all the decisions. I couldn't work. I wasn't able to be myself. I was letting someone else take over. I didn't have any control over it. I didn't know how to stop it. I was unsure that if anything really happened I could actually make it on my own or not.

The separation precipitates a redefinition of self for the significant other. Without other resources for self-validation, and with the coupled identity now publicly challenged, the significant other begins a restructuring of the private sphere.

This restructuring occurs not only in the social realm but also entails a form of restructuring that is physical, tangible, and symbolic of the break in the coupled identity. For instance, if the initiator has been the one to leave, at some point the significant other begins reordering the residence they shared to suit the needs of one adult rather than two. Furniture is rearranged or thrown out. Closets and drawers are reorganized. A thorough house-cleaning may be undertaken. As the initiator has moved to a new location that reinforces his singularity, the significant other transforms the home that validated the coupling into one that likewise objectivates the new definition. Changes in the physical appearance of either or both partners may be a part of the symbolic restructuring of the private sphere. Weight losses, changes of hair style, or changes in clothing preferences further symbolize the yielding of the mutual identity and the move toward autonomy.

Should the significant other be the one to leave, the move into a new location aids in the redefinition of self as an autonomous individual. For example, the necessity of surviving in a new environment, the eventual emergence of a new set of friends that define and relate to the significant other as a separate being instead of as half of a couple, and the creation of a new residence without the other person are all mechanisms which reinforce autonomy and a definition of singularity.

Though the initiator has long been involved in objectivating a separate reality, frequently for the significant other this stage is just beginning. Seldom does the secret of the troubled marriage become shared with others by this partner until it can no longer be deferred. Although the initiator actively has sought objectivation, the significant other has avoided it. Confronted with actual separation, however, the significant other responds by taking the subjectively experienced meanings and moving them to the objective level—by confiding in others, perhaps in writing, in letters or in diaries—any means that helps the other deal with the new reality.

There are some who must be told of the separation—children, parents, best friends. Not only are the two partners reconstructing their own reality, but they now must reconstruct the reality for others. Conversation provides the mechanism for reconstruction, simultaneously creating common definitions and working as a major objectivating apparatus. The longer the conversation goes on, the more massively real do the objectivations become to the partners. The result is a stabilization of the objectivated reality, as the new definition of uncoupledness continues to move outward.

Uncoupling precipitates a reordering of all other significant relationships. As in coupling, where all other relationships are reperceived and regrouped to account for and support the emergence of *the* significant other, in uncoupling the reordering supports the singularity of each partner. Significant relationships are lost, as former friends of the couple now align with one or the other or refuse to choose between the two. Ties with families of orientation, formerly somewhat attenuated because of the coupling, are frequently renewed. For each of the partners, pressure exists to stabilize characterizations of others and of self so that the world and self are brought toward consistency. Each partner approaches groups that strengthen the new definition each has created, and avoids those that weaken it. The groups with which each partner associates help co-define the new reality.

OBJECTIVATION: THE PUBLIC SPHERE

The uncoupling is further objectivated for the participants as the new definition is legitimized in the public sphere. Two separate households demand public identification as separate identities. New telephone listings, changes of mailing address, separate checking accounts, and charge accounts, for example, all are mechanisms by which the new reality becomes publicly reconstructed.

The decision to initiate legal proceedings confirms the uncoupling by the formal negotiation of a heretofore informally negotiated definition. The adversary process supporting separate identities, custody proceedings,

the formal separation of the material base, the final removal of the rings all act as means of moving the new definition from the private to the public sphere. The uncoupling now becomes objectivated not only for the participants and their close intimates, but for casual acquaintances and strangers.

Objectivation acts as a constraint upon whatever social identity has been constructed. It can bind a couple together, or hinder their recoupling, once the uncoupling process has begun. Perhaps this can better be understood by considering the tenuous character of the extramarital affair. The very nature of the relationship is private. The coupling remains a secret shared by the two and seldom becomes objectivated in the public realm. Thus, the responsibility for the maintenance of that coupling usually rests solely with the two participants. When the relationship is no longer self-validating for one of the participants, the uncoupling does not involve a reconstruction of reality for others. The constraints imposed by the objectivation of a marital relationship which function to keep a couple in a marriage do not exist to the same extent in an affair. The fragility of the coupling is enhanced by its limited objectivation.

Berger and Kellner (1964:6) note that the "degree of objectivation will depend on the number and intensity of the social relationships that are its carriers." As the uncoupling process has moved from a nonshared secret held within the initiator to the realm of public knowledge, the degree of objectivation has increased. The result is a continuing decline in the precariousness of the newly constructed reality over time.

DIVORCE: A STAGE IN THE PROCESS

Yet a decrease in precariousness is not synonymous with a completion of the uncoupling process. As marriage, or coupling, is a dramatic act of redefinition of self by two strangers as they move from autonomous identities to the construction of a joint biography, so uncoupling involves yet another redefinition of self as the participants move from mutual identity toward autonomy. It is this redefinition of self, for each participant, that completes the uncoupling. Divorce, then, may not be the final stage. In fact, divorce could be viewed as a nonstatus that is at some point on a continuum ranging from marriage (coupling) as an achieved status, to autonomy (uncoupling), likewise an achieved status. In other words, the uncoupling process might be viewed as a status transformation which is complete when the individual defines his salient status as "single" rather than "divorced." When the individual's newly constructed separate subworld becomes nomos-building—when it creates for the individual a sort of order in which he can experience his life as making sense—the uncoupling process is completed.

The completion of uncoupling does not occur at the same moment for each participant. For either or both of the participants, it may not occur until after the other has created a coupled identity with another person. With that step, the tentativeness is gone.

> When I learned of his intention to remarry, I did not realize how devastated I would be. It was just awful. I remember crying and crying. It was really a very bad thing that I did not know or expect. You really aren't divorced while that other person is still free. You still have a lot of your psychological marriage going—in fact, I'm still in that a little bit because I'm still single.

For some, the uncoupling may never be completed. One or both of the participants may never be able to construct a new and separate subworld that becomes self-validating. Witness, for example, the widow who continues to call herself "Mrs. John Doe," who associates with the same circle of friends, who continues to wear the wedding ring and observes wedding anniversaries. For her, the coupled identity is still a major

mechanism for self-validation, even though the partner is gone.

In fact, death as a form of uncoupling may be easier for the significant other to handle than divorce. There exist ritual techniques for dealing with it, and there is no ambiguity. The relationship is gone. There will be no further interaction between the partners. With divorce, or any uncoupling that occurs through the volition of one or both of the partners, the interaction may continue long after the relationship has been formally terminated. For the significant other—the one left behind, without resources for self-validation—the continuing interaction between the partners presents obstacles to autonomy.

> There's a point at which it's over. If your wife dies, you're a lot luckier, I think, because it's over. You either live with it, you kill yourself, or you make your own bed of misery. Unlike losing a wife through death, in divorce, she doesn't die. She keeps resurrecting it. I can't get over it, she won't die. I mean, she won't go away.

CONTINUITIES

Continuities are linkages between the partners that exist despite the formal termination of the coupled identity. Most important of these is the existence of shared loved ones—children, in-laws, and so on. Though in-laws may of necessity be excluded from the separately constructed subworlds, children can rarely be and, in their very existence, present continued substantiation of the coupled identity.

In many cases continuities are actively constructed by one or both of the participants after the formal termination of the relationship. These manufactured linkages speak to the difficulty of totally separating that common biography, by providing a continued mechanism for interaction. They may be constructed as a temporary bridge between the separated subworlds, or they may come to be a permanent interaction pattern. Symbolically, they seem to indicate caring on the part of either or both of the participants.

The wife moves out. The husband spends his weekend helping her get settled—hanging pictures, moving furniture.

The husband moves out, leaving his set of tools behind. Several years later, even after his remarriage, the tools are still there, and he comes to borrow them one at a time. The former wife is planning to move within the same city. The tools are boxed up, ready to be taken with her.

The wife has moved out, but is slow to change her mailing address. Rather than marking her forwarding address on the envelopes and returning them by mail, the husband either delivers them once a week or the wife picks them up.

The wife moves out. The husband resists dividing property with her that is obviously hers. The conflict necessitates many phone calls and visits.

The husband moves out. Once a week he comes to the house to visit with the children on an evening when the wife is away. When she gets home, the two of them occasionally go out to dinner.

A nice part of the marriage was shared shopping trips on Sunday afternoons. After the divorce, they still occasionally go shopping together.

The holidays during the first year of separation were celebrated as they always had been—with the whole family together.

During a particularly difficult divorce, the husband noted that he had finally succeeded in finding his wife a decent lawyer.

Continuities present unmeasurable variables in the uncoupling process. In this paper, uncoupling is defined as a reality socially constructed by the participants. The stages that mark the movement from a coupled identity to separate autonomous identities are characterized, using divorce for an ideal-type analysis. Yet, there is no intent to portray uncoupling as a compelling linear process from which there is no turning back. Such conceptualization would deny the human factor inherent in reality construction. Granted, as the original secret is moved from private to public, becoming increasingly objectivated, reconstructing the coupled identity becomes more and more difficult.

Each stage of objectivation acts as the closing of a door. Yet at any stage the process may be interrupted. The initiator may not find mechanisms of self-validation outside the coupling that reinforce his autonomy. Or the self-validation found outside the coupling may be the very stuff that allows the initiator to stay *in* the relationship. Or continuities may intervene and reconstruction of the coupled identity may occur, despite the degree of objectivation, as in the following case.

Ellen met Jack in college. They fell in love and married. Jack had been blind since birth. He had pursued a college career in education and was also a musician. Both admired the independence of the other. In the marriage, she subordinated her career to his and helped him pursue a masters degree, as well as his musical interests. Her time was consumed by his needs—for transportation and the taping and transcribing of music for the musicians in his group. He was teaching at a school for the blind by day and performing as a musician at night. They had a son, and her life, instead of turning outward, as his, revolved around family responsibilities. She gained weight. Jack, after twelve years of marriage, left Ellen for his high school sweetheart. Ellen grieved for a while, then began patching up her life. She got a job, established her own credit, went back to college, and lost weight. She saw a lawyer, filed for divorce, joined Parents Without Partners, and began searching out singles groups. She dated. Throughout, Jack and Ellen saw each other occasionally and maintained a sexual relationship. The night before the divorce was final, they reconciled.

The uncoupling never was completed, though all stages of the process occurred, including the public objectivation that results from the initiation of the legal process. Ellen, in constructing an autonomous identity, became again the independent person Jack had first loved.[3] This, together with the continuities that existed between the two, created the basis for a common definition of the coupling as savable.

DISCUSSION

Berger and Kellner describe the process by which two individuals create a coupled identity for themselves. Here, we have started from the point of the coupled identity and examined the process by which people move out of such relationships. Using interview data, we have found that, although the renegotiation of separate realities is a complex web of subtle modifications, clear stages emerge which mark the uncoupling process. The emergent stages are like benchmarks which indicate the increasing objectivation of the changing definitions of reality, as these definitions move from the realm of the private to the public.

Beginning within the intimacy of the dyad, the initial objectivation occurs as the secret of the troubled marriage that the initiator has held is shared with the significant other. With this, the meaning has begun to move from the subjective to the objective. Definition negotiation begins. While attempting to negotiate a common definition, the initiator acts to increase the validation of his identity and place in the world by use of accompanying reconstructions of reality. The autonomy of the initiator increases as he finds self-validation outside the marriage and an ideology that supports the uncoupling. The increased autonomy of the initiator brings the significant other to accept a definition of the marriage as troubled, and they enter into the stage of "trying." The process

continues, as counseling and separation further move the new definition into the public sphere.

The telling of others, the symbolic physical signs of the uncoupling, and the initiation of formal legal proceedings validate the increasing separation of the partners as they negotiate a new reality which is different from that constructed private sphere which validated their identity as a couple. Eventually, a redefinition of the mutual identity occurs in such a way that the joint biography is separated into two separate autonomous identities. As Berger and Kellner state that marriage is a dramatic act of redefinition of self by two individuals, so uncoupling is characterized by the same phenomenon. Self-realization, rather than coming from the coupledness, again comes from outside sources. Significant conversation again finds its source in nonoverlapping circles. The new definition of the relationship constructed by the participants has, in interaction with others, become common property.

Language is crucial to this process. Socially constructed worlds need validation. As conversation constantly reconfirms a coupled identity, so also does it act as the major validating mechanism for the move to singularity, not by specific articulation, but by the way in which it comes to revolve around the uncoupled identity as taken for granted.

The notion that the stages uncovered do broadly apply needs to be further confirmed. We need to know whether the process is invariant regardless of the heterosexuality, homosexuality, or social class of couples. Does it also apply for close friends? In what ways does the sex of the interviewer bias the data? Additionally, the stages in the process should be confirmed by interviews with both partners in a coupling. Due to the delicacy of the subject matter, this is difficult. In only one instance were both partners available to be interviewed for this study. Notwithstanding these limitations, the findings which emerge deserve consideration.

Most significant of these is the existence of an underlying order in a phenomenon generally regarded as a chaotic and disorderly process. Undoubtedly the discovery of order was encouraged by the methodology of the study. The information was gained by retrospective analysis on the part of the interviewees. Certainly the passage of time allowed events to be reconstructed in an orderly way that made sense. Nonetheless, as was previously noted, the interviewees were all at various stages in the uncoupling process—some at the "secret" stage and some five years hence. Yet, the stages which are discussed here appeared without fail in every case and have been confirmed repeatedly by the other means described earlier.

In addition to this orderliness, the examination of the process of uncoupling discloses two other little-considered aspects of the process that need to be brought forth and questioned.

One is the caring. Generally, uncoupling is thought of as a conflict-ridden experience that ends as a bitter battle between two adversaries intent on doing each other in. Frequently, this is the case. Yet, the interviews for this study showed that in all cases, even the most emotion generating, again and again the concern of each of the participants for the other revealed itself. Apparently, the patterns of caring and responsibility that emerge between the partners in a coupling are not easily dispelled and in many cases persist throughout the uncoupling process and after, as suggested by the concept of continuities.

A second question that emerges from this examination of uncoupling is related to Berger and Kellner's thesis. They state that, for adults in our society, marriage is a significant validating relationship, one that is nomos-building. Marriage is, in fact, described as "a crucial nomic instrumentality" (1964:4). Though Berger and Kellner at the outset do delimit the focus of their analysis to marriage as an ideal type, the question to

be answered is, To what degree is this characterization of marriage appropriate today?

Recall, for example, the quote from one interviewee: "I was never psychologically married. I always felt strained by attempts that coupled me into a marital unit. I was just never comfortable as 'Mrs.' " The interviews for this study suggest that the nomos-building quality assumed to derive from marriage to the individual should be taken as problematic rather than as given. Gouldner (1959) suggests that the parts of a unit vary in the degree to which they are interdependent. His concept of functional autonomy may be extended to illuminate the variable forms that marriage, or coupling, may take and the accompanying degree of nomos. A relationship may exist in which the partners are highly interdependent, and the coupled identity does provide the major mechanism for self-validation, as Berger and Kellner suggest. Yet it is equally as likely that the participants are highly independent, or "loosely coupled" (Weick, 1976; Corwin, 1977), wherein mechanisms for self-validation originate *outside* the coupling rather than from the coupling itself. The connection between the form of the coupling, the degree to which it is or is not nomos-building, and the subsequent implications for uncoupling should be examined in future research.

NOTES

1. For a sensitive and thought-provoking examination of these as integral components of divorce, see Willard Waller's beautiful qualitative study, *The Old Love and the New.*
2. This statement must be qualified. There are instances when the partners enter a stage of trying with shared definitions of the marriage as savable. The conditions under which the coupling can be preserved have to be negotiated. If they can arrive at a common definition of the coupling that is agreeable to both, the uncoupling process is terminated. But this analysis is of uncoupling, and there are two alternatives: (1) that they enter with common definitions of the marriage as sav-

able but are not able to negotiate the conditions of the coupling so that the self-validation function is preserved or (2) that they enter the period of trying with opposing definitions, as stated here.

3. Waller interprets this phenomenon by using Jung's conceptualization of the container and the contained, analogous to the roles of initiator and significant other, respectively, in the present discussion. Notes Waller, "Or the contained, complicated by the process of divorcing, may develop those qualities whose lack the container previously deplored" (Waller:163–168).

REFERENCES

Berger, Peter L. and Hansfried Kellner, 1964, "Marriage and the Construction of Reality," *Diogenes*, 46:1–23.

Berger, Peter L. and Thomas Luckmann, 1966, *The Social Construction of Reality*. New York: Doubleday.

Bohanon, Paul, 1971, *Divorce and After*. Garden City, N.Y.: Anchor.

Corwin, Ronald G., 1976, "Organizations as Loosely Coupled Systems: Evolution of a Perspective," Paper presented, Seminar on Educational Organizations as Loosely Coupled Systems. Palo Alto, Calif.

Davis, Murray S., 1973, *Intimate Relations*. New York: Free Press.

Epstein, Joseph E., 1975, *Divorce: The American Experience*. London: Jonathan Cape.

Goode, William J., 1956, *Women in Divorce*. New York: Free Press.

Gouldner, Alvin A., 1959, "Organizational Analysis," in R. K. Merton, L. Bloom, and L. S. Cottrell, Jr., eds. *Sociology Today*. New York: Basic Books, pp. 400–428.

Krantzler, Mel, 1973, *Creative Divorce*. New York: New American Library.

Nichols, Jack, 1975, *Men's Liberation: A New Definition of Masculinity*. New York: Penguin.

Sullivan, Judy, 1974, *Mama Doesn't Live Here Anymore*. New York: Pyramid.

Waller, Willard, 1930, *The Old Love and the New*. Carbondale: Southern Illinois University Press.

Walum, Laurel Richardson, 1977, *The Dynamics of Sex and Gender: A Sociological Perspective*. Chicago: Rand McNally.

Weber, Max, 1930, *The Protestant Ethic and the Spirit of Capitalism*, translated by Talcott Parsons. New York: Charles Scribner's Sons.

Weick, Karl E., 1976, "Educational Organizations as Loosely Coupled Systems," *Administrative Science Quarterly*, 21:1–19.

Weiss, Robert, 1975, *Marital Separation*. New York: Basic Books.

29

Social Determinants of
Bystander Intervention in Emergencies

BIBB LATANÉ
JOHN M. DARLEY

Almost 100 years ago, Charles Darwin wrote: "As man is a social animal, it is almost certain that he would . . . from an inherited tendency be willing to defend, in concert with others, his fellow-men; and be ready to aid them in any way, which did not too greatly interfere with his own welfare or his own strong desires" (*The Descent of Man*). Today, although many psychologists would quarrel with Darwin's assertion that altruism is inherited, most would agree that men will go to the aid of others even when there is no visible gain for themselves. At least, most would have agreed until a March night in 1964. That night, Kitty Genovese was set upon by a maniac as she returned home from work at 3:00 AM. Thirty-eight of her neighbors in Kew Gardens came to their windows when she cried out in terror; but none came to her assistance, even though her stalker took over half an hour to murder her. No one even so much as called the police.

Since we started our research on bystander response to emergencies, we have heard about dozens of such incidents. We have also heard many explanations: "I would assign this to the effect of the megalopolis in which we live, which makes closeness very difficult and leads to the alienation of the individual from the group," contributed a psychoanalyst. "A disaster syndrome," explained a sociologist, "that shook the sense of safety and sureness of the indi-

viduals involved and caused psychological withdrawal from the event by ignoring it." "Apathy," others claim. "Indifference." "The gratification of unconscious sadistic impulses." "Lack of concern for our fellow men." "The Cold Society." These explanations and many more have applied to the surprising failure of bystanders to intervene in emergencies—failures which suggest that we no longer care about the fate of our neighbors.

But can this be so? We think not. Although it is unquestionably true that the witnesses in the incidents above did nothing to save the victim, "apathy," "indifference," and "unconcern" are not entirely accurate descriptions of their reactions. The 38 witnesses of Kitty Genovese's murder did not merely look at the scene once and then ignore it. Instead they continued to stare out of their windows at what was going on. Caught, fascinated, distressed, unwilling to act but unable to turn away, their behavior was neither helpful nor heroic; but it was not indifferent or apathetic either.

Actually, it was like crowd behavior in many other emergency situations; car accidents, drownings, fires, and attempted suicides all attract substantial numbers of people who watch the drama in helpless fascination without getting directly involved in the action. Are these people alienated and indifferent? Are the rest of us? Obviously not. It seems only yesterday we were being called overconforming. But why, then, do we not act?

Paradoxically, the key to understanding these failures of intervention may be found exactly in the fact that so surprises us about them: so many bystanders fail to intervene. If we think of 38, or 11, or 100 individuals, each looking at an emergency and callously deciding to pass by, we are horrified. But if we realize that each bystander is picking up cues about what is happening and how to react to it from the other bystanders, understanding begins to emerge. There are several ways in which a crowd of onlookers can make each individual member of that crowd less likely to act.

DEFINING THE SITUATION

Most emergencies are, or at least begin as, ambiguous events. A quarrel in the street may erupt into violence or it may be simply a family argument. A man staggering about may be suffering a coronary, or an onset of diabetes, or he simply may be drunk. Smoke pouring from a building may signal a fire, but on the other hand, it may be simply steam or airconditioner vapor. Before a bystander is likely to take action in such ambiguous situations, he must first define the event as an emergency and decide that intervention is the proper course of action.

In the course of making these decisions, it is likely that an individual bystander will be considerably influenced by the decisions he perceives other bystanders to be taking. If everyone else in a group of onlookers seems to regard an event as nonserious and the proper course of action as nonintervention, this consensus may strongly affect the perceptions of any single individual and inhibit his potential intervention.

The definitions that other people held may be discovered by discussing the situation with them, but they may also be inferred from their facial expressions or behavior. A whistling man with his hands in his pockets obviously does not believe he is in the midst of a crisis. A bystander who does not respond to smoke obviously does not attribute it to fire. An individual, seeing the inaction of others, will judge the situation as less serious than he would if alone.

But why should the others be inactive? Probably because they are aware that other people are also watching them. The others are an audience to their own reactions. Among American males, it is considered desirable to appear poised and collected in times of stress. Being exposed to the public view may constrain the actions and expressions of emotion of any individual as he tries to avoid possible ridicule and embarrassment. Even though he may be truly concerned and upset about the plight of a victim, until he decides what to do, he may maintain a calm demeanor.

If each member of a group is, at the same time, trying to appear calm and also looking around at the other members to gauge their reactions, all members may be led (or misled) by each other to define the situation as less critical than they would if alone. Until someone acts, each person sees only other nonresponding bystanders and is likely to be influenced not to act himself. A state of "pluralistic ignorance" may develop.

It has often been recognized that a crowd can cause contagion of panic leading each person in the crowd to overreact to an emergency to the detriment of everyone's welfare. What we suggest here is that a crowd can also force inaction on its members. It can suggest by its passive behavior that an event is not to be reacted to as an emergency, and it can make any individual uncomfortably aware of what a fool he will look for behaving as if it is.

Where There's Smoke, There's (Sometimes) Fire[1]

In this experiment we presented an emergency to individuals either alone or in groups of three. It was our expectation that the constraints on behavior in public combined with social influence processes would lessen the likelihood that members of three-person groups would act to cope with the emergency.

College students were invited to an interview to discuss "some of the problems involved in life at an urban university." As they sat in a small room waiting to be called for the interview and filling out a preliminary questionnaire, they faced an ambiguous but potentially dangerous situation. A stream of smoke began to puff into the room through a wall vent.

Some subjects were exposed to this potentially critical situation while alone. In a second condition, three naive subjects were tested together. Since subjects arrived at slightly different times, and since they each had individual questionnaires to work on, they did not introduce themselves to each other or attempt anything but the most rudimentary conversation.

As soon as the subjects had completed two pages of their questionnaires, the experimenter began to introduce the smoke through a small vent in the wall. The "smoke," copied from the famous Camel cigarette sign in Times Square, formed a moderately fine-textured but clearly visible stream of whitish smoke. It continued to jet into the room in irregular puffs, and by the end of the experimental period, it obscured vision.

All behavior and conversation were observed and coded from behind a one-way window (largely disguised on the subject's side by a large sign giving preliminary instructions). When and if the subject left the experimental room and reported the smoke, he was told that the situation "would be taken care of." If the subject had not reported the smoke within 6 minutes from the time he first noticed it, the experiment was terminated.

The typical subject, when tested alone, behaved very reasonably. Usually, shortly after the smoke appeared, he would glance up from his questionnaire, notice the smoke, show a slight but distinct startle reaction, and then undergo a brief period of indecision, perhaps returning briefly to his questionnaire before again staring at the smoke. Soon, most subjects would get up from their chairs, walk over to the vent and investigate it closely, sniffing the smoke, waving their hands in it, feeling its temperature, etc. The usual Alone subject would hesitate again, but finally would walk out of the room, look around outside, and, finding somebody there, calmly report the presence of the smoke. No subject showed any sign of panic, most simply said: "There's something strange going on in there, there seems to be some sort of smoke coming through the wall. . . ." The median subject in the Alone condition had reported the smoke within 2 minutes of first noticing it. Three-quarters of the 24 people run in this condition reported the smoke before the experimental period was terminated.

Because there are three subjects present and available to report the smoke in the Three Naive Bystanders condition as compared to only one subject at a time in the Alone condition, a simple comparison between the two conditions is not appropriate. We cannot compare speeds in the Alone condition with the average speed of the three subjects in a group because, once one subject in a group had reported the smoke, the pressures on the other two disappeared. They could feel legitimately that the emergency had been handled and that any action on their part would be redundant and potentially confusing. Therefore, we used the speed of the first subject in a group to report the smoke as our dependent variable. However, since there were times as many people available to respond in this condition as in the Alone condition, we would expect an increased likelihood that at least one person would report the smoke by chance alone. Therefore, we mathematically created "groups" of three scores from the Alone condition to serve as a baseline.[2]

In contrast to the complexity of this procedure, the results were quite simple. Subjects in the three-person-group condition were markedly inhibited from reporting the smoke. Since 75% of the Alone subjects reported the smoke, we would expect over 98% of the three-person groups to include at least one reporter. In fact, in only 38% of the eight groups in this condition did even one person report ($p < .01$). Of the 24 people run in these eight groups, only one person reported the smoke within the first 4 minutes before the room got noticeably unpleasant. Only three people reported the smoke within the entire experimental period. Social inhibition of reporting was so strong that the smoke was reported faster when only one person saw it than when groups of three were present ($p < .01$).

Subjects who had reported the smoke were relatively consistent in later describing their reactions to it. They thought the smoke looked somewhat "strange." They were not sure exactly what it was or whether it was dangerous, but they felt it was unusual enough to justify some examination. "I wasn't sure whether it was a fire, but it looked like something was wrong." "I thought it might be steam, but it seemed like a good idea to check it out."

Subjects who had not reported the smoke were also unsure about exactly what it was, but they uniformly said that they had rejected the idea that it was a fire. Instead, they hit upon an astonishing variety of alternative explanations, all sharing the common characteristic of interpreting the smoke as a nondangerous event. Many thought the smoke was either steam or airconditioning vapors, several thought it was smog, purposely introduced to simulate an urban envi-

ronment, and two actually suggested that the smoke was a "truth gas" filtered into the room to induce them to answer the questionnaire accurately! Predictably, some decided that "it must be some sort of experiment" and stoically endured the discomfort of the room rather than overreact.

The results of this study clearly support the prediction. Groups of three naive subjects were less likely to report the smoke than solitary bystanders. Our predictions were confirmed—but this does not necessarily mean that our explanation of these results is the correct one. As a matter of fact, several alternative explanations center around the fact that the smoke represented a possible danger to the subject himself as well as to others in the building. For instance, it is possible that the subjects in groups saw themselves as engaged in a game of "chicken" in which the first person to report would admit his cowardliness. Or it may have been that the presence of others made subjects feel safer, and thus reduced their need to report.

To rule out such explanations, a second experiment was designed to see whether similar group inhibition effects could be observed in situations where there is no danger to the individual himself for not acting. In this study, male Columbia University undergraduates waited either alone or with a stranger to participate in a market research study. As they waited they heard a woman fall and apparently injure herself in the room next door. Whether they tried to help and how long they took to do so were the main dependent variables of the study.

The Fallen Woman[3]

Subjects were telephoned and offered $2 to participate in a survey of game and puzzle preferences conducted at Columbia by the Consumer Testing Bureau (CTB), a market research organization. When they arrived, they were met at the door by an attractive young woman and taken to the testing room. On the way, they passed the CTB office, and through its open door they were able to see a desk and bookcase piled high with papers and filing cabinets. They entered the adjacent testing room, which contained a table and chairs and a variety of games, and they were given questionnaires to fill out. The representative told subjects that she would be working next door in her office for about 10 minutes while they were completing the questionnaire and left by opening the collapsible curtain which divided the two rooms. She made sure that subjects were aware that the curtain was unlocked and easily opened and that it provided a means of entry to her office. The representative stayed in her office, shuffling papers, opening drawers, and making enough noise to remind the subjects of her presence. Four minutes after leaving the testing area, she turned on a high fidelity stereophonic tape recorder.

The Emergency. If the subject listened carefully, he heard the representative climb up on a chair to reach for a stack of papers on the bookcase. Even if he were not listening carefully, he heard a loud crash and a scream as the chair collapsed and she fell to the floor. "Oh, my God, my foot...I...I...can't move...it. Oh...my ankle," the representative moaned. "I...can't get this...thing ...off me." She cried and moaned for about a minute longer, but the cries gradually got more subdued and controlled. Finally she muttered something about getting outside, knocked over the chair as she pulled herself up and thumped to the door, closing it behind her as she left. The entire incident took 130 seconds.

The main dependent variable of the study, of course, was whether the subjects took action to help the victim and how long it took them to do so. There were actually several modes of intervention possible: a subject could open the screen dividing the two rooms, leave the testing room and enter

the CTB office by the door, find someone else, or most simply, call out to see if the representative needed help. In one condition, each subject was in the testing room alone while he filled out the questionnaire and heard the fall. In the second condition, strangers were placed in the testing room in pairs. Each subject in the pair was unacquainted with the other before entering the room and they were not introduced.

Across all experimental groups, the majority of subjects who intervened did so by pulling back the room divider and coming into the CTB office (61%). Few subjects came the round-about way through the door to offer their assistance (14%), and a surprisingly small number (24%) chose the easy solution of calling out to offer help. No one tried to find someone else to whom to report the accident.

Since 70% of Alone subjects intervened, we should expect that at least one person in 91% of all two-person groups would offer help if members of a pair had no influence upon each other. In fact, members did influence each other. In only 40% of the groups did even one person offer help to the injured woman. Only eight subjects of the 40 who were run in this condition intervened. This response rate is significantly below the hypothetical baseline ($p < .001$). Social inhibition of helping was so strong that the victim was actually helped more quickly when only one person heard her distress than when two did ($p < .01$).

When we talked to subjects after the experiment, those who intervened usually claimed that they did so either because the fall sounded very serious or because they were uncertain what had occurred and felt they should investigate. Many talked about intervention as the "right thing to do" and asserted they would help again in any situation.

Many of the nonintervenors also claimed that they were unsure what had happened (59%), but had decided that it was not too serious (46%). A number of subjects reported that they thought other people would or could help (25%), and three said they refrained out of concern for the victim—they did not want to embarrass her. Whether to accept these explanations as reasons or rationalizations is moot—they certainly do not explain the differences among conditions. The important thing to note is that noninterveners did not seem to feel that they had behaved callously or immorally. Their behavior was generally consistent with their interpretation of the situation. Subjects almost uniformly claimed that in a "real" emergency they would be among the first to help the victim.

These results strongly replicate the findings of the Smoke study. In both experiments, subjects were less likely to take action if they were in the presence of others than if they were alone. This congruence of findings from different experimental settings supports the validity and generality of the phenomenon; it also helps rule out a variety of alternative explanations suitable to either situation alone. For example, the possibility that smoke may have represented a threat to the subject's personal safety and that subjects in groups may have had a greater concern to appear "brave" than single subjects does not apply to the present experiment. In the present experiment, nonintervention cannot signify bravery. Comparison of the two experiments also suggests that the absolute number of nonresponsive bystanders may not be a critical factor in producing social inhibition of intervention; pairs of strangers in the present study inhibited each other as much as did trios in the former study.

Other studies we have done show that group inhibition effects hold in real life as well as in the laboratory, and for members of the general population as well as college students. The results of these experiments clearly support the line of theoretical argument advanced earlier. When bystanders to

an emergency can see the reactions of other people, and when other people can see their own reactions, each individual may, through a process of social influence, be led to interpret the situation as less serous than he would if he were alone, and consequently be less likely to take action.

These studies, however, tell us little about the case that stimulated our interest in bystander intervention: the Kitty Genovese murder. Although the 38 witnesses to that event were aware, through seeing lights and silhouettes in other windows, that others watched, they could not see what others were doing and thus be influenced by their reactions. In the privacy of their own apartments, they could not be clearly seen by others, and thus inhibited by their presence. The social influence process we have described above could not operate. Nevertheless, we think that the presence of other bystanders may still have affected each individual's response.

DIFFUSION OF RESPONSIBILITY

In addition to affecting the interpretations that he places on a situation, the presence of other people can also alter the rewards and costs facing an individual bystander. Perhaps most importantly, the presence of other people can reduce the cost of not acting. If only one bystander is present at an emergency, he carries all of the responsibility for dealing with it; he will feel all of the guilt for not acting; he will bear all of any blame others may level for nonintervention. If others are present, the onus of responsibility is diffused, and the individual may be more likely to resolve his conflict between intervening and not intervening in favor of the latter alternative.

When only one bystander is present at an emergency, if help is to come it must be from him. Although he may choose to ignore them out of concern for his personal safety, or desire "not to get involved," any pressures to intervene focus uniquely on him. When there are several observers present, however, the pressures to intervene do not focus on any one of the observers; instead, the responsibility for intervention is shared among all the onlookers and is not unique to any one. As a result, each may be less likely to help.

Potential blame may also be diffused. However much we wish to think that an individual's moral behavior is divorced from consideration of personal punishment or reward, there is both theory and evidence to the contrary. It is perfectly reasonable to assume that under circumstances of group responsibility for a punishable act, the punishment or blame that accrues to any one individual is often slight or nonexistent.

Finally, if others are known to be present, but their behavior cannot be closely observed, any one bystander may assume that one of the other observers is already taking action to end the emergency. If so, his own intervention would only be redundant—perhaps harmfully or confusingly so. Thus, given the presence of other onlookers whose behavior cannot be observed, any given bystander can rationalize his own inaction by convincing himself that "somebody else must be doing something."

These considerations suggest that even when bystanders to an emergency cannot see or be influenced by each other, the more bystanders who are present, the less likely any one bystander would be to intervene and provide aid. To test this suggestion, it would be necessary to create an emergency situation in which each subject is blocked from communicating with others to prevent his getting information about their behavior during the emergency.

A Fit to Be Tied[4]

A college student arrived in the laboratory, and was ushered into an individual room from which a communication system would enable him to talk to other participants (who were actually figments of the tape recorder). Over the intercom, the subject was told that the experimenter was concerned with the kinds of personal problems faced by normal college students in a high-pressure, urban environment, and that he would be asked to participate in a discussion about these problems. To avoid embarrassment about discussing personal problems with strangers, the experimenter said, several precautions would be taken. First, subjects would remain anonymous, which was why they had been placed in individual rooms rather than face-to-face. Second, the experimenter would not listen to the initial discussion himself, but would only get the subject's reactions later by questionnaire.

The plan for the discussion was that each person would talk in turn for 2 minutes, presenting his problems to the group. Next, each person in turn would comment on what others had said, and finally there would be a free discussion. A mechanical switching device regulated the discussion, switching on only one microphone at a time.

The Emergency. The discussion started with the future victim speaking first. He said he found it difficult to get adjusted to New York and to his studies. Very hesitantly and with obvious embarrassment, he mentioned that he was prone to seizures, particularly when studying hard or taking exams. The other people, including the one real subject, took their turns and discussed similar problems (minus the proneness to seizures). The naive subject talked last in the series, after the last prerecorded voice.

When it was again the victim's turn to talk, he made a few relatively calm comments, and then, growing increasingly loud and incoherent, he continued:

> I er I think I I need er if if could er er somebody er er er er er er er give me a little er give me a little help here because I er I'm er er

h-h-having a a a a real problem er right now and I er if somebody could help me out it would er er s-s-sure be sure be good . . . because er there er er a cause I er I uh I've got a a one of the er sie . . . er er things coming on and and and I could really er use some help so if somebody would er give me a little h-help uh er-er-er-er-er c-could somebody er er help er uh uh uh (choking sounds). . . . I'm gonna die er er I'm . . . gonna die er help er er seizure (chokes, then quite).

The major independent variable of the study was the number of people the subject believed also heard the fit. The subject was led to believe that the discussion group was one of three sizes: a two-person group consisting of himself and the victim; a three-person group consisting of himself, the victim, and the other person; or a six-person group consisting of himself, the victim, and four other persons.

The major dependent variable of the experiment was the time elapsed from the start of the victim's seizure until the subject left his experimental cubicle. When the subject left his room, he saw the experimental assistant seated at the end of the hall, and invariably went to the assistant to report the seizure. If 5 minutes elapsed without the subject's having emerged from his room, the experiment was terminated.

Ninety-five percent of all the subjects who ever responded did so within the first half of the time available to them. No subject who had not reported within 3 minutes after the fit ever did so. This suggests that even had the experiment been allowed to run for a considerably longer period of time, few additional subjects would have responded.

Eighty-five percent of the subjects who thought they alone knew of the victim's plight reported the seizure before the victim was cut off; only 31% of those who thought four other bystanders were present did so. Everyone of the subjects in the two-person condition, but only 62% of the subjects in the six-person condition ever reported the emergency. To do a more detailed analysis of the results, each subject's time score was transformed into a "speed" score by taking the reciprocal of the response time in seconds and multiplying by 100. Analysis of variance of these speed scores indicates that the effect of group size was highly significant ($p < .01$), and all three groups differed significantly one from another ($p < .05$).

Subjects, whether or not they intervened, believed the fit to be genuine and serious. "My God, he's having a fit," many subjects said to themselves (and we overheard via their microphones). Others gasped or simply said, "Oh." Several of the male subjects swore. One subject said to herself, "It's just my kind of luck, something has to happen to me!" Several subjects spoke aloud of their confusion about what course of action to take: "Oh, God, what should I do?"

When those subjects who intervened stepped out of their rooms, they found the experimental assistant down the hall. With some uncertainty but without panic, they reported the situation. "Hey, I think Number 1 is very sick. He's having a fit or something." After ostensibly checking on the situation, the experimenter returned to report that "everything is under control." The subjects accepted these assurances with obvious relief.

Subjects who failed to report the emergency showed few signs of the apathy and indifference thought to characterize "unresponsive bystanders." When the experimenter entered her room to terminate the situation, the subject often asked if the victim was all right. "Is he being taken care of?" "He's all right, isn't he?" Many of these subjects showed physical signs of nervousness; they often had trembling hands and sweating palms. If anything, they seemed more emotionally aroused than did the subjects who reported the emergency.

Why, then, didn't they respond? It is not our impression that they had decided not to respond. Rather, they were still in a state of indecision and conflict concerning whether to respond or not. The emotional behavior of those nonresponding subjects was a sign of their continuing conflict, a conflict that other subjects resolved by responding.

The fit created a conflict situation of the avoidance-avoidance type. On the one hand, subjects worried about the guilt and shame they would feel if they did not help the person in distress. On the other hand, they were concerned not to make fools of themselves by overreacting, not to ruin the ongoing experiment by leaving their intercoms, and not to destroy the anonymous nature of the situation, which the experimenter had earlier stressed as important. For subjects in the two-person condition, the obvious distress of the victim and his need for help were so important that their conflict was easily resolved. For the subjects who knew that there were other bystanders present, the cost of not helping was reduced and the conflict they were in was more acute. Caught between the two negative alternatives of letting the victim continue to suffer or rushing, perhaps foolishly, to help, the nonresponding bystanders vacillated between them rather than choosing not to respond. This distinction may be academic for the victim, since he got no help in either case, but it is an extremely important one for understanding the causes of bystanders' failures to help.

Although subjects experienced stress and conflict during the emergency, their general reactions to it were highly positive. On a questionnaire administered after the experimenter had discussed the nature and purpose of the experiment, every single subject found the experiment either "interesting" or "very interesting" and was willing to participate in similar experiments in the future. All subjects felt that they understood what the experiment was all about and indicated that they thought the deceptions were necessary and justified. All but one felt they were better informed about the nature of psychological research in general.

CONCLUSION

We have suggested two distinct processes which might lead people to be less likely to intervene in an emergency if there are other people present than if they are alone. On the one hand, we suggested that the presence of other people may affect the interpretations each bystander puts on an ambiguous emergency situation. If other people are present at an emergency, each bystander will be guided by their apparent reactions in formulating his own impressions. Unfortunately, their apparent reactions may not be a good indication of their true feelings. It is possible for a state of "pluralistic ignorance" to develop, in which each bystander is led by the apparent lack of concern of the others to interpret the situation as being less serious than he would if alone. To the extent that he does not feel the situation is an emergency, he will be unlikely to take any helpful action.

Even if an individual does decide that an emergency is actually in process and that something ought to be done, he still is faced with the choice of whether he himself will intervene. Here again, the presence of other people may influence him—by reducing the costs associated with nonintervention. If a number of people witness the same event, the responsibility for action is diffused, and each may feel less necessity to help.

"There's safety in numbers," according to an old adage, and modern city dwellers seem to believe it. They shun deserted streets, empty subway cars, and lonely dark walks in dark parks, preferring instead to go where others are or to stay at home. When faced with stress, most individuals seem less afraid when they are in the presence of others than when they are alone.

A feeling so widely shared should have some basis in reality. Is there safety in number? If so, why? Two reasons are often suggested: individuals are less likely to find themselves in trouble if there are others about, and even if they do find themselves in trouble, others are likely to help them deal with it. While it is certainly true that a victim is unlikely to receive help if nobody knows of his plight, the experiments above cast doubt on the suggestion that he will be more likely to receive help if more people are present. In fact, the opposite seems to be true. A victim may be more likely to get help, or an emergency be reported, the fewer the people who are available to take action.

Although the results of these studies may shake our faith in "safety in numbers," they also may help us begin to understand a number of frightening incidents where crowds have heard but not answered a call for help. Newspapers have tagged these incidents with the label, "apathy." We have become indifferent, they say, callous to the fate of suffering of others. Our society has become "dehumanized" as it has become urbanized. These glib phrases may contain some truth, since startling cases such as the Genovese murder often seem to occur in our large cities, but such terms may also be misleading. Our studies suggest a different conclusion. They suggest that situational factors, specifically factors involving the immediate social environment, may be of greater importance in determining an individual's reaction to an emergency than such vague cultural or personality concepts as "apathy" or "alienation due to urbanization." They suggest

that the failure to intervene may be better understood by knowing the relationship among bystanders rather than that between a bystander and the victim.

NOTES

1. A more complete account of this experiment is provided in Latané and Darley (1968). Keith Gerritz and Lee Ross provided thoughtful assistance in running the study.
2. The formula for calculating the expected proportion of groups in which at least one person will have acted by a given time is $1-(1-p)^n$ where p is the proportion of single individuals who acted by that time and n is the number of persons in the group.
3. This experiment is more fully described in Latané and Rodin (1969).
4. Further details of this experiment can be found in Darley and Latané (1968).

REFERENCES

Darley, J. M., and Latané, B. Bystander intervention in emergencies: Diffusion of responsibility. *Journal of Personality and Social Psychology,* 1968, 8, 377–383.

Latané, B., and Darley, J. M. Group inhibition of bystander intervention. *Journal of Personality and Social Psychology,* 1968, 10, 215–221.

Latané, B., and Rodin, J. A lady in distress: Inhibiting effects of friends and strangers on bystander intervention. *Journal of Experimental Social Psychology,* 1969, 5, 189–202.

30

Situated Actions and Vocabularies of Motive

C. WRIGHT MILLS

The major reorientation of recent theory and observation in sociology of language emerged with the overthrow of the Wundtian notion that language has as its function the "expression" of prior elements within the individual. The postulate underlying modern study of language is the simple one that we must approach linguistic behavior, not by referring it to private states in individuals, but by observing its social function of coordinating diverse actions. Rather than expressing something which is prior and in the person, language is taken by other persons as an indicator of future actions.[1]

Within this perspective there are suggestions concerning problems of motivation. It is the purpose of this paper to outline an analytic model for the explanation of motives which is based on a sociological theory of language and a sociological psychology.[2]

As over against the inferential conception of motives as subjective "springs" of action, motives may be considered as typical vocabularies having ascertainable functions in delimited societal situations. Human actors do vocalize and impute motives to themselves and to others. To explain behavior by referring it to an inferred and abstract "motive" is one thing. To analyze the observable lingual mechanisms of motive imputation and avowal as they function in conduct is quite another. Rather than fixed elements "in" an individual, motives are the terms with which interpretation of conduct *by social actors* proceeds. This imputation and avowal of motives by actors are social phenomena to be explained. . . .

First, we must demarcate the general conditions under which such motive imputation and avowal seem to occur.[3] Next, we must give a characterization of motive in denotable terms and an explanatory paradigm of why certain motives are verbalized rather than others. Then, we must indicate mechanisms of the linkage of vocabularies of motive to systems of action. What we want is an analysis of the integrating, controlling, and specifying function a certain type of speech fulfils in socially situated actions.

The generic situation in which imputation and avowal of motives arise, involves, first, the *social* conduct or the (stated) programs of languaged creatures, i.e., programs and actions oriented with reference to the actions and talk of others; second, the avowal and imputation of motives is concomitant with the speech form known as the "question." Situations back of questions typically involve *alternative* or *unexpected* programs or actions which phases analytically denote "crises."[4] The question is distinguished in that it usually elicits another *verbal* action, not a motor response. The question is an element in *conversation*. Conversation may be concerned with the factual features of a situation as they are seen or believed to be or it may seek to integrate and promote a set of diverse social actions with reference to the situation and its normative pattern of expectations. It is in this latter assent and dissent phase of conversation that persuasive and dissuasive speech and vocabulary arise. For men live in immediate acts of experience and their attentions are directed outside themselves until acts are in some way frustrated. It is then that awareness of self and of motive occur. The "question" is a lingual index of such conditions. The avowal and imputation of motives are features of such conversations as arise in "question" situations.

Motives are imputed or avowed as answers to questions interrupting acts or programs. Motives are words. Generically, to what do they refer? They do not denote any elements "in" individuals. They stand for anticipated situational consequences of questioned conduct. Intention or purpose (stated as a "program") *is* awareness of anticipated consequence; motives are names for consequential situations, and surrogates for actions leading to them. Behind questions are possible alternative actions with their terminal consequences. "Our introspective words for motives are rough, shorthand descriptions for certain typical patterns of discrepant and conflicting stimuli."[5]

The model of purposive conduct associated with Dewey's name may briefly be stated. Individuals confronted with "alternative acts" perform one or the other of them on the basis of the differential consequences which they anticipate. This nakedly utilitarian schema is inadequate because: (a) the "alternative acts" of *social* conduct "appear" most often in lingual form, as a question, stated by one's self or by another; (b) it is more adequate to say that individuals act in terms of anticipation of *named* consequences.

Among such names and in some technologically oriented lines of action there may appear such terms as "useful," "practical," "serviceable," etc., terms so "ultimate" to the pragmatists, and also to certain sectors of the American population in these delimited situations. However, there are other areas of population with different vocabularies of motives. The choice of lines of action is accompanied by representations, and selection among them, of their situational termini. Men discern situations with particular vo-

cabularies, and it is in terms of some delimited vocabulary that they anticipate consequences of conduct.[6] Stable vocabularies of motives link anticipated consequences and specific actions. There is no need to invoke "psychological" terms like "desire" or "wish" as explanatory, since they themselves must be explained socially.[7] Anticipation is a subvocal or overt naming of terminal phases and/or social consequences of conduct. When an individual names consequences, he elicits the behaviors for which the name is a redintegrative cue. In a *societal* situation, implicit in the names for consequences is the social dimension of motives. Through such vocabularies, types of societal controls operate. Also, the terms in which the question is asked often will contain both alternatives: "Love or Duty?", "Business or Pleasure?" Institutionally different situations have different *vocabularies of motive* appropriate to their respective behaviors.

This sociological conception of motives as relatively stable lingual phases of delimited situations is quite consistent with Mead's program to approach conduct socially and from the outside. It keeps clearly in mind that "both motives and actions very often originate not from within but from the situation in which individuals find themselves. . . ."[8] It translates the question of "why"[9] into a "how" that is answerable in terms of a situation and its typal vocabulary of motives, i.e., those which conventionally accompany that type situation and function as cues and justifications for normative actions in it.

It has been indicated that the question is usually an index to the avowal and imputation of motives. Max Weber defines motive as a complex of meaning, which appears to the actor himself or to the observer to be an adequate ground for his conduct.[10] The aspect of motive which this conception grasps is its intrinsically social character. A satisfactory or adequate motive is one that satisfies the questioners of an act or program, whether it be the other's or the actor's. As a word, *a motive tends to be one which is to the actor and to the other members of a situation an unquestioned answer to questions concerning social and lingual conduct.* A stable motive is an ultimate in justificatory conversation. The words which in a type situation will fulfil this function are circumscribed by the vocabulary of motives acceptable for such situations. Motives are accepted justifications for present, future, or past programs or acts.

To term them justification is *not* to deny their efficacy. Often anticipations of acceptable justifications will control conduct. ("If I did this, what could I say? What would they say?") Decisions may be, wholly or in part, delimited by answers to such queries.

A man may begin an act for one motive. In the course of it, he may adopt an ancillary motive. This does not mean that the second apologetic motive is inefficacious. The vocalized expectation of an act, its "reason," is not only a mediating condition of the act but it is a proximate and controlling condition for which the term "cause" is not inappropriate. It may strengthen the act of the actor. It may win new allies for his act.

When they appeal to others involved in one's act, motives are strategies of action. In many social actions, others must agree, tacitly or explicitly. Thus, acts often will be abandoned if no reason can be found that others will accept. Diplomacy in choice of motive often controls the diplomat. Diplomatic choice of motive is part of the attempt to motivate acts for other members in a situation. Such pronounced motives undo snarls and integrate social actions. Such diplomacy does not necessarily imply intentional lies. It merely indicates that an appropriate vocabulary of motives will be utilized—that they are conditions for certain lines of conduct.[11]

When an agent vocalizes or imputes motives, he is not trying to *describe* his experienced social action. He is not merely stating "reasons." He is influencing others—and himself. Often he is finding new "reasons"

which will mediate action. Thus, we need not treat an action as discrepant from "its" verbalization, for in many cases, the verbalization is a new act. In such cases, there is not a discrepancy between an act and "its" verbalization, but a difference between two disparate actions, motor-social and verbal.[12] This additional (or "*ex post facto*") lingualization may involve appeal to a vocabulary of motives associated with a norm with which both members of the situation are in agreement. As such, it is an integrative factor in *future* phases of the original social action or in other acts. By resolving conflicts, motives are efficacious. Often, if "reasons" were not given, an act would not occur, nor would diverse actions be integrated. . . .

NOTES

1. See C. Wright Mills, "Bibliographical Appendices," Section I, 4: "Sociology of Language" in *Contemporary Social Theory*, Ed. by Barnes, Becker & Becker, New York, 1940.
2. See G. H. Mead, "Social Psychology as Counterpart of Physiological Psychology," *Psychol. Bul.*, VI: 401–408, 1909; Karl Mannheim, *Man and Society in an Age of Reconstruction*, New York, 1940; L. V. Wiese-Howard Becker, *Systematic Sociology*, part I, New York, 1932; J. Dewey, "All psychology is either biological or social psychology," *Psychol. Rev.*, vol. 24: 276.
3. The importance of this initial task for research is clear. Most researches on the verbal level merely ask abstract questions of individuals, but if we can tentatively delimit the situations in which certain motives *may* be verbalized, we can use that delimitation in the construction of *situational* questions, and we shall be *testing* deductions from our theory.
4. On the "question" and "conversation," see G. A. DeLaguna, *Speech: Its Function and Development*, 37 (and index), New Haven, 1927. For motives in crises, see J. M. Williams, *The Foundations of Social Science*, 435 ff, New York, 1920.
5. K. Burke, *Permanence and Change*, 45, New York, 1936. I am indebted to this book for several leads which are systematized into the present statement.

6. See such experiments as C. N. Rexroad's "Verbalization in Multiple Choice Reactions," *Psychol. Rev.*, Vol. 33: 458, 1926.

7. Cf. J. Dewey, "Theory of Valuation," *Int. Ency. of Unified Science*, New York, 1939.

8. K. Mannheim, *Man and Society*, 249, London, 1940.

9. Conventionally answerable by reference to "subjective factors" within individuals. R. M. MacIver, "The Modes of the Question Why," *J. of Soc. Phil.*, April, 1940. Cf. also his "The Imputation of Motives," *Amer. J. Sociol.*, July 1940.

10. *Wirtschaft und Gesellschaft*, 5, Tubingen, 1922, " 'Motiv' heisst ein Sinnzusammenhang, Welcher dem Handelnden selbst oder dem Beobachtenden als sinnhafter 'Grund' eines Verhaltens in dem Grade heissen, als die Beziehung seiner Bestandteile von uns nach den durchschnittlichen Denk- und Gefühlsgewohnheiten als typischer (wir pflegen in sagen: 'richtiger') Sinzusammenhang bejaht Wird."

11. Of course, since motives are communicated, they may be lies; but, this must be proved. Verbalizations are not lies merely because they are socially efficacious. I am here concerned more with the social function of pronounced motives, than with the sincerity of those pronouncing them.

12. See F. Znaniecki, *Social Actions*, 30, New York, 1936.

PART FOUR

Institutional Social Psychology

This book began with the statement that the field of social psychology is vast. It has been further said that there are important connections between the individual and the larger social system of society that are essential to social psychology as a discipline. Without a clear understanding of the structural influences on human behavior, one cannot fully comprehend the gamut of issues within the discipline's purview.

In addition to the microscopic social processes that are explored within social psychology, there are macroscopic factors that are considered as well. In the earlier sections of this volume, the focus was primarily on the individual, the dyad, and the small group. These represent the relevant areas of analysis of the microscopic brand of social psychology. Various forms of collective action, the social forces that accompany major societal institutions (the family, religion, politics, military, work, etc.), and modernization within society represent the areas of analysis of the macroscopic social psychology discussed here.

The macroscopic approach recognizes the important connection between individuals and social systems. Although sometimes referred to as socially structured psychology, here we group this approach under the general category of institutional social psychology. This domain suggests a link between the micro and the macro, since not all social processes can be analyzed and understood merely on the microscopic level. In essence, at times an integrative understanding of larger social processes and the individual is necessary to better comprehend human conduct or action.

An important area within macro social psychology is the broad topic of collective action. For years, social scientists have tried to understand the motivations for behavior within large groups. Primarily within the academic domain of sociology rather than psychology, the subject of collective action has been addressed through the related areas of collective behavior and social movements. Collective behavior normally refers to a form of collective action that is relatively spontaneous or unplanned and emerges out of a particular set of environmental conditions. The behavior of crowds at athletic events, panics that seem to grip the collective psychology of a society, and crazes or fads that consume the collective conscience are all of interest to those who study collective behavior.

A related area has come to be known as social movements. Unlike collective behavior, social movements normally involve less spontaneous action and more

purposeful behavior. However, like collective behavior, social movements are motivated by a particular set of environmental or structural factors that make the collective
action viable and conducive. Like those who study collective behavior, those who
examine social movements are also interested in collective action. Labor organizations, new religious movements, and forms of collective action that center on a
particular social issue such as war or the environment are all of interest to the social
psychologist who studies social movements.

Collective behavior and social movements, although very different conceptually,
do share some common ground. First, both involve individual behavior with larger
social processes. That is, individual behavior is required for collective action to take
place. Second, forms of both collective behavior and social movement can result in
some type of social change that ultimately will influence individuals. Society is made
up of individuals who will experience the consequences of collective action.

Third, it is likely that collective behavior will be present within a social movement, although the emergence of collective behavior does not necessarily need a social
movement. This means that collective behavior is often a component of a social
movement, since it may offer a way of expressing the movement's goals, but forms of
collective behavior such as a panic do not necessarily require the backing of a social
movement. Finally, both types of collective action can involve rebellion against or
rejection of certain established, institutionalized aspects of society or culture. Nothing
is permanent within the larger structure of society. While culture may be a constant,
societies, countries, states, and communities change given the right combination of
internal and external forces.

Other important areas of institutional social psychology include what have been
referred to within sociology as social institutions, which are intangible entities within
society to which people belong. The influence of social institutions goes beyond mere
membership, however, for there are social forces coming from social institutions that
guide human conduct. Although social institutions such as the family, religion, work,
the military, and government are all macro in nature, the microscopic connection
becomes clear when examining a single nuclear family, a personal religious experience, the alienation of a lone worker, the life of a soldier, or the role of the ordinary
citizen within a governed society. Although social institutions are massive, intangible
entities within society, they have tangible, individual dimensions because individuals
make up larger social systems. Attempts have been made to draw parallels between
the experience of individuals and the experiences of larger social systems.

Yet another aspect of institutional social psychology that deserves mention is
modernization. An ever-present aspect of any society is social change. Much of what
constitutes social change is beyond the control of the individual, but the individual
must remain mutable and respond to various innovations and alterations in society.
This can lead to changing social selves and searching for identity within a shifting
social environment. Some change is purposeful, as is sometimes seen in collective
action (social movements); at times, societies and their social institutions are sometimes resistant to and fearful of change, not knowing what the future might hold.
Whatever the case, individuals must cope with the changes within society, and this is
not always easy. The process of social change caused by modernization underscores
the need to understand not only the larger social processes but also the microscopic
impact of social change.

Taken together, collective action, social institutions, and modernization demonstrate the important linkages between the collectivities within society and the individual experience. One cannot fully understand the role of social psychology within society without clearly recognizing the institutional influences on human behavior.

THE SELECTIONS

The selections found within this section all speak to the social psychological impact of social systems on individual behavior. Each addresses a different area of institutional social psychology, from collective action to the social psychology of modernization. Keeping with this theme, each also attempts to demonstrate how social systems and institutional aspects of societal influence help us to understand human behavior.

The first selection, "The Crowd" by Gustave LeBon, is a classical piece excerpted from a larger work. Within this brief treatment of collective action in the form of collective behavior, LeBon describes the phenomenon that has come to be known as "crowd psychology." Crowds, according to LeBon, adopt a crowd mind. Published in 1896, this excerpt describes the behavior of crowds from the "social contagion" perspective of collective behavior. The theme of social contagion suggests that individuals within crowds lose all ability to behave rationally because they are overcome by the hysteria and excitement inherent in such masses. Many years later, Social psychologist and symbolic interactionist Herbert Blumer also discussed this approach.

The second selection, Norris R. Johnson's "Panic and Breakdown of Social Order," also addresses the topic of collective behavior. Unlike LeBon, however, Johnson adopts a more contemporary approach in explaining instances of collective action within society. Using detailed case studies, he argues, contrary to LeBon and other advocates of the social contagion theory, that episodes of collective behavior may actually elicit rational, intentional, and thoughtful action. Johnson illustrates how the emergent norm theory of collective behavior, rather than examples of monolithic, individualistic crowds, is perhaps a better explanatory tool for collective action, since society is based on a premise of social order and social structure.

Continuing with the theme of collective action, Jan Fritz, in "Communities: Making Them Work," applies the clinical sociological perspective to sociology and social psychology. She demonstrates how sociological knowledge can assist a person to identify community issues and advocate community change. While supporting an applied approach, Fritz describes and provides relevant examples of community mobilization, collective action, conflict intervention, and consultation.

The next three selections also deal with the usefulness of social psychology as applied to social institutions. In "The Military Academy as an Assimilating Institution," Sanford M. Dornbusch discusses the influence of a highly structured environment, which is reinforced by the military establishment, on individual behavior. Dornbusch also examines the impact of the environment on one's ability to adjust to a total institution and the roles and statuses one has to contend with as a military academy cadet.

The next two selections address different institutions: work and the world of professional experts. William E. Thompson, in "Hanging Tongues: A Sociological Encounter with the Assembly Line," details his symbolic interactionist participant observation study in a large Midwestern meat-processing plant. He addresses such components of the social psychology of work as monotony, danger, strain, and workers' coping mechanisms. Further analysis reveals the impact of consumerism, which may create financial traps, and the workers' attempt to maintain self-worth in spite of the work's demoralizing aspects.

"The Social Construction of Deviance" by Donileen R. Loseke and Spencer E. Cahill addresses certain professions here, "experts" on the battered spouse phenomenon. Loseke and Cahill provide a critical examination of the types of accounts (justifications and excuses) that are used by experts to explain the behavior of domestic violence victims. The authors conclude that members of the knowledge class (the so-called experts on battered wives) work to create their own clientele by providing accounts for victim behavior, even when the responses to domestic violence are not "abnormal" but are defined as such by experts. Domestic violence victims are further depicted by experts as not capable of existing without their "expert" assistance and intervention.

Peter L. Berger, in "Towards a Sociological Understanding of Psychoanalysis," provides another discussion of professionalization and experts within society while combining modernization themes. Berger outlines how psychoanalysis as both a profession and a vast array of related institutional forces became a pervasive entity on the American cultural landscape. Part of this pervasiveness may be found in the day-to-day adoption of Freudian terminology to explain behavior, the emergence and continued dominance of psychology and psychiatry within criminal justice and law, and the impact of psychoanalytic thought through the process of modernization and industrialization. Berger provides a lucid critique of psychoanalysis from a sociological perspective.

In the final selection, Arthur G. Neal provides a social psychological account of the impact of modernization. "Psychological Modernity" speaks to the state of mind that has emerged due to "contemporary historical circumstance." Neal examines two areas of the social psychological impact of modernization—freedom and control, and inventing the future—in order to illustrate how humans have grown to cope with change and our creation of the future.

FOR FURTHER READING

Alfred McClung Lee. *Sociology for Whom?*, Second Edition. Syracuse: Syracuse University Press, 1986.

Gary T. Marx. *Undercover: Police Surveillance in America.* Berkeley: University of California Press, 1988.

David L. Miller. *Introduction to Collective Behavior.* Belmont, CA: Wadsworth Publishing Company, 1985.

Anthony Pratkanis and Elliot Aronson. *Age of Propaganda: The Everyday Use and Abuse of Persuasion.* New York: W. H. Freeman, 1991.

Stephen K. Sanderson. *Macrosociology: An Introduction to Human Societies.* New York: Harper and Row, Publishers, 1988.

The Crowd

GUSTAVE LEBON

It being impossible to study here all the successive degrees of organization of crowds, we shall concern ourselves more especially with such crowds as have attained to the phase of complete organization. In this way we shall see what crowds may become, but not what they invariably are. It is only in this advanced phase or organization that certain new and special characteristics are superposed on the unvarying and dominant character of the race; then takes place that turning already alluded to of all the feelings and thoughts of the collectivity in an identical direction. It is only under such circumstances, too, that what I call above the *psychological law of the mental unity of crowds* comes into play.

Among the psychological characteristics of crowds there are some that they may present in common with isolated individuals, and others, on the contrary, which are absolutely peculiar to them and are only to be met with in collectivities. It is these special characteristics that we shall study, first of all, in order to show their importance.

The most striking peculiarity presented by a psychological crowd is the following: Whoever be the individuals that compose it, however like or unlike be their mode of life, their occupations, their character, or their intelligence, the fact that they have been transformed into a crowd puts them in possession of a sort of collective mind which makes them feel, think, and act in a manner quite different from that in which each individual of them would feel, think, and act were he in a state of isolation. There are certain ideas and feelings which do not come into being, or do not transform themselves into acts except in the case of individuals forming a crowd. The psychological crowd is a provisional being formed of heterogeneous elements, which for a moment are combined, exactly as the cells which constitute a living body form by their reunion a new being which displays characteristics very different from those possessed by each of the cells singly. . . .

Different causes determine the appearance of these characteristics peculiar to crowds, and not possessed by isolated individuals. The first is that the individual forming part of a crowd acquires, solely from numerical considerations, a sentiment of invincible power which allows him to yield to instincts which, had he been alone, he would perforce have kept under restraint. He will be the less disposed to check himself from the consideration that, a crowd being anonymous, and in consequence irresponsible, the sentiment of responsibility which always controls individuals disappears entirely.

The second cause, which is contagion, also intervenes to determine the manifestation in crowds of their special characteristics, and at the same time the trend they are to take. Contagion is a phenomenon of which it is easy to establish the presence, but that it is not easy to explain. It must be classed among those phenomena of a hypnotic order, which we shall shortly study. In a crowd every sentiment and act is contagious, and contagious to such a degree that an individual readily sacrifices his personal interest to the collective interest. This is an aptitude very contrary to his nature, and of which a man is scarcely capable, except when he makes part of a crowd.

A third cause, and by far the most important, determines in the individuals of a crowd special characteristics which are quite contrary at times to those presented by the isolated individual. I allude to that suggestibility of which, moreover, the contagion mentioned above is neither more nor less than an effect. . . .

It is for these reasons that juries are seen to deliver verdicts of which each individual juror would disapprove, that parliamentary assemblies adopt laws and measures of which each of their members would disapprove in his own person. Taken separately, the men of the Convention were enlightened citizens of peaceful habits. United in a crowd, they did not hesitate to give their adhesion to the most savage proposals, to guillotine individuals most clearly innocent, and, contrary to their interests, to renounce their inviolability and to decimate themselves.

It is not only by his acts that the individual in a crowd differs essentially from himself. Even before he has entirely lost his independence, his ideas and feelings have undergone a transformation, and the transformation is so profound as to change the miser into a spendthrift, the sceptic into a believer, the honest man into a criminal, and the coward into a hero.

The conclusion to be drawn from what precedes is, that the crowd is always intellectually inferior to the isolated individual, but that, from the point of view of feelings and of the acts these feelings provoke, the crowd may, according to circumstances, be better or worse than the individual. All depends on the nature of the suggestion to which the crowd is exposed.

32

Panic and the Breakdown of Social Order
Popular Myth, Social Theory, Empirical Evidence

NORRIS R. JOHNSON

Within four miles of this point and one decade of this moment, three dramatic examples of a social phenomenon assumed to reflect a breakdown of social order have occurred. I want to use those episodes—all of which have been described as forms of panic—to make some points about social order and its breakdown, the general theme of these meetings, about theories of collective behavior, and briefly about sociology as well.

On Memorial Day weekend of 1977, more than 160 people died fleeing a fire at the Beverly Hills Supper Club, just across the river from here. On the plaza outside Riverfront Coliseum, just a few blocks distant, 11 young people were killed in December of 1979 as part of a surge into a rock concert. And just two years ago, in March of 1985, anxious depositors precipitated a statewide bank run by queuing outside the Cincinnati branches of Home State Savings Bank, including the branch not far from Fountain Square, to withdraw funds threatened by the bank's reported losses.

Not enamored of the on-the-spot analyses and media discussions which relied on discredited views of collective behavior, I hoped to examine them more thoroughly within a contemporary approach related to the breakdown of social order. My plan here is to summarize my studies of the three events, subjecting the popular myths and the social theory to the test of a confrontation with data. I will go from these case studies to a more general discussion of social organization in such gatherings. However, I will present no statistical analysis to support my interpretation of the data, which I will offer as hypotheses *suggested* rather than hypotheses *tested*. More thorough documentation appears in other papers (Johnson, 1987a, 1987b).

SOCIAL THEORY

Almost all nonsociologists and, I suspect, many sociologists would explain these three events as examples of panic. This is in spite of the fact that many scholars, including "Henry" Quarantelli and Russ Dynes have repeatedly reported on the myths concerning panic (see Keating, 1982). As usually defined, individual panic would include a "reaction involving terror, confusion, and irrational behavior, precipitated by a threatening situation" (Goldenson, 1984), often including physical symptoms as well, and panic as a social phenomenon is defined as simply an aggregate of such responses.

My own approach, which rejects the idea of panic, grows from sociology's fundamental concern with social order, and its core assumption that social order is a product of a normative order and a social structure. Together, they both constrain individual action and permit orderly interaction. Following Turner and Killian's (1972) emergent norm theory of collective behavior, these three incidents are viewed as examples of individualistic crowds responding to a situation in which the social order has broken down. Behavior can then become highly selfish and aggressive, not as a result of irrational panic, but of emergent definitions of the situation as one in which norms of civility no longer apply, and to compete for individual advantage is legitimate. I prefer the term *unregulated competition* as the descriptive label.

My research was also guided by an approach that views flight from a burning building and similar occurrences simply as competition produced by an aggregate of rational, individual acts in response to the reward structure of the situation (see Mintz, 1951; Brown, 1965; Kelley et al., 1965). Rushing to exit a burning building or to withdraw funds from a shaky bank is a reasonable response. When many act in that way, competition for the exits or for the cash held by the bank results. These two sets of ideas directed me to look for evidence for rational responses in the face of a threatened loss and for perceptions of collective support for pursuit of individual interests. In short, it is not only rational to rapidly exit a burning building, but the general norms which lead us to step aside and let others go first no longer apply.

By examining three disparate instances, the intent in this paper is to assess the evidence for the emergence of competition unregulated by social forces.

POPULAR MYTH

My analysis begins with the Home State Savings Bank run, the most recent of the events, and ends with the earliest, the Beverly Hills fire. By reversing the chronology I, at the same time, order the events on the basis of the extent to which competitive action was apparent. In this way the nature of the competition may be more apparent.

■ *The Home State Bank Run.* Bank runs are usually viewed by social scientists as well as others as examples of panic; this one was no exception. A typical comment in this instance was a statement attributed to the bank president: "Most of it was inflicted by the depositors themselves. It was the panic of the individual depositors . . . that led to the situation" (Ivanovich and Rowe, 1985). When the run spread beyond Home State to other institutions insured in the same way, another banking official also adopted the panic argument when he said, "It was a panic situation, similar to 1929. People destroy themselves" (Kemme, 1985).

■ *The Who Concert Surge.* On the morning after the deaths at the Coliseum the newspaper's lead story reported, "Eleven youths were killed and eight seriously injured at Riverfront Coliseum last night in a human stampede through the arena's doors before the start of The Who rock group concert . . . " (Cincinnati Enquirer, Dec. 4, 1979). The "stampede" metaphor became the basis for understanding the tragedy. Most interpretations presented to the media by scholars were based on classical crowd theory dating back to Le Bon and are illustrated by an interpretation quoted in the first day story. "When many people get together, they become subject to what is called 'crowd behavior.' They do all kinds of behavior which, if they'd think, they would not do. The group itself develops some sort of amorphous personality and individual thinking ceases" (Garloch, 1979). A complementary account added the effect of the youth of the crowd members, who were "at an age at which intimacy is so critical" and the "magnetizing," emotion-arousing effect of rock music (Garloch, 1979). The disinhibiting effect of drugs was added to the interpretation by the media, leading a national columnist (Royko, 1979) to refer to the young people as barbarians who "stomped 11 persons to death . . . (after) . . . having numbed their brains on weeds, chemicals, and Southern Comfort. . . ."

■ *The Beverly Hills Flight.* Media reports concerning the effect of panic on the Beverly Hills tragedy were less consensual. One local paper headlined, "Panic set in as patrons saw, smelled fire" and the story quoted a member of club management as saying, "When the smoke thickened, it caused a lot of the older people to panic" (Stein, 1977). And under a subheadline, "Stampeding and panic blocked the escape route for many in the Cabaret Room," a county official reported that "people apparently panicked and stampeded toward what they thought were exits but were not exits" (Bunting, 1977).

Official reports issued after investigation of the fire were also mixed. The initial grand jury report blamed those present, although this interpretation was always in dispute. The report asserted that the smoke and flames pouring into the main showroom created "panic among those who had not yet exited the room from the exits which were still available" (Lawson, 1984:271). Later, a special prosecutor reviewing the grand jury's findings disagreed (Lawson, 1984:276).

EMPIRICAL EVIDENCE

The theories with which I began my investigation did not lead to expectations of the emotional, irrational behavior of panic. They did lead to expectations of competition unregulated by social constraints. The competition was seen as emerging among threatened individuals who lacked confidence that others would follow norms of civil behavior. With confirming evidence for their lack of confidence, and with social support for their individualism, they would act in selfish disregard of others.

— *The Home State Bank Run.* The bank run is included briefly here, although my source of "data" is limited to newspaper accounts and a few informal interviews. The data on the two other incidents are in a different form.

The most important data are: (1) that Home State did lose an enormous sum of money in a failed investment, a loss so great

that court appointed experts concluded that the bank would have been insolvent even without the run[1] (Kennedy, 1985), and (2) lines at the bank were orderly, with no evidence of competition among those in the queues. Officials at first assured depositors they would not lose money, but soon refused to reaffirm that promise (Rawe, 1985). Thus, the bank was in trouble, and a case could be made that withdrawal of funds was a prudent decision for a depositor.

Accounts of their actions by those in line did appear to reflect rational assessments of risks and alternative responses. One woman concluded that even if others did not withdraw their funds, her loss would be so great that it was best for her to do so, and another depositor, admitting the risk was probably minimal, still chose to move his money to another bank (Garloch, 1985). Withdrawing funds presented hardly any cost to the *individual* depositor; thus, a low risk of loss was sufficient to lead many to do so.

Those considering withdrawals were aware that they could contribute to the risk for depositors generally, but assumed that, regardless of their own actions, others would continue to remove their deposits. News accounts and direct information of lines at the bank provided confirming evidence. Some depositors checked the length of the lines daily to determine whether to join in (Byczkowski and Eckberg, 1985). A banking official caught the essence of the depositors' logic when he said, "The reason for the run . . . was that people felt that if they were last in line, they wouldn't get their money" (Kemme, 1985).

When the insurance fund was widely recognized as being a private fund not supported by the state, withdrawals from other privately insured banks began with redeposits into those that were federally insured (through the Federal Savings and Loan Insurance Corporation [FSLIC]). These other banks were not threatened by lost investments but by a lost faith in the insurance system itself. But to suggest the depositors' actions were not rational because they increased the threat to all depositors is to assume that they should have greater concern for other depositors and for the social fabric than did local merchants or the other banks. Merchants were refusing to accept even cashiers' checks drawn on Home State, and other banks were themselves attempting to leave the private insurance fund and join the FSLIC.

This evidence is anecdotal only, but it shows action that reflected a reasonable concern and competition that was regulated by queuing norms. This interpretation is supported by a more systematic study of another bank run in which researchers likewise concluded that even the most anxious withdrawers were cooperative and orderly (Mann et al., 1976).

■ *The Who Concert Surge.*[2] The Who Concert surge at first appears to be very different from the bank run. Rather than people in an orderly queue patiently awaiting their turns with the tellers, there were hundreds who rushed toward the entrances. My data are from transcripts of interviews with people present at the surge. The interviews were conducted by police investigators and made available by the Cincinnati Police Division.

The evidence contained in those transcripts is not congruent with theory and is in clear conflict with popular interpretations of stampeding barbarians reported in the newspapers. It shows more cooperative than competitive behavior. When the transcripts were coded for three categories of helping behavior—giving, receiving, and observing help—approximately 40% of the patrons interviewed reported helping behavior in each of the coded categories. When the three indicators are combined, more than three-fourths of those interviewed reported evidence of prosocial activity in one of the three forms. Only seven respondents reported the reverse, i.e., observing others showing a lack of concern for their fellows in

the crowd, and six of those also reported observing others engaged in helping behavior. Thus, just *one* respondent reported *only* self-interested, competitive behavior.

Although, as expected, much helping was of those to whom one was bonded in primary groups, strangers figured in three-fourths of the reports both of receiving help and of providing help, indicating that general norms of civility had not broken down. As reported in a letter to the local newspaper, "Total strangers probably saved my life" (Cincinnati Enquirer, Dec. 10, 1979, p. A-14). Most of the helping by and of strangers was also socially structured by sex role expectations. Most of the women interviewed reported being helped, and almost twice as many men gave as received help.

Although acts of ruthless competition were at best rare, there *were* reports of people "climbin' over people ta get in" (Police Division, II, A; see footnote 2 for citation style). But both the analysis of coded transcripts and the interpretation drawn from studying the material in the transcribed interviews indicate that most persons continued to try to help others so long as it was possible. If a total disregard for norms of civil behavior developed—and there is hardly any evidence that it did—it was only after cooperation was no longer possible.

Most accounts of this event assume that the competition was for favorable locations within the arena. Analysis of the transcripts indicates that the competition was generally for an *escape* from the crush rather than to view the concert. All, save four, of the transcripts from patrons included some reference to themselves or others trying to get *out* of the crush. Entering the Coliseum was the only likely escape (Police Division, II, T). As a letter to the evening paper asserted, "To us, the door to the Coliseum was no longer to a concert, but to survival and safety" (Cincinnati Post, Dec. 14, 1979, p. 14).

Because of problems of communicating to the rear of the gathering and to the police, those near the rear were unaware of developments ahead of them, and police officers viewed efforts to open additional doors as gate-crashing. The result was that people in the rear continued to surge forward, and the policemen and private security guards continued their routine rule-enforcing activity.

The overall situation was perceived as routine. Patrons and policemen agreed that the generally uninhibited behavior and the crush prior to the deaths were not unusual. Even the stumbling into the Coliseum by nearly unconscious people did not alert security guards, who attributed it to drinking and drugs (Police Division II, I). The expected behavior—the situational norms—included competition for favorable locations near the doors, but it was a regulated competition of the form occurring at other rock concerts and similar to that found at bargain basement sales. Although different in form from that at the bank run, the behavior *was* normatively regulated and not unexpected.

— *The Beverly Hills Flight.* Movement toward the exits from the Beverly Hills Supper Club began in an orderly fashion when the need to evacuate the building was announced. Within the Cabaret Room, the main showroom in which all except two of the deaths occurred, the initial reaction was a calm, adaptive response. As described by one patron, "So we got up and there was no panic. We turned around and we walked straight back . . . up the aisle . . . to a doorway" (L20; see footnote 2 for citation style).

A somewhat different initial response occurred in an upstairs banquet room in which a warning of the fire was not received until the only known exit, a staircase that led almost directly to the source of the fire, was no longer usable. There, one woman describing her own hysteria said, "Somebody screamed 'everyone out' . . . and then somebody hollered again, 'get out, get out, this place is on fire.' Well there was just pandemonium . . . " (B42). But numbers of calming

remarks by other group members and the appearance of an employee with directions to an alternate exit prevented chaos. The employee directed the groups through the dark, down narrow service stairs and out through the kitchen. In the words of one who followed him, "We didn't panic, and we went out cool, just like a fire drill, like when I was in the Navy . . . It was done beautiful" (S-89).

Transcripts of approximately 450 interviews conducted in a Kentucky State Police (KSP) investigation of the fire were available for analysis. The transcripts were coded for use of phrases such as "calm," "orderly," "not pushing," or "like a fire drill" to describe the action of the fleeing crowd. More than one-third of the patrons used at least one such term, and less than one-half that many used a conflicting term such as "panic," "hysterical," or some behavioral description such as "pushing" or "rushing."

The reactions of others to the emotional responses that did occur were not congruent with images of "circular reaction" or "contagion," the terms used in textbook descriptions, but were more often efforts to counter the response. For instance, one woman confronted with a hysterical person in front of her, responded with "No honey, this is not the time to become hysterical," and calmly talked her out the door (19). Several similar reports were of efforts by people to calm members of their own groups such as the report from the second floor rooms which said, "A few people jumped up and sort of panicked but (he mentioned himself and three other men by name) told the people quickly and quietly not to panic and we can all get out of here safely" (L6).

Just as within the concert crowd, the extent of helping behavior indicates that the response, at least initially, was not ruthlessly competitive. Overall, only 18% volunteered that they gave some form of help—no direct question was asked—and 13% report receiving help. But many who reported neither giving nor receiving help were in situations in which help was not required, so the importance of help is underestimated by those data. Transcripts were also coded for four categories of degree of difficulty encountered in escaping from the building, and among those having the greatest difficulty exiting, 36% reported receiving help; only 77% of those in the lowest category of exit difficulty received help. In the same manner, those most likely to give help were those who were themselves most threatened; 40% of those with the greatest difficulty exiting reported helping others escape from the burning building.

The response of employees was to assist their customers in escaping the fire. Their helping responses ranged from simply pointing customers toward exits to crawling beneath the smoke back into the building to try to rescue others. Overall, two-thirds of the employees reported helping others, and one-third were coded as going beyond simply assisting those for whom they were most directly responsible. Only three of 95 employees were categorized as showing a panic response, and those only after exits were blocked. Additionally, one-third of the patrons reported being helped by employees, and the transcripts abound with quotations from grateful patrons who credited employees with getting them to safety.[3]

Considering that one-half of the employees were less than 25 years old—nearly one-third were 21 or younger—and that these cocktail waitresses and busboys without direction or prior training continued to perform, even expand their roles, leads us at least to question the popular interpretation of the behavior of the same age group at the concert.

Patrons did report the emergence of competition as the situation became more threatening. One report from the Cabaret Room noted that after an initially calm movement toward an exit, "We got about three-quarters of the way up. At this point we saw a heavy amount of smoke coming in these front entrances here. . . . At that point then we started getting the pushing and the panicking attitudes" (T8/T8A). One person, just at the doorway when the flames came into the room, said, "I heard people scream, these women behind me in line, and I just looked back for a split second and I saw the flames at the door of the Cabaret Room . . . and that is when the people really started pushing and shoving . . . " (S56). But reports of helping behavior also continue. A middle-aged woman, with a girl lying across her chest when rescuers were trying to get to her, reported, "I hoisted the girl up. . . . I felt there was still life there so I pushed her up to this guy and we got her out of there. After they pulled her out, I got up there and they pulled me out" (A6).

THEORETICAL SUMMARY AND CONCLUSION

Little evidence is provided for the unregulated competition postulated by theory, and even less evidence emerged for the emotional, maladaptive behavior expected by classical panic theory and popular myth. Support for organizational breakdown theory—the ideas with which I began—requires evidence both that the general societal norms governing interaction no longer prevailed and that the social relations within existing groups had disintegrated. This concluding section presents evidence of a functioning social structure and behavior conforming to general societal norms of civil behavior and cooperation.

Limits to Competition

The extent of competition varied among the three examples and, over time, within each. Competition was greatest within the Beverly Hills fire in the final moments before escape became impossible, and least within the bank run, compatible with ideas of rational individual responses to perceived risk. But probably at no time, even when the fire threat was greatest, was there a total disregard for others, particularly for others to whom one had social bonds.

The postulate of individual rationality does provide a partial explanation for the bank run, assuming that those who perceived the loss as probable formed the queues, and those who thought the threat minimal waited. The competition was to be first in line, but it was minimized by differential perception of risk and regulated by queuing norms. The sense of greatest urgency did not spread until it was too late to produce ruthless competition; the banks were closed.

The response within Beverly Hills was similar. With an initial variation in perceived risk, there is much evidence that people politely permitted others, even strangers, to proceed in front of them. Within most of the club, the threat was never sufficient to enough people to break down norms of civility. But the situation began to change as the fire threat grew and lines formed in front of the exits—then both the perception of risk and competition increased.

A different queuing norm was observed outside the concert. The gradual sorting and shifting of people as later arrivals tried to slip through the crowd toward the doors, and the dense crowd competing for entrance were both expected. In fact, the unreserved seating structured competition in that way. Later, when safety, even survival was threatened, competition for escape emerged near the front but those in the rear continued to push forward as was routine.

Both organizational breakdown and individualistic approaches which predict unregulated competition underestimate the strength of the forces constraining behavior and prevent the competitive rather than cooperative action. In all of these situations, norms of civil behavior prevailed. In addition, more specific role expectations were maintained within both the concert crowd

and the supper club exit. In both, congruent with sex role expectations, men provided help for women, and in several cases, the physically impaired were helped by those more fit.

The Social Organization of Gatherings

In addition to being constrained by general societal norms, two of the gatherings show a relatively complex internal organization. The micro-structure of assemblies in which panic is assumed to have occurred is rarely considered. In fact, discussions of most forms of collective behavior have assumed an absence of ties of one participant to another. Over the past decade, however, work by some sociologists (e.g., Weller and Quarantelli, 1973; Aveni, 1977; McPhail, 1985; Johnson and Feinberg, forthcoming), has focused on the group structure of crowds. The evidence here demonstrates a comparable organization within these gatherings.

Small Groups

In these gatherings, those present generally came with others, usually with members of primary groups. In fact, not one person interviewed from the concert arrived alone, and only one person interviewed was at the supper club alone on the night of the fire. The typical unit in Beverly Hills was a two-person group, but also common were four-person groups, usually two couples, or groups of more than seven. The most frequent grouping of those interviewed from the concert gathering (36%) was also a two-person, husband and wife, group, followed by other family groups, usually siblings, and same sex friendship groups. This group structuring produced solidary bonds and role obligations among many.

There is no evidence for the breakdown of primary group bonds resulting in the abandonment of a spouse, a parent, a child, a date, or a friend, in order to save oneself. As I have detailed elsewhere (Johnson, 1987b), throughout the Beverly Hills interviews are reports of a concern by one primary group member for another and multiple reports of group members exiting together, often hand-in-hand. The presence in the casualty list of numerous examples of multiple last names with the same address is additional, stark evidence that many of those who died did so along with family members.

Secondary Associations

Social organization existed at another level as well. Forty percent of those in the supper club were in secondary groups. In one banquet room, approximately 370 employees of financial institutions were attending a banquet. In the upstairs rooms where immediate panic was most imminent, everyone was in one of two groups of approximately 100 members each, perhaps partially responsible for their safe exit under extremely poor conditions. In addition, many smaller groups, both formal and informal, were in attendance. People in these groups were almost twice as likely to report helping others as those who were not a part of such groups, possibly reflecting group bonds.

The larger groups were themselves made up of smaller units. Within the banking group, many tables were occupied by co-workers from the same firms or branches, and friendship groups within the large out-of-town groups shared tables within the Cabaret Room. One executive who alerted the people at his table said, "There were 10 people at our table, all either members of the Board of Directors . . . or employees and their wives and their husbands. . . . Of course . . . we were waiting for our whole table to get out, and we all got out about the same time . . . " (A00). Many others reported from the Empire Room that they were seated at tables with others from their workplace, and

both there and in the Crystal Rooms the frequent use of names of others in descriptions of the escape indicates the presence of social bonds.

Within the few interviews constituting the data from the concert, there is only minimal evidence for comparable secondary group ties. Most were in small friendship groups, but at least one large group came from out-of-town by bus, and there is evidence of the presence of several informal groups of high school students. Interviews do report a concern for other group members lost in the crush and of searching for them in the confusion that ensued.

There is some evidence that helping outside the concert might have grown from ephemeral groups which emerged during the prolonged period of waiting for the doors to open (Police Division, II, V; III, M), and I suspect that similar groupings emerged in the lines outside the banks. Whether general societal norms of civil behavior may be strengthened by these casual bonds and thus operate to prevent unregulated competition is a hypothesis worth pursuing.

Formal Organizational Roles

The final evidence for the continuing operation of social organization is the impact of roles occupied in other social structures, a typical finding in disaster research. Within the supper club, physicians, nurses, firefighters, and others present as patrons immediately began performing in their occupational roles. Several physicians provided instructions for filtering or staying beneath the smoke during the exit and later treated survivors, assisted by nurses also present. One firefighter directed others, including his wife, from the building and was himself killed trying to help still others, and another crawled back into the building searching for survivors. A nurse saturated a number of napkins with water as she began her exit and distributed them to others along the way.

There is also suggestive evidence that supervisors within the banking group assumed responsibility for the safe exit of those for whom they were responsible in another social structure, and clear evidence that employees with a bus tour tried to herd toward the exits from the showroom the elderly people on their tour (S256). The formal role behavior of employees of the club was reported earlier.

Interviews conducted by police detectives as part of a criminal investigation are not designed to extract information concerning the social bonds among people present in these situations. Thus, specific hypotheses involving the presence of ties cannot be tested; however, the frequent unsolicited mentions of such bonding and its constraining effect on those involved provides a powerful suggestion for future research.

CONCLUSION

Throughout the analysis I was struck not by the breakdown of social order but by its strength and persistence; not by the irrational, individual behavior of popular myth, but by the socially structured, socially responsible, and adaptive actions of those affected. Ruthless competition did not occur, and it did not occur because a functioning social order prevented it. General societal norms continued to constrain individual behavior, and formal roles in groups continued to be performed. Both primary and secondary group ties continued to influence individual behavior, and transitory small groups were emerging to reinforce societal norms. As a result, action was not based on individual concerns alone, but for general civility and a concern for others as well. The competition that did develop was a regulated competition, and it was for the safety of groups

rather than between individuals. I may not have demonstrated this to your satisfaction without submitting my interpretations to more rigorous tests, but I present my conclusions nevertheless, reminding you of Shel Stryker's remarks on this same honorific occasion eight years ago in which he pointed out the latitude given the speaker to go beyond the evidence (Stryker, 1979:175).

A very different approach to collective behavior has emerged in recent years from the work of Clark McPhail and his students (McPhail and Wohlstein, 1983; Miller, 1985) which focuses on temporary human gatherings. Social forms ordinarily labelled as, e.g., acting crowds or panics, are analyzed as routine concerted action. Within that framework these events would be seen as ordinary social behavior—attempting to enter an arena, exit a supper club, or withdraw money from a bank—under adverse and deteriorating circumstances. The data presented here suggest that might be the most fruitful approach.

Finally, the conclusion of these studies—that the social order constrains individual behavior and thus places limits on competition—is a fundamental sociological premise and surely should not surprise us. I am, however, constantly amazed at the regularity with which we sociologists must remind ourselves of the nature of social order, of the essence of our discipline, and the insights of its founders. That we frequently do not take our own models seriously probably contributes to the fact that others do not as well.

NOTES

1. Three former officials of Home State have been convicted on various charges stemming from the bank failure.
2. This analysis is based on material in files maintained by the Cincinnati Police Division. Transcripts of 46 interviews conducted with those present by police investigators, and 10 statements given by patrons at a City Council hearing were

included in the files. In addition, six extended interviews with patrons included within newspaper articles were analyzed. The undated police report is divided into three parts, designed by Roman numeral, following a Summary section. Each part is sectioned by labelled file dividers. Citations are to these parts and sections without pagination. The Beverly Hills analysis which follows is based on transcripts of 445 interviews from the Kentucky State Police investigation. KSP transcripts are designed with a letter/number combination beginning with A1 (and A1A if a joint interview, usually with husband and wife), and are cited in that form. See Johnson, 1987a and 1987b for discussion of the data and the analysis.

3. The employee role implies a responsibility for their customers, but here it appears that the employees, who had no training for emergencies, immediately expanded their roles to include a responsibility for, first, the safety of their own customers, and the other people in the building. A graduate student is currently examining in more detail the responses of the employees as part of a thesis related to the concept of role expansion.

REFERENCES

Aveni, Adrian, 1977. "The no-so-lonely crowd: Friendship groups in collective behavior." *Sociometry* 40:96–9.

Brown, Roger, 1965. *Social Psychology*. New York: Free Press.

Bunting, Ken, 1977. "For the survivors, it was a night of terror." *Cincinnati Post*, May 30, p. 3.

Byczkowski, John J. and John Eckberg, 1985. "Depositors withdraw funds." *Cincinnati Enquirer*, March 15, p. C-4.

Cincinnati Enquirer, 1979. December 4, p.1.

_____, 1979. December 10.

Cincinnati Post, 1979. December 14.

Garloch, Karen, 1979. "Crowds capable of developing own personalities, expert says." *Cincinnati Enquirer*, December 5.

_____, 1985. "Withdrawals continue at Home State." *Cincinnati Enquirer*, March 8, p. B-7.

Goldenson, Robert M. (ed.), 1984. *Longman Dictionary of Psychology and Psychiatry*. New York: Longman.

Ivanovich, David and D. Rowe, 1985. "Home State sale talks under way." *Cincinnati Post*, March 9, p. 1A.

Johnson, Norris R., 1987a. "Panic at The Who concert 'stampede': An empirical assessment." Paper read at the meetings of the Southern Sociology Society. Atlanta.

_____, 1987b. "Fire in a crowded theater: A descriptive analysis of the emergence of panic." Paper read at the meetings of the American Sociological Association. Chicago.

Johnson, Norris R. and William E. Feinberg, forthcoming. "Crowd structure and process: Theoretical framework and computer simulation model." *Advances in Group Processes: Theory and Research*. E. Lawler (ed). Greenwich, CT: JAI Press.

Keating, John P., 1982. "The myth of panic." *Fire Journal*, May, p. 57-62.

Kelley, Harold H., J. Condry, Jr., A. Dahlke, and A. Hill, 1965. "Collective behavior in a simulated panic situation." *Journal of Experimental and Social Psychology* 1:20–54.

Kemme, Steve, 1985. "New insurance more secure, official says." *Cincinnati Enquirer*, March 18, p. A-5.

Kennedy, Rich, 1985. "Home State in trouble before run." *Cincinnati Post*, March 13, p. 1.

Lawson, Robert G., 1984. *Beverly Hills: The Anatomy of a Nightclub Fire*. Athens: Ohio University Press.

Mann, Leon, Trevor Nagel, and Peter Dowlin, 1976. "A study of economic panic: The 'run' on the Hindmarsh Building Society." *Sociometry* 39:223–35.

McPhail, Clark and R. Wohlstein, 1983. "Individual and collective behaviors within gatherings, demonstrations, and riots." *Annual Review of Sociology* 9:579–600.

McPhail, Clark, 1985. "The social organization of demonstrations." Paper read at the meetings of the American Sociological Association. Washington.

Miller, David L., 1985. *Introduction to Collective Behavior*. Belmont, CA: Wadsworth.

Mintz, Alexander, 1951. "Non-adaptive group behavior." *Journal of Abnormal and Social Psychology* 46:1550–59.

Police Division, City of Cincinnati, undated. *Final Report Concerning the Eleven Deaths Which Pre-*

ceded The 'Who' Rock Concert Held at Riverfront Coliseum. Cincinnati, OH: City of Cincinnati.

Rawe, Rick, 1985. "Official can't assure full recovery by depositors." *Cincinnati Post*, March 14, p. 6C.

Royko, Mike, 1979. "The new barbarians: A glimpse of the future." *Cincinnati Post*, December 6.

Stein, Jerry, 1977. "Panic set in as patrons saw, smelled fire." *Cincinnati Post*, May 30, p. 25.

Stryker, Sheldon, 1979. "The profession: Comments from an interactionist's perspective." *Sociological Focus* 12:175–86.

Turner, Ralph A. and L. Killian, 1972. *Collective Behavior*, 2nd. ed. Englewood Cliffs, NJ: Prentice Hall.

Weller, Jack E. and E. L. Quarantelli, 1973. "Neglected characteristics of collective behavior." *American Journal of Sociology* 79:665–85.

33

Communities: Making Them Work

JAN FRITZ

An article in *Community Jobs* (1983), the national newspaper for those interested in community change, profiled three people who work for social justice. One of them, an environmental writer for a Kentucky newspaper, advised college students to put more energy into finding jobs that are consistent with their values. In other words, he said, find organizations that are out to solve the world's problems.

Many sociologists face the same dilemma; they want to use their skills to work for social justice. Those who are teachers make sure that the content of some or all of their courses touches upon or focuses on social justice issues. Others contribute by conducting research that will help change initiatives succeed; still others work within or outside academic institutions to make those changes happen. In some cases the sociologist explores all these avenues of social change. This chapter gives you some background on current interests in the area of community and introduces you to some of the clinical sociologists who work on behalf of the community.

ESTABLISHING A DEFINITION OF COMMUNITY

Many of the founders of scientific sociology—including Auguste Comte, Ferdinand Tönnies, Emile Durkheim, and Karl Marx—were fascinated by the idea of community. Those who wrote at the time of the Industrial Revolution were concerned about the different kind of community that was developing around them, and some went on to talk about its alienating effects.

Tönnies described this as a change from *Gemeinschaft* ("community" in German) to *Gesellschaft* ("society"). The first refers to a form of social relations in which the individual is embedded in a matrix of tightly knit primary groups, such as family, church, and kinship networks. Characteristic of preindustrial societies, it can still be found in some rural areas of industrial societies. The second refers to a more businesslike form of social relations—often associated in art, literature, and political rhetoric with urban life—in which primary bonds have been all but replaced by impersonal, contractural secondary relationships.

By and large, small-town life in the United States is treated with nostalgia; big-city life is associated with all the evils of the modern age. In sociology, Tönnies established the idea that this shift meant a crucial "loss of community" with negative consequences for individuals and society in general.

The question whether we have lost "community" is still not settled. According to Barry Wellman (1979), there are three main points of view on this subject. The "community-lost view" holds that tightly knit primary groups have been replaced by impersonal, contractual secondary relationships. The "community-saved view" contradicts the first by pointing out the survival of primary-group relationships, particularly among poor people and minorities, in even the largest cities. The "community-liberated view" finds that primary-group relationships still exist and are highly valued but that they are now based on work and friendship rather than geography. The feeling of belonging now comes from social networks people have formed by choice rather than from neighborhoods. By "community liberated," then, Wellman emphasizes how a person chooses his or her own community.

Just as scholars hold divergent opinions about whether we are suffering from a loss of community, they also may define the concept in differing ways. It might be helpful, in establishing a definition for use here, to look at the four kinds of communities identified by Calvin Redekop (1975):

1. The *geographic community* refers to an aggregate of people situated in a rather definite ecological area. In this view of community, there is a strong tie between the social system that develops and the territorial unit.
2. In the *spiritual community* people are not bound together geographically but by a solidarity that comes through friendship, religious belief, tradition, and/or language. Examples of this kind of community include the Jewish, intellectual, and religious communities.
3. The *purposive community* refers to those who live, work, or meet together because of common objectives or purposes. Members of a corporation, a mental hospital, or a college are referred to as communities in this sense. A purposive community has a geographical base, but this factor is not the basic characteristic of this kind of community.
4. The *intentional community* is quite different from the other three. In this case, the collective is formed for its own sake—to become a community. This is the aim of most contemporary communal move-

ments, as well as classical Christian communes such as the Shakers.

When sociologists give a general definitions of community, they usually refer to and build upon what Redekop has defined as the geographical community. We follow this approach by defining a community as *a collection of people within a geographic area among whom there is some degree of mutual identification, interdependence, loyalty, and common social organization of activities.* The clearest examples of communities in this sense of the term are villages, neighborhoods, and small towns.

THE NATURE OF CONTEMPORARY COMMUNITIES

As sociologists from Comte's time till our own have observed, industrialization drastically changed living patterns, first in Europe and then in the United States. According to the U.S. Bureau of the Census (1981), the percentage of our population living in *urban areas* of at least 2500 inhabitants grew from 6% in 1800 to 51% in 1920. Concerned about this change from a predominantly rural and small-town population to an urban society, many Americans came to villify the city as the cause of ever-growing social problems.

University of Chicago sociologists developed a novel *sociological* approach to the study of urban life . . . They discovered that "the city" was really a conglomeration of *natural areas,* each with its own community, problems, and life styles. These include wealthy areas, ghettos, ethnic neighborhoods, slums, and commercial areas. They investigated the processes by which natural areas form—the *segregation* of distinctive groups into separate areas; *invasion* of new groups into existing areas; and *succession,* the process by which natural areas change character as they are invaded by different groups (Park, Burgess, and Mc-Kenzie1925).

They investigated land-use patterns and their ecological relationship to natural areas, developing a highly influential theory of city growth. Louis Wirth (1928), a pioneering clinical sociologist, also explored *urbanism* as a distinctive way of life characterized by sophistication, individual freedom, change orientation, and diversity at the cost of the sort of *Gemeinschaft* relationships characteristic of rural life styles.

Since World War II, the structure of American communities has undergone a further shift from centralized, densely populated cities to *metropolitan areas*, which are defined by the Census Bureau as counties or groups of counties with one or more central cities of at least 50,000 population, a density of at least 1000 people per square mile, and outlying areas whose social and economic life are linked to that of the urban centers. By this definition there are some 318 "standard metropolitan statistical areas" in the United States today. Nearly 69 million Americans live in the 20 largest such areas, according to the 1980 Census.

The rapid growth of metropolitan areas was made possible by the mass production of automobiles and the government-sponsored creation of modern highway networks enabling "commuters" to live anywhere within 50–100 miles away from the urban workplace. While this allowed the middle class to achieve the "American dream" of owning their own home and land, it increasingly concentrated the poor in the rundown inner cities and enabled business and industry to sprawl beyond the old commercial centers.

This pattern is known as the *megalopolis*, an area of urban and suburban development often covering hundreds of miles, such as "Bos-wash," stretching between Boston and Washington, D.C., on the East Coast, or the urbanized belt from just north of Los Angeles to the Mexican border on the West Coast.

Five-sixths of the U.S. population may live in such areas by the end of the century.

In the past few years as well, growth has shifted both from the old industrial centers of the Northeast and Midwest to the Sunbelt of the Southwest and West Coast, and from densely populated urban communities to more "suburban" communities spreading throughout what were previously rural areas outside the metropolis. This trend affects mainly the more affluent sectors of the population—those who can afford the increasingly high prices of suburban homes and are able to commute to work—or those who can find jobs in offices, retail, or service businesses no longer tied to centralized industry and commerce.

Each of these trends in the American community has contributed to the conditions sociologists since Tönnies have described as "loss of community." That is, we find an increasingly mobile population living outside traditional—rural and small-town—patterns of primary relationship. More and more people either choose to be, or find themselves to be, anonymous both where they reside and where they work.

At least, that is how it *seems* on the face of it. As mentioned, however, sociologists continue to find older forms of primary-group belonging alive and well in both city and suburb. In addition, they have observed the emergence of alternative "network" structures in which people create their own community relationships in conformity with the demands of present-day life styles. Let us turn, then, to a consideration of what this term "community" means outside the small town, on which our ideas are so strongly modeled.

THE MOBILIZATION OF THE COMMUNITY

City dwellers often participate in many levels of social organization—the block, the neighborhood, the section, as well as the city as a whole—each of which may fit our definition of a community. Each unit is a "collective representation" that exists in the minds of the inhabitants rather than as a geographic region. A physical barrier such as a bridge, a road, or a railroad track may be used to define the edge of a community, but the boundary may also be the north side of a particular street, if that is how people view it. It is the *labeling of the area as a community* that has real consequences.

We stereotype sectors of a large community (such as a major city) because this helps us understand the complex whole. In so doing, we cannot possibly be completely accurate; yet we may grow up believing in the truth of our stereotypes. For instance, we see one section as rich, another as integrated, and a third as only for poor people. These stereotypes may be so strong that, while we are proud to tell what city we are from, we may be less willing, or even embarrassed, to name our neighborhood because of what it "means" to be from there (Milgram 1972).

Each of us identifies more strongly at any particular time with one or another level of community organization. For some, the whole town is important; for others, it is the specific block or neighborhood. External realities, like a crime wave or a natural disaster, are among the factors that help increase identification with a community.

As this identification grows, so may a strong desire to control the forces that shape the lives of the inhabitants of the community. Under what circumstances and in which communities does this *mobilization,* or desire for control over one's own community, develop? Let us now examine the conditions under which mobilization of a community takes place, and investigate the relationship between these conditions and what is referred to as "community development."

Many kinds of projects fall under the label community development (Christenson and Robinson, 1980:3). A state government official might think of flood disaster relief or new roads. A local public official might talk

of industrial development or revitalization of an area in the central part of the city. A community activist might think about making jobs, training opportunities, and housing available to the poor, or organizing against construction of a nuclear power plant. Environmentalists might talk of slowing commercial development and preserving natural areas, while an agent from the Cooperative Extension Service might discuss educational programs or organization of groups to study community needs. All these activities have been categorized as community development.

According to the United Nations (1963:4), *community development* is

> the process by which the efforts of the people themselves are united with those of governmental authorities to improve the economic, social, and cultural conditions of communities, to integrate these communities into the life of the nation, and to enable them to contribute fully to national progress. This complex of processes is, therefore, made up of two essential elements: the participation by the people themselves in efforts to improve their level of living, with as much reliance as possible on their own initiative; and the provision of technical and other services in ways which encourage initiative, self-help, and mutual help and make these more effective. It is expressed in programmes designed to achieve a wide variety of improvements.

The problem with this UN definition is that it stresses the nation-state as the context of development and suggests that what is deemed desirable by governmental authorities corresponds to the needs, interests, and values of all groups of people in the society. This definition also excludes any consideration of conflict or dissension. A more sociological approach would simply define community development in terms of *action on the part of some group to change programmatically economic, cultural, social, or environmental conditions of that community.*

In recent years, in developed and developing countries, there has been growing interest in community development. But as Roberts (1979:xiii) has noted, the aim has not always been to encourage the involvement of citizens: "In many cases, such as the American Model Cities programs, these workers were employed to serve the interests of the employing agencies rather than to facilitate real participation by the people."

In writing about the new directions in community development, urban affairs expert Hans Spiegel (1980:230) has discussed the current trend toward more decentralization and neighborhood-oriented programs. He says that this trend "represents a golden opportunity for community development." As this golden opportunity develops, however, it will be important to emphasize continually the basic commitment to facilitating citizen participation. This becomes particularly important in troubled economic times as practitioners who work, for instance, for such organizations as public utilities and those who are community activists may find it difficult to remain within the same organizations and continue talking together.

The sociological approach to community development sees it as a process beginning when community groups or members recognize that there is some kind of tension but does not have a real grasp of the problem. The next step is to learn about the problem and then formulate a set of goals or objectives. This might be done with the help of a clinical sociologist or other practitioner, who will facilitate thorough empirical investigation of problems and assessment of community resources, pinpoint weaknesses or skills (such as organization, communication, problem solving, and recordkeeping) that need to be learned, and then help community members formulate specific goals or objectives. Only after these steps have been taken should the community act and evaluate the extent to which goals have actually been met—and the degree to which action has reduced or not reduced tensions.

If a community moves too quickly from the initial phase of "tension" to action without systematically going through the intermediary stages, there may be unsatisfactory results. This frequently has been the case. When clinical sociologists or social scientists with similar training are involved, the chances increase for successful problem solving by the community.

COLLECTIVE ACTION

Another element the sociologist contributes to the community development process is the concept of the *social movement* as a mobilizing force in community change. Most community development experts exclude from consideration those social movements that go through a process that leads to violent confrontation. But other forms of collective behavior—such as demonstrations, celebrations, boycotts, presenting demands, and symbolic acts—can give voice to tensions and concerns among community groups whose needs and interests are not effectively represented or considered in the formal community development process.

According to Neil Smelser (1962), six conditions usually exist before there is an episode of collective behavior. The first of these six factors is *structural conduciveness*. The organization of the community—for instance, a good communication network and an open administration—sets the stage for certain forms of collective activity.

When the structure of a society is conducive to collective behavior, *social strain* becomes a precipitating factor. Strain may develop from a sudden disruption to the existing order (a tornado), from persistent and increasing value conflicts (as between economic classes or religious groups), or when some event takes place and the culture offers no guidelines for responding (seepage from a nuclear facility).

Before a collective action takes place, a *generalized belief* usually develops to explain the social strain and anticipate consequences. In the case of radioactive seepage, for instance, there may arise a belief that the facility was improperly designed and that the radioactivity will cause cancer and birth defects. Then something may happen—a *precipitating event*—that confirms the generalized belief. Now *mobilization of the participants* may take place, and that activity may or may not be under the influence of a leader.

The last factor that Smelser discusses is *social control.* Control often is used to stop or redirect a collective action or eliminate its causes. It may also backfire, however, provoking a situation, as sometimes happened when the police attempted to halt civil rights or peace marchers in the 1960s. The form of control very much influences the direction, timing, and outcome of collective activity.

Even when a number of these conditions are met, a community may not take collective action. This does not necessarily mean that a group does not have desire for change. Rather, the reason may lie in the relative prosperity of the community. In general, more prosperous communities often start with a higher feeling of confidence in their own power to influence change.

In the next two sections of this chapter we explore ways in which clinical sociologists encourage community action through research and consultation.

COMMUNITY RESEARCH

Sociologists are scientists trained in qualitative and quantitative research methods. For example, you will find sociologists conducting indepth interviews with community organizers about the strategies they use,

videotaping meetings to study effective negotiating strategies, working as participant observers in rural communities about to become boom towns, or using sophisticated computer techniques to analyze data that have been collected about demographic trends.

Often, those who describe themselves as "applied sociologists" limit their activity to such research. Academically oriented community researchers may study interaction patterns, institutions, norms, and roles for no other reason than to learn about them or test theoretical hypotheses. Clinical sociologists go beyond this, concerning themselves also with application. They study an area because an individual, organization, or community can benefit from an analysis of the situation, and because the research will help further the planning process or help decide a course of action.

When the intent is to have an impact on the planning process, it is generally felt that it will take more than one study to have that effect. As Lindblom and Cohen (1979:5–6) have noted:

> It may be that the principal impact of policy-oriented studies, say, on inflation, race, conflict, deviance or foreign policy—including those specifically designed to advise a specific policy maker at a particular time—is through their contribution to a cumulating set of incentives (many studies with like results) for a general reconsideration by policy makers of their decision-making framework, their operating political or social philosophy, or their ideology.

Douglas Biklen (1983), author of *Community Organizing*, says that "when researchers amass enough evidence, in study after study, they can topple a whole way of thinking, but it is a slow process."

To enable you to examine this process, we review here two research projects: a case study of the social impact of a flood, and a study of black participation in Georgia local electoral politics.

The Buffalo Creek Flood

The devastating Buffalo Creek, West Virginia flood occurred on February 26, 1972. A huge dam owned by the local coal company (an absentee landlord) collapsed. Water traveling in waves 20 and 30 feet high swallowed Buffalo's Creek's 16 small towns, leaving more than 125 people dead and over 4000 homeless.

Sociologist Kai Erikson (1976:193–94) was called in by the survivors' law firm to evaluate the personal and social impact of the flood. He stressed the loss of community caused by the disaster and talked about the special importance of community to the people of Buffalo Creek:

> The community in general can be described as the focus for activities that are normally regarded as the exclusive property of the individuals. It is the community that cushions pain, the community that provides a context for intimacy, the community that represents morality and serves as the repository for old traditions.

Some 18 months after the flood, 615 survivors were interviewed by psychiatrists; more than 90% were found to be emotionally disturbed, suffering from confusion, despair, and hopelessness. Crime, alcoholism, and the use of drugs increased after the flood; many people lost their morale, mental health, and respect for the law. For the survivors, the disaster showed that everything and everybody was unreliable. Erikson concluded that this would be a very difficult base from which to build a new community. Erikson's research was of primary use to the survivors' insurance company, but also would be of help to those who work with the survivors of natural disasters and to community planners.

Black Participation in Georgia Local Electoral Politics

Clinical sociologist Brian Sherman (1982) was a consultant with the Voting Rights Study Group in Atlanta (see Chapter 2). On behalf of the Study Group he designed and conducted research that documented the continuing problems of minority access to government that still exists in Georgia.

Sherman (1982:3) collected data from 60 counties for this study. The county was the unit of analysis because it is the "most important level for local political activity in Georgia" and because the county is the arena in which most residents can see for themselves their impact on, or exclusion from, the political process that affects their everyday lives.

Despite the abolition of the white primary, literacy tests, and the poll tax, Sherman found many barriers that still prevent blacks from participating fully in the political process. Among these practices were the manipulation of absentee ballots, voting by noneligible whites, voting by the deceased, purging of voter lists, switching to at-large representation, uncooperativeness on the part of white registrars, and a refusal to appoint black poll watchers. In this situation, the whites in power avoid blatant and overt racial intimidation and excessive legal violations; covert tactics are used and what is done is explained as being in the interest of "good government."

Sherman noted that whites have not tried to reach an accommodation with the black community for joint political action. He concluded that it was very important, then, for blacks to develop the experience, organization, contacts, and expertise for full political participation. As a start in this direction, Sherman recommended that a clearinghouse for information be established as an aid for black candidates in election campaigns and for use in voting rights court cases.

Sherman (1982:34) thinks that the Voting Rights Act has had a tremendous impact in Georgia:

> Blacks do register, vote, run for office and occasionally win an election. Without the Voting Rights Act, they would not have been able to do this in Georgia. As the details of this survey have demonstrated, white resistance is still both strong and successful. The continuation of the Voting Rights Act is necessary if blacks are to maintain their achievements and make future political gains.

Sherman was invited to testify before a U.S. congressional committee about the results of his study, and now is research director for the Voter Education Project in Atlanta. After every national census count, lines between voting districts are redrawn to reflect population shifts. Sherman's present job allows him to consult with black groups in southern states about local reapportionment plans. If a black group feels that the white power structure in the community has developed a discriminatory reapportionment plan, Sherman will investigate and contact the U.S. Department of Justice. He points out the defects of the plan and gives an analysis of the community situation showing possible reasons for the development of a discriminatory plan.

Sherman's research in particular is a good example of *action research*—it calls for attention, recognition, and action. It is the kind of work that can transform public consciousness if it is done well, is supported by other studies, and catches the attention of the public and policy makers. This is work of the kind C. Wright Mills, author of *The Sociological Imagination* and *The Power Elite*, would have liked. Mills encouraged his students to take on important research topics—the kind that would provide analysis but also influence the world.

COMMUNITY CONSULTATION

A *consultant*, according to community clinical psychologists O'Neill and Trickett (1982), is *someone who intervenes, who works with a system focus rather than an individual focus and whose advice may be accepted or rejected as the client chooses.* According to this definition, the consultant is a resource and has no permanent role in the system to which he or she acts as an adviser.

Consultation has become a professional activity for members of every social and behavioral discipline and other fields such as business, education, and nursing. Probably the most complete listing of the characteristics of a good consultant is that developed by Ronald Lippitt and Gordon Lippitt (1978). They identify three areas of competence:

1. *Knowledge,* including a thorough grounding in the behavioral sciences; knowledge of systems, human personality, and oneself; and an understanding of philosophical systems as foundations for value systems.
2. *Skill areas,* including communication, teaching, counseling; ability to form relationships and work with groups in planning and implementing change, and ability to conduct research and diagnose problems.
3. *Attitude areas,* including open-mindedness, courage, and the possession of a humanistic value system.

Professional consultants work in many different kinds of settings and use different models of consultation. These models can generally be linked to one of two perspectives—*social control* or *influence.* Gamson (1968), in discussing these perspectives, shows how each deals with conflict. The social-control perspective emphasizes the continuity and functioning of the system and sees conflict as disruptive and requiring control. The social-influence perspective sees conflict as a useful condition that allows change to occur.

Consultants' work should be viewed in relation to these perspectives. If one employs a social-control perspective, the powerful may maintain control through the assistance of the consultant. On the other hand, the powerless can benefit when an influence perspective is used.

CONFLICT INTERVENTION

One major form of community-level consultation is *conflict intervention*. Since the 1960s a growing body of professionals—social scientists, group facilitators, lawyers, and labor leaders—has been refining and applying strategies to deal with problems such as racial struggles, housing-project disputes, and school controversies. Consultants who work in this growing field of community conflict intervention certainly are concerned with questions of social control and influence.

Conflict intervention is generally viewed as a process in which a *third party* (an outsider) enters into a conflict in order to influence its outcome in what is felt to be a desirable direction. According to clinical sociologist James Laue (1981b:3), who has been working in this field for 20 years: "Because intervention always alters the power configuration of the conflict, all interveners are advocates—for either a specific party, a particular outcome or a preferred process of conflict intervention."

There has been increasing use of the four major techniques of conflict intervention— negotiation, conciliation, mediation, and arbitration—in this country and Europe, and to a more limited extent in Asia, Latin America, Africa, and the Pacific basin. The areas of application include family and neighborhood disputes, consumer disputes, intraorganizational and interorganizational relations, racial and other intergroup conflicts, federal-state-local relations, environ-

mental disputes, and international conflict (Laue 1981b:7).

In order to understand the work of a community consultant better, we take a look at James Laue's work as a mediator. A *mediator* is an impartial individual who is acceptable at some level to all the disputants. The mediator assists the parties in reaching mutually satisfactory solutions to their differences and does this without having any formal power and without being able to impose penalties.

Laue, Director of the Center for Metropolitan Studies at the University of Missouri-St. Louis, was invited to be the mediator for the development of a Negotiated Investment Strategy (NIS) for the test city of Gary, Indiana. NIS is an experimental approach to getting government and private groups to work together on setting priorities for a community. NIS assumes that there are legitimate differences among these groups and attempts to negotiate agreements.

The NIS model has six essential parts (Berry, Kunde, and Moore 1982:44):

1. An impartial mediator
2. Three negotiating teams representing the public and private sectors of the city, the state, and the federal government, each of which is small initially but is subject to later expansion to assure representation of important interests
3. An opportunity of informal exchange of information before formal proposals are written
4. Formal face-to-face negotiating sessions with all teams present
5. A written agreement containing mutual commitments
6. A public review and adoption of the agreement with monitoring of subsequent performance by each party and by the mediator

The NIS model is distinct from other intergovernmental reform efforts in its use of an impartial "outside" mediator. James Laue facilitated an 8-month process in Gary, Indiana, that involved the mayor, the governor, and U.S. Steel, Gary's major employer and taxpayer. In his role as mediator, Laue provided structure and discipline for the entire process. As an outside mediator, he was expected to encourage new behavior from participants, several of whom had strained relations before entering the process.

The results of the long negotiations were striking (Berry, Kunde, and Moore 1982:53):

> The final agreement contained commitments from each of the three levels of government (and, in some cases, the private sector) on some 33 specific objectives in six major areas: downtown development, transportation, recreation, housing, industrial/commercial development, and health care. A seventh area—crime and public safety—was identified for future work.

A year after the agreement was signed, Laue and his mediating staff gave a progress report indicating which objectives had been met and on which only some or no action had been taken. The mediators have continued to monitor implementation and have been working with the Chicago Federal Regional Council in reviewing the status of the Gary Agreement for future action.

The most significant achievement in the Gary negotiation process was the improved relationship between the city, state, and U.S. Steel. A framework for cooperation was established that should prove helpful to all parties in the future.

THE SOCIOLOGIST IN THE COMMUNITY

In addition to these well-established roles of action researcher and consultant, the sociologist may take skills and knowledge out into the community to organize the community's resources to meet the needs of its people. An exemplary case of a clinical sociologist pursuing this option is that of Veronica Maz. A sociology professor at Georgetown University in Washington, D.C., she left teaching 15 years ago to work with the hungry and homeless of the nation's capitol.

In 1969, along with the late Reverend Horace B. McKenna, a Jesuit priest, and other community members, Maz co-founded an organization known as SOME (So Others Might Eat) to provide free food, counseling, and health care. Operating the soup kitchen, she gradually became aware of the numbers of destitute women in the city and the lack of services for them. In 1976 she decided to do something about it.

She started the House of Ruth by putting down a $1 deposit to rent an old rooming-house for women who were destitute or homeless. Eight women who had been sheltered in a nearby park became its first residents.

By 1978 the original 35-bed House of Ruth had expanded to include an annex for 30 battered women and two thrift shops. Dr. Maz, now with a $30,000 grant from the Cafritz Foundation, also established two "second stage" shelters to which women from the main house could move and pay rent while still living in a situation of mutual support. She had, as well, convinced the District of Columbia to fund her Madison Center, a 65-bed facility for homeless women. All of this was accomplished through donations, contributions, and the efforts of Dr. Maz and her volunteers. A newspaper editorial that year saluted her work and said that she stood as a working definition of courage.

By 1982 Veronica Maz was in the news again. In September of that year, McKenna's Wagon—a truck that brings food to the destitute of the city—rolled onto the streets of Washington D.C. The wagon was the newest project of Dr. Maz's soup kitchen for children, Martha's Table. The soup kitchen, which runs a lunch line for adults in addition to the children's facility, provides daily meals for about 100 destitute and homeless persons.

Some of the food on the wagon is purchased for five cents a pound from the Capital Area Community Food Bank in northeast Washington. Much of the food comes from donations—church members give sandwiches, pastries are donated by a bakery, and individuals working on Capitol Hill and living in the community give food regularly. Amazingly, McKenna's Wagon operates on a budget of just over $100 a week. This money comes from donations to Martha's Table by area residents, churches, and community groups.

The House of Ruth (or Friends of Ruth) is now established in 35 states; Dr. Maz hopes to expand McKenna's Wagon and the children's center in the same way. Her most recent accomplishment is the establishment of the National Institute, part of Martha's Table, which conducts one-day workshops around the country showing community activists how they can start a soup kitchen or a shelter. Maz also has gotten the Washington Redskins to endorse Martha's Table; the football players visit the center and hold events where items are sold and the proceeds given to the program.

What Veronica Maz has done is to take her knowledge and skills as a clinical sociologist out into the community to create new community-based institutions that meet people's needs. Her work stands as a fine example of the possibilities for clinical sociologists in the community.

CONCLUSION

There has been a surge of interest in developing effective community organizations on the part of citizens, foundations, and the government. Community scholars seem to agree that, in the next decade, neighborhood organizations will increase in number and importance. There will be many more block organizations, tenant groups, neighborhood councils, suburban civic associations, and local beautification, restoration, and ecology groups. The decentralization of municipal government also is expected to continue. All of which means that private and public neighborhood groups will probably gain political power.

This power will not be equally distributed. The growth of effective neighborhood organizations is expected to take place mainly in middle-class areas. Unless there is governmental commitment and funding, organizational efforts among the poor will not keep pace.

All these developments spell expanded opportunities for sociologists working at the community level. During this period, the role of clinical sociologists is expected to continue to grow in both community research and community consultation. Among other activities, sociologists will help communities explore alternative economic institutions, such as worker and consumer cooperatives, food-buying clubs, or neighborhood credit unions, and will help them develop new mechanisms for dispute resolution. . . .

READINGS AND REFERENCES

Berry, Daniel, James Kunde, and Carl Moore. "Negotiated Investment Strategy: Improving Intergovernmental Effectiveness by Improving Intergroup Relations" *Journal of Intergroup Relations* 10, no. 2 (Summer 1982: 42–57).

Biklen, Douglas P. *Community Organizing Theory and Practice.* Englewood Cliffs, N.J.: Prentice-Hall, 1983.

Christenson, James A., and Jerry W. Robinson, Jr., eds. *Community Development in America.* Ames, Iowa: Iowa State University Press, 1980.

Community Jobs. "Working for More Than a Living." 6, no. 4 (May 1982): 3–5.

Cox, Fred M., John L. Erlich, Jack Rothman, and John E. Tropman, eds. *Tactics and Techniques of Community Practice.* Itasca, Ill.: Peacock, 1977.

Erikson, Kai J. *Everything in Its Path.* New York: Simon and Schuster, 1976.

Etzkowitz, Henry, and Gerald M. Schaflander. "A Manifesto for Sociologists: Institution-formation–A new Sociology." *Social Problems* 15, no. 4 (Spring 1968): 399–407.

Finsterbush, Kurt, and C. P. Wolf, eds. *Methodology of Social Impact Assessment.* Stroudsburg, Pa.: Dowden, Hutchinson and Ross, 1977.

Frederich, Carl J., ed. *Community.* New York: Liberal Arts Press, 1959.

Gamson, W.A. *Power and Discontent.* Homewood, Ill.: Dorsey Press, 1968.

Laue, James H. "Conflict Intervention." In Olsen and Micklin, ed., *Handbook of Applied Sociology,* 67–90. New York: Praeger, 1981.

——. "The Development of Community Conflict Intervention." *Journal of Intergroup Relations* 9 (Summer 1981): 3–11.

Laue, James H., ed. "Intervening in Community Conflicts—II." Special Issue. *Journal of Intergroup Relations* 10, no. 2 (Summer 1982).

Lindblom, Charles, and David Cohen. *Useable Knowledge: Social Science and Social Problem Solving.* New Haven: Yale University Press, 1979.

Lippett, Ronald, and Gordon Lippitt. *The Consulting Process in Action.* La Jolla, Calif.: University Associates, 1978.

Littrell, Donald W. *The Theory and Practice of Community Development.* Columbia, Mo.: University of Missouri-Columbia, 1976.

Milgram, Stanley. "The Idea of Community." Book review of the *The Social Construction of Communities. Science* 178 (November 1972): 494–495.

Nelson, Lowrey, Charles E. Ramsey, and Coolie Verner. *Community Structure and Change.* New York: Macmillan, 1960.

O'Neill, Patrick, and Edison J. Trickett. *Community Consultation.* San Francisco: Jossey-Bass. 1982.

Poplin, Dennis E. *Communities: A Survey of Theories and Methods in Research.* 2ed. New York: Macmillan, 1979.

Park, Robert E., Ernest W. Burgess, and Robert D. Mackenzie, eds. *The City.* Chicago: University of Chicago Press, 1925.

Redekop, Calvin. "Communal Groups: Inside or Outside the Community?" In Jack Klinton, ed., *The American Community, Creation and Revival,* 135–161. Aurora, Ill.: Social Science and Sociological Resources, 1975.

Roberts, Hayden. *Community Development: Learning and Action.* Toronto: University of Toronto Press, 1979.

Sherman, Brian. *Half a Foot in the Door–Black Participation in Georgia Electoral Politics: Sixteen Years after the Voting Rights Act.* Atlanta, Ga.: Voting Rights Study Group, 1982.

Smelser, Neil J. *Theory of Collective Behavior.* New York: Free Press, 1962.

Spiegel, Hans B. C. "New Directions." In Christenson and Robinson, eds., *Community Development in America,* 220–233. Ames, Iowa: Iowa State University Press, 1980.

Suttles, Gerald D. *The Social Construction of Communities.* Chicago: University of Chicago Press, 1972.

Tönnies, Ferdinand. *Community and Society.* Translated by C. P. Loomis. New York: Harper & Row, 1963. (Originally published 1887.)

UN Ad Hoc Group of Experts on Community Development. *Community Development and National Development.* New York: United Nations, 1963.

U.S. Bureau of the Census. *Statistical Abstract of the United States: 1980.* 101st ed. Washington D.C.: U.S. Government Printing Office, 1980.

Wellman, Barry. "The Community Question: The Intimate Network of East Yorkers." *American Journal of Sociology* 84 (1979): 1201–1231.

Wirth, Louis. "Urbanism as a Way of Life." *American Journal of Sociology* 44 (July 1938): 1–24.

34

The Military Academy as an Assimilating Institution

Sanford M. Dornbusch

The function of a military academy is to make officers out of civilians or enlisted men. The objective is accomplished by a twofold process of transmitting technical knowledge and of instilling in the candidates an outlook considered appropriate for members of the profession. This paper is concerned with the latter of these processes, the assimilating function of the military academy. Assimilation is viewed as "a process of interpenetration and fusion in which persons and groups acquire the memories, sentiments, and attitudes of other persons and groups, and, by sharing their experience and history, are incorporated with them in a common cultural life. . . . The unity thus achieved is not necessarily or even normally like-mindedness; it is rather a unity of experience and of orientation, out of which may develop a community of purpose and action."[1]

Data for this study consist almost entirely of retrospective material, based on ten months spent as a cadet at the United States Coast Guard Academy. The selective nature of memory obviously may introduce serious deficiencies in the present formulation. Unfortunately, it is unlikely that more objective evidence on life within the Academy will be forthcoming. Cadets cannot keep diaries, are formally forbidden to utter a word of criticism of the Academy to an outsider, and are informally limited in the matters which are to be discussed in letters or conversations. The lack of objective data is regrettable, but

the process of assimilation is present here in an extreme form. Insight into this process can better be developed by the study of such an explicit, overt case of assimilation.

The Coast Guard Academy, like West Point and Annapolis, provides four year of training for a career as a regular officer. Unlike the other service academies, however, its cadet corps is small, seldom exceeding 350 cadets. This disparity in size probably produces comparable differences in the methods of informal social control. Therefore, all the findings reported here may not be applicable to the other academies. It is believed, however, that many of the mechanisms through which this military academy fulfills its assimilating function will be found in a wide variety of social institutions.

THE SUPPRESSION OF PRE-EXISTING STATUSES

The new cadet, or "swab," is the lowest of the low. The assignment of low status is useful in producing a correspondingly high evaluation of successfully completing the steps in an Academy career and requires that there be a loss of identity in terms of pre-existing statuses. This clean break with the past must be achieved in a relatively short period. For two months, therefore, the swab is not allowed to leave the base or to engage in social intercourse with non-cadets. This complete isolation helps to produce a unified group of swabs, rather than a heterogeneous collection of persons of high and low status. Uniforms are issued on the first day, and discussions of wealth and family background are taboo. Although the pay of the cadet is very low, he is not permitted to receive money from home. The role of the cadet must supersede other roles the individual has been accustomed to play. There are few clues left which will reveal social status in the outside world.[2]

It is clear that the existence of minority-group status on the part of some cadets would tend to break down this desired equality. The sole minority group present was the Jews, who, with a few exceptions, had been informally excluded before 1944. At that time 18 Jews were admitted in a class of 162. Their status as Jews made them objects of scrutiny by the upper classmen, so that their violations of rules were more often noted. Except for this "spotlight," however, the Jews reported no discrimination against them—they, too, were treated as swabs.

LEARNING NEW RULES AND ADJUSTMENT TO CONFLICTS BETWEEN RULES

There are two organized structures of rules which regulate the cadet's behavior. The first of these is the body of regulations of the Academy, considered by the public to be the primary source of control. These regulations are similar to the code of ethics of any profession. They serve in part as propaganda to influence outsiders. An additional function is to provide negative sanctions which are applied to violations of the second set of expectations, the informal rules. Offenses against the informal rules are merely labeled as breaches of the formal code, and the appropriate punishment according to the regulations is then imposed. This punitive system

conceals the existence of the informal set of controls.

The informal traditions of the Academy are more functionally related to the existing set of circumstances than are the regulations, for although these traditions are fairly rigid, they are more easily forgotten or changed than are the formal regulations. Unlike other informal codes, the Academy code of traditions is in part written, appearing in a manual for entering cadets.

In case of conflict between the regulations and tradition, the regulations are superseded. For example, it is against the regulations to have candy in one's room. A first classman orders a swab to bring him candy. Caught en route by an officer, the swab offers no excuse and is given 15 demerits. First classmen are then informally told by the classmate involved that they are to withhold demerits for this swab until he has been excused for offenses totaling 15 demerits. Experience at an Academy teaches future officers that regulations are not considered of paramount importance when they conflict with informal codes—a principle noted by other observers.[3]

Sometimes situations arise in which the application of either form of control is circumvented by the commanding officer. The following case is an example. Cadets cannot drink, cannot smoke in public, can never go above the first floor in a hotel. It would seem quite clear, therefore, that the possessor of a venereal disease would be summarily dismissed. Cadets at the Academy believed that two upper-class cadets had contracted a venereal disease, were cured, and given no punishment. One of the cadets was an outstanding athlete, brilliant student, and popular classmate. Cadets were told that a direct appeal by the commanding officer to the Commandant of the Coast Guard resulted in the decision to hush up the entire affair, with the second cadet getting the same treatment as his more popular colleague. The event indicated the possibility of individualization of treatment when rules are violated by officers.

THE DEVELOPMENT OF SOLIDARITY

The control system operated through the class hierarchy. The first class, consisting of cadets in their third or fourth year at the Academy, are only nominally under the control of the officers of the Academy. Only one or two officers attempt to check on the activities of the first classmen, who are able to break most of the minor regulations with impunity. The first class is given almost complete control over the rest of the cadet corps. Informally, certain leading cadets are even called in to advise the officers on important disciplinary matters. There are one or two classes between the first classmen and the swabs, depending on the existence of a three- or four-year course. These middle classes haze the swabs. Hazing is forbidden by the regulations, but the practice is a hallowed tradition of the Academy. The first class demands that this hazing take place, and since they have the power to give demerits, all members of the middle classes are compelled to haze the new cadets.

As a consequence of undergoing this very unpleasant experience together, the swab class develops remarkable unity. For example, if a cadet cannot answer an oral question addressed to him by his teacher, no other member of his class will answer. All reply, "I can't say, sir," leaving the teacher without a clue to the state of knowledge of this student compared to the rest of the class. This group cohesion persists throughout the Academy period, with first classmen refusing to give demerits to their classmates unless an officer directly orders them to do so.

The honor system, demanding that offenses by classmates be reported, is not part of the Coast Guard Academy tradition. It seems probable that the honor system, if enforced, would tend to break down the social solidarity which the hazing develops within each class.

The basis for interclass solidarity, the development of group feeling on the part of the entire cadet corps, is not so obvious. It occurs through informal contacts between the upper classmen and swabs, a type of fraternization which occurs despite the fact it traditionally is discouraged. The men who haze the swab and order him hazed live in the same wing of the dormitory that he does. Coming from an outside world which disapproves of authoritarian punishment and aggressiveness, they are ashamed of their behavior. They are eager to convince the swab that they are good fellows. They visit his room to explain why they are being so harsh this week or to tell of a mistake he is making. Close friendships sometimes arise through such behavior. These friendships must be concealed. One first classman often ordered his room cleaned by the writer as a "punishment," then settled down for an uninterrupted chat. Such informal contacts serve to unite the classes and spread a "we-feeling" through the Academy.

In addition, the knowledge of common interests and a common destiny serves as a unifying force that binds together all Academy graduates. This is expressed in the identification of the interest of the individual with the interest of the Coast Guard. A large appropriation or an increase in the size of the Coast Guard will speed the rate of promotion for all, whether ensign or captain. A winning football team at the Academy may familiarize more civilians with the name of their common alma mater. Good publicity for the Coast Guard raises the status of the Coast Guard officer.

The Coast Guard regulars are united in their disdain for the reserves. There are few reserve officers during peacetime, but in wartime the reserve officers soon outnumber the regulars. The reserves do not achieve the higher ranks, but they are a threat to the cadets and recent graduates of the Academy.

The reserves receive in a few months the rank that the regulars reach only after four grueling years. The Academy men therefore protectively stigmatize the reserves as incompetents. If a cadet falters on the parade ground, he is told, "You're marching like a reserve." Swabs are told to square their shoulders while on liberty, "or else how will people know you are not a reserve?" Myths spring up—stories of reserve commanders who must call on regular ensigns for advice. The net effect is reassurance that although the interlopers may have the same rank, they do not have equal status.

Another out-group is constituted by the enlisted men, who are considered to be an inferior ability and eager for leadership. Segregation of cadets and enlisted men enables this view to be propagated. Moreover, such segregation helps to keep associations within higher status social groups. There is only one leak in this insulating dike. The pharmacist mates at sick bay have direct contact with the cadets, and are the only enlisted personnel whom cadets meet on an equal basis. The pharmacist mates take pleasure in reviling the Academy, labeling it "the p—k factory." Some of the cadets without military experience are puzzled by such an attitude, which is inconsistent with their acquired respect for the Academy.

THE DEVELOPMENT OF A BUREAUCRATIC SPIRIT

The military services provide an excellent example of the bureaucratic structure. The emphasis is upon the office with its sets of rights and duties, rather than on the man. It is a system of rules with little regard for the individual case. The method of promotion within the Coast Guard perfectly illustrates this bureaucratic character. Unlike the Army or Navy, promotions in the Coast Guard up to the rank of lieutenant-commander do not even depend on the evaluation of superior officers. Promotion comes solely according to seniority, which is based on class standing at the Academy. The 50th man in the 1947 class will be lieutenant-commander before the 51st man, and the latter will be promoted before the 1st man in the 1948 class.

The hazing system contributes directly to acceptance of the bureaucratic structure of the Coast Guard, for the system is always viewed by its participants as not involving the personal character of the swab or upper classman. One is not being hazed because the upper classman is a sadist, but because one is at the time in a junior status. Those who haze do not pretend to be superior to those who are being hazed. Since some of those who haze you will also try to teach you how to stay out of trouble, it becomes impossible to attribute evil characteristics to those who injure you. The swab knows he will have his turn at hazing others. At most, individual idiosyncrasies will just affect the type of hazing done.[4]

This emphasis on the relativity of status is explicitly made on the traditional Gizmo Day, on which the swabs and their hazers reverse roles. The swabs-for-a-day take their licking without flinching and do not seek revenge later, for they are aware that they are under the surveillance of the first classmen. After the saturnalia, the swabs are increasingly conscious of their inability to blame particular persons for their troubles.

Upper classmen show the same resentment against the stringent restrictions upon their lives, and the manner in which they express themselves indicates a feeling of being ruled by impersonal forces. They say, "You can't buck the System." As one writer puts it, "The best attitude the new cadet can have is one of unquestioning acceptance of tradition and custom."

There is a complete absence of charismatic veneration of the Coast Guard heroes of the past and present. Stirring events are recalled, not as examples of the genius of a particular leader, but as part of the history of the great organization which they will serve.

A captain is a cadet thirty years older and wiser. Such views prepare these men for their roles in the bureaucracy.

NEW SATISFACTIONS IN INTERACTION

A bureaucratic structure requires a stable set of mutual expectations among the occupants of offices. The Academy develops this ability to view the behavior of others in terms of a pre-ordained set of standards. In addition to preparing the cadet for later service as an officer, the predictability of the behavior of his fellows enables the cadet to achieve a high degree of internal stability. Although he engages in a continual bustle of activity, he always knows his place in the system and the degree to which he is fulfilling the expectations of his role.

Sharing common symbols and objects, the cadets interact with an ease of communication seldom found in everyday life. The cadet is told what is right and wrong, and, if he disagrees, there are few opportunities to translate mental reservations into action. The "generalized other" speaks with a unitary voice which is uncommon in modern societies. To illustrate, an upper classman ordered a swab to pick up some pieces of paper on the floor of a washroom. The latter refused and walked away. There were no repercussions. The swab knew that, if he refused, the upper classman would be startled by the choice of such an unconventional way of getting expelled from the Academy. Wondering what was happening, the upper classman would redefine his own behavior, seeing it as an attack on the high status of the cadet. Picking up litter in a washroom is "dirty work," fit only for enlisted men. The swab was sure that the upper classman shared this common universe of discourse and never considered the possibility that he would not agree on the definition of the situation.

Interaction with classmates can proceed on a level of confidence that only intimate friends achieve in the outside world. These men are in a union of sympathy, sharing the same troubles, never confiding secrets to upper classmen, never criticizing one another to outsiders. Each is close to only a few but is friendly with most of the men in his class.

When interacting with an upper classman in private, a different orientation is useful. The swab does not guess the reason why he is being addressed, but instead assumes a formal air of deference. If the upper classman says, "Aw cut it out," the swab relaxes. In this manner the role of the upper classman is explicitly denoted in each situation.

In addition to providing predictability of the behavior of others, the Academy provides a second set of satisfactions in the self-process. An increase in the cadet's self-esteem develops in conjunction with identification in his new role. Told that they are members of an elite group respected by the community, most cadets begin to feel at ease in a superordinate role. One may be a low-ranking cadet, but cadets as a group have high status. When cadets visit home for the first time, there is a conflict between the lofty role that they wish to play and the role in which their parents are accustomed. Upon return to the Academy, much conversation is concerned with the way things at home have changed.

This feeling of superiority helps to develop self-confidence in those cadets who previously had a low evaluation of themselves. It directly enters into relationships with girls, with whom many boys lack self-confidence. It soon becomes apparent that any cadet can get a date whenever he wishes, and he even begins to feel that he is a good "catch." The cadet's conception of himself is directly influenced by this new way of viewing the behavior of himself and others. As one cadet put it, "I used to be shy. Now I'm reserved."

SOCIAL MOBILITY

A desire for vertical social mobility on the part of many cadets serves as one means of legitimizing the traditional practices of the Academy. The cadets are told that they will be members of the social elite during the later stages of their career. The obstacles that they meet at the Academy are then viewed as the usual barriers to social mobility in the United States, a challenge to be surmounted.

Various practices at the Academy reinforce the cadets' feeling that they are learning how to enter the upper classes. There is a strong emphasis on etiquette, from calling cards to table manners. The Tactics Officer has been known to give long lectures on such topics as the manner of drinking soup from an almost empty bowl. The cadet must submit for approval the name of the girl he intends to take to the monthly formal dance. Girls attending the upper-class college in the vicinity are automatically acceptable, but some cadets claim that their dates have been rejected because they are in a low status occupation such as waitress.

Another Academy tradition actively, though informally, encourages contact with higher status girls. After the swabs have been completely isolated for two months, they are invited to a dance at which all the girls are relatives or friends of Coast Guard officers. A week later the girls at the nearby college have a dance for the swabs. The next week end finds the swab compelled to invite an acceptable girl to a formal reception. He must necessarily choose from the only girls in the area whom he knows, those that he met during the recent hours of social intercourse.

JUSTIFICATION OF INSTITUTIONAL PRACTICES

In addition to the social mobility theme which views the rigors of Academy life as obstacles to upward mobility, there is a more open method of justifying traditionally legitimated ways of doing things. The phrase, "separating the men from the boys" is used to meet objections to practices which seem inefficient or foolish. Traditional standards are thus redefined as further tests of ability to take punishment. Harsh practices are defended as methods by which the insincere, incompetent, or undisciplined cadets are weeded out. Cadets who rebel and resign are merely showing lack of character.[5]

Almost all cadets accept to some extent this traditional view of resignations as admissions of defeat. Of the 162 entering cadets in 1944, only 52 graduated in 1948. Most of the 110 resignations were entirely voluntary without pressure from the Academy authorities. Most of these resignations came at a time when the hazing was comparatively moderate. Cadets who wish to resign do not leave at a time when the hazing might be considered the cause of their departure. One cadet's history illustrates this desire to have the resignation appear completely voluntary. Asked to resign because of his lack of physical coordination, he spent an entire year building up his physique, returned to the Academy, finished his swab year, and then joyously quit. "It took me three years, but I showed them."

Every cadet who voluntarily resigns is a threat to the morale of the cadet corps, since he has rejected the values of the Academy. Although cadets have enlisted for seven years and could theoretically be forced to remain at the Academy, the usual procedure is to isolate them from the swabs and rush acceptance of their resignation. During the period before the acceptance is final, the cadets who have resigned are freed from the usual duties of their classmates, which action effectively isolates them from cadets who might be affected by their contagious disenchantment.

REALITY SHOCK

Everett C. Hughes has developed the concept of "reality shock," the sudden realization of the disparity between the way a job is envisaged before beginning work and the actual work situation.[6] In the course of its 75-

year history the Coast Guard Academy has wittingly or unwittingly developed certain measures to lessen reality shock in the new ensign. The first classmen, soon to be officers, are aided in lessening the conflict between the internalized rules of the Academy world and the standards for officer conduct.

On a formal level the first classmen are often reminded that they are about to experience a relative decline in status. On their first ship they will be given the most disagreeable duties. The first classmen accept this and joke about how their attitudes will change under a harsh captain. On a more concrete level, first classmen are given week-end leaves during the last six months of their stay at the Academy. These leaves allow them to escape from the restrictive atmosphere of the nearby area. It is believed wise to let them engage in orgiastic behavior while still cadets, rather than suddenly release all controls upon graduation.

Rumors at the Academy also help to prepare the cadets for their jobs as officers. Several of the instructors at the Academy were supposed to have been transferred from sea duty because of their incompetence. Such tales protect the cadets from developing a romantic conception of the qualities of Coast Guard officers, as well as providing a graphic illustration of how securely the bureaucratic structure protects officers from their own derelictions. In addition, many stories were told about a junior officer whose career at the Academy had been singularly brilliant. He had completely failed in his handling of enlisted men because he had carried over the high standards of the Academy. The cadets were thus oriented to a different conception of discipline when dealing with enlisted personnel.

CONCLUSION

The United States Coast Guard Academy performs an assimilating function. It isolates cadets from the outside world, helps them to identify themselves with a new role, and thus changes their self-conception. The manner in which the institution inculcates a bureaucratic spirit and prevents reality shock is also considered in this analysis.

The present investigation is admittedly fragmentary. Much of the most relevant material is simply not available. It is also clear that one cannot assume that this analysis applied completely to any other military academy. However, as an extreme example of an assimilating institution, there is considerable material which can be related to other institutions in a comparative framework.

NOTES

1. Robert E. Park and Ernest W. Burgess, *Introduction to the Science of Sociology* (Chicago: University of Chicago Press, 1921), pp. 735, 737.
2. Cf. Arnold Van Gennep, *Les Rites de Passage* (Paris: Emile Nourry, 1909). Translated by Everett C. Hughes in *Anthropology-Sociology 240, Special Readings* (Chicago: University of Chicago Bookstore, 1948), Pt. II, p. 9.
3. Ralph H. Turner, "The Navy Disbursing Officer As a Bureaucrat," *American Sociological Review*, XII (June 1946), 344 and 348; Arnold Rose, " The Social Structure of the Army," *American Journal of Sociology*, LI (March 1946), 361.
4. Compare this viewpoint with that expressed in Hugh Mullan, "The Regular Service Myth," *American Journal of Sociology*, LIII (January 1948), 280, where hazing is viewed as the expression of "pent-up sadism." Such individualistic interpretations do not take into account the existence of an institutional structure, or else they give psychological interpretation to social processes.
5. "At each step of the ceremonies he feels that he is brought a little closer, until at last he can feel himself a man among men." A. R. Radcliffe-Brown, *The Andaman Islanders* (Glencoe, Illinois: The Free Press, 1948), p. 279.
6. Miriam Wagenschein, Reality Shock. Unpublished M.A. thesis, Department of Sociology, University of Chicago, 1950.

35

Hanging Tongues: A Sociological Encounter with the Assembly Line

WILLIAM E. THOMPSON

This qualitative sociological study analyzes the experience of working on a modern assembly line in a large beef plant. It explores and examines a special type of assembly line work which involves the slaughtering and processing of cattle into a variety of products intended for human consumption and other uses.

Working in the beef plant is "dirty work," not only in the literal sense of being drenched with perspiration and beef blood, but also in the figurative sense of performing a low status, routine, and demeaning job.[1] Although the work is honest and necessary in a society which consumes beef, slaughtering and butchering cattle is generally viewed as an undesirable and repugnant job. In that sense, workers at the beef plant share some of the same experiences as other workers in similarly regarded occupations (for example, ditchdiggers, garbage collectors, and other types of assembly line workers).

Demeaning work has been studied in several different contexts. For example, while on sabbatical leave from his college presidency, Coleman (1974) worked in a variety of low status jobs and wrote about the experiences of workers such as dishwashers and ditchdiggers. Terkel (1974) interviewed a multitude of people whose occupations fit into the category of "dirty work." Garson (1975) investigated low status, monotonous, and often demeaning work situations. Her study included typists, keypunchers, and factory workers, among others. She also interviewed people who worked on an assembly line in a tuna processing plant and whose work was similar to the work in the beef plant of this study. Garson did not observe the tuna workers for any period of time, nor perform the work herself, but was able to portray the attitudes of the workers about their jobs.

Some studies have focused on one type of "dirty work." Perry (1978), a social scientist, observed and worked alongside garbage collectors in San Francisco. He described not only their daily work activities, but also the way workers coped with the demeaning aspects of their work and managed to maintain their self-esteem. Perry found that these garbage collectors overcame the stigma commonly associated with their jobs partially by forming a co-op type of ownership in which they purchased shares. Therefore, the "dirty workers" were actually part-owners.

Other studies relevant to this analysis have been conducted on assembly line work in major automobile plants. Walker and Guest (1952), Chinoy (1955), Georgakas and Surkin (1978), King (1978), and Linhart (1981) vividly describe the experiences of automobile assembly line workers. Linhart's study, conducted in France, demonstrates that the drudgery and dehumanization experienced by auto assembly line workers are not confined to America.

Beef industry workers have also been studied previously. Meara (1974) describes how American meatcutters and Turkish butchers retain their sense of honor while performing "dirty work." But the meat-cutters in Meara's study worked in grocery stores, not large-scale assembly lines. Further, her subjects worked with what beef plant workers view as the "finished product." Meatcutters in a grocery store are far removed from the actual slaughter process where live cattle come in one door and hanging sides of beef go out the other. Her Turkish subjects were butchers who owned their own butcher shops, and basically cut meat to order for their customers. Consequently, there is little similarity between their work and the work performed in the beef plant in this research.

This study attempts to extend the range of sites of occupational research. In addition to studying a previously explored occupational setting, it is hoped that this study will also add to the conceptual and theoretical understanding of this type of work.

Couched within the symbolic interactionist perspective, this study focuses on the daily activities of the workers. These activities must meet the work demands of their employer and enable the workers to construct and perpetuate a social world of work in a way meaningful to them. Specifically, this study analyzes how workers interact with one another on the job, how they cope with the strains of the work, how they maintain a sense of self-worth, and how they develop and maintain informal norms in regard to consumer spending. These spending patterns lead to a financial trap which prevents most workers from leaving the employ of the plant.

THE SETTING

The setting for the field work was a major beef processing plant in the Midwest. At the time of the study, the plant was the third largest branch of a corporation which operated ten such plants in the United States. It employed approximately 1800 people. In ad-

dition to slaughtering and processing cattle for beef, the plant also produced pet food, leather for the wholesale market, and a variety of pharmaceutical supplies which were derived from various glands and organs of cattle. This particular plant had operated for twelve years and was considered a stable and important part of the community in which it was located.

The beef plant was organizationally separated into two divisions: Slaughter and Processing. This study focused on the Slaughter division in the area of the plant known as the *kill floor*. A dominant feature of the kill floor was the machinery of the assembly line itself. The line was comprised of an overhead stainless steel rail which began at the slaughter chute and curved its way around every work station in the plant. Every work station contained specialized machinery for the job performed at that place on the line. Dangling from the rail were hundreds of stainless steel hooks pulled by a motorized chain. Virtually every part of the line and all of the implements (tubs, racks, knives, etc.) were made of stainless steel. The walls were covered with a ceramic tile and the floor was made of sealed cement. There were floor drains located at every work station, so that at the end of each work segment (at breaks, lunch, and shift's end) the entire kill floor could be hosed down and cleaned for the next work period.

Another dominant feature of the kill floor was the smell. Extremely difficult to describe, yet impossible to forget, this smell combined the smells of live cattle, manure, fresh beef blood, and internal organs and their contents. This smell not only permeated the interior of the plant, but was combined on the outside with the smell of smoke from various waste products being burned and could be smelled throughout much of the community. This smell contributed greatly to the general negative feelings about work at the beef plant, as it served as the most distinguishable symbol of the beef plant to the rest of the community. The single most often asked question of me during the research by those outside the beef plant was, "How do you stand the smell?" In typical line workers' fashion, I always responded, "What smell? All I smell at the beef plant is money."

Approximately 350 employees worked on the "A" shift on "Slaughter" and were the subjects observed for this research. The most intensive observation focused on the twelve members of the particular work crew to which I was assigned. Of the 350 employees, approximately one-third were Mexican-Americans, two-thirds were white, and two individuals were Native Americans. No blacks worked on this shift. Only five women worked on the "A" shift: a nurse, a secretary, and three federal inspectors; all the line workers were male. A few blacks and several women worked in the Process division. The explanation given for the lack of women lineworkers in " Slaughter" was the hard physical labor and the nature of the jobs associated with slaughtering. Although pursued, an adequate explanation for the lack of blacks in the slaughter division was never provided.

METHOD

The method of this study was nine weeks of full-time participant observation as outlined by Schatzman and Strauss (1973) and Spradley (1979; 1980). To enter the setting, the researcher went through the standard application process for a summer job. No mention of the research intent was made, though it was made clear that I was a university sociology professor. After initial screening, a thorough physical examination, and a helpful reference from a former student and part-time employee of the plant, the author was hired to work on the *Offal*[2] crew in the Slaughter division of the plant.

Due to the nature of the work, it was impossible to use any hardware, such as cameras or tape recorders, or to take field notes during the work period. Mental notes of observations and interviews were made throughout each work shift, and logged in a journal at the end of each working day. The researcher gained full acceptance by fellow employees, was treated like any other worker, and encountered very little difficulty in obtaining answers to virtually all research questions pursued. An effort was made to meet, observe, and interact with as many of the 350 employees on the "A" shift as possible. Admittedly, however, the bulk of the information came from the twelve crew members in Offal.

The use of covert research methods in sociology has been questioned from an ethical standpoint. Humphreys' use of covert participant observation in *Tearoom Trade* (1970) brought a variety of ethical questions to the forefront. This study is not nearly as controversial as Humphreys', in the sense that no laws were broken, no false pretenses of other research purposes were used, and the subjects' personal and private lives were not probed. Still, the overall question of whether researchers should observe and study people who are not informed of the research intent is relevant. In his classic work on sociological field observer roles, Gold (1958) describes four legitimate techniques for field research. In this study, I utilized Gold's role of "complete participant" in which I concealed my research intent in order to become a full-fledged member of the group under study. In this case, I am satisfied that doing the research in such a manner was not only legitimate, but the only way to fulfill the research purposes. As Garson (1975:149) points out:

> It is very difficult to see people doing their jobs. It's easy to visit the front office of a factory. And it's not too hard to stop workers at the factory gate. The difficult problem is watching the work itself.

Fearful of industrial espionage and interruption of work activities, it is extremely doubtful that plant management would have approved a research project of this nature. Further, even if amenable, there would be no way to interact with the line workers and clearly comprehend their experiences without simply being one of them. Since it was known by all the members of the crew with which I worked that I was a professor, it is quite possible that some guessed that I was conducting research. In fact, more than one worker suggested it. And, at least two or three, only partly in jest, suggested, "You ought to write a book about this."

In order to protect the anonymity of the plant and the workers, no direct references are made that would necessarily identify either the plant or any of its workers.

THE WORK

The physical exhaustion of assembly line work at the beef plant was extreme. Certain jobs on the line required more physical exertion than others, but the strain of assembly line work went beyond physical exhaustion. As a worker on the line at Ford put it, "The work is always physically exhausting . . . but the real punishment is the inevitability of the line" (King, 1978:201). The inevitability of the line indeed; the line speed on the kill floor was 187. That means that 187 head of cattle were slaughtered per hour. At any particular work station, each worker was required to work at that speed. Thus, at my work station, in the period of one hour, 187 beef tongues were mechanically pulled from their hooks; dropped into a large tub filled with water; had to be taken from the tub and hung on a large stainless steel rack full of hooks; branded with a "hot brand" indicating they had been inspected by a USDA inspector; and then covered with a small plastic bag. The rack was taken to the cooler, replaced with an empty one, and the process began again.

It would be logical to assume that if a person worked at a steady, continuous pace of handling 187 tongues per hour, everything would go smoothly; not so. In addition to hanging, branding, and bagging tongues, the worker at that particular station also cleaned the racks and cleaned out a variety of empty stainless steel tubs used to hold hearts, kidneys, and other beef organs. Thus, in order to be free to clean the tubs when necessary, the "tongue-hanger" had to work at a slightly faster pace than the line moved. Then, upon returning from cleaning the tubs, the worker would be behind the line (*in a hole*) and had to work much faster to catch up with the line. Further, one fifteen minute break and a thirty minute lunch break were scheduled for an eight-hour shift. Before the "tongue-hanger" could leave his post for one of these, all tongues were required to be properly disposed of, all tubs washed and stored, and the work area cleaned.

The first two nights on the job, I discovered the consequences of working at the line speed (hanging, branding, and bagging each tongue as it fell in the tub). At the end of the work period when everybody else was leaving the work floor for break or lunch, I was furiously trying to wash all the tubs and clean the work area. Consequently, I missed the entire fifteen minute break and had only about ten minutes for lunch. By observing other workers, I soon caught on to the system. Rather than attempting to work at a steady pace consistent with the line speed, the norm was to work sporadically at a very frenzied pace, actually running ahead on the line and plucking tongues from the hooks before they got to the station. With practice, I learned to hang two or three tongues at a time, perform all the required tasks, and then take an unscheduled two or three minute break until the line caught up with me. Near break and lunch everybody worked at a frantic pace, got ahead of the line, cleaned the work areas, and even managed to add a couple of minutes to the scheduled break or lunch.

Working ahead of the line seems to have served as more than merely a way of gaining a few minutes of extra break time. It also seemed to take on a symbolic meaning. The company controlled the speed of the line. Seemingly, that took all element of control over the work process away from the workers. As Garson (1975:140) indicates, "The main advantage of the auto assembly line to an employer is not speed but control." However, when the workers refused to work at line speed and actually worked faster than the line, they not only added a few minutes of relaxation from the work while the line caught up, but they symbolically regained an element of control over the pace of their own work.

Occasionally, the line broke down. Mixed emotions accompanied such an occurrence. On the one hand, the workers were happy. While the problem was being solved, we were being paid by the company for doing nothing. Foremen and supervisors viewed the breakdown quite differently, of course, and maintenance crews were pressured to work at a frenzied speed to get the line back in motion. On the other hand, even the line workers could not be totally pleased with a breakdown. The Slaughter crew worked on a quota of killing between 1350 and 1500 steers in an eight-hour shift. Invariably, when the line was repaired after being down for a short period, the line speed was generally increased to compensate for the *down time*. Thus, although a brief unscheduled break was enjoyed, when work resumed one usually was forced to work faster and harder to make up for it.

WORKER SOCIAL RELATIONS

Worker social relations were complex. As could be expected, the various roles occupied by workers in the plant greatly influenced the types of interaction which occurred among them. The major occupational roles at the beef plant were manager, foreman, nurse, federal meat inspector, and line worker. The hierarchial structure of personnel was clear-cut from the company's viewpoint. Plant superintendent, general manager, and other executives were, of course, at the top of the status hierarchy. However, since their offices were separated from the work floor (and they rarely ventured there), their interaction with labor personnel was virtually non-existent. When interaction did occur, it was usually on a one-way basis—there was a clear superordinate/subordinate relationship.

Management's link to labor personnel was the foreman. He personified management on the work floor. His main duties were to assign jobs to his crew members and supervise their work activities. In addition, however, the foreman was often required to perform physical labor. Thus, he had to know all the jobs performed by his crew. Should a worker be absent or have to leave the line unexpectedly, the foreman was required to take over his responsibilities. The foreman often fulfilled the laborer role and worked alongside the rest of the crew. Ironically, though higher in status and "in charge" of the crew, the foreman periodically performed all the duties of a laborer at lower pay.

Foremen worked on monthly salaries, whereas laborers worked for hourly wages. When laborers worked overtime, they were paid "time-and-a-half." When foremen worked overtime, it was gratis to the company. This pay differential was usually compensated for at the end of the year when profit-sharing dividends of foremen far exceeded those of laborers. Since foremen's dividends were based on the production of their crews, they tended to push their crews to the maximum. The foreman role was somewhat analogous to that of the "overseer" on slave plantations in the antebellum South (Stampp, 1956). He did not have the status nor reap the benefits of the company owner, yet became the "driver" of those who produced the work and profits. In a sociological sense, the foreman at the beef plant emerged as the classic example of "marginal man" (Stonequist, 1937); he was in fact neither management nor labor, and not fully accepted by either.

The general attitudes of the laborers toward the foremen were those of dislike and mistrust. Even when certain workers knew a foreman on a friendly basis in a social context outside the plant, their relations inside the plant were cool. A scenario I personally saw acted out on several occasions by several different workers involved a foreman stopping to talk to a worker in a non-work related, seemingly friendly conversation. The worker would be smiling and conversing congenially, yet the moment the foreman turned to walk away, the worker would make an obscene gesture (usually involving the middle finger) behind the foreman's back, so that all other workers could clearly see. The overt submission and yet covert show of disrespect was reminiscent of the "puttin' on ole massa" technique practiced by slaves toward their masters in the pre-Civil War South (Osofsky, 1969).[3]

Social relations between laborers were marked by anonymity. While virtually all the workers on the kill floor knew each other on sight and knew who performed what job, it was not uncommon for two workers who had worked alongside each other for ten years to know only each other's first names—and that only because it was written on a piece of plastic tape on the front of their hard hats. As Berger points out, " . . . technological production brings with it *anonymous social* relations" [italics in original] (Berger, et al., 1974:31). Similarly, an auto assembly line worker lamented, "I've been here for over a year, and I hardly know the first names of the men in the section where I work" (Walker and Guest, 1952:77). The nature of the work on an assembly line almost negates the possibility for social interaction during the work, and consequently creates a certain anonymity among the workers.

Though anonymous, the workers also shared a sense of unity. Work on the line could best be described as "uncooperative teamwork." Because the assembly line demanded coordinated teamwork to some extent, the work became "one for all." Yet, at the same time, since each worker had a separate specialized task, the work became "every man for himself." Workers occasionally helped each other *out of the hole* when they fell behind, but it was done more because it slowed their own work, than because they wanted to help a fellow worker. Still, the help was appreciated and almost always reciprocated.

Beyond sharing labor occasionally, a more subtle sense of unity existed among the workers; a sense that "we are all in this together." Just as an auto worker indicated, "The monotony of the line binds us together" (King, 1978:201), the beef plant workers apparently shared a common bond. The workers referred to themselves as *beefers* and each individual *beefer* shared something in common with all others. The hard work, danger of the job, and ambivalence toward the company and its management, all seemed to unite the workers in spirit. The line workers in the beef plant constituted an "occupational culture" as described by Reimer (1979:24) in his study of construction workers.

Although through profit-sharing and participation in stock options the workers technically shared in the ownership of the plant, they tended to view themselves as apart from it. Management and the plant in general were always referred to as "they", while the workers referred to themselves as "we." As indicated by Schutz (1967), this contrast between the "we-relationship" and "they-relationship" has tremendous impact upon social relations. As shown by the classic "Hawthorne Experiment," employee social relations often take precedence over production, efficiency, and promise of material rewards (Roethslinger, 1941).

Another uniting element regarding worker social interaction was the process of sharing meaningful symbols. Language emerged as one of the most important symbols at the beef plant (Mead, 1934). As Hummel (1977) suggests, in most bureaucratic organizations a language exists to facilitate communication among those within the organization and to exclude those outside it. As Reimer (1979:78) points out, "For a worker to be fully integrated into a work group and its culture, he must literally know how to communicate in the language of the group." A brief description of the slaughter process in the argot of a *beefer* will illustrate the point:

> After *herders* send in the beef, a *knocker* drops them. The *shackler* puts them on the chain so the *head droppers, splitters, boners, trimmers,* and the rest of the *chain gang* can do their jobs. As long as *the man* doesn't reject a lot and you don't run into a lot of *down time,* it's easy to *stay out of the hole* and get some *sunshine time* at the end of the shift.

Despite special argot, the excessive noise from the machinery and the requirement that all employees wear ear plugs made nonverbal gestures the primary form of communication. Exaggerated gestures and shrill whistles were used to get a fellow worker's attention. The "thumbs up" sign indicated everything was alright, whereas "thumbs down" meant one was *in the hole.* One of the most interesting means of non-verbal communication was to beat knives against the stainless steel tables and tubs used throughout the plant. This clanging signified either that a break in the line was coming or that the men on slaughter had quit "knocking". The first person on the line to see the upcoming gap would begin clanging his knife against metal; the next worker picked up on this, and so on down the line, until the entire line was clanging unbelievably loudly. My work station was situated so that when the clanging began it was exactly 35 minutes until the end of the line would reach me. Since there were no clocks on the kill floor and talk was virtually impossible, this procedure served as an important time indicator for all workers in regard to breaks, lunch and quitting time. This ability to communicate a sense of time to fellow workers also served to symbolically regain an element of control that management had taken from the workers by virtue of not installing any clocks on the kill floor.

Two other worker roles existed on the slaughter side of the plant: the nurse, and the federal meat inspectors. The nurse was one of five women on the Slaughter side of the plant on our particular shift. She was approximately 25 years old and considered quite attractive. Needless to say, she received a great deal of attention from the approximately 350 male workers on that shift. The nurse's office was located between the work floor and the lunch room, so that workers walked directly by it on the way to and from breaks and meals. Workers invariably peered in the little glass window on the nurse's door and often dropped in just to say "hi."

Due to working around excessive amounts of beef blood, even the slightest cut on a worker had to be treated in order to avoid infection. This provided an excellent alibi for the workers to make frequent visits to the nurse. On the other hand, trips to the nurse meant time away from the line. Therefore, workers had to be careful not to get too many cuts and spend too much time in the nurse's office, or a foreman would be suspicious. Each visit to the nurse for treatment was documented and crew foremen periodically reviewed the records of their crew members.

While the nurse was considered attractive, and many sexually suggestive comments were made about her among the workers, she was overtly treated with a great deal of respect. I never heard any rude comments made to her or in her presence perhaps because the importance of her role in the plant was recognized by all, including management, foremen, workers, and inspectors.

The federal meat inspector emerged as the most autonomous role in the plant. While inspectors occupied a significant place in the plant's operational system, they were in a sense outside of and above all the plant personnel. Employed by the federal government, their authority superceded even that of plant management. Their decision to reject a product or order something destroyed was unquestioned. Thus, they held a great deal of potential power. This power was not accompanied with respect however. Virtually every encounter a worker had with an inspector took on negative connotations. The only circumstance causing occupants of the two roles to interact was the rejection by the inspector of the laborer's work. Thus, each encounter with an inspector meant more work for the laborer, plus probably an unpleasant encounter with the foreman. Workers typically viewed the inspectors as arrogant and pompous—or as one worker put it—"a royal pain in the ass." It was extremely uncommon to see workers and inspectors interact in anything other than an official context. Inspectors ate in a separate lunchroom and dressed in a separate locker room. Their clean white uniforms made them immediately distinguishable from the laborers whose "white" uniforms had long since become khaki colored from the constant staining of beef blood and the process of being washed in the plant laundry. Only a new worker whose uniform had not yet been laundered could possibly be confused with an inspector at first glance. Inspectors also wore a badge on their shirt pocket for identification.

Because I had previously had one of the inspectors as a student, I had occasion to interact with him in a different context than most workers. This inspector indicated to me that inspectors tended to view workers negatively. They saw workers as overpaid, careless, and often sneaky—constantly trying to subvert the federal standards that were supposed to be maintained. Further, he indicated that there was more than a little resentment toward the workers in regard to wages. The workers' starting wage exceeded the starting wage of an inspector by approximately $2.50 per hour. This resentment could be manifested by forcing workers to do a job more than once. All in all, the interactional process between workers and inspectors can be summarized as "mutually hostile."

COPING

One of the difficulties of work at the beef plant was coping with three aspects of the work: monotony, danger, and dehumanization. While individual workers undoubtedly coped in a variety of ways, some distinguishable patterns emerged.

Monotony

The monotony of the line was almost unbearable. At my work station, a worker would hang, brand, and bag between 1,350 and 1,500 beef tongues in an eight-hour shift. With the exception of the scheduled 15 minute break and a 30 minute lunch period (and sporadic brief gaps in the line), the work was mundane, routine, and continuous. As in most assembly line work, one inevitably drifted into daydreams (e.g., Garson, 1975; King, 1978; Linhart, 1981). It was not unusual to look up or down the line and see workers at various stations singing to themselves, tapping their feet to imaginary music, or carrying on conversations with themselves. I found that I could work with virtually no attention paid to the job, with my hands and arms almost automatically performing their tasks. In the meantime, my mind was free to wander over a variety of topics, including taking mental notes. In visiting with other workers, I found that daydreaming was the norm. Some would think about their families, while others fantasized about sexual escapades, fishing, or anything unrelated to the job. One individual who was rebuilding an antique car at home in his spare time would meticulously mentally rehearse the procedures he was going to perform on the car the next day.

Daydreaming was not inconsequential, however. During these periods, items were most likely to be dropped, jobs improperly performed, and accidents incurred. Inattention to detail around moving equipment, stainless steel hooks, and sharp knives invariably leads to dangerous consequences. Although I heard rumors of drug use to help fight the monotony, I never saw any workers take any drugs nor saw any drugs in any workers' possession. It is certainly conceivable that some workers might have taken something to help them escape the reality of the line, but the nature of the work demanded enough attention that such a practice could be ominous.

Danger

The danger of working in the beef plant was well known. Safety was top priority (at least in theory) and management took pride in the fact that only three employee on-the-job deaths had occurred in 12 years.[4] Although deaths were uncommon, serious injuries were not. The beef plant employed over 1,800 people. Approximately three-fourths of those employed had jobs which demanded the use of a knife honed to razor-sharpness. Despite the use of wire-mesh aprons and gloves, serious cuts were almost a daily occurrence. Since workers constantly handled beef blood, danger of infection was ever-present. As one walked along the assembly line, a wide assortment of bandages

on fingers, hands, arms, necks, and faces could always be seen.

In addition to the problem of cuts, workers who cut meat continuously sometimes suffered muscle and ligament damage to their fingers and hands. In one severe case, I was told of a woman who worked in processing for several years who had to wear splints on her fingers while away from the job to hold them straight. Otherwise, the muscles in her hand would constrict her fingers into the grip position, as if holding a knife.

Because of the inherent danger of the plant in general, and certain jobs in the plant in particular, workers were forced to cope with the fear of physical harm.[5] Meara (1974) discovered that meatcutters in her study derived a sense of honor from the serious cuts and injuries they incurred doing their work, but this did not seem to be the case at the beef plant. Although workers were willing to show their scars, they did not seem to take much pride in them. Any time a serious accident occurred (especially one which warranted the transport of the victim to the hospital in an ambulance) news of the event spread rapidly throughout the plant.

When I spoke with fellow workers about the dangers of working in the plant, I noticed interesting defense mechanisms. As noted by Shostak (1980), the workers talked a great deal about workers being injured on the job. After a serious accident, or when telling about an accident or death which occurred in years past, the workers would almost immediately disassociate themselves from the event and its victim. Workers tended to view those who suffered major accidents or death on the job in much the same way that non-victims of crime often view crime victims as either partially responsible for the event, or at least as very different from themselves (Barlow, 1981). "Only a part-timer," "stupid," "careless" or something similar was used, seemingly to reassure the worker describing the accident that it could not happen to him. The reality of the situation was that virtually all the jobs on the kill floor were dangerous, and any worker could have experienced a serious injury at any time.

The company management was very much aware of the danger and posted signs everywhere as constant reminders to wear all safety equipment and to be careful at all times. Yet, speed and efficiency clearly took precedence over caution in actual practice. To fall behind the speed of the line meant one had to work extra fast to catch up. In haste to keep up production, worker safety often took a back seat to speed in performing tasks. As in the auto industry, "the single goal of the company was to increase profit by getting more work out of each individual worker" (Georgakas and Surkin, 1978:60).

The nurse indicated that accidents seemed to increase near the end of a shift and near the end of the week when fatigue combined with the attempt to hurry-up and get finished produced several injuries. It was also her opinion that accidents on the job might be significantly related to workers' problems at home.[6] She pointed out that invariably when she was treating an accident victim, they would describe to her how problems with a spouse, finances, etc., had temporarily distracted them and helped bring about the accident.

Dehumanization

Perhaps the most devastating aspect of working at the beef plant (worse than the monotony and the danger) was the dehumanizing and demeaning elements of the job. In a sense, the assembly line worker became a part of the assembly line. The assembly line is not a tool used by the worker, but a machine which controls him/her. A tool can only be productive in the hands of somebody skilled in its use, and hence, becomes an extension of the person using it. A machine, on the other hand, performs specific tasks, thus its operator becomes an extension

of it in the production process. Further elaboration on the social and psychological distinction between tools and machines has been discussed in the ecology literature (for example, Bookchin, 1972). When workers are viewed as mere extensions of the machines with which they work, their human needs become secondary in importance to the smooth mechanical functioning of the production process. In a bureaucratic structure, when "human needs collide with systems needs the individual suffers" (Hummel, 1977:65).

Workers on the assembly line are seen as interchangeable as the parts of the product on the line itself. An example of one worker's perception of this phenomenon at the beef plant was demonstrated the day after a fatal accident occurred. I asked the men in our crew what the company did in the case of an employee death (I wondered if there was a fund for flowers, or if the shift was given time off to go to the funeral, etc.). One worker's response was: "They drag off the body, take the hard hat and boots and check 'em out to some other poor sucker, and throw him in the guy's place." While employee death on the job was not viewed quite that coldly by the company, the statement fairly accurately summarized the overall result of a fatal accident, and importance of any individual worker to the overall operation of the production process. It accurately summarized the workers' perceptions about management's attitudes toward them.

The dehumanization process affected the social relations of workers, as well as each worker's self-concept. Hummel (1977:2) indicates that bureaucracy and its technical means of production give birth to a " . . . new species of inhuman beings." As noted by Perry (1978:7), "there are dire consequences for someone who feels stuck in an occupation that robs him of his personhood or, at best, continually threatens his personhood for eight hours a day." However, workers on the line strove in a variety of ways to maintain their sense of worth. As pointed out by Perrow (1979:4), the bureaucratic structure of the complex organization never realizes its "ideal" form because " . . . it tries to do what must be (hopefully) forever impossible—to eliminate all unwanted extraorganizational influence upon the behavior of its members." Reimer (1979) showed that construction workers view deviance as a fun part of their work. So, too, *beefers* strained to maintain their humanity, and hence, their sense of self-esteem through horseplay (strictly forbidden), daydreaming, unscheduled breaks, social interaction with other employees, and occasional sabotage.

SABOTAGE

It is fairly common knowledge that assembly line work situations often lead to employee sabotage or destruction of the product or equipment used in the production process (Garson, 1975; Balzer, 1976; Shostak, 1980). This is the classic experience of alienation as described by Marx (1964a,b). This experience has been most eloquently expressed by an assembly line worker in Terkel's research, who stated:

> Sometimes out of pure meanness, when I make something I put a little dent in it. I like to do something to make it really unique. Hit it with a hammer. I deliberately fuck it up to see if it'll get by, just so I can say I did it (Terkel, 1974:9–10).

At the beef plant I quickly learned that there was an art to effective sabotage. Subtlety appeared to be the key. "The art lies in sabotaging in a way that is not immediately discovered," as a Ford worker put it (King, 1978:202). This seemed to hold true at the beef plant as well.

Although sabotage did not seem to be a major problem at the beef plant, it did exist, and there appeared to be several norms (both formal and informal) concerning what was acceptable and what was not. The greatest

factor influencing the handling of beef plant products was its status as a food product intended for human consumption. Thus, the formal norms were replete with USDA and FDA regulations and specifications. Foremen, supervisors, and federal inspectors attempted to insure that these norms were followed. Further, though not an explicitly altruistic group, the workers realized that the product would be consumed by people (even family, relatives, and friends), so consequently, they rarely did anything to actually contaminate the product.

Despite formal norms against sabotage, some did occur. It was not uncommon for workers to deliberately cut chunks out of pieces of meat for no reason (or for throwing at other employees). While regulations required that anything that touched the floor had to be put in tubs marked "inedible," the informal procedural norms were otherwise. When something was dropped, one usually looked around to see if an inspector or foreman noticed. If not, the item was quickly picked up and put back on the line.

Several explanations might be offered for this type of occurrence. First, since the company utilized a profit-sharing plan, when workers damaged the product, or had to throw edible pieces into inedible tubs (which sold for pet food at much lower prices), profits were decreased. A decrease in profits to the company ultimately led to decreased dividend checks to employees. Consequently, workers were fairly careful not to actually ruin anything. Second, when something was dropped or mishandled and had to be rerouted to "inedible", it was more time-consuming than if the product had been handled properly and kept on the regular line. In other words, if no inspector noticed, it was easier to let it go through on the line. There was a third, and seemingly more meaningful explanation for this behavior, however. It was against the rules to do it, it was a challenge to do it, and thus it was fun to do it.

The workers practically made a game out of doing forbidden things simply to see if they could get away with it. As Perrow (1975:40) indicates, "One of the delights of the organizational expert is to indicate to the uninitiated the wide discrepancy between the official hierarchy (or rules for that matter) and the unofficial ones." Similarly, new workers were routinely socialized into the subtle art of rulebreaking as approved by the line workers. At my particular work station, it was a fairly common practice for other workers who were covered with beef blood to come over to the tub of swirling water designed to clean the tongues, and as soon as the inspector looked away, wash their hands, arms, and knives in the tub. This procedure was strictly forbidden by the rules. If witnessed by a foreman or inspector, the tub had to be emptied, cleaned, and refilled, and all the tongues in the tub at the time had to be put in the "inedible" tub. All of that would be a time-consuming and costly procedure, yet the workers seemed to absolutely delight in successfully pulling off the act. As Balzer (1976:90) indicates:

> Since a worker often feels that much if not all of what he does is done in places designated by the company, under company control, finding ways to express personal freedom from this institutional regimentation is important.

Thus, artful sabotage served as a symbolic way in which the workers could express a sense of individuality, and hence, self-worth.

THE FINANCIAL TRAP

Given the preceding description and analysis of work at the beef plant, why did people work at such jobs? Obviously, there are a multitude of plausible answers to that question. Without doubt, however, the key is money. The current economic situation, the lack of steady employment opportunities (especially for the untrained and poorly edu-

cated), combined with the fact that the beef plant's starting wage exceeded the minimum wage by approximately $5.50 per hour emerge as the most important reasons people went to work there.

Despite the high hourly wage and fringe benefits, however, the monotony, danger, and hard physical work drove many workers away in less than a week. During my study, I observed much worker turnover. Those who stayed, displayed an interesting pattern which helps explain why they did not leave. Every member of my work crew answered similarly my questions about why they stayed at the beef plant. Each of them took the job directly after high school, because it was the highest paying job available. Each of them had intended to work through the summer and then look for a better job in the fall. During that first summer on the job they fell victim to what I label the "financial trap."

The "financial trap" was a spending pattern which demanded the constant weekly income provided by the beef plant job. This scenario was first told to me by an employee who had worked at the plant for over nine years. He began the week after his high school graduation, intending only to work that summer in order to earn enough money to attend college in the fall. After about four weeks' work he purchased a new car. He figured he could pay off the car that summer and still save enough money for tuition. Shortly after the car purchase, he added a new stereo sound system to his debt; next came a motorcycle; then the decision to postpone school for one year in order to continue working at the beef plant and pay off his debts. A few months later he married; within a year purchased a house; had a child; and bought another new car. Nine years later, he was still working at the beef plant, hated every minute of it, but in his own words "could not afford to quit." His case was not unique. Over and over again, I heard stories about the same process of falling into the "financial trap." The youngest and newest of our crew had just graduated high school and took the job for the summer in order to earn enough money to attend welding school the following fall. During my brief tenure at the beef plant, he purchased a new motorcycle, a new stereo, and a house trailer. When I left, he told me he had decided to postpone welding school for one year in order "to get everything paid for." I saw the financial trap closing in on him fast; he did too.

Besides hearing about it from my fellow crew members, this financial trap was confirmed for me by the nurse who indicated she had heard the same type of stories from literally hundreds of employees at the plant. All intended to work a few months, make some quick money, and leave. However, they developed spending patterns which simply would not allow them to leave. Deferred gratification was obviously not the norm for the "beefers." While not specifically referring to it as such, research by Walker and Guest (1952), Garson (1975), and Shostak (1980) indicate similar financial traps may exist in other types of factory work.

SUMMARY AND CONCLUSIONS

There are at least three interwoven phenomena in this study which deserve further comment and research.

First is the subtle sense of unity which existed among the line workers. Because of excessive noise, the use of earplugs, and the relative isolation of some work areas from others, it was virtually impossible for workers to talk to one another. Despite this, workers developed a very unsophisticated (yet highly complex) system of non-verbal symbols to communicate with one another. Hence, in a setting which would apparently eliminate it, the workers' desire for social interaction won out and interaction flourished. Likewise, the production process was devised in such a way that each task was

somewhat disconnected from all others, and workers had a tendency to concern themselves only with their own jobs. Yet, the line both symbolically and literally linked every job, and consequently every worker, to each other. As described earlier, a system of "uncooperative teamwork" seemed to combine simultaneously a feeling of "one-for-all, all-for-one, and every man for himself." Once a line worker made it past the first three or four days on the job which "weeded out" many new workers, his status as a *beefer* was assured and the sense of unity was felt as much by the worker of nine weeks as it was by the veteran of nine years. Because the workers maintained largely secondary relationships, this feeling of unification is not the same as the unity typically found on athletic teams, in fraternities, or among various primary groups. Yet it was a significant social force which bound the workers together and provided a sense of meaning and worth. Although their occupation might not be highly respected by outsiders, they derived mutual self-respect from their sense of belonging.

A second important phenomenon was the various coping methods employed by workers in a dehumanizing environment to retain their sense of humanity and self-worth. "There are high human costs in dirty work for the person who performs it" (Perry, 1978:6). Either intentionally or inadvertently, the assembly line process utilized at the beef plant tended to reduce the laborers to the level of the machinery with which they worked. On assembly lines, workers are typically regarded as being as interchangeable as the parts of the machines with which they work. As an auto worker put it, "You're just a number to them—they number the stock, and they number you" (Walker and Guest 1952:138). Attempts to maximize efficiency and increase profits demand the sacrifice of human qualities such as uniqueness, creativity, and the feeling of accomplishment and self-worth. Meara (1974) found that one of the sources of honor for the meatcutters in her study was that, despite the fact that their job was viewed as undesirable, it was commonly acknowledged that it was a skilled craft and thus allowed control of their work. As she indicates:

> Occupations provide honorable and dishonorable work. Those who participate in a generally dishonored kind of work have the opportunity to find honor in being able successfully to cope with work which others may define as dirty. Honor is diminished when autonomy in the work is restricted by others in ways not perceived to be inherent in the nature of the work (Meara, 1974:279).

The workers in the beef plant experienced very little autonomy as a result of the assembly line process. Therefore, their sense of honor in their work had to come from other sources.

The beef plant line workers developed and practiced a multitude of techniques for retaining their humanness. Daydreaming, horseplay and occasional sabotage protected their sense of self. Further, the prevailing attitude among workers that it was "us" against "them" served as a reminder that, while the nature of the job might demand subjugation to bosses, machines, and even beef parts, they were still human beings.

Interestingly, the workers' rebellion against management seemed to lack political consciousness. There was no union in the plant, and none of the workers showed any interest in the plant becoming organized. Despite all the problems of working at the plant, the wages were extremely good, so that the income of workers in the plant was high, relative to most of the community. Even the lowest paid line workers earned approximately $20,000 per year. Thus, the high wages and fringe benefits (health insurance, profit-sharing, etc.) seemed to override the negative aspects of the daily work. This stands in stark contrast with research in similar occupations (Garson, 1975; Linhart, 1981).

A third significant finding was that consumer spending patterns among the beefers seemed to "seal their fate" and make leaving the beef plant almost impossible. A reasonable interpretation of the spending patterns of the beefers is that having a high income/low status job encourages a person to consume conspicuously. The prevailing attitude seemed to be "I may not have a nice job, but I have a nice home, a nice car, etc." This conspicuous consumption enabled workers to take indirect pride in their occupations. One of the ways of overcoming drudgery and humiliation on the job was to surround oneself with as many desirable material things as possible off the job. These items (cars, boats, motorcycles, etc.) became tangible rewards for the sacrifices endured at work.

The problem, of course, is that the possession of these expensive items required the continual income of a substantial paycheck which most of these men could only obtain by staying at the beef plant. These spending patterns were further complicated by the fact that they were seemingly "contagious." Workers talked to each other on breaks about recent purchases, thus reinforcing the norm of immediate gratification. A common activity of a group of workers on break or lunch was to run to the parking lot to see a fellow worker's new truck, van, car or motorcycle. Even the seemingly more financially conservative were usually caught up in this activity and often could not wait to display their own latest acquisitions. Ironically, as the workers cursed their jobs, these expensive possessions virtually destroyed any chance of leaving them.

Working at the beef plant was indeed "dirty work." It was monotonous, difficult, dangerous, and demeaning. Despite this, the workers at the beef plant worked hard to fulfill employer expectations in order to obtain financial rewards. Through a variety of symbolic techniques, they managed to overcome the many negative aspects of their work and maintain a sense of self respect about how they earned their living.

NOTES

1. For an excellent overview of this concept of "dirty work" and its impact upon those who perform it, see Hughes, 1971; Braverman, 1974; Meara, 1974 and Perry, 1978.

2. Interestingly, not a single line worker in *Offal* knew what the word meant or stood for (I did not ask the foreman). Workers who had been in *Offal* for as long as twelve years did not know the meaning of the term. Officially pronounced as "Off-all", it was often pronounced by the workers as "awful."

3. The analogies to slavery are not meant to imply that the workers are slaves, the foremen overseers, and the management slaveowners. The laborers voluntarily went to work at the beef plant and were well-compensated financially for having done so. The analogy is used merely to analyze social relations between various work roles.

4. One of the deaths occurred during the second week of my study when a crane operator's skull was crushed between the frame of the crane and a steel support beam.

5. For example, one of the most dangerous jobs in the plant was that of *shackler* who reached down and placed a chain around the back leg of a kicking 2,000 lb. steer only seconds after it had been slaughtered. This worker was constantly being kicked or battered with flying steel chains and hooks. The *shackler* was paid 10¢ per hour more than other workers on the kill floor, because of the extremely dangerous nature of the job.

6. Though I had no mechanism for testing this hypothesis, it seemed plausible. In my opinion the relation between on-the-job accidents and off-the-job events should be studied. Shostak (1980) implies that non-work related problems may relate to stress on the job for blue collar workers.

REFERENCES

Balzer, Richard. 1976, *Clockwork: Life In and Outside an American Factory*. Garden City: Doubleday.

Barlow, Hugh. 1981. *Introduction to Criminology* (2nd ed.). Boston: Little, Brown.

Berger, Peter, Brigitte Berger, and Hansfield Kellner. 1974. *The Homeless Mind: Modernization and Consciousness*. New York: Random House-Vintage Books.

Bookchin, Murray. 1972. "A technology of life." Pp. 247–259 in Theodore Roszak (ed.). *Sources: An Anthology of Contemporary Materials Useful for Preserving Personal Sanity While Braving the Great Technological Wilderness*. New York: Harper and Row.

Braverman, Harry. 1974. *Labor and Monopoly Capital: The Degradation of Work in the Twentieth Century*. New York: Monthly Review Press.

Chinoy, Ely. 1955. *Automobile Workers and the American Dream*. Garden City: Doubleday.

Coleman, John R. 1974. *Blue-Collar Journal: A College President's Sabbatical*. Philadelphia: Lippincott.

Garson, Barbara. 1975. *All the Livelong Day: The Meaning and Demeaning of Routine Work*. Garden City: Doubleday.

Georgakas, Don and Marvin Surkin. 1978. "Niggermation in auto company policy and the rise of black caucuses." Pp. 58–65 in Kenneth Henry (ed.), *Social Problems: Institutional and Interpersonal Perspectives* Glenview, Illinois: Scott, Foresman.

Gold, Raymond. 1958. "Roles in sociological field observations." *Social Forces* 36:217–223.

Hughes, Everett C. 1971. *The Sociological Eye: Selected Papers*. Chicago: Aldine Atherton.

Hummel, Ralph P. 1977. *The Bureaucratic Experience*. New York: St. Martin's Press.

Humphreys, Laud. 1970. *Tearoom Trade: Impersonal Sex in Public Places*. Chicago: Aldine.

King, Rick. 1978. "In the sanding booth at ford." Pp. 199–205 in John and Erna Perry (eds.), *Social Problems in Today's World*. Boston: Little, Brown.

Linhart, Robert (translated by Margaret Crosland). 1981. *The Assembly Line*. Amherst: University of Massachusetts Press.

Marx, Karl. 1964a. *Economic and Philosophical Manuscripts of 1844*. New York: (1844) International Publishing.

_____. 1964b. *The Communist Manifesto*. New York: Washington Square Press (1848).

Mead, George H. 1934. *Mind, Self, and Society*. Chicago: University of Chicago Press.

Meara, Hannah. 1974. "Honor in dirty work: The case of American meatcutters and Turkish butchers." *Sociology of Work and Occupations* 1:259–82.

Osofsky, Gilbert (ed.). 1969. *Puttin' on Ole Massa.* New York: Harper & Row.

Perrow, Charles. 1979. *Complex Organizations: A Critical Essay* (2nd ed.) Glenview, Illinois: Scott, Foresman.

Perry, Stewart F. 1978. *San Francisco Scavengers: Dirty Work and the Pride of Ownership.* Berkeley: University of California Press.

Reimer, Jeffery. 1979. *Hard Hats: The Work World of Construction Workers.* Beverly Hills: Sage.

Roethslinger, F. J. 1941. *Management and Morale.* Cambridge: Harvard University Press.

Schatzman, Leonard and Anselm L. Strauss. 1973. *Field Research.* Englewood Cliffs: Prentice-Hall.

Schutz, Alfred. 1967. *The Phenomenology of the Social World.* Evanston, Illinois: Northwestern University Press.

Shostak, Arthur. 1980. *Blue Collar Stress.* Reading, Mass.: Addison-Wesley.

Spradley, James P. 1979. *The Ethnographic Interview.* New York: Holt, Rinehart, and Winston.

_____. 1980. *Participant Observation.* New York: Holt, Rinehart, and Winston.

Stampp, Kenneth M. 1956. *The Peculiar Institution: Slavery in the Ante-Bellum South.* New York: Random House-Vintage Books.

Stonequist, E. V. 1937. *The Marginal Man.* New York: Scribner.

Terkel, Studs. 1974. *Working: People Talk About What They Do All Day and How They Feel About What They Do.* New York: Pantheon.

Walker, Charles R. and Robert H. Guest. 1952. *The Man on the Assembly Line.* Cambridge: Harvard Press.

36

The Social Construction of Deviance
Experts on Battered Women

DONILEEN R. LOSEKE
SPENCER E. CAHILL

Like previous examinations of wife assault, this article is primarily concerned with the question of why battered women remain in relationships with abusive mates. However, we focus not on the behavior of battered women per se but on the experts who ask this question. The question "Why do they stay?" implicitly defines the parameters of the social problem of battered women. By asking this question, the experts imply that assaulted wives are of two basic types: those who leave their mates and those who do not. Not only are possible distinctions among assaulted wives who remain with their mates implicitly ignored, but so, too, are the unknown number of assaulted wives who quickly terminate such relationships. By focusing attention on those who stay, the experts imply that assaulted wives who remain with their mates are more needy and deserving of public and expert concern than those who do not. In fact, some of the experts have explicitly defined battered women as women who *remain* in relationships containing violence (Ferraro and Johnson, 1983; Pizzey, 1979; Scott, 1974; Walker, 1979).

Moreover, the experts' common and overriding concern with the question of why assaulted wives stay reveals their shared definition of the normatively expected response to the experience of battering. To ask why assaulted wives remain with their mates is to imply that doing so requires explanation. In general, as Scott and Lyman (1968) have noted, normatively expected behavior does not require explanation. It is normatively unanticipated, untoward acts which require what Scott and Lyman term an "account." By asking why battered women stay, therefore, the experts implicitly define leaving one's mate as the normatively expected response to the experience of wife assault. Staying, on the other hand, is implicitly defined as deviant, an act "which is perceived (i.e., recognized) as violating expectations" (Hawkins and Tiedeman, 1975:59).

In other words, once the experts identify a woman as battered, normative expectations regarding marital stability are reversed. After all, separated and divorced persons are commonly called upon to explain why their relationships "didn't work out" (Weiss, 1975). It is typically marital stability, "staying," which is normatively expected and marital instability, "leaving," which requires an account. However, as far as the experts on battered women are concerned, once wife assault occurs, it is marital stability which requires explanation.

In view of the experts' typifications of relationships within which wife assault occurs, this reversal of normative expectations seems only logical. Although research indicates that the severity and frequency of wife assault varies considerably across couples (Straus et al., 1980), the experts stress that, *on the average,* wife assault is more dangerous for victims than is assault by a stranger (U.S.

Department of Justice, 1980). Moreover, most experts maintain that once wife assault has occurred within a relationship, it will become more frequent and severe over time (Dobash and Dobash, 1979), and few believe that this pattern of escalating violence can be broken without terminating the relationship.[1] It is hardly surprising, therefore, that the experts on battered women define "leaving" as the expected, reasonable, and desirable response to the experience of wife assault.[2] Staying, in contrast, is described as "maladaptive choice behavior" (Waites, 1977–78), "self-destruction through inactivity" (Rounsaville, 1978), or, most concisely, "deviant" (Ferraro and Johnson, 1983). For the experts, battered women who remain with their mates pose an intellectual puzzle: Why are they so unreasonable? Why do they stay?

To ask such a question is to request an account. Experts who provide answers to this question are, therefore, offering accounts on behalf of battered women who remain with their mates. According to Scott and Lyman (1968), two general types of accounts are possible: justifications and excuses. A justification is an account which acknowledges the actor's responsibility for the behavior in question but challenges the imputation of deviance ("I did it, but I didn't do anything wrong"). An excuse, on the other hand, acknowledges the deviance of the behavior in question but relieves the actor of responsibility for it ("I did something wrong, but it wasn't my fault").

Clearly, these different types of accounts elicit different kinds of responses. If the behavior in question is socially justifiable, then the actor was behaving reasonably, as normatively expected. The actor's ability or competence to manage everyday affairs without interference is not called into question (Garfinkel, 1967:57). In contrast, excusing behavior implies that the actor cannot manage everyday affairs without interference. Although the behavior is due to circumstances beyond the actor's control, it is admittedly deviant. By implication, assistance from others may be required if the actor is to avoid behaving similarly in the future. In order to fully understand the experts' responses to battered women who remain with their mates, it is necessary, therefore, to determine which type of account they typically offer on behalf of such women.

THE EXPERTS' ACCOUNTS

Experts on battered women are a diverse group. This diversity is reflected in the emphasis each expert places on various accounts, in the number of accounts offered, and in how series of accounts are combined to produce complex theoretical explanations. Despite such diversity, however, there is a sociologically important similarity among the experts' accounts. None of the experts argues that "staying" is justifiable. "Staying" is either explicitly or implicitly defined as unreasonable, normatively unexpected, and, therefore, deviant. By implication, the accounts offered by the experts are excuses for women's deviant behavior, and they offer two basic types.[3] Battered women are said to remain with their mates because of external constraints on their behavior or because of internal constraints. In either case, the accounts offered by the experts acknowledge the deviance of staying but relieve battered women of responsibility for doing so.

External Constraints

Almost all contemporary experts on battered women maintain that staying is excusable due to external constraints on women's behavior (Dobash and Dobash, 1979; Freeman, 1979; Langley and Levy, 1977; Martin, 1976; Pagelow, 1981a,b; Pizzey, 1979; Ridington, 1977–78; Roy, 1977; Shainess, 1977).

Why does she not leave? The answer is simple. If she has children but no money and no place to go, she has no choice. (Fleming, 1979:83)

Clearly, such accounts are based on the assumption that battered women who stay are economically dependent upon their mates. If a woman has no money and no place to go, she cannot be held responsible for the unreasonable act of staying. She has no choice.

Although this excuse is the most prevalent in the literature on battered women, further elaboration is necessary. In its simplest form, such an account can be easily challenged: What about friends, family, the welfare system, and other social service agencies? In response to such challenges, experts must offer accounts which will excuse women for not taking advantage of such assistance. Experts meet these challenges with at least two further accounts of external constraints. First, experts claim that most battered women are interpersonally isolated. Even if they are not, family and friends are said to typically blame women for their problems instead of providing assistance (Carlson, 1977; Dobash and Dobash, 1979; Fleming, 1979; Hilberman and Munson, 1977–78; Truninger, 1971). Second, experts claim that social service agencies typically provide little, if any, assistance. In fact, experts maintain that the organization of agencies (bureaucratic procedures and agency mandates to preserve family stability) and the behavior of agency personnel (sexism) discourage battered women who attempt to leave (Bass and Rice, 1979; Davidson, 1978; Dobash and Dobash, 1979; Higgins, 1978; Martin, 1976, 1978; McShane, 1979; Pizzey, 1979; Prescott and Letko, 1977; Truninger, 1971). In other words, the experts maintain that battered women can expect little assistance in overcoming their economic dependency.

Although the external constraint type of excuse acknowledges that staying is unreasonable, it relieves battered women of the responsibility for doing so. Battered women who remain with their mates are portrayed as "more acted upon than acting" (Sykes and Matza, 1957:667). The implication, of course, is that women would leave (i.e., they would be reasonable) if external constraints could be overcome. The experts provide a warrant, therefore, for intervention in battered women's everyday affairs. In order to act reasonably, and leave, battered women must overcome the external constraint of economic dependency, which they cannot do without the assistance of specialized experts.

Despite the prevalence of external constraint accounts in the literature on battered women, most experts consider such excuses insufficient. Instead of, or in addition to, such accounts, the experts maintain that battered women face a second type of constraint on their behavior.

Internal Constraints

Some experts have proposed that biographically accumulated experiences may lead women to define violence as "normal" and "natural" (Ball, 1977; Gelles, 1976; Langley and Levy, 1977; Lion, 1977). Likewise, according to some experts, women define violence as a problem only if it becomes severe and/or frequent "enough"[4] (Carlson, 1977; Gelles, 1976; Moore, 1979; Rounsaville and Weissman, 1977–78). If violence is not subjectively defined as a "problem," then women have no reason to consider leaving.

For the most part, experts have focused their attention on documenting internal constraints which are said to prevent women from leaving their mate *even when* violence is subjectively defined as a problem. Experts suggest two major sources of such internal constraints: femininity and the experience of victimization.

To many experts, the primary source of internal constraints is the femininity of battered women. Attributes commonly regarded as "feminine" are automatically attributed to battered women, especially when these characteristics can conceivably account for why such women might remain with their mates. For example, women who stay are said to be emotionally dependent upon their mates (Dobash and Dobash, 1979; Fleming, 1979; Freeman, 1979; Langley and Levy, 1977; Moore, 1979; Pizzey, 1979; Roy, 1977); to have a poor self-image or low self-esteem (Carlson, 1977; Freeman, 1979; Langley and Levy, 1977; Lieberknecht, 1978; Martin, 1976; Morgan, 1982; Ridington, 1977–78; Star et al., 1979; Truninger, 1971); and to have traditional ideas about women's "proper place."[5] In isolation or in combination, these so-called feminine characteristics are said to internally constrain women's behavior. According to the experts, women find it subjectively difficult to leave their mates even when violence is defined as a problem.

Internal constraints are also said to follow from the process of victimization itself. According to the experts, battered women not only display typically feminine characteristics, but they also develop unique characteristics due to the victimization process. For example, some experts have argued that once a woman is assaulted she will fear physical reprisal if she leaves (Lieberknecht, 1978; Martin, 1979; Melville, 1978). Other physical, emotional, and psychological after-effects of assault are also said to discourage battered women from leaving their mates (Moore, 1979; Roy, 1977). Indeed, battered women are sometimes said to develop complex psychological problems from their victimization. These include the "stress-response syndrome" (Hilberman, 1980), "enforced restriction of choice" (Waites, 1977–78), "learned helplessness" (Walker, 1979), or responses similar to those of the "rape trauma syndrome" (Hilberman and Munson, 1977–78). A symptom common to all such diagnostic categories is that sufferers find it subjectively difficult to leave their mates.

As with external constraint excuses, these internal constraint accounts also acknowledge the deviance of remaining in a relationship containing violence while, at the same time, relieving battered women of responsibility for doing so. They function in this way, as excuses, because the various internal constraints attributed to battered women are identified as beyond their personal control. Clearly, battered women are not responsible for their gender socialization or for the physical violence they have suffered. In other words, both external and internal constraint accounts portray battered women who stay with their mates as more acted upon than acting. What women require, "for their own good," is assistance in overcoming the various barriers which prevent them from acting reasonably. Thus, both types of accounts offered by the experts on behalf of battered women who stay provide grounds for expert intervention in these women's everyday affairs.

As Scott and Lyman (1968) have pointed out, the criteria in terms of which accounts are evaluated vary in relation to the situation in which they are offered, the characteristics of the audience, and the identity of the account provider. In the present context, the identity of the account provider is of particular interest. Experts who speak on behalf of others are expected to do so on the basis of uncommon knowledge. If, therefore, the evidence which the experts offer in support of their accounts for why battered women stay fails to confirm the expectation of uncommon knowledge, then their claim to be speaking and acting on such women's behalf is open to question.

THE EVIDENCE FOR EXPERTS' ACCOUNTS

How do experts obtain their knowledge about the experiences and behavior of battered women? In order to explore the experts' claim to uncommon knowledge, we address three questions: From whom is evidence obtained (the issue of generalizability)? By what means is evidence obtained (the issue of validity)? How consistently does the evidence support the accounts offered (the issue of reliability)?

Generalizability

Experts on battered women claim to have knowledge of the experiences and behavior of women who remain in relationships containing violence. Yet, while there is general agreement that many battered women suffer in silence, with few exceptions the experts have studied only those assaulted wives who have come to the attention of social service agencies, many of whom have already left their mates.[6] Women who contact social service agencies have decided that they require expert intervention in their private affairs, and there is good reason to believe that such women differ from women who have *not* sought assistance.

The decision to seek professional help is typically preceded by a complex process of problem definition, and this process is invariably more difficult and of longer duration when the problem involves the behavior of a family member (Goffman, 1969; Schwartz, 1957; Weiss, 1975; Yarrow et al., 1955). Only as a last resort are professional helpers contacted (Emerson and Messinger, 1977; Kadushin, 1969; Mechanic, 1975). Since it is primarily the experiences of women who have reached the end of this help-seeking process which provide evidence for experts' accounts, the generalizability of this evidence is questionable.

Validity

When not simply stating their own perceptions of battered women, experts obtain their evidence in one of two ways. They sometimes question other experts, and they sometimes directly question women. Clearly, others' perceptions, whether expert or not,

are of uncertain validity. However, even the evidence based on battered women's responses to the question "Why do you stay?" is of doubtful validity.

To ask a battered woman to respond to this question is to request that she explain her apparently deviant behavior. This leaves her two alternatives. She can either justify her staying ("I love him"; "He's not all bad"; "The kids need him"), or she can excuse her behavior. Since experts have predefined staying as undeniably deviant, it is unlikely that they will honor a justification. Indeed, some experts on battered women have explicitly characterized justifications for staying as "rationalizations," accounts which are self-serving and inaccurate (Ferraro and Johnson, 1983; Waites, 1977–78). Given the experts' presuppositions about the behavior of "staying" and the typical desire of persons to maintain "face" (Goffman, 1955), it is likely that the only accounts the experts will know—excuses—are subtly elicited by the experts who question battered women.[7]

It is hardly surprising, therefore, that the experts on battered women offer remarkably similar accounts of why women stay. This is particularly visible in the evidence which supports the external constraint accounts. By almost exclusively interviewing women who turn to inexpensive or free social service agencies and then constructing an interactional situation which is likely to elicit a particular type of account, experts practically ensure that their presuppositions about external constraints are confirmed.[8] In brief, the validity of the experts' evidence is doubtful.

Reliability

Another important question is whether the evidence the experts obtain through interviewing and observation is consistent with evidence obtained using other methods. For example, if the economic dependency (external constraint) excuse is to avoid challenge, it must be supplemented by the additional excuses of unresponsive friends, family members, and social service agencies. Yet, some evidence undermines the excuse that social service agencies and providers discourage battered women from leaving their mates. Pagelow (1981a) found little relationship between her measures of "agency response" and the amount of time battered women had remained with their mates. Hofeller (1982) found that many battered women self-reported being either "completely" or "somewhat" satisfied with the efforts of social service agencies on their behalf.[9]

As with the excuse of unresponsive social service agencies, available evidence conflicts with various internal constraint accounts offered by the experts. For example, available evidence does not support assertions that battered women hold traditional beliefs about "women's proper place," or that these beliefs internally constrain women from leaving their mates. Walker (1983) reports that battered women perceive themselves to be *less* traditional than "other women," and the results of experimental studies conducted by Hofeller (1982) and Rosenbaum and O'Leary (1981) indicate that women who have *not* been victims of wife assault hold more traditional attitudes than women who are victims. Moreover, Pagelow (1981a) reports that her measures of "traditional ideology" did not help explain the length of time battered women remained with their mates.

The experts have also maintained that the low self-esteem assumed to be common to women in general is exacerbated by the process of victimization, producing a powerful internal constraint on the behavior of battered women. Yet in their now classic review of research evidence regarding sex differences in self-esteem, Maccoby and Jacklin (1974:15) labeled as a popular myth the commonsense deduction that "women, knowing that they belong to a sex that is devalued . . . must have a poor opinion of themselves."

Contrary to this commonsense deduction, sex differences in self-esteem have rarely been found in experimental studies, and when they have, women's self-esteem is often higher than men's. In addition, at least two studies contained in the literature on battered women refute the statement that battered women have lower self-esteem than women who have not experienced assault (Walker, 1983; Star, 1978).

In short, the evidence provided to support expert claims about battered women is, by scientific standards, less than convincing. In fact, it appears as if the experts' accounts are presupposed and then implicitly guide both the gathering and interpretation of evidence. In constructing their accounts, the experts have employed the commonsense practice of automatically attributing to individual women (in this case, battered women) sets of traits based on their sex. As females, battered women are automatically assumed to be economically and emotionally dependent upon their mates, to have low self-esteem, and to hold traditional attitudes and beliefs. Methodologies which might yield conflicting evidence are seldom used, and when seemingly conflicting evidence is uncovered it is often explained away. For example, Walker (1983:40) implicitly argues that battered women have an inaccurate perception of themselves. She interprets the finding that battered women consider themselves to be in control of their own behavior as a "lack of acknowledgment that her batterer *really* is in control" (emphasis added). Likewise, Pagelow (1981a) discredits seemingly conflicting evidence by challenging her own measures; the presupposed accounts are not questioned. In other words, the interpretive force of the "master status" of sex "overpowers" evidence to the contrary (Hughes, 1945:357). What the experts on battered women offer in support of their accounts for why women remain is not uncommon knowledge, therefore, but professional "folklore" which, however sophisticated, remains folklore (Zimmerman and Pollner, 1970:44).

The sociologically intriguing issue is not, however, the "truthfulness" of accounts. In a diverse society, a variety of different vocabularies of motive (Mills, 1940) are available for making sense out of the complex interrelationships between actor, biography, situation, and behavior. Under such circumstances, "What is reason for one man is mere rationalization for another" (Mills, 1940:910). Any attempt to ascertain battered women's "true" motives would therefore be an exercise in what Mills termed "motive-mongering." What is of sociological interest is that the experts' accounts are not based upon uncommon knowledge but upon commonsense deductions best described as folklore. Clearly, this should raise questions about both the experts' claim to be speaking on battered women's behalf and their claim to have the right to intervene in such women's private affairs.

Given the experts' claim to be speaking and acting in battered women's "best interests," the sociologically important issue is the relative plausibility of the particular vocabulary of motive used by the experts. According to the experts, their primary concerns are the condemnation and elimination of wife assault, tasks which are likely to require specialized expertise. The vocabulary of motive which supports this agenda is one of highlighting "constraints" on women's behavior which must be overcome in order for them to behave reasonably—that is, in order for them to leave. But such a vocabulary is not the only plausible way to make sense of women's behavior.

AN ALTERNATIVE
VOCABULARY OF MOTIVE

Prior to the 1970s, the problems of battered women received little attention. In contrast, the contemporary experts have portrayed women as little more than victims. The tendency has been to define both battered women and their relationships with their mates almost exclusively in terms of the occurrence and effects of physical and emotional assault. Battered women are simply defined as assaulted wives who remain with assaultive mates (Ferraro and Johnson, 1983; Pizzey, 1979; Scott, 1974; Walker, 1979), and their relationships are portrayed as no more than victimizing processes. Such a focus leads to what Barry (1979) has termed "victimism," knowing a person only as a victim. One effect of the victimism practiced by the experts on battered women is that possible experiential and behavioral similarities between battered women and other persons are overlooked. However, even a cursory review of the sociological literature on marital stability and instability suggests that, at least in regard to their reluctance to leave their mates, battered women are quite similar both to other women and to men.

This literature consistently indicates that marital stability often outlives marital quality. Goode (1956) found that such stability was only sometimes due to the obvious, objective costs of terminating the relationship ("external constraints"). Contrary to predictions that relationships will terminate when apparent "costs" outweigh apparent "benefits," it is not at all unusual for relationships to be sustained even when outsiders perceive costs to be greater than benefits. Although experts on battered women have argued that leaving a relationship means that a woman's status will change from "wife" to "divorcee" (Dobash and Dobash, 1979; Truninger, 1971), a variety of family sociologists have noted that terminating a relationship is far more complex than is suggested by the concept of "status change." Over time, marital partners develop an "attachment" to one another (Weiss, 1975), a "crescive bond" (Turner, 1970), a "shared biography" (McLain and Weigert, 1979). As a result, each becomes uniquely irreplaceable in the eyes of the other. Such a personal commitment to a specific mate has been found to persist despite decreases in marital partners' liking, admiration, and/or respect for one another (Rosenblatt, 1977; Weiss, 1975). Battered women who remain in relationships which outsiders consider costly are not, therefore, particularly unusual or deviant.

Moreover, the sociological literature on marital stability and instability suggests that the process of separation and divorce, what Vaughan (1979) terms "uncoupling," is typically difficult. One indication of the difficulty of this process is the considerable time uncoupling often takes (Cherlin, 1981; Goode, 1956; Weiss, 1975). It is also typical for a series of temporary separations to precede a permanent separation (Lewis and Spanier, 1979; Weiss, 1975; Vaughan, 1979). In brief, the lengthy "leaving and returning" cycle said to be characteristic of battered women is a typical feature of the uncoupling process. Further, the guilt, concern, regret, bitterness, disappointment, depression, and lowered perception of self attributed to battered women are labels for emotions often reported by women and men in the process of uncoupling (Spanier and Castro, 1979; Weiss, 1975).

Although the experts attribute unusual characteristics and circumstances to battered women who remain with their mates, the reluctance of battered women to leave can be adequately and commonsensically expressed in the lyrics of a popular song: "Breaking up is hard to do." It can also be expressed in the more sophisticated vocabulary of sociological psychology: Individuals who are terminating intimate relationships "die one of the deaths that is possible" for them (Goffman, 1952). The sociological literature on marital stability and instability does suggest, therefore, an alternative to the vocabulary of battered women's motives provided by the experts on battered women. Because a large portion of an adult's self is

typically invested in their relationship with their mate, persons become committed and attached to this mate as a uniquely irreplaceable individual. Despite problems, "internal constraints" are experienced when contemplating the possibility of terminating the relationship with the seemingly irreplaceable other. Again, if this is the case, then women who remain in relationships containing violence are not unusual or deviant; they are typical.

Some experts on battered women have reported evidence which supports this alternative characterization of the motives of women who remain. Gaylord (1975) reports that half of his sample of battered women claimed to be satisfied with their relationships, and Dobash and Dobash (1979) note that, apart from the violence, battered women often express positive feelings toward their mates. Moreover, Ferraro and Johnson (1983) report that battered women typically believe that their mates are the only person they could love, and Walker (1979) reports that battered women often describe their mates as playful, attentive, exciting, sensitive, and affectionate. Yet, because of the victimism they practice, experts on battered women often fail to recognize that such findings demonstrate the multi-dimensionality of battered women's relationships with their mates. Indeed, some of these experts have explicitly advised that battered women's expressions of attachment and commitment to their mates not be believed:

> The statement that abused wives love their husbands need not be taken at face value. It may represent merely a denial of ambivalence or even unmitigated hatred. (Waites, 1977–78:542)
>
> The only reasons the woman does not end the marriage are dependence—emotional or practical—and fear of change and the unknown. These are often masked as love or so the woman deludes herself. (Shainess, 1977:118)

Such expressions of commitment and attachment are *justifications* for why a person might remain with [her] mate. To honor such a justification would be to acknowledge that staying in a relationship which contains violence is not necessarily deviant. In order to sustain their claim to expertise, therefore, the experts on battered women cannot acknowledge the possible validity of this alternative, "justifying" vocabulary of motive even when it is offered by battered women themselves. In other words, the experts discredit battered women's interpretations of their own experiences in order to sustain the claim that such women require their "expert" assistance.

CONCLUSIONS

This case study of the social construction of deviance by a group of experts illustrates how members of the knowledge class create a new clientele for their services. In effect, experts discredit the ability of a category of persons to manage their own affairs without interference. The actors in question are portrayed as incapable of either understanding or controlling the factors which govern their behavior. In order for them to understand their experiences and gain control over their behavior, by implication, they require the assistance of specialized experts. Because the category of actors which compose such a clientele are characterized as unreasonable and incompetent, any resistance they offer to the experts' definitions and intervention is easily discredited. For example, battered women's attempts to justify staying with their mates are often interpreted by the experts as further evidence of such women's unreasonableness and incompetence. Experts are able to sustain their claims to be speaking and acting on others' behalf, therefore, despite the protests of those on whose behalf they claim to be speaking and acting.

We do not mean to suggest that experts' potential clientele do not benefit from

experts' efforts. For example, the experts on battered women have played a major role in focusing public attention on the plight of the victims of wife assault. In doing so, they have helped to dispel the popular myth that these women somehow deserved to be assaulted. In turn, this has undoubtedly encouraged the general public, the police, the courts, and various social service agencies to be more responsive and sensitive to the needs of such women. Yet, battered women may pay a high price for this assistance.

The experts on battered women define leaving one's mate as the normatively expected, reasonable response to the experience of wife assault. By implication, staying with one's mate after such an experience requires explanation. In order to explain this unreasonable response, the experts have provided accounts, that is, ascribed motives to battered women which excuse such deviance. As Blum and McHugh (1971:106) have noted, "observer's ascription of motive serves to formulate . . . persons." In offering accounts on behalf of battered women who stay, the experts propose a formulation of the type of persons such women are. For example, the experts characterize this type of person as "oversocialized into feminine identity" (Ball and Wyman, 1977–78), "bewildered and helpless" (Ball, 1977), "immature" and lacking clear self-identities (Star et al., 1979), "overwhelmingly passive" and unable to act on their own behalf (Hilberman and Munson, 1977–78), and cognitively, emotionally, and motivationally "deficient" (Walker, 1977–78). Moreover, these women are described as suffering from the "battered wife syndrome" (Morgan, 1982; Walker, 1983), and, consequently, they are "society's problem" (Martin, 1978). Clearly, the identity of battered women is a deeply discrediting one.

In summary, once a woman admits that she is a victim of wife assault, her competence is called into question if she does not leave. She is defined as a type of person who requires assistance, a person who is unable to manage her own affairs. As a result, the experts on battered women have constructed a situation where victims of wife assault may lose control over their self-definitions, interpretations of experience, and, in some cases, control over their private affairs. In a sense, battered women may now be victimized twice, first by their mates and then by the experts who claim to speak on their behalf.

NOTES

1. There has been little systematic study of the possibility of change in relationships. Walker (1979) reports that her pessimism is based on clinical experience. See Coleman (1980) for a more optimistic prognosis.
2. Of course, this commonsense deduction is also based on the common, although often unspoken, assumption that humans are "rational actors." If the basis of human motivation is a desire to maximize rewards and minimize costs, then why would a battered woman remain in such an obviously "costly" relationship?
3. A third type of explanation for why victims of wife assault remain with their mates is seldom found in the literature on battered women and, therefore, will not be reviewed here. This type of explanation is based on a systems theory analysis of family interactions. Straus (1974) suggests the empirical applicability of such an approach, and Denzin (1983) provides a phenomenological foundation. Erchak (1981) used this approach to explain the maintenance of child abuse, and Giles-Sims (1983) has used this to explain the behavior of battered women.
4. Empirical testing of the association between leaving and childhood experiences has not confirmed this theory (Pagelow, 1981a; Star, 1978; Walker, 1977–78). Likewise, empirical testing of the association between leaving and "severity/frequency" has also not supported theory. See Pagelow (1981b) for a complete discussion.
5. "Traditional ideology" includes such beliefs as: divorce is a stigma (Dobash and Dobash, 1979; Langley and Levy, 1977; Moore, 1979; Roy, 1977); the children need their father (Dobash and Dobash, 1979); the woman assumes responsibility for the actions of her mate (Fleming, 1979; Lang-

ley and Levy, 1977; Martin, 1976); or feels embarrassed about the family situation (Ball and Wyman, 1977–78; Fleming, 1979; Hendrix et al., 1978).
6. Exceptions are Gelles (1976), Hofeller (1982), and Rosenbaum and O'Leary (1981), who included matched samples of persons not receiving services, and Prescott and Letko (1977), who used information from women who responded to an advertisement in *Ms.* magazine.
7. The situation is more complicated when women who have left are asked why *did* you stay? Or, as Dobash and Dobash (1979:47) asked: "Why do you think you stayed with him as long as you did?" In such situations, the question asks women to retrospectively reconstruct their personal biographies based on their current circumstances and understandings.
8. However, Rounsaville (1978) found that "lack of resources" did not distinguish between women who had left and women who had not left.
9. The "satisfaction" of victims with social services varies considerably by the type of agency (Hofeller, 1982; Prescott and Letko, 1977).

REFERENCES

Ball, Margaret. 1977. "Issues of violence in family casework." *Social Casework* 58(1):3–12.
Ball, Patricia G., and Elizabeth Wyman. 1977–78. "Battered wives and powerlessness: What can counselors do?" *Victimology* 2(3, 4):545–552.
Barry, Kathleen. 1979. *Female Sexual Slavery*. New York: Avon.
Bass, David, and Janet Rice. 1979. "Agency responses to the abused wife." *Social Casework* 60 (June):338–342.
Blum, Alan, and Peter McHugh. 1971. "The social ascription of motives." *American Sociological Review* 36 (February):98–109.
Carlson, Bonnie E. 1977. "Battered women and their assailants." *Social Work* 22 (November):455–460.
Cherlin, Andrew J. 1981. *Marriage, Divorce, Remarriage*. Cambridge, Mass.: Harvard University Press.
Coleman, Karen Howes. 1980. "Conjugal violence: What 33 men report." *Journal of Marital and Family Therapy* 6 (April):207–214.

Davidson, Terry. 1978. *Conjugal Crime*. New York: Hawthorne.

Denzin, Norman K. 1983. "Towards a phenomenology of family violence." Paper presented at the meetings of the American Sociological Association, Detroit, August.

Dobash, R. Emerson, and Russell Dobash. 1979. *Violence Against Wives: A Case Against the Patriarchy*. New York: Free Press.

Emerson, Robert M., and Sheldon L. Messinger. 1977. "The micropolitics of trouble." *Social Problems* 25 (December):121–134.

Erchak, Gerald M. 1981. "The escalation and maintenance of child abuse: A cybernetic model." *Child Abuse and Neglect* 5:153–157.

Ferraro, Kathleen J., and John M. Johnson. 1983. "How women experience battering: The process of victimization." *Social Problems* 30 (February):325–339.

Fleming, Jennifer Baker. 1979. *Stopping Wife Abuse*. Garden City, N.Y.: Anchor.

Freeman, M. D. A. 1979. *Violence in the Home*. Westmead, England: Saxon House.

Garfinkel, Harold. 1967. *Studies in Ethnomethodology*. Englewood Cliffs, N.J.: Prentice-Hall.

Gaylord, J. J. 1975. "Wife battering: A preliminary survey of 100 cases." *British Medical Journal* 1:194–197.

Gelles, Richard J. 1976. "Abused wives: Why do they stay?" *Journal of Marriage and the Family* 38(4):659–668.

Giles-Sims, Jean. 1983. *Wife Battering: A Systems Approach*. New York: Guilford Press.

Goffman, Erving. 1952. "On cooling the mark out: Some aspects of adaptation to failure." *Psychiatry* 15 (November):451–463.

_____. 1955. "On face-work: An analysis of ritual elements in social interaction." *Psychiatry* 18 (August):213–231.

_____. 1969. "Insanity of place." *Psychiatry* 32 (November):352–388.

Goode, William J. 1956. *After Divorce*. Glencoe, Ill.: Free Press.

Hawkins, Richard, and Gary Tiedeman. 1975. *The Creation of Deviance: Interpersonal and Organizational Determinants*. Columbus, Ohio: Charles E. Merrill.

Hendrix, Melva Jo, Gretchen E. Lagodna, and Cynthia A. Bohen. 1978. "The battered wife." *American Journal of Nursing* 78 (April):650–653.

Higgins, John G. 1978. "Social services for abused wives." *Social Casework* 59 (May):266–271.

Hilberman, Elaine. 1980. "Overview: The 'Wife-beater's wife' reconsidered." *American Journal of Psychiatry* 137 (November):1336–1346.

_____, and Kit Munson. 1977–78. "Sixty battered women." *Victimology* 2(3, 4):460–470.

Hofeller, Kathleen H. 1982. *Social, Psychological, and Situational Factors in Wife Abuse*. Palo Alto, Calif.: R. and E. Associates.

Hughes, Everett. 1945. "Dilemmas and contradictions of status." *American Journal of Sociology* 50 (March):353–359.

Kadushin, Charles. 1969. *Why People Go to Psychiatrists*. New York: Atherton.

Langley, Roger, and Richard C. Levy. 1977. *Wife Beating: The Silent Crisis*. New York: Pocket Books.

Lewis, Robert A., and Graham B. Spanier. 1979. "Theorizing about the quality and stability of marriage," pp. 268–294 in Wesley R. Burr, Reuben Hill, F. Ivan Nye, and Ira L. Reiss (eds), *Contemporary Theories About the Family*, Vol. 1. New York: Free Press.

Lieberknecht, Kay. 1978. "Helping the battered wife." *American Journal of Nursing* 78 (April):654–656.

Lion, John R. 1977. "Clinical aspects of wifebattering," pp. 126–136 in Maria Roy (ed.), *Battered Women: A Psychosociological Study of Domestic Violence*. New York: Van Nostrand Reinhold.

MacCoby, Eleanor Emmons, and Carol Nagy Jacklin. 1974 *The Psychology of Sex Differences*. Stanford, Calif.: Stanford University Press.

McLain, Raymond, and Andrew Weigert. 1979. "Toward a phenomenological sociology of family: A programmatic essay," pp. 160–205 in Wesley R. Burr, Reuben Hill, F. Ivan Nye, and Ira L. Reiss (eds.), *Contemporary Theories About the Family*, Vol. 2. New York: Free Press.

McShane, Claudette. 1979. "Community services for battered women." *Social Work* 24 (January):34–39.

Martin, Del. 1976. *Battered Wives*. San Francisco: Glide Publications.

_____. 1978. "Battered women: Society's problem," pp. 111–142 in Jane Roberts Chapman and Margaret Gates (eds.), *The Victimization of Women*. Beverly Hills, Calif.: Sage Publications.

_____. 1979. "What keeps a woman captive in a violent relationship? The social context of battering," pp. 33–58 in Donna M. Moore (ed.), *Battered Women*, Beverly Hills, Calif.: Sage Publications.

Mechanic, David. 1975. "Sociocultural and social psychological factors affecting personal responses to psychological disorder." *Journal of Health and Social Behavior* 16(4):393–404.

Melville, Joy. 1978. "Women in refuges," pp. 293–310 in J. P. Martin (ed.), *Violence and the Family*. New York: John Wiley.

Mills, C. Wright. 1940. "Situated actions and vocabularies of motive." *American Sociological Review* 5 (December):904–913.

Moore, Donna M. 1979. "An overview of the problem," pp. 7–32 in Donna M. Moore (ed.), *Battered Women*. Beverly Hills, Calif.: Sage Publications.

Morgan, Steven M. 1982. *Conjugal Terrorism: A Psychological and Community Treatment Model of Wife Abuse*. Palo Alto, Calif.: R. and E. Associations.

Pagelow, Mildred Dailey. 1981a. *Woman-Battering: Victims and Their Experiences*. Beverly Hills, Calif.: Sage Publications.

_____. 1981b. "Factors affecting women's decisions to leave violent relationships." *Journal of Family Issues* 2 (December): 391–414.

Pizzey, Erin. 1979. "Victimology interview: A refuge for battered women." *Victimology* 4(1):100-112.

Prescott, Suzanne, and Carolyn Letko. 1977. "Battered women: A social psychological perspective," pp. 72–96 in Maria Roy (ed.), *Battered Women: A Psychosociological Study of Domestic Violence* New York: Van Nostrand Reinhold.

Ridington, Jillian. 1977–78. "The transition process: A feminist environment as reconstructive milieu." *Victimology* 2(3, 4):563–575.

Rosenbaum, Alan, and K. Daniel O'Leary. 1981. "Marital violence: Characteristics of abusive couples." *Journal of Consulting and Clinical Psychology* 49(1):63–71.

Rosenblatt, Paul C. 1977. "Needed research on commitment in marriage," pp. 73–86 in George Levinger and Harold L. Raush (eds.), *Close Relationships: Perspectives on the Meaning of Intimacy*. Amherst: University of Massachusetts.

Rounsaville, Bruce J. 1978. "Theories in marital violence: Evidence from a study of battered women." *Victimology* 21(1, 2):11–31.

Rounsaville, Bruce, and Myrna M. Weissman. 1977–78. "Battered women: A medical problem requiring detection." *International Journal of Psychiatry in Medicine* 8(2):191–202.

Roy, Maria. 1977. "A current survey of 150 cases," pp. 25–44 in Maria Roy (ed.). *Battered Women: A Psychosociological Study of Domestic Violence*. New York: Van Nostrand Reinhold.

Schwartz, Charlotte Green. 1957. "Perspectives on deviance: Wives' definitions of their husbands' mental illness." *Psychiatry* 20(3): 275–291.

Scott, Marvin B., and Stanford, M. Lyman. 1968. "Accounts." *American Sociological Review* 33 (December):46–62.

Scott, P. D. 1974. "Battered wives." *British Journal of Psychiatry* 125 (November):433–441.

Shainess, Natalie. 1977. "Psychological aspects of wifebattering," pp. 111–118 in Maria Roy (ed.), *Battered Women: A Psychosociological Study of Domestic Violence*. New York: Van Nostrand Reinhold.

Spanier, Graham, and Robert F. Castro. 1979. "Adjustment to separation and divorce: An analysis of 50 case studies." *Journal of Divorce* 2 (Spring):241–253.

Star, Barbara. 1978. "Comparing battered and non-battered women." *Victimology* 3(1, 2):32–44.

_____, Carol G. Clark, Karen M. Goetz, and Linda O'Malia. 1979. "Psychosocial aspects of wife battering." *Social Casework* 60 (October):479–487.

Straus, Murray A. 1974. "Forward," pp. 13–17 in Richard J. Gelles, *The Violent Home*. Beverly Hills, Calif.: Sage Publications.

_____, Richard J. Gelles, and Suzanne Steinmetz. 1980. *Behind Closed Doors: Violence in the American Home*. Garden City, N.Y.:Anchor.

Sykes, Gresham, and David Matza. 1957. "Techniques of neutralization: A theory of delinquency." *American Sociological Review* 22 (December):664–669.

Truninger, Elizabeth. 1971. "Marital violence: The legal solutions." *Hastings Law Journal* 23 (November):259–276.

Turner, Ralph. 1970. *Family Interaction*. New York: John Wiley.

U.S. Department of Justice. 1980. *Intimate Victims: A Study of Violence Among Friends and Relatives*. Washington, D.C.:U.S. Government Printing Office.

Vaughan, Diane. 1979. "Uncoupling: The process of moving from one lifestyle to another." *Alternative Lifestyles* 2 (November):415–442.

Waites, Elizabeth A. 1977–78. "Female masochism and the enforced restriction of choice." *Victimology* 2(3, 4):535–544.

Walker, Lenore E. 1977–78. "Battered women and learned helplessness." *Victimology* 2(3, 4):525–534.

_____. 1979. *The Battered Woman*. New York: Harper & Row.

_____. 1983. "The battered woman syndrome study," pp. 31–48 in David Finkelhor, Richard J. Gelles, Gerald T. Hotaling, and Murray A. Straus (eds.), *The Dark Side of Families*. Beverly Hills, Calif.: Sage Publications.

Weiss, Robert. 1975. *Marital Separation*. New York: Basic Books.

Yarrow, Marian Radke, Charlotte Green Schwartz, Harriet S. Murphy, and Leila Calhoun Desy. 1955. "The psychological meaning of mental illness in the family." *Journal of Social Issues* 11(4):12–24.

Zimmerman, Don, and Melvin Pollner. 1970. "The everyday world as a phenomenon," pp. 80–104 in Jack Douglas (ed.), *Understanding Everyday Life*. Chicago: Aldine.

37

Towards a Sociological Understanding of Psychoanalysis

PETER L. BERGER

Psychoanalysis has become a part of the American scene. It is taken for granted in a way probably unparalleled anywhere else in the world. This can be asserted without hesitation even if one means psychoanalysis in its narrower, proper sense, that is, as a form of psychotherapy practiced both within and beyond the medical establishment. But psychoanalysis in this narrower sense constitutes only the institutional core of a much broader phenomenon. Within this core we find the highly organized structures of psychoanalytically oriented psychiatry, with its networks of hospitals, research agencies and training centers, the various psychoanalytic associations (both those which deny and those which admit nonmedical practice), and wide sectors of clinical psychology. The prestige and privilege of this institutional complex in American are already a remarkable matter, not least for the sociologist. Yet, if we take psychoanalysis in a more general sense, that is, as an assortment of ideas and activities derived in one way or another from the Freudian revolution in psychology, then we find ourselves confronted in this country with a social phenomenon of truly astounding scope.[1]

Surrounding the institutional core of psychoanalysis there is a ring of satellite organizations and activities that may be called, loosely, the counseling and testing complex. Here we find entire professions, young in age and quite peculiar to this country, the most important among them being social casework, which only in America has taken on the character of psychotherapeutic activity.[2] The counseling and testing complex, increasingly professionalized in its staff, extends into large areas of the total institutional structure of the society, its heaviest sedimentation being in the areas of welfare organization, both public and private, education, and personnel administration.[3] Yet even this much more extended perspective by no means exhausts our phenomenon. For we are not dealing only, or even primarily, with institutions and organizations. More importantly, psychoanalysis has become a cultural phenomenon, a way of understanding the nature of man and an ordering of human experience on the basis of this understanding. Psychoanalysis has given birth to a psychological model that has influenced society far beyond its own institutional core and the latter's fringe. American law, especially in such new branches as juvenile and domestic relations courts, but by no means only there, is increasingly permeated with psychoanalytically derived conceptions.[4] American religion, both in its thought and in its institutional activities, has been deeply influenced by the same psychological model.[5] American literature, both "high" and "low," would be unthinkable today without it. The media of mass communication are filled with materials derived from the same source. Most importantly, everyday life, as expressed in the common speech, has been invaded by the terminology and interpretative schemes of psychoanalysis. Terms such as "repression," "frustration," "needs" and "rationalization," not to mention the key concept of "unconscious," have become matter-of-course expressions in broad strata of the population. While we cannot be sure how far this linguistic usage is merely rhetorical and how far it has actually influenced the conduct it purports to describe, we are probably on safe ground if we assume that at least three areas of everyday life have been significantly affected by psychoanalytically derived ideas—sexuality, marriage and child-rearing. Both the so-called sexual revolution and the so-called family renascence in America have been accompanied by a flood of psychoanalytically inspired interpretations, which, by the nature of such processes, have increasingly become self-interpretations of those engaged in these activities. If we accept Robert Musil's observation that ninety per cent of human sex life consists of talk, then we may add that in America this has become more and more Freudian talk. And if we may believe John Rechy's novel, *City of Night,* even the young male prostitutes on Times Square worry about their narcissism.

A phenomenon of such magnitude becomes part of what Alfred Schutz has called the world-taken-for-granted, that is, it belongs to those assertions about the nature of reality that every sane person in a society believes as a matter of course. Only a madman would have denied the existence in medieval Europe of demoniacal possession; demoniacal possession was a self-evident fact of everyday life. Today, only a madman would assert this once self-evident fact as against, say, the germ theory of disease. Sane people in our society take the germ theory of disease for granted and act accordingly, although, naturally, most of them have to defer to experts for proof of this theory. It would seem that a number of root assertions of psychoanalysis have come to be taken for granted in a similar way. Thus, the question-

ing of the existence of the unconscious in a gathering of college-educated Americans is likely to be as much a self-certification of derangement as would be the questioning of the germ theory of disease. Insofar as college-educated Americans interpret themselves, they know themselves to be equipped with an unconscious as a sure fact of experience and, what is more, they also have quite specific notions as to how this appendage is furnished. For example, they are predisposed to admit the existence of unconscious guilt and to anticipate its eventual eruption. And only in America could James Baldwin have converted this predisposition into a political strategy.

Sociology, like psychoanalysis, occupies a fairly unique position in the American cultural situation. There is probably a common reason behind the cultural prominence of these two disciplines of collective introspection. Be this as it may, it would be very surprising if they had not influenced each other. As we know, the mutual influence has been massive.[6] There has been a strong sociological undercurrent in the development of psychoanalytic theory in this country, especially in the neo-Freudian schools, which have transformed the gloomy vision of the great Viennese pessimist into a bright, uplift and social-engineering-oriented program of secularized Methodism. The influence in the other direction has been no less remarkable, although American sociology is still probably less influenced by psychoanalytic theory than its sister discipline, cultural anthropology. What is very interesting, however, is the range of this theoretical acculturation within the field of sociology. Although individual sociologists differ in their views concerning the feasibility of integrating psychoanalytic ideas with sociological theory, those who have a strongly positive opinion pretty much cover the spectrum of contemporary positions in the field. Thus Talcott Parsons, who has gone very far in incorporating psychoanalytic conceptions within his sociological system, shares this predilection with some of his sharpest critics.[7] Whatever else may be in dispute between the currently dominant structural-functional school and its antagonists, the propriety of the sociological employment of psychoanalysis is not. Those sociologists who have kept aloof from psychoanalysis, for instance those who prefer to draw upon George Herbert Mead rather than Freud for the psychological underpinnings of their sociological work, have generally done so without directly questioning the validity of the interdisciplinary intermarriage.

If one is married, one may describe precisely this or that facet of the marriage partner's conduct, but the apprehension of the latter's total *gestalt* becomes ever more difficult. A similar difficulty of perception has been the result of the American liaison between psychoanalysis and sociology. Thus we have excellent analyses by sociologists of specific, partial aspects of the psychoanalytic phenomenon. There is a whole literature which concerns itself with various social dimensions of the psychotherapeutic enterprise. There are studies of the social distribution of various psychiatrically relevant conditions, intensive analyses of the social structure of the mental hospital (these investigations now adding up to a sort of sub-discipline within the sub-discipline of medical sociology), studies of attitudes towards various psychotherapeutic procedures in different social strata, and studies of the social processes going on in the course of psychotherapy.[8] In recent years much of this work has been generously subsidized by the National Institute of Mental Health, as well as by private foundations. Far be it from us to disparage these studies, which have greatly enriched our knowledge of many facets of the phenomenon and in some cases have yielded insights of much wider theoretical import (as, for example, the work of August Hollingshead and Erving Goffman).[9] All the same, there remains an enormous gap when it comes to the sociological analysis of the phenomenon as a whole. Three recent attempts at such analysis which have achieved a measure of comprehensiveness are Richard LaPiere's *The Freudian Ethic*, Eric Larrabee's *The Self-Conscious Society* and Philip Rieff's *Freud—The Mind of the Moralist*.[10] LaPiere's work is burdened with a heavy political bias (because the author looks upon Freudianism as some sort of socialistic subversion of American free enterprise—hardly a helpful suggestion), Larrabee's does not go much beyond description, and Rieff's is in the main an exegetical enterprise, with some general observations on what its author calls "the emergence of psychological man" in the concluding chapter.

Obviously, the present paper cannot even begin to fill this gap. What is does attempt, however, is to outline some of the presuppositions for the needed task of sociological analysis and to venture some very tentative hypotheses on the possible results of such an analysis. The first presuppositions are negative. It goes without saying that a sociological analysis will have to bracket, or avoid passing scientific judgment on, the practical utility of the various psychotherapeutic activities. The sociologist, qua sociologist, can be of no assistance to distressed individuals hesitating before the multiplicity of healing cults available on the market today, just as he can be of no assistance in the choice of the many religious or quasi-religious *Weltanschauungen* which are engaged in pluralistic competition in our society. In addition, a sociological analysis of our phenomenon will have to bracket the question of the scientific validity of the psychological model under scrutiny. This might be a task for sociological theory or social psychology, but it is an unnecessary burden for the study of the empirical phenomenon itself. The sociologist, qua sociologist, need not serve as arbiter among competing psychologies, just as, to return to the previous analogy, the sociologist of religion does not have to concern himself with the question of whether God exists. It should be strongly emphasized that this bracketing can occur even if the sociologist believes, as most American sociologists evidently do, that the psychoanalytic understanding of man is somehow true. Ideas do not succeed in history by virtue of their truth but by virtue of their relationship to specific social processes. This, as it were, root platitude of the sociology of knowledge makes it imperative that a phenomenon such as ours be investigated in an attitude of rigid abstinence from epistemological judgments about it.

The most important positive presupposition for such a sociological analysis is that it proceed within a frame of reference that is itself sociological. This means that sociological modes of analysis must be pushed to their own intrinsic limits and not be blocked by limits stipulated by another discipline. This procedure excludes the common practice of American sociologists of conceding extraterritorial preserves to the psychologists within the sociological universe of discourse (a courtesy, by the way, rarely reciprocated by the psychologists). Whatever may be the methodological merits of other disciplines, the sociologist cannot allow the scope of his work to be dictated by the latter. Thus, in different areas of investigation, the sociologist cannot allow the jurist or the theologian to put up "no trespassing" signs on territory that, by the rules of his own game, is legitimate sociological hunting ground. In terms of the phenomenon that interests us here, the sociologist cannot concede to the psychologist exclusive rights to that vast area we commonly call psychological. It was precisely the great achievement of George Herbert Mead to show how the sociologist may enter this area without abandoning the presuppositions of his own discipline.

This is hardly the place to argue in what sense a sociological psychology may be constructed on the basis of Mead's work. Two crucial propositions of a sociological approach to psychological phenomena must, however, be explicated (in this context, of necessity, in an abbreviated and axiomatic fashion). The first proposition asserts that there is a dialectical relationship between social structure and psychological reality, the second that there is, similarly, a dialectical relationship between psychological reality and any prevailing psychological model. It must be emphasized that, in either proposition, psychological reality does not mean some givenness that may be uncovered or verified by scientific procedures of one kind or another. Psychological reality means the way in which human beings in a specific situation subjectively experience themselves. The dialectical relationship between psychological reality, in this sense, and social structure is already implied in the fundamental Meadian theory of the social genesis of the self. A particular social structure generates certain socialization processes that, in their turn, serve to shape certain socially recognized identities, with whatever psychological configuration (cognitive and emotive) appertains to each of these identities. In other words, society not only defines but shapes psychological reality. Just as a given psychological reality originates in specific social processes of identity production, so the continued existence and subjective plausibility of such a psychological reality depend upon specific social processes of identity confirmation. Self and society, as Mead understood, are inextricably interwoven entities. The relationship between the two, however, is a dialectical rather than a mechanistic one, because the self, once formed, is ready in its turn to react upon the society that shaped it. This understanding, which we would regard as fundamental to a sociological psychology, provides the sociologist with his logical starting point in the investigation of any psychological phenomenon—to wit, the analysis of the social structures of the situation in question.

The second proposition concerns the relationship of this psychological reality with whatever theories have been concocted to explain it. Since human beings are apparently destined not only to experience but also to explain themselves, we may assume that every society provides a psychological model (in some cases possibly more than one) precisely for this purpose of self-explanation. Such a psychological model may take any number of forms, from highly differentiated intellectual constructions to primitive myths. And once more we have here a dialectical relationship. The psychological reality produces the psychological model, insofar as the latter is an empirical description of the former. But the psychological reality is in turn produced by the psychological model, because the latter not only describes but defines the former, in that creative sense of definition intended in W. I. Thomas' famous statement that a situation defined as real in a society will be real in its consequences, that is, will become reality as subjectively experienced by the members of that society. Although we have jumped many steps of argumentation here, it may be clear that our second proposition follows of necessity from our first; both propositions spring from the same underlying understanding of the structuring of consciousness as a social process. As far as the second proposition, an important one for our phenomenon, is concerned, it may at least partially be paraphrased by saying that psychological models operate in society as self-fulfilling prophecies.

The phenomenon that interests us here is a particular psychological model, acculturated and institutionalized in American society in particular ways. The sociological analysis must then revolve around the question of what social structures, with their appropriate psychological realities, this particular psychological model corresponds to (or, if one wishes to use a Weberian term, with what social structures this model may

have an elective affinity). Before we turn to some hypothetical reflections on this question, however, it will be advisable to clarify the character of the psychological model a little further. Now, it must be emphasized very strongly that in the characterization to follow it is not our intention to reduce the various psychoanalytic theories to some sort of common denominator. Indeed, at this point we are not primarily interested in theories at all, but in the much broader socio-cultural configuration outlined in our opening remarks, a configuration that has its historical origin and its theoretical as well as institutional core in the psychoanalytical movement, but which is no longer co-extensive with this movement. The following, then, is an attempt to isolate some key propositions of a psychological model operative in the taken-for-granted world of everyday life in our society, a phenomenon that (perhaps *faute de mieux*) we would designate as psychologism: [11]

Only a relatively small segment of the total self is present to consciousness. The unconscious is the matrix of decisive mental processes. The conscious self is moved out of these unknown depths into actions the true meaning of which it does not understand. Men are typically ignorant of their own motives and incapable of interpreting their own symbolizations. Specific and scientifically verifiable hermeneutic procedures have to be applied for such interpretation. Sexuality is a key area of human conduct. Childhood is the key phase of human biography. The ongoing activity of the self may be understood in terms of the operation of scientifically ascertainable mechanisms, of which the two most important are repression and projection. Culture may be understood as the scene of interaction between unconscious motor forces and consciously established norms.

What structural developments have a bearing on the success of this psychological model in our society? In the argument to follow we are strongly indebted to Arnold

Gehlen's and Thomas Luckmann's contributions to a social psychology of industrial society. [12]

The fundamental structurizing force in modern society is industrialization. In rationalizing and fragmenting the processes of production industrialization has autonomized the economic area of the institutional fabric. This autonomous economic area has then become progressively segregated from the political institutions on the one hand and from the family on the other. The former segregation does not concern us here. The segregation between the economic complex and the family, however, is very relevant for our considerations, for it is closely connected with the emergence of a quite novel social phenomenon—the sphere of the private. A modern industrial society permits the differentiation between public and private institutional spheres. What is essential for the psychological reality of such a society is that its members experience this dichotomization as a fundamental ordering principle of their everyday life. Identity itself then tends to be dichotomized, at the very least, in terms of a public and a private self. Identity, in this situation, is typically uncertain and unstable. In other words, the psychological concomitant of the structural patterns of industrial society is the widely recognized phenomenon of identity crisis. Or in even simpler words, individuals in this sort of society do not know for certain who they are, or more accurately, do not know to which of a number of selves which they experience they should assign priority status. Some individuals solve the problem by identifying themselves primarily in terms of their public selves. This solution, however, can be attractive only to those whose roles in the public sphere (usually this means occupational roles) allow such identification in the first place. Thus one might perhaps decide that one's real self is identical with one's role as a top business executive or as some kind of professional. This option is not very se-

ductive for the great masses of people in the middle and lower echelons of the occupational system. The typical option for them has been to assign priority to their private selves, that is, to locate the "real me" in the private sphere of life. Thus an individual may say, "Don't judge me by what I do here—on Madison Avenue I only play a role—but come home with me to Darien and I'll show you who I *really* am."

This privatization of identity has its ideological dimension and its psychological difficulties. If the "real me" is to be located in the private sphere, then the activities of this sphere must be legitimated as decisive occasions for self-discovery. This legitimation is provided by interpreting sexuality and its solemnization in the family as precisely the crucial tests for the discovery (we would say, the definition) of identity. Expressions of this are the ideologies of sexualism and familism in our society, ideologies that are sometimes in competition (say, *Playboy* magazine against the *Ladies' Home Journal*) and sometimes merge into synthesis (the sensible-sex-for-young-couples constellation). The psychological difficulties stem from the innate paucity of firm social controls in the private sphere. The individual seeking to discover his supposedly real self in the private sphere must do so with only tenuous and (in terms of his total life) limited identity-confirming processes to assist him. There appears then the need for identity-maintenance agencies in the private sphere. The family is, of course, the principal agency for the definition and maintenance of private identity. However, for many reasons that cannot be developed here, the family alone is insufficient. Other social formations must fill this gap. These are the agencies designed to meet the psychological needs of the identity market. Variously organized, some of these agencies are old institutions transformed to fulfill new functions, such as the churches, while others are institutional novelties, such as the psychotherapeutic organizations that interest us here. All reflect the over-all character of the private identity market, that of a social sphere poor in control mechanisms (at least as compared with the sphere of public institutions) and permissive of a considerable measure of individual liberty. The various identity-marketing agencies thus tend to be voluntary, competitive and consumer-oriented, at least insofar as their activity is restricted to the private sphere.

If we now turn briefly to the public sphere, with its central economic and political institutions, we are confronted with yet another structural consequence of industrialization—the prevalence of bureaucratic forms of administration. As Max Weber showed long ago, bureaucracy is one of the main results of the profound rationalizations of society necessitated by modern industrial capitalism. Bureaucracy, however, is much more than a form of social organization. Bureaucracy also entails specific modes of human interaction. Broadly speaking, one may say that bureaucracy tends to control by manipulative skill rather than by outright coercion. The bureaucrat is thus not only a sociological but also a psychological type. The psychological reality brought about by bureaucratically administered institutions has been studied by a good number of recent sociologists, the concepts of some of them having actually gained broad popular familiarity; we need only mention David Riesman's "other-directed character" and William Whyte's "organization man" by way of illustration.

With this excursus of sociologizing behind us it is not difficult to return to the phenomenon that concerns us here. In view of the structural configuration and its psychological concomitants just outlined one would like to say, "If Freud had not existed, he would have had to be invented." Institutionalized psychologism, as derived directly or indirectly from the psychoanalytic movement, constitutes an admirably designed response to the needs of this particular socio-historical situation. Unlike some other social entities involved in the modern identity crisis (such as the churches on the one hand and political fanaticisms on the other), institutionalized psychologism straddles the dividing line between the public and private spheres, thus occupying an unusually strategic position in our society. In the private sphere, it appears as one of the agencies supplying a population of anxious consumers with a variety of services for the construction, maintenance and repair of identities. In the public sphere, it lends itself with equal success to the different economic and political bureaucracies in need of non-violent techniques of social control. The same psychological practitioner (psychiatrist, clinical psychologist, psychiatric social worker, or what-have-you) can in one role assist the privatized suburbanite in the interior decorating of his sophisticated psyche, and in another role assist him (let us assume that he is an industrial relations director) in dealing more effectively with actual or potential troublemakers in the organization. If one may put it this way, institutionalized psychologism is in a probably unique position to commute along with its clientele. It is capable of doing just what institutionalized religion would like to do and is increasingly unable to do—to accompany the individual in both sectors of his dichotomized life. Thus the symbols of psychologism become overarching collective representations in a truly Durkheimian sense—and that in a cultural context singularly impoverished when it comes to such integrating symbols.

Sociological analysis, however, can penetrate even further into the phenomenon, to wit, it can clarify the social roots of the psychological model itself. Thus we can now go back to our characterization of this model and ask how its central themes relate to the social situation in which the model has been so eminently successful. We would suggest, first of all, that a psychological model that has as its crucial concept a notion of the unconscious may be related to a social situation in which there is such complexity in the fabric of roles and institutions that the individual is no longer capable of perceiving his society in its totality. In other words, we would argue that the opaqueness of the psychological model reflects the opaqueness of the social structure as a whole. The individual in modern society is typically acting and being acted upon in situations the motor forces of which are incomprehensible to him. The lack of intelligibility of the decisive economic processes is paradigmatic in this connection. Society confronts the individual as mysterious power, or in other words, the individual is unconscious of the fundamental forces that shape his life. One's own and the others' motives, meanings and identities, insofar as they are comprehensible, appear as a narrow foreground of translucency, the background of which is provided by the massive structures of a social world that is opaque, immensely powerful and potentially sinister. The interpretation of one's own being in terms of the largely submerged Freudian iceberg is thus subjectively verified by one's ongoing experience of a society with these characteristics.

As the crucial psychologistic concept of the unconscious fits the social situation, so do the other themes used in our previous characterization of the model. The theme of sexuality fits the requirements of the social situation in which the essential self is located in the private sphere. In consequence, the identity-defining functions of contemporary sexual myths are legitimated by psychologism on various levels of intellectual sophistication. Again, the theme of childhood serves to establish the primacy of the private sphere in the hierarchy of self-definitions. This theme has been particularly significant in the psychologistic legitimation of contemporary familism, and ideology that interprets the family as the most "healthy" locale of identity affirmation. The understanding of the self as an assemblage of psychological mechanisms allows the individual to deal with himself with the same technical, calculating and "objective" attitude that is the attitude *par excellence* of industrial production. Indeed, the term "productivity" has easily found its way from the language of the engineer to that of the psychologist. In consequence, psychologism furnishes the (*nota bene*) "scientific" legitimation of both inter- and intra-personal manipulation. Furthermore, the interpretation of culture as a drama between individual "needs" and social realities is a fairly accurate reflection of the ongoing balancing act between "fulfillment" and "frustration" in the everyday life of individuals in a high-level consumers' society. In consequence, psychologism again provides a "scientific" legitimation to the adjustment technology without which such a society could hardly get along.

Finally, psychologism provides a peculiar combination of soberness and fantasy that would seem to correspond to profound aspirations of people living in a highly rationalized society. On the one hand, psychologism presents itself as a science and as a technique of rational control. On the other hand, however, psychologism makes possible once more the ancient fascination with mystery and magic. Indeed, one is tempted to speak here of a form of neo-mysticism. Once more the true self is to be discovered through a descent into the presumed depths of one's own being, and, even if the ultimate discovery is not that of the divine (at least not anywhere this side of Jungianism), it still has the old flavor of the *numinous*. Psychologism thus brings about a strange reversal of the disenchantment and demythologization of modern consciousness. The other world, which religion located in a transcendental reality, is now introjected within human consciousness itself. It becomes that other self (the more real, or the healthier, or the more mature self, or however it may be called by the different schools) which is the goal of the psychologistic quest.

Our considerations here have had to be distressingly abbreviated. And, we would emphasize once more, our argument has been tentative and hypothetical in its intention. Hopefully, though, we have been able to indicate the scope of the analytic task to be undertaken. Thomas Szasz, in his recent study of psychiatric influences on American law, has spoken of the emergence of the "therapeutic state." It may well be that the latter is but one aspect of the emergence of a "psychological society." It is all the more important that the full weight of sociological understanding be brought to bear on this monumental phenomenon.

NOTES

1. *Cf.* George Wilbur and Werner Muensterberger (eds.), *Psychoanalysis and Culture* (New York: International Universities Press, 1951); Benjamin Nelson (ed.), *Freud and the 20th Century* (New York: Meridian Books, 1957); John Sutherland (ed.), *Psychoanalysis and Contemporary Thought* (New York: Grove Press, 1959); C. P. Oberndorf, *A History of Psychoanalysis in America* (New York: Harper and Row, 1964).

2. *Cf.* Gordon Hamilton, *Theory and Practice of Social Case Work* (New York: Columbia University Press, 1940).

3. *Cf.* Martin Gross, *The Brain Watchers* (New York: New American Library, 1963).

4. *Cf.* Thomas Szasz, *Law, Liberty and Psychiatry* (New York: The Macmillan Co., 1963).

5. *Cf.* Samuel Klausner, *Psychiatry and Religion* (New York: Free Press, 1964).

6. Hendrik Ruitenbeek (ed.), *Psychoanalysis and Social Science* (New York: Dutton and Co., 1962),

particularly the articles by Talcott Parsons and John Seeley.

7. *Cf.*, for example, the treatment of the relationship between society and personality in Talcott Parsons, *The Social System* (Glencoe, Ill.: Free Press, 1951), with that in Maurice Stein *et al.* (eds.), *Identity and Anxiety* (Glencoe, Ill: Free Press, 1960).

8. *Cf.*, as examples of these, William Rushing, *The Psychiatric Professions* (Chapel Hill: University of North Carolina Press, 1964); John Seeley *et al.*, *Crestwood Heights* (New York: Basic Books, 1956); J. L. Moreno (ed.), *Group Psychotherapy* (New York: Beacon Press, 1945).

9. August Hollingshead and Frederick Redlich, *Social Class and Mental Illness* (New York: Wiley, 1958); Erving Goffman, *Asylums* (Garden City, N.Y.: Doubleday-Anchor Books, 1961), and *Stigma* (Englewood Cliffs, N.J.: Prentice-Hall, 1963).

10. Richard LaPiere, *The Freudian Ethic* (New York: Duell, Sloan & Pearce, Inc., 1959); Eric Larrabee, *The Self-Conscious Society* (Garden City, N.Y.: Doubleday, 1960); Philip Rieff, *Freud—The Mind of the Moralist* (Garden City, N.Y.: Doubleday-Anchor Books 1961). For a European study of the diffusion of psychoanalysis, *cf.* Serge Moscovici, *La psychoanalyse—son image et son public* (Paris: Presses Universitaires de France, 1961).

11. The authors of a sociological study of religious best sellers have suggested "mentalism" for roughly the same complex of phenomena in the area of popular culture, but this is at least as ambiguous a term as "psychologism." *Cf.* Louis Schneider and Sanford Dornbush, *Popular Religion* (Chicago: University of Chicago Press, 1958).

12. *Cf.* Arnold Gehlen, *Die Seele im technischen Zeitalter* (Hamburg: Rowohlt, 1957); Thomas Luckmann, *Das Problem der Religion in der modernen Geselschaft* (Freiburg: Rombach, 1963).

38

Psychological Modernity

ARTHUR G. NEAL

Basic human concerns have special meanings within the context of modern society. A sense of social purpose, a sense of personal control, and a sense of belonging increasingly depend on deliberate choices and rational decisions. Traditions as blueprints for behavior have been weakened with industrial and technological developments, and new forms of freedom have emerged. If we knew who we were collectively and if we knew where we headed historically, the study of social psychology would be less necessary than it now is. We no longer have a society in which the places of individuals in the broader scheme of social affairs are clear and definite. The stability of social ties that characterized our historical past has been broken, and increases in our freedom of movement have increasingly uprooted us. The result is greater psychological dependence on our individual resources in times of trouble.

Psychological modernity refers to modern forms of consciousness (Berger, Berger, and Kellner, 1973). The concept is not the same as the older idea of social change as progress, or the notion of being up to date. We have no clear gauges for measuring progress; determining what is up to date and hence appropriate is largely a matter of opinion. When we speak of psychological modernity we are referring primarily to the states of mind that have developed in response to contemporary historical circumstances. The growth of cities, the magnitude of bureaucracies, and the pervasiveness of technological environ-ments are among the frameworks of modern social life.

The time dimension of psychological modernity is reflected in knowing how we got to where we are now, knowing where we are now, and knowing where we are going. Coping with the changing conditions of our society, responding to the changes occurring within ourselves, and elaborating on the meaning of social events are among the many aspects of modern awareness. In effect, modernity is the stage or the social setting in which we enact the drama of freedom and control as we seek to invent our futures.

FREEDOM AND CONTROL

An emphasis on the voluntaristic element in human conduct is clearly evident in the research of psychologists and sociologists. A great deal of research has been directed toward studies of selective perception, decision making, interpersonal attraction, and the formation of commitments. Clearly people do make many kinds of choices in everyday life; yet the concept of freedom is largely missing from the vocabulary of social psychologists. On purely philosophical grounds, convincing arguments could be made for freedom as an illusion. But from the standpoint of human experiences, people are free if they think they are free, or, correspondingly, freedom is lacking if people feel that they are deprived or that they are prevented from doing the kinds of things they want to do.

George Hillery and his associates (1971; 1977; 1979) have investigated empirically several aspects of freedom in the experiences of individuals. The primary contribution of their research findings has been to clarify the major forms of freedom by making the distinction between the individual and society and the distinction between personal choices and social constraints. The three main types of freedom to emerge from these research studies are personal freedom, conditional freedom, and disciplined freedom. The forms of freedom are expressed in the perceived options available, the perceived capacities for making choices, and the willingness to make personal sacrifices for attaining what one wants.

Personal freedom is the most unencumbered of all the forms of freedom. It exists under those conditions in which individuals feel free to do what they want to do without any limitations or constraints. Freedom in such cases permits spontaneous behavior and is more likely to be found within the spheres of privacy than within other areas of life (Schwartz, 1968). In many respects personal freedoms are the residuals of social living: they constitute the options that remain after obligations have been fulfilled. The sense of personal freedom frequently reaches its highest level of intensity under those circumstances in which individuals are released from a heavy set of social commitments. The weekend pass for the enlisted soldier during the course of basic training, the time for college students following final exams, and the vacation for the factory worker who does not enjoy his or her job are among the situations sometimes promoting an exhilarating sense of freedom. The popularity of the TGIF (Thank God It's Friday) parties in our society perhaps reflects the lack of intrinsic rewards for many people in the activities of everyday life. . . .

Conditional freedom stems from group processes and "refers to the notion that other people or things are important in determining the manner in which an individual lives" (Hillery, Dudley, and Morrow, 1977:694). This form of freedom is conditioned by many circumstances—by the people in the individuals' life, by the limits of social resources, and by the perceived capacities of individuals to act in accordance with their wishes. All social groups impose restrictions on their members by setting limits on the range of behavior that they will tolerate or consider appropriate. For example, if you are living in a college dormitory, your own freedoms are likely to be limited by your roommate and by the need to negotiate for the use of physical space. Living in a college dormitory, in a military barrack, or in a commune makes certain options available while precluding others. Being married, working for a corporation, or belonging to a church permits the pursuit of certain valued goals and objectives while preventing the pursuit of certain others. Social life involves making compromises; conditional forms of freedom require aligning personal goals and interests with the objectives of social groups and the rules for regulating conduct. Nearly all social groups provide some latitude for their members while at the same time setting up boundaries around the range of permitted behavior.

The third form of freedom to emerge from the research of Hillery and his associates is *disciplined freedom*. This refers to the willingness of individuals to make sacrifices to attain some desired goal. Getting what we want out of life involves sharing and sacrificing. We make concessions to others and invest personal resources in the attainment of group goals.

The disciplined form of freedom is reflected in personal commitments, in dedication to social causes, and in linkages of self-fulfillment with group accomplishments. The disciplined form of freedom as noted by Hillery in his studies of monasteries, communes, and cooperatives bears an affinity to the earlier observations made by

Emile Durkheim (1951) on altruistic suicide. ... In extreme cases individuals may seek self-fulfillment through voluntarily sacrificing their lives for a social cause. A well-known historical example is the Japanese Kamikaze fliers of World War II. The pilots volunteered for suicide missions knowing fully in advance that their lives would be lost in carrying out the assigned mission. The linkage of self-fulfillment with self-destruction is perhaps the most extreme form of sacrifice possible in the exercise of disciplined freedom. Very few of us would be willing to make the kind of sacrifice made by the Kamikaze pilots; but such an unwillingness is also likely to reflect a lack of strong commitments.

Emotional investments and a sense of commitment are necessary for attaining most of the goals in life; but if the demands become too great or if the sacrifices become too burdensome, we are likely to change our minds and to move in other directions. Pursuing a career, developing a love affair, enhancing the qualities of family life, and acquiring material goods are typical expressions of freedom. For most people, however, such freedoms are likely to take conditional rather than disciplined forms. It is not the type of activity that determines the type of freedom but the emotional investments that social actors make. ... Extreme commitments are more likely to be found in moral crusades and social movements than in other types of activities. Whatever the case may be, exercises of conditional and disciplined freedom tend to establish social identities and to reflect what it is that people expect to get out of life.

Inventing the Future

One of the primary characteristics of the twentieth century is the emphasis in the more highly developed societies on collecting, organizing, and interpreting knowledge in the various forms (Lane, 1966). The modern concerns with advancing new forms of knowledge derive from the recognition that humans shape their own destinies, and that they do so with the information they have at their disposal, however incomplete or inadequate that information may be. The pursuit of knowledge in modern society does not stem from an emphasis on knowledge as something to be valued as an end within itself, but from the concerns for finding solutions to clearly identifiable problems. People extract additional meanings from the world around them in order to enhance basic values and objectives.

The quest for additional knowledge is reflected in the growth of specialized areas of inquiry. For example, a hundred years ago there was no one in the entire world who thought of himself or herself as a social psychologist. Social psychology had not yet been invented as a specialized area of academic inquiry. There were people, of course, who wrote about and reflected on many of the problems about which social psychologists are still concerned. But systematic inquiry into the subject matter of social psychology is primarily an outgrowth of the twentieth century.

It has been said that more than 90 percent of the scientists the world has ever known are alive today (Heilbronner, 1960), suggesting that we are living in a world in which knowledge is proliferating in many different directions at the same time. Just as we have turned our attention outward to the exploration of space, we also are turning our attention inwardly to examine the subjective qualities of life (Blauner, 1964). Within this context we may reasonably expect a great deal of interest in experimenting with new forms of social organization and social living. To the extent that this is so, humans appear to have the capacity and the freedom to shape their own destinies within certain limits, and these limits may be very broad indeed. Human awareness and intentions enter into the matrix of social causation, along with many other factors, in shaping the course of social events.

While we need not agree with the full implications of Alvin Toffler's (1971) description of social change as future shock, it is clear that many people do view the overall drift of societies as chaotic, unpredictable, and bereft of purpose. Under these conditions it is difficult for the individual to engage in long-range planning with a reasonable degree of confidence. Instead the individual often responds by developing a limited time perspective, by emphasizing the here and now, and by accepting the hedonistic view that one should live for today and let tomorrow take care of itself. To a significant degree, faith in long-term planning of one's life is dependent on being able to see the interrelatedness of events and to make social predictions with a reasonable degree of confidence.

This generation is making a sharp separation between self and society, but it is a separation that cannot be sustained adequately on purely theoretical grounds. The individual is both a producer and a product of social life in its varied forms. The performances that give shape to behavior are in part socially imposed and in part self-generated. Individuals act out of an awareness of others, necessarily take each other into account, and have their own behaviors shaped and modified in the process. Humans are indeed adaptable creatures, and their futures are shaped by the cumulative effects of the decisions made by many people. According to C. Wright Mills (1959: 174),

> within an individual's biography and with a society's history, the social task of reason is to formulate choices, to enlarge the scope of human decisions in the making of history. The future of human affairs is not merely some set of variables to be predicted. The future is what is to be decided—within the limits, to be sure, of historical possibility. But this possibility is not fixed; in our time the limits seem very broad indeed.

This quote is a fitting conclusion to our venture into social psychological inquiry. It was selected from Mills' discussion of reason and freedom. In his view, history has not yet completed its exploration of the limits of human nature, nor completed experimentation on the many possible relationships between the individual and society. Mills was essentially correct in this point of view. Realities are constructed at many levels of human action and are always changing social conditions. The futures of individuals and societies are created out of hopes and aspirations, out of committed lines of action, and out of the consequences that follow from the decision-making process.

REFERENCES

Berger, Peter, Brigitte Berger, and Hansfried Kellner. 1973. *The Homeless Mind,* New York: Vintage Books.

Blauner, Robert. 1964. *Alienation and Freedom.* Chicago: University of Chicago Press.

Durkheim, Emile. 1951. *Suicide.* Glencoe, Ill.: The Free Press.

Heilbronner, Robert L. 1960. *The Future as History.* New York: Harper & Row.

Hillery, George A., Jr. 1971. "Freedom and Social Organization," *American Sociological Review* 36 (February): 51–64.

Hillery, George A., Jr., Charles J. Dudley, and Paula C. Morrow. 1977. "Toward a Sociology of Freedom," *Social Forces* 55 (March): 685–700.

Hillery, George A., Jr., Charles J. Dudley, and Thomas P. Thompson. 1979. "A Theory of Integration and Freedom," *Sociological Quarterly* 20 (Autumn): 551–564.

Lane, Robert E. 1966. "The Decline of Politics and Ideology in a Knowledgeable Society," *American Sociological Review* 31 (October): 649–662.

Mills, C. Wright. 1959. *The Sociological Imagination.* New York: Oxford University Press.

Schwartz, Barry. 1968. "The Social Psychology of Privacy," *American Journal of Sociology* 73 (May): 741–752.

Toffler, Alvin. 1971. *Future Shock,* New York: Bantam Books.

Correlation Table

The Correlation Table on pages 338 and 339 may be used as a guide to further readings in the field of social psychology.

The horizontal axis represents additional Social Psychology texts (see key on page 340). The vertical axis represents chapters from these texts. The numbers within the chart indicate the selections in this book that correspond to these text chapters. Blanks indicate either "no applicable reading" or "no chapter."

	1	2	3	4	5	6	7	8
1	1, 2, 6	1, 2	2, 3, 4	1, 2, 6	1, 2	1, 2	1, 2, 3, 4	1, 2, 3, 4, 6, 7
2	7	9, 11	9, 11	9, 12, 13, 14	5	3, 4, 8	6, 7	12, 13
3	3, 4, 5, 29	10, 12, 13, 25	—	16, 18	3, 4, 6, 7	5, 38	9, 11, 16, 25	9, 11, 14, 25, 26
4	8, 10, 12, 13, 17	8, 18, 19, 29	—	4, 10, 14	8, 21	9, 12, 13	12, 13, 14	10, 14
5	11, 19	17, 31, 32, 33, 34	10	24, 26	9, 11, 14	8, 9, 14, 30, 36	21, 24	15, 17
6	16, 18	5	17, 25, 26	27, 28	18, 24	18, 29	10	18
7	9, 14	3, 4, 6	18, 36	27, 28	8, 17	19, 26	5, 14	29
8	15, 20	—	31, 32	3, 8, 19	19, 26	25, 27, 28	27, 28	26
9	21, 22, 25, 26, 30	—	34	29	9, 12, 13, 25	3, 4, 6, 7	8, 18, 36	27, 28
10	23, 34	—	—	18, 36	10, 14	—	29	8, 18, 20
11	27, 28	—	—	17	27, 28	—	5, 24	24, 26
12	17	—	—	25, 26	29	—	3, 17, 26	31, 32, 33, 34, 38
13	31, 32, 33, 34	—	—	31, 32, 38	36	—	31, 32, 33, 34	36, 37
14	5, 17	—	—	33, 36, 37	17, 18	—	19, 26	—
15	35	—	—	35	8, 34	—	31, 38	—
16	36, 37, 38	—	—	—	31, 32, 33	—	22	—
17	—	—	—	—	—	—	37	—

9	10	11	12	13	14	15	16
5, 11, 16, 25	1, 2, 5	1, 2, 3, 4, 5, 21	1, 2, 5, 20	1, 2, 3, 4, 6, 7	1, 2, 6	1, 2, 14	1, 2, 3, 4, 5, 6, 7
15, 16, 26	3, 4	9, 11, 14, 15, 16, 25	7	10, 14, 16, 25	3, 4, 18, 29	6, 7	21
25, 27, 28	5, 16, 25	8, 17, 18	11	12, 13, 14	17, 34	16, 18, 25	30
27	9, 11	22, 23, 24	17	3, 4	10, 26	12, 13, 21, 22, 26	12, 13, 14
2, 10, 36	12, 16, 21, 30	11, 26, 27, 28, 34	16, 18	22, 37	12, 13	9, 11, 14	10, 14
7, 22, 23, 24	23, 31, 32, 33, 34	18, 32, 36	8, 12, 13, 30, 36	24, 34	16, 18, 24, 36	5	36, 37
8, 36, 37	8, 18, 19	19, 26	11, 21	3, 18, 31	9, 14, 25	10	5, 9, 16, 25
—	36, 37, 38	29	9, 15, 21	36, 37	5, 11, 16	8, 18, 24	3, 18, 34
—	—	—	11	3, 4, 17, 18	24	11, 21	27, 28
—	—	—	25	23, 36, 37	15, 29	3, 17	3, 4, 17, 31, 32, 33
—	—	—	24, 34	16, 24	8, 23, 36	3, 18, 34	18, 36
—	—	—	17, 35, 38	2, 18, 36	8, 23, 24, 26	27	12
—	—	—	24, 27, 28	27, 28	8, 18, 36	27, 28	10, 26
—	—	—	8, 18, 19	29	27	29	16, 4, 36
—	—	—	7, 22, 26	33	27, 28	36	31, 33, 38
—	—	—	—	—	10, 14	10, 26	22, 26
—	—	—	—	—	8, 11, 30	1	—

Key:

1. Michael C. Kearl and Chad Gordon. *Social Psychology: Shaping Identity, Thought, and Conduct.* Boston: Allyn and Bacon, 1992.
2. James A. Schellenberg. *An Invitation to Social Psychology.* Boston: Allyn and Bacon, 1992.
3. James A. Schellenberg. *Exploring Social Behavior: Investigations in Social Psychology.* Boston: Allyn and Bacon, 1992.
4. Robert A. Baron and Donn Byrne. *Social Psychology: Understanding Human Interaction,* Sixth Edition. Boston: Allyn and Bacon, 1991.
5. Cookie White Stephan and Walter G. Stephan. *Two Social Psychologies,* Second Edition. Belmont, CA: Wadsworth, 1990.
6. Elliot Aronson. *The Social Animal,* Sixth Edition. New York: W. H. Freeman, 1992.
7. Reuben M. Baron and William G. Graziano. *Social Psychology.* Chicago: Holt, Rinehart and Winston, 1991.
8. John C. Brigham. *Social Psychology,* Second Edition. New York: HarperCollins, 1991.
9. Steve Duck. *Human Relationships,* Second Edition. Newbury Park, CA: Sage, 1992.
10. John P. Hewitt. *Self and Society: A Symbolic Interactionist Social Psychology,* Fifth Edition. Boston: Allyn and Bacon, 1991.
11. Jack Levin and William C. Levin. *The Human Puzzle: An Introduction to Social Psychology.* Belmont, CA: Wadsworth, 1988.
12. Alfred R. Lindesmith, Anselm L. Strauss, and Norman K. Denzin. *Social Psychology,* Seventh Edition. Englewood Cliffs, NJ: Prentice Hall, 1991.
13. David G. Meyers. *Social Psychology,* Third Edition. New York: McGraw-Hill, 1990.
14. John Sabini. *Social Psychology.* New York: W. W. Norton and Company, 1992.
15. David J. Schneider. *Introduction to Social Psychology.* New York: Harcourt Brace Jovanovich, 1988.
16. David O. Sears, Letitia Anne Peplau, and Shelley E. Taylor. *Social Psychology,* Seventh Edition. Englewood Cliffs, NJ: Prentice Hall, 1991.